Fodor's 2010

NEW YORK CITY

Fodor's Travel Publications   New York, Toronto, London, Sydney, Auckland

www.fodors.com

Be a Fodor's Correspondent

Your opinion matters. It matters to us. It matters to your fellow Fodor's travelers, too. And we'd like to hear it. In fact, we need to hear it.

When you share your experiences and opinions, you become an active member of the Fodor's community. That means we'll not only use your feedback to make our books better, but we'll publish your names and comments whenever possible. Throughout our guides, look for "Word of Mouth," excerpts of your unvarnished feedback.

Here's how you can help improve Fodor's for all of us.

Tell us when we're right. We rely on local writers to give you an insider's perspective. But our writers and staff editors—who are the best in the business—depend on you. Your positive feedback is a vote to renew our recommendations for the next edition.

Tell us when we're wrong. We're proud that we update most of our guides every year. But we're not perfect. Things change. Hotels cut services. Museums change hours. Charming cafés lose charm. If our writer didn't quite capture the essence of a place, tell us how you'd do it differently. If any of our descriptions are inaccurate or inadequate, we'll incorporate your changes in the next edition and will correct factual errors at fodors.com immediately.

Tell us what to include. You probably have had fantastic travel experiences that aren't yet in Fodor's. Why not share them with a community of like-minded travelers? Maybe you chanced upon a beach or bistro or B&B that you don't want to keep to yourself. Tell us why we should include it. And share your discoveries and experiences with everyone directly at fodors.com. Your input may lead us to add a new listing or highlight a place we cover with a "Highly Recommended" star or with our highest rating, "Fodor's Choice."

Give us your opinion instantly at our feedback center at www.fodors.com/feedback. You may also e-mail editors@fodors.com with the subject line "New York City Editor." Or send your nominations, comments, and complaints by mail to New York City Editor, Fodor's, 1745 Broadway, New York, NY 10019.

Yours truly, and travelers like you are the heart of the Fodor's community. Make our community richer by sharing your experiences. Be a Fodor's correspondent.

Tim Jarrell, Publisher

FODOR'S NEW YORK CITY 2010

Editors: Maria Teresa Hart (lead editor); Erica Duecy (restaurants and hotels editor); and Jennifer Paull

Editorial Contributors: Alia Akkam, Lynne Arany, Alexander Basek, Nina Callaway, Nicole Crane, Michelle Delio, Jen Laskey, Meryl Pearlstein, Sandra Ramani, John Rambow, Jacqueline Terrebonne

Production Editor: Astrid deRidder

Maps & Illustrations: Mark Stroud, David Lindroth, cartographers; Bob Blake, Rebecca Baer, map editors; William Wu, information graphics

Design: Fabrizio LaRocca, creative director; Guido Caroti, Siobhan O'Hare, art directors; Tina Malaney, Chie Ushio, Ann McBride, Jessica Walsh, designers; Melanie Marin, senior picture editor

Cover Photo: (Empire State Building): Gabriel J. Jimenez/eStock Photo

Production Manager: Angela McLean

ISBN 978-1-4000-0837-7

ISSN 0736-9395

SPECIAL SALES

This book is available at special discounts for bulk purchases for sales promotions or premiums. Special editions, including personalized covers, excerpts of existing books, and corporate imprints, can be created in large quantities for special needs. For more information, write to Special Markets/Premium Sales, 1745 Broadway, MD 6-2, New York, New York 10019, or e-mail specialmarkets@randomhouse.com.

AN IMPORTANT TIP & AN INVITATION

Although all prices, opening times, and other details in this book are based on information supplied to us at press time, changes occur all the time in the travel world, and Fodor's cannot accept responsibility for facts that become outdated or for inadvertent errors or omissions. So **always confirm information when it matters**, especially if you're making a detour to visit a specific place. Your experiences—positive and negative—matter to us. If we have missed or misstated something, **please write to us.** We follow up on all suggestions. Contact the New York City editor at editors@fodors.com or c/o Fodor's at 1745 Broadway, New York, NY 10019.

PRINTED IN SINGAPORE

10 9 8 7 6 5 4 3 2 1

CONTENTS

Fodor's Features

ABOUT THIS BOOK

Our Ratings

Sometimes you find terrific travel experiences and sometimes they just find you. But usually the burden is on you to select the right combination of experiences. That's where our ratings come in.

As travelers we've all discovered a place so wonderful that its worthiness is obvious. And sometimes that place is so unique that superlatives don't do it justice: you just have to be there to know. These sights, properties, and experiences get our highest rating, **Fodor's Choice**, indicated by orange stars throughout this book.

Black stars highlight sights and properties we deem **Highly Recommended**, places that our writers, editors, and readers praise again and again for consistency and excellence.

By default, there's another category: any place we include in this book is by definition worth your time, unless we say otherwise. And we will.

Disagree with any of our choices? Care to nominate a place or suggest that we rate one more highly? Visit our feedback center at www.fodors.com/feedback.

Budget Well

Hotel and restaurant price categories from ¢ to $$$$ are defined in the opening pages of the respective chapters. For attractions, we always give standard adult admission fees; reductions are usually available for children, students, and senior citizens. Want to pay with plastic? **AE, D, DC, MC, V** following restaurant and hotel listings indicate whether American Express, Discover, Diners Club, MasterCard, and Visa are accepted.

Restaurants

Unless we state otherwise, restaurants are open for lunch and dinner daily. We mention dress only when there's a specific requirement and reservations only when they're essential or not accepted—it's always best to book ahead.

Hotels

Hotels have private bath, phone, TV, and air-conditioning and operate on the European Plan (aka EP, meaning without meals), unless we specify that they use the Continental Plan (CP, with a Continental breakfast), Breakfast Plan (BP, with a full breakfast), or Modified American Plan (MAP, with breakfast and dinner), or are all-inclusive (AI, including all meals

and most activities). We always list facilities but not whether you'll be charged an extra fee to use them.

Many Listings

★	Fodor's Choice
★	Highly recommended
✉	Physical address
✛	Directions
⌂	Mailing address
☎	Telephone
🖷	Fax
⊕	On the Web
✍	E-mail
🎟	Admission fee
☉	Open/closed times
Ⓜ	Metro stations
▭	Credit cards

Hotels & Restaurants

🏨	Hotel
⇗	Number of rooms
☖	Facilities
⦿	Meal plans
✕	Restaurant
⬿	Reservations
⦥	Smoking
🍸	BYOB
✕🏨	Hotel with restaurant that warrants a visit

Outdoors

⅄	Golf
⛺	Camping

Other

ⓒ	Family-friendly
⇨	See also
✉	Branch address
☞	Take note

Experience
New York City

NEW YORK CITY TODAY

New York, New York. It's hard living here when the economy's up, and it's even harder when the economy is going down. New Yorkers are trying to make do with a new normal that includes a financial sector on the skids and a cooling real-estate market. So, please excuse us if we're gruff—or make that even gruffer than normal.

Those anxieties go all the way to the top: just like the rest of us, Mayor Michael Bloomberg is concerned about keeping his job. After shepherding the city through years of dizzying expansion after 9/11, Mayor Bloomberg campaigned in October of 2008 to extend the term limits for Mayor and city council, allowing him to run a third time. New Yorkers are divided on the possibility of a third term. While Bloomberg was undoubtedly popular when the money was rolling in, now that they view his last two terms with a critical eye, some see his push to run again as hubristic.

Whoever is elected will face a new set of difficulties, including MTA Budget shortfalls and a shrinking tax base. Many of the city's linchpin industries, including finance, real estate, hospitality and the arts are going through periods of contraction. Difficulties in the finance sector in particular ripple through the city. When bonuses are small—or layoffs are plentiful—fewer apartments are purchased, people eat out less, and seats at Broadway shows go unfilled.

A big focus is also on the real estate here. In Manhattan rents have fallen from their 2007 peaks. Condo buildings conceived during the boom are coming to completion in a completely different market. The Williamsburg and Greenpoint waterfront in Brooklyn is full of half-empty or half-finished projects. Citywide, pioneering gentrifiers worry that their neighborhoods might not stay so nice during a downturn. Despite the doom and gloom, prices here still outstrip most U.S. cities: the average cost of an apartment citywide is $669,000, down 10 percent from a year ago. The price in Manhattan for a condo continues to climb, but sales volume is down a staggering 55 percent compared to the same time last year.

No matter the economy, people still get hungry, so locals are still eating out...just not so much at places with $50 entrées. But price aside, there are exciting meals

WHAT WE'RE TALKING ABOUT

The most recent season of *Top Chef* was filmed here, and the city's foodies watched for sightings of NYC's culinary stars. Nonfoodies enjoy comparing the (fake) luxurious lifestyles of the cast of *Gossip Girl* with the (slightly less fake) luxurious lifestyles of the cast of *The City*.

It may get harder to partake in our typical vices. First cigarette smoking was attacked and now Governor David Paterson took on sodas and sugary drinks by proposing a 15% "obesity tax." It didn't pass, but one measure that did—posting the calories of foods in chain restaurants—means NYC junk

food lovers are still being taken to task.

Could there be a silver lining in this economy? Rents are dropping across the board and many landlords are giving incentives like the first month's rent free to entice tenants. Some renters are even bold

to be had. Heck, you can even have an eight-course meal with Tom Colicchio, Mr. Top Chef himself, at his restaurant Craft as part of his recent "Tom Tuesday Dinner" promotion. More cheaply, you can try to spot David Chang while slurping from a bowl of noodles at the Momofuku Noodle Bar or simply eat your weight in French fries at Pommes Frites. There's something for everyone to eat, and plenty of restaurants have promotions to lure diners on slower nights, so keep an eye out for those. Since strong cocktails are a necessity during these trying times, New York's bars have risen to the task by serving delicious, complex drinks at White Star, Death & Co., and the Clover Club.

Meanwhile, in the world of the performing arts, long-running shows are closing, but things aren't totally dire. There are bargain tickets galore to the surviving plays and musicals, and Off-Broadway shows are ascendant in popularity and quality. Plus, we still have *Law & Order* (filming just about everywhere in the city on any given day) as well as *Gossip Girl* and *30 Rock* at the Silvercup Studios in Queens. Musically, there's everything from

indie troubadour Beirut at the Brooklyn Academy of Music to Billy Joel playing the last concert at Shea Stadium. And if those don't appeal, there are countless other venues from Red Hook to Morningside Heights.

They say if you can make it here you can make it anywhere. In a New York that's in flux between identifying as a "luxury city" (as Mayor Bloomberg called it) and a becoming town with the same struggles as the rest of America, "making it" feels like an even bigger accomplishment. Luckily, New Yorkers are a proud bunch, and we're happy to share all the tips and tricks we've learned. Welcome.

—Alexander Basek

enough to renegotiate the terms of their current leases—hello, new roommate!

Don't cry for them, Argentina—Broadway has seen quite a few shows drop the curtain for good, including *Gypsy*, *Spamalot*, *Spring Awakening*, *Hairspray*, *Young Frankenstein*

and *Grease*. Now's the time to catch a performance while you still can.

Hotels are slashing their rates so much here that even New Yorkers are taking the opportunity to sample luxurious digs for the weekend. Don't be surprised if the couple across

the hall from you has traveled up north…from Greenwich Village.

—*Alexander Basek*

NEW YORK CITY PLANNER

Weather This

New York City weather, like its people, is a study in extremes. Much of winter brings bone-chilling winds and an occasional traffic-snarling snowfall, but you're just as likely to experience mild afternoons sandwiched by cool temperatures.

In late spring and early summer, streets fill with parades and sidewalk concerts and Central Park has free performances. Late August temperatures sometimes claw skyward, giving many subway stations the feel and bouquet of dingy saunas (no wonder the Hamptons are so crowded). This is why September brings palpable excitement, with stunning yellow-and-bronze foliage complementing the dawn of a new cultural season. Between October and May, museums mount major exhibitions, most Broadway shows open, and formal opera, ballet, and concert seasons begin.

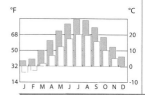

Getting Around

Without a doubt, the best way to explore New York is on foot. No matter what neighborhood you're headed to, you'll get a better sense of it by wandering around; you can check out the architecture, pop into cool-looking shops and cafés, and observe the walk-and-talk of the locals. Our easy grid pattern makes it hard to get lost for more than a few blocks—and if you do, you'll find New Yorkers are surprisingly helpful with directions.

The days when New York's subways were dangerous are long gone. Now, the city's network of underground trains is the most efficient way to get around. (City buses are equally cheap, but can take forever to navigate through traffic, especially crosstown.) The subway is by no means flawless: good luck understanding loudspeaker announcements on all but the newest trains; the floors are sticky; stations are sweltering in summer; and platforms are grimy year-round. In other words, it's quite obvious that the subway is over 100 years old. Still, for now $2 gets you to almost any neighborhood in Manhattan or the outer boroughs, and lines that service the most popular destinations are generally clean, with maps and signs that clearly state where you're going. It gets crowded during rush hours, when you'll likely find that all the subway car seats are taken—and have to join your fellow riders in the particular New York sport of "strap-hanging."

If you've got a long way to go and would rather be comfortable than thrifty, hail one of the ubiquitous yellow cabs that troll New York's streets around the clock. A December 2006 hike in taxi fares means that a 20-minute ride can now set you back more than $10. But you'll get to look at the scenery as you go and talk to the driver (who might be from as far away as Bangladesh or Ukraine). Avoid trying to hail a cab between 4 and 4:30 PM, unless you want to do a lot of futile street-side arm waving; it's when the drivers change shifts.

Our Streets

The map of Manhattan is, for the most part, easy to follow: north of 14th Street, streets are laid out in a numbered grid pattern. Numbered streets run east and west (crosstown), and broad avenues, most of them also numbered, run north (uptown) and south (downtown). The main exception is Broadway, which runs the entire length of Manhattan on a diagonal. Below 14th Street, street patterns get chaotic. In the West Village, West 4th Street intersects West 11th Street, Greenwich Street runs roughly parallel to Greenwich Avenue, and Leroy Street turns into St. Luke's Place for one block and then becomes Leroy again. There's an East Broadway and a West Broadway, both of which run north–south and neither of which is an extension of Broadway, leaving even locals scratching their heads.

Street Smarts

Avoid deserted blocks in unfamiliar neighborhoods. A brisk, purposeful pace helps deter trouble wherever you go. New York City is a safe city, but it's still a city, so keep jewelry out of sight on the street; better yet, leave valuables at home. Don't wear gold chains or large jewelry, even if it's fake.

When in bars or restaurants, never hang your purse or bag on the back of a chair or put it underneath the table.

Never leave any bags unattended, and expect to have you and your possessions inspected thoroughly in such places as airports, sports stadiums, museums, and city buildings. Police officers stationed by subway token booths also reserve the right to check your bags before you pass through the turnstile to enter the platform.

Politely ignore panhandlers on the streets and subways, people who offer to hail you a cab (they often appear at Penn Station, the Port Authority, or the airport), and limousine and gypsy cab drivers who (illegally) offer rides priced according to how desperate you look.

Knockoff wristwatches will keep excellent time until you're about an hour away from the vendor, so don't bother with them; ditto for pirated DVDs. Trust us, they work poorly and, not for nothing, their sale is highly illegal.

If you wander into a cold snap, do as the locals do and buy an inexpensive hat or scarf from a sidewalk vendor. Similarly, if it rains, scan the mouths of subway stairwells for umbrella salesmen who materialize so quickly you'll think the raindrops hydrated them into existence.

Our Hours

Subways and buses run around the clock, and so do plenty of businesses—including restaurants, pharmacies, copy shops, and even fitness clubs (there's no wait for a treadmill at 4 AM). Other shops and services have more extensive hours than you'll find elsewhere in the United States; for example, there are quite a few places where you can get groceries—or get your hair and nails done—at 11 PM. In general, though, you can safely assume that most shops are open seven days a week, from about 10 to 7 Monday–Saturday, and noon to 6 on Sunday. Bars generally close at 4 AM, though some after-hours clubs are open later.

Two Ways to Save

Consider buying a CityPass, a group of tickets to six top-notch attractions in New York: the Empire State Building, the Guggenheim Museum, the American Museum of Natural History, the Museum of Modern Art, the Metropolitan Museum of Art (including the Cloisters), and Circle Line Cruises or admission to Liberty and Ellis Island. The $74 pass, which saves you half the cost of each individual ticket, is good for nine days from first use.

Discount coupons are available at the city's official tourism marketing bureau, **NYC & Company** (⊕ *www.nycvisit. com*), near Times Square.

WHAT'S WHERE

1 Lower Manhattan.
Heavy-duty landmarks anchor the southern tip: Wall Street and the Financial District; the breezy waterfront parks of Battery Park City and historic South Street Seaport; ferry terminals dispatching boats out to Ellis Island and the Statue of Liberty; and the gradually evolving construction site at Ground Zero, where thousands flock daily to pay their respects.

2 Chinatown and Little Italy. Between Broome Street and Columbus Park (to the north and south) and the Bowery and Broadway (to the east and west), these touristy areas teem with street vendors selling knockoff handbags and "Faux-lex" watches. Brave the crowds and explore some of the less traveled streets to find vestiges of what makes these neighborhoods special: Chinese herb shops, exceptional noodle joints, Italian cafés, and gelaterias.

3 SoHo, NoLita and TriBeCa. The only struggling creative types in SoHo these days are sidewalk merchants hawking canvases, handmade jewelry, and T-shirts; the superluxe shops dominate here. To the east, NoLita has more tiny boutiques and restaurants. South and west of SoHo are the streets of TriBeCa, broader and, also,

quieter, because hardly anyone can afford to live here.

4 The East Village and the Lower East Side. Once an edgy neighborhood of artists and punks, now filled with combination of artists, fashionable lawyers, and students, the East Village centers around the scruffy but beloved Tompkins Square Park. The neighborhood is one of the city's best for eating, both in terms of variety and quality. To the south, the rapidly gentrifying Lower East Side (bounded by the Bowery, Clinton, Houston, and Delancey streets), draws hipsters with live-music clubs, independent clothing shops, wine-and-tapas bars, and health-food joints.

5 Greenwich Village and the Meatpacking District. Happily, artists with rent-controlled apartments, out-and-proud gays, jazz musicians, and university students are as much in evidence in the Village today as they ever were. From 14th Street south to Houston and from the Hudson River east to 5th Avenue, the blocks are a jumble of jazz clubs, funky restaurants, former speakeasies, and rainbow flags. Farther west, the once blue-collar Meatpacking District has evolved into a clubbing and late-night restaurant scene for the young and scantily clad.

6 Chelsea. Like its namesake London district, our Chelsea has a small-town personality, albeit with big-city prices. Its leafy streets (which stretch from 14th to the upper 20s) are lined with renovated brownstones and spacious art galleries; its avenues (from 6th to the Hudson) brim with restaurants, bakeries, bodegas, and men's clothing stores. Chelsea has supplanted the Village as the center of gay life in the city.

7 Union Square, Murray Hill and Gramercy. Bustling Union Square Park, bounded by 14th and 17th streets, Broadway, and Park Avenue, hosts the city's best greenmarket four times a week. On the 14th Street edge are broad stone steps where break-dancers and other performers busk for onlookers. North, up Broadway, is Madison Square Park, beloved for its outdoor summer jazz concerts. Nearby are the preening mansions and town houses of Gramercy in the East 20s, and of Murray Hill in the East 30s.

8 Times Square and Midtown West. Once profoundly seedy, Times Square today is homogenous, over-the-top razzle-dazzle. Neon, scrolling tickers, and massive TV screens coat building facades, and street preachers and musicians man the corners. It's so hectic that ducking into a chain restaurant seems relatively restful, and heading west to a Broadway show feels downright genteel.

9 Rockefeller Center and Midtown East. Near Rockefeller Center, justly famous for its tree and rink, are ultra-swanky Saks, Tiffany & Co., Henri Bendel, and Bergdorf Goodman, among others. St. Patrick's Cathedral, on 5th Avenue, is a key landmark. Heading south will bring you to the stately New York Public Library (and the adjacent Bryant Park), Grand Central Terminal, and the Chrysler Building.

10 The Upper East Side. North of 59th Street, between 5th and Park avenues, the Upper East Side is home to more millionaires than any other part of the city. Historic-district designation has kept the tony mansions and apartment buildings intact and largely uninterrupted by "plebeian" structures. Tucked into this stretch of 5th are the Museum Mile and, a block east, Madison Avenue's haute boutiques.

11 The Upper West Side. In the shadow of ornate prewar buildings, sidewalks burst with stroller-pushing caregivers, dog-walkers, joggers, and students. By day the dominant draw is the American Museum of Natural History; by night, Lincoln Center. Way north sits the eminently walkable Columbia University campus and the grounds of the Cathedral Church of St. John the Divine, with catacombs and wandering peacocks.

12 Harlem. A hotbed of African-American and Hispanic-American culture for almost a century, Harlem still sizzles today. The brownstone-lined blocks between about 110th and 145th streets—many of which languished in the '70s and '80s—are being refurbished: Bill Clinton moved his post-presidency offices here in 2001. Chic boutiques and restaurants are popping up, while music venues from the 1920s and '30s are still in full swing.

13 Brooklyn and the Outer Boroughs. Brooklyn, our largest borough, counts among its stars Coney Island, Prospect Park, and the Brooklyn Botanic Gardens. Its ultradistinct neighborhoods include the hipster Neverland Williamsburg and the Italian-American Carroll Gardens. Staten Island harbors a commuter-transporting ferry and Queens has pocket communities of Greeks, Indians, and Dominicans (among others), as well as Flushing Meadows and Citi Field. The Bronx was best known for the old Yankee Stadium—it's likely the new one will remain famous, too—but Arthur Avenue's Italian restaurants, the New York Botanical Garden, and the Bronx Zoo are no slouches.

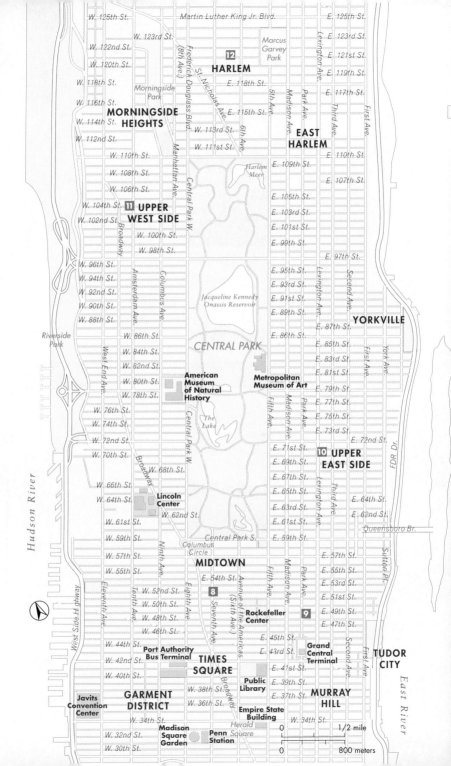

NEW YORK CITY
TOP ATTRACTIONS

Metropolitan Museum of Art

(A) The largest art museum in the western hemisphere, the Met is—naturally—a mecca for art lovers of all stripes. Treasures from all over the world and every era of human creativity comprise its expansive collection. It's easy to get dizzy circling all the Dutch master canvases, bronze Rodins, and ancient Greek artifacts—but if you need a breather, you can always retire to the Temple of Dendur or the rooftop café.

Times Square

(B) Times Square is the most frenetic part of New York City: a cacophony of flashing lights, honking horns, and shoulder-to-shoulder crowds that many New Yorkers studiously avoid. But if you like sensory overload, the chaotic mix of huge underwear billboards, flashing digital displays, on-location television broadcasts, and outré street performers it will give you your fix. If you're a quieter sort, it will almost certainly give you a headache.

Empire State Building

(C) From the 86th-floor observatory, which towers 1,050 feet above the city, you can see up to 80 mi away on a clear day (and it's heated and air-conditioned, unlike the deck 16 stories farther up). The views at night are equally stunning, with the glittering city lights French architect Le Corbusier once called "a Milky Way come down to earth." If you're afraid of heights, gazing at the building from afar will still deliver a dose of dazzle—especially after dark, when it's illuminated by colored lights that correspond to different holidays and events.

Museum of Modern Art

(D) Described as a "modernist dream world" after its $425 million face-lift in 2004, MoMA has since become as famous for its architecture as for its collections. Yoshio Taniguchi, the Japanese architect

responsible for the redesign, created newly spacious, soaring-ceiling galleries suffused with natural light, where masterpieces like Monet's *Water Lilies,* Picasso's *Les Demoiselles d'Avignon,* and van Gogh's *Starry Night* can get the oohs and aahs they deserve. The museum's restaurant next door, the Modern, is nearly as breathtaking.

Brooklyn Bridge

(E) "A drive-through cathedral" is how critic James Wolcott described this, one of New York's noblest and most recognized landmarks. Spanning the East River, the Brooklyn Bridge connects the island of Manhattan to the borough of Brooklyn (once an independent city, and still worth a visit in its own right). A leisurely hour's stroll on the pedestrian walkway (which you'll share with bicyclists and in-line skaters) is an essential New York experience. Traffic is beneath you, and the views along the East River

and of Manhattan's Financial District are some of the best anywhere.

Statue of Liberty

(F) Presented to the United States in 1886 as a gift from France, Lady Liberty is a near-universal symbol of freedom and democracy, standing 152 feet high atop an 89-foot pedestal on Liberty Island. You can get a taste of the thrill millions of immigrants must have experienced as you approach Liberty Island on the ferry from Battery Park.

American Museum of Natural History

(G) The towering, spectacularly reassembled dinosaur skeletons that greet you when you enter this museum are practically worth the (suggested) price of admission. But there's tons more, including exhibits of ancient civilizations, anim
both stuffed and living (don't miss
Butterfly Conservatory Octob
hall of oceanic creatures
94-foot model of a blue w

shows at the adjoining Rose Center for Earth and Space.

Central Park

(H) The literal and spiritual center of Manhattan, Central Park has 843 acres of meandering paths, tranquil lakes, ponds, and open meadows. For equestrians, softball and soccer players, strollers, ice- and roller skaters, rock climbers, bird-watchers, boaters, picnickers, and outdoor performers, it's an oasis of fresh air and greenery that lets them forget—at least for a little while—the hustle and congestion of the city.

Bronx Zoo

(I) One urban jungle deserves another. Only at the world's largest urban zoo is there room for gorillas to lumber around a 6.5-acre simulated rain forest, or tigers and lions to roam nearly 40 acres of open meadows.

SoHo

(J) The elegant cast-iron buildings, cobblestone streets, art galleries, chic boutiques, and swanky hotels make this a wonderful area in which to shop, drink, and dream of a more glamorous life.

NEW YORK CITY WITH KIDS

Though much of New York revolves around the distinctly adult pursuits of making and spending money, it's also a great city for kids. Our top activities include:

American Museum of Natural History. The hands-down favorite for both visiting and local kids, this museum's many exhibits could entertain most children for a week. The dinosaurs alone are worth the trip, as is the live Butterfly Conservatory that runs each year from October to May. There's also an IMAX theater, ancient-culture displays, and wildlife dioramas with taxidermied creatures that hit the right mix of fascinating and creepy.

Bronx Zoo. The country's largest metropolitan wildlife park is home to more than 4,000 animals, including endangered and threatened species. Plan to spend a whole day here, so your kids don't have to choose between Congo Gorilla Forest and the Siberian cats at Tiger Mountain. Be sure to check out the World of Darkness, a black-lighted indoor exhibit of nocturnal creatures. On Tuesday from April through October the zoo runs special tours for young children.

Central Park Zoo. Three climatic regions—Rain Forest, Temperate Territory, and Polar Circle—are represented at this bite-size zoo. The rain-forest frogs, red pandas, and performing sea lions are all nifty—but the showstopper is the underwater viewing window into the polar bear pool.

Children's Museum of Manhattan. Interactive exhibits in this five-floor museum change frequently—but they're always fun. As well as visiting with TV friends like Dora the Explorer, your little ones can build castles in the sand laboratory, and—in warm weather—race boats on a zigzagging outdoor watercourse.

New York Aquarium. Alongside the creaky amusements of Coney Island, this aquarium is home to more than 10,000 marine species, including walrus, giant sea turtles, sand-tiger sharks, and sea otters.

New York Botanical Garden. Fifty gardens and plant collections fill this gorgeous 250-acre space; there are flowering rose and water-lily gardens in the warm months, and hothouses full of tropical flowers in winter. Don't miss the Children's Adventure Garden and its boulder maze.

Rose Center for Earth and Space. The appropriately space-age design of the new Hayden Planetarium (and its accompanying cosmos museum) has made waves among architects—but the thrilling daily space shows inside are a big bang with kids. The complex is part of the American Museum of Natural History, though planetarium tickets are sold separately.

Sony Wonder Technology Lab. The line to get into this futuristic fantasy world might be long (as well as having great interactive exhibits, the museum has free entry). But don't worry—a slightly freaky talking robot will keep your kids entertained while they wait. Inside, there are more robots and image and sound labs where kids can record their own digital music, movies, and games.

South Street Seaport Museum. The fleet of historic square-riggers with looming masts might be the first thing to catch your children's eyes—but there's much more going on here, including weekend concerts, performances by storytellers and shanty-singers, and special guided tours for families.

NEW YORK CITY LIKE A LOCAL

The phrase "in a New York minute" is clichéd for a reason: in this wonderful, frenetic, and overwhelming city, things really do change in a flash. Even for those of us who live here, keeping up with the latest trends in fashion, art, music, food, and nightlife can be exhausting.

Thankfully, there are a few tricks to navigating this city—unspoken, hard-won bits of knowledge that help us locals get the most out of our hometown without driving ourselves crazy. And at the risk of compromising our New York credibility (after all, we consider ourselves members of an exclusive club, and guard our secrets accordingly), we've decided to share those tricks here. Just don't tell anyone we told you.

Getting Around Like a Local

First, when distance is involved, take the subway. Skip the horse-drawn carriages that wait for fares around Central Park; a jaunt in one will leave you exposed to the elements; stalled in exhaust-filled traffic; guilt-ridden about the poor, plodding horse; and broke. Pedicabs aren't much use either, except for the novelty value.

When hailing a taxi, recognize which cabs to avoid flagging down. Don't wave at cars whose rooftop lights aren't illuminated; these already have passengers inside. Taxis whose roof lights are only lighted at the edges—not the center— are off-duty, and will rarely pick you up unless your destination is on their way to the garage.

Think twice about getting into a cab whose driver has cut across three lanes of traffic to get to you; if he's willing to risk his life and the lives of others just to pick you up, he might not suddenly morph into a model of safe driving once you're inside. Then again, he might be the only sure bet to get you to the airport when you're running late.

Once you're in a cab, know your passenger rights. Although your driver will likely career at high speeds while simultaneously cursing, leaning on his horn, and chattering into his cell-phone headset, you're entitled to ask him to slow down. You're also allowed to ask him to turn off his phone or blaring car radio, and if he doesn't comply, refrain from tipping him. Cabbies make their money from tips, so for any typical ride tack on 15% to 20% to your fare.

Lastly, hailing a cab between the hours of 4 and 6 PM is near impossible. It's rush hour, when every workaday New Yorker is trying to get home, and available taxis are very scarce, and they're all but nonexistent between 4 and 4:30 when the driver shifts change, so don't even waste your time trying to find one—head right for the subway or else hoof it.

Speaking of walking, it's crucial that you be aware of the implicit rules of the New York City sidewalk. Most importantly, when walking here, move quickly. Realize that New Yorkers are like sharks: if they stop moving forward, they die (or else bite your head off). Unless you're holding the hand of a small child, single file is the rule; walking two or three abreast will cause locals to jostle, sideswipe, and growl at you. Stopping on the sidewalk to take pictures of each other or consult your guidebook will also put you at risk for being hip-checked. If you need a moment to consult your map or text-message a friend, make like you're on the highway: pull over and get out of the way.

Dining Like a Local

The first rule of New York eating is, forget the heavy breakfast—at least on weekdays. Although weekend brunches are popular—as the lines in front of morning restaurants on Saturday and Sunday attest—when the rest of the city is on the clock, it's better to get up and go. Grab a cup of joe and a muffin from a café, a deli, or one of the ubiquitous sidewalk carts (they're passably good), and walk around while you eat. This will give you more valuable exploring time (trust us, there's too much to see to waste the whole morning lingering over omelets), and will also help you save money for the most important meal of the day: dinner.

While we're on the subject, you should plan to eat dinner later than you ordinarily would—if you want to experience the real New York dining scene, that is. Most New York restaurants are empty at around 6 PM and don't fill up until at least 7:30 or 8, so if you eat early, you'll have your pick of tables. Prime-time dinner reservations—between 8 and 10 o'clock—are the hardest to score, but will ensure that you're surrounded by chic dining companions.

Of course, if you can't get a good reservation (and you don't have young kids in tow), you can always do what many savvy locals do: eat at the bar. You'll get the same great food and people-watching, plus you'll get to feel like an insider while other folks are still waiting for a table.

Going Out Like a Local

There's one major rule New Yorkers abide by when hitting the nightspots: avoid, avoid, avoid the big clubs on Friday and Saturday nights. The only people you're likely to see then are other visitors, the pickup artists trying to scam them, and kids too young to know better. Locals and A-listers go clubbing on Tuesday, Wednesday, and Thursday—on weekends you'll either find them at smaller, low-key bars and lounges, or huddled in their apartments with Netflix and takeout Chinese.

When you do hit one of the superswanky spots in Chelsea or the Meatpacking District, don't over- or underdress. If you're female, don't confuse "dressy" with "formal"; leave the cocktail dress at home and go for something casually sexy: tight designer jeans, a classy-yet-revealing top, a fabulous handbag, and expensive heels are almost always a safe bet. If you're a guy, don't imagine that you can dress like the hip-hop artists you see on MTV; Pharrell may get past the doormen wearing slouchy jeans, sneakers, and a hoodie, but he's Pharrell. You—and pardon us for making assumptions here, it's what we exclusive-club types tend to do—are not.

SITTING IN A TV AUDIENCE

Tickets to tapings of TV shows are free, but can be very hard to come by on short notice. Most shows accept advance requests by e-mail, phone, or online—but for the most popular shows, like *The Daily Show with Jon Stewart,* the request backlog is so deep you might even have to wait a few months before they'll accept any new ones. Same-day standby tickets are often available—but be prepared to wait in line for several hours, sometimes starting at 5 or 6 AM, depending on how hot the show is, or the wattage of that day's celebrity guests.

The Shows

The Daily Show with Jon Stewart. The smirking, amiable, and incisive Jon Stewart pokes fun at news headlines on this half-hour cable show. The program tapes from Monday through Thursday; you can request advance tickets by e-mailing the studio or by checking the calendar on the Web site. For standby tickets, show up well before the 5:45 PM doors-open time. Audience members must be 18 or older. ⊠*733 11th Ave., between W. 51st and W. 52nd Sts., Midtown West* ☎*212/586–2477* ⊕*www.thedaily show.com* ✉ *requesttickets@thedaily show.com* Ⓜ *C, E to 50th St.*

The Martha Stewart Show. Master baker, craft-maker, and champion of all "good things," Martha Stewart hosts her show with a live studio audience and various celebrity guests. The program generally tapes weekdays at both 10 AM and 2 PM. You can request tickets through the Martha Stewart Web site. Often, show producers are recruiting for groups of people (like nurses, new moms, or brides-to-be) and if you fit that category, your chances of scoring tickets increase. Occasionally, two hours prior to showtime, standby tickets are given out. Audience members must be at least 10 years old. ⊠*221 W. 26th St., between 7th and 8th Ave., Chelsea* ☎*212/727–1234* ⊕*www.marthastewart.com* Ⓜ *C or 1 to 23rd St.*

Good Morning America. Diane Sawyer, Robin Roberts, Chris Cuomo, and Sam Champion host this early-morning news and entertainment standby. *GMA* airs live, weekdays from 7 AM to 9 AM, and ticket requests (online only) should be sent four to six months in advance. ⊠*7 Times Sq., at W. 44th St. and Broadway, Midtown West* ☎*212/456–7384* ⊕*www.abcnews.go.com/GMA* Ⓜ *1, 2, 3, 7, N, Q, R, W, S to 42nd St./Times Sq.*

Late Night with Jimmy Fallon. We still miss Conan O'Brien, but Jimmy Fallon has a few things going for him, namely "Slow Jamming the News" with the Roots. For tickets, call the **Ticket Information Line** (☎*212/664–3056*) for a maximum of four tickets in advance. Single standby tickets are available on taping days—Monday through Friday—at the West 49th Street side of 30 Rockefeller Plaza; arrive before 9 AM. You must be 17 years or older. ⊠*NBC Studios, 30 Rockefeller Plaza, between W. 49th and W. 50th Sts., Midtown West* Ⓜ *B, D, F, V to 47th–50th Sts./Rockefeller Center.*

The Late Show with David Letterman. Letterman's famously offbeat humor and wacky top-10 lists have had fans giggling for more than two decades. Call 212/247–6497 starting at 11 AM on tape days—Monday through Thursday—for standby tickets. For advance tickets (two maximum), you can submit a request online or fill out an application in person at the theater. You must be 18 or older to sit in the audience. ⊠*Ed Sullivan Theater, 1697 Broadway, between*

W. 53rd and W. 54th Sts., Midtown West ☏212/975–5853 ⊕ www.lateshow.cbs.com Ⓜ 1, C, E to 50th St.; B, D, E to 7th Ave.

Live! with Regis and Kelly. The sparks fly on this morning program, which books an eclectic roster of guests. Standby tickets become available weekdays at 7 AM at the **ABC Studios** (⊠ 7 Lincoln Sq., corner of W. 67th St. and Columbus Ave., Upper West Side). Otherwise, write for tickets (four tickets maximum) a full year in advance or fill out a form online. Children under 10 aren't allowed in the audience. ✑ Live Tickets, Ansonia Station, Box 230-777, 10023 ☏212/456–3054 Ⓜ 1 to 66th St./Lincoln Center.

Saturday Night Live. Influential from the start, *SNL* continues to captivate audiences. Standby tickets—only one per person—are distributed at 7 AM on the day of the show at the West 49th Street entrance to 30 Rockefeller Plaza. You may ask for a ticket for either the dress rehearsal (8 PM) or the live show (11:30 PM). Requests for advance tickets (two per applicant) must be submitted by e-mail only in August to snltickets@nbcuni.com; recipients are determined by lottery. You must be 16 or older to sit in the audience. ⊠ NBC Studios, Saturday Night Live, 30 Rockefeller Plaza, between W. 49th and W. 50th Sts., Midtown West ☏212/664–3056 Ⓜ B, D, F, V to 47th–50th Sts./Rockefeller Center.

Today. America's first morning talk–news show airs weekdays from 7 AM to 10 AM in the glass-enclosed, ground-level NBC studio across from its original home at 30 Rockefeller Plaza. You may well be spotted on TV by friends back home while you're standing behind anchors Meredith Vieira and Matt Lauer (if you bring a funny sign, you're more likely to catch the cameraman's attention). ⊠ Rockefeller Plaza at W. 49th St., Midtown West Ⓜ B, D, F, V to 47th–50th Sts./Rockefeller Center.

TIPS

Prepare to have your pockets and bags checked before you enter. You may be told you can't bring your camera inside. Snapping a shot during a show, even with a camera phone, is forbidden.

Wear layers: TV studios blast the air-conditioning.

Sitting in a TV audience can be more boring than watching the show at home. You'll have to wait intermittently while sets are changed and stars' makeup refreshed; if your seats are in back, you may feel far from the action.

Audience laughter is carefully orchestrated. There will be "Applause" signs signaling when to clap and staffers gesturing for you to laugh louder.

NEW YORK CITY FOR FREE

If you think everything in New York costs too much, well, you're right—almost. In fact, the city has tons of free attractions and activities; you just need to know where to look for them. Choose from our list of favorite freebies, below.

Outdoor Fun

Walk across the Brooklyn Bridge for a spectacular view of the Financial District, Brooklyn, the seaport, and Manhattan.

Ride the Staten Island ferry to see the Statue of Liberty, Ellis Island, and the southern tip of Manhattan from the water. Check out the spiffy Whitehall terminal in Manhattan, completed in 2005 after a $200 million renovation. The ferry is popular as an inexpensive date spot—the cafeteria onboard is a surprisingly inexpensive place to buy beer and snacks. Ⓜ *1 to South Ferry; 4, 5 to Bowling Green.*

Catch a free movie screening in Bryant Park in summertime. A tradition since 1992, watching films alfresco surrounded by tall Midtown buildings is a summertime rite of passage for New Yorkers. Bring a blanket and a picnic basket, and be prepared to stake out a good spot on the lawn well in advance. The park runs from 40th to 42nd streets between 5th and 6th avenues; movie schedules are posted on ⊕ *www.bryantpark.org.* Ⓜ *B, D, F, V to 42nd St.*

Wander Battery Park City's waterfront promenade; the breeze and passing boats will make you forget you're in the gritty city, though the view of the Statue of Liberty will remind you that you couldn't be anywhere but New York. Ⓜ *4, 5 to Bowling Green; 1 to South Ferry.*

Kayak on the Hudson; the Downtown Boathouse gives free lessons and paddling tours. There's even an indoor-swimming-pool program to hone kayaking skills in winter months. The boats are distributed on a first-come, first-served basis, so cloudy days and early mornings are the best times to avoid the crowds. ⊠ *Pier 40 at Houston St.* ⊕ *www.downtownboathouse.org* Ⓜ *B, D, F, V to 47th–50th Sts./ Rockefeller Center.*

Taste the goods at the Union Square greenmarket (on Monday, Wednesday, Friday, and Saturday), where farmers offer samples of their organically grown produce, artisanal cheeses, and fresh bread. The greenmarket, a hip outing for all, is often filled with families shopping for dinner, famous chefs choosing ingredients, and foodies stalking Food Network hosts.

Stroll the Coney Island boardwalk for some old-school kitsch (before it's redeveloped into swanky condos). There are also plenty of annual events for free here, including the outrageous Mermaid Parade and the Fourth of July hot-dog-eating contest. Ⓜ *B, F, N, Q to Stillwell Ave.*

Check out the street performers around New York's parks: break-dancing crews in Union Square, ragtime duets in Central Park, nutty unicyclists in Washington Square. Buskers in the subway are better than you'd expect—in order to perform, they must first be vetted by an MTA committee, with the top performers assigned to the busiest subway stops.

Smell the cherry blossoms in spring at the Central Park Conservatory; the pathways beneath the blossoming trees are gorgeous, and much closer than the botanical gardens in the outer boroughs. ⊠ *5th Ave. at 105th St.* Ⓜ *6 to 103rd.*

Music, Theater and Dance

Watch tango dancers and jazz musicians *outside* Lincoln Center at the annual month-long Out of Doors festival, held in August. It includes more than 100 performances of spoken word, beat boxing, and bigwigs like Dave Brubeck and Arlo Guthrie. Ⓜ*1 to 66th St./Lincoln Center.*

Hit Central Park Summerstage for big-name performers like Afrobeat bandleader Seun Kuti and Columbia's own Vampire Weekend.

Catch rising stars in classical music, drama, and dance at the Juilliard School's free student concerts (check ⊕ *www.juilliard. edu* for a calendar of events). Free tickets are available at the Juilliard box office for theater performances; there's also a line for standby an hour before the show. Smaller acts don't require tickets beforehand. ✉*144 W. 65th St.* Ⓜ*1 to 66th St./ Lincoln Center.*

Entertain thyself at Shakespeare in the Park, one of New York City's most beloved events—80,000 watch each year. It's been going strong since 1962, and shows usually feature celebrities earning their olde English acting chops. Get in line early at the Public Theater for a shot at tickets, or head to the Delacorte Theater in Central Park. ✉*425 Lafayette St.* Ⓜ*6 to Astor Pl.*

Get gratis giggles at the Upright Citizens Brigade Theatre's comedy shows. The theater has moved a few times since 1999, but the improv comedy, inspired by Chicago's Second City, remains sharp regardless of location. Professional comedians, including UCB cofounder and Saturday Night Live alumna Amy Poehler, are sprinkled in with amateurs during the shows. ✉*307 W. 26th St.* ⊕*www.ucbtheatre.com* Ⓜ*A, C, E to 23rd St.*

Art, Lit and Architecture

Visit the Metropolitan Museum of Art; if you'll believe it, the $20 entry fee is really a suggested donation. You can pay as much, or as little, as you wish. Smaller donations may get some eye-rolling from the cashier, but it's a small price to pay for access to world-famous works. ✉*1000 5th Ave. at 80th St.* ⊕ *www.metmuseum.org* Ⓜ*6 to 86th St.*

Browse through the galleries scattered throughout the city. Chelsea's full of expensive galleries with superstar artists, though things get edgier the closer you get to the West Side Highway; you'll also find a busy, if self-involved, art scene in Williamsburg, Brooklyn.

Marvel at Grand Central Terminal's spectacular main concourse; the ceiling painted with the constellations of the zodiac is one of the city's treasures. Ⓜ*4, 5, 6 to Grand Central/42nd St.*

Attend a reading at one of the city's hundreds of bookstores. Night owls shouldn't feel left out—they can attend readings of their own at bars like the Half King in Chelsea or Pete's Candy Store in Brooklyn.

Explore the new MoMA on Friday between 4 and 8 PM, when the $20 entry fee is waived during Target Free Friday Nights. Tickets are not available in advance, so plan to wait in line. ✉*11 W. 53rd St., between 5th and 6th Aves.* ⊕ *www.moma.org* Ⓜ*E, V to 5th Ave./53rd St.; B, D, F to 47-50th St./Rockefeller Center.*

CHOW DOWN CHINATOWN WALK

The knockoffs lining Canal Street only represent the surface of Chinatown, but many New Yorkers rarely venture past this; cultural differences and a language barrier can be intimidating to the uninitiated. Thankfully the language of food is universal, so spend the day strolling while partaking in local snacks. By the end of this walk, you'll be both a confident Chinatown explorer and blissfully sated!

Classic Chinatown: Canal Street, Tai Chi, and Bubble Tea

Start out at Canal Street, the most bustling strip in Chinatown. After running this gauntlet of knockoff handbags and perfumes, head one block south to the tidy, English-labeled **Dragon Land Bakery** (125 Walker St.) to indulge in Chinese baked goods such as a brioche-like sweet bean bun. Pastry in-hand, turn right at Mulberry St. to stroll past produce carts piled high. At the corner of Bayard St. you'll find **Columbus Park,** where you can spot people warming up with Tai Chi or playing "Chinese chess." Cross down on Mott St. and take a left on Pell. To the right is Doyers St., a dogleg dubbed "the Bloody Angle" because of gang warfare at the beginning of the 20th Century. It's home to the neighborhood's oldest dim sum restaurant, **Nam Wah Tea Parlor** (13 Doyers). Loop around on Bowery. At Bayard, there's usually a small stand selling Hong Kong cakes: light, sweet balls that taste like mini pancakes. They're irresistible at 15 for a dollar. If you need something to wash them down, head back half a block on Bayard to **Vivi Bubble Tea** (49 Bayard Street), a cheerful storefront selling bubble tea (tea or fruit drinks with tapioca balls) and popcorn chicken dusted with flavorings like basil or curry. Fortified, cross up north onto Elizabeth Street where you'll continue to spot seafood markets crowding the sidewalks; weave around the buckets of twitchy crabs.

Sweet and Sour Strolling

On Hester, just off Elizabeth, you'll find **Munchies Paradise** candy store (167 Hester). Help yourself to samples from dried squid to a dozen kinds of fermented plums, then get a bag of your favorites for on-the-go snacking. Continue north on Mott to the **Banh Mi Saigon Bakery** (138-01 Mott St.). Inside, it's a classic Chinatown mashup: jewelry store up front/lunch counter at the back selling Banh Mi Vietnamese sandwiches—baguettes with pickled vegetables, cilantro, and assorted meats. On Grand, you may smell the **Kam Wo** tea store (211 Grand St.) before you even set foot inside. The medicinal loose teas and soups stocked here are prescribed to improve vision or soothe aching joints.

The Sights—and Smells—of Chinatown

On the corner of Grand and the Bowery is the **Tu Quyn Pharmacy** (230 Grand), displaying an impressive selection of durian, a spiky fruit with a strong odor, available for the adventurous to sample. Continuing on Grand you'll pass the **Ocean Star** (250 Grand St.), a slightly more spacious seafood market to explore if you're traveling in a group. Finally, cross Chrystie St. and rest your feet at **Vanessa's Dumpling House** (118A Eldridge) with ample seating and inexpensive options like sesame fried bread stuffed with Peking Duck for less than $3.   —Alexander Basek

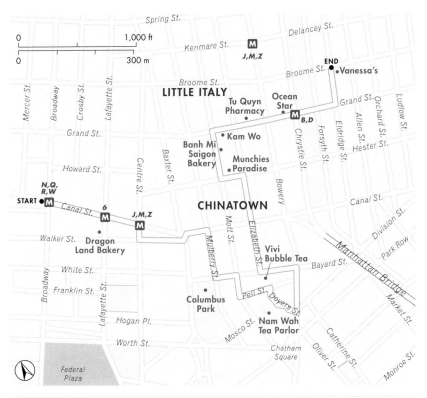

Where to Start:	Canal Street, especially if you want to shop first.
Length:	2 mi (about 3 hours with lots of stops for nibbling)
Where to Stop:	Columbus Park is nice for sitting if the weather is good; Nam Wah is worth seeing if the weather is not.
Best Time to Go:	Noon on the dot, when the foods are fresh and the lines are shortest.
Worst Time to Go:	Sunday afternoons, when the crowds are oppressive, or on hot days, when the asphalt and fish markets are odiferous.
Highlights:	Munchies Paradise, Banh Mi Saigon Bakery, Columbus Park

SIGHTSEEING NEW YORK CITY

Taking a guided tour is a good idea, even if you generally prefer flying solo. For one thing, it will help you get your bearings in this often overwhelming city; for another, it's a great way to investigate out-of-the-way areas where you might not venture on your own, or learn about a particular facet of the city's history, inhabitants, or architecture.

Boat Tours

In good weather a **Circle Line Cruise** (*Pier 83 at W. 42nd St., Midtown West 212/563–3200 www.circleline42.com*) around Manhattan island is one of the best ways to get oriented in the city. Once you've finished the three-hour, 35-mi circumnavigation, you'll have a good sense of where things are and what you want to see next. The cruises run at least once daily; the cost is $31 per person (there's also a shorter, "semi-Circle" option available for $27).

If you're after a more historical experience, the *Shearwater* (*North Cove Marina, Lower Manhattan 10280 212/619–0885 www.shearwatersailing.com*), an 82-foot yacht dating from the 1920s, sails from the North Cove Marina at the World Financial Center and makes two-hour public sails from mid-April through mid-October during the day, at sunset, and for Sunday brunch. Reservations can only be made a maximum of two weeks in advance, and are advised. Fares start at $45.

Bus Tours

Gray Line New York (*777 8th Ave., between 47th and 48th Sts., Midtown 1 www.graylinenewy*mber of "hop-on, hop-r bus tours in various ng a downtown Man-er Manhattan loop, a

Brooklyn loop, and evening tours of the city. Packages include entrance fees to attractions.

Walking Tours

The wisecracking PhD candidates of **Big Onion Walking Tours** (*212/439–1090 www.bigonion.com*) lead themed tours such as "Irish New York" and "Jewish Lower East Side," as well as famous multiethnic eating tours and guided walks through every neighborhood from Harlem to the Financial District and Brooklyn. Tours run daily and cost $15; there's a slight additional fee for the eating tours.

The knowledgeable **Joyce Gold** (*212/242–5762 www.nyctours.com*) has been conducting neighborhood walking tours since 1976. Her theme walks like "Gangs of New York and the Bloody Five Points," and "Hell Ain't Hot: This Here's Hell's Kitchen," run on weekends and cost $15.

The **Municipal Art Society** (*212/935–3960, 212/439–1049 recorded information www.mas.org*) conducts a series of daily walking tours, which emphasize the architecture and history of particular neighborhoods. The cost is $15 per person.

New York City Cultural Walking Tours (*212/979–2388 www.nycwalk.com*) have covered such topics as buildings' gargoyles and the Millionaire's Mile of 5th Avenue. Tours run every Sunday from March to December; private tours can be scheduled throughout the week at $60 per hour with.

The **Urban Park Rangers** (*866/692–4295 www.nycgovparks.org*) conduct free weekend walks and workshops.

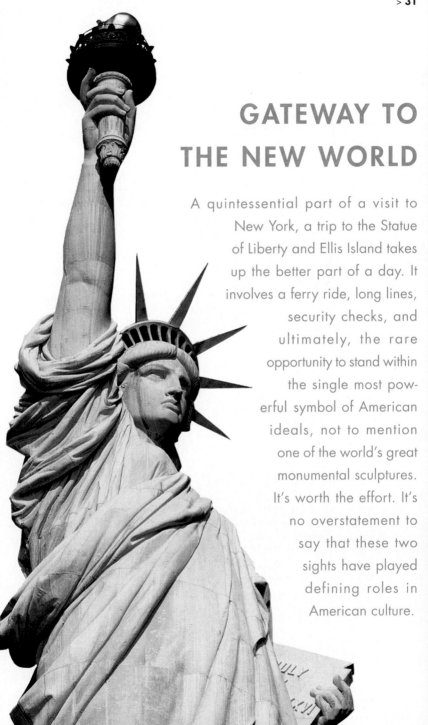

GATEWAY TO THE NEW WORLD

A quintessential part of a visit to New York, a trip to the Statue of Liberty and Ellis Island takes up the better part of a day. It involves a ferry ride, long lines, security checks, and ultimately, the rare opportunity to stand within the single most powerful symbol of American ideals, not to mention one of the world's great monumental sculptures. It's worth the effort. It's no overstatement to say that these two sights have played defining roles in American culture.

THE STATUE OF LIBERTY

Impressive from the shore, the Statue of Liberty is majestic in person and up close. For millions of immigrants, the first glimpse of America was the Statue of Liberty. You get a taste of the thrill they must have experienced as you approach Liberty Island on the ferry from Battery Park and witness the statue grow from a vaguely defined figure on the horizon into a towering, stately colossus.

What's Here

The statue itself stands atop an 89-foot pedestal designed by American Richard Morris Hunt, with Emma Lazarus's sonnet "The New Colossus" ("Give me your tired, your poor, your huddled masses yearning to breathe free . . ."). This massive pedestal section is now the only area to which visitors have access, and only with timed tickets and after an extensive security check.

Inside the pedestal is an informative and entertaining museum. Highlights include the torch's original glass flame that was replaced because of water damage (the current flame is 24-karat gold and lit at night by floodlights), full-scale copper replicas of Lady Liberty's face and one of her feet, Bartholdi's alternative designs for the statue, and a model of Eiffel's intricate framework.

The observatory platform is a great place for a photo op; you're 16 stories high with all of Lower Manhattan spread out in front of you. You'll then descend to the promenade at the bottom of the base, where you're still four stories high. Be aware that to reach the platform you'll need to walk up 26 steps from the elevator drop-off point.

Liberty Island has a pleasant outdoor café for refueling as well as a large cafeteria. The gift shop sells trinkets little better than those available from street vendors.

Know Before You Go

You're allowed access to the museum only as part of one of the free tours of the promenade (which surrounds the base of the pedestal) or the observatory (at the pedestal's top). The tours are limited to 3,000 participants a day. To guarantee a spot on one of the tours, you must order tickets ahead of time—they can be reserved up to one year in advance, by phone or over the Internet. There are a limited amount of same-day standby tickets available at the Castle Clinton and Liberty State Park ticket offices.

Once you reach the island, there are no tickets available. And without a ticket, there is absolutely no admittance into the museum or observatory. You can get a good look at the statue's inner structure on the observatory tour through glass viewing windows that look straight into the statue. Be sure to try the view from several different viewing spots to get the whole interior. There has been no access to the torch since 1916, however the park service now offers limited access by lottery to the statue's crown.

Liberty Highlights

■ The surreal chance to stand next to, and be dwarfed by, the original glass torch and the copper cast of Lady Liberty's foot.

■ The vistas of New York from the observatory platform.

■ The rare opportunity to look up the skirt of a national monument.

Statue Basics

☎ 212/363-3200,
212/269-5755
ferry information;
877/523-9849 ticket
reservations

🌐 www.statuecruises.com

🎫 Free; ferry $12.00
round-trip

🕐 Daily 9 AM–5:00; extended
hours in summer.

Liberty helicopters

VIEWS OF THE CROWN
Some unique ways to see
Lady Liberty:

**Rise in the Ritz-Carlton
New York Battery Park:**
A swank cocktail lounge 14
stories high with straight
sight lines to the statue.

Liberty Helicopter: Sightseeing tours that fly over the
crown and torch (⇨ Chapter
1, Sightseeing Tours).

Kayak: Free kayak tours of
the harbor depart from the
NYC Downtown Boathouse
(See Smart Travel Tips,
Sports & the Outdoors).

FAST FACT: To move
the Statue of Liberty from
its initial home on a Paris
rooftop to its final home
in the New York Harbor,
the statue was broken
down into 350 individual
pieces and packed in
214 crates. It took four
months to reassemble it.

FAST FACT: The
face of Lady Liberty
is actually a likeness
of sculptor Frederic-
Auguste Bartholdi's
mother—quite a tribute.

FAST FACT: *Liberty Enlightening
the World*, as the statue is officially
named, was presented to the United
States in 1886 as a gift from France
to celebrate the centennial of the
United States, a symbol of unity
and friendship between the two
countries. The 152-foot-tall figure
was sculpted by Frederic-Auguste
Bartholdi and erected around an
iron skeleton engineered by Gustav
Eiffel (the same Eiffel who would
later create the Eiffel Tower).

Foundation of
the pedestal to
torch: 305′6″

Heel to top
head: 111′6″

ELLIS ISLAND

Chances are you'll be with a crowd of international tourists as you disembark at Ellis Island. Close your eyes for a moment and imagine the jostling crowd 100 times larger. Now picture that your journey has lasted weeks at sea and that your daypack contains all your worldly possessions, including all your money. You're hungry, tired, jobless, and homeless. This scenario just begins to set the stage for the story of the millions of poor immigrants who passed through Ellis Island at the turn of the 20th century. Between 1892 and 1924, approximately 12 million men, women, and children first set foot on U.S. soil at the Ellis Island federal immigration facility. By the time the facility closed in 1954, it had processed ancestors of more than 40% of Americans living today.

What's Here

The island's main building, now a national monument, reopened in 1990 as the Ellis Island Immigration Museum, containing more than 30 galleries of artifacts, photographs, and taped oral histories. The centerpiece of the museum is the white-tile Registry Room (also known as the Great Hall). It feels dignified and cavernous today, but photographs show that it took on a multitude of configurations through the years, always packed with humanity undergoing one form of screening or another. While you're there, take a look out the Registry Room's tall, arched windows and try to imagine what passed through immigrants' minds as they viewed lower Manhattan's skyline to one side and the Statue of Liberty to the other.

Along with the Registry Room, the museum's features include the ground-level Railroad Ticket Office, which has several interactive exhibits and a three-dimensional graphic representation of American immigration patterns; the American Family Immigration Center, where for a fee you can search Ellis Island's records for your own ancestors; and, outside, the American Immigrant Wall of Honor, where the names of more than 600,000 immigrant Americans are inscribed along a promenade facing the Manhattan skyline.

The gift shop has a selection of international dolls, candies, and crafts. You can also personalize a number of registry items here as well.

Making the Most of Your Visit

Because there's so much to take in, it's a good idea to make use of the museum's interpretive tools. Check at the visitor desk for free film tickets, ranger tour times, and special programs.

Consider starting your visit with a viewing of the free film *Island of Hope, Island of Tears.* A park ranger starts off with a short introduction, then the 25-minute film takes you through an immigrant's journey from the troubled conditions of European life (especially true for ethnic and religious minorities), to their nervous arrival at Ellis Island, and their introduction into American cities. The film is a primer into all the exhibits and will deeply enhance your experience.

The audio tour ($6) is also worthwhile: it takes you through the exhibits, providing thorough, engaging commentary interspersed with recordings of immigrants themselves recalling their experiences.

Ellis Island Highlights

- Surveying the Great Hall.

- The moving film *Island of Hope, Island of Tears.*

- Listening to the voices of actual immigrants who risked their lives to come to America.

- Reading the names on the American Immigrant Wall of Honor.

- Researching your own family's history.

Ellis Island Basics

☎ 212/363–3200 Ellis
  Island; 212/561–4500
  Wall of Honor
  information
⊕ www.ellisisland.org
🎟 Free; ferry $12.00
  round-trip
⊙ Daily 9–5:00; extended
  hours in summer.

IMMIGRANT HISTORY TIMELINE

Starting in the 1880s, troubled conditions throughout Europe persuaded both the poor and the persecuted to leave their family and homes to embark on what were often gruesome journeys to come to the golden shores of America.

1880s 5.7 million immigrants arrive in U.S.

1892 Federal immigration station opens on Ellis Island in January.

1901–1910 8.8 million immigrants arrive in U.S.; 6 million processed at Ellis Island.

1907 Highest number of immigrants (860,000) arrives in one year, including a record 11,747 on April 17.

1910 75% of the residents of New York, Chicago, Detroit, Cleveland, and Boston are now immigrants or children of immigrants.

1920s Federal laws set immigration quotas based on national origin.

1954 Ellis Island immigration station is closed.

Ellis Island: New arrivals line up to have their papers examined. ca. 1880 – 1910.

FAST FACT: Some immigrants who passed through Ellis Island later became household names. A few include Charles Atlas (1903, Italy); Irving Berlin (1893, Russia); Frank Capra (1903, Italy); Bob Hope (1908, England); Knute Rockne (1893, Norway); and Baron Von Trapp and his family (1938, Germany).

FAST FACT: In 1897, a fire destroyed the original pine immigration structure on Ellis Island, including all immigration records dating back to 1855.

FAST FACT: Only third-class, or "steerage," passengers were sent to Ellis Island. Affluent first- and second-class passengers, who were less likely to be ill or become wards of the state, were processed on board and allowed to disembark in Manhattan.

Four immigrants and their belongings, on a dock, look out over the water; view from behind.

PLANNING

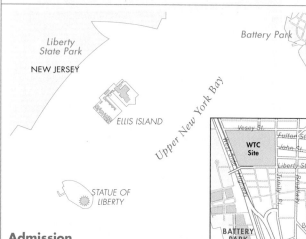

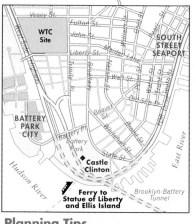

Admission

There's no admission fee for either sight, but the ferry ride, run by Statue Cruises, costs $12.00 ($20.00 with an audio tour). Ferries leaving from **Battery Park** (See Chapter 2) every half hour take you to both islands. (Note that large packages and oversize bags and backpacks aren't permitted on board.) Reserve tickets in advance online—you'll still have to wait in line, both to pick up the tickets and to board the ferry, but you'll be able to pick up a Monument Pass allowing you access to the pedestal of the statue, the museum, and the statue's interior structure. There is no fee for the Monument Pass and you cannot enter inside the statue without it.

Where to Catch the Ferry

Broadway and Battery Pl., Lower Manhattan Ⓜ Subway: 4, 5 to Bowling Green.

When in New Jersey

Directly on the other side of the Hudson River from Battery Park, Liberty State Park is an impressive stretch of green with ample parking and quick ferries to the monuments. Lines are almost never an issue here, something that can't be said about the New York side.

Planning Tips

Buy tickets in advance. This is the only way to assure that you'll have tickets to actually enter the Statue of Liberty museum and observatory platform.

Be prepared for intense security. At the ferry security check, you will need to remove your coat; at the statue, you will need to remove your coat as well as your belt, watch, and any metal accessories. At this writing, no strollers, large umbrellas, or backpacks are allowed in the statue.

Check ferry schedules in advance. Before you go, check www.statuecruises.com.

Keep in mind that even though the last entry time for the monument is at 4:30 PM, **the last ferry to the Statue of Liberty and Ellis Island is at 3:30 PM.** You need to arrive by at least 3 PM (to allow for security checks and lines) if you want to make the last ferry of the day.

Lower Manhattan

WITH CHINATOWN AND TRIBECA

WORD OF MOUTH

"While Canal Street is a 'main drag' of Chinatown, try Mott St. or Mulberry St. south of Canal for the smaller shops and restaurants that most people would associate with Chinatown."

—ellenem

GETTING ORIENTED

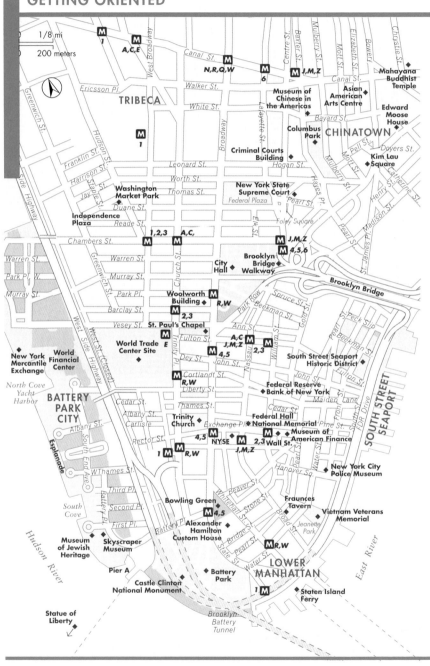

AMBROSE

MAKING THE MOST OF YOUR TIME

Visit Lower Manhattan during business hours on a weekday to capture the district's true vitality—but expect to be jostled on the crowded sidewalks if you stand still too long—or walk too slowly. On weekends you could feel like a lone explorer in a canyon of buildings. The neighborhood all but shuts down in the evening; conclude your visit by watching the sunset on the Hudson River.

GETTING HERE

Many subway lines service this area. The Fulton Street Broadway–Nassau station, serviced by nine different subway lines, puts you within walking distance of City Hall, South Street Seaport, and the World Trade Center site (⇨ *Ground Zero essay in this chapter*).

If Chinatown is your downtown destination, don't even think of driving here—the area's cramped streets and heavy congestion make this an exceptionally tough place to navigate. The subway is a better idea, with the J, M, N, R, Q, W, Z, and 6 (Canal Street) and the B and D (Grand Street) all serving the area. The 1 subway line stops in the heart of TriBeCa (Franklin Street).

WORD OF MOUTH (WWW.FODORS.COM/FORUMS)

"Ground Zero is what you expect. A large building site surrounded by hawkers and gawkers. I didn't want to go there. Much more moving is St. Paul's [Chapel]. Firefighters and rescue workers used it as a base in the tragic days after 9/11 and there are small memorials and exhibitions inside. It's extremely heart wrenching but I would advise people to visit there to get an uplifting example of what the human spirit can achieve and rescue from utter tragedy. We were all moved to tears by it."

—MacSporran

FODOR'S CHOICE

Brooklyn Bridge
Columbus Park
South Street Seaport
Washington Market Park

TOP ATTRACTIONS

Kim Lau Square
New York Stock Exchange
Staten Island Ferry

TOP EXPERIENCES

Visiting Ground Zero
Taste-testing Chinatown's dim sum
Touring Ellis Island (⇨ Ch. 1)
Strolling TriBeCa's Harrison Street
Relaxing on Pier 17's deck at South Street Seaport

BEST FOR KIDS

Castle Clinton
Seaport Museum
Washington Market Park

NEARBY MUSEUMS (⇨ CH. 14)

Asian American Arts Centre
Museum of American Finance
Museum of Jewish Heritage
National Museum of the American Indian
New York City Police Museum
Skyscraper Museum

AREA SHOPS (⇨ CH. 17)

Century 21
City Store

WHERE TO EAT (⇨ CH. 18)

Delmonico's
Harry's Steak

Sightseeing
★★★★★
Nightlife
★
Dining
★★
Lodging
★★
Shopping
★

Updated by
Michelle Delio

Pirates, rogue politicians, upwardly mobile go-getters, robber barons, scrappy entrepreneurs, and roaming packs of pigs scouring the streets for garbage: no, this is not the group photo for any given presidential administration. Rather, this is the citizenry that built and inhabited the southern tip of Manhattan in various eras, and in varying combinations.

Lower Manhattan, or in the parlance of New Yorkers emphatically giving directions to tourists, "all the way downtown," has long been where the action—or transaction—is. Back when the neighborhood was the village of New Amsterdam (1626–47), its roguish director-general, Peter Minuit, did the quintessential deal on behalf of the Dutch, trading knives, tools, and cloth to an Algonquian tribe, the Canarsees, for all of Manhattan (the market price of $24 is more or less an urban myth). In 1789, a year before New York City would lose its title as America's capital, George Washington was sworn in as the nation's first president at Federal Hall, where, two years later, Congress would ratify the Bill of Rights.

Little is left from Manhattan's colonial era, however: apart from a precious few structures built in the 1700s, the 19th-century brick facades of South Street Seaport are about as old as it gets here. As you'll notice immediately, the neighborhood has largely given way to the sometimes intimidating (and on weekends, seemingly deserted) skyscraper-lined canyons of Wall Street and lower Broadway. Bounded by the East and Hudson rivers to the east and west, respectively, and by Chambers Street and Battery Park to the north and south, this is an area you can fully and best appreciate by walking its streets.

You'll want to see what's here, but above all you'll want to see what's not, most notably in that empty but evolving gulf among skyscrapers: Ground Zero. As you tour the area, refer to our feature in this chapter to deepen your understanding of the devastation rendered by the brutal 9/11 attacks and get a glimpse of the future plans for the site.

The southern tip has often served as a microcosm for a city that offers as many first shots as it does second chances, so it's appropriate that it's the key point of departure for the Statue of Liberty and Ellis Island *(⇨ our feature in Chapter 1)*. This experience should never be underestimated as too touristy a way to spend a day. Like nothing else, the excursion will remind you that we're a city of immigrants and survivors.

The city's downtown neighborhoods give you a close-up view of some of the many cultures of Manhattan. Tucked to the west, south of Canal Street, residential TriBeCa has a quieter vibe and still owes much of its cred to Robert De Niro, whose investments in the area include the TriBeCa Grill and the nonprofit TriBeCa Film Center. Unlike nearby SoHo and NoLita's in-your-face commercial presence, TriBeCa keeps more to itself with self-assurance and urban grace. And although TriBeCa's money is hidden away behind grand industrial facades, you can get a taste of it at one of the posh neighborhood restaurants or when the stars turn out for the annual TriBeCa Film Festival in spring.

Chinatown, by contrast, is a living, breathing, anything-but-quiet ethnic enclave: a quarter of the city's 400,000 Chinese residents live here above storefronts crammed with souvenir shops and restaurants serving every imaginable regional Chinese cuisine, from modest dumplings to sumptuous Hong Kong feasts. What started as a 7-block area has morphed into more than 40 blocks above and below Canal Street with tea shops, restaurants, Buddhist temples, herbalists, acupuncturists, and pungent open-air markets.

THE FINANCIAL DISTRICT, THE SEAPORT, AND THE WORLD TRADE CENTER AREA

THREE WAYS TO EXPLORE

THE BATTERY'S DOWN

The best piece of navigational advice about the city still resides in the tune, "New York, New York" (the one from the musical *On the Town*): "The Bronx is up and the Battery's down." But once you head down (take the 4 or 5 train to the Bowling Green stop at Broadway and Battery Place; the 1 train to South Ferry, or the R or W train to Whitehall) you'll want a clue about what's actually down here.

Perhaps mercifully, after all your walking as well as standing on buses and trains with no available seats, Battery Park has plenty of places to sit, including two tiers of wood benches that line the promenade facing New York Harbor. On a reasonably clear day you'll be able to see Governors Island, a former Coast Guard installation now managed by the National Park Service; a hilly Staten Island in the distance; the Statue of Liberty; Ellis Island; and the old railway terminal in Liberty State Park, on the mainland in Jersey City, New Jersey. On crystal-clear days you can see all the way to Port Elizabeth's cranes, which seem to mimic Lady Liberty's stance.

Your key point of interest within the park is **Castle Clinton National Monument,** once a fort intended as a defense against the British, though the castle's cannons were never fired in war. The building saw far more

Where can I find...?

COFFEE	Financier Patisserie 62 Stone St. Swell joe, pastries, and soups.	Klatch Coffee Bar 9-11 Maiden La. Caffeine addicts and vegans will be pleased.
A QUICK BITE	Adrienne's Pizza Bar 54 Stone St. Quality slices, right in the Financial District.	Chinatown Ice Cream Factory 65 Bayard St. Sample almond cookie, green tea, or mango flavors.
COCKTAILS	Church Lounge 2 6th Ave., near White St. Attracts a celeb crowd with 30+ signature cocktails.	Rise 2 West St. Statue of Liberty views from the Ritz-Carlton's 14th floor.

action in later centuries as an opera house, an aquarium, and a processing center for immigrants. In 2005 the Bosque gardens by landscape artist Piet Oudulf were opened, as was the Spiral Fountain, with 35 illuminated and interactive jets. Adjoining Battery Park on this western side is Robert F. Wagner Jr. Park, which has public bathrooms and a restaurant-café.

Perhaps most relevant for your purposes, within Castle Clinton is the ticket office for ferries to the Statue of Liberty and Ellis Island; catch the ferries to both at the west end of the park.

The northern tip of Battery Park skims **Bowling Green,** New York's first public park. In the 18th century New Yorkers rioted periodically in the park. The most notable brouhaha involved the knocking down and beheading of a statue of King George III that was once the park's centerpiece. The statue was melted into bullets used in the Revolutionary War. But you can still see traces of the riot; every 12th post on the fence that surrounds the park is a bit mangled. These spikes were once surmounted by gold crowns, which the mob gleefully wrenched off during the riot. On Bowling Green's south side a warren of blocks contain additional remnants of New York's colonial history, including **Fraunces Tavern,** established in 1762 and still serving meals (try the apple pie). George Washington was fond of the tavern, and the American Revolution was in part planned here. History buffs will want to view the American Revolution/early New York City collections in the Fraunces Tavern Museum, which includes four 19th-century buildings in addition to the 18th-century Fraunces Tavern building. See the listing below for details.

SHOW ME THE MONEY

Late in the evening of December 15, 1989, sculptor Arturo Di Modica left a 7,000-pound surprise gift for NYC under the Christmas tree in front of the New York Stock Exchange—his bronze *Charging Bull* statue. The bull quickly became the icon of Wall Street. Ask New Yorkers who don't frequent the downtown area where the statue is and they'll usually tell you it's somewhere on Wall Street near the stock exchange. But the statue actually resides in **Bowling Green,** where it was moved after police complained it was blocking traffic in its original location. Since the city never commissioned it, the bull is still officially dubbed a "temporary installation."

After you pose for snapshots with the bull, head northeast to **Wall Street,** one of the most famous thoroughfares in the world. The epicenter of Wall Street is—you guessed it—the **New York Stock Exchange,** at the intersection of Wall and Broad streets. The stock exchange traces its beginnings back to a group of brokers who, in 1792, shortly after Alexander Hamilton issued the first bonds in an attempt to raise money to cover Revolution-caused debt, were in the habit of meeting under a buttonwood tree that once grew on Wall Street. The exchange itself isn't open to visitors, but there is a related museum at the **Federal Hall National Memorial.**

Look at the facade of 23 Wall Street, just across from the exchange. The deep pockmarks and craters were created on September 16, 1920, when, at noon, a horse-drawn wagon packed with explosives detonated in front of the building, killing 33 people and injuring 400. Those responsible were never apprehended and no one ever claimed credit for what was the worst terrorist attack on American soil until the Oklahoma City bombing on April 19, 1995.

Marking Wall Street's far west end is **Trinity Church,** whose parish was founded by King William III of England in 1697. Trinity's burial ground serves as a resting place for a half-dozen notables, including Alexander Hamilton.

THE STREET OF SHIPS

It's hard to see history in Lower Manhattan's rebuilt and bustling streets. But at **South Street Seaport** history is right in your face. The seaport was created to time-warp visitors back to the days when NYC was a bustling nautical town, and it succeeds in part. Its spiffy little fleet does bring you back to the 19th century, when tall ships sailed from South Street, a time when pirates—Captain Kidd had a house near the wharves—and merchants walked the cobblestone streets and warehouses held treasures from exotic ports. What the seaport, in all its scrubbed tourist beauty, does not include among its careful restorations are the gambling houses, brothels, and saloons that were once so common in this area. The infamous Kit Burns once had his "Sportsman's Hall" tavern at 273 Water Street (now a luxury apartment building),

---

BROOKLYN BRIDGE FACTS

- Overall length: 6,016 feet

- Span of twin Gothic-arch towers: 1,595½ feet

- Distance from top of towers to East River: 272 feet

- Distance from roadway to the water: 133 feet

- Number of times the line "If you believe that, I've got a bridge to sell you" is used referring to the Brooklyn Bridge: Infinite

where the popular amusement was watching as big wharf rats were turned loose in a pit to fight.

TOP ATTRACTIONS

Fodor'sChoice
★
Brooklyn Bridge. "A drive-through cathedral" is how the critic James Wolcott describes one of New York's noblest and most recognized landmarks, which spans the East River and connects Manhattan to Brooklyn. A walk across the bridge's promenade—a boardwalk elevated above the roadway and shared by pedestrians, in-line skaters, and bicyclists—takes about 40 minutes from the heart of Brooklyn Heights to Manhattan's civic center. It's well worth traversing for the astounding views. The roadway is supported by a web of steel cables, hung from the towers and attached to block-long anchorages on either shore. Ⓜ *1, 5, 6 to Brooklyn Bridge/City Hall; J, M, Z to Chambers St.; A, C to High St.-Brooklyn Bridge.*

Federal Hall National Memorial. It's a museum now, but this site has a most notable claim: George Washington was sworn in here as the first president of the United States in 1789, when the building was Federal Hall of the new nation. When we lost capital rights to Philadelphia in 1790, Federal Hall reverted to New York's City Hall, then was demolished in 1812 when the present City Hall was completed. The museum within covers 400 years of New York City's history, with a focus on the life and times of what is now the city's Financial District. You can spot this building easily—it was modeled on the Parthenon, and a statue of George Washington is planted quite obtrusively on the steps. ✉ *26 Wall St., at Nassau St., Lower Manhattan* ☎ *212/825–6870* 🆓 *Free* ⊙ *Weekdays 9–5* Ⓜ *2, 3, 4, 5 to Wall St.; A, C to Broadway/Nassau; J, M, Z to Broad St.*

New York Stock Exchange (NYSE). Unfortunately you can't tour it, but it's certainly worth ogling. At the intersection of Wall and Broad streets, the exchange is impossible to miss. The neoclassical building, designed by architect George B. Post., opened on April 22, 1903, has six Corinthian columns supporting a pediment with a sculpture entitled *Integrity Protecting the Works of Man,* featuring a tribute to the then-sources of American prosperity: Agriculture and Mining to the left of Integrity; Science, Industry, and Invention *to the right The Exchange was* one of the world's first air-conditioned buildings. ✉ *11 Wall St. Lower Manhattan* Ⓜ *2, 3, 4, 5 to Wall St.; J, M, Z to Broad St.*

Fodor'sChoice
★
South Street Seaport Historic District. Had this charming cobblestone corner of the city not been declared a historic district in 1977, we have no doubt you'd be glancing indifferently at yet more hyperdeveloped skyscrapers in this spot rather than at the city's largest concentration of early-19th-century commercial buildings. If you've been to either Boston's Quincy Market or Baltimore's Harborplace, you may feel a flash of déjà vu—the same company leased, restored, and adapted the

SHOP SMART

Ignore the lure of the Seaport mall's chain stores. Focus instead on the Seaport Museum's gift shop, a fun repository of local history and nautical goods. Inside the mall, the Metropolitan Museum of Art Store, NY Yankees Clubhouse Shop, and the Van der Plas Gallery also stock local flair.

A mix of old and new: Lower Manhattan's bright lights combine with the seaport's historic ships.

existing buildings, preserving the commercial feel of centuries past. The result blends a quasi-authentic historic district with a homogenous shopping mall.

At the intersection of Fulton and Water streets, the gateway to the seaport, is the **Titanic** Memorial, a small white lighthouse that commemorates the sinking of the RMS *Titanic* in 1912. Beyond the lighthouse, Fulton Street turns into a busy pedestrian mall. On the south side of Fulton is the seaport's architectural centerpiece, **Schermerhorn Row,** a redbrick terrace of Georgian- and Federal-style warehouses and countinghouses built from 1811 to 1812. Some upper floors house gallery space, and the ground floors are occupied by upscale shops, bars, and restaurants.

Also at 12 Fulton Street is the main lobby of the **South Street Seaport Museum** (☎ *212/748–8600* ⊕ *www.southstseaport.org* ⊙ *Apr.–Oct., Tues.–Sun. 10–6; Nov.–Mar., Fri.–Mon. 10–5*), which hosts walking tours, hands-on exhibits, and fantastic creative programs for children, all with a nautical theme. You can purchase tickets ($10) at either 12 Fulton Street or Pier 16 Visitors Center.

Cross South Street, once known as the Street of Ships, under an elevated stretch of the FDR Drive to **Pier 16,** where historic ships are docked, including the *Pioneer,* a 102-foot schooner built in 1885; the *Peking,* the second-largest sailing bark in existence; the iron-hulled *Wavertree*; and the lightship *Ambrose.* The Pier 16 ticket booth provides information and sells tickets to the museum, ships, tours, and exhibits. Pier 16 is the departure point for various seasonal cruises.

To the north is **Pier 17**, a multilevel dockside shopping mall with national chain retailers such as Express and Victoria's Secret, among others. Weathered-wood decks at the rear of the pier make a splendid spot from which to sit and contemplate the river, with views as far north as Midtown Manhattan and as far south as the Verrazano–Narrows Bridge. ⊠ *South Street Seaport, Lower Manhattan* ☎ *212/732–7678 events and shopping information* ⊕ *www.southstreetseaport.com* ⊠ *$5 to ships, galleries, walking tours, Maritime Crafts Center, films, and other seaport events* Ⓜ *2, 3, 4, 5, A, C, J, M, Z to Fulton St./Broadway Nassau.*

> **HIGH NOON ON THE HARBOR**
>
> The *Titanic* Memorial once stood on the roof of the old Seaman's Church Institute, a meeting place for merchant seaman docked in New York. Until 1967 the ball at the top of the lighthouse slid down the pole at noon to signal the time to the ships in the harbor.

Staten Island Ferry. About 70,000 people ride the ferry every day, and you should be one of them. Without having to pay a cent, you get great views of the Statue of Liberty, Ellis Island, and the southern tip of Manhattan. You'll pass tugboats, freighters, and cruise ships—a reminder that this is still a working harbor. The boat embarks from the Whitehall Terminal at Whitehall and South streets near the east end of Battery Park. The ferry provides transport to Staten Island, one of the city's boroughs. But if you don't want to visit Staten Island you can usually remain onboard for the return trip. Occasionally a boat is taken out of service for a while; if you're told to disembark, walk down the main gangplank (the same one you used when you came aboard), enter the terminal, and catch the next boat back to the city. Ⓜ *1 to South Ferry; R, W to Whitehall St.; 4, 5 to Bowling Green.*

ALSO WORTH SEEING

City Hall. You just might spot news crews jockeying on the front steps as they attempt to interview city officials, which is perhaps all you want to know about City Hall. But if the history of local politics is truly your thing, the hall is open for tours. Among the highlights within are the Victorian-style **City Council Chamber,** the **Board of Estimate Chamber,** with colonial paintings and church-pew-style seating; and the **Governor's Room,** which includes a writing table that George Washington used in 1789 when New York was the U.S. capital. If nothing else, take a moment to snap a photo of the austere columned exterior. ⊠ *City Hall Park, Lower Manhattan* ☎ *212/639–9675* ⊠ *Free* ⊙ *Tours weekdays; reservations required 2 wks in advance* Ⓜ *R, W to City Hall; 4, 5, 6 to Brooklyn Bridge/City Hall; J, M, Z to Chambers St.*

Federal Reserve Bank of New York. With its imposing mix of sandstone, limestone, and ironwork, the reserve looks the way a bank ought to: strong and impregnable. The gold ingots in the subterranean vaults here are worth roughly $140 billion—reputedly a third of the world's gold reserves. Hour-long tours (conducted five times a day and requiring reservations made at least five days in advance) include a visit to the gold vault, the trading desk, and "FedWorks," a multimedia exhibit center where you can track hypothetical trades. Visitors must show an officially issued photo ID, such as a driver's license or passport, and will pass through scanning equipment to enter the building; the Fed advises showing up 20 minutes before your tour to accommodate security screening. Photography is not permitted. ✉ *33 Liberty St., between William and Nassau Sts., Lower Manhattan* ☎ *212/720–6130* ⊕ *www.newyorkfed.org* ✆ *Free* ◷ *1-hr tour by advance reservation, weekdays 9:30–2:30* Ⓜ *A, C to Broadway/Nassau; J, M, Z, 2, 3, 4, 5 to Fulton St.*

⟳ **Fraunces Tavern.** In his pre-presidential days as a general, George Washington celebrated the end of the Revolutionary War here in 1783, delivering a farewell address to his officers upon the British evacuation of New York. Today the former tavern is a museum covering two floors above a restaurant and bar.

> **FRAUNCES WHO?**
>
> Fraunces Tavern was the hostelry of Samuel Fraunces, George Washington's steward and one of the colonial era's most prominent black New Yorkers.

It has two fully furnished period rooms—including the Long Room, site of Washington's address—and other modest displays of 18th- and 19th-century American history. The museum also hosts family programs (such as crafts workshops), lectures, and concerts. ✉ *54 Pearl St., at Broad St., Lower Manhattan* ☎ *212/425–1778* ⊕ *www.frauncestavern museum.org* ✆ *$4* ◷ *Sept.–June, Tues.–Fri. noon–5, Sat. 10–5; July and Aug., Tues.–Sat. 10–5* Ⓜ *R, W to Whitehall St.; 4, 5 to Bowling Green; 1 to South Ferry; J, M, Z to Broad St.*

St. Paul's Chapel. For more than a year after the World Trade Center attacks, the chapel's fence served as a shrine for visitors seeking solace. People from around the world left tokens of grief and support, or signed one of the large drop cloths that hung from the fence. After having served as a 24-hour refuge where rescue and recovery workers could eat, pray, rest, and receive counseling, the chapel, which amazingly suffered no damage, reopened to the public in fall 2002. The ongoing exhibit, titled "Unwavering Spirit: Hope & Healing at Ground Zero," honors the efforts of rescue workers in the months following September 11. Open since 1766, St. Paul's is the oldest public building in continuous use in Manhattan. ✉ *209 Broadway, at Fulton St., Lower Manhattan* ☎ *212/233–4164* ⊕ *www.saintpaulschapel.org* ◷ *Mon.–Sat. 10–5:45, Sun. 8–3:45* Ⓜ *2, 3, 4, 5, A, C, J, M, Z to Fulton St.*

Trinity Church. Alexander Hamilton is buried under a white-stone pyramid in the church's graveyard, not far from a monument commemorating steamboat inventor Robert Fulton (buried in the Livingston family vault with his wife). The church (the third on this site) was designed in 1846 by Richard Upjohn. Its most notable feature is the set of enormous bronze doors designed by Richard Morris Hunt to recall Lorenzo Ghiberti's doors for the Baptistery in Florence, Italy. *Trinity Root*, a 12½-foot-high, 3-ton sculpture by Steven Tobin cast from the sycamore tree struck by debris on 9/11 behind St. Paul's Chapel, was installed in front of the church on September, 11, 2005. A museum outlines the

Continued on page 55

GROUND ZERO
THE WORLD TRADE CENTER SITE

Every New Yorker has a story about September 11th: what they saw, where they were when it happened, who they worried about, who they lost.

In its perpetual aftermath, no two people look at the tragedy the same way. Perhaps the only thing that elicits unanimous agreement, then and now, is the sentiment voiced that day by then-Mayor Rudolph Giuliani: "The number of casualties will be more than any of us can bear, ultimately."

What will you experience when you visit Ground Zero? Quite simply, we can't tell you. Perhaps more so than anything we've tried to describe in our guides, you just have to be there to know.

But here's what we can tell you.

■ Approximately 50,000 people worked in the north tower (1 World Trade Center) and south tower (2 World Trade Center), and another 40,000 visited the 16-acre complex every day. Beneath the towers was a mall with nearly 100 stores and restaurants. The entire complex—hosting more than 430 companies from 28 countries—was so large it had its own zip code—10048.

■ Each 110 stories tall (though at 1,368 feet, the north tower was six feet taller), the towers were triumphs of mid-20th-century engineering. Their construction began in 1968, and they officially opened in 1973. Avoiding the thick interior columns typically used at the time, the architects gave each building an exterior skeleton made up of 244 slim steel columns and an inner "core" tube that supported the weight of the tower and housed its elevators and stairwells.

■ On September 11, 2001, terrorist hijackers steered two jets into the World Trade Center's twin towers, demolishing them and five outlying buildings and killing 2,749 people.

■ Both planes were Boeing 767s. American Airlines Flight 11 hit the north tower at 494 mph. United Airlines Flight 175 hit the south tower at 586 mph. Researchers speculate that the higher speed of United 175 may have caused the south tower to fall first, even though it was hit second.

■ Why *did* the towers fall? A three-year federal study revealed several reasons. The airplanes damaged the exterior columns, destroying core supports for at least three of the north tower's floors and up to six of the south tower's floors. Ensuing fires, fed by tens of thousands of gallons of fuel, further weakened the buildings. The collapse of the most heavily damaged floors then triggered a domino effect, causing the towers to crumple at an estimated speed of about 125 mph. The collapse of the towers released dust clouds filled with toxins, including jet fuel, cement, glass, fiberglass, and asbestos.

■ Dubbed Ground Zero, the fenced-in 16-acre work site that emerged from the rubble has come to symbolize the personal and historical impact of the attack. A steel "viewing wall" now encircles the site, bound on the north and south by Vesey and Liberty streets, and on the east and west by Church and West streets. Along the east wall are panels that detail the history of lower Manhattan and the WTC site before, during, and after September 11. There are also panels bearing the names of those who perished on 9/11/01 and during the 1993 World Trade Center attack.

Left: Ground Zero today. Center: Pedestrians flee as the south tower falls. Right: Views of the World Trade Center before the September 11 attacks.

■ After years of delays, the process of filling the massive void at Ground Zero is well under way. Ground has been broken on the World Trade Center Memorial and Museum, the 1,776-foot Freedom Tower, and Santiago Calatrava's soaring new transportation hub. Plans for three distinct new towers, all by famous architects, have also been unveiled.

UNDERSTANDING THE DEVASTATION

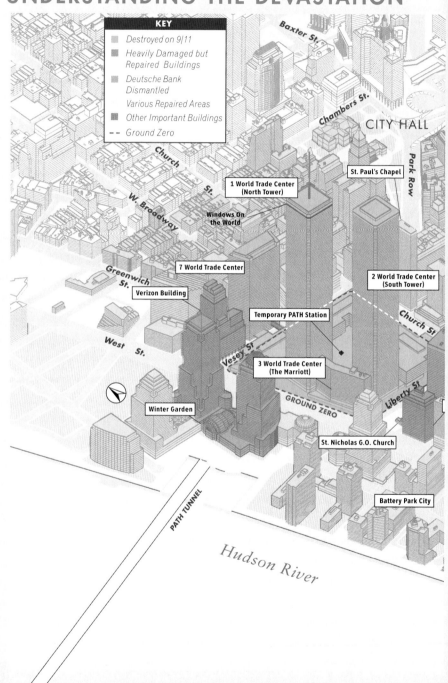

KEY
- Destroyed on 9|11
- Heavily Damaged but Repaired Buildings
- Deutsche Bank Dismantled
- Various Repaired Areas
- Other Important Buildings
- -- Ground Zero

Baxter St.

Chambers St.

CITY HALL

Park Row

Church St.

W. Broadway

St. Paul's Chapel

1 World Trade Center
(North Tower)

Windows On
the World

7 World Trade Center

2 World Trade Center
(South Tower)

Greenwich
St.

Verizon Building

Temporary PATH Station

Church St.

West St.

Vesey St.

3 World Trade Center
(The Marriott)

Winter Garden

GROUND ZERO

Liberty St.

St. Nicholas G.O. Church

PATH TUNNEL

Battery Park City

Hudson River

In the days after 9/11, police barricades permitted only residents and emergency personnel to go south of 14th Street. A second line of barriers blocked access below Houston Street to all but residents, and only emergency workers were permitted south of a National Guard perimeter running from Chambers Street to the Brooklyn Bridge.

1 WORLD TRADE CENTER (The North Tower)

The first hijacked jet, American Airlines Flight 11, crashed into the north tower at 8:46 AM, cutting through floors 93 to 99. Evidence suggests that all three building stairwells became impassable from the 92nd floor up. The tower collapsed at 10:28 AM. Cantor Fitzgerald, a brokerage firm headquartered between the 101st and 105th floors, lost 658 of its 1,050 employees. At the Windows on the World restaurant (floors 106 and 107), 100 patrons and 72 staff members perished.

2 WORLD TRADE CENTER (The South Tower)

The second hijacked jet, United Airlines Flight 175, hit the south tower at 9:03 AM, crashing through the 77th to 85th floors. The plane banked as it hit, so portions of the building remained undamaged on impact floors. Consequently, one stairwell initially remained passable from at least the 91st floor down. The tower collapsed at 9:58 AM.

3 WORLD TRADE CENTER (The Marriott)

Located between the north and south towers, the New York Marriott World Trade Center was completely destroyed in the attacks. Before the towers fell, hundreds of people evacuated through the hotel's lobby. The building had an ominous history. In 1993, damage from the first World Trade Center bombing shut the hotel down for a year and a half. Part of the World Trade Center Site Memorial will cover the area previously occupied by the hotel.

7 WORLD TRADE CENTER
This 47-story building was struck by large chunks of falling debris from the north and south towers. Mayor Giuliani's emergency command center—which he would never get to use on 9/11—was on the 23rd floor. The building remained standing despite suffering structural damage, but fires broke out and burned unchecked for seven hours, eventually causing the building to collapse at 5:20 PM. The new 52-story 7 World Trade Center opened in May 2006.

VERIZON BUILDING
As 7 World Trade Center collapsed, a 60-foot-tall pile of its rubble fell against the Verizon Building, severely damaging the switching center and cutting off phone service to Lower Manhattan. The impact also took a heavy toll on the art deco building's east facade, south-facing wall, foundation walls, and two structural columns; repair workers have replaced 1,800 windows, 520,000 exterior bricks, and 22,500 cinder blocks—many by hand.

NEW YORK STOCK EXCHANGE AND AMERICAN STOCK EXCHANGE
The New York Stock Exchange (NYSE) remained closed for six days after the attacks (including 9/11). When trading resumed on September 17, the Dow Jones industrial average dropped 684.81 points, or 7.13 percent. The American Stock Exchange (Amex) was damaged on September 11, and for two weeks Amex stocks and exchange-traded funds were traded on the NYSE floor. During that time, Amex options were traded on the floor of the Philadelphia Stock Exchange.

ST. PAUL'S CHAPEL
Though it's directly across from the World Trade Center site, St. Paul's sustained no major damage in the attacks. After September 11, the chapel was host to an eight-month volunteer relief effort for Ground Zero recovery workers, providing food, shelter, and medical care. St. Paul's has long been a sanctuary for those with heavy burdens—George Washington worshipped here on his inauguration day.

WINTER GARDEN
The 10-story glass-domed Winter Garden, home to the World Financial Center's Arts & Events Program, was severely damaged in the attacks. The atrium reopened in September 2002 after extensive repairs, which included the installation of 2,000 windows and 1.2 million pounds of stone. The venue hosts a year-round series of free exhibitions, festivals, and performances.

DEUTSCHE BANK BUILDING

Falling World Trade Center debris cut a 15-story gash in the north facade of the Deutsche Bank Building, which has been unoccupied since 9/11. Various negotiations delayed deconstruction of the badly damaged and contaminated building until March 2006. As of this writing, the complex demolition, which required removing World Trade Center dust and contaminants from the building, gutting it, and then disassembling it, was to be completed by the end of 2009.

90 WEST STREET

The terra-cotta and limestone exterior of this Cass Gilbert–designed 1907 office building, one block away from the south tower, was damaged by fire and falling debris. Now renovated and restored, 90 West Street has been converted into apartments.

ST. NICHOLAS GREEK ORTHODOX CHURCH

Tiny St. Nicholas Greek Orthodox Church was buried in rubble and completely destroyed. The church will be rebuilt on a site near its former location.

PATH/SUBWAY LINE

About 1,000 feet of the tunnels used by the Metropolitan Transit Authority's 1 subway trains collapsed after the towers fell, closing Cortlandt Street station. The Port Authority of New York and New Jersey's World Trade Center PATH train station was also damaged in the attacks. After the first plane hit, PATH workers began evacuating the WTC station and rerouting inbound trains. The last train evacuated people from the platform before leaving the station; after the evacuation, an empty train picked up the remaining station workers and carried them to safety. The entire evacuation was completed 48

From left to right: View of the burning towers from Washington Square Park. (Top) One of two pedestrian bridges that connected the World Financial Center to the WTC. (Bottom) Firefighters search the WTC rubble on September 12, 2001. Part of the facade of one of the towers rises above the Ground Zero debris. (Top) A November 11, 2001, peace vigil near Ground Zero. (Bottom) Protesters demonstrate against military retaliation in the days following September 11.

minutes before the first tower fell. In November 2003, PATH opened a temporary station at the World Trade Center. The best way to view the WTC site is by riding the PATH from Exchange Place.

BATTERY PARK CITY

Many people fled across the Hudson River to New Jersey on boats commanded by volunteer captains. One ferry line alone reported evacuating nearly 30,000 people. The community's 9,000 residents were left homeless, and almost half of the renters never returned.

THE FUTURE OF GROUND ZERO

■ "Reflecting Absence," the World Trade Center memorial designed by Michael Arad and Peter Walker, will be set in an oak-filled plaza. Water will cascade down into two subterranean reflecting pools outlining the twin towers' original footprints, and then tumble down into smaller square holes at the center of each pool. A museum and visitors center will be built below the plaza surface. The current plan is to open the memorial on the tenth anniversary of 9/11—9/11/11.

■ The memorial plaza will be bordered by four distinct new skyscrapers: the Freedom Tower (Tower 1) and Towers 2, 3, 4, all designed by famous architects (David M. Childs, Norman Foster, Richard Rogers, and Fumihiko Maki, respectively). Santiago Calatrava's lofty transit hub, which will replace the current temporary PATH station, was inspired by the image of a child releasing a dove; it features a roof that will open to the sky every September 11. The site will also include a performing arts center designed by Frank Gehry. At this writing, ground has been broken on the Freedom Tower and PATH terminal, which are expected to open in 2011 and 2013, respectively.

■ For more information on the new structures, visit www.lowermanhattan.info and www.buildthememorial.org.

VISITING THE SITE

WHEN TO GO: There are no special viewing hours, and the site seldom feels crowded. Early weekday mornings, when many tourists and locals are still working on their first cups of coffee, are good times to go.

GETTING THERE: Subway: 1, R, W to Rector St.; 2, 3, 4, 5, A, C, J, M, Z to Fulton St./Broadway-Nassau; E to World Trade Center/Church St. PATH: any line to World Trade Center stop.

BEST ROUTE: The corner of Vesey and Church streets, near PATH and subway stations, is a good starting point for viewing Ground Zero; walk clockwise around the site. The main viewing area is on Liberty Street, but you'll have a better view from the two pedestrian bridges to the World Financial center, as well as from inside the World Financial Center itself. During your walk, refer to the map above for an idea of the site's future layout; at press time, the foundations for the Freedom Tower and one of the memorial pools were visible.

TOURS: New York City Vacation Packages (888/692–8701, www.nycvp.com, $19) conducts several guided tours of lower Manhattan, including the World Trade Center site, each week. The **Tribute WTC Visitor Center** (212/422–3520, www.tributewtc.org, $10), a project of the September 11 Families Association, leads walking tours of Ground Zero several times daily. **Talking Street** tours (212/586–8687, www.talkingstreet.com, $5.95) converts your cell phone into a tour guide, calling out 16 stops at and around Ground Zero; portions of the profits go to the World Trade Center Memorial Foundation.

church's history; a daily tour is given at 2. ⊠*74 Trinity Pl., Broadway at head of Wall St., Lower Manhattan* ☎*212/602–0800* ⊕*www.trinitywallstreet.org* ⊘ *Weekdays 7–6, Sat. 8–4, Sun. 7–4; churchyard Nov.–Apr., daily 7–4; May–Oct., weekdays 7–5, Sat. 8–3, Sun. 7–3* Ⓜ*4, 5 to Wall St.; R, W to Rector St.*

Vietnam Veterans Memorial. At the center of a triangular plaza sits this 14-foot-high, 70-foot-long rectangular memorial. Passages from news dispatches from the wartime period and the letters of military service people are etched into its wall of greenish glass. The Walk of Honor memorializes 1,741 New Yorkers who lost their lives in the war. ⊠*End of Coenties Slip between Water and South Sts., adjacent to 125 Broad St., Lower Manhattan* Ⓜ*1 to South Ferry; R, W to Whitehall St.; J, M, Z to Broad St.*

Woolworth Building. Until 40 Wall Street stole the title in 1930, the 792-foot Woolworth Building, opened in 1913, was the world's tallest building. Make a quick stop in the lobby to check out the stained-glass skylight and sculptures set into the portals to the left and right: one represents an elderly F. W. Woolworth counting his nickels and dimes, another depicts the architect, Cass Gilbert, cradling in his arms a model of his creation. ⊠*233 Broadway, between Park Pl. and Barclay St., Lower Manhattan* Ⓜ*2, 3 to Park Pl.; R, W to City Hall.*

> **TALL TALE**
>
> Trinity Church was the city's tallest building until 1890, when the New York World Building took the title (currently held by the Empire State Building). Don't look too hard for the former New York World Building, however: it bit the dust in 1955 to make way for automobile access to the Brooklyn Bridge.

CHINATOWN AND TRIBECA

THREE WAYS TO EXPLORE

A STREET THAT DEFINES THE COMMUNITY

For a quick taste of Chinatown, head to Mott Street, Chinatown's main thoroughfare. This is where the first Chinese immigrants (mostly men) settled in tenements in the late 1880s. Today the street is dense with restaurants, hair salons and barbershops, bakeries, tea parlors, and souvenir shops, most of them lying below Canal Street. If you plan it right, you can create a movable feast, starting with soup dumplings, a specialty from Shanghai, and continuing with Peking duck, a yellow custard cake, and a jasmine bubble tea, each at a different place. Or, you can have it all come to you at **Ping's Seafood**, with dim sum for lunch. The few blocks above Canal overflow with food markets selling vegetables and fish (some still alive and squirming). Walk carefully, as the sidewalks can be slick from the ice underneath the eels, blue crabs, snapper, and shrimp that seem to look back at you as you pass by. A good place to get oriented or arrange a walking tour is the **Museum of Chinese in the Americas.**

CLOSE UP

Gangs of Five Points

"Debauchery has made the very houses prematurely old," novelist Charles Dickens wrote in 1842 after visiting Five Points. Although his prose was a bit purple, historians agree that the description of this former Lower Manhattan neighborhood was accurate.

In the mid-19th century the Five Points area was perhaps the city's most notorious and dangerous neighborhood. The confluence of five streets—Mulberry, Anthony (now Worth), Cross (now Park), Orange (now Baxter), and Little Water (no longer in existence)—had been built over a drainage pond that had been filled in the 1820s. When the buildings began to sink into the mosquito-filled muck, middle-class residents abandoned their homes. Buildings were chopped into tiny apartments that were rented to the poorest of the poor, who at this point were newly emancipated slaves and Irish immigrants fleeing famine.

Newspaper accounts at the time tell of robberies and other violent crimes on a daily basis. And with corrupt political leaders like William "Boss" Marcy Tweed more concerned with lining their pockets than patrolling the streets, keeping order was left to the club-wielding hooligans portrayed in *Gangs of New York.*

But the neighborhood, finally razed in the 1880s to make way for Columbus Park, has left a lasting legacy. In the music halls where different ethnic groups begrudgingly came together, the Irish jig and the African-American shuffle combined to form a new type of fancy footwork called tap dancing.

MOVIE-PERFECT BUT WITH A SHADY PAST

To the right off restaurant-lined Pell Street is alley-size **Doyers Street,** the site of early-20th-century gang wars and today a favorite location for film shoots. At this juncture, Tobey McGuire and Kirsten Dunst had a heart-to-heart talk in *Spider-Man 2,* and Woody Allen used it in two of his films, *Alice* and *Small Time Crooks.* Quirky, angled and authentic, this curving roadway is where you can find Chinatown's oldest teahouse, dating from 1920, **Nom Wah Tea Parlor.** There's also a relatively hidden and grungy underground passage, formerly a storage place for liquor and now lined with Chinese travel agencies and other very low-tech businesses (don't expect to see signs in English). The street makes a sharp angle (according to legend, it was built this way by Chinatown merchants to thwart straight-flying ghosts who brought bad luck; history says it's because the street was once the entryway to brewer Heinreich Doyers's elegant home.) before it reaches the **Bowery,** a point known as "Bloody Angle" because of the visibility-challenged victims' inability to anticipate a gang's attacks from the corner. The Bowery itself was once lined with theaters and taverns, but earned a reputation well into the late 20th century as the city's skid row. Today it's a busy commercial thoroughfare. The oldest row building in New York City, the **Edward Mooney House,** is located on 18 Bowery on the corner of Pell Street. Erected in 1785 by Edward Mooney, the house was a residence until the 1820s and was at one time or another a hotel,

Getting decked out for the carnival of colors and sounds that is the Chinese New Year's parade in Chinatown.

tavern, pool hall, restaurant, and bank. Today, it's a historic landmark and is open to the public.

STAR POWER AND STELLAR LOOKS

Walking the photogenic streets of TriBeCa, full of cast-iron factories as well as a time-defying stretch of Federal row houses on Harrison Street, you can understand why everyone from Robert De Niro to J.F.K. Jr have bought apartments here. The two-block-long Staple Street is a favorite of urban cinematographers with its connecting overhead walkway. At 60 Hudson Street is the art-deco Western Union Building—try to sneak a peek at its magnificent lobby.

TOP ATTRACTIONS

Fodor'sChoice **Columbus Park.** People-watching is the thing in this .park. If you swing
★ by in the morning, you'll see men and women practicing tai chi; the afternoons bring intense games of mah-jongg. In the mid-19th century the park was known as Five Points—the point where Mulberry Street, Anthony (now Worth) Street, Cross (now Park) Street, Orange (now Baxter) Street, and Little Water Street (no longer in existence) intersected—and was notoriously ruled by dangerous Irish gan⌐ the 1880s a neighborhood-improvement campaign brough⌐ park's creation. Ⓜ *N, Q, R, W, 6 to Canal St.*

Kim Lau Square. Ten streets converge at this l⌐¹ crisscrossed at odd angles by pedestrian walk island in this busy area is the **Kim Lau Arch,** hon⌐ ties in American wars. A statue on the square's east⌐

Chinatown & Tribeca Dining

BUDGET DINING

Bubby's, American,
120 Hudson St.

Financier Patisserie,
Café, 62 Stone St.

**Great New York
Noodletown,** Chinese,
28 Bowery

Jing Fong, Chinese, 20
Elizabeth St., 2nd fl.

Joe's Shanghai,
Chinese, 9 Pell St.

Kitchenette, American,
156 Chambers St, near
Greenwich St.

Nha Trang, Vietnamese,
87 Baxter St.;
148 Centre St.

XO Kitchen, Chinese,
148 Hester St.

MODERATE DINING

The Harrison, American,
355 Greenwich St.

Mai House, Vietnamese,
186 Franklin St.

Matsugen, Japanese,
241 Church St.

Odeon, Bistro,
145 West Broadway

Ping's Seafood,
Chinese, 22 Mott St.

EXPENSIVE DINING

Chanterelle, French,
2 Harrison St.

Delmonico's, Steak-
house, 56 Beaver St.

to a Quin Dynasty official named Lin Ze Xu, the Fujianese minister who sparked the Opium War by banning the drug. Ⓜ*4, 5, 6 to Brooklyn Bridge/City Hall.*

FodorsChoice **Washington Market Park.** This landscaped recreation space with a gazebo
★ and playground—ideal for permitting the kids to blow off steam—
ↂ was named after the great food market that once sprawled over the area. Across the street at the elementary school are a stout red tower resembling a lighthouse and a fence with iron ship figures—reminders of the neighborhood's dockside past. There's a small greenmarket here on Wednesday and Saturday. ⊠ *Greenwich St. between Chambers and Duane Sts., TriBeCa* Ⓜ *1, 2, 3 to Chambers St.*

ALSO WORTH SEEING

Mahayana Buddhist Temple. You'll be able to say you saw New York's largest Buddha here at the largest Buddhist temple in Chinatown; it's at the foot of the Manhattan Bridge Arch on the Bowery. A donation of $2 is requested. There's a great gift shop on the second floor. Before its incarnation as a place of worship in 1996, this was the Rosemary, an adult-movie theater. ⊠ *133 Canal St., at the Bowery, Chinatown* ☎ *212/343–9592* ⏰ *Daily 8 AM–5 PM* Ⓜ *4, 5, 6 to Brooklyn Bridge/City Hall.*

SoHo & Little Italy

WORD OF MOUTH

"For SoHo, I recommend a walk down Broadway south of Houston Street. There are many stores in this area, including [Prada], Bloomingdale's...Pearl River Mart, etc. You can also wander along Spring and Prince towards West Broadway. At Spring and Thompson St. you will find Kee's Chocolates—fabulous."

—Proenza_Preschooler

GETTING ORIENTED

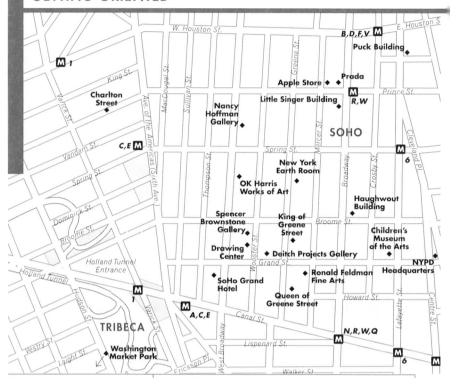

<table>
<tr><td>

FODOR'S CHOICE

Greene Street
St. Patrick's Old Cathedral

TOP ATTRACTIONS

Apple Store (⇨ Ch. 17)
Pearl River Mart (⇨ Ch. 17)
San Gennaro Shrine

TOP EXPERIENCES

Architecture-ogling stroll along
Greene Street
Browsing SoHo's boutiques
Grazing Grand Street's grocers
Indulging in extreme pampering at Bliss Spa

</td><td>

MAKING THE MOST OF YOUR TIME

If you're coming to shop in SoHo and NoLita, plan to arrive after 11 AM, as most shops open late and stay open until early evening. If art is your thing, avoid Sunday, because most galleries are closed. SoHo is almost always a madhouse (unless it's raining), but weekdays are somewhat less frenetic. NoLita is calmer and less crowded. Little Italy represents a very small area nowadays—just four blocks. You can see it all in a half hour, or you can spend an afternoon exploring the grocery stores and the tacky-but-amusing Italian-theme T-shirts, bumper stickers, and assorted tchotchkes, capped off with a meal at one of Mulberry Street's almost-authentic Italian-American restaurants. If you come in mid-September, during the San Gennaro festival (a huge street fair in honor of the patron saint of Naples) you—along with thousands upon thousands of other people—can easily spend an entire day and night exploring the many food and souvenir booths and playing games of chance.

</td></tr>
</table>

3

NEARBY MUSEUMS (⇨ CH. 14)

Children's Museum of the Arts
New York City Fire Museum

AREA SHOPS (⇨ CH. 17)

Agent Provocateur
Bellora
De Vera
Kirna Zabête
Les Petits Chapelais
Marc Jacobs
MarieBelle
Marni
McNally Jackson
Moss
Pearl River Mart
Prada
Pylones
R by 45rpm
Santa Maria Novella
Stuart Moore

GETTING HERE

SoHo is roughly bounded by Houston Street, Canal Street, 6th Avenue, and Lafayette Street. To the east, NoLita grows daily but lies pretty much between Houston, the Bowery, Kenmare, and Lafayette. There are plenty of subways that service the area; take the 6 or A, C, E to Spring Street; the R, W to Prince Street; or the B, D, F, V to Broadway-Lafayette.

WORD OF MOUTH

"Sunday. Our Soho day. Based largely on Fodorite advice, we [had] brunch at Balthazar. The décor is perfect—it really did feel as if we were in a classic French brasserie. Much cheaper than going to Paris, and no jet lag. Well fortified, we head out to Spring Street for a spot of shopping/browsing through Kate's Paperie, Sur la Table, down to Pearl River, and then (more walking) past enticing windows." —SB_Travlr

Sightseeing
★★★
Nightlife
★★★
Dining
★★★
Lodging
★★
Shopping
★★★★★

Updated by
Michelle Delio

SoHo (South of Houston) and NoLita (North of Little Italy) are shopper's paradises, supertrendy, painfully overcrowded on the weekends, often overpriced, and undeniably glamorous. Not too long ago though, these neighborhoods were quiet warrens of artists' lofts and galleries, and the only reason to visit was to go gallery hopping. Checking out the art is still a big reason to come to SoHo, but shopping has for the most part supplanted the quest for visual stimulation. In between whipping your credit card out of your wallet and feverishly searching for a café with empty seats, do take a few seconds to savor what other passersby may miss: the neighborhood's Belgian brick cobblestones and turn-of-the-20th-century lampposts.

And then—just east of Broadway—you'll find the remains of what once was a thriving, lively community of Italian Americans: the tangle of streets that make up Little Italy. A few nostalgic blocks surrounding Mulberry Street between NoLita and ultrabusy Canal Street are all that remain of the vast community that once dominated the area, but what remains is still a cheerful salute to all things Italian, with red, green, and white street decorations on permanent display and specialty grocers and cannelloni makers dishing up delights. (If you want to see a current and far less nostalgic Little Italy, head up to Arthur Avenue in the Bronx.)

SOHO

THREE WAYS TO EXPLORE

SHOP TILL YOU DROP

The stretch of Broadway between Houston and Broome streets is a flurry of pedestrian traffic with retail giants like H&M, Banana Republic, and Victoria's Secret, as well as smaller city favorites like Scoop NYC and Zara. ■TIP➜Unless you're in dire need of something specific, skip the mass marketers and check out the stores that may be less familiar to you—they

> **SOHO WAS HELL**
>
> SoHo once had the less trendy moniker "Hell's Hundred Acres," so named because the crowded slums were repeatedly beset by frequent fires, but it boomed after the Civil War, when the neighborhood came to be known simply as the Eighth Ward.

offer some of the city's most elegant and interesting fashions. To the west or east in SoHo are boutiques from established contemporary designers like Vivienne Tam, Nanette Lepore, Nicole Miller, and Barbara Bui. In NoLita on Elizabeth, Mulberry, and Mott streets, you'll mix with models and magazine editors at one-off shops by young designers just starting to make their marks. There, amid lingering remnants of the neighborhood's immigrant past, custom-designed jewelry, hand-sewn dresses, trendy home furnishings, and high-concept lighting fill the storefronts. When you're ready to "drop" you can hit Bliss SoHo Spa (568 Broadway, 2nd Fl., between Prince St. and Houston St.) for a muscle-soothing Ginger Rub massage. Just be warned, this type of pampering isn't the "walk in" variety, so book at least a month ahead on www.blissworld.com, or you can just enjoy the spa store with it's lotions and potions to enjoy back at your hotel.

THE ARTS SCENE AND DESIGN: A LEGACY

Even if you're not in the market for a $1,000 skirt, the 23,000-square-foot **Prada** design store is worth a stop to check out the Rem Koolhaas design. ■TIP➜Try something on just to experience the drama of the dressing room, just as hyperdesigned as the rest of the space. A showcase of everything wired, the **Apple Store** is a tech-head's Nirvana. Showcasing new Mac products, it's a place to learn about everything from photography to the care of your PowerBook or iPod. Edgy in the '70s and '80s, SoHo still retains some of the artists' galleries that brought the neighborhood to the forefront of the city's art scene at the time. Several of SoHo's better exhibition spaces, including **Deitch Projects**, the **Drawing Center**, and **Spencer Brownstone**, are clustered in the vicinity of Greene and Wooster streets near Grand and Canal. Many a rainy day can be spent enjoying the often outré collections showcased inside, no purchase necessary.

CAST IRON, COBBLESTONES AND ARCHITECTURAL MASTERPIECES

SoHo has the world's greatest concentration of cast-iron buildings, built in response to fires that wiped out much of lower Manhattan in the mid-18th century. Although it's hard to single out any one block, as almost

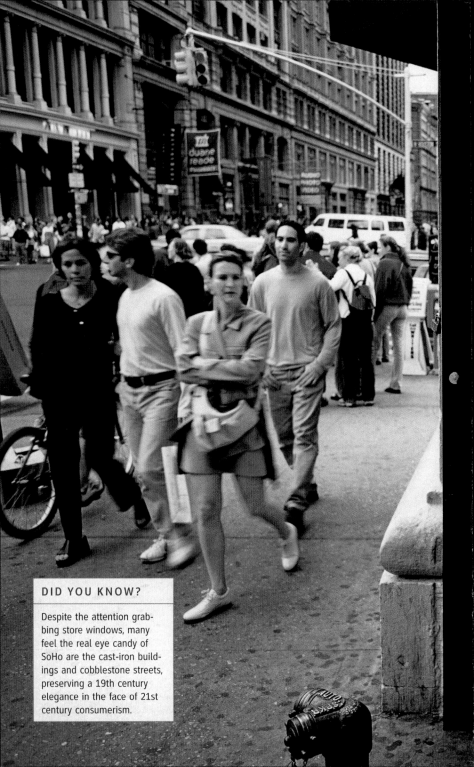

DID YOU KNOW?

Despite the attention grabbing store windows, many feel the real eye candy of SoHo are the cast-iron buildings and cobblestone streets, preserving a 19th century elegance in the face of 21st century consumerism.

all have gorgeous examples of the various cast-iron styles (Italianate, Victorian Gothic, Greek Revival), Greene Street has two standouts, the **Queen of Greene Street** and the **King of Greene Street.** Even the lampposts in this neighborhood are architectural gems, with their turn-of-the-20th-century bishop's-crook style, adorned with cast-iron curlicues from their bases to their curved tops; they're the perfect complement to the paving stones below. Other notable buildings are the Beaux-Arts **Little Singer Building** and the **Haughwout Building** on Broadway, and the 1885 Romanesque Revival **Puck Building,** a former magazine headquarters and now a busy event space.

TOP ATTRACTIONS

Fodor'sChoice **King of Greene Street.** This five-story Renaissance-style 1873 building has
★ a magnificent projecting porch of Corinthian columns and pilasters. Today the King is painted a brilliant shade of ivory. ⊠ *72–76 Greene St., between Spring and Broome Sts., SoHo* Ⓜ *R, W to Prince St.*

Queen of Greene Street. The regal grace of this 1873 cast-iron beauty is exemplified by its dormers, columns, window arches, projecting central bays, and Second Empire–style roof. ⊠ *28–30 Greene St., between Grand and Canal Sts., SoHo* Ⓜ *J, M, N, Q, R, W, Z, 6 to Canal St.*

ALSO WORTH SEEING

Charlton Street. The city's longest stretch of Federal-style redbrick row houses from the 1820s and '30s runs along the north side of this street, which is west of 6th Avenue and south of West Houston Street. The high stoops, paneled front doors, leaded-glass windows, and narrow dormer windows are all intact. Nearby King and Vandam streets have more historic houses. Much of this area was once the site of a mansion called Richmond Hill; in the late 18th century Richmond Hill was set in what is described as a beautiful wild meadow with glimpses of the nearby city and the "hamlet" of Greenwich Village, which served variously as George Washington's headquarters and the home of Abigail Adams and Aaron Burr. Ⓜ *1 to Houston St; C, E to Spring St.*

Haughwout Building. Perhaps best known for what's no longer inside—the world's first commercial passenger elevator, invented by Elisha Graves Otis—the building's exterior is still well worth a long look. Nicknamed the Parthenon of Cast Iron, this five-story, Venetian palazzo–style structure was built in 1857 to house department-

KIDS IN SOHO & LITTLE ITALY

This is primarily a grown-up section of town, unless you're raising dedicated shoppers, but there are things for the kids to do here. Check out the programs and events at SoHo's Children's Museum of the Arts (⇨ *Chapter 14*) and the interactive if overtly commercial Scholastic Store (also in SoHo at 557 Broadway). Steam can be blown off at Little Italy's DeSalvio Playground at the corner of Spring and Mulberry streets— it's far from fancy, but the kids may enjoy clambering on red, white, and green equipment.

Where can I find...?

COFFEE	Aroma Espresso Bar 145 Greene St. Find out why locals skip Star- bucks to come here.	Once Upon a Tart 135 Sullivan St. Great name with the goods to back it up.
A QUICK BITE	Lombardi's 32 Spring St. Killer pizza. Take a leap of faith with the clam pie.	Ceci-Cela 55 Spring St. Éclairs, crèmes brûlées, and truffles? Oui.
COCKTAILS	Fanelli's 94 Prince St. A true neighborhood bar.	MercBar 151 Mercer St. Chic locals, excellent martinis.

store merchant E. V. Haughwout's china, silver, and glassware store. Each window is framed by Corinthian columns and rounded arches. ✉ *488–492 Broadway, at Broome St., SoHo* Ⓜ *6 to Spring St.; R, W to Prince St.*

Little Singer Building. Ernest Flagg's 1904 masterpiece reveals the final flower of the cast-iron style with a delicate facade covered with curlicues of wrought iron. The central bay windows are recessed, allowing the top floor to arch over like a proscenium. The L-shape building's second facade is around the corner on Prince Street. ✉ *561 Broadway, SoHo* Ⓜ *R, W to Prince St.*

LITTLE ITALY

TWO WAYS TO EXPLORE

HOUSEWARES, FOOD SHOPS AND THE MOB

Around Grand Street near Mulberry and Mott are a number of fine family-run Italian grocers, including the fifth-generation **DiPalo's Fine Foods** (amazing cheese and cured meats—don't just stand there salivating, ask for a sample!), fourth-generation **Alleva** (the mozzarella and the fried rice balls are among the best eats in NYC), and **Piemonte Ravioli** (pick up some dried pasta to make at home). Try to avoid visiting just before dinner when the locals all seem to shop—you'll have a much less frenzied experience and more chance to taste the goods. (DiPalo's in particular has long lines most days.) Established in 1910, **E. Rossi & Co.** sells music, espresso makers, and other essential items for Italian homes, and they're always happy to talk about the neighborhood. At the corner of Hester and Mulberry streets stands what was once **Umberto's Clam House** (now Ristorante Da Gennaro), where in 1972 mobster Joey Gallo was gunned down by mob hit men during dinner. Although this was Little Italy's most notorious whack job, there are less well-known mob spots here, like John "The Dapper Don" Gotti's former Manhattan headquarters on 247 Mulberry Street in NoLita.

THE HEART OF LITTLE ITALY

St. Patrick's Old Cathedral (⊠ *263 Mulberry St.*) was established in 1809 and described by the *New York Gazette* as "a grand and beautiful church, which may justly be considered one of the greatest ornaments of our city." Step inside this Gothic Revival church, once the scene of race riots, vehement anti-Catholic protests, and other less savory bits of NYC history, and you'll see a peaceful space which has grandeur that far exceeds what you might expect to find in this neighborhood.

> ### MULBERRY SIZZLES
>
> Crowded with restaurants, cafés, bakeries, imported-food shops, and souvenir stores, the few blocks of Mulberry Street between Canal and Broome streets are where Little Italy still lives. Although the waiters inviting you to dine are mostly Albanian and not Italian, there's still a festive air about; try to snag an outdoor table. In September, Mulberry Street becomes the giant Feast of San Gennaro, a crowded 11-day festival that sizzles with the smell of sausages and onions. This is by far the city's most extensive annual street fair.

TOP ATTRACTION

National Shrine of San Gennaro. A replica of the grotto at Lourdes is the high point of this church's richly painted interior. Every September the church—officially known as the Most Precious Blood Church (⊠ *109 Mulberry St.*) sponsors the Feast of San Gennaro. ⊠ *113 Baxter St., near Canal St., Little Italy* ☎ *212/768–9320 festival information, 212/226–6427 church* ☻ *Masses Sat. noon, 5:30; Sun. noon, 2 (Vietnamese)* Ⓜ *N, Q, R, W, 6 to Canal St.; J, M, Z to Canal St.*

Fodor'sChoice
★
St. Patrick's Old Cathedral. If you've watched *The Godfather,* you've peeked inside St. Patrick's Old Cathedral—the interior shots of the infamous Baptism scene were filmed here. The unadorned exterior of the cathedral gives no hint to the splendors within, including a 1868 Henry Erben pipe organ. the enormous marble altar surrounded by hand-carved niches (reredos) housing an extraordinary collection of sacred statuary and other assorted Gothic exuberance. There's a maze of mortuary vaults underneath the Cathedral (older residents of Little Italy recall playing hide and seek in the vaults), and the outdoor cemetery is the final resting place for notable New Yorkers including the Venerable Pierre Toussaint, an African-American who was born a slave in Haiti, made his fortune as a hairdresser in New York, and whose many charitable works have resulted in his consideration for sainthood. Also interred here is Bishop Hughes—better known during his time as "Dagger John," a nickname he earned for the distinctive pointed cross he always scrawled after his name and his fiery temperament. ⊠ *263 Mulberry St., corner of Mott and Prince Sts, Little Italy* ☎ *212/226–8075* ☻ *Hours may vary, usually open 9* AM*–5* PM Ⓜ *N, R to Prince St.; 6 to Bleecker St.*

The stark, simple interior of OK Harris Works of Art illustrates the typical gallery space in SoHo.

ALSO WORTH SEEING

New York City Police Headquarters. Seen in Martin Scorsese's *Gangs of New York,* this magnificent 1909 Edwardian baroque structure with a striking copper dome served as the headquarters of the New York City Police Department until 1973. Designed to "impress both the officer and the prisoner with the majesty of the law," it was converted into luxury condos in 1988 and is known today as the Police Building Apartments. Big-name residents have included Cindy Crawford, Winona Ryder, and Steffi Graf. ⊠*240 Centre St., between Broome and Grand Sts., Little Italy* Ⓜ*6 to Spring St.; J, M, Z to Bowery.*

GALLERIES

Deitch Projects. This energetic enterprise composed of two gallery spaces shows works from the global art scene, as well as performance groups such as the Citizens Band. Artists on view have included Cecily Brown, Ryan McGinness, and Kihinde Wiley. ⊠*76 Grand St., between Greene and Wooster Sts., SoHo* ☎*212/343–7300* ⊕*www.deitch.com* Ⓜ*C, E to Spring St.* ⊠*18 Wooster St., between Grand and Canal Sts., SoHo* ☎*212/343–7300* Ⓜ*A, C, E to Canal St.*

Drawing Center. At this nonprofit organization the focus is on contemporary and historical drawings seen nowhere else. Works often push the envelope on what's considered drawing; many projects are commissioned especially by the center. A second gallery is across the street at 40 Wooster Street. ⊠*35 Wooster St., between Broome and Grand Sts., SoHo* ☎*212/219–2166* ⊕*www.drawingcenter.org* Ⓜ*A, C, E to Canal St.*

Dining at Glance in SoHo & Little Italy

AT A GLANCE

BUDGET DINING
Lombardi's, Pizza,
32 Spring St.

MarieBelle, Café,
484 Broome St.

MODERATE DINING
Balthazar, Brasserie,
80 Spring St.

Blue Ribbon, New
American, 97 Sullivan St.

Blue Ribbon Sushi, Japanese, 119 Sullivan St.

Hundred Acres,
New American,
38 MacDougal St.

La Esquina, Mexican,
203 Lafayette St., at
Kenmare St.

Peasant, Italian, 194
Elizabeth St.

Public, Eclectic,
210 Elizabeth St.

Tasting Room,
New American, 264
Elizabeth St.

Woo Lae Oak, Korean,
148 Mercer St.

EXPENSIVE DINING
Aquagrill, Seafood,
210 Spring St.

Lure, Seafood,
142 Mercer St.

Savoy, American,
70 Prince St.

Nancy Hoffman. Contemporary painting, sculpture, drawing, prints, and photographic works by an impressive array of international artists are on display here. Gallery artists range from Rupert Deese, known for his conceptual shaped canvases, to Yuko Shiraishi, whose abstract oil paintings explore different tones of a single color. ✉ *429 West Broadway, between Prince and Spring Sts., SoHo* ☎ *212/966–6676* ⊕ *www. nancyhoffmangallery.com* Ⓜ *C, E to Spring St.; R, W to Prince St.*

New York Earth Room. Walter de Maria's 1977 avant-garde work consists of 140 tons of gently sculpted soil (22 inches deep) filling 3,600 square feet of space of a second-floor gallery maintained by the Dia Art Foundation. You cannot touch, tread on, tease, or otherwise molest the dirt, nor can you take its photo. If you like the work, check out de Maria's *Broken Kilometer,* a few blocks away at 393 West Broadway. ✉ *141 Wooster St., between W. Houston and Prince Sts., SoHo* ☎ *212/473–072* ⊕ *www.earthroom.org* ✉ *Free* ☉ *Open Wednesday through Sunday, noon to 6 pm (closed 3:00-3:30)* Ⓜ *R, W to Prince St.; B, D, F, V to Broadway-Lafayette.*

OK Harris Works of Art. This SoHo stalwart hosts a wide range of visual arts: paintings, digitally enhanced photographs, trompe-l'oeil reliefs, and sculptures. The gallery closes from mid-July to early September. ✉ *383 West Broadway, between Spring and Broome Sts., SoHo* ☎ *212/431–3600* ⊕ *www.okharris.com* Ⓜ *C, E to Spring St.*

Ronald Feldman Fine Arts. Founded in 1971, this gallery represents more than 30 international contemporary artists. It has a large selection of Andy Warhol prints, paintings, and drawings. ✉ *31 Mercer St., between Grand and Canal Sts., SoHo* ☎ *212/226–3232* ⊕ *www.feldmangallery. com* Ⓜ *J, M, N, Q, R, W, Z, 6 to Canal St.*

East Village & the Lower East Side

WORD OF MOUTH

"I have to say [the Tenement Museum] is one of the most interesting museums I have ever seen, especially in NYC. You can NOT begin to imagine how people coming to the U.S. lived back then. You must see this place. It was sad, humbling, but very, very interesting. I would heartily recommend!"

—skikat9

GETTING ORIENTED

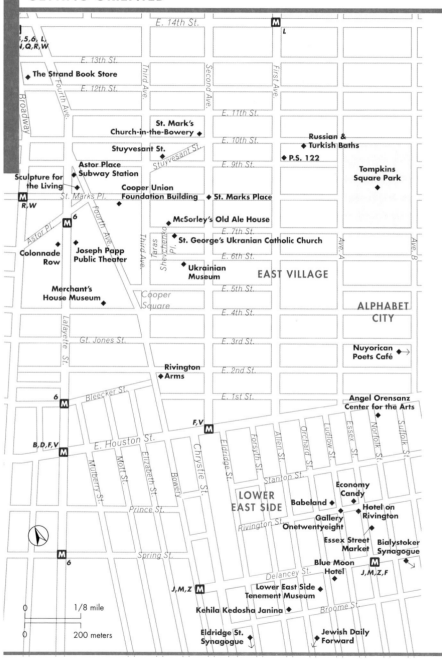

1,5,6, L,
N,Q,R,W

E. 14th St.

M L

E. 13th St.

Third Ave.

Second Ave.

First Ave.

◆ The Strand Book Store

E. 12th St.

Broadway

Fourth Ave.

E. 11th St.

St. Mark's
Church-in-the-Bowery ◆

E. 10th St.

Russian &
◆ Turkish Baths

Stuyvesant St.

Stuyvesant St.

◆ P.S. 122

Astor Place
◆ Subway Station

E. 9th St.

Tompkins
Square Park
◆

Sculpture for
the Living ◆

St. Marks Pl.

Cooper Union
Foundation Building   ◆ St. Marks Place

Fourth Ave.

M
R, W

M
6

Ave. A

Ave. B

Astor Pl.

McSorley's Old Ale House ◆

E. 7th St.

Colonnade
Row ◆

Joseph Papp
Public Theater

Third Ave.

Taras Shevchenko Pl.

◆ St. George's Ukranian Catholic Church

E. 6th St.

EAST VILLAGE

◆ Ukrainian
Museum

Merchant's
House Museum ◆

Cooper
Square

E. 5th St.

**ALPHABET
CITY**

Lafayette St.

E. 4th St.

Gt. Jones St.

E. 3rd St.

Nuyorican
Poets Café →

Rivington
◆ Arms

E. 2nd St.

6 M

Bleecker St.

E. 1st St.

Angel Orensanz
Center for the Arts

F, V
M

B, D, F, V
M

E. Houston St.

Mott St.

Elizabeth St.

Bowery

Chrystie St.

Eldridge St.

Forsyth St.

Allen St.

Orchard St.

Ludlow St.

Essex St.

Norfolk St.

Suffolk St.

Stanton St.

Mulberry St.

Prince St.

**LOWER
EAST SIDE**

Babeland ◆

Rivington St.

Gallery
Onetwentyeight

Economy
Candy

◆ Hotel on
Rivington

M
6

Spring St.

Essex Street
Market

Bialystoker
Synagogue

Blue Moon
Hotel

M
J,M,Z,F

0   1/8 mile

Delancey St.

J,M,Z M

Lower East Side
Tenement Museum

0   200 meters

Kehila Kedosha Janina ◆

Broome St.

Eldridge St.
Synagogue

Jewish Daily
Forward

MAKING THE MOST OF YOUR TIME

Houston Street, which runs the entire width of this part of Manhattan, somewhat neatly divides the area south of 14th Street and east of 4th Avenue and the Bowery into the East Village (above) and the Lower East Side (below). So many communities converge in these neighborhoods that each block seems like a new neighborhood unto itself.

The East Village lets loose on weekend nights, when reservations fill up and bar-hoppers converge. Visiting on weekdays makes for a more low-key experience, when establishments attract mostly locals shuffling on errands and visitors enjoying the mellow shopping and café vibe. Weekend days see the street life at its most vibrant, with brunch spots like EU and Max Brenner's filled with lingering patrons, and boutiques shoppers trying on vintage dresses.

The Lower East Side is not an early riser any day of the week. Although there's plenty to see during the day, nightfall offers a different vision: blocks that were previously empty rows of pulled-down gratings transform into clusters of throbbing bars. When shopping, be aware that a number of traditional food and clothing establishments close on Saturday to observe the Jewish Sabbath and, on Sunday, Orchard Street below Houston becomes a pedestrian-only strip where street vendors set up their stands outside the many "bargain district" clothing and specialty shops. On the increasingly trendy streets around Rivington and Stanton, stores, bars, and cafés buzz all week but are less crowded by day.

GETTING HERE

Driving is not recommended, as parking here is very difficult. A better choice is to take the R or W subway line to 8th Street or the 6 to Astor Place. To reach Alphabet City, take the L to 1st Avenue or the F or V to 2nd Avenue. Head southeast from the same stop on the F or V; or take the F to Delancey or the J, M, Z to Essex Street.

FODOR'S CHOICE

St. Marks Place

TOP ATTRACTIONS

Alphabet City
Astor Place subway station
Eldridge Street Synagogue
Russian & Turkish Baths

TOP EXPERIENCES

People-watching on
St. Marks Place
Stopping for a beer at McSorley's

BEST FOR KIDS

Tompkins Square Park
Lower East Side Tenement
Museum (⇨ Ch. 14)

NEARBY MUSEUMS (⇨ CH. 14)

Lower East Side Tenement
Museum
Merchant's House Museum
New Museum
Ukrainian Museum

AREA SHOPS (⇨ CH. 17)

Foley & Corinna
Las Venus
Other Music
Patricia Field
Screaming Mimi's

Sightseeing
★★
Nightlife
★★★★★
Dining
★★★★★
Lodging
★★
Shopping
★★★★

The high concept of "La Bohème meets hipsters in vintage clothing," better known as the musical *Rent,* accurately pegs the East Village as a community of artists, activists, and other social dissenters. Spend some time wandering these bohemian side streets, and you'll be struck by the funky pastiche of ethnicities whose imprints are visible in the neighborhood's restaurants, shops, and, of course, people. A smattering of painted walls and hookah bars belie the area's radical roots.

Updated by
Meryl D.
Pearlstein

Another defining point in the neighborhood's history, American punk was born here at the now-defunct CBGB; the punk rock/indie scene is kept alive at the many small music venues both here and on the Lower East Side. A walk along the lively but somewhat homogenized St. Mark's Place will evoke this once-gritty and counter-culture scene. But the arrival of a Trader Joes and several glass-and-chrome condos signal a tamer neighborhood has taken hold.

The Lower East Side, the historic "Gateway to America" for many seeking a better life, has seen waves of Irish, German, Jewish, Hispanic, and Chinese immigrants: a legacy of tough times and survival instincts that has been movingly captured in the Lower East Side Tenement Museum *(⇨ Chapter 14).* Today a cool arts and nighttime scene, some distinctively modern high-rises, and the ultracontemporary New Museum exist alongside buildings and cultural centers staunchly rooted in the past.

EAST VILLAGE

THREE WAYS TO EXPLORE

ASTOR PLACE: ANCHORED IN TIME

Stop a moment at Astor Place, the triangle formed by the intersections of East 8th Street, Lafayette Street, Astor Place, and 4th Avenue. The area seems frozen in time, in a way, with both a university and an arts community holding on to the idealism of the neighborhood's past. On any given day you can see students from NYU or Cooper Union shooting a film or sketching a scene; political groups soliciting signatures; and punks and rockers boldly evincing the city's bohemian subculture. A few blocks north is the **Strand**, an enormous bookstore where you can spend hours among its "18 miles of books."

Distinctive architecture and design are also part of this area's legacy. On East 4th Street off Lafayette is the **Merchant's House Museum,** an example of upscale residential Manhattan life in the 19th century, and open for a self-guided tour. Although now in a sorry state, **Colonnade Row,** around the corner along Lafayette Street, is marked by marble Corinthian columns in front of a sweep of Greek Revival mansions once home to millionaires John Jacob Astor and Cornelius Vanderbilt. You'll have to look closely to see them, through the soot and above the mix of theaters and restaurants and other retail that now fill their lower levels.

Out of sync with this somewhat idealistic and artsy setting is the **Sculpture for Living** building, a much-maligned glass-and-steel tower of million-dollar apartments. The building's name and shape seem to ironically reference what had previously been Astor Place's focal point, **the Alamo,** a giant spinning cube on the central traffic island. New York City's first public abstract sculpture, the cube defiantly remains a hangout for skateboarders and tattooed kids. At the entrance to the **Astor Place Subway Station** is a cast-iron replica of the Beaux-Arts kiosks that covered most subway entrances in the early 20th century.

STREETS WITH A CHARACTER OF THEIR OWN

The East Village is an area of nonconformity, and its streets are no different. East 6th Street between 2nd and 3rd avenues is known as Little India. Spilling around the corners to each of the avenues, Bangladeshi and Indian restaurants offer inexpensive, authentic dining choices, some with musicians visible through their glass windows. Two blocks east, the strip between Avenues A and B has an eclectic assortment of South American and other international (and generally affordable) restaurants.

East 7th Street between 2nd and 3rd avenues is dominated by **St. George's Ukrainian Catholic Church,** the meeting place for the local Ukrainian community and the site of an annual Ukrainian folk festival in spring. Incongruously, the block also has an odd assortment of brewpubs, including the grizzly **McSorley's Old Ale House** which remains unchanged in both menu and decor over its 100-plus-year-old history, but it now allows women to partake in the revelry.

One block north is **St. Marks Place,** aka 8th Street between 3rd Avenue and Avenue A. Over the years, beatniks, artists, and punk rockers have congregated at this hub of the East Village scene. Today the block between 2nd and 3rd avenues feels like a shopping arcade for Goths and the vinyl-pants set. It's crammed with body piercing and tattoo salons; shops selling cheap jewelry, sunglasses, incense, and caustic T-shirts; restaurants and bars; plus the city's only food automat, BAMN! And if you've craving Asian food, there seems to be a new restaurant opening here every day.■ TIP➜ Many claim that the egg cream was hatched at Gem Spa (⊠ 131 2nd Ave. ☎ 212/995–1866), a 24-hour newsstand at the corner of St. Marks and 2nd Avenue. Cold milk, seltzer, and chocolate or vanilla syrup combine to make this peculiarly New York drink, which comes in two sizes: $2 for a small, $2.50 for a large.

One block north and a proverbial world away in look and feel is Stuyvesant Street, a strip of historic redbrick row houses and the oldest street in Manhattan, laid out along a precise east–west axis (other streets in the city follow the island's geographic orientation). Fitting in perfectly is **St. Mark's-in-the-Bowery Church,** a charming 1799 fieldstone country church that occupies the former site of Dutch governor Peter Stuyvesant's family chapel.

THE CITY'S BOHEMIA

East of 1st Avenue is nicknamed **Alphabet City,** with avenues designated by letters instead of numbers. Alphabet City was once a burned-out area of slums and drug haunts, but has gentrified somewhat and is pretty safe today. The area has a young, artistic rawness about it, and the energy flows strongly in the late hours in the tiny bars and innovative restaurants around Avenues A, B, and C. At the center of the crowded tenements is **Tompkins Square Park,** a popular hangout with playgrounds, green expanses, and active dog runs. The Avenue A side has one of the city's most interesting arrays of inexpensive ethnic restaurants, Internet cafés, collectibles shops, and low-rent bars. The area has a strong artistic bent, with numerous sculpture-filled community gardens and the popular Friday-night poetry slam at the **Nuyorican Poets Café** on East 3rd Street between Avenues B and C. At 151 Avenue B, on the west side of the park, stands a brownstone where jazz saxophonist Charlie Parker lived in the '50s.

TOP ATTRACTIONS

Alphabet City. The north–south avenues east of 1st Avenue, from Houston Street to 14th Street, are all labeled with letters, not numbers, which give this area its nickname, Alphabet City. With the exception of Avenue D, it is now fairly gentrified, with colorful community gardens dotting the area. The many reasonably priced restaurants with their bohemian atmosphere on Avenues A, B, and C, and the cross streets in between, attract all kinds. A close-knit Puerto Rican community makes its home around Avenue C, with predominantly Latino shops and bodegas, plus a "Nuyorican" café and music venue. Avenue A along the park has a wide variety of ethnic cafés and bars, and Avenue B likewise has a growing restaurant scene. Also called Loisaida Avenue (a Spanglish

Vibrant vintage clothing boutiques and pop culture shops display the funky, freewheeling vibe of the East Village.

creation meaning Lower East Side), Avenue C has a few fun spots like **Sunburnt Cow** and **Esperanto.** ⊠ *East Village* Ⓜ*6 to Astor Pl.; L to 1st Ave.; F, V to 2nd Ave.*

Astor Place Subway Station. At the beginning of the 20th century, almost every Interborough Rapid Transit (IRT) subway entrance resembled the ornate cast-iron replica of a Beaux-Arts kiosk that covers the stairway leading to the uptown No. 6 train here. Inside, plaques of beaver emblems line the tiled station walls, a reference to the fur trade that contributed to John Jacob Astor's fortune. Milton Glaser, a Cooper Union graduate, designed the station's murals. ⊠*On traffic island at E. 8th St. and 4th Ave., East Village* Ⓜ*6 to Astor Pl.*

McSorley's Old Ale House. Joseph Mitchell immortalized this spot, which claims to be one of the city's oldest, in *The New Yorker.* Opened in 1854, it didn't admit women until 1970. Fortunately, it now offers separate restrooms. The mahogany bar, gas lamps, potbelly stove, and yellowing newspaper clips are originals. Try to visit on a weekday before 7 PM so you can enjoy one of the two McSorley's ales and a cheese plate with onions in relative peace. Be warned: on weekends this place is a zoo, and there can be a line to get in day or night. ⊠*15 E. 7th St., between 2nd and 3rd Aves., East Village* ☎*212/473–9148* Ⓜ*6 to Astor Pl.*

Russian & Turkish Baths. It's clear from the older Soviet types devouring blintzes and Baltika beer served in the lobby that this is no cushy, uptown spa. But the three-story public bathhouse, which dates to 1892, isn't about pampering as much as hearty, Slavic-style cleansing. There's a eucalyptus steam room, a Finnish sauna, pull-chain showers, and an

CLOSE UP

Keep Your Eyes Peeled

The East Village's reputation for quirkiness is evidenced not only among its residents and sites but also in the many incongruous structures that somehow coexist so easily that they can go almost unnoticed. Keep your eyes open as you explore the streets. You never know what might turn up:

■ The Hells Angel's Headquarters tucked into a residential block of 3rd Street between 1st and 2nd avenues, surrounded by a bevy of showstopping bikes.

■ The architectural "joke" on New York City atop the Red Square building on Houston Street at Norfolk, where a statue of Lenin points to the sky and a clock has lost its notion of time.

■ The shingled Cape Cod–style house perched on the apartment building at the northwest corner of Houston and 1st Avenue, one of the city's many unique rooftop retreats. It's best viewed from the east.

■ Two nearly hidden but airy "marble" cemeteries (New York Marble Cemetery and the New York City Marble Cemetery), hold remains in marble-lined vaults thought to prevent the spread of miasma. They can be visited at select times during the year at 2nd Avenue at 2nd Street and at 2nd Street and 1st Avenue.

ice-cold plunge pool (45°F), and you're encouraged to alternate cooking in the hot rooms with plunges in the cold pool to stimulate circulation, a bathing cultures staple. Traditional massages and scrubs are offered without appointment, including the detoxifying Platza (Oak Leaf Treatment; $35), in which a Russian strongman or -woman swats your soapy skin with an oak-leaf broom. Except for a few single-sex hours per week on Wednesday, Thursday, and Sunday, the baths are coed, with bathing suits or shorts worn, and felt hats (alleged to decrease lightheadedness) for the seriously old-school. ✉ *268 E. 10th St., between 1st Ave. and Ave. A, East Village* ☎ *212/674–9250* ⊕ *www.russianturkishbaths.com* ✉ *$30* ⊙ *Weekdays noon–10, Sat., 9* AM*–10* PM*, Sun. 8* AM*–10* PM Ⓜ *L to 1st Ave.*

Fodor'sChoice **St. Marks Place.** The longtime hub of the edgy East Village, St. Marks
★   Place is the name given to idiosyncratic East 8th Street between 3rd Avenue and Avenue A. During the 1950s, beatniks Allen Ginsberg and Jack Kerouac lived and wrote in the area; the 1960s brought Bill Graham's Fillmore East, Andy Warhol's the Dom, the Electric Circus nightclub, and hallucinogenic drugs. The studded, pink-haired and shaved-head punk scene followed, continuing today along with pierced rockers and teenage Goths. The blocks between 2nd and 3rd avenues have time-tested alternative-clothing boutiques and Asian restaurants galore. At 80 St. Marks Place, near 1st Avenue, is the Pearl Theatre Company, which performs classic plays from around the world. The handprints, footprints, and autographs of such past screen luminaries as Joan Crawford, Ruby Keeler, Joan Blondell, and Myrna Loy lie in its sidewalk. At 96–98 St. Marks Place (between 1st Avenue and Avenue A) stands the building that was photographed for the cover of Led Zeppelin's *Physical*

Where can I find...?

COFFEE	Black Hound New York 170 2nd Ave. Coffee and "Busy Bee Cake" in a New York minute.	D'espresso 100 Stanton St. Italian-style coffee, plus the pastries to match.
A QUICK BITE	Katz's Delicatessen 205 E. Houston St. Yes, yes, yes, Meg Ryan had her big scene right here.	Il Laboratorio del Gelato 95 Orchard St. Seasonal flavors make this gelato la crème de la crème.
COCKTAILS	Cake Shop 152 Ludlow St. A kickin' blend of music, drinks, and coffee.	McSorley's Old Ale House 15 E. 7th St. "McSurly" service? Who cares? It's about the beer.

Graffiti album. The cafés between 2nd Avenue and Avenue A attract customers late into the night. Ⓜ 6 to Astor Pl.

Tompkins Square Park. This leafy spot amid the East Village's crowded tenements is a release valve. The park fills up with locals year-round, partaking in picnics, drum circles, the playground, and two dog runs. The Charlie Parker Jazz Festival, honoring the former park-side resident and noted jazz saxophonist, packs the park in late August. But it wasn't always so rosy. In 1988 police followed then-mayor David Dinkins's orders to clear the many homeless who had set up makeshift homes here, and homeless rights and antigentrification activists fought back with sticks and bottles. The park was reclaimed and reopened in 1992 with a midnight curfew, still in effect today. ✉ *Bordered by Aves. A and B and E. 7th and E. 10th Sts., East Village* Ⓜ 6 to Astor Pl.; L to 1st Ave.

ALSO WORTH SEEING

Colonnade Row. Marble Corinthian columns on the second level front this shabby-but-grand sweep of four Greek Revival mansions (originally nine) constructed in 1833, with stonework by Sing Sing penitentiary prisoners. These once-elegant homes served as residences to millionaires John Jacob Astor and Cornelius Vanderbilt until they moved uptown. Today they house apartments, stores, and restaurants, and the northernmost building is the home of the Astor Place Theatre and *Blue Man Group.* ✉ *428–434 Lafayette St., between Astor Pl. and E. 4th St., East Village* Ⓜ 6 to Astor Pl.

St. Mark's Church in-the-Bowery. This charming 1799 fieldstone country church stands on what was once Governor Peter Stuyvesant's *bouwerie,* or farm. St. Mark's is Manhattan's oldest continually used Christian site, and both Stuyvesant and Commodore Perry are buried here in vaults. Be sure to check out the gorgeous modern stained-glass windows on the balcony, which replaced the more traditional windows like those on the ground level, after a fire in the late '70s. Over the years St. Mark's has hosted many progressive arts events including readings by poet Carl Sandburg and dance performances by Martha Graham and Merce Cunningham. It is considered quite an honor to perform in this multi-use church, and the tradition has continued with Danspace, the Poetry Project, and the Ontological Hysteric-Theater, which give performances throughout the year. ⊠*131 E. 10th St., at 2nd Ave., East Village* ☎*212/674–6377* Ⓜ *6 to Astor Pl.; L to 3rd Ave.*

Sculpture for Living. A few steps down from the Public Theater near Cooper Union sits this residential skyscraper, an anomaly among the predominantly low-rise, traditional architecture of this neighborhood. The curving glass building was designed by postmodern architect Charles Gwathmey (known for his addition to the Guggenheim Museum). ⊠*7 E. 7th St., at 3rd Ave., East Village* Ⓜ *6 to Astor Pl.; R, W to 8th St./Broadway.*

Stuyvesant Street. This diagonal slicing through the block bounded by 2nd and 3rd avenues and East 9th and 10th streets is unique in Manhattan: it's the oldest street laid out precisely along an east–west axis. Among the handsome 19th-century redbrick row houses are the Federal-style **Stuyvesant-Fish House** (⊠*21 Stuyvesant St., East Village*), built as a wedding gift for a great-great-granddaughter of the Dutch governor Peter Stuyvesant, and **Renwick Triangle,** an attractive group of Anglo-Italianate brick and brownstone residences, which face Stuyvesant and East 10th streets. Ⓜ*6 to Astor Pl.*

LOWER EAST SIDE

THREE WAYS TO EXPLORE

THE HISTORIC LOWER EAST SIDE: GATEWAY TO AMERICA

Directly south of the East Village, on the other side of Houston Street, is the traditional Lower East Side, a juxtaposition of old and new worlds, where a hot nightlife scene is growing amid aged businesses that hark back to the area's immigrant heritage. The historic heart of the Lower East Side is Orchard Street, the center of New York's fabric and garment district at the turn of the 20th century. At the **Lower East Side Tenement Museum** (⇨ *Chapter 14*) five different tours draw you into Irish, German, Polish, Jewish, and Sicilian family life of the period. Some of the old building fronts remain, as do dated clothing shops (the so-called Bargain District), but younger fashion-furious boutiques and other cool shops have started to move in as well. Further proof of the surprising gentrification occurring here are the new **Blue Moon Hotel,** retrofitted across the street in a five-story tenement, and the all-glass high-rise **Hotel on Rivington** with the sleek restaurant Thor.

THE REMNANTS OF THE FIRST JEWISH IMMIGRANT COMMUNITY IN THE CITY

Several historic synagogues, their gorgeous facades squeezed among the tenements, are still in use. The **Eldridge Street Synagogue** was the first Orthodox synagogue erected by the large number of Eastern European Jews who settled on the Lower East Side in the late 1880s. Its main sanctuary has just completed a glorious restoration allowing the synagogue to become a permanent museum and home to its practicing orthodox congregation. The only Romaniote (Greek Jewish) synagogue in the western hemisphere, **Kehila Kedosha Janina** also functions as a museum to this obscure branch of Judaism. The city's oldest synagogue, dating to 1850, is now the funky **Angel Orensanz Center for the Arts**, named for the sculptor who purchased the synagogue when it fell into disrepair. This originally German synagogue was modeled after the Cathedral of Cologne and now hosts exhibits and dramatically lighted events such as the wedding of Sarah Jessica Parker and Matthew Broderick. The busiest of the Lower East Side synagogues today is the orthodox **Bialystoker Synagogue** with its dramatic blue-sky, clouds-and-stars ceiling; scenes from the Zodiac; and "hidden" balcony door (you can open it), which was once used by the Underground Railroad to hide slaves during the synagogue's former days as a Methodist church.

Starting on Houston Street and heading south along Essex, Allen, and Orchard streets, you can munch on traditional pickles, bialys, knishes, and strudel as you walk by buildings with Hebrew letters and antique Jewish books in the windows. The indoor **Essex Street Market** took the place of the pushcarts that once dominated Hester Street and has a colorful assortment of fish markets, butchers, and Latino shops. (Note that it's not open on Sunday.)

CENTER FOR THE CULTURALLY HIP

The epicenter of the trendy, gentrified Lower East Side falls along parallel Rivington and Stanton streets, between Orchard and Essex streets, and the section of Ludlow Street that crosses them. Among the restaurants, boutiques, and bars are stores that fluctuate from hip to historic, like **Babeland**, a women-oriented sex shop, and **Economy Candy**, every kids' fantasy and a pseudo-general store literally crammed to the rafters with barrels of nuts and shelves of old-time and current candy favorites.

TOP ATTRACTIONS

Eldridge Street Synagogue. This was the first Orthodox synagogue erected by the large number of Eastern European Jews who settled in the Lower East Side in the late 19th century. The exterior is a striking mix of Romanesque, Gothic, and Moorish motifs. Inside is an exceptional hand-carved ark of mahogany and walnut, a sculptured wooden balcony, jewel-tone stained-glass windows, stenciled walls, and an enormous brass chandelier. A much-anticipated and massive renovation of this beloved synagogue was completed in late 2007. The synagogue can be viewed as part of a tour, and begins at the small museum downstairs where interactive "touch tables" teach all ages about Eldridge Street and

East Village & Lower East Side Dining

BUDGET DINING

Kampuchea, Cambodian, 78 Rivington St., at Allen St.

Katz's Delicatessen, Deli, 205 E. Houston St., at Ludlow St.

Mexicana Mama, Mexican, 47 E. 12th St., bet. B'way and University Pl.

Momofuku Noodle Bar, Japanese, 171 1st Ave., bet. E. 10th and E. 11 Sts.

Piola, Pizza, 48 E. 12th St., bet. B'way and University Pl.

Schiller's Liquor Bar, Bistro, 131 Rivington St., at Norfolk St.

Una Pizza Napoletana, Pizza, 349 E. 12th St., at 2nd Ave.

Veniero's Pasticceria, Café, 342 E. 11th St., near 1st Ave.

MODERATE DINING

Apiary, New American, 60 3rd Ave

Chinatown Brasserie, Chinese, 380 Lafayette St., at Great Jones St.

Five Points, American, 31 Great Jones St., bet. Lafayette St. and Bowery

Gnocco, Italian, 337 E. 10th St., bet. Aves. A and B

Il Buco, Italian, 47 Bond St., bet. the Bowery and Lafayette St.

'inoteca, Italian, 98 Rivington St., at Ludlow St.

Jewel Bako, Japanese, 239 E. 5th St., near 2nd Ave.

Prune, New American, 54 E. 1st St., bet. 1st and 2nd Aves.

Rayuela, Latin, 165 Allen St.

wd~50, New American, 50 Clinton St., bet. Rivington and Stanton Sts.

EXPENSIVE DINING

Momofuku Ko, Japanese, 163 1st Ave

the Lower East Side. Family programs add to the community experience. ✉*12 Eldridge St., between Canal and Division Sts., Lower East Side* ☎*212/219–0888* ⊕*www.eldridgestreet.org* 🎫*$5* ☉ *Sun.–Thurs. 10–4; tours on the half hr 10:30* AM–3:30 PM Ⓜ*F to E. Broadway; B, D to Grand St.*

★ **Gallery Onetwentyeight.** Inside the jewel-box space, artist Kazuko Miyamoto directs crisp and provocative group shows. ✉*128 Rivington St., between Essex and Norfolk Sts., Lower East Side* ☎*212/674–0244* ⊕*www.galleryonetwentyeight.org* Ⓜ*F to Delancey St.; J, M, Z to Essex St.*

Rivington Arms. In a town house with a quirky and casual mind-atmosphere, this gallery shows young, emerging artists. Look for the photographic-sound works of collective Lansing-Dreiden and portrait paintings by Mathew Cerletty. ✉*4 E. 2nd St., at the Bowery, Lower East Side* ☎*646/654–3213* ⊕*www.rivingtonarms.com* Ⓜ*F to Delancey St.; J, M, Z to Essex St.*

Greenwich Village & Chelsea

WORD OF MOUTH

"I would recommend simply walking the area. There is the beautiful Washington Square Mews one block north of [Washington] Square with cobblestone and old carriage house to blocks of wonderful brownstones and limestones and other streets with some of the best specialty shops in the city"

—amanda amanda

GETTING ORIENTED

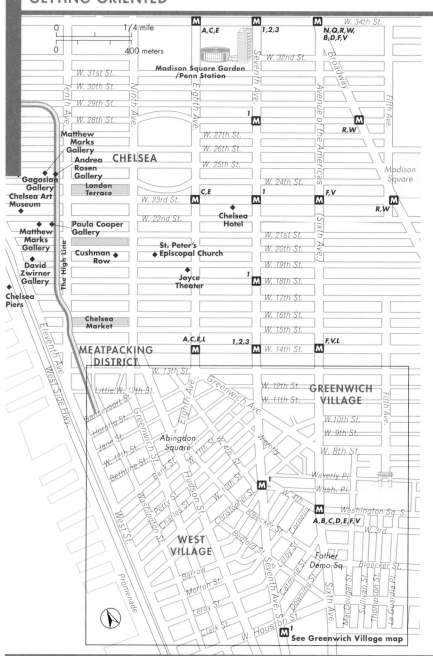

MAKING THE MOST OF YOUR TIME

Weekday afternoons the streets of the West Village are nearly empty. Because of the many artists, students, and writers who live here, you'll have just enough company at the cafés and shops to make you feel like an insider instead of a tourist. To truly appreciate the Meatpacking District, make a 9 PM or later dinner reservation at a hot restaurant, then hit the bars to see where the glitterati are this week. If shopping is your pleasure, weekdays are great; come after noon, though, or you'll find most spots shuttered.

Chelsea has a dual life: typical gallery hours are Tuesday–Saturday 10–6, but at night the neighborhood changes into a party town with gay bars and difficult-to-enter clubs that don't rev up until after 10.

GETTING HERE

The West 4th Street subway stop—serviced by the A, B, C, D, E, F, and V—puts you in the center of Greenwich Village. Farther west, the 1 train has stops on West Houston Street and Christopher Street/Sheridan Square. The A, C, E, and 1, 2, 3, and L trains stop at 14th Street for both the Meatpacking District and Chelsea. The latter is further served by the C, E, 1, F, and V lines at the 23rd Street stop and the 1 stops at 28th Street. The L train connects Union Square on 14th Street to the Meatpacking District at 8th Avenue and 14th Street. 14th Street and 23rd Street are both also served by the PATH trains.

WORD OF MOUTH (WWW.FODORS.COM/FORUMS)

"Weave your way through the West Village and definitely go down Bleecker Street (all the way down) for amazing bakeries, cheese shops and grab a slice of cake at Amy's or a dessert and coffee/hot chocolate with homemade whipped cream at Rocco's."   —amanda amanda

FODOR'S CHOICE

Chelsea Market
Washington Square Park

TOP ATTRACTIONS

Chelsea Hotel
Cushman Row
Gay Street
Patchin Place
75½ Bedford Street

TOP EXPERIENCES

Gallery-hopping in Chelsea
Wandering along Bedford, Barrow, Grove, and Commerce streets
Clubbing in the Meatpacking District

BEST FOR KIDS

Chelsea Piers
The High Line
Hudson River Park

NEARBY MUSEUMS (⇨ CH. 14)

Chelsea Art Museum
Forbes Galleries
Rubin Museum of Art

AREA SHOPS (⇨ CH. 17)

Aedes De Venustas
Books of Wonder
Bottle Rocket
Fisch for the Hip
Flight 001
Loehmann's
Mxyplyzyk

5

Sightseeing
★★★
Nightlife
★★★★★
Dining
★★★★★
Lodging
★★★
Shopping
★★★★

Updated by
Meryl D.
Pearlstein

Long the home of writers, artists, bohemians, and bon vivants, the West Village is a singular section of the city. High-rises and office towers have no business among the small curving streets, peculiar alleys, and historic town houses here, although a new boom in distinctive apartment living by designer architects has emerged around the west edges of the Village north to Chelsea. Primarily residential, the area also has many specialty restaurants, cafés, and boutiques with a warm and charming neighborhood vibe. Tiny as they might be, restaurants like The Little Owl and P*ong invite you to linger as do larger restaurants with outside dining areas.

Fertile doesn't even begin to describe the West Village's yield of creative genius. In the late 1940s and early 1950s, abstract expressionist painters Franz Kline, Jackson Pollock, Mark Rothko, and Willem de Kooning congregated here, as did Beat writers Jack Kerouac, Allen Ginsberg, and Lawrence Ferlinghetti. The '60s brought folk musicians and poets, notably Bob Dylan. NYU students keep the idealistic spirit of the neighborhood alive, but polished professionals have also moved into the high-rent town houses. The Meatpacking District, in the far northwest part of the Village, has cobblestone streets whose original meatpacking tenants are being replaced by a different kind of meat-market life: velvet-rope clubs, trendy restaurants, and trendy-chic shops.

Overlapping the Meatpacking District to the north, stylish Chelsea has usurped SoHo as the world's contemporary-art-gallery headquarters (an extensive gallery list and map at the end of this chapter will help you find your way). The west edge of the neighborhood has high-profile galleries housed in cavernous converted warehouses that are easily identified by their ultracool, glass-and-stainless-steel doors. Other former warehouses, unremarkable by day, pulsate through the night as the city's hottest nightclubs. Chelsea has also replaced the West Village as the heart of the city's gay community. One-of-a-kind boutiques and gay-friendly shops are scattered among unassuming grocery stores and other remnants of Chelsea's immigrant past.

GREENWICH VILLAGE AND THE MEATPACKING DISTRICT

FIVE WAYS TO EXPLORE

PARKS, STATELY LIVING AND ARCHITECTURAL NOTABLES

At **Washington Square Park** the city's central business artery, 5th Avenue, ends, and the student-bohemian feel of the Village begins. Circle the recently spruced-up open square, but don't expect to find a bench or fountain-side seat not occupied by New York University students, professors, pigeon-feeders, or idlers of all sorts. On the park's north side is the grand **Washington Memorial Arch**, which looks upon the **Row**, two blocks of lovingly preserved Greek Revival and Federal-style town houses.

Residences are sometimes tucked away in little enclaves in the Village. **Washington Mews** and **MacDougal Alley** are two cobblestone private streets just above the park. **Grove Court**, a cluster of brick-front homes, seems like a precursor to today's gated communities. West of 6th Avenue on 10th Street is the wrought-iron gateway to a tiny courtyard called **Patchin Place.** Around the corner is another alley filled with homes, **Milligan Place.**

The beautiful blocks of 19th-century redbrick town houses that predominate in the Village are occasionally marked by attempts at nonconformity. At **18 West 11th Street** sits a home with a modern, angled bay window, a building erected to replace the town house inadvertently blown up by the antiwar group the Weathermen in 1970. The triangle formed by West 10th Street, 6th Avenue, and Greenwich Avenue originally held a market, a jail, and the magnificent towered courthouse that is now the **Jefferson Market Library.** Where Christopher Street crosses Waverly Place is the triangular-shape 1831 brick **Northern Dispensary building.**

A SINGULAR STREET

Christopher Street has long been the symbolic heart of New York's gay and lesbian community. On this street, among cafés, lifestyle boutiques, and clothing shops, is one of the city's most acclaimed off-Broadway theaters, the **Lucille Lortel,** where major off-Broadway playwrights like David Mamet, Eugene Ionesco, and Edward Albee have their own markers in the sidewalk. There's also an active nightlife scene, anchored by the **Duplex** piano bar and cabaret at the corner of 7th Avenue. At **51–53 Christopher Street,** the historic Stonewall riots marked the beginning of the gay rights movement. Across the street is a green triangle

5

named **Christopher Park,** where commemorative statues of gay and lesbian companions mingle with real-live visitors. Far west, where Christopher Street continues to the river, a fountain and a landscaped pier with benches mark a stop in **Hudson River Park,** part of the city's greenway.

YOU'RE GUARANTEED TO GET LOST HERE

West of 7th Avenue South, the Village turns into a picture-book town of twisting tree-lined streets, quaint houses, and tiny restaurants. Streets cross back and forth, and Greenwich Street and Greenwich Avenue bear no relation to each other. In a seemingly random way, West 4th inexplicably crosses West 10th and West 11th streets.

The area where Grove and Bedford streets intersect is among the most beautiful in the Village. These streets still feel like 19th-century New York, with simple redbrick homes from the early part of the century as well as a clapboard home and even a home built to resemble a Swiss chalet. Commerce Street, the location of the historic **Cherry Lane Theatre,** is undoubtedly one of the city's most romantic lanes. Minetta Lane, a "hidden" alley dating from the city's speakeasy history, lies between Washington Square Park and 6th Avenue and is now home to the innovative **Minetta Lane Theatre** and **Minetta Tavern.**

A STREET THAT DEFINES A NEIGHBORHOOD

If you walk from one end of Bleecker Street to another, you can pass through a smattering of everything Village: NYU buildings, used-record stores, Italian cafés and food shops, charming restaurants and bakeries, and funky boutiques, plus a park with a playground and tables and benches. Because of all the shops and crowds, Bleecker Street between 6th and 7th avenues seems more of a vibrant Italian neighborhood today than the city's eponymous Little Italy. On this extended block you can grab an espresso and *zuppa inglese,* check out century-old butcher shops, and sample some of the city's best thin-crust pizza. West of 7th Avenue, you can also find fashion and home-furnishings boutiques featuring antiques, eyeglasses, shoes, and designer clothing.

To absorb some of the area's idealism and spirituality, stop at **Our Lady of Pompeii Church** at Bleecker and Carmine, where Mother Cabrini, a naturalized Italian immigrant who became the first American saint, often prayed. At 119 MacDougal Street is **Caffe Reggio,** one of the Village's first coffeehouses, pretty much unchanged since it opened in 1927. Partly because of the proximity of NYU, the streets in the area also attract a young crowd to its theaters, cabarets, and jazz clubs. Two of the best for getting your jazz on are the **Blue Note** at West 3rd near 6th Avenue and the **Village Vanguard** on 7th Avenue South just below West 11th Street, considered by many to be "the Carnegie Hall of jazz."

GLAM, NIGHTLIFE, AND THE CITY THAT NEVER SLEEPS

The **Meatpacking District** is concentrated in a few blocks of the West Village, between the Hudson River and 9th Avenue, from Little West 12th Street to West 14th Street, with some fringe activity heading toward West 16th Street. This burgeoning cobblestoned area is a meat market by morning, and a metaphorical one at night, when the city's trendiest frequent the equally trendy restaurants and bars here. Attracting a late-day shopping crowd, affluent-angled retailers and services line West

CLOSE UP

Bleecker Street's "Little Italy"

Little Italy can be besieged by slow-moving crowds, touristy shops, and desperate restaurant owners who call at you like shooting-gallery barkers at Coney Island. With its crowded cafés, bakeries, pizza parlors, and old-world merchants, Bleecker Street between 6th and 7th avenues seems more vital as a true Italian neighborhood.

For an authentic Italian bakery experience, step into **Rocco's** (No. 243) for wonderful cannoli, cream puffs, and cookies packed up or order an espresso to linger over the treats.

Step into the past at the old-style butcher shops, such as **Ottomanelli & Sons** (No. 285) and **Faicco's Sausage Store** (No. 260), where Italian locals have gotten their pork custom cut since 1900.

The sweet (or stinky) smell of success seems nowhere more evident than at **Murray's Cheese** (No. 254), at Cornelia Street. The original shop, opened in 1940 by Murray Greenberg (not Italian), was not much larger than the display case that stocked the stuff. Now it's a fromage fiend's emporium, with everything from imported crackers to bamboo cutting boards. Samples of cheese, gelato, salami, and other goodies are frequently offered.

In a town that's fierce about its pizza, some New Yorkers swear by **John's Pizzeria** (No. 278). But be forewarned: they don't deal in individual slices—whole thin-crust pies only. Got diet-breaking guilt? Head east to Carmine Street and Our Lady of Pompeii Church, where Mother Cabrini, a naturalized Italian immigrant and the first American saint, often prayed.

5

14th Street and include hair-cutting extortionist **Sally Hershberger** (whose cuts cost about $800) and the boutiques of fashion designers **Alexander McQueen** and **Stella McCartney.** For one of the city's most extensive and expensive shoe departments, visit **Jeffrey,** the district's pioneer retailer.

The city's recent crop of slick megarestaurants seem to have found their homes in the streets between Little West 12th and West 16th, with huge Asian-food and -style "temples" like **Buddakan** (16th Street and 9th Avenue), **Morimoto** (16th Street and 10th Avenue), **Matsuri** (16th Street and 9th Avenue), and **Buddha Bar** (Little West 12th between 9th Avenue and Washington Street). Equally sexy but somewhat smaller, **Spice Market** has a rich Southeast Asian design, Merkato 55 tumbles through African flavors, and late-night hot spot **Pastis** is a wall-to-wall version French bistro scene. The scene-y **Hotel Gansevoort** is brilliant purple at night and has a rooftop pool and bar. From the top you can look down at the pool at the private SoHo House, used in *Sex and the City*. A notable exception among all the glitz is the rough-and-tumble **Hogs and Heifers,** on 13th Street, a neighborhood drinking hole infamous for its bra-covered bar and the movie *Coyote Ugly,* based on it.

TOP ATTRACTIONS

Gay Street. A curved, one-block lane lined with small row houses, Gay Street is named after Sydney Howard Gay, managing editor of the long-defunct *New York Tribune,* who lived here during the Civil War with his wife and fellow abolitionist, Lucretia Mott. In the 1930s this darling thoroughfare and nearby Christopher Street became famous nationwide when, from No. 14, Ruth McKenney wrote her somewhat zany autobiographical stories published in *The New Yorker* and later in *My Sister Eileen,* based on what happened when she and her sister moved to Greenwich Village from Ohio. Also on Gay Street, Howdy Doody was designed in the basement of No. 12. ⊠ *Between Christopher St. and Waverly Pl., Greenwich Village* Ⓜ *1 to Christopher St./Sheridan Sq.; A, B, C, D, E, F, V to W. 4th St.*

Patchin Place. This little cul-de-sac off West 10th Street between Greenwich and 6th avenues has 10 diminutive 1848 row houses. Around the corner on 6th Avenue is a similar dead-end street, **Milligan Place,** with five small homes completed in 1852. The houses in both quiet enclaves were originally built for waiters who worked at 5th Avenue's high-society Brevoort Hotel, long since demolished. Later Patchin Place residents included writers Theodore Dreiser, e.e. cummings, Jane Bowles, and Djuna Barnes. Milligan Place became popular among playwrights, including Eugene O'Neill. Ⓜ *A, B, C, D, E, F, V to W. 4th St.*

75½ Bedford Street. Rising real-estate rates inspired the construction of New York City's narrowest house—just 9½ feet wide—in 1873. Built on a lot that was originally a carriage entrance of the Isaacs-Hendricks House next door, this sliver of a building was home to actor John Barrymore and poet Edna St. Vincent Millay. ⊠ *75½ Bedford St., between Commerce and Morton Sts., Greenwich Village* Ⓜ *A, B, C, D, E, F, V to W. 4th St.*

Fodor'sChoice ★ Ⓒ **Washington Square Park.** NYU students, street musicians, skateboarders, jugglers, chess players, and those just watching the grand opera of it all generate a maelstrom of activity in this physical and spiritual heart of the Village. The newly restored 9½-acre park had inauspicious beginnings as a cemetery, principally for yellow fever victims—an estimated 10,000–22,000 bodies lie below. At one time, plans to renovate the park called for the removal of the bodies; however, local resistance prevented this from happening. In the early 1800s the park was a parade ground and the site of public executions; bodies dangled from a conspicuous Hanging Elm that still stands at the northwest corner of the square. Today playgrounds attract parents with tots in tow, dogs go leash-free inside the popular dog runs, and everyone else seems drawn toward the large central fountain.

The triumphal European-style **Washington Memorial Arch** stands at the square's north end, marking the start of 5th Avenue. In 1889 Stanford White designed a wood-and-papier-mâché arch, originally situated a half block north, to commemorate the 100th anniversary of George Washington's presidential inauguration. The arch was reproduced in Tuckahoe marble in 1892, and the statues—*Washington as General Accompanied by Fame and Valor* on the left, and *Washington*

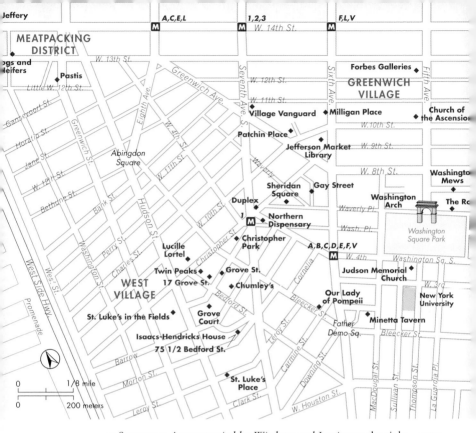

as *Statesman Accompanied by Wisdom and Justice* on the right—were added in 1916 and 1918, respectively. ⊠ *5th Ave. between Waverly Pl. and 4th St., Greenwich Village* Ⓜ *A, B, C, D, E, F, V to W. 4th St.*

ALSO WORTH SEEING

Chumley's. A speakeasy during the Prohibition era, this still-secret tavern behind an unmarked door on Bedford Street has been closed for structural reasons for a few years. Inside, however, it retains its original ambience with oak booths, a fireplace once used by a blacksmith, and a sawdust-strewn floor. For years Chumley's attracted a literary clientele (John Steinbeck, Ernest Hemingway, Edna Ferber, Simone de Beauvoir, and Jack Kerouac), and the book covers of their publications still proudly adorn the walls. There's another "secret" entrance in Pamela Court, accessed at 58 Barrow Street around the corner. Watch for the bar's reopening; it's one-of-a-kind. ⊠ *86 Bedford St., near Barrow St., Greenwich Village* ☎ *212/675–4449* Ⓜ *A, B, C, D, E, F, V to W. 4th St.*

Northern Dispensary. Edgar Allan Poe was a frequent patient at the triangular dispensary, built in 1831 as a private medical clinic for indigent Villagers. The weird Georgian brick building has *one* side on *two* streets (Grove and Christopher streets where they meet) and *two* sides facing *one* street—Waverly Place, which splits in two directions. Sadly you can't visit the interior. ✉*165 Waverly Pl., Greenwich Village* Ⓜ*A, B, C, D, E, F, V to W. 4th St.*

St. Luke's Place. Steeped in New York City history and shaded by graceful gingko trees, this street officially called Leroy Street has 15 classic Italianate brownstone and brick town houses (1851–54). Novelist Theodore Dreiser wrote *An American Tragedy* at No. 16, and poet Marianne Moore resided at No. 14. Mayor Jimmy Walker (first elected in 1926) lived at No. 6; the lampposts in front are "mayor's lamps," which were sometimes placed in front of the residences of New York mayors. This block is often used as a film location: No. 12 was shown as the Huxtables' home on *The Cosby Show* (although on the show it was in Brooklyn), and No. 4 was the setting of the Audrey Hepburn movie *Wait Until Dark*. Before 1890 the playground on the south side of the street near Hudson was a graveyard where, according to legend, the dauphin of France—the lost son of Louis XVI and Marie Antoinette—is buried. ✉*Between Hudson St. and 7th Ave. S, Greenwich Village* Ⓜ*1 to Houston St.*

Washington Mews. A rarity in Manhattan, this private gated street is lined on one side with the former stables of the houses on the Row on Washington Square North. ✉*Between 8th St. and Washington Sq. N, between 5th Ave. and University Pl., Greenwich Village* Ⓜ*A, B, C, D, E, F, V to W. 4th St.*

IF THERE'S STILL TIME

Christopher Park. You might have to share a bench in this tiny park with George Segal's life-size sculptures of a lesbian couple. A gay male couple is also captured in mid-chat nearby. ✉*Bordered by W. 4th, Grove, and Christopher Sts., Greenwich Village* Ⓜ*1 to Christopher St./Sheridan Sq.*

Jefferson Market Library. After Frederick Clarke Withers and Calvert Vaux's towered Third Judicial Courthouse was constructed in 1877, critics variously termed its hodgepodge of styles Venetian, Victorian, or Italian. Villagers, noting the alternating wide bands of red brick and narrow strips of granite, dubbed it the "lean bacon style." Now a library, the veritable Victorian Gothic castle was the site of the murder trial of architect Stanford White at the beginning of the 20th century. ✉*425 6th Ave., at 10th St., Greenwich Village* ☎ *212/243–4334* Ⓜ*A, B, C, D, E, F, V to W. 4th St./Washington Sq.; 1 to Christopher St.*

The Row. Built from 1833 through 1837, this series of beautifully preserved Greek Revival row houses along Washington Square North, between University Place and MacDougal Street, once belonged to merchants and bankers, then writers and artists such as John Dos Passos and Edward Hopper. ✉*1–13 and 19–26 Washington Sq. N, between University Pl. and MacDougal St., Greenwich Village* Ⓜ*A, B, C, D, E, F, V to W. 4th St./Washington Sq.*

Twin Peaks. In 1925 financier Otto Kahn gave money to a Village eccentric named Clifford Daily to remodel an 1835 house for artists'

DID YOU KNOW?

Once teeming with more than 200 slaughterhouses, the meatpacking district has done an abrupt 180 in the last two decades to become the epicenter of all things hot.

use. The building was whimsically altered with stucco, half-timbers, and the addition of a pair of steep roof peaks. The result: an imitation Swiss chalet. *⊠102 Bedford St., between Grove and Christopher Sts., Greenwich Village* Ⓜ*1 to Christopher St./Sheridan Sq.*

CHELSEA

TWO WAYS TO EXPLORE

THE CONTEMPORARY ARTS

North of the Meatpacking District, Chelsea is the nexus of the American art scene with a thriving gallery culture that spans from 20th to 27th streets, primarily between 10th and 11th avenues. The range of contemporary art on display includes almost every imaginable medium and style; if it's going on in the art world, it'll be in one of the 300 or so galleries here. Standouts include the enormous **David Zwirner Gallery** on West 19th Street, across from the amazing Frank Gehry–designed IAC office building; the **Robert Miller Gallery** on West 26th Street, whose proprietor is a titan in the New York art world and represents the estate of Diane Arbus among others; and the galleries of **Gagosian** and **Matthew Marks**, both showing the latest in painting, photography, and sculpture. For a taste of the artistic past, there's the **Chelsea Art Museum** on West 22nd Street, housed in a former Christmas ornament factory. If it's performing arts that you're more interested in, the **Joyce Theater** on 8th Avenue and 19th Street showcases modern dance troupes like Pilobolus, Elisa Monte Dance, and Momix.

ARCHITECTURAL ICONS

The neighborhood's history is on display a few blocks east on West 23rd Street at the legendary **Chelsea Hotel,** one of the best-known reminders of the street's heyday as a gathering point for the literati and creatures of counterculture. Equally distinguished long-term digs can be found on West 20th Street in the **Cushman Row** town houses, dating from the 1820s, and at **London Terrace** on West 23rd Street, home to such notables as Isaac Mizrahi and Annie Leibovitz and the hot restaurant Bette. Regardless of whether they rent or own, nearly all neighborhood residents make frequent pilgrimages to block-long **Chelsea Market** at 15th Street between 9th and 10th avenues, the former National Biscuit Company Building, now filled with gourmet and specialty stores, restaurants, bakeries, florists, and the headquarters of the Food Network.

THE CUPCAKE CRAZE

Magnolia Bakery (⊠*401 Bleecker St., at W. 11th St.* ☎*212/462–2572*), made infamous by a scene in *Sex and the City,* kicked off an urbanite hunger for buttercream that still hasn't been sated more than 10 years, and two more locations, later. The bakeries that followed in its success, Buttercup Bakeshop, Billy's, and Sugar Sweet Sunshine, have been bringing the sugar buzz to other neighborhoods, and that cupcake colony continues to expand throughout the Upper East Side, Upper West Side, Midtown, Chelsea, and the Lower East Side.

TOP ATTRACTIONS

Chelsea Hotel. The shabby aura of the hotel is part of its bohemian allure. This 12-story Queen Anne–style neighborhood landmark (1884) became a hotel in 1905, although it has always catered to long-term tenants with a tradition of broad-mindedness and creativity. Its literary roll call of live-ins is legendary: Mark Twain, Eugene O'Neill, O. Henry, Thomas Wolfe, Tennessee Williams, Vladimir Nabokov, Mary McCarthy, Brendan Behan, Arthur Miller, Dylan Thomas, and William S. Burroughs. In 1966 Andy Warhol filmed a group of fellow artists in eight rooms; the footage was included in *The Chelsea Girls* (1967). The hotel was also seen on-screen in *I Shot Andy Warhol* (1996) and in *Sid and Nancy* (1986), a dramatization of the real-life murder of Nancy Spungen, stabbed to death here by punk rocker boyfriend Sid Vicious. Read the commemorative plaques outside, then check out the eclectic collection of art in the lobby, some donated in lieu of rent. ⊠ *222 W. 23rd St., between 7th and 8th Aves., Chelsea* ☎ *212/243–3700* ⊕*www. hotelchelsea.com* Ⓜ*1, C, E to 23rd St.*

Fodor's Choice ★ ☺ **Chelsea Market.** In the former Nabisco plant, where the first Oreos were baked in 1912, nearly two dozen food wholesalers flank what is possibly the city's longest interior walkway in a single building—from 9th to 10th avenues. You can snack your way from one end to the other, nibbling Fat Witch brownies, Ronnybrook farmer's cheese, Amy's sourdough, or just watch the bread being made as it perfumes the halls. The market's funky industrial design—a tangle of glass and metal creates the awning and art, artifacts, and a factory pipe converted into an indoor waterfall—complements the eclectic assortment of bakers, butchers, florists, grocers, cafés, and wine merchants inside. ⊠ *75 9th Ave., between W. 15th and W. 16th Sts., Chelsea* ☎*212/243–6005* ⊕*www.chelsea market.com* ☉*Mon.–Sat. 7–10, Sun. 8–8* Ⓜ*A, C, E, L to 14th St.*

☺ **Chelsea Piers.** A phenomenal example of adaptive reuse, this sports-and-entertainment complex along the Hudson River between 17th and 23rd streets (entrance on 23rd) is the size of four 80-story buildings lying flat. There's pretty much every kind of sports activity going on inside and out from golf to ice-skating, roller skating, rock climbing, swimming, kayaking, bowling, gymnastics, and basketball. Plus there's a spa, film studios, and a brewery, and it's the jumping-off point for some of the city's varied water tours and dinner cruises. Trips on the river via private yacht can be arranged by **Surfside 3 Marinemax Marina** (☎*212/336–7873*). Lunch cruises, dinner cruises, and cabaret sails can be reserved on **Bateaux New York** or **Spirit of New York,** which both leave from Pier 61 (☎*866/211–3805*). ⊠*Piers 59–62 on Hudson River from 17th to 23rd Sts.; entrance at 23rd St., Chelsea* ☎*212/336–6666* ⊕*www.chelseapiers.com* Ⓜ*C, E to 23rd St.*

5

DID YOU KNOW? The *Titanic* was scheduled to arrive at Chelsea Piers on April 16, 1912. Fate intervened and the "unsinkable" ship struck an iceberg on April 14 and went down. Of the 2,200 passengers aboard, 675 were rescued by the Cunard liner *Carpathia,* which arrived at Chelsea Piers eight days later.

Out and On Display: George Segal's sculptures of two gay couples in Christopher Park illustrate gay pride in Greenwich Village.

Check out Chelsea Piers' historical photos on the wall between Piers 60 and 61.

Cushman Row. Built in 1840, this string of homes between 9th and 10th avenues represents some of the country's most perfect examples of Greek Revival row houses. Original details include small wreath-encircled attic windows, deeply recessed doorways with brownstone frames, and striking iron balustrades and fences. Note the pineapples, a traditional symbol of welcome, on top of the black iron newels in front of No. 416. ⊠ *406–418 W. 20th St., between 9th and 10th Aves., Chelsea* Ⓜ *C, E to 23rd St.*

The High Line. Once a 1.5-mi elevated railroad track carrying freight trains, this space is now being transformed into Manhattan's newest green retreat in the spirit of Paris's Promenade Plantée. A long "walking park" with occasional benches, views of the Hudson River, and the Manhattan skyline, the High Line is set above the west end of the Village, reaching up to 30th Street, with scattered access points. The first section is scheduled to open spring 2009 and stretches from Gansevoort to 20th Streets. Future plans include water features, children's attractions, viewing platforms, sundecks, and performance areas. Check the Web site for announcements and openings. ⊠ *10th Ave. from Gansevoort St. to 30th St., Greenwich Village and Chelsea* ⊕ *www.thehighline.org* Ⓜ *L to 8th Ave.*

Contemporary art finds a home in the Pace Wildenstein Gallery, one of many such spaces in Chelsea.

GALLERIES

Alan Klotz Gallery. Fine 19th- and 20th-century and contemporary photography is the focus of the exhibitions here. Shows range from the modern photo-realistic domestic scenes by Melissa Ann Pinney to the more playful portraits of photojournalist Jonathan Torgovnik. Also here are extensive collections from some of history's most important photographers, including Josef Sudek, Berenice Abbott, and Eugene de Salignac. ✉*511 W. 25th St., Suite 701, between 10th and 11th Aves., Chelsea* ☎*212/741–4764* ⊕*www.klotzgallery.com* Ⓜ*C, E to 23rd St.*

Andrea Rosen. The gallery showcases artists on the cutting edge, such as sculptor Andrea Zittel, Felix Gonzalez-Torres, and painter and installation artist Matthew Ritchie. ✉*525 W. 24th St., between 10th and 11th Aves., Chelsea* ☎ *212/627–6000* ⊕*www.andrearosengallery.com* Ⓜ*C, E to 23rd St.*

ATM Gallery. On an industrial cobblestone block just off the West Side Highway, this gallery is now located in a larger space. Eleven artists, six from Japan, are represented here in a gallery that began in the East Village in 2002. ✉*621 W. 27th St., between 11th and 12th Aves., Chelsea* ☎*212/375–0349* ⊕*www.atmgallery.com* Ⓜ*C, E to 23rd St.*

Casey Kaplan. Founded in 1995, this gallery represents 17 contemporary artists from Europe and the Americas. Casey Kaplan presents sophisticated and ambitious exhibitions of works by such artists as Liam Gillick, Trisha Connelly, Carsten Höllen, and Brian Jungen. ✉*525 W. 21st*

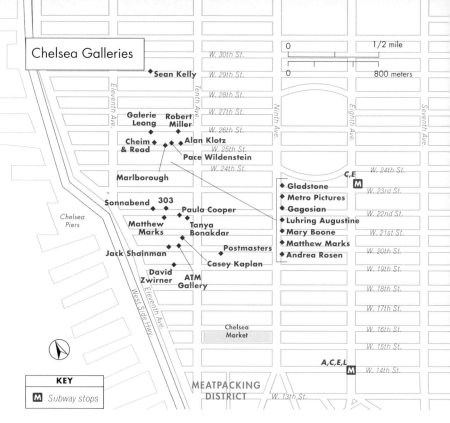

Chelsea Galleries

W. 30th St.
Sean Kelly
W. 29th St.
W. 28th St.
Galerie Leong
Robert Miller
W. 27th St.
W. 26th St.
Cheim & Read
Alan Klotz
W. 25th St.
Pace Wildenstein
W. 24th St.
Marlborough
Gladstone
C, E
W. 24th St.
Metro Pictures
W. 23rd St.
Sonnabend
303
Gagosian
Paula Cooper
Luhring Augustine
W. 22nd St.
Matthew Marks
Tanya Bonakdar
Mary Boone
W. 21st St.
Chelsea Piers
Matthew Marks
Postmasters
W. 20th St.
Jack Shainman
Andrea Rosen
Casey Kaplan
W. 19th St.
David Zwirner
ATM Gallery
W. 18th St.
W. 17th St.
Chelsea Market
W. 16th St.
W. 15th St.
A, C, E, L
W. 14th St.
KEY
M Subway stops
MEATPACKING DISTRICT
W. 13th St.

0   1/2 mile
0   800 meters

Eleventh Ave. Tenth Ave. Ninth Ave. Eighth Ave. Seventh Ave. West Side Hwy. Eleventh Ave.

St., *between 10th and 11th Aves., Chelsea* ☎212/645–7335 ⊕*www. caseykaplangallery.com* Ⓜ*C, E to 23rd St.*

Cheim & Read. This prestigious gallery represents artists such as Louise Bourgeois, William Eggleston, Joan Mitchell, Jenny Holzer, Donald Baechler, and Jack Pierson. ⊠*547 W. 25th St., between 10th and 11th Aves., Chelsea* ☎212/242–7727 ⊕*www.cheimread.com* Ⓜ*C, E to 23rd St.*

David Zwirner. Proving his finger is on the pulse of contemporary art, Zwirner shows works in all mediums by such emerging artists as Luc Tuymans, Stan Douglas, Thomas Ruff, Diana Thater, and Yutaka Sone. ⊠*525 W. 19th St., between 10th and 11th Aves., Chelsea* ☎212/727–2070 ⊕*www.davidzwirner.com* Ⓜ*C, E to 23rd St.*

Gagosian. This enterprising modern gallery has two large Chelsea branches and a third on the Upper East Side, one in Beverly Hills, plus one in London. All present works by heavy hitters, such as sculptor Richard Serra, the late pop-art icon Roy Lichtenstein, and Willem de Kooning. ⊠*555 W. 24th St., at 11th Ave., Chelsea* ☎ 212/741–1111 ⊠ *522 W. 21st St., between 10th and 11th Aves., Chelsea* ☎212/741–1717 ⊕ *www.gagosian.com* Ⓜ*C, E to 23rd St.*

Galerie Lelong. This large gallery presents challenging installations and art, as well as many Latin American artists. Look for Alfredo Jaar,

Chelsea Galleries 101

Good art, bad art, edgy art, downright disturbing art—it's all here waiting to please and provoke in the contemporary art capital of the world. For the uninitiated, the concentration of nearly 300 galleries within a seven-block radius can be overwhelming, and the sometimes cool receptions upon entering and deafening silence, intimidating. Art galleries are not exactly famous for their customer-service skills, but they're free, and you don't need a degree in art appreciation to stare at a canvas or any installation.

There's no required code of conduct, although most galleries are library-quiet and cell phones are seriously frowned upon. Don't worry, you won't be pressured to buy anything; staff will probably be doing their best to ignore you.

Galleries are generally open Tuesday through Saturday from 10 AM to 6 PM.

Gallery-hop on a Saturday afternoon—the highest traffic day—if you want company. You can usually find a binder with the artist's résumé, examples of previous work, and exhibit details (usually including prices) at the front desk. If not, ask. You can also ask if there's information you can take with you.

You can't see everything in one afternoon, so if you have specific interests, plan ahead. Find gallery information and current exhibit details at ⊕ www.galleryguide.org (you can pick up a free print copy of the publication at any gallery desk). Sift further through your choices by checking the "Art Guide" in Friday's "Weekend" section of the New York Times. You can also learn more about the galleries and the genres and artists they represent at ⊕ www.artincontext.org.

—Jacinta O'Halloran

Andy Goldsworthy, Cildo Meireles, Ana Mendieta, Hélio Oiticica, Sean Scully, and Petah Coyne. ✉ 528 W. 26th St., between 10th and 11th Aves., Chelsea ☎ 212/315–0470 Ⓜ C, E to 23rd St.

Gladstone Gallery. The international roster of artists in this gallery's two locations includes sculptor Anish Kapoor, photographer Sharon Lockhart, and multimedia artists Matthew Barney and Richard Prince. ✉ 515 W. 24th St., between 10th and 11th Aves.,Chelsea ☎ 212/206–9300 ⊕ ✉ 530 W. 21st St., between 10th and 11th Aves., Chelsea ☎ 212/206–7606 ⊕ www.gladstonegallery.com Ⓜ C, E to 23rd St.

Jack Shainman. Both emerging and established artists are shown here, such as Subodh Gupta, a young sculptor from India, and Kerry James Marshall, who deals with African-American issues. You might find works by Phil Frost, whose imagery is derived from graffiti, or Zwelethu Mthethwa, a South African photographer. ✉ 513 W. 20th St., between 10th and 11th Aves., Chelsea ☎ 212/645–1701 ⊕ www.jackshainman. com Ⓜ C, E to 23rd St.

Luhring Augustine. Since 1985 owners Lawrence Luhring and Roland Augustine have worked with established and emerging artists from Europe, Japan, and America. ✉ 531 W. 24th St., between 10th and

Where can I find...?

COFFEE	Donut Pub 203 W. 14th St. Care for an apple fritter with your coffee? Pull up a stool.	Joe the Art of Coffee 141 Waverly Pl. Java with swirled milk almost too beautiful to glup down.
A QUICK BITE	Three Tarts 164 9th Ave. Elegant sweets in pocket-sized portions.	Peanut Butter & Co 240 Sullivan St. From smooth to crunchy to superfunky.
COCKTAILS	Velour Bar 297 10th Ave. Gallerygoers winding down and nightclubbers warming up.	Flatiron Lounge 37 W. 19th St. Art deco hangout, mini-martini flights.

11th Aves., Chelsea ☎212/206–9100 ⊕www.luhringaugustine.com Ⓜ C, E to 23rd St.

Marlborough. With galleries in London, Monaco, and Madrid, the Marlborough empire also operates two of the largest and most influential galleries in New York City. The Chelsea location (the other's in Midtown) shows the latest work of modern artists, with a special interest in sculptural forms, such as the large-scale work of Michele Oka Doner. Red Grooms, Richard Estes, and Fernando Botero are just a few of the 20th-century luminaries represented. ✉545 W. 25th St., between 10th and 11th Aves., Chelsea ☎212/463–8634 ⊕www.marlboroughgallery. com Ⓜ C, E to 23rd St.

Mary Boone. A hot SoHo gallery during the 1980s, this venue now resides both in Midtown and in the newer flash point of Chelsea. Boone continues to show established artists such as Barbara Kruger and Eric Fischl, as well as newcomers. ✉541 W. 24th St., between 10th and 11th Aves., Chelsea ☎212/752–2929 ⊕www.maryboonegallery.com Ⓜ C, E to 23rd St.

Matthew Marks. A white-hot venue for both the New York and international art crowd, openings at any of the three Matthew Marks galleries are always an interesting scene. Swiss artist Ugo Rondinone made his U.S. debut here, as did Andreas Gursky. Nan Goldin, Ellsworth Kelly, Brice Marden, Katharina Fritsch, and a cast of illustrious others also show here. ✉523 W. 24th St., between 10th and 11th Aves., Chelsea ☎212/243–0200 Ⓜ C, E to 23rd St. 522 W. 22nd St., between 10th and 11th Aves., Chelsea ☎212/243–0200 ⊕ www.matthewmarks.com Ⓜ C, E to 23rd St. 521 W. 21st St., between 10th and 11th Aves., Chelsea ☎212/243–0200 Ⓜ C, E to 23rd St..

Metro Pictures. The hottest talents in contemporary art shown here include Cindy Sherman, whose provocative photographs have brought her international prominence. ✉*519 W. 24th St., between 10th and 11th Aves., Chelsea* ☎*212/206–7100* Ⓜ *C, E to 23rd St.*

Pace Wildenstein. The Midtown specialist in 20th- and 21st-century art now has two spaces in Chelsea. The West 25th Street location can fit the largest sculpture and installations. Their roster concentrates on upper-echelon artists, sculptors, and photographers, including Elizabeth Murray, Chuck Close, Sol LeWitt, and Robert Rauschenberg. ✉*534 W. 25th St., between 10th and 11th Aves., Chelsea* ☎*212/929–7000* Ⓜ *C, E to 23rd St. 545 W. 22nd St., between 10th and 11th Aves., Chelsea* ☎*212/989–4258* ⊕*www.pacewildenstein.com* Ⓜ*C, E to 23rd St.*

Paula Cooper. SoHo pioneer Paula Cooper moved to Chelsea in 1996 and enlisted architect Richard Gluckman to transform a warehouse into a dramatic space with tall ceilings and handsome skylights. Now she has three galleries that showcase the minimalist sculptures of Carl André, the dot paintings of Yayoi Kusama, and the provocative photos of Andres Serrano, among other works. ✉*534 W. 21st St., between 10th and 11th Aves., Chelsea* ☎*212/255–1105* Ⓜ*C, E to 23rd St. 521 W. 21st St., 2nd fl., between 10th and 11th Aves., Chelsea* ☎*212/255–5247* Ⓜ*C, E to 23rd St. 465 W. 23rd St., at 10th Ave., Chelsea* ☎*212/255–4499* Ⓜ*C, E to 23rd St.*

Postmasters. Postmasters shows new and established conceptual artists, with one room devoted to multimedia shows. Recent exhibits have included Claude Wampler's *Pomerania*—a series of photographs, sculptures, video, and drawings examining the artist's relationship with her pet Pomeranian. ✉*459 W. 19th St., between 9th and 10th Aves., Chelsea* ☎*212/727–3323* ⊕*www.postmastersart.com* Ⓜ *C, E to 23rd St.*

Robert Miller. Miller, a titan of the New York art world, represents some of the biggest names in modern painting and photography, including Diane Arbus and the estates of Lee Krasner and Alice Neel. ✉*524 W. 26th St., between 10th and 11th Aves., Chelsea* ☎*212/366–4774* ⊕*www.robertmillergallery.com* Ⓜ *C, E to 23rd St.*

Sean Kelly. Drop in to this large space for works by top contemporary American and European artists including Marina Abramovic, Robert Mapplethorpe, Antony Gormley, Joseph Kosuth, and James Casebere. ✉*528 W. 29th St., between 10th and 11th Aves., Chelsea* ☎*212/239–1181* ⊕*www.skny.com* Ⓜ*1 to 28th St.; C, E to 23rd St.*

Sonnabend. This pioneer of the SoHo art scene continues to show important contemporary artists in its Chelsea space, including Jeff Koons, Ashley Bickerton, and British art duo Gilbert & George. ✉*536 W. 22nd St., between 10th and 11th Aves., Chelsea* ☎*212/627–1018* Ⓜ*C, E to 23rd St.*

Tanya Bonakdar. This gallery presents such contemporary artists as Uta Barth, whose blurry photos challenge ideas about perception, and Ernesto Neto, a Brazilian artist who has made stunning room-size installations of large nylon sacks filled with spices. ✉*521 W. 21st St., between 10th and 11th Aves., Chelsea* ☎*212/414–4144* ⊕*www.tanyabonakdargallery.com* Ⓜ*C, E to 23rd St.*

5

Greenwich Village & Chelsea Dining

BUDGET DINING

Fatty Crab, Malaysian, 643 Hudson St., bet. Gansevoort and Horatio Sts.

Mexicana Mama, Mexican, 525 Hudson St., nr. Charles St.

Moustache, Middle Eastern, 90 Bedford St.

P*ONG, Dessert, 150 W. 10th St., at Waverly Pl.

R.U.B. BBQ, Barbecue, 208 W. 23rd St.

Vento, Italian, 675 Hudson St.

MODERATE DINING

Arturo's, Pizza, 106 W. Houston St.

August, Mediterranean, 359 Bleecker St.

Barbuto, Italian, 775 Washington St.

Bar Q, Asian, 308 Bleecker St.

Blue Ribbon Bakery, Bistro, 35 Downing St.

Do Hwa, Korean, 55 Carmine St.

Del Posto, Italian, 85 10th Ave.

Elettaria, New American, 33 W 8th St.

Gonzo, Italian, 140 W. 13th St.

The Little Owl, New American, 90 Bedford St.

Lupa, Italian, Bleecker St., bet. 6th and 7th Aves.

Paris Commune, Brasserie, 99 Bank St.

Pastis, Brasserie, 9 9th Ave.

Perry St., New American, 176 Perry St.

Tía Pol, Spanish, 205 10th Ave.

Vento, Italian, 675 Hudson St.

EXPENSIVE DINING

Babbo, Italian, 110 Waverly Pl.

Blue Hill, New American, 75 Washington Pl.

Buddakan, Asian, 75 9th Ave.

Centro Vinoteca, Italian, 74 7th Ave. S., at Barrow St.

dell'anima, Italian, 38 8th Ave.

Gotham Bar & Grill, American, 12 E. 12th St.

Scarpetta, Italian, 355 W14th St.

Spice Market, Asian, 403 W. 13th St.

Wallsé, Austrian, 344 W. 11th St.

---

303. International cutting-edge artists shown here include photographers Doug Aitken and Thomas Demand and installation artist–painter Karen Kilimnik. 303 is closed in August and weekends between July 5 and Labor Day. ⊠ *525 W. 22nd St., between 10th and 11th Aves., Chelsea* ☎ *212/255–1121* ⊕ *www.303gallery.com* Ⓜ *C, E to 23rd St.*

Union Square

INCLUDING GRAMERCY PARK, FLATIRON DISTRICT & MURRAY HILL

WORD OF MOUTH

"I think the best [market] is on Saturday at Union Square. You will find fresh fruit, granola, baked goods, organic milk, eggs, yogurt, fresh flowers, salad ingredients, jams, honey—everything you need. Walk around the square first and enjoy the scene, and get the groceries at the end of the day so the dairy doesn't spoil."

—bugswife1

GETTING ORIENTED

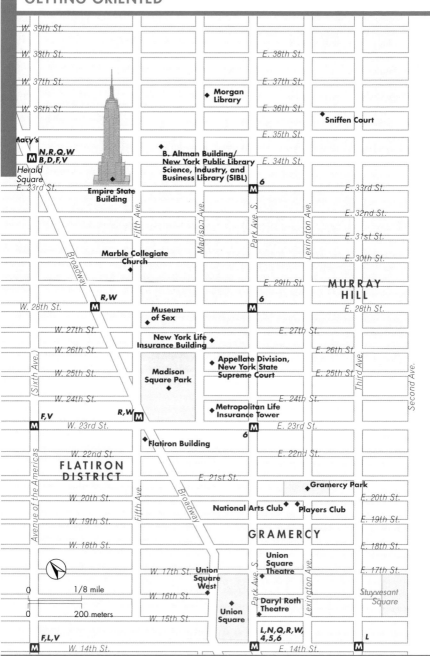

W. 39th St.

W. 38th St.

W. 37th St.

W. 36th St.

W. 33rd St.

Macy's

**N,R,Q,W
B,D,F,V**

Herald
Square

E. 38th St.

E. 37th St.

E. 36th St.

Morgan
Library

E. 35th St.

Sniffen Court

B. Altman Building/
New York Public Library
Science, Industry, and
Business Library (SIBL)

E. 34th St.

6

Empire State
Building

E. 33rd St.

E. 32nd St.

Fifth Ave.

Madison Ave.

Park Ave. S.

Lexington Ave.

E. 31st St.

E. 30th St.

Marble Collegiate
Church

E. 29th St.

**MURRAY
HILL**

Broadway

R,W

W. 28th St.

6

E. 28th St.

W. 27th St.

Museum
of Sex

E. 27th St.

W. 26th St.

New York Life
Insurance Building

E. 26th St.

Third Ave.

Second Ave.

W. 25th St.

Appellate Division,
New York State
Supreme Court

E. 25th St.

Madison
Square Park

W. 24th St.

E. 24th St.

F,V

R,W

Metropolitan Life
Insurance Tower

W. 23rd St.

6

E. 23rd St.

Avenue of the Americas
(Sixth Ave.)

W. 22nd St.

Flatiron Building

E. 22nd St.

**FLATIRON
DISTRICT**

E. 21st St.

W. 20th St.

Gramercy Park

E. 20th St.

Fifth Ave.

Broadway

W. 19th St.

National Arts Club

Players Club

E. 19th St.

W. 18th St.

GRAMERCY

E. 18th St.

0   1/8 mile

W. 17th St.

Union
Square
West

Union
Square
Theatre

E. 17th St.

Park Ave. S.

Lexington Ave.

W. 16th St.

Daryl Roth
Theatre

Stuyvesant
Square

0   200 meters

W. 15th St.

Union
Square

F,L,V

W. 14th St.

**L,N,Q,R,W,
4,5,6**

E. 14th St.

L

MAKING THE MOST OF YOUR TIME

Union Square is lively round-the-clock. Many establishments in the area are open late, and everyone seems to hang out on wide, concrete steps on the south end of Union Square Park, especially on weekends. During warmer months, protesters handing out pamphlets share space with young street groups who put on semiregular dance shows. The fabulous greenmarket is filled with local produce four days a week. The area is also popular with theatergoers and fine-diners.

6

GETTING HERE

Both Union Square/14th Street and Herald Square/34th Street are major subway hubs, connected by the N, Q, R, and W lines. Any of these trains can bring you right to the center of the action. For Madison Square Park, take the local R or W to 23rd Street. You can reach the Empire State Building via the B, D, F, N, Q, R, V, or W lines to 34th Street or the 6 to 33rd Street. The 6 also has stops at 23rd and 28th streets.

WORD OF MOUTH (WWW.FODORS.COM/FORUMS)

"My favorite part [of Macy's]? The escalator. I LOVED the clankety-clank of the wooden escalator (metal treads hitting against wooden walls.) LOVED it. The sound reminded me of a wooden roller coaster. I'm just riding and smiling…Rode all the way up. Took the elevator back down."   —starrs

STILL TRUE TODAY

"In the early 1800s, when [builder Sam Ruggles bought Gramercy Park], the area was far north of the city. His contemporaries derided his dream of turning this woodland tract into an English-type residential square and dubbed it 'Sam Ruggles' Vacant Lot.' The men of little vision lived to eat their words."   —*Fodor's New York City, 1988*

Sightseeing
★★★★

Nightlife
★

Dining
★★★★

Lodging
★★★

Shopping
★★★★

Updated by
Meryl D.
Pearlstein

Union Square refers to an area of the city anchored by Union Square Park, which resides between 14th and 17th streets and Broadway and Park Avenue South. If you're in this area on a Tuesday, Thursday, or Sunday, you've missed one of the best parts of being here, the expansive and colorful farmers' market. But don't despair if you're here on a nonmarket day: skateboarders keep the pace moving, artists and craftsmen add to the ambience, and vendors of all kinds lobby for your attention. NYU students, nannies with their charges, chess players, visitors, and locals feed the energy of this open space.

The haste and hullabaloo of the city calms considerably as you stroll through the mostly residential neighborhoods of Murray Hill and Gramercy Park to the east. Just above Union Square and to the west, the Flatiron District and the remnants of Ladies' Mile (as it was known in the late 1880s) continue the shopping and commercial buzz.

Murray Hill stretches from 30th to 40th streets between 5th and 3rd avenues. A charming, quiet neighborhood, it has tree-lined and townhouse-filled streets and some high-profile haunts: the Morgan Library and Museum with its vast book stacks and rare manuscripts, and King Kong's favorite hangout, the Empire State Building.

Dignified Gramercy Park, named for its 1831 gated garden square ringed by historic buildings and private clubs, is an early example of the city's creative urban planning. Even though you can't unpack your picnic in the exclusive residents-only park, you can bask in its historic surroundings and artistic significance. Beautiful Greek Revival, Italianate, Gothic Revival, and Victorian Gothic buildings flank its sides. Off its southern edge is a small street honoring Washington Irving, where you can find one of the city's most charming inns, the Inn at Irving Place, and a number of casual restaurants. Just north of the park is Ian

Schrager's cooler-than-cool reincarnation of the Gramercy Park Hotel on Lexington Avenue.

The Flatiron District—anchored by Madison Square Park on the north and Union Square to the south—is one of the city's busiest neighborhoods, particularly along 5th Avenue and Park Avenue South. In some ways it should still be called Ladies' Mile: the area is a favorite for spotting models because of the number of agencies and photography studios here. You can also see charming shops, some of the city's coolest hotels and trendiest restaurants, and an elegant turn-of-the-20th-century skyline that's brilliantly lighted at night.

TWO WAYS TO EXPLORE

PARK LIFE AND A TASTE OF CULTURE

The energy of **Union Square** reaches its peak during its greenmarket on Monday, Wednesday, Friday, and Saturday, when more than 25 farms and food purveyors set up shop on the square's north and west sides to peddle everything from produce to meat, fresh fish to baked goods; all of it makes for great grazing. For those who prefer a sit-down environment, the area also offers up some intriguing restaurants, including Danny Meyer's **Union Square Café** and the spicy **Mesa Grill.** On nearby Irving Place, **Pete's Tavern,** dating from 1864, maintains its claim as the oldest original bar in the city. Two famous writers, O. Henry (*Gift of the Magi*), and Ludwig Bemelmans (*Madeline*) were "inspired" here, probably from the amazing eggnog or Pete's House Ale.

Although Union Square is a "passive park," meaning there are no sports, there are playgrounds and a dog run. It's also a great place for music and off-off-Broadway theater. One block to the east, on Irving Place, **Irving Plaza** posts a list of upcoming concerts under its marquee, spanning the likes of Tom Jones and Willie Nelson to DJ Shadow. The **Vineyard Theatre,** where *Avenue Q* began, is here, as well as the **Daryl Roth Theatre** and the **Union Square Theatre,** both on 15th Street and both offering innovative and sometimes participatory theater. Union Square's most love-it-or-hate-it feature is the *Metronome* art sculpture with its bank of cascading numbers. Half art installation, half timepiece, it sits above the former Virgin Megastore and is actually a clock that counts both time elapsed and time remaining in the day. At noon and midnight, huge bursts of steam emerge, turning into trickles throughout the day. The birthplace of some more-venerated 20th-century art, **33 Union Square West,** now occupied by the new Puma concept store, once held Andy Warhol's Factory.

A few blocks north of Union Square along Irving Place, the hustle and flow fades into serenity with the look-but-don't touch primness of **Gramercy Park.** The park oozes urbane theatrical and artistic ambience, surrounded by the tony likes of the **Players Club (technically just called "The Players")** and the **National Arts Club,** both established to indulge and encourage a passion for the arts.

ARCHITECTURE AT ITS MOST ELABORATE

Rimming **Madison Square Park** is some of Manhattan's most impressive skyline. In the northeast corner, the gold-top **New York Life Insurance** building was the tallest in the city when it opened in 1903. The elaborately carved Beaux-Arts structure one block down at East 25th Street, is the **Appellate Division, New York State Supreme Court,** with its main entrance tucked onto the side street. The imposing **Metropolitan Life Insurance Tower,** between East 23rd and 24th streets, is another classically inspired spire. One of the buildings most emblematic of New York City, the charming and historic **Flatiron Building** is a limestone-and-terra-cotta vessel sailing its prowlike shape uptown from its berth on 23rd Street. With the surrounding towers lighted in various colors, Madison Square Park positively glows at night. The park has been recently flanked with triangular concrete "parks" with flowers and outdoor seating. It's a great place to spend some time and enjoy a burger or frozen custard from the wonderful **Shake Shack**, where there's usually a grateful queue that wraps around the tree-lined path.

At the edge of Murray Hill, at 33rd St. and 5th Ave., looms the inimitable **Empire State Building.** Canonized in postcards, books, and on film, the building reaches toward the sky with its majestic spire, which is lighted up at night according to an elaborate calendar of dates and corresponding colors. An excellent view can be had from the steps of the Italian-Renaissance-style **B. Altman Building** one block north. From there, it's a quick walk up Madison Avenue to the **Morgan Library and Museum** (⇨ Ch. 14), with its impressive collection of rare books and manuscripts. A mile south on 5th Avenue at 27th Street, the **Museum of Sex** (⇨ Ch. 14) sits behind an unassuming facade, giving little hint of its salacious interior.

6

TOP ATTRACTIONS

Fodor's Choice
★
☺

Empire State Building. Bittersweet though it is, this landmark is once again the city's tallest building. Its pencil-slim silhouette, recognizable virtually worldwide, is an art deco monument to progress, a symbol for New York City, and a star in some great romantic scenes, on- and off-screen. Its cinematic résumé—the building has appeared in more than 200 movies—means that it remains a fixture of popular imagination, and many visitors come to relive favorite movie scenes. You might just find yourself at the top of the building with *Sleepless in Seattle* look-alikes or even the building's own *King Kong* impersonator.

Built in 1931 at the peak of the skyscraper craze, this 103-story limestone giant opened after a mere 13 months of construction. The framework rose at an astonishing rate of 4½ stories per week, making the Empire State Building the fastest-rising skyscraper ever built. Many floors were left completely unfinished so tenants could have them custom designed.

■ TIP ➔ Thanks to advance ticketing on the Internet, you can speed your way to the observatory on the 86th floor. If this is your first visit, rent a headset with an audio tour from Tony, a fictional but "authentic" native New Yorker, available in eight languages. The 86th-floor observatory

(1,050 feet high) is outdoors and spans the building's circumference. This is the deck to go to, to truly see the city. Don't be shy about going outside into the wind (even in winter) or you'll miss half the experience. Bring quarters for the high-powered binoculars: on clear days you can see up to 80 mi. If it rains, you can view the city between the clouds and watch the rain travel sideways around the building from the shelter of the enclosed walkway. The advantage of paying the extra $15 to go to the indoor 102nd floor is that this observatory affords an easy and less-crowded circular walk-around from which to view the city. It also feels more removed and quieter. Express tickets can be purchased for front-of-the-line admission for an extra $45.

Time your visit for early or late in the day—morning is the least crowded time, and at night the city lights are dazzling. A good strategy is to go up just before dusk and witness nightfall. ⊠*350 5th Ave., at E. 34th St., Murray Hill* ☎*212/736–3100 or 877/692–8439* ⊕*www.esbnyc. com* ✉*$19* ⊙*Daily 8* AM*–2* AM; *last elevator up leaves at 1:15* AM Ⓜ *B, D, F, N, Q, R, V, W to 34th St./Herald Sq.; 6 to 33rd St.*

Although some parents blanch when they discover both how much it costs and how it lurches, the second-floor **NY SKYRIDE** is a favorite of the seven- and eight-year-old set. The ride presents a movie, motion, and sights, rolled up into New York's only aerial virtual-tour simulator. ☎*212/279–9777 or 888/759–7433* ⊕*www.skyride.com* ✉*$25.50; $38 combo SKYRIDE and observatory* ⊙*Daily 10–10.*

Flatiron Building. When completed in 1902, the Fuller Building, as it was originally known, caused a sensation. Architect Daniel Burnham made ingenious use of the triangular wedge of land at 23rd Street, 5th Avenue, and Broadway, employing a revolutionary steel frame, which allowed for the building's 22-story, 286-foot height. Covered with a limestone and white terra-cotta skin in the Italian Renaissance style, the building's shape resembled a clothing iron, hence its nickname. When it became apparent that the building generated strong winds, gawkers would loiter at 23rd Street hoping to catch sight of ladies' billowing skirts. Local traffic cops had to shoo away the male peepers—one purported origin of the phrase "23 skidoo." There is a small display of historic building and area photos in the lobby. ⊠*175 5th Ave., bordered by E. 22nd and E. 23rd Sts., 5th Ave., and Broadway, Flatiron District* Ⓜ *R, W to 23rd St.*

Macy's. Sure, you can shop in Macy's in other cities, but there's a say-you-did-it appeal to walking that indoor city block between 6th (where it meets Broadway) to 7th Avenue, from 34th to 35th streets, verifying that yes, it is indeed the world's largest store (11 floors, 2 million square feet of selling space). In that spirit, chance a ride on one of the narrow wooden escalators you can find tucked among its metallic brethren: installed in 1902, they were the first escalators ever used in an American store. ■TIP➔If you're in town in April, visit Macy's during its flower show, when the store is blanketed with banks of tulips, sprouting orchids, and more than 30,000 varieties of flowers and plants. During Thanksgiving, Macy's world-famous balloons float down the avenue, stopping in front of the store for performances by a variety of celebs, bands, and dancers. The store's Christmastime windows are a must-see, sparking a *Mirac[l]* Street spirit. ⊠ *W. 34th St. between Broadway at 6th and 7th [Au]. Murray Hill* ☎ *212/695–4400* ⊕ *www.macys.com* ☯ *Hrs vary seasonally; Mon.–Sat. 10–9:30, Sun. 11–8* Ⓜ *B, D, F, N, Q, R, V, W to 34th St./Herald Sq.; 1, 2, 3 to 33rd St.*

The first Macy's Thanksgiving Day Parade in 1924 was called "Macy's Christmas Day Parade" although it took place on Thanksgiving. It included camels, goats, elephants, and donkeys. The parade is the world's second-largest consumer of helium after the U.S. government. Each year balloons are floated through the parade. Due to a helium shortage in 1958, however, the balloons were brought down Broadway on cranes.

Fodor'sChoice
★

The Strand. Serious bibliophiles flock to this monstrous book emporium with some 2 million volumes (the store's slogan is "18 Miles of Books"). The stock includes both new and secondhand books plus thousands of collector's items. A separate rare-book room is on the third floor at 826 Broadway (accessible through the main store). A second store is near South Street Seaport. Check out the basement, with discounted, barely touched reviewers' copies of new books, organized by author. ■TIP→ Don't be too goal oriented or you might end up frustrated. The beauty of the Strand is that you'll never quite leave with what you came for, and treasures will essentially find you. ⊠ *828 Broadway, at E. 12th St., Union Square* ☎ *212/473–1452* ☯ *Mon.–Sat. 9:30 AM–10:30 PM, Sun. 11–10:30* Ⓜ *L, N, Q, R, W, 4, 5, 6 to Union Sq./14th St.*

Union Square. A park, farmers' market, meeting place, and site of rallies and demonstrations, this pocket of green space sits in the center of a bustling residential and commercial neighborhood. The name "Union" originally signified that two main roads—Broadway and 4th Avenue—crossed here, but it took on a different meaning in the late 19th and early 20th centuries, when the square became a rallying spot for labor protests; many unions, as well as fringe political parties, moved their headquarters nearby. Since 9/11, antiwar groups have led their public campaigns here. Statues in the park include George Washington, Abraham Lincoln, and the Marquis de Lafayette sculpted by Frederic Auguste Bartholdi, creator of the Statue of Liberty. Plaques in the sidewalk on the southeast and southwest sides chronicle the park's history from the 1600s to 1800s.

Union Square is at its best on Monday, Wednesday, Friday, and Saturday (8–6), when the largest of the city's **greenmarkets** brings farmers and food purveyors from the tristate area. Browse the stands of fruit and vegetables, flowers, plants, fresh-baked pies and breads, cheeses, cider, New York State wines, fish, and meat. Between Thanksgiving and Christmas, artisans sell unique gift items in candy-cane-stripe booths at the square's southwest end.

New York University dormitories, theaters, and cavernous commercial spaces occupy the handsomely restored 19th-century commercial buildings that surround the park. The run of diverse architectural styles on the building at 33 Union Square West, the **Decker Building,** is as imaginative as its former contents: this was once home to Andy Warhol's

6

Empire State Building

At night the Empire State Building illuminates the Manhattan skyline with a colorful view as awe-inspiring from a distance as the view from the top. The colors at the top of the building are changed regularly to reflect seasons, events, and holidays, so New Yorkers and visitors from around the world always have a reason to look at this icon in a new light.

The building's first light show was in November 1932, when a simple searchlight was used to spread the news that New York–born Franklin Delano Roosevelt had been elected president of the United States. Douglas Leigh, sign designer and mastermind of Times Square's kinetic billboard ads, tried to brighten up prospects at the "Empty State Building" after the Depression by negotiating with the Coca-Cola Company to occupy the top floors. He proposed that Coca-Cola could change the lights of the building to serve as a weather forecast and then publish a small guide on its bottles to decipher the colors. Coca-Cola loved this idea but the deal fell through due to Pearl Harbor, when the U.S. government needed office space in the building.

In 1956 the revolving "freedom lights" were installed to welcome people to America; then in 1964 the top 30 floors of the building were illuminated to mark the New York World's Fair. Douglas Leigh revisited the lights of the ESB in 1976 when he was made chairman of City Decor to welcome the Democratic Convention. He introduced the idea of color lighting, and so the building's tower was ablaze in red, white, and blue to welcome the convention and to mark the celebration of the American Bicentennial. The color lights were a huge success and they remained red, white, and blue for the rest of the year.

Leigh's next suggestion of tying the lights to different holidays, a variation on his weather theme for Coca-Cola, is the basic scheme still used today. In 1977 the lighting system was updated to comply with energy conservation programs and to allow for a wider range of colors. Leigh further improved this new system in 1984 by designing an automated color-changing system so vertical fluorescents in the mast could be changed with the flick of a switch, the only automated portion of the building's lighting system to date. With a schedule that changes each year, the lights honor national holidays, the multiethnic population of New York, special local and national events, and charitable causes. The city's greatest night-light dims respectfully, however, to allow for migrating birds that could otherwise be distracted. For a full lighting schedule, click on *www.esbnyc.com*.

—Jacinta O'Halloran

studio. The redbrick-and-white-stone **Century Building** (⊠ *33 E. 17th St., Flatiron District*), built in 1881, on the square's north side, is now a Barnes & Noble bookstore, with original cast-iron columns. The building at 17th Street and Union Square East, now housing the New York Film Academy and the Union Square Theater, was the final home of **Tammany Hall,** an organization famous in its day as a corrupt and powerful political machine. Two blocks south at Union Square East and 15th Street is the former U.S.

> **LABOR DAY IS BORN**
>
> On September 5, 1882, more than 10,000 New York City union workers took an unpaid day off to march from City Hall to Union Square in the city's first Labor Day parade. The day was celebrated with picnics, speeches, and concerts. Twelve years later Congress passed an act making the first Monday in September a legal holiday to celebrate workers.

Savings Bank, now the Daryl Roth Theatre. ⊠ *E. 14th to E. 17th Sts., between Broadway and Park Ave. S, Flatiron District* Ⓜ *L, N, Q, R, W, 4, 5, 6 to Union Sq./14th St.*

ALSO WORTH SEEING

🕙 **B. Altman Building/New York Public Library–Science, Industry, and Business Library (SIBL).** In 1906 department-store magnate Benjamin Altman gambled that his fashionable patrons would follow him uptown from his popular store in the area now known as the Ladies' Mile Historic District. His new store, one of the first of the grand department stores on 5th Avenue, was designed to blend with the mansions nearby. Note in particular the beautiful entrance on 5th Avenue. In 1996 the New York Public Library set up a high-tech library here. A 33-foot-high atrium unites the building's two floors, the lending library off the lobby and the research collections below. Downstairs a wall of electronic ticker tapes and TVs tuned to business-news stations beam information and instructions to patrons. Tours are offered Tuesday and Thursday at 2. ⊠ *188 Madison Ave., between E. 34th and E. 35th Sts., Murray Hill* ☏ *212/592–7000* ⊕ *www.nypl.org* ☉ *Tues.–Thurs. 10–8, Fri. and Sat. 11–6* Ⓜ *6 to 33rd St.*

Madison Square Park. The benches of this elegant tree-filled park afford great views of some of the city's oldest and most charming skyscrapers (the Flatiron Building, the Metropolitan Life Insurance Tower, the New York Life Insurance Building, and the Empire State Building) and serve as a perfect vantage point for people-, pigeon-, dog-, or squirrel-watching. Baseball was invented across the Hudson in Hoboken, New Jersey, but the city's first baseball games were played in this 7-acre park in 1845. On the north end an imposing 1881 statue by Augustus Saint-Gaudens memorializes Civil War naval hero Admiral Farragut. An 1876 statue of Secretary of State William Henry Seward (the Seward of the term "Seward's folly"—as Alaska was originally known) sits in the park's southwest corner, though it's rumored that the sculptor placed a reproduction of the statesman's head on a statue of Abraham

Where can I find...?

COFFEE	71 Irving Pl. Coffee & Tea Bar 71 Irving Pl. Owners roast their own beans—always a good sign.	Spoon 17 W. 20th St. Caterers who also kno a thing or two about coffe
A QUICK BITE	City Bakery 3 W. 18th St. Signature "pretzel croissants" and super thick hot chocolate.	Shake Shack in Madison Square Park A true contender for New York's best burger.
COCKTAILS	Cibar 56 Irving Pl. Martinis, quiet, candlelit basement.	Molly's Pub and Shebeen 287 3rd Ave. Superfriendly, super Irish, and amazing pints.

Lincoln's body. ⊠ *E. 23rd to E. 26th Sts., between 5th and Madison Aves., Flatiron District* Ⓜ *R, W to 23rd St.*

IF THERE'S STILL TIME

Appellate Division Courthouse. Sculpted by Frederick Ruckstuhl, figures representing "Wisdom" and "Force" flank the main portal of this imposing Beaux-Arts courthouse, built in 1899. Melding the structure's purpose with artistic symbolism, statues of great lawmakers line the roof balustrade, including Moses, Justinian, and Confucius. In total, sculptures by 16 artists adorn the ornate building, a showcase of themes relating to law. This is one of the most important appellate courts in the country: it hears more than 3,000 appeals and 6,000 motions a year, and also admits approximately 3,000 new attorneys to the bar each year. Inside the courtroom is a stunning stained-glass dome set into a gilt-covered ceiling. All sessions are open to the public. ⊠ *27 Madison Ave., entrance on E. 25th St., Flatiron District* ☎ *212/340–0400* ⊙ *Weekdays 9–5* Ⓜ *R, W, 6 to 23rd St.*

Metropolitan Life Insurance Company Tower. When it was added in 1909, the 700-foot tower resembling the campanile of St. Mark's in Venice made this 1893 building the world's tallest. The clock's four faces are each three stories high, and their minute hands weigh half a ton each. The clock chimes on the quarter hour. The building and its art deco loggias have appeared in such films as *Radio Days* and *The Fisher King.* ⊠ *1 Madison Ave., between E. 23rd and E. 24th Sts., Flatiron District* Ⓜ *R, W, 6 to 23rd St.*

Union Square Dining

BUDGET DINING

City Bakery, Café,
3 W. 18th St.

Eisenberg's Sandwich Shop, Café, 174 5th Ave.

Gahm Mi Oak, Korean,
43 W. 32nd St.

Ilili, Eastern,
236 5th Ave.

Republic, Asian,
37 Union Sq. W.

Turkish Kitchen,
Turkish, 386 3rd Ave.

MODERATE DINING

Artisanal, Brasserie,
2 Park Ave.

Blue Smoke, Barbecue,
116 E. 27th St., bet.
Lexington and Park Aves.

Boqueria, Spanish,
53 W. 19th St.

Craftbar, New American,
900 Broadway

Harry's Steak and Harry's Café, Steakhouse, 1 Hanover Sq.

Hill Country, Barbecue,
30 W. 26th St.,

Irving Mill, American,
116 E. 16th St., bet.
Union Square E and
Irving Pl.

Les Halles, Brasserie,
411 Park Ave. S

Tamarind, Indian,
41–43 E. 22nd St.

Tocqueville, New
American, 1 E 15th St.

Wildwood, Barbecue,
225 Park Ave. S

EXPENSIVE DINING

A Voce, Italian,
41 Madison Ave.

BLT Fish, Seafood,
21 W. 17th St.

BLT Prime, Steak house,
111 E. 22nd St., bet.
Lexington and Park Aves.

**Country and The Café
at Country,** American,
90 Madison Ave.,
at 29th St.

Craft, New American,
43 E. 19th St.

Eleven Madison Park,
New American,
11 Madison Ave.

Gramercy Tavern,
American, 42 E. 20th St.

Primehouse New York,
Steak house,
381 Park Ave. S,
at 27th St.

Tabla, Indian,
11 Madison Ave.

Union Square Cafe,
American, 21 E. 16th St.

Veritas, American,
43 E. 20th St.

Midtown

INCLUDING TIMES SQUARE & ROCKEFELLER CENTER

WORD OF MOUTH

"Christmastime is the best time to visit the city... Fifth Avenue is always done up in decorations and makes for some beautiful window shopping. Same for Rockefeller Center... for a beautiful ground-floor view of [Rockefeller Center's] rink and skaters, get a reservation for a meal at the Sea Grill."

—lisettemac

GETTING ORIENTED

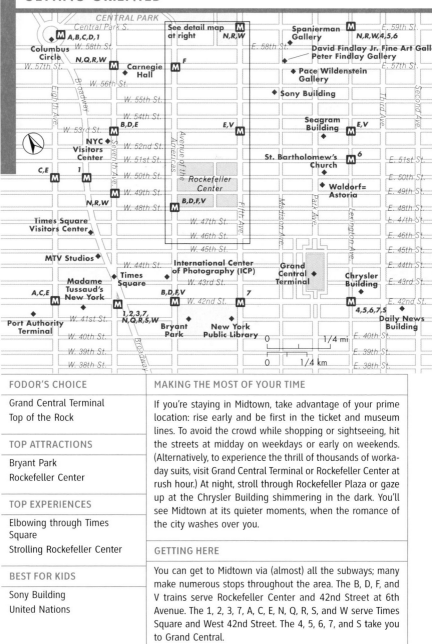

FODOR'S CHOICE

Grand Central Terminal

Top of the Rock

TOP ATTRACTIONS

Bryant Park

Rockefeller Center

TOP EXPERIENCES

Elbowing through Times Square

Strolling Rockefeller Center

BEST FOR KIDS

Sony Building

United Nations

MAKING THE MOST OF YOUR TIME

If you're staying in Midtown, take advantage of your prime location: rise early and be first in the ticket and museum lines. To avoid the crowd while shopping or sightseeing, hit the streets at midday on weekdays or early on weekends. (Alternatively, to experience the thrill of thousands of worka-day suits, visit Grand Central Terminal or Rockefeller Center at rush hour.) At night, stroll through Rockefeller Plaza or gaze up at the Chrysler Building shimmering in the dark. You'll see Midtown at its quieter moments, when the romance of the city washes over you.

GETTING HERE

You can get to Midtown via (almost) all the subways; many make numerous stops throughout the area. The B, D, F, and V trains serve Rockefeller Center and 42nd Street at 6th Avenue. The 1, 2, 3, 7, A, C, E, N, Q, R, S, and W serve Times Square and West 42nd Street. The 4, 5, 6, 7, and S take you to Grand Central.

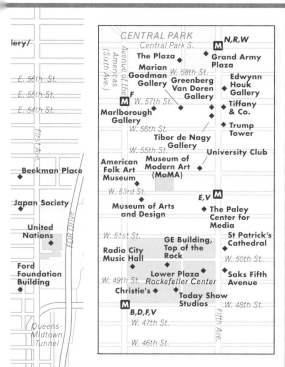

CENTRAL PARK

Central Park S.

N,R,W

The Plaza

Grand Army Plaza

Marian Goodman Gallery

W. 58th St.

Greenberg Van Doren Gallery

Edwynn Houk Gallery

W. 57th St.

Tiffany & Co.

Marlborough Gallery

W. 56th St.

Trump Tower

Tibor de Nagy Gallery

W. 55th St.

University Club

American Folk Art Museum

Museum of Modern Art (MoMA)

W. 53rd St.

E,V

Museum of Arts and Design

The Paley Center for Media

W. 51st St.

GE Building, Top of the Rock

St Patrick's Cathedral

Radio City Music Hall

W. 50th St.

W. 49th St.

Lower Plaza Rockefeller Center

Saks Fifth Avenue

Christie's

Today Show Studios

W. 48th St.

B,D,F,V

W. 47th St.

W. 46th St.

Avenue of the Americas (Sixth Ave.)

First Ave.

Fifth Ave.

Beekman Place

Japan Society

United Nations

Ford Foundation Building

Queens-Midtown Tunnel

EDR Drive

lery/

E. 56th St.

E. 55th St.

E. 54th St.

NEARBY MUSEUMS (⇨ CH. 14)

American Folk Art Museum
Dahesh Museum of Art
International Center of Photography
Japan Society
Madame Tussaud's New York
Museum of Arts and Design
Museum of Modern Art
The Paley Center for Media

AREA SHOPS (⇨ CH. 17)

American Girl Place
Apple Store
Bergdorf Goodman
Bloomingdale's
Chanel
Christian Dior
F.A.O. Schwarz
Gucci
Prada
Saks Fifth Avenue
Takashimaya New York
Toys "R" Us

7

WORD OF MOUTH (WWW.FODORS.COM/FORUMS)

"…The shopping, restaurants, and bar scene are a lot of fun so long as you don't go north into Times Square." —NYer1979

"I understand the idea of a New Yorker wanting to avoid Times Square, the glitz, the lights, the noise, and all that accompanies it. You live in a big city and you love the shelter of your neighborhood. But most of us live in the shelter of neighborhoods and we spend the big bucks to go to New York to experience what we don't have at home—and that is the glitz, the lights, and the noise. If we wanted the quiet and the dull and the mundane, many of us would just stay home." —Neopolitan

STILL TRUE TODAY

"Times Square is the object of what seems to New Yorkers like a never-ending battle for upgrading."
—Fodor's New York City, 1988

Sightseeing
★★★★★
Nightlife
★★
Dining
★★★★
Lodging
★★★★★
Shopping
★★★★★

Updated by
Michelle Delio

Washington D.C.'s got its Mall chockablock with landmarks, and we've got ours: Midtown, mobbed with more massive urban monuments—Rockefeller Center, Times Square, and Grand Central Terminal among them—than any other part of the city.

The funny thing is—and this is true for many a landmark—there doesn't appear at first glance to be a whole lot to *do* at these places. Rockefeller Center cameos in a lion's share of the movies filmed about New York, but beyond the spectacle of the rink and *Today* show early risers, its charms are not immediately obvious. Grand Central is a commuter hub and an architecture buff's dream, but the building's individual diversions don't cry out to visitors as must-sees. And then there's Times Square, a triple threat: no great shopping, few notable restaurants, and meager cultural offerings.

So what's the secret? What brings people here? It's simple: all three are destinations in themselves. There's something so inexhaustibly classy about Rockefeller Center that you're happy just being here. Times Square, as excruciatingly crowded and unpleasant as it often is, has an undeniable gravitational pull, even to locals who firmly believe Times Square is not really part of NYC. And Grand Central—well, just trust us on this one: if stepping into the main concourse doesn't give you a chill, you're in need of a serious de-jading. And if that's the case, we've got an immediate antidote: look up at the ceiling.

TWO WAYS TO EXPLORE

MIDTOWN'S ARCHITECTURE

Soaring skyscrapers frame an architectural playground, a mind-boggling patchwork of styles spanning two centuries that coalesce into one of the world's great urban landscapes. No painting or sculpture compares with the artistic beauty of Midtown itself. Modern glass towers coexist with 19th-century limestone mansions; pocket-size parks and peaceful plazas provide sanctuary amid steel towers that climb high into the clouds.

Art deco is perhaps Midtown's most distinctive style. Its principles of symmetry and geometric angularity, coupled with Machine Age materials of steel and aluminum, governed such mega-achievements of the 1920s and '30s as the **Chrysler Building** (considered one of the great art deco masterpieces) and **Rockefeller Center,** and decorated such Jazz Age landmarks as the **Waldorf=Astoria Hotel** and **Beekman**

> ### RATS WITH WINGS
>
> Woody Allen may have called them "rats with wings" and we may associate them with the refuse of urban living, but there's a natural reason pigeons live here: skyscrapers mimic the sea cliffs that are the natural habitat of these domesticated rock doves.

Tower, all located in the 40s east of 6th Avenue. Should you be continuing up 6th, you'll hit a landmark piece of art deco architecture, **Radio City Music Hall,** with its distinctive pink-and-blue neon sign. If you're continuing downtown, get a taste of Greek and Roman 20th-century neoclassicism and walk along East 42nd Street to the Beaux-Arts masterpieces **Grand Central Terminal** and nearby **New York Public Library,** two brilliantly designed public spaces, as beautiful as they are functional.

A great place to see the coexistence of New York's old and new is on Park Avenue, where the Byzantine dome of **St. Bartholomew's Church** reclines two blocks south of the bronze-and-glass **Seagram Building,** designed by modernist innovator Mies van der Rohe. For an even sharper contrast, try to glimpse two remaining 19th-century mansions (at No. 9–11 and No. 13–15 West 54th Street) from the upper levels of the **Museum of Modern Art**; in fact, all of the museum's cleverly placed windows frame similar juxtapositions of urban settings.

Moving north, relive the 1980s at the dark glass **Trump Tower** (⊠ *725 5th Ave., at E. 56th St.*). Its ostentatious atrium flaunts that decade's unbridled luxury, with expensive boutiques and gaudy brass everywhere. The "Donald" resides above in a penthouse (with an elevator that famously descends from his bedroom to his office), and the famous boardroom from the TV show *The Apprentice* is also above. Step into the '90s at the flagship **Louis Vuitton–Moët Hennessy Tower,** an arced glass skyscraper that's both conspicuous and elegant, just like the handbags sold by the resident French luxury-goods giant. Finally, return to the 21st century with the glitzy display that is **Times Square**: its blend of culture and consumerism, architecture and advertising, makes it a glittering high-tech lasso looping in gawking tourists and theatergoers into one giant bottlenecked bundle.

CULTURE HIGH AND LOW

Whether you want to see a Broadway show, visit world-class museums, or tour a television studio, Midtown is the place to be. You can score good seats to some of the hottest Broadway shows for half the going rate at the TKTS booth at the Marriott Marquis Hotel. Although people think of Broadway as the heart of the theater scene, few theaters actually line the thoroughfare. To see some of Broadway's grand old dames, head west on 45th Street. Here you can see a bevy of Broadway beauties, including the **Booth,** the **Schoenfeld,** the **Jacobs,** the **Music Box** and the **Imperial.** On the southern side of 45th Street you can find t'

Where can I find...?

COFFEE	Fika 41 W. 58th St. Coffee break with a Swedish twist.	Macchiato Espresso Bar 141 E. 44th St. Popular for morning cups, light lunches.
A QUICK BITE	Kati Roll Company 49 W. 39th St. Indian food wrapped up burrito-style.	John's Pizzeria 260 W. 44th Best pizza in nabe, hands down.
COCKTAILS	Campbell Apartment 15 Vanderbilt Ave. Grand Central's not-so-humble abode makes a mean Manhattan.	P. J. Clarke's 915 3rd Ave. New York's most famous Irish bar, and for good reason.

pedestrians-only **Shubert Alley,** distinguished by colorful posters advertising the latest hit plays and musicals, and the **Shubert Theatre,** one of Broadway's most lustrous gems. Head west along 44th Street to see its neighbors, the **Helen Hayes,** the **Broadhurst,** the **Majestic,** and the **St. James.** Tucked among them, at No. 243, is **Sardi's,** the legendary Broadway watering hole, and nearby is the former speakeasy **'21' Club** with its row of jockeys out front, once the ultimate retreat for New York high society.

Just to the north is **Carnegie Hall,** the world-famous performance venue for classical music, and jazz venues **Birdland** and the **Iridium.** Also in Times Square are the **MTV Studios** at Broadway and 45th Street. Upstairs is the MTV TRL studio, and if you're there around 3 PM you'll see the barricades go up to impose some structure on the hordes of excited teenagers who gather here hoping to catch a glimpse of their favorite singer.

TOP ATTRACTIONS

☺ **Bryant Park.** An oasis amid skyscrapers, this is one of Manhattan's most popular parks. Lining the perimeter of the sunny central lawn, tall London plane trees cast welcome shade over stone terraces, formal flower beds, gravel pathways, and kiosks selling everything from sandwiches to egg creams. In the afternoon the garden tables scattered about fill with lunching office workers and folk enjoying the park's free Wi-Fi (signs show you how to log on). In summer you can check out live jazz and comedy concerts and free outdoor film screenings on Monday at dusk. At the east side of the park, near a squatting bronze cast of Gertrude Stein, is the stylish Bryant Park Grill, which has a rooftop garden, and e adjacent open-air Bryant Park Café, open April 15–October 15. ι February and early September giant white tents spring up here for ne New York fashion shows. On the south side of the park is an old-fashioned **carousel** (🎠 *$2*) where kids can ride fanciful rabbits and frogs instead of horses.Come late October the park rolls out the artificial frozen "**pond**" (🕙 *Late Oct.–mid-Jan., Sun.–Thurs. 8 am–10 PM, Fri. and Sat. 8 AM–midnight*) for ice-skating. Rental for skates and locker will run you $20 ($10 for skates, $10 for a lock to close your "free" locker). Surrounding the ice rink are the Christmas market–like stalls of the **Holiday Shops** (🕙 *Late Nov.–Jan. 1*), selling handcrafted and designer goods from around the world. ✉ *6th Ave. between W. 40th and W. 42nd Sts., Midtown West* ☎ *212/768–4242* ⊕ *www.bryantpark. org* 🕙 *Oct.–Apr., daily 7–7; May–Sept., weekdays 7 AM–8 PM, weekends 7 AM–11 PM* Ⓜ *B, D, F, V to 42nd St.; 7 to 5th Ave.*

Fodor'sChoice
★ **Grand Central Terminal.** Grand Central is not only the world's largest (76 acres) and the nation's busiest (500,000 commuters and subway riders use it daily) railway station, but also one of the world's greatest public spaces ("justly famous," as critic Tony Hiss noted, "as a crossroads, a noble building…and an ingenious piece of engineering"). A massive four-year renovation completed in October 1998 restored the 1913 landmark to its original splendor—and then some.

You can best admire Grand Central's exquisite Beaux-Arts architecture from its ornate south face on East 42nd Street, modeled after a Roman triumphal arch. Crowning the facade's Corinthian columns and 75-foot-high arched windows, a graceful clock keeps time for hurried commuters. In the central window stands an 1869 bronze statue of Cornelius Vanderbilt, who built the station to house his railroad empire. Step inside past the glimmering chandeliers of the waiting room to the majestic **main concourse,** 200 feet long, 120 feet wide, and 120 feet (roughly 12 stories) high, modeled after a Roman bath. Overhead, a celestial map of the twinkling fiber-optic constellations covers the robin's egg–blue ceiling. During rush hour you'll be swept into the tides and eddies of human traffic, which swirl around the central information kiosk, a popular meeting place. Experience the thrill, then escape up the sweeping staircases at either end, where balconies house three upscale restaurants. Any would make an enjoyable perch from which to survey the concourse, but for a real taste of the station's early years, head beyond the western staircase to the Campbell Apartment, a clubby cocktail lounge housed in the restored private offices and salon of 1920s tycoon John W. Campbell.

Despite its grandeur, Grand Central still functions primarily as a railroad station. Underground, more than 60 ingeniously integrated railroad tracks lead trains upstate and to Connecticut via Metro-North Commuter Rail. The subway connects here as well. The **Municipal Art Society** (✉ *457 Madison Ave., between 50th and 51st Sts., Midtown East* ☎ *212/935–3960* ⊕ *www.mas.org*) leads architectural tours of the terminal that begin here on Wednesday at 12:30. Reservations are required and a $10 donation is suggested. *Main entrance* ✉ *E. 42nd St. at Park Ave., Midtown East* ☎ *212/935–3960* ⊕ *www.grandcentral terminal.com* Ⓜ *4, 5, 6, 7, S to 42nd St./Grand Central.*

Radio City Music Hall. This icon of New York City was built to enchant everyone who stepped inside its doors. Shortly after the stock market

7

CLOSE UP

Grand Meals

If you're looking for a great meal around Grand Central, head to one of these go-to restaurants.

Amid the hustle and bustle of Grand Central Station is the elegant **Grand Central Oyster Bar & Restaurant** (✉ *89 E. 42nd St., at Vanderbilt Ave.* ☎ *212/490–6650*). This sprawling space, with a tiled-vaulted ceiling, brings a sense of grandeur to a chaotic transportation hub. Famous for its architecture and decor—the Oyster Bar's impressive raw bar and fresh seafood are the real reason customers have been returning for the past 90 years.

If you want to indulge yourself, stop at the stylish **Michael Jordan's The Steakhouse** (✉ *Grand Central Terminal, 23 Vanderbilt Ave.* ☎ *212/655–2300*) located on the balcony of Grand Central Station. The prime dry-aged rib eye or the succulent 2½-pound

lobster are reason enough to dine here. But if you don't have time to sit for a meal, pull up a stool at the restaurant's bustling bar and have a drink off the impressive wine list.

For classic Italian cuisine, head to **Naples 45** (✉ *200 Park Ave. , at 45th St.* ☎ *212/972–7001*). This spacious restaurant with an open kitchen feels friendly and casual. The comforting menu of pizzas and pastas will please any and all palates.

If you're looking for a see-and-be-seen scene, dine at the sleek **Prime-house New York** (✉ *381 Park Ave. S* ☎ *212/824–2600*) steak house. The Caesar salad and steak tartare are prepared table-side, and dry-aged prime cuts, ranging from hanger steak to porterhouse for two are featured on the menu. Make sure to call ahead for reservations.

crash of 1929, John D. Rockefeller wanted to create a symbol of hope in what was a sad, broke city. He selected a piece of real estate in an area of Manhattan then known as "the speakeasy belt," and partnered with the Radio Corporation of America to build a grand theater, a place where everyday people could see the finest entertainment at sensible prices. Every inch of the interior was designed to be extraordinary. RCA head David Sarnoff named their creation "Radio City Music Hall." When it opened, some said it was so grand there was no need for performances, people would get more than their money's worth by simply by sitting there and enjoying the space. Despite being the largest indoor theater in the world with its city-block long marquee, it feels warm and intimate. Although there are performances and media events here year-round, most people (more than a million visitors every year, in fact) want to attend the Radio City Christmas Spectacular. Make reservations as early as possible, especially if you want to attend near the Christmas holidays or on weekends. The shows tend to sell out, but you can usually find tickets up until at least mid-October. Happily there are no bad seats at Radio City Music Hall, so if you are booking late, grab what you can get. Tickets—about $42–$100 per person for the 90-minute show—can be purchased at the Radio City Music Hall, Madison Square Garden, or the Beacon Theatre Box Offices; on the Web at *www.radiocity.com*; by phone on the Christmas Spectacular hot line *212/307–1000*; or at Ticketmaster. ⊠*1260 6th Ave., at W. 51st St., Midtown* ☏*212/307–7171* ⊕*www.radiocity.com* Ⓜ *B, D, F, V to 47th—50th St./Rockefeller Center; N, R to 49th St.*

Rockefeller Center. If Times Square is New York's crossroads, Rockefeller Center is its communal gathering place, where the entire world converges to snap pictures, skate on the ice rink, peek in on a taping of the *Today* show at NBC Studios, shop, eat, and take in the monumental art deco structures and public sculptures from the past century. Totaling 49 shops, 28 restaurants (1.4 million square feet in all), the complex runs from 47th to 52nd streets between 5th and 7th avenues. Special events and huge pieces of art dominate the central plazas in summer, and in December an enormous twinkling tree towers above (visit ⊕ *www.rockefellercenter.com* for a schedule).

At the complex's center is the sunken **Lower Plaza,** site of the world's most famous ice-skating rink October through April (it's a café in summer). Skaters swoop or stumble across the ice while crowds gather above on the Esplanade to watch the spins and spills. Hovering above, the gold-leaf statue of the fire-stealing Greek hero **Prometheus**—Rockefeller Center's most famous sculpture—forms the backdrop to zillions of photos. Carved into the wall behind it, a quotation from Aeschylus reads PROMETHEUS, TEACHER IN EVERY ART, BROUGHT THE FIRE THAT HATH PROVED TO MORTALS A MEANS TO MIGHTY ENDS. The Lower Plaza provides access to the marble-lined corridors underneath Rockefeller Center, which house restaurants (everything from the high-end Sea Grill to pizza parlors), a post office, and clean public restrooms—a rarity in Midtown. ⊠*Between 5th and 6th Aves. and W. 49th and W. 50th Sts., Midtown West* ☏*212/332–7654 for the rink* Ⓜ *B, D, F, V to 47th–50th Sts./Rockefeller Center.*

Rising up on the Lower Plaza's west side is the 70-story (850-foot-tall) art deco **GE Building,** a testament to modern urban development. Here Rockefeller commissioned and then destroyed a mural by Diego Rivera upon learning it featured Vladimir Lenin. He replaced it with the monumental *American Progress* by José María Sert, still on view in the lobby, flanked by additional murals by Sert and English artist Frank Brangwyn. While in the lobby, pick up a free "Rockefeller Center Visitor's Guide" at the **information desk** (☏ *212/332–6868*). Sixty-five floors up, the glittering **Rainbow Room** (opened in 1934) brings the Rockefeller era to life with dancing and big-band music. The GE Building also houses **NBC Studios** (☏ *212/664–7174*), whose news tapings, visible at street level, attract gawking crowds. For ticket information for NBC shows or the 70-minute studio tour, visit the NBC Experience Store at the building's southeast corner. ⊠*30 Rockefeller Plaza, between 5th and 6th Aves. at 49th St., Midtown*

ABOUT THE TREE

A holiday tradition began in 1931 when workers clearing away the rubble for Rockefeller Center erected a 20-foot-tall balsam. It was two years into the Great Depression, and the 4,000 men employed at the site were grateful to finally be away from the unemployment lines. The first official tree-lighting ceremony was held in 1933.

The high-steppin' Rockettes show off their signature moves at Radio City Music Hall.

West ✉*NBC Studio Tour $18.50* ☞*Children under 6 not permitted* ☉*Tours depart every 30 mins Mon.–Sat. 8:30–5:30, Sun. 9:30–4:30* Ⓜ *B, D, F, V to 47th–50th Sts./Rockefeller Center.*

Fodor's Choice
★

Top of the Rock. Rockefeller Center's multifloor observation deck, first opened in 1933, and closed in the early 1980s, reopened in 2005. Arriving just before sunset affords a view of the city that morphs before your eyes into a dazzling wash of colors, with a bird's-eye view of the tops of the Empire State Building, the Citicorp Building, and the Chrysler Building, and sweeping views northward to Central Park and south to the Statue of Liberty. Transparent elevators lift you to the 67th-floor interior viewing area, then an escalator leads to the outdoor deck on the 69th floor for sightseeing through nonreflective glass safety panels. Then, take another elevator or stairs to the 70th floor for a 360-degree outdoor panorama of New York City on a deck that is only 20 feet wide and nearly 200 feet long. Reserved-time ticketing eliminates long lines. Indoor exhibits include films of Rockefeller Center's history and a model of the building. Especially interesting is a Plexiglas screen on the floor with footage showing Rock Center construction workers dangling on beams high above the streets; the brave can even "walk" across a beam to get a sense of what it might have been like to erect this skyscraper. The local consensus is that the views from the Top of the Rock are better than those from the Empire State Building, in part because the Empire State is part of the skyline here. ✉*Entrance on 50th St., between 5th and 6th Aves., Midtown West* ☎877/692–7625 *or* 212/698–2000 ⊕*www.topoftherocknyc.com* 🎫*$17.50* ☉*Daily*

Iconic ice skating under the sculpture of Prometheus is a NYC rite of pasage for many local and visiting families.

8–midnight; last elevator at 11 PM Ⓜ *B, D, F, V to 47th–50th Sts./ Rockefeller Center.*

ALSO WORTH SEEING

★ **Chrysler Building.** A monument to modern times and the mighty automotive industry, the former Chrysler headquarters wins many a New Yorker's vote for the city's most iconic and beloved skyscraper (the world's tallest for 40 days until the Empire State Building stole the honor). Architect William Van Alen, who designed this 1930 art deco masterpiece, incorporated car details into its form: American eagle gargoyles sprout from the 61st floor, resembling car-hood ornaments used on 1920s Chryslers; winged urns festooning the 31st floor reference the car's radiator caps. Most breathtaking is the pinnacle, whose tiered crescents and spiked windows radiate out like a magnificent steel sunburst. View it at sunset to catch the light gleaming off the tip. Even better, observe it at night, when its peak illuminates the sky like the backdrop to a Busby Berkeley musical. The inside is off-limits apart from the amazing time-capsule lobby replete with chrome "grillwork," intricately patterned wood elevator doors, marble walls and floors, and an enormous ceiling mural saluting transportation and the human endeavor. ✉*405 Lexington Ave., at E. 42nd St., Midtown East* Ⓜ *4, 5, 6, 7, S to 42nd St./Grand Central.*

New York Public Library (NYPL) Humanities and Social Sciences Library. The "Library with the Lions" is a1911 masterpiece of Beaux-Arts design and one of the great research institutions in the world, with 6 million books, 12 million manuscripts, and 2.8 million pictures. But you

Keeping It Real in Times Square

How to act like a local in Times Square? Look as if you want to leave. The local art of walking in Times Square, "slalom," involves zigzagging around the slow crowds that gather like obstacles. Avoid looking overtly at the billboards, and whatever you do, don't snap pictures. Display an ironic detachment: you don't really want to be here; you're just passing through.

Why the snide comments? Just take yourself to Times Square. Looking at giant Applebee's, M&M's World, and Toys "R" Us with its Ferris wheel, it's hard to imagine the old "naughty, bawdy, gaudy" Times Square portrayed in the musical *42nd Street*. New Yorkers often like to reminisce on the Times Square where glitz and grime converged, rich and poor shimmied together on the dance floor, sailors chased after chorus girls (and, unsuccessful, headed to nearby brothels), and young men and women from Smalltown, USA, arrived with a suitcase full of dreams.

Times Square's status as the city's nightlife playground began in 1895, when Oscar Hammerstein opened the Olympia Theatre (an over-the-top folly that closed in 1898), the first of many entertainment venues, from theaters and movie palaces to porn cinemas and strip clubs, for which the thoroughfare would grow notorious. Its fate as Manhattan's entertainment capital was sealed on October 27, 1904 with the opening of the city's first subway line, which included a station at 42nd Street: people from all walks of life had easy access to its risqué brand of entertainment.

Over the next century, Times Square rose and fell with the times, functioning like a circus mirror in which New York saw itself exaggerated. During the Roaring Twenties, its Roseland Ballroom introduced many New Yorkers to Ella Fitzgerald, Duke Ellington, and Benny Goodman, while hundreds of speakeasies opened on Broadway in the wake of Prohibition. During the Depression, the great theaters converted into cheaper burlesques, movie houses, and peep shows.

The mostly harmless street hustlers and peep shows, which coexisted in relative peace with the swank restaurants and remaining legitimate theaters through the post–WWII era and into the 1960s, grew more insidious in the 1970s as urban flight to the suburbs left behind a breeding ground for crime. Magnifying the general plight of New York, Times Square descended into a dark stage of prostitution and drug dealing, whose raffish denizens were portrayed in Martin Scorsese's 1976 film *Taxi Driver.* When Robert De Niro's character Travis Bickle talks of wanting to wash away the scum and lowlifes of the city, he echoed most New Yorkers' sentiments.

After a Herculean cleanup begun in the 1980s and 1990s, Bickle got his wish, to an extent he could not ever have imagined. The 49-story Marriott Marquis hotel trampled five historic theaters. Viacom brought the MTV and Nickelodeon television networks to Broadway. Times Square today is a family-friendly, open-air promenade of familiar brand names in theme park–like settings, from ESPN Zone to the world's largest McDonald's.

It's all great fun for a while— especially if you're with kids (whose hands you must *never* release because of the undertow-like crowds)—but the entertainment quickly wears thin as

you realize it's just another vehicle for corporate advertising. Times Square the neighborhood is now "Times Square" the marketing concept, as perfectly composed, and as soulless, as the waxwork celebrity figures at Madame Tussaud's museum, which incidentally is a few feet away on West 42nd Street.

While nobody's really nostalgic (no matter what they may say) for the derelict Times Square of the '70s and '80s, at least that Times Square still reflected (however grotesquely) the challenges all the city's residents were facing. New Yorkers pride themselves on their survivor's ability to tough out the harshness of city living. For decades, Times Square embodied that toughness ("if I can make it here, I can make it anywhere"). The thoroughfare reflected everything that was wonderful about New York: freedom of expression, progressive ideas, live-and-let-live attitude, the ability of a world of cultures and classes to coexist on top of each other, and—more than anything—the triumph of great ideas, talent, and the almighty dollar.

Out in the open, underneath the bright-lighted billboards, it was clear as day what New York City had to offer newcomers, take it or leave it.

Times Square Visitors Center. Newly reopened after a $1.8 million renovation, this visitors center is a savvy place to take shelter and get your bearings when the crowds threaten to suck you into an undertow. Stop by for multilingual kiosks, Metro-Cards, interactive Google Earth map tables, sightseeing and theater tickets, and (most important!) free restrooms. ✉ *1560 Broadway, between 46th and 47th Sts., Midtown West* ☎ *212/768–1560* ⊕ *www.timessqare. nyc.org* ⊗ *Daily 8–8* Ⓜ *1, 2, 3, 7, N, Q, R, W, S to 42nd St./Times Sq.*

don't have to crack a book to make it worth visiting: an hour or so at this National Historic Landmark is a peaceful (and free!) alternative to Midtown's bustle, along with some pretty incredible architecture, especially when combined with a stroll through adjacent **Bryant Park.** Buy a drink at a park kiosk, then head to the library's grand 5th Avenue entrance to people-watch from the block-long marble staircase, then check out the opulent interior.

The library's bronze front doors open into **Astor Hall,** which leads to several special exhibit galleries and, to the left, a stunning periodicals room with wall paintings of New York publishing houses. Walk up the sweeping double staircase to a second-floor balconied corridor overlooking the hall, with panels highlighting the library's development. Make sure to continue up to the magisterial **Rose Main Reading Room**—297 feet long (almost two full north–south city blocks), 78 feet wide, and just over 51 feet high; walk through to best appreciate the rows of oak tables and the extraordinary ceiling of this space. Several additional third-floor galleries show rotating exhibits on typography, literature, bookmaking, and maps (past exhibits have included old New York restaurant menus and a 1455 Gutenberg Bible). Free one-hour tours leave Tuesday–Saturday at 11 and 2 from Astor Hall. There are women's rooms on the ground floor and third floor, and a men's room on the third floor. ✉ *5th Ave. between E. 40th and E. 42nd Sts., Midtown West* ☎ *212/930–0800, 212/869–8089 for exhibit information* ⊕ *www.nypl. org* ⊙ *Mon. and Thurs.–Sat. 11–6, Sun. 1–5, Tues. and Wed. 11–7:30; exhibitions until 6* Ⓜ *B, D, F, V to 42nd St.; 7 to 5th Ave.*

THE NAME GAME

Thanks to a donation of a cool $100 million from Wall Street financier Stephen A. Schwarzman, the New York Public Library will likely be sporting a new name. The ample gift is set to kick off a billion-dollar renovation, which is projected to be complete in 2014, after which it'll be christened the Stephen A. Schwarzman Building. Assuming that the city's Landmarks Preservation Commission doesn't object, the new name will be discreetly carved into the building facade near the main entrance.

★ ⟳ **United Nations Headquarters.** Officially an "international zone" and not part of the United States, the U.N. Headquarters is a working symbol of global cooperation. Built between 1947 and 1961, the headquarters sit on a lushly landscaped, 18-acre tract on the East River, fronted by flags of member nations.

The main reason to visit is the 45-minute guided tour (given in 20 languages), which includes the **General Assembly** and major council chambers, though some rooms may be closed on any given day. The tour includes displays on war, nuclear energy, and refugees, and passes corridors overflowing with imaginatively diverse artwork. Free tickets to assemblies are sometimes available on a first-come, first-served basis before sessions begin; pick them up in the General Assembly lobby. If you just want to wander around, the grounds include a beautiful riverside promenade, a rose garden with 1,400 specimens, and sculptures donated by member nations. The complex's buildings (the slim, 505-foot-tall green-glass **Secretariat Building**; the much smaller, domed **General**

Assembly Building; and the **Dag Hammarskjöld Library**) evoke the influential French modernist Le Corbusier (who was on the team of architects that designed the complex) and the surrounding park and plaza remain visionary. Inside, the **Delegates Dining Room** (☎212/963–7625) is open for an international buffet lunch weekdays ($25; jackets required for men, no jeans or sneakers; reservations required at least one day in advance, no children under 12 years old). The public concourse, beneath the visitor entrance, has a coffee shop, gift shops, a bookstore, and a post office where you can mail letters with U.N. stamps. If you want to have a meal in the Delegates Dining Room, be sure to bring a photo ID and make a reservation as far in advance as possible. *Visitor entrance* ✉*1st Ave. at E. 46th St., Midtown East* ☎*212/963–8687* ⊕*www.un.org* 🎫*Tour $13* ☞*Children under 5 not admitted* ⊙*Tours weekdays 9:30–4:45, weekends 10–4:30, no weekend tours Jan. and Feb.; tours in English leave General Assembly lobby every 30 mins; Delegates Dining Room, 11:30–2:30* Ⓜ *4, 5, 6, 7, S to 42nd St./Grand Central.*

IF THERE'S STILL TIME

Ⓒ **Daily News Building.** One of the city's most unusual lobbies resides in Raymond Hood's art deco and modernist tower. An illuminated 12-foot globe revolves beneath a black glass dome. Around it, spreading across the floor like a giant compass and literally positioning New York at the center of the world, bronze lines indicate mileage to various international destinations. ✉*220 E. 42nd St., between 2nd and 3rd Aves., Midtown East* Ⓜ *4, 5, 6, 7, S to 42nd St./Grand Central.*

The Plaza. With two sides of Central Park *and* 5th Avenue at its doorstep, this world-famous 19-story 1907 building claims one of Manhattan's prize real-estate corners. Henry Hardenbergh, who built the Dakota on Central Park West, here concocted a birthday-cake effect of highly ornamented white-glazed brick topped with a copper-and-slate French mansard roof. The original hotel was home to Eloise, the fictional star of Kay Thompson's children's books, and has appeared in many movies, including Alfred Hitchcock's *North by Northwest, Plaza Suite,* and *Home Alone 2.* After a $400 million renovation, the Plaza reopened in early 2008. The legendary Palm Court, Oak Room, Oak Bar, and Grand Ballroom are all back, as are new high-end shops, luxury hotel rooms, and condo hotel units. ✉*5th Ave. at W. 59th St., Midtown West* ☎*212/759–3000* Ⓜ *N, R, W to 5th Ave./59th St.*

St. Bartholomew's Church. Known to locals as St. Bart's, this handsome 1919 limestone-and-salmon-color brick church represents a generation of Midtown Park Avenue buildings long since replaced by modernist behemoths and contemporary glass-and-steel towers. It's a pleasant surprise to stumble upon its triple-arched Romanesque portal and see the intricately tiled Byzantine dome set against the skyscrapers, then have a bite at its

BART ON SCREEN

St. Bart's should have a SAG card: It has had roles in the movies *Arthur* and *Maid in Manhattan,* among others, and has also showed up on episodes of *Sex and the City* and *Law & Order.*

7

A statue of Atlas stands across the street from the looming, Gothic St. Patrick's Cathedral.

popular outdoor café open in good weather. St. Bart's also sponsors major music events throughout the year, including the summer's Festival of Sacred Music, with full-length masses and other choral works; an annual Christmas concert; and an organ recital series that showcases the church's 12,422-pipe organ, the city's largest. The church has been associated with VIPs in many capacities, including weddings. ✉ *109 E. 50th St., at Park Ave., Midtown East* ☎*212/378–0222, 212/378–0248 for concert information* ⊕*www.stbarts.org* ⊘*Daily 8–6* Ⓜ *6 to 51st St./Lexington Ave.; E, V to Lexington–3rd Aves./53rd St.*

St. Patrick's Cathedral. The country's largest Catholic cathedral (seating approximately 2,400) this 1859–79 Gothic edifice is among New York's most striking churches (note the 330-foot spires). Among the statues in the alcoves around the nave is a modern depiction of the first American-born saint, Mother Elizabeth Ann Seton. The 5th Avenue steps are a convenient, scenic rendezvous spot. Sunday Masses can overflow with tourists; off-hours are significantly more peaceful. Many of the funerals for fallen New York City police and firefighters after 9/11 were held here. ✉*5th Ave. between E. 50th and E. 51st Sts., Midtown East* ☎*212/753–2261 rectory* ⊕*www.ny-archdiocese.org* ⊘*Daily 8* AM*–8:45* PM Ⓜ *E, V to 5th Ave./53rd St.*

Seagram Building. Ludwig Mies van der Rohe, a pioneer of modern architecture, built this boxlike bronze-and-glass tower in 1958. The austere facade belies its wit: I-beams, used to hold buildings up, here are merely attached to the surface, representing the *idea* of support. The Seagram Building's innovative ground-level plaza, extending out to the sidewalk, has since become a common element in urban skyscraper design. ✉*375 Park Ave., between E. 52nd and E. 53rd Sts., Midtown*

Irish pride takes the streets and sweeps up Fifth Avenue in the annual St. Patrick's Day Parade.

East ✉️*Free* 🕐*Tours Tues. at 3* Ⓜ *6 to 51st St./Lexington Ave.; E, V to Lexington–3rd Aves./53rd St.*

🅒 **Sony Building.** Designed by Philip Johnson in 1984, the Sony Building's rose-granite columns and its giant-size Chippendale-style pediment made the skyscraper an instant landmark. The first-floor public arcade includes electronics stores, an upscale kosher restaurant, a café, and an atrium filled with children and adults playing chess. ✉️*550 Madison Ave., between E. 55th and E. 56th Sts., Midtown East* 🕐*Daily 7*AM*–11*PM Ⓜ*E, V to 5th Ave./53rd St.*

FRUGAL FUN

Have kids in tow? The free **Sony Wonder Technology Lab** in the Sony Building (✉️*550 Madison Ave., between E. 55th and E. 56th Sts., Midtown East* ☎*212/833–8100* ⊕ *www.sonywondertechlab.com* 🕐*Tues.–Sat. 10–5, Sun. noon–5; last entrance 30 mins before closing*) lets them program robots, edit music videos, or take a peek inside the human body. Admission is free but call at least seven days ahead for reservations, as it's very popular.

University Club. Among the best surviving works of McKim, Mead & White, New York's leading turn-of-the-20th-century architects, this 1899 pink Milford granite palace was built for an exclusive club of degree-holding men. (The crests of various prestigious universities hang above its windows.) The club's popularity declined as individual universities built their own clubs and as gentlemen's clubs became less important to the New York social scene. Still, the nine-story Italian High Renaissance Revival building (the facade looks as though it's three sto-

The view of Midtown from across the Hudson River shows the skyline punctuated by the Empire State Building.

ries) stands out, grand as ever, among the shiny 5th Avenue shops. ✉*1 W. 54th St., at 5th Ave., Midtown West* Ⓜ *E, V to 5th Ave./53rd St.*

GALLERIES

David Findlay Jr. Fine Art. This gallery concentrates on American 19th- and 20th-century painters from Winslow Homer to Robert Rauschenburg to op artist Richard Anuszkiewicz. ✉*41 E. 57th St., 11th fl., between 5th and Madison Aves., Midtown East* ☎*212/486–7660* ⊕*www.findlay art.com* Ⓜ *N, R, W to 5th Ave.*

Edwynn Houk. The impressive stable of 20th-century photographers here includes Sally Mann, Lynn Davis, and Elliott Erwitt. The gallery also has prints by masters Edward Weston and Alfred Stieglitz. ✉*745 5th Ave., between E. 57th and E. 58th Sts., Midtown East* ☎*212/750–7070* ⊕*www.houkgallery.com* Ⓜ *N, R, W to 5th Ave.*

Greenberg Van Doren. This gallery exhibits the works of young artists as well as retrospectives of established masters. You can purchase works here by Georgia O'Keeffe, Ed Ruscha, and Robert Motherwell, among others. ✉*730 5th Ave., at E. 57th St., Midtown East* ☎*212/445–0444* ⊕*www.agvdgallery.com* Ⓜ*N, R, W to 5th Ave.*

Marian Goodman. The excellent contemporary art here includes Jeff Wall's staged photographs presented on light boxes, South African artist William Kentridge's video animations, and Gerhard Richter's paintings. ✉*24 W. 57th St., between 5th and 6th Aves., Midtown West* ☎*212/977–7160* ⊕*www.mariangoodman.com* Ⓜ *F to 57th St.*

Rockefeller vs. Rivera

As Rockefeller Center neared completion in 1932, John D. Rockefeller Jr. still needed a mural to grace the lobby of the main building. The industrialist's taste dictated that the subject of the 63-foot-by-17-foot mural was to be grandiose: "human intelligence in control of the forces of nature." He hired an artist known for his grand vision, Mexican painter Diego Rivera.

With its depiction of massive machinery moving mankind forward, Rivera's *Man at the Crossroads* seemed exactly what Rockefeller wanted. Everything was going fine until someone noticed that near the center of the mural was a portrait of Soviet Premier Vladimir Lenin surrounded by red-kerchiefed workers. Rockefeller, who was building what was essentially a monument to capitalism, was less than thrilled. When Rivera was accused of willful propagandizing, the artist famously replied, "All art is propaganda."

Rivera refused to remove the offending portrait (although, as an olive branch, he did offer to add an image of Abraham Lincoln). In early 1934, as Rivera was working on the unfinished work, representatives for Rockefeller informed him that his services were no longer required. Within a half hour, tar paper had been hung over the mural. Despite negotiations to move it to the Museum of Modern Art, Rockefeller was determined to get rid of the mural once and for all. Not content to have it painted over, he ordered ax-wielding workers to chip away the entire wall.

Rockefeller ordered the mural replaced by a less offensive one by José María Sert. (This one did include Lincoln.) But Rivera had the last word. He re-created the mural in the Palacio de Bellas Artes in Mexico City, adding a portrait of Rockefeller among the champagne-swilling swells ignoring the plight of the workers.

Marlborough. With its latest branch in Chelsea, Marlborough has raised its global visibility up yet another notch. The gallery represents modern artists such as Michele Oka Doner, Magdalena Abakanowicz, and Israel Hershberg. Look for sculptures by Tom Otterness—his whimsical bronzes are found in several subway stations. ✉*40 W. 57th St., between 5th and 6th Aves., Midtown West* ☎*212/541–4900* ⊕*www.marlboroughgallery.com* Ⓜ *F to 57th St.*

Pace Wildenstein. The giant gallery—now in Chelsea as well—focuses on such modern and contemporary painters as Julian Schnabel, Mark Rothko, and New York School painter Ad Reinhardt. ✉*32 E. 57th St., between Park and Madison Aves., Midtown East* ☎*212/421–3292* ⊕*www.pacewildenstein.com* Ⓜ *N, R, W to 5th Ave.*

Peter Findlay. Covering 19th- and 20th-century works by European artists, this gallery shows pieces by Mary Cassatt, Paul Klee, and Alberto Giacometti. ✉*41 E. 57th St., 8th fl., at Madison Ave., Midtown East* ☎*212/644–4433* ⊕*www.findlay.com* Ⓜ *N, R, W to 5th Ave.*

Spanierman. This venerable gallery deals in 19th- and early-20th-century American painting and sculpture, their inventory list and scholarship is amazing, and they frequently sell to museums looking to broaden their own

Midtown Dining

AT A GLANCE

BUDGET DINING
Burger Joint, Burger,
118 W. 57th St.

Meskerem, Ethiopian,
468 W. 47th St.

MODERATE DINING
Marseille, Mediterranean, 630 9th Ave.

Mia Dona, Mediterranean, 206 E 58th St.

Mint, Indian,
150 E. 50th St.

Sosa Borella, Italian,
832 8th Ave., bet. 50th
and 51st Sts.

Sushi Yasuda, Japanese,
204 E. 43rd St.

Toloache, Mexican,
251 W. 50th St.,
nr. Broadway

Virgil's Real BBQ, Barbecue, 152 W. 44th St.

EXPENSIVE DINING
Abboccato, Italian,
136 W. 55th St.

Adour Alain Ducasse,
Modern French,
2 E. 55th St.

Aquavit and Aquavit
Café, Scandinavian,
65 E. 55th St.

Bar Americain, Brasserie, 152 W. 52nd St.

Becco, Italian,
355 W. 46th St.

Ben Benson's Steakhouse, Steak house,
123 W. 52nd St.

BLT Steak, Steak house,
106 E. 57th St.

Brasserie Ruhlmann,
Brasserie, 45 Rockefeller
Plaza

Churrascaria
Plataforma, Brazilian,
316 W. 49th St.

db bistro moderne,
French, 55 W. 44th St.

Esca, Seafood,
402 W. 43rd St.

Four Seasons,
American, 99 E. 52nd St.

Gordon Ramsay at
the London and Maze,
French, 51 W. 54th St.
bet. 6th and 7th Aves.

Kuruma Zushi,
Japanese, 7 E. 47th St.

L'Atelier de Joël
Robuchon, French,
57 E. 57th St.

Le Bernardin, French,
155 W. 51st St.

Le Cirque, French,
151 E. 58th St.

Michael Jordan's The
Steakhouse NYC, Steak
house, 23 Vanderbilt Ave.

The Modern and Bar
Room, French,
9 W. 53rd St.

Oyster Bar, Seafood,
E. 42nd St. at
Vanderbilt Ave.

Palm, Steak house,
250 W. 50th St.

Shun Lee Palace,
Chinese, 155 E. 55th St.

Sparks Steakhouse,
Steak house, 210 E.
46th St.

'21' Club, American,
21 W. 52nd St.

Uncle Jack's Steakhouse, Steak house,
440 9th Ave.

---

collections. ⊠*45 E. 58th St., between Park and Madison Aves., Midtown East* ☎*212/832–0208* ⊕*www.spanierman.com* Ⓜ *N, R, W to 5th Ave.*

Tibor de Nagy. Founded in 1950, this gallery shows work by 20th-century artists such as Biala, Nell Blaine, Jane Freilicher, and Shirley Jaffee. Instrumental in bringing many of America's finest Abstract Expressionist artists to public attention in the mid-20th century, the gallery now shows abstract and realistic work. It's closed weekends June through mid-August, and closes up completely from mid-August to Labor Day. ⊠*724 5th Ave., between W. 56th and W. 57th Sts., Midtown West* ☎*212/262–5050* ⊕*www.tibordenagy.com* Ⓜ*N, R, W to 5th Ave.*

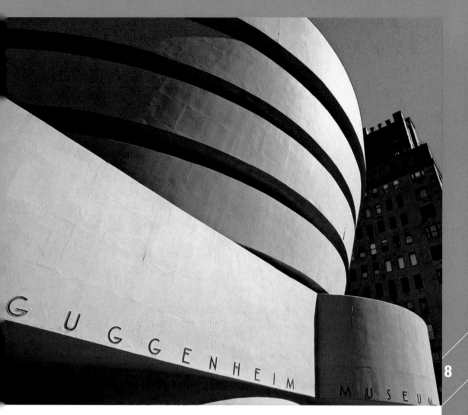

The Upper East Side

WORD OF MOUTH

"There can be so many WOW moments in New York. As one poster mentioned, the first time the skyline comes into view. The Statue of Liberty. The view of Central Park from the roof garden of the Metropolitan Museum."

—lisettemac

GETTING ORIENTED

St. Nicholas Russian
Orthodox Cathedral

E. 97th St.

6

E. 96th St.

El Museo
del Barrio

Museum of the
City of New York

E. 95th St.

E. 94th St.

E. 93rd St.

Jewish Museum

E. 92nd St.

Cooper-Hewitt
National Design Museum

E. 91st St.

E. 90th St.

E. 89th St.

Gracie
Mansion

Solomon R. Guggenheim
Museum

E. 88th St.

E. 87th St.

Henderson Place
Historic District

4, 5, 6

E. 86th St.

Schaller
& Weber

Neue Galerie
New York

E. 85th St.

Carl Schurz
Park

YORKVILLE

E. 84th St.

E. 83rd St.

Goethe Institute

E. 82nd St.

Crawford
Doyle

E. 81st St.

Metropolitan
Museum of Art

E. 80th St.

E. 79th St.

Mitchell-Innes &
Nash Gallery

Maison
du Chocolat

E. 78th St.

Leo Castelli
Gallery

6

E. 77th St.

Gagosian Gallery

E. 76th St.

The Carlyle Hotel

Whitney Museum of
American Art

E. 75th St.

Jane Kahan
Gallery

E. 74th St.

E. 73rd St.

Knoedler & Co.
Gallery

E. 72nd St.

Sotherby's

Frick
Collection

Hirschl & Adler
Gallery

E. 71st St.

Asia Society
and Museum

E. 70th St.

Americas
Society

E. 69th St.

6

E. 68th St.

E. 67th St.

Temple
Emanu-El

China Institute
Gallery

Wildenstein
& Co.
Gallery

B, Q

E. 64th St.

E. 63rd St.

E. 62nd St.

Mount Vernon Hotel
Museum and Garden

Metropolitan
Club

E. 61st St.

Serendipity 3

Roosevelt Island
Tramway

E. 60th St.

Bloomingdale's

Queensboro Bridge

E. 59th St.

N, R, W

N, R, W,
4, 5, 6

E. 58th St.

CENTRAL PARK

Fifth Ave.

Madison Ave.

Park Ave.

Lexington Ave.

Third Ave.

Second Ave.

First Ave.

York Ave.

East End Ave.

FDR Dr.

East River

Roosevelt
Island

East River

0   1/4 mile

0   400 meters

MAKING THE MOST OF YOUR TIME

The Upper East Side lends itself to a surprising variety of simple but distinct itineraries: Regimented hopping up and down Museum Mile; languorous gallery grazing (⇨ gallery listings at the end of this chapter); window-shopping on Madison Avenue; and, perhaps the hands-down year-round favorite for twentysomething locals, bar-hopping on 2nd Avenue.

There are a number of nail salons, and both men and women enjoy a soak and a buff, betraying a semi-true neighborhood stereotype—the pampered Upper East Sider. The cluster of salons means you can shop around quickly for a reasonably priced predinner manicure or that well-deserved post–Museum Mile foot rub to join in the indulgence.

GETTING HERE

Take the Lexington Avenue 4 or 5 express train to 59th or 86th Street. The 6 local train also stops at 68th, 77th, and 96th streets. If you're coming from Midtown, the F train will let you out at Lexington Avenue at 63rd Street. From the Upper West Side, take one of the crosstown buses, which are the M66, M72, M79, M86, and M96. You can also take the N, R, or W trains to 59th St. and Lexington Avenue.

WORD OF MOUTH (WWW.FODORS.COM/FORUMS)

"I like the neighborhood that the Carlyle is in, being very chi-chi poo-poo and quiet. It is a pleasure to walk down Madison Ave. on a Sunday morning past all the great boutiques." — marginal_margiela

STILL TRUE TODAY

"One of the most extraordinary buildings in New York is the Solomon R. Guggenheim Museum at 88th Street. The six-story spiral structure designed by the late Frank Lloyd Wright is alone worth a visit." —Fodor's New York City, 1989

FODOR'S CHOICE

Gracie Mansion

TOP ATTRACTIONS

Metropolitan Museum of Art (⇨ Ch. 14)

Mount Vernon Hotel Museum and Garden

TOP EXPERIENCES

Lingering at the Carlyle

Window-shopping on Madison

NEARBY MUSEUMS (⇨ CH. 14)

Asia Society and Museum
China Institute Gallery
Cooper-Hewitt National Design Museum
El Museo del Barrio
Frick Collection
Goethe Institut
Jewish Museum
Museum of American Illustration
Museum of the City of New York
National Academy
Neue Galerie New York
Solomon R. Guggenheim Museum
Whitney Museum

AREA SHOPS (⇨ CH. 17)

Calvin Klein
Fred Leighton
Giorgio Armani
Michael Kors
Nina Griscom
Oscar de la Renta
Roberto Cavalli
Valentino
Vera Wang

8

Sightseeing
★★★

Nightlife
★★

Dining
★★★

Lodging
★★

Shopping
★★★★

Updated by
John Rambow

To many New Yorkers the Upper East Side connotes old money and high society. Alongside Central Park, between 5th and Lexington avenues, up to East 96th Street, the trappings of wealth are everywhere apparent: posh buildings, Madison Avenue's flagship boutiques, and doormen in braided livery.

While a glance up and down the manicured grass meridian of Park Avenue may conjure scenes from *Bonfire of the Vanities* or *Gossip Girl*, there are more than palatial apartments, elite private schools, and highfalutin clubs up here—starting with world-class museums. The Metropolitan Museum of Art, the Guggenheim, and many others lie on and around "Museum Mile" (⇨ *Chapter 14*), as do a number of worthy art galleries (⇨ *list at the end of this chapter*). For a local taste of the luxe life, hit up the platinum-card corridor that is Madison Avenue for its lavish boutiques, marble-counter cafés, and the epitome of class, the **Carlyle Hotel.**

Venture east of Lexington Avenue and you encounter a less wealthy— and more diverse—Upper East Side, one inhabited by couples seeking some of the last affordable places to raise a family south of 100th Street, and recent college grads getting a foothold in the city (on weekend nights, 2nd Avenue resembles a miles-long fraternity and sorority reunion). One neighborhood particularly worth exploring is northeast-lying Yorkville, especially between 78th and 86th streets, east of 2nd Avenue. Once a remote hamlet with a large German population, its remaining ethnic food shops, 19th-century row houses, and, one of the city's best-kept secrets, Carl Schurz Park, make for a good half-day's exploration.

TWO WAYS TO EXPLORE

NEW YORK'S LAP OF LUXURY

Walking up Madison Avenue between East 60th and East 82nd Street is like stepping into the pages of a glossy magazine. Many fashion houses have their flagships here and showcase their lush threads in equally exquisite settings. Compared with the megastores of Midtown, Madison Avenue feels quieter; it's significantly less crowded and more conducive to leisurely shopping (window or otherwise). Beyond clothing, the boutiques here carry baubles to satisfy anyone's champagne wishes, whether it's a box of truffles at **La Maison du Chocolat,** an intriguing read at **Crawford Doyle Booksellers,** or a piece of contemporary silver tableware at **Christofle** (⊠*680 Madison Ave.,* ☎*212/308–9390*). When your feet grow tired, grab a seat at a glitzy café and take in the fashion show on the sidewalk. End the day in style with dinner at **Café Boulud** or a drink at one of the neighborhood's sleek lounges or bars.

A NEIGHBORHOOD IN EVERY BLOCK

The Upper East Side is more than just an enclave for the wealthy. In fact, a great way to experience Manhattan's hodgepodge of communities is to walk east from 5th Avenue to the East River—zigzagging to include both avenues and side streets—and watch the neighborhoods change. One good place to start is along lavish East 65th Street, passing the Romanesque **Temple Emanu-El;** the double town house at No. 47 built for Sara Delano Roosevelt and her son, Franklin; and the acclaimed French restaurant **Daniel** across the street. End several blocks and a world away at the 18th-century **Mount Vernon Hotel Museum and Garden.** Another good route starts at 1040 5th Avenue, at East 85th Street, the former home of Jacqueline Kennedy Onassis, which overlooks the reservoir that now bears her name. Heading east beyond Park Avenue, the town houses and boutiques give way to the quaint secondhand stores and the residential high-rises of **Yorkville** (the one at 185 East 85th appeared in the opening credits of the TV show *The Jeffersons*). Few remaining shops recall the neighborhood's German and Hungarian immigrant past (which earned 2nd Avenue the nickname "Goulash Avenue"); one delicious reminder is the 1937 food shop **Schaller & Weber** (⊠1654 2nd Ave., at East 86th Street), where you can pick up homemade bratwurst or imported stollen, cookies, and other goodies. From here, continue east to see the official mayoral residence, **Gracie Mansion**, and the serene riverside **Carl Schurz Park.**

8

TOP ATTRACTIONS

☾ **Carl Schurz Park.** Above the East River, this park, named for a German immigrant who was a prominent newspaper editor in the 19th century, is so tranquil you'd never guess you're directly above FDR Drive. Walk along the promenade, where you can take in views of the river and the Roosevelt Island Lighthouse across the way; to the north are Randalls and Wards islands and newly renamed RFK Bridge (aka the Triborough Bridge)—as well as the more immediate sight of locals pushing strollers, riding bikes, or exercising their dogs. If you're visiting with kids, there's a very worthwhile playground at the 84th Street end with climbing equipment, swings, and other diversions for toddlers and older children. If you enter the park at its 86th Street entrance or you're exiting there, you'll find yourself approaching the grounds of a Federal-style wood-frame house that belies the grandeur of its name—Gracie Mansion.

Fodor'sChoice
★

The official mayor's residence, **Gracie Mansion** (✉ *Carl Schurz Park, East End Ave. opposite 88th St., Upper East Side* ☎ *212/570–4751* 💲*$7* 🕙 *45-min guided tours by advance reservation only; Wed. 10–2* Ⓜ *4, 5, 6 to 86th St.*) was built in 1799 by shipping merchant Archibald Gracie, with an enlargement in 1966. Tours of the highly impressive interior—which must be scheduled in advance and take place under limited hours— take you through its history and colorful rooms furnished over centuries and packed with American objets d'art. Nine mayors have lived here since it became the official residence in 1942, but New York City's current mayor, Michael Bloomberg, broke with tradition; he chose to stay in his own 79th Street town house, though he uses this house for meetings and functions. ■ TIP→ If you exit the park at 86th Street, cross East End Avenue for a stroll through Henderson Place, a miniature historic district of 24 connected Queen Anne–style houses in a dead end. The small redbrick houses, built in 1881 "for persons of moderate means," have turrets marking the corner of each block and symmetrical roof gables, pediments, parapets, chimneys, and dormer windows. ✉ *Carl Schurz Park spans East End Ave. to the East River, E. 84th to E. 90th Sts., Upper East Side* Ⓜ *4, 5, 6 to 86th St.*

☺ **Mount Vernon Hotel Museum and Garden.** Built in 1799, this former carriage house became a day hotel (a sort of country club) in 1826. Now restored and owned by the Colonial Dames of America, it provides a glimpse of the days when the city ended at 14th Street and this area was a country escape for New Yorkers. The 45-minute tour passes through the eight rooms that display furniture and artifacts of the Federal and Empire periods. Many rooms have real artifacts like clothes, hats, and fans that children can handle. The adjoining garden, designed in an 18th-century style, hosts classic music concerts Tuesday in June and July at 6 PM (extra charge). ✉ *421 E. 61st St., between York and 1st Aves., Upper East Side* ☎ *212/838–6878* ⊕ *www.mvhm.org* 💲*$8* 🕙 *Sept.–July, Tues.–Sun. 11–4* Ⓜ *4, 5, 6, F, N, R, W to 59th St./Lexington Ave.*

ALSO WORTH SEEING

Metropolitan Club. The grandest of the überexclusive clubs abutting Central Park, this Italian Renaissance–style edifice was commissioned by J. P. Morgan in the 1890s when a friend was denied membership to the Union League Club (the "new money" of bankers was too vulgar for New York society at the time). Morgan's grandiose result outdid the other clubs in magnificence, with lordly gates and an ornate lounge overlooking Central Park. Today's members include leaders of foreign countries, presidents of major corporations, and former U.S. president Bill Clinton. ✉ *1 E. 60th St., near 5th Ave., Upper East Side* Ⓜ *N, Q, R, W to 5th Ave.*

Where can I find...?

COFFEE	Sant Ambroeus 1000 Madison Ave., by 77th St. The best cappuccino this side of Milan.	Two Little Red Hens 1652 2nd Ave., by 85th St. First-rate joe and the cupcakes to match.
A QUICK BITE	Payard 1032 Lexington Ave., at 73rd St. Croissants as they're meant to be: flakey and light.	Totonno's 1544 2nd Ave., by 80th St. No slices, but the best white pizza you'll ever eat.
COCKTAILS	Bemelmans Bar 35 E. 76th St., by Madison Ave. Classy but unpretentious.	Tin Lizzie 1647 2nd Ave., by 85th St. Just-out-of-college vibe, with very reasonable tabs.

Although **Roosevelt Island** (the 2-mi-long East River slice of land that parallels Manhattan from East 48th to East 85th streets) is now a quasi-suburb of 10,000 people, the vestiges of its infamous asylums, hospitals, and prisons make this an offbeat trip for the historically curious. At the south tip is the **Renwick Ruin,** the eerie remains of a smallpox hospital built in the Gothic Revival style. On a small park at the island's north tip is a lighthouse built in 1872 by island convicts. Most of what's in between (new condominiums and a modern-day hospital) is fairly banal, but riverside esplanades provide nice panoramas of Manhattan. You can get here by subway, but more fun is the five-minute ride on the **Roosevelt Island Tramway,** the only commuter cable car in North America, which lifts you 250 feet in the air, with impressive views of Queens and Manhattan. A visitor center, made from an old trolley kiosk, stands to your left as you exit the tram. Red buses service the island, 25¢ a ride. ⊠ *Tramway entrance at 2nd Ave. and either 59th St. or 60th St., Upper East Side* ☎ *212/832–4555* ⊕ *www.rioc.com, island corporation, www.rihs.us, historical society* 🎫 *$2 (subway Metrocard accepted)* ⊙ *Sun.–Thurs. 6 AM–2 AM, Fri. and Sat. 6 AM–3:30 AM; leaves every 15 mins* Ⓜ *F to Roosevelt Island.*

GALLERIES

Many Upper East Side art galleries reside in town houses or upper stories on Madison Avenue. Although their often limited hours and location lend an exclusive air (sometimes they're identified only by the lettering near the buzzer—which you must ring to be let in), once inside, the atmosphere is generally welcoming, even if you're not in the market for a Pollock painting.

Gagosian Gallery. Nicknamed Mr. Go Go for his aggressive approach to art dealing, Larry Gagasian represents some of the most talked-about and playful of contemporary artists. Works by Damian Hirst, Andy

AT A GLANCE

Upper East Side Dining

MODERATE DINING

Alloro, Italian,
307 E 77th St.

Café d'Alsace,
Brasserie, 1695 2nd Ave.

Maya, Mexican,
1191 1st Ave.

EXPENSIVE DINING

Café Boulud, French,
20 E. 76th St.

Daniel, French,
60 E. 65th St.

David Burke & Donatella, New American,
133 E. 61st St.

Le Pain Quotidien,
1270 1st Ave., at 68th St.; 252 E. 77th St., nr. 2nd Ave.; 1131 Madison Ave., nr. 84th St.; 833 Lexington Ave., nr. 64th St.

Park Avenue
Summer/Autumn/
Winter/Spring,
American, 100 E. 63rd St., at Park Ave.

Payard Pâtisserie & Bistro, Bistro,
1032 Lexington Ave.

Sfoglia, Italian,
1402 Lexington Ave.

Warhol, Tracy Emin, and Jeff Koons have all been exhibited in this massive, multi-level penthouse gallery, one of the three Gagosian spaces in New York alone. ⊠*980 Madison Ave., at E. 77th St., Upper East Side* ☎*212/744–2313* ⊕*www.gagosian.com* Ⓜ*6 to 77th St.*

Jane Kahan. This welcoming gallery represents very lofty works. Besides ceramics by Picasso and modern master tapestries, one of this gallery's specialties, you'll see works by late-19th- and early-20th-century modern artists such as Fernand Léger, Joan Miró, and Marc Chagall. ⊠*922 Madison Ave., 2nd fl., between E. 73rd and E. 74th Sts., Upper East Side* ☎*212/744–1490* ⊕*www.janekahan.com* Ⓜ*6 to 77th St.*

Leo Castelli. Castelli was one of the most influential dealers of the 20th century. He helped foster the careers of many important artists, including one of his first discoveries, Jasper Johns. The gallery continues to show works by Roy Lichtenstein, Ed Ruscha, Jackson Pollock, and other heavies. ⊠*18 E. 77th St., between 5th and Madison Aves., Upper East Side* ☎*212/249–4470* ⊕*www.castelligallery.com* Ⓜ*6 to 77th St.*

Sotheby's. Occupying its own 10-story building, this branch of the storied U.K. auction house puts on display many of the items it will be auctioning. A sizeable portion of these are extremely high-profile: a copy of the Magna Carta, Fabergé eggs, rare Tiffany lamps, and Norman Rockwell's 1943 painting *Rosie the Riveter* have all been sold through this Sotheby's. ⊠*1334 York Ave., atd E. 72nd St., Upper East Side* ☎*212/606–7000* ⊕*www.sothebys.com* Ⓜ*6 to 77th St.*

Wildenstein & Co. This branch of the Wildenstein art empire was the first to take root in New York; its reputation for brilliant holdings was cemented by the acquisition of significant museum-quality collections. Look for French impressionist exhibitions. ⊠*19 E. 64th St., between 5th and Madison Aves., Upper East Side* ☎*212/879–0500* ⊕*www.wildenstein. com* Ⓜ*6 to 68th St./Hunter College; F to 63rd-Lexington Ave.*

Central Park

WORD OF MOUTH

"For anybody reading this who has never been to NYC before, listen carefully: get up early, and walk in Central Park on the weekend. Do it. As soon as you take two steps inside, you realize that you are going to LOVE New York with all your heart and soul, and that you want to have her babies."

— MacSporran

OUR BACKYARD

HOW A SWAMP BECAME AN OASIS

1855 Using eminent domain, New York City acquires 843 acres of undeveloped swamp for the then-obscene sum of $5 million, displacing 1,600 people living there.

1857 Frederick Law Olmsted becomes superintendent of a park that does not yet exist. He spends days clearing dirt and evicting squatters and evenings working with architect friend Calvert Vaux on what will become the Greensward plan. The plan is the winning entry in the city's competition to develop a design for the park.

The Panic of 1857 creates widespread unemployment. Thousands of workers begin the task of moving five million cubic yards of dirt and planting more than five million trees, plants, and shrubs. Beleaguered by bureaucrats, Olmsted and Vaux unsuccessfully submit their resignations several times.

1873 The Greensward plan is completed. It has been the basic blueprint for Central Park ever since.

Twenty-five million people use Central Park each year; on an average spring weekend day, a quarter-million children and adults flood these precincts from all over Manhattan, frolicking in the 21 playgrounds, bellying up the 150 drinking fountains (water not guaranteed), and collapsing on more than 9,000 benches, which would span seven miles if you lined them up. There are more than 50 monuments and sculptures in the park, but many more ways to make your own fun.

⟨30⟩ THINGS WE LOVE TO DO IN CENTRAL PARK

1 Take a rowboat out on the Lake

2 Watch the sea lions play at feeding time

3 Walk around the Reservoir

4 Ice-skate at Wollman Rink

5 Watch rollerbladers show off

6 Go bird watching at the Ramble

7 Lie in the grass at Sheep Meadow

8 Rent a bike at the Boathouse

9 Sit on the hill behind the Met Museum

10 See a free concert or play

11 Catch a softball game

12 Clap for the jugglers

13 Remember John Lennon at Strawberry Fields

14 Run through an icy playground sprinkler

15 Rent a gondola and a gondolier

16 Cross the park on the bridle path

17 Stand under the gnarly 72nd Street pergola

18 Hear the Delacorte Clock's musical chimes

19 Crunch the snow before anyone else

20 Pilot a tiny boat at Conservatory Water

21 Stroll through Shakespeare Garden

22 Fish at Harlem Meer

23 Watch dogs play

24 Smell the Conservatory Garden tulips

25 Shoot photos from Bow Bridge

26 Ride the Carousel; wave at everyone

27 People-watch at Bethesda Fountain

28 Picnic on the Great Lawn

29 Pet the bronze Balto statue

30 Climb to the top of Belvedere Castle

(top left) Monarch butterfly pollinates at Conservatory Garden (top center) Hansom driver between fares (top right) Chrysanthemums near Sheep Meadow (center) The skyline with some of the park's 26,000 trees (bottom) Park skaters in the 1860s.

PARK BASICS

Several entrances lead into the park. You can enter from the east, west, south, and north by paved pedestrian walkways, just off Fifth Avenue, Central Park North (110th St.), Central Park West, and Central Park South.

Four roads, or transverses, cut through the park from east to west—66th, 79th, 86th, and 96th streets. The East and West drives are both along the north–south axis; Center Drive enters the south edge of the park at Sixth Avenue and connects with East Drive around 66th Street.

Three Visitor Centers—the Dairy (just south of the 66th St. transverse), Belvedere Castle (just north of the 79th Street transverse), and the Charles A. Dana Discovery Center (at the top of the park at Central Park North)—have directions, park maps, event calendars, and volunteers who can guide you.

Central Park's reputation for danger is a remnant of bleaker days. An awareness of one's surroundings and common sense should suffice to protect the wary, but it's still not a good idea to wander through the park alone at night..

TOURS

The **Central Park Conservancy** gives nine different free walking tours of the park on Wednesday, Saturday, and Sunday, based on the season. The walks provide a perfect opportunity to explore the Ramble without getting lost, become well versed in the park's history, or get clued into "hidden" aspects you might otherwise have missed. Most tours are 60 to 90 minutes, and custom tours are also available.

WHERE AM I?

Along the main loop and some smaller paths, lampposts are marked with location codes. Posts bear a letter—always "E" (for east) or "W" (for west)—followed by four numbers. The first two numbers tell you the nearest cross street. The second two tell you how far you are from either 5th Avenue or Central Park West (depending on whether it's an "E" or "W" post). So E7803 means you're near 78th Street, three posts in from 5th Avenue. For street numbers above 99, the initial "1" is omitted, for example, E0401 (near 104th Street, one post in from 5th Avenue).

PERFORMERS AND THE PARK: SOULMATES

It was inevitable that Central Park, conceived to give so much and ask little in return, would attract artists and arts lovers who feel the same way.

Be they superstars like Paul Simon, Diana Ross, or Barbra Streisand or one of the amateur musicians, animal handlers, or jugglers who delight passersby, they all share the urge to entertain and give back to the city, the park, and its visitors.

Information on scheduled events is provided, but if you can't catch one, don't fret: you'll be rewarded by the serendipitous, particularly on summer and autumn days. Just keep your ears peeled for the music, applause, and laughter. The Central Park Conservancy, in cooperation with other arts patrons, drives a series of free events, including the Harlem Meer Performance Festival and the Great Lawn performances by the Metropolitan Opera and New York Philharmonic. One standout is SummerStage, which yields a cornucopia of international performers.

Perhaps the brass ring of park performances is the more than four-decade-old Shakespeare in the Park, which wows about 80,000 New Yorkers and visitors during any given summer. Free tickets (two per person) are given out starting at 1 PM for the performance that evening, but you need to line up by midmorning or earlier depending on the show. The wait is worth it, though, as casts are often studded with the likes of Meryl Streep, Philip Seymour Hoffman, Natalie Portman, Morgan Freeman, Denzel Washington, and Kevin Kline.

GOINGS ON

Central Park Film Festival: Five nights at end of summer; Rumsey Playfield, near E. 72nd St. entrance.

Harlem Meer Performance Festival: Late May–early Sept., Sun.; at Dana Discovery Center, near Lenox Ave. entrance.

New York Grand Opera: Performances Aug.–Sept.; Naumburg Bandshell; mid-park near 72nd St.

New York Philharmonic: Two performances in June or July; Great Lawn.

Shakespeare in the Park: Late May–early Sept., Tues.–Sun. evenings.

Storytelling: June–Sept., Sat. 11 AM; Hans Christian Andersen Statue.

SummerStage: Late May or June–early Sept.; Rumsey Playfield. Big-name, up-and-coming, and international musicians perform here, sometimes for free.

Swedish Cottage Marionette Theatre: Since 1947, puppeteers have entertained in this 1876 Swedish schoolhouse. $8 adults/$5 kids. Tue.–Sun. hours vary; reservations required.

(center) N.Y. Philharmonic associate conductor Xian Zhang (right) Shakespeare's *Much Ado About Nothing*

FROM 59TH TO 72ND ST.

 The busy southern section of Central Park is where most visitors get their first impression. Artists line the entrances off Central Park South, and drivers of horse carriages await passengers. But no matter how many people congregate in this area, you can always find a spot to picnic, ponder, or just take in the beauty, especially on a sunny day.

At the southeast corner of the park, you will come upon one of its prettiest areas, the **Pond**. Swans and ducks cruise on its calm waters, and if you follow the shore line to Gapstow Bridge and look southward, you'll see much of New York City's skyline: to the left (east) are the peak-roofed Sherry-Netherland Hotel, the black-and-white CBS Building, the Chippendale-style top of the Sony Building, and the black-glass Trump Tower. In front of you is the château-style Plaza Hotel.

Opening in late October, **Wollman Memorial Rink** sits inside the park against a backdrop of Central Park South skyscrapers. You can rent skates there, buy snacks, and have a perfect city-type outing. There's a lively feeling here with lots of great music playing and a

terrace so you can watch if you're not into skating.

The **Friedsam Memorial Carousel**, also known as the Central Park Carousel, was built in 1908. It has 58 nearly life-size hand-carved horses and remains a favorite among young and old. Its original Wurlitzer organ plays calliope waltzes, polkas, and standards. Even if you don't need visitor infomation, the **Dairy** is worth a stop for its Swiss-chalet exterior.

If you saw the film *Madagascar*, you may recognize the Central Park Zoo, officially known as the **Central Park Wildlife Center**. Here, the polar bears play at the Polar Circle, monkeys frolic in the open-air Temperate Territory, and the Rain Forest showcases flora and fauna that you wouldn't expect to see in Manhattan. An unusual exhibit is the ant colony—even New York City's zoo has a sense of humor. Stick around to see the sea lion feedings (call for times) and to watch the animal statues dance to a variety of nursery rhymes at the **Delacorte Musical Clock** just outside, on the hour and half-hour from 8 AM to 6 PM.

Wedged between the zoo and the clock is **The Arsenal**, the second-oldest building in the park. Inside

are rotating exhibits that often cover park history and landscape art.

North of the clock is **Tisch Children's Zoo**, where kids can pet and feed sheep, goats, rabbits, cows, and pigs. Enter through the trunk of a make-believe tree and arrive at The Enchanted Forest, filled with huge "acorns," a climbable "spider web," and hoppable "lily pads."

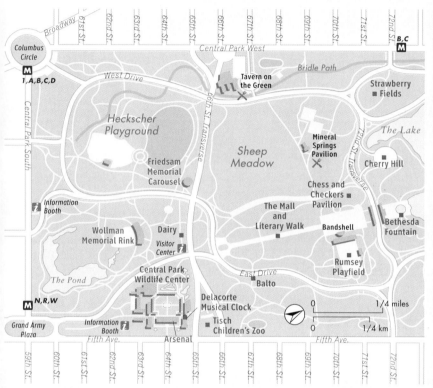

Perhaps more pettable than any of the zoo's occupants is a decidedly more inert creature, perched on a rockpile at East Drive and 67th Street: **Balto**. Shiny in places from constant touching, this bronze statue commemorates a real-life sled dog who led a team of huskies that carried medicine for 674 mi across perilous ice to Nome, Alaska, during a 1925 diphtheria epidemic.

The Mall, at the intersection of Central Drive and East Drive, is arguably the most elegant area of Central Park. In the beginning of the 20th century, it was the place to see and be seen. Today, these formal walkways are still a wonderful place to stroll, meander, or sit and take in the "parade" under a canopy of the largest collection of American elms in North America. The mall's

southern end, known as **Literary Walk**, is lined with statues of authors and artists such as Robert Burns and William Shakespeare.

(from left to right) Riding on the outside track (recommended) of the Carousel; Getting in a workout on a park drive loop; The Mall, where Dustin Hoffman's character famously teaches his son to ride a bike in Kramer vs. Kramer.

The large expanse to the west of the Mall is known as **Sheep Meadow**, the only "beach" that some native New Yorkers have ever known. Join in on a Frisbee or football game, admire the tenacity of kite flyers, or indulge simultaneously in the three simplest meadow pleasures of them all—picnicking, sunbathing, and languorously consuming the newspaper.

There's a reason why the ornate **Bethesda Fountain**, off the 72nd Street transverse, shows up in so many movies set in New York City: the view from the staircase above is one of the most romantic in the city. The statue in the center of the fountain, The Angel of the Waters, designed by Emma Stebbins, is surrounded by four figures symbolizing Temperance, Purity,

Health, and Peace. There's a good amount of New York–style street entertainment here, too, with break dancers, acrobats, and singers all vying for your spare change. It's also a great place to meet, sit, stretch after a long run, and admire the beautiful lake beyond with its swans and boaters. For a glimpse of the West Side skyline and another view of the lake, walk slightly west to **Cherry Hill**.

Originally a watering area for horses, this circular plaza has a small wrought-iron-and-gilt fountain. It's particularly beautiful in the spring when the cherry trees are in full pink-and-white bloom.

Across from the Dakota apartment building on Central Park West is **Strawberry Fields,** named for the Beatles' 1967 classic, "Strawberry Fields Forever." This informal memorial to John Lennon is sometimes called the "international garden of peace," and fans make pilgrimages to walk its curving paths, reflect among its shrubs, trees, and flower beds, play guitar, and lay flowers on the black-and-white "Imagine" mosaic. On December 8, hundreds of Beatles fans mark the anniversary of Lennon's death by gathering here.

(top from left to right) Seals cavorting at the zoo; Artist painting the oft-rendered Gapstow bridge, which spans the northeast end of the Pond; Cutting through the park is a classic midday timesaver and post-work respite; Meeting up and chilling out at world-famous Bethesda Fountain (center left); Nighttime at Wollman Rink serves up twinkling skyscrapers and skaters of all abilities (center right); The late John Lennon and his widow, Yoko Ono, often visited the site of what would become Strawberry Fields.

FROM 72ND ST. TO THE RESERVOIR

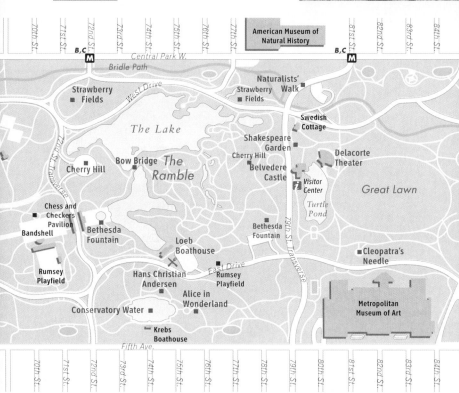

Playgrounds, lawns, jogging and biking paths, and striking buildings populate the midsection of the park. You can soak up the sun, have a picnic, or even play in a pick-up basketball or baseball game by the Great Lawn; get your cultural fix at the Metropolitan Museum of Art; or train for the next New York City Marathon along the Reservoir.

A block from Fifth Avenue, just north of the 72nd Street entrance, is a peaceful section of the park where you'll find the **Conservatory Water**, named for a conservatory that was never built. Generations of New Yorkers have grown up racing radio-controlled model sailboats here. It's a tradition that happens each Saturday at 10 AM from spring through fall. Smaller boats are available for rent. At the north end is the **Alice in Won-**derland statue; on the west side of the pond, a bronze statue of **Hans Christian Andersen**, the Ugly Duckling at his feet, is the site of Saturday storytelling hours during summer.

At the brick neo-Victorian **Loeb Boathouse** on the park's 18-acre Lake, you can rent a rowboat, kayak, or a bicycle as well as ride in an authentic Venetian gondola. The attached café is a worthy pit stop.

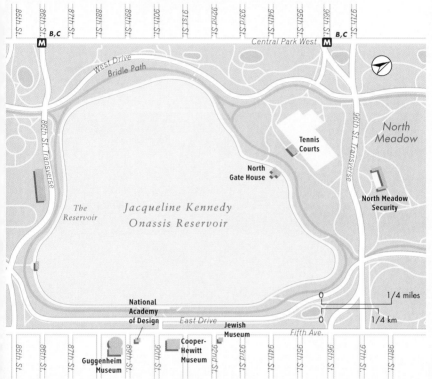

Designed to resemble upstate New York's Adirondack Mountain region, the **Ramble** covers 38 acres and is laced with twisting, climbing paths. This is prime bird-watching territory, since it's a rest stop along a major migratory route and a shelter for many of the more than 230 species of birds that have been sighted in the park; bring your binoculars. Because the Ramble is so dense and isolated,

however, don't wander here alone, or after dark. Head south through The Ramble and you'll come to the beautiful cast-iron **Bow Bridge**, spanning part of the Lake between the Ramble and Bethesda Fountain. From the center of the bridge, you can get a sweeping view of the park as well as of the apartment buildings on both the East Side and the West Side.

North of the Ramble atop Vista Rock, **Belvedere Castle** is the second-highest natural point in the park. If you can't get tickets for Delacorte Theater, you can climb to one of the castle's

(from left to right) Belvedere means "beautiful view" in Italian, a clue to why we climb to the top of Belvedere Castle; Birders, photographers, and couples of all ages are drawn to Bow Bridge; Red-eared slider turtles frolic in Turtle Pond, at the base of Belvedere Castle.

three terraces and look down on the stage. You'll also get a fantastic view of the Great Lawn—it's particularly beautiful during the fall foliage months—and of the park's myriad bird visitors. Since 1919 the castle has served as a U.S. Weather Bureau station, and meteorological instruments are set on top of the tower. If you enter the Castle from the lower level, you can visit the Henry Luce Nature Observatory, which has nature exhibits, children's workshops, and educational programs.

Somewhat hidden behind Belvedere Castle, **Shakespeare Garden** is an informal jumble of flowers, trees, and pathways, inspired by the flora mentioned in Shakespeare's plays and poetry. Bronze plaques throughout the garden bear the bard's lines mentioning the plants.

The Great Lawn hums with action on weekends, on warm days, and on most summer evenings, when its baseball fields and picnic grounds fill with city folks and visitors alike. Its 13 acres have endured millions of footsteps, thousands of ball games, hundreds of downpours, dozens of concerts, fireworks displays, and even a papal mass. On a beautiful day, everyone seems to be here.

Chancing upon the 70-ft-tall **Cleopatra's Needle** always feels a bit serendipitous and delightfully jarring, even to the most cynical New Yorkers. This weathered hieroglyphic-covered obelisk began life in Heliopolis, Egypt, around 1500 BC, but has only a little to do with Cleopatra—it's just New York's nickname for the work. It was eventually carted off to Alexandria by the Romans in 12 BC, and

it landed here on January 22, 1881, when the khedive of Egypt made it a gift to the city.

At the southwest corner of the Great Lawn is the fan-shaped **Delacorte Theater**, home to the summer Shakespeare in the Park festival.

If you want to take in several sites in a single brisk jaunt, consider walking the **Naturalists' Walk**. On this path you can wind your way

toward the Swedish Cottage, the Shakespeare Garden, and Belvedere Castle on a landscaped nature

(top, from left to right) A female Canada goose and goslings on Turtle Pond; Cyclists make good use of the bike paths; Bikers as well as joggers boost their egos by outpacing the hansom carriages; Racing boats at Conservatory Water (center) In the 1930s, a flock of mutant sheep was evicted from what would later be known as Sheep Meadow.

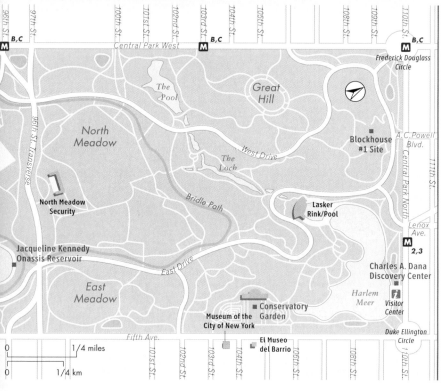

walk with spectacular rock outcrops, a stream that attracts bird life, a woodland area with various native trees, stepping-stone trails, and, thankfully, benches.

North of the Great Lawn and the 86th Street transverse is a popular gathering place for New Yorkers and visitors alike, the Jacqueline Kennedy Onassis Reservoir. Rain or shine, you'll see runners of all ages and paces heading counterclockwise around the 1.58-mi cinder path that encircles the water. The path in turn is surrounded by hundreds of trees that burst into color in the spring and fall. The 106-acre reservoir, finished in 1862, was a source of fresh water for Manhattanites. It holds more than a billion gallons, but it's no longer used for drinking water; the city's main reservoirs are upstate. From the top of the stairs at 90th Street just off 5th Avenue you have a 360-degree panorama of the city's exciting skyscrapers and often-brilliant sunsets. On the south side, there are benches so you can rest and recharge.

FROM THE RESERVOIR TO 110TH ST.

 More locals than tourists know about the wilder-looking, less-crowded northern part of Central Park, and there are hidden gems lurking here that enable even the most tightly wound among us to decompress, at least for a short while.

Walking along Fifth Avenue to 105th Street, you'll see a magnificent wrought-iron gate—once part of the 5th Avenue mansion of Cornelius Vanderbilt II—that marks the entrance to the **Conservatory Garden**. As you walk through it, you enter a different world, a quiet place that's positively idyllic for reading and slowing down. The Italian-style Central Garden is a beauty, with an expansive lawn, a strikingly simple fountain, and a wisteria-draped pergola that just oozes romance.

The French-inspired **North Garden** is a colorful place with plants placed into elaborate patterns. Springtime is magical—thousands of tulips come to life in a circle around the garden's striking Untermyer Fountain and its three bronze dancers; in the fall, chrysanthemums take their place. The English-style **South Garden** conjures up images from the classic children's book *The Secret Garden*. The garden is a beautiful hodgepodge of trees, bushes, and flowers that bloom year-round. A free tour is conducted on Saturday at 11 AM, from April through October.

Yes, there are fish in Central Park. At **Harlem Meer,** the third-largest body of water in Central Park, you can borrow fishing poles (identification required) from mid-April through October and try your hand at catching the largemouth bass, catfish, golden shiners, and bluegills that are stocked in the water's 11 acres. You can also learn about the upper park's geography, ecology, and history at the Victorian-style **Charles A. Dana Discovery Center.**

Although only a shell of this stone building remains, **Blockhouse #1** serves as a historical marker: the structure was built in 1814 as a cliffside fortification against the British. The area is deserted and dense with trees, so go as a group here.

(left) A pensive raccoon in the park's northern reaches (center); Indulging in a park favorite, soccer, near East Meadow (right); A jogger makes her counterclockwise progress along the Reservoir.

CONTACT INFORMATION

Central Park Conservancy
☎ 212/310–6600 (park events); 212/360–2726 (walking tours)
⊕ www.centralparknyc.org

Central Park SummerStage
☎ 212/360–2756
⊕ www.summerstage.org

Central Park Wildlife Center (Central Park Zoo)
☎ 212/439–6500
⊕ www.centralparkzoo.org

Central Park Visitor Centers
☎ 212/794–6564
⊕ www.nycgovparks.org
☎ 212/639–9675

Charles A. Dana Discovery Center
☎ 212/860–1370
Delacorte Theater
☎ 212/539–8750
⊕ www.publictheater.org

Loeb Boathouse, Boathouse Restaurant
☎ 212/517–2233
⊕ www.thecentral parkboathouse.com

Swedish Cottage Marionette Theatre
☎ 212/988–9093

Wollman Memorial Rink
☎ 212/439–6900
⊕ www.wollmanskating rink.com

PALE MALE: IF YOU CAN MAKE IT HERE...

Telescoping the nest from within the park; Pale Male returns home; watching the brood like a hawk; Pale Male's progeny.

Since 1993, the red-tailed hawk Pale Male has sired and raised 23 offspring in a nest on the 12th floor of 927 Fifth Avenue, near 74th St. and one of the city's toniest co-ops. Despite his upscale digs, life hasn't always been easy. He's lost mates (current partner Lola is his fourth), eggs, chicks, and even his home. In 2004, the co-op trashed Pale Male and Lola's nest and blocked their return. Under pressure from the news media and protesters (some holding signs that urged passing drivers to "Honk-4-Hawks"), the board relented less than a month later. A platform was installed to hold the nest, and Pale Male and Lola returned and began to rebuild. Today the hawks' numbers are growing—in 2005 Pale Male's son Junior and his mate, Charlotte, hatched two chicks in their nest at the Trump Parc building.

The Upper West Side

INCLUDING MORNINGSIDE HEIGHTS

WORD OF MOUTH

"Absolutely loved staying on the UWS. Everything is right at your fingertips from the grocery store across the street, the bakery and liquor store, Zabar's, and a ton of restaurant options. Also, Central Park is very close, as is the River."

—AustinTraveler

GETTING ORIENTED

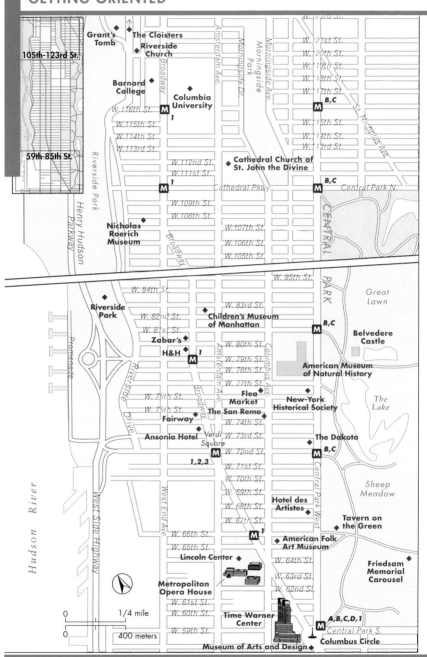

105th–123rd St.

59th–85th St.

Grant's Tomb

The Cloisters

Riverside Church

Barnard College

Columbia University

W. 116th St.

W. 115th St.

W. 114th St.

W. 113th St.

W. 123rd St.

W. 121st St.

W. 120th St.

W. 119th St.

W. 118th St.

W. 117th St.

B,C

W. 115th St.

W. 114th St.

W. 113th St.

Amsterdam Ave.

Broadway

Morningside Dr.

Morningside Park

Morningside Ave.

St. Nicholas Ave.

Cathedral Church of St. John the Divine

W. 112nd St.

W. 111st St.

Cathedral Pkwy.

W. 109th St.

W. 108th St.

B,C

Central Park N.

Nicholas Roerich Museum

W. 107th St.

W. 106th St.

W. 105th St.

Riverside Park

Henry Hudson Parkway

Broadway

CENTRAL PARK

W. 85th St.

Great Lawn

Riverside Park

W. 84th St.

W. 83rd St.

W. 82nd St.

W. 81st St.

Zabar's

H&H

Children's Museum of Manhattan

B,C

Belvedere Castle

Promenade

Riverside Drive

W. 80th St.

W. 79th St.

W. 78th St.

W. 77th St.

Amsterdam Ave.

Columbus Ave.

American Museum of Natural History

Flea Market

New-York Historical Society

The Lake

W. 76th St.

W. 75th St.

The San Remo

Fairway

Ansonia Hotel

Verdi Square

W. 74th St.

W. 73rd St.

W. 72nd St.

1,2,3

W. 71st St.

W. 70th St.

The Dakota

B,C

Sheep Meadow

Hudson River

West End Ave.

West Side Highway

Broadway

Central Park West

W. 69th St.

W. 68th St.

W. 67th St.

Hotel des Artistes

Tavern on the Green

W. 66th St.

W. 65th St.

Lincoln Center

American Folk Art Museum

W. 64th St.

W. 63rd St.

W. 62nd St.

Friedsam Memorial Carousel

Metropolitan Opera House

W. 61st St.

W. 60th St.

Time Warner Center

W. 59th St.

A,B,C,D,1

Central Park S.

Columbus Circle

Museum of Arts and Design

1/4 mile

400 meters

0

0

MAKING THE MOST OF YOUR TIME

Broadway is hands down the most walkable and interesting thoroughfare on the Upper West Side, due largely to its broad sidewalks and aggressive mélange of retail stores, restaurants, and apartment buildings. If you head north from the Lincoln Center area until about 81st Street (about 0.75 mi) you'll get a feel for the neighborhood's local color, particularly above 72nd Street; up here you'll encounter residents of every conceivable age and ethnicity either shambling or sprinting (New Yorkers wouldn't know a medium pace if they tripped over it, quite literally), street vendors hawking used and newish books, and such beloved landmarks as the 72nd Street subway station, the Beacon Theater, the produce mecca Fairway (the cause of perhaps the most perpetually crowded block in creation), and Zabar's, the food spot that launches a memorable assault on all five of your senses—and your wallet.

Should you venture farther uptown you'll encounter a high concentration of apartments and the families that complain about outgrowing them, along with a smattering of decent and enduring restaurants. If you're intrigued by having the city's only Ivy League school close at hand, hop the 1 train to 116th Street and emerge on the east side of the street, which puts you smack in front of Columbia University and its Graduate School of Journalism. Pass through the gates and up the walk for a look at a cluster of buildings so elegant you'll understand why it's an iconic NYC setting.

GETTING HERE

The A, B, C, D, and 1 subway lines will take you to Columbus Circle. From there, the B and C lines run along Central Park (stopping at 72nd, 81st, 86th, 96th, 103rd, and 110th streets). The 1 train runs up Broadway, stopping at 66th, 72nd, 79th, 86th, 96th, 103rd, 110th, 116th, and 125th streets. The 2 and 3 trains, which also go along Broadway, stop at 72nd and 96th.

FODOR'S CHOICE

Columbia University

TOP ATTRACTIONS

American Museum of Natural History (⇨ Ch. 14)

Riverside Park

TOP EXPERIENCES

Walking Broadway

Grazing Zabar's

Strolling the Riverside Park boat basin

NEARBY MUSEUMS (⇨ CH. 14)

American Folk Art Museum

American Museum of Natural History

Children's Museum of Manhattan

New-York Historical Society

Nicholas Roerich Museum

AREA SHOPS (⇨ CH. 17)

Allan & Suzi

Betsey Johnson

Design Within Reach

H&H Bagels

Intermix

Kiehl's Since 1851

L'Artisan Parfumeur

Sean

Vintage New York

Westsider Rare & Used Books

Z'Baby Company

10

Updated by
John Rambow

Sightseeing ★★★

Nightlife ★★

Dining ★★

Lodging ★

Shopping ★★★★

Residents of the Upper West Side (which lies between West 59th and West 110th streets) will proudly tell you that they live in one of the last real neighborhoods in the city. That's highly debatable (as is most everything in NYC), but people actually do know their neighbors in this primarily residential section of Manhattan, and some small owner-operated businesses still flourish. On weekends stroller-pushing parents cram the sidewalks and shoppers jam the gourmet food emporiums and eclectic stores that line Broadway and Columbus Avenue. Those who aren't shopping are likely to be found in Riverside Park, the neighborhood's communal backyard. Lively avenues, quiet tree-lined side streets, and terrific restaurants and museums, all in a relatively compact area, make this the perfect neighborhood in which to experience life the way the locals do.

Most people think the area north of 106th Street and south of 125th Street on the West Side is just an extension of the Upper West Side. But technically it's called Morningside Heights, and it's largely dominated by Columbia University, along with the cluster of academic and religious institutions—Barnard College, St. Luke's Hospital, and the Cathedral of St. John the Divine, to name a few. Within the gates of the Columbia or Barnard campuses or inside the hushed St. John the Divine, New York City takes on a different character. This is an *uptown* student neighborhood—less hip than the Village, but friendly, fun, and intellectual.

THREE WAYS TO EXPLORE

LIVE LIKE A NEW YORKER

The upper 70s and lower 80s of the Upper West Side depict a very livable, bourgeois New York. Families and young couples settled here, attracted to the peaceful streets combined with the best accessories of urban living: museums and performance centers, plentiful stores, restaurants, gourmet markets, and parks. You could shop and eat your way up and down this stretch of Broadway and Columbus Avenue for hours, turning along tree-lined side streets of gorgeous brownstones. Museum lovers should stroll right up Central Park West—passing the **Dakota** and other elegant residences—to reach the **American Museum of Natural History** and the **New-York Historical Society.** Need a rest? Go for a spot of tea at **Alice's Teacup** (✉ *102 W. 73rd St.* ☎ *212/799–3006*) or assemble a picnic at **Zabar's** (✉ *80th St at Broadway*) and bring it to nearby **Riverside Park.**

> ### SPRING FEVER
>
> In 1915 the infamous "Typhoid Mary" Mallon was arrested at her place of employment, the Sloan Women's Hospital near Columbia University, where she was working as a cook after city officials had forbidden her from doing so many years before. Mallon didn't believe she carried typhoid fever, since she was never sick from it, but she may have passed on more than 50 cases of the virus, 3 of which resulted in death.

LIVE LIKE A COLUMBIA STUDENT

Feeling a world away (actually, only 50 blocks) from the hustle of Midtown, Morningside Heights moves at the scholarly pace of its many schools, including **Columbia University** and **Barnard College.** Both campuses have beautiful buildings, but the area's architectural winner is the **Cathedral Church of St. John the Divine,** the world's largest Gothic-style cathedral. And when you get hungry, well…with students come great cheap eats: you could root out some of the city's best bagels (plenty of candidates on Broadway), peruse a local newspaper at an old-school diner, or sample the authentic Mexican cooking on Amsterdam Avenue.

ENJOY A LITTLE NIGHT MUSIC

Have a night on the town without heading south of Central Park. The Upper West Side is New York's epicenter of the performing arts, especially classical music. Juilliard and other music schools reside here, but the acoustic star is **Lincoln Center** (⇨ *Chapter 15*), a 16-acre collective of concert halls that draws the world's greatest musicians, dancers, and other performers. In early 2009 the Center finished major renovations to its Alice Tully Hall and to many of its exteriors, making the complex much more a part of the neighborhood. Its sparkling main plaza (✉ *W. 63rd St. at Columbus Ave, Upper West Side*) is a thrilling place to wander through when free from construction. You can often snag same-day tickets, too. Sharing the neighborhood's energetic vibe are busy **Columbus Circle** and the adjacent 55-story **Time Warner Center.** Locals sneer at the skyscraper complex's mall-like atmosphere, but it includes a great collection of shops, Jazz at Lincoln Center, and a blue-chip lineup of restaurants, including **Per Se, Café Gray,** and **Porter House New York.**

10

TOP ATTRACTIONS

Fodor'sChoice **Columbia University.** Wealthy, pri-
★ vate, Ivy League, New York's first
college has a pedigree that has
always attracted students. But for a
visitor, the why-go resides within its
campus, bucolic and quietly energetic at once. The main entrance is
at 116th Street and Broadway, site
of the Columbia Graduate School
of Journalism. After walking past
the "J-School" on your right, follow the herringbone-pattern brick
pathway of College Walk to the
main quadrangle, the focal point
for campus life. (When you eventually leave, exit through the quad's
south gate to West 11th Street's Frat
Row, where brownstones housing
Columbia's frats display quirky
signs of collegiate pride.) Dominat-
ing the quad's south side is **Butler
Library** (1934), modeled after the Roman Pantheon, which holds the
bulk of the university's 8 million books. Looking north, you'll see **Low
Memorial Library,** its steps presided over by Daniel Chester French's
statue *Alma Mater.* Low is one of the few buildings you can enter (on
weekdays), either to check out the former Reading Room and marble
rotunda or pick up a map or take a campus tour at the **visitor center.**
(Alternatively, you can visit Columbia's Web site ahead of time for
a podcast and map covering architectural highlights.) North of the
quad (near a cast bronze of August Rodin's *Thinker*) is the interde-
nominational **St. Paul's Chapel,** an exquisite little Byzantine-style dome
church with salmon-color Guastavino tile vaulting inside. (This same
design can be seen in Grand Central Terminal and many other buildings
throughout the city.) Right across Broadway from Columbia's main gate
lies the brick-and-limestone campus of women-only **Barnard College**
(☎ 212/854–2014), which also gives tours. ✉*Morningside Heights*
☎*212/854–4900* ⊕*www.columbia.edu* ☉ *Visitor center weekdays
9–5. Tours begin at 1 weekdays from Room 213, Low Library* Ⓜ *1 to
116th St./Columbia University.*

☾ **Riverside Park.** Walking around concrete and skyscrapers all day, you can
easily miss the expansive waterfront park just blocks away. Riverside
Park—bordering the Hudson from 58th to 156th streets—dishes out a
dose of tranquillity. Its original sections, designed by Olmsted and Vaux
of Central Park fame and laid out between 1873 and 1888, are often
outshone by Olmsted's "other" park. But with its waterfront bike and
walking paths and lighter crowds, Riverside Park holds its own.

One of the park's loveliest attributes is a half-mile waterfront **promenade,** a rare spot in Manhattan where you can walk right along the

---

MAN'S BEST FRIEND

The ZIP code 10024—roughly the
Upper West Side from West 77th
to West 91st Street—has more
dogs per capita than any other
in the country. You can see dogs
of all pedigrees being walked,
but the best place to watch the
pooches is the enclosed dog
run in Theodore Roosevelt Park
behind the Museum of Natural
History. (In such dog runs everyone's best friends can play off
leash.) Dog owners can pick up a
gift for Fido around the corner at
Canine Ranch (✉ *452A Columbus Ave., between 81st and 82nd
Sts.* ☎ *212/787–7387*), a doggie
boutique and "barkery."

Where can I find...?

COFFEE	Hungarian Pastry Shop 1030 Amsterdam Ave. Encourages lingering over a Danish with the Columbia set.	Zabar's Café 2245 Broadway, at 80th St. Brewed with the beans from store next door.
A QUICK BITE	Bouchon Bakery 19 Columbus Circle, Time Warner Center Boulangerie sandwiches.	Gray's Papaya 2090 Broadway, at 72nd St. Go to counter, say "two with everything, medium papaya."
COCKTAILS	Emerald Inn 205 Columbus Ave., at 69th St. Longtime neighborhood bar near Lincoln Center.	Hi-Life Bar and Grill 477 Amsterdam Ave., at 82nd St. 1940s movie decor.

river's edge. Reach it by heading through an underpass beneath the West Side Highway at the park's entrance at West 72nd Street and Riverside Drive (look for the **statue of Eleanor Roosevelt**). The promenade takes you past the **79th Street Boat Basin,** where you can watch a flotilla of houseboats bobbing in the water. Above it, a ramp leads to the **Rotunda,** home in summer to the Boat Basin Café, an open-air spot for a burger, a beer, and river views.

At the end of the promenade **and up** a staircase, a community garden explodes with flowers. Cresting a hill along Riverside Drive at West 89th Street stands the Civil War **Soldiers' and Sailors' Monument** (1902, designed by Paul M. Duboy), an imposing 96-foot-high circle of white-marble columns. ⊠ *W. 58th to W. 156th Sts. between Riverside Dr. and Hudson River, Upper West Side* Ⓜ *1, 2, 3 to 72nd St.*

ALSO WORTH SEEING

10

Cathedral Church of St. John the Divine. The largest Gothic-style cathedral in the world, even with its towers and transepts still unfinished, this divine behemoth comfortably asserts its bulk in the country's most vertical city. Episcopal in denomination, it acts as a sanctuary for all, giving special services that include a celebration of New York's gay and lesbian community as well as the annual Blessing of the Bikes, when cyclists of all faiths bring their wheels for a holy-water benediction. The cathedral hosts **musical performances** (⊕*www.stjohndivine.org*) and has held funerals and memorial services for such artists as Duke Ellington, Jim Henson, George Balanchine, James Baldwin, and Alvin Ailey. At the end of 2008 a renovation intended to fix damage from a 2001 fire left the church looking newly scrubbed.

Built in two long spurts starting in 1892, the cathedral remains only two-thirds complete. What began as a Romanesque-Byzantine structure under the original architects George Heins and Christopher Grant

Lafarge shifted (upon Heins's death in 1911) to French Gothic under the direction of Gothic Revival purist Ralph Adams Cram. You can spot the juxtaposition of the two medieval styles by comparing the finished Gothic arches, which are pointed, with the still-uncovered arches, which are rounded in the Byzantine style.

To get the full effect of the cathedral's size, approach it from Broadway on West 112th Street. Above the 3-ton central bronze doors is the intricately carved **Portal of Paradise,** which depicts St. John witnessing the Transfiguration of Jesus, and 32 biblical characters. Then step inside to the cavernous nave. Over 600 feet long, it holds some 5,000 worshippers, while the 162-foot-tall dome crossing could comfortably contain the Statue of Liberty (minus its pedestal). Turn around to see the **Great Rose Window,** made from more than 10,000 pieces of colored glass, the largest stained-glass window in the United States.

> ## HOLY HOUSE CATS
>
> On the first Sunday of October, the Cathedral Church of St. John the Divine is truly a zoo. In honor of St. Francis, the patron saint of animals, the church holds its usual Sunday service with a twist: the service is attended by men, women, children, dogs, cats, rabbits, hamsters, and the occasional horse, sheep, or ant farm. In past years, upward of 3,500 New Yorkers have shown up to have their pets blessed. A procession is led by such guest animals as elephants, camels, llamas, and golden eagles. Seats are first-come, first-served.

At the end of the nave, surrounding the altar, are seven chapels expressing the cathedral's interfaith tradition and international mission—with menorahs, Shinto vases, and dedications to various ethnic groups. The **Saint Saviour Chapel** contains a three-panel bronze altar in white-gold leaf with religious scenes by artist Keith Haring (his last work before he died in 1990).

Outside in the cathedral's south grounds, don't miss the eye-catching **Peace Fountain.** It depicts the struggle of good and evil in the form of the archangel Michael decapitating Satan, whose head hangs from one side. Encircling it are whimsical animals cast in bronze from pieces sculpted by children. ✉ *1047 Amsterdam Ave., at W. 112th St., Morningside Heights* ☎ *212/316–7540, 212/662–2133 box office, 212/932–7347 tours* ⊕ *www.stjohndivine.org* 🎫 *Tours $5* ⊙ *Mon.—Sat. 7–6, Sun. 7–7; tours Tues.–Sat. at 11 and 1, Sun at 2. A vertical tour with a climb of 124 feet to top is given on Sat. at noon and 2 (reservations required; $15). Sun. services at 9, 11, and 6* Ⓜ *1 to 110th St./Cathedral Pkwy.*

Columbus Circle. This busy traffic circle at Central Park's southwest corner anchors the Upper West Side and makes a good starting place for exploring the neighborhood if you're coming from south of 59th Street. The central 700-ton granite monument (capped by a marble statue of Christopher Columbus) serves as a popular meeting place.

To the west looms the **Time Warner Center,** its 80-story twin glass towers designed by skyscraper architect David M. Childs. The concave front of its lower floors envelops Columbus Circle's curve, while the upper towers mirror the angle of Broadway and the lines of the city's street grid. Its first three floors house stores that include Sephora, Williams-Sonoma, Borders, and Coach. The third and fourth floors have restaurants, including outrageously priced and acclaimed sushi restaurant Masa (a meal for two starts at $800), plus Thomas Keller's takeout-friendly Bouchon Bakery, and Gray Kunz's Café Gray. Above are luxury condos, offices, Thomas Keller's somewhat less accessible restaurant Per Se, and the Mandarin Oriental Hotel, whose restaurant and bar make a bird's-eye perch for surveying the city below.

> ### AT THE ANSONIA
>
> You'd have to stare at the sidewalk to miss the turrets, sloped roof, and filigreed iron balconies of the Ansonia Hotel (Broadway between 73rd and 74th streets), a Beaux-Arts throwback famous for its many interesting residents. Babe Ruth, Igor Stravinsky, and Theodore Dreiser all lived there, and Bette Midler got her start singing in the gay Continental Baths that once occupied the basement. (Her accompanist was Barry Manilow.)

The performing arts center **Jazz at Lincoln Center** (☎*212/258–9800* ⊕*www.jalc.org*) is also in the complex.

Just north of Columbus Circle, the **Trump International Hotel and Tower** fills the wedge of land between Central Park West and Broadway; it's home to the self-named Jean Georges restaurant, where the celebrity chef works his culinary magic. On the circle's south side, at 2 Columbus Circle, is the former Huntington Hartford building, built in 1964. In 2008 it reopened as the new home of the **Museum of Arts and Design** (⇨*Chapter 14*) after extensive renovation that clad its exterior in lots of zigzags and narrow slits of glass. Ⓜ *A, B, C, D, 1 to 59 St./ Columbus Circle.*

The Dakota. One of the first residences built on the Upper West Side, the château-style Dakota (1884) remains an architectural fixture with its picturesque gables, gaslights, copper turrets, and a central courtyard. Celebrity residents have included Boris Karloff, Rudolf Nureyev, José Ferrer, Rosemary Clooney, Lauren Bacall, Leonard Bernstein, Gilda Radner, and Connie Chung, but none more famous than John Lennon, who in 1980 was shot and killed at the Dakota's gate by Mark Chapman, a deranged fan. ⊠*1 W. 72nd St., at Central Park W, Upper West Side* Ⓜ *B, C to 72nd St.*

Grant's Tomb *(General Grant National Memorial)* . Walk through upper Riverside Park and you're sure to notice this towering granite mausoleum (1897), the final resting place of Civil War general and two-term president Ulysses S. Grant and his wife, Julia Dent Grant. But who's buried here, as the old joke goes? Nobody—they're *entombed* in a crypt beneath a domed rotunda, surrounded by photographs and Grant memorabilia. Once a more popular sight than the Statue of Liberty, this pillared Classical Revival edifice feels more like a relic of yesteryear. The words engraved on the tomb, LET US HAVE PEACE, recall Grant's speech to the Republican convention upon his presidential nomination. Surrounding the memorial are swoopy benches covered with colorful mosaic tiles.

10

Upper West Side Dining

BUDGET DINING

Barney Greengrass, Deli, 541 Amsterdam Ave.

Big Nick's, Diner, 2175 Broadway

Bouchon Bakery, Café, 10 Columbus Circle

Kefi, Greek, 222 W. 79th St., bet. Broadway and Columbus Ave.

MODERATE DINING

Bar Boulud, French, 1900 Broadway, bet 63rd and 64th St.

Dovetail, American, 103 W. 77th St.

Telepan, American, 72 W. 69th St.

EXPENSIVE DINING

Asiate, Asian, 80 Columbus Circle

Café Luxembourg, Brasserie, 200 W. 70th St.

'Cesca, Italian, 164 W. 75th St

Eighty One, Modern American, 45 W 81st St.

Jean Georges, French, 1 Central Park W.

Per Se, American, 10 Columbus Circle

Picholine, Mediterranean, 35 W. 64th St.

Porter House, Steakhouse, 10 Columbus Circle

Tavern on the Green, American, in Central Park at W. 67th St.

Made in the 1970s as a public art project, they are now as beloved as they are incongruous with the grand memorial they surround. ✉ *Riverside Dr. at W. 122nd St., Morningside Heights* ☎ *212/666–1640* ⊕ *www.nps.gov/gegr* 🎟 *Free* ☉ *Daily 9–5; 20-min tours at 10, noon, and 2* Ⓜ *1 to 116th St. or 125th St.*

Harlem

WORD OF MOUTH

"We ate dinner at Lenox Lounge in Harlem and it was fantastic! Soul food at its best. I had the rib/seafood combo (ribs, shrimp, mac & cheese, with yams), very very good! . . . The atmosphere here gives you that '70's feel."

—louise1928

GETTING ORIENTED

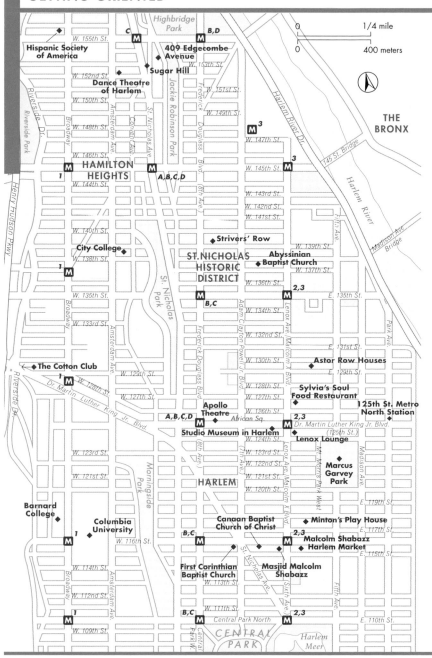

W. 155th St.

C   B,D

Highbridge Park

Hispanic Society of America

409 Edgecombe Avenue

W. 153rd St.

Sugar Hill

W. 152nd St.

Dance Theatre of Harlem

W. 150th St.

W. 151st St.

W. 149th St.

W. 148th St.

3

W. 147th St.

W. 146th St.

HAMILTON HEIGHTS

1

A,B,C,D

3

W. 145th St.

W. 144th St.

W. 143rd St.

W. 142nd St.

W. 141st St.

City College

W. 140th St.

Strivers' Row

W. 139th St.

ST. NICHOLAS HISTORIC DISTRICT

W. 138th St.

1

Abyssinian Baptist Church

W. 137th St.

W. 136th St.

2,3

E. 135th St.

B,C

W. 135th St.

W. 134th St.

W. 133rd St.

W. 132nd St.

The Cotton Club

W. 130th St.

Astor Row Houses

E. 129th St.

1

W. 129th St.

W. 128th St.

Sylvia's Soul Food Restaurant

W. 127th St.

Apollo Theatre

W. 126th St.

125th St. Metro North Station

A,B,C,D

African Sq.

2,3

Dr. Martin Luther King Jr. Blvd. (125th St.)

Studio Museum in Harlem

W. 124th St.

Lenox Lounge

W. 123rd St.

W. 122nd St.

W. 121st St.

HARLEM

W. 120th St.

Marcus Garvey Park

Barnard College

Columbia University

1

W. 116th St.

Canaan Baptist Church of Christ

Minton's Play House

E. 117th St.

B,C

2,3

Malcolm Shabazz Harlem Market

E. 115th St.

W. 114th St.

First Corinthian Baptist Church

Masjid Malcolm Shabazz

W. 113th St.

W. 112nd St.

B,C

2,3

W. 111th St.

1

Central Park North

W. 109th St.

CENTRAL PARK

Harlem Meer

THE BRONX

145 St. Bridge

Harlem River

Madison Ave. Bridge

1/4 mile

400 meters

Riverside Dr.

Henry Hudson Pkwy.

Riverside Park

Broadway

Amsterdam Ave.

St. Nicholas Ave.

Convent Ave.

Jackie Robinson Park

Frederick Douglass Blvd.

(8th Ave.)

St. Nicholas Park

Adam Clayton Powell Jr. Blvd.

Lenox Ave./Malcolm X Blvd.

Mt. Morris Park West

Dr. Martin Luther King Jr. Blvd.

Morningside Park

(8th Ave.)

(7th Ave.)

St. Nicholas Ave.

(Sixth Ave.)

Central Park W.

Lenox Ave./Malcolm X Blvd.

Madison Ave.

Park Ave.

Fifth Ave.

E. 135th St.

E. 131st St.

E. 119th St.

E. 110th St.

7th Ave.

MAKING THE MOST OF YOUR TIME

One underhyped simple pleasure in Harlem is shopping: you can make your way along 125th Street, where brands like H&M coexist with local favorites like Carol's Daughter, filled with tantalizing body sprays, soaps, and essential oils. While you're at it, visit the Studio Museum in Harlem, which showcases contemporary works of Harlem's burgeoning artist community.

The city's north–south avenues take on different names in Harlem: 6th Avenue is called Malcolm X Boulevard *and* Lenox Avenue (its former name); 7th Avenue is Adam Clayton Powell Jr. Boulevard; and 8th Avenue is Frederick Douglass Boulevard. West 125th Street, the major east–west street, is sometimes called Dr. Martin Luther King Jr. Boulevard.

GETTING HERE

The 2 and 3 subway lines stop on Lenox Avenue; the 1 goes along Broadway; and the A, B, C, and D trains travel along St. Nicholas and 8th avenues. And yes, as the song goes, the A train is still among the quickest ways to Harlem.

SAFETY

In this past decade, Harlem's crime rate has decreased far below the heights it reached in the 1980s and early '90s. It is still advisable, however, to use common sense when walking around. Stay close to main commercial areas like 125th Street and Lenox Avenue if you visit at night, and enjoy the side streets and parks during daylight hours.

WORD OF MOUTH (WWW.FODORS.COM/FORUMS)

"My favorite restaurant in Harlem is Amy Ruth's. You'll have amazing, authentic soul food. It's frequented by locals and tourists alike (last time we were there, Al Sharpton was sitting at the next table)." —Gekko

TOP ATTRACTIONS

Abyssinian Baptist Church
Canaan Baptist Church of Christ
Strivers' Row
Sugar Hill

TOP EXPERIENCES

A jazz session at Lenox Lounge
Attending a gospel service
Spotting Bill Clinton
Walking 125th Street

BEST FOR KIDS

Marcus Garvey Park

NEARBY MUSEUMS (⇨ CH. 14)

Hispanic Society of America
Studio Museum in Harlem

AREA SHOPS (⇨ CH. 17)

H&M
M.A.C.

WHERE TO EAT (⇨ CH. 18)

Amy Ruth's
Miss Mamie's Spoonbread Too
Native

SNAPSHOT-WORTHY

Apollo Theatre
First Corinthian Baptist Church
Masjid Malcolm Shabazz
Strivers' Row

Sightseeing
★★
Nightlife
★★★★
Dining
★★★
Lodging
★★
Shopping
★

Updated by
John Rambow

Harlem is known throughout the world as a center of culture, music, and African-American life. Today's Harlem, however, is a very different Harlem from that of 15 years ago, when many considered it too dangerous to visit and with little to offer in the way of cultural attractions, business, or residential life. Today more and more renovated and new buildings join such historic jewels as the Apollo Theatre, architecturally splendid churches, and cultural magnets like the Studio Museum in Harlem and the Schomburg Center for Research in Black Culture.

As overcrowded apartments and expensive rents downtown make Harlem a more and more attractive area, black (and, increasingly, white) professionals and young families are restoring many of Harlem's classic brownstone and limestone buildings. This new growth has brought much new life and commerce to the community, but it has also priced out some longtime residents.

Back in 2001, former president Bill Clinton's selection of 55 West 125th Street as the site of his New York office was an inspiration to businesses considering a move to Harlem; now the busy thoroughfare sprouts outposts of Starbucks, Old Navy, the Body Shop, MAC Cosmetics, American Apparel, and H&M. Outside the shops, the sidewalk is a continuous traffic jam of people, offering a concentrated glimpse of neighborhood life. Pedestrians compete with street-side hawkers selling bootleg CDs and DVDs, books, and homemade essential oils in nondescript bottles.

THREE WAYS TO EXPLORE

FIND RELIGION IN HARLEM

Some of Harlem's most interesting religious buildings—especially its Baptist churches—stand on 116th Street. You can admire the ornate

11

theatrical facade of the giant **First Corinthian Baptist Church,** or fill your soul with the mellifluous gospel music of the **Canaan Baptist Church of Christ's** choir during a Sunday service. Take a hint from the parishioners and follow up with the smothered chicken and waffles at **Amy Ruth's.** After lunch, walk by the plain but colorful **Masjid Malcolm Shabazz**—a mosque primarily attended by West Africans and African-Americans. Finish at **Malcolm Shabazz Harlem Market,** where you can stock up on jewelry, African masks, and caftans at good prices.

RELIVE THE JAZZ AGE

Many of Harlem's historic jazz venues (mostly found on 125th Street) are still active, so you can pay respect to the legends like Duke Ellington and Louis Armstrong, then listen to a legend-in-the-making. A giant digital marquee announces the **Apollo Theatre,** where jazz and funk godfather James Brown debuted in 1956 and was laid out in splendor following his death in 2006. Around the corner, the **Lenox Lounge** buzzes with action; eat here and be transported back in time; or enjoy a swing concert or gospel brunch at the **Cotton Club** (⊠*656 W. 125th St., off West Side Hwy.*), which continues the tradition of the celebrated original (closed in 1935). Continue the pilgrimage at the **Minton's Playhouse** (⊠*206 W. 118th St.*), the birthplace of bebop, where Thelonious Monk was house pianist in the 1940s. It reopened in 2006 after being closed since 1974.

Do a little preconcert shopping along 125th Street for herbal pedicures at Carol's Daughter or snakeskin belts at Men's Walker Shoes. Or check out the exhibitions of contemporary African-American-oriented artworks at the **Studio Museum in Harlem.**

HUNT THE GHOSTS OF THE HARLEM RENAISSANCE

Take the subway up to the 140s and lower 150s (between Edgecombe and Convent avenues) and you can find yourself on a rocky bluff above lower Harlem. Here, in the enclaves of **Sugar Hill** and **Hamilton Heights,** the Harlem elite of the late 1800s and early 1900s could literally "look down on" their neighbors. Some blocks will require more imagination than others to re-create their former glory (especially Edgecombe Avenue, where many leaders of the Harlem Renaissance once resided) but the brownstones of Convent Avenue and adjacent **Hamilton Terrace** remain in mint condition. Finish your walk at **Strivers' Row,** a pair of posh blocks that have attracted well-to-do African-Americans since 1919.

TOP ATTRACTIONS

Abyssinian Baptist Church. This 1923 Gothic-style church holds one of Harlem's richest legacies, dating to 1808 when a group of parishioners defected from the segregated First Baptist Church of New York City and established the first African-American Baptist church in New York State. Among its legendary pastors was Adam Clayton Powell Jr., a powerful orator and civil rights leader and the first black U.S. congressman. Today sermons by pastor Calvin Butts III are fiery and the seven choirs are excellent. Because of its services' popularity, the church maintains separate lines for parishioners and tourists. Dress your best, and get there

Where can I find...?

COFFEE	Hue-Man Bookstore & Cafe 2319 Frederick Douglass Blvd., near 125th St. Good joe and fun bookstore.	Patisserie des Ambassades 2200 Frederick Douglass Blvd. Classic combo of pastries and java.
A QUICK BITE	Uptown Juice Bar 54 W. 125th St. Tasty veggie fare; snacks; "detoxifying" juices.	Make My Cake 121 St. Nicholas Ave. Calling all red velvet cake aficionados!
COCKTAILS	The Den 2150 5th Ave., near 132nd St. Hidden gem, specialty drinks.	Lenox Lounge 288 Lenox Ave., near 125th St. Quintessential Harlem jazz spot.

early on Sunday holidays. ⊠*132 Odell Clark Pl., W. 138th St., between Adam Clayton Powell Jr. Blvd., 7th Ave., and Malcolm X Blvd., Lenox Ave./6th Ave., Harlem* 🖃*212/862–7474* ⊕*www.abyssinian.org* ☉ *Sun. services at 9 and 11* Ⓜ*2, 3 to 135th St.*

Canaan Baptist Church of Christ. The heavenly gospel music during Sunday-morning services makes up for this church's concrete-box-like exterior (visitors may enter once parishioners are seated). Pastor emeritus Wyatt Tee Walker worked with Dr. Martin Luther King Jr. (who delivered his famous "A Knock at Midnight" sermon here). ⊠*132 W. 116th St., between Malcolm X Blvd., Lenox Ave./6th Ave., and Adam Clayton Powell Jr. Blvd., 7th Ave., Harlem* 🖃*212/866–0301 Services Sun. at 10:45* Ⓜ*2, 3 to 116th St.*

Hamilton Heights. To taste this neighborhood's Harlem Renaissance days, walk down tree-lined Convent Avenue, detouring onto adjacent **Hamilton Terrace,** and see a time capsule of elegant stone row houses in mint condition. (Until 2008, Hamilton Grange, founding father Alexander Hamilton's Federal-style mansion, stood at 287 Convent Avenue. Now closed for refurbishment, the clapboard structure, owned by the National Park Service, has been moved around the corner to Saint Nicholas Park. It's scheduled to reopen for tours in late 2009: visit *www.nps.gov/hagr* for updates). Continue down Convent Avenue and see the Gothic spires (1905) of **City College** loom seemingly out of nowhere. Meander through the Oxford-inspired campus (try to spot the rebellious sycamore that "ate" the KEEP OFF THE GRASS sign) before heading east through the park to Strivers' Row. ⊠*Convent Ave. between 138th and 150th Sts., Harlem* Ⓜ*A, B, C, D to 145th St.*

Strivers' Row. Some of the few remaining private service alleys that once ran behind the city's town houses (where deliveries would arrive via horse and cart) lie behind these elegant 1890s Georgian and neo-Italian homes, visible through iron gates. Note the gatepost between No. 251 and 253 on West 138th Street that says, "Private Road. Walk Your

Horses." When the houses failed to sell to whites, the properties on these blocks were sold to African-American doctors, lawyers, and other professionals. The Row earned its enduring nickname in the 1920s from less affluent Harlemites who felt its residents were "striving" to become well-to-do. ✉ *W. 138th and W. 139th Sts. between Adam Clayton Powell Jr. and Frederick Douglass Blvds., Harlem* Ⓜ *B, C to 135th St.*

ALSO WORTH SEEING

First Corinthian Baptist Church. One of the most ornate structures in Harlem, this church kicked off its life in 1913 as the Regent Theatre, one of the country's early movie palaces that replaced the nickelodeons. Its elaborately columned and arched facade loosely resembles the Doges' Palace in Venice. The Regent was sold to the church in 1964. ✉ *1912 Adam Clayton Powell Jr. Blvd., 7th Ave., Harlem* ☎ *212/864–5976* ⊘ *Services Sun. at 10:45* Ⓜ *2, 3 to 116th St.*

🕐 **Marcus Garvey Park.** At the center of this historic, tree-filled public square, atop a 70-foot-high outcrop of Manhattan schist (the same bedrock that anchors our skyscrapers) stands a 47-foot cast-iron **watch-tower** (Julius Kroel, 1865), the last remnant of a citywide network used to spot and report fires in pretelephone days. Around it, an **Acropolis** provides great views of Manhattan, and of the handsome neoclassical row houses of **Mount Morris Park Historic District,** which extends west from the park. ✉ *Interrupts 5th Ave. between W. 120th and W. 124th Sts., Madison Ave. to Mt. Morris Park W, Harlem* ⊕ *www.east-harlem. com/parks_mg.htm* Ⓜ *2, 3 to 125th St.*

Masjid Malcolm Shabazz *(Mosque).* Talk about religious conversions. In the mid-'60s the Lenox Casino was transformed into this house of worship and cultural center, and given bright yellow arches and a huge green onion dome that loudly proclaims its presence in a neighborhood of churches. Once functioning as Temple No. 7 under the Nation of Islam with a message of pro-black racism, the mosque was bombed after the assassination of Malcolm X, who had preached here. It was then rebuilt and renamed for the name Malcolm took at the end of his life, El-Hajj Malik Shabazz; its philosophy now is one of inclusion. These days the Sunni congregation has a large proportion of immigrants from Senegal, many of whom live in and around 116th Street. Next door is Graceline Court, a 16-story luxury condominium building that opened in 2008. Note how it cantilevers somewhat awkwardly over the mosque. ✉ *102 W. 116th St., at Malcolm X Blvd., Lenox Ave./6th Ave., Harlem* ☎ *212/622–2200* Ⓜ *2, 3 to 116th St.*

Sugar Hill. Standing on the bluff of Sugar Hill overlooking Jackie Robinson Park, outside **409 Edgecombe Avenue,** you'd never guess that here resided such influential African-Americans as NAACP founder W.E.B. DuBois and Supreme Court Justice Thurgood Marshall, or that farther north at **555 Edgecombe,** writers Langston Hughes and Zora Neale Hurston and jazz musicians Duke Ellington, Count Basie, and others lived and played (unless you catch the Sunday jazz concerts here from 4 to 6:30 PM in Apartment 3F; see ⊕ *www.parlorentertainment.com*). Harlem's society hill from the 1920s to the 1950s is today another

CLOSE UP

D.I.Y. Harlem Gospel Tours

The typical "gospel tour" includes only a 20-minute stop at a church to hear some of the sermon and the gospel music. Then you're off (via bus) to another Harlem sight or to a soul-food brunch. Prices range from $35 to $80. The tours are an expeditious, if not authentic, way to experience a bit of Harlem.

Tours garner mixed reactions from church officials and parishioners. Some see it as an opportunity to broaden horizons and encourage diversity. But others find tours disruptive and complain that tourists take seats away from regular parishioners (churches regularly fill to capacity). If you decide to go on one of these tours, remember that parishioners do not consider the service, or themselves, to be tourist attractions. Also, dress nicely. Harlem churchgoers take the term "Sunday best" to heart and are impressively decked out. Be as quiet as possible and avoid taking photos or videos.

For a rich gospel-church experience, do your own tour. The following are some of the uptown churches with gospel choirs:

Abyssinian Baptist Church is one of the few churches that does not allow tour groups. Services are at 9 and 11. **Canaan Baptist Church of Christ** has services at 10:45. **Convent Avenue Baptist Church** (⊠ *420 W. 145th St., between Convent and St. Nicholas Aves., Harlem* ☎ *212/234–6767* ⊕ *www.conventchurch.org*) has services at 8, 11, and 6. **First Corinthian Baptist Church** has services at 10:45.

Greater Refuge Temple (⊠ *2081 Adam Clayton Powell Jr. Blvd., at 124th St., Harlem* ☎ *212/866–1700*) has services at 11. **Memorial Baptist Church** (⊠ *141 W. 115th St., between Adam Clayton Powell Jr. and Malcolm X Blvds., Harlem* ☎ *212/663–8830* ⊕ *www.mbcvisionharlem.org*) has services at 8 and 11.

partly cleaned-up "evolving" neighborhood, on its way to regentrification. Walk over to Hamilton Heights for a better-preserved taste of the Harlem Renaissance years. ■TIP➔If you're here after 9:30 PM, drop by the basement jazz club St. Nick's Pub (⊠ *773 St. Nicholas Ave., near 148th St.* ☎ *212/283–9728*), a laid-back local fixture that's been around for ages. Bring some bills to stuff into the tip jar that circulates, grab a drink, and enjoy the late-night jam sessions. ⊠ *Bounded by 145th and 155th Sts. and Edgecombe and St. Nicholas Aves., Harlem* Ⓜ *A, B, C, D to 145th St.*

Brooklyn

WORD OF MOUTH

"Seems to me, I've seen, over the years, reviews of some Brooklyn-locale steakhouses that rivaled anything in Manhattan. Is this so? Bring it on, folks—what's the report?" —Raeona

"Peter Luger Steak House is worth every penny! Be forewarned: They don't take credit cards." —Howard

GETTING ORIENTED

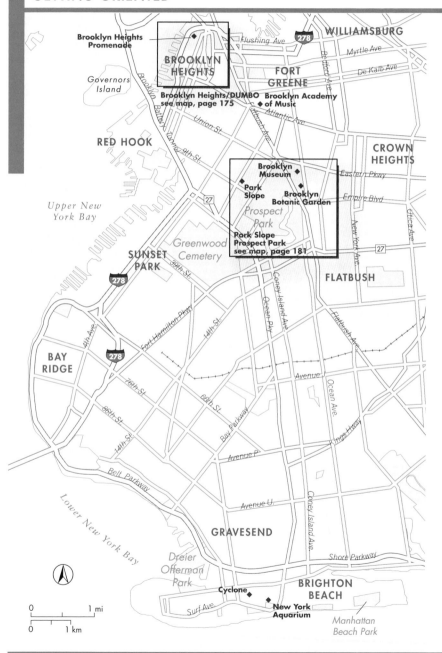

Brooklyn Heights
Promenade

**BROOKLYN
HEIGHTS**

Governors
Island

**Brooklyn Heights/DUMBO
see map, page 175**

**FORT
GREENE**

**Brooklyn Academy
of Music**

RED HOOK

**CROWN
HEIGHTS**

*Upper New
York Bay*

**Brooklyn
Museum**

**Park
Slope**

**Brooklyn
Botanic Garden**

*Prospect
Park*

**Park Slope
Prospect Park
see map, page 181**

*Greenwood
Cemetery*

**SUNSET
PARK**

FLATBUSH

**BAY
RIDGE**

GRAVESEND

Lower New York Bay

*Dreier
Offerman
Park*

Cyclone

**BRIGHTON
BEACH**

**New York
Aquarium**

*Manhattan
Beach Park*

WILLIAMSBURG

Myrtle Ave

De Kalb Ave

Eastern Pkwy

Empire Blvd

0   1 mi
0   1 km

12

MAKING THE MOST OF YOUR TIME

The best way to enter this borough is by its most majestic bridge. Walking across the wooden pedestrian path of the Brooklyn Bridge—a classic New York experience—takes about 30 minutes, all worth it for the panoramic views of the skylines and the harbor. It's also a great way to transition from the bustle of Manhattan into Brooklyn's slower pace. After you exit onto Cadman Plaza, walk southwest to poke around Brooklyn Heights, a charming neighborhood of posh 19th-century brownstone homes, or walk north into the hip neighborhood of DUMBO to grab a slice at legendary Grimaldi's Pizza. To get to Brooklyn's sights more quickly, take the 2 or 3 train to the Eastern Parkway/Brooklyn Museum stop. The museum, the Botanic Garden, the Children's Museum, and Prospect Park are all close, and a weekend trolley makes it easy to combine attractions.

GETTING HERE

To get to Williamsburg, take the L train from 14th Street to Bedford Avenue, the first stop in Brooklyn. You can reach Brooklyn Heights by the 2 or 3 train to Clark Street, the M or R to Court Street, or the 4 or 5 to Borough Hall. To get to DUMBO, take the F train to York Street or walk from Brooklyn Heights. The F to 7th Avenue will take you to the center of Park Slope. From there, walk uphill to reach Prospect Park or walk north on 7th Avenue to sample the shops. The hipper boutiques and eateries are two long blocks west, on 5th Avenue. Closer subway stops to 5th Avenue include M or R to Union Street. To reach the Brooklyn Museum, Brooklyn Botanic Garden, and Prospect Park take the 2 or 3 train to Eastern Parkway/Brooklyn Museum. Coney Island is the last stop on the D, F, N, and Q trains, and the Q or B will take you to Brighton Beach. Allow a good part of the day for these trips, since it takes about an hour to reach the ocean from Manhattan.

Sightseeing
★★★
Nightlife
★★★★
Dining
★★★★
Lodging
★
Shopping
★★★

Updated
by Nina
Callaway

Hardly Manhattan's wimpy sidekick, Brooklyn is the largest and most populous of all the boroughs, with more than 2.5 million residents. If it were an independent city, it would be the fourth-largest in the country. Diverse neighborhoods share a down-to-earth character: neighborly chats take place on the steps of brownstones, family-owned businesses preserve their heritages, and patrons at restaurants and bars are happy to eat and drink rather than "see and be seen." It's largely Brooklyn that has lent New York its streetwise and sincere personality, famously captured in films such as *Do the Right Thing, Moonstruck,* and *Brighton Beach Memoirs.*

THREE WAYS TO EXPLORE

LOCAL LANDMARKS AND PERFECT PARKS
In the midst of urban bustle, Brooklyn is full of green getaways and natural attractions. Relax like real Brooklynites by packing a picnic lunch and heading to **Prospect Park**'s lush Long Meadow. Or, find its hidden nooks and surprises, like the zoo, the ravine, and great summer concerts. Next door is the breathtaking **Brooklyn Botanic Garden.** Take an unexpected detour to **Green-Wood Cemetery**, where you can walk along its hills and lakes or hunt for the headstones of V.I.P.s among the R.I.P.s. And no tour of Brooklyn would be complete without a pilgrimage to **Coney Island**, where the boardwalk, hot dogs, and amusement parks have thrilled generations of New Yorkers.

BOUTIQUE BONANZA
Manhattan is slowly being taken over by chain stores, but Brooklyn's boutique scene is thriving. It's easy to spend an afternoon looking at ladylike knits or punchy, bright-color sundresses, chuckling at ironic home items (resin deer antlers, anyone?), or simply discovering new

designers. Start off in Williamsburg at **Future Perfect**, a modern-home-decor-lover's dream, then hop over to other Brooklyn spots like **Catbird**, **Jumelle**, or **Noisette**. In Park Slope, stroll down 5th and 7th avenues for a more sophisticated range. And over in Carroll Gardens, combine boutique hopping with lunch at one of the celebrated restaurants on **Smith Street.**

EPICURE'S PARADISE

Eating your way through Brooklyn is one of the best ways to experience the mix of old, new, and immigrant cultures that make the borough so vibrant. Carroll Gardens perhaps best epitomizes this mix; here 50 years of Italian heritage meet a more recent and highly acclaimed restaurant scene on Smith Street. Take the F train to Bergen and stroll south on Smith to standout eateries like **Grocery** or **Saul**, then walk off your meal along leafy Court Street, stopping at one of its bakeries for dessert. (Try **Monteleone & Cammareri** for authentic Italian pastries and breads.) For more international adventures, head to **Brighton Beach** for smoked fish at elaborate Russian palaces beneath the train tracks or browse the Central Asian eateries on Brighton Beach Avenue. (**Café Kashkar** is a local fave.) In Sunset Park, wallet-friendly fare from Latin America (clustered on 5th Avenue) and East Asia (on 8th Avenue) compete for your taste buds' time. **Ba Xuyen**, on 8th Avenue between 42nd and 43rd streets, vies for the title of New York's best bahn mi (Vietnamese hero sandwiches), while **Tacos Matamoros**, at 5th Avenue and 45th Street, is full of locals eating authentic and adventurous tacos and tortas.

WHAT IT COSTS				
¢	$	$$	$$$	$$$$
AT DINNER	under $10	$10–$17	$18–$24	$25–$35	over $35

Price per person for a median main course or equivalent combination of smaller dishes. Note: if a restaurant offers only prix-fixe (set-price) meals, it has been given the price category that reflects the full prix-fixe price.

BROOKLYN HEIGHTS

Brooklyn's toniest neighborhood offers residents something wealthy Manhattanites will never have: a stunning view of the Manhattan skyline from the **Brooklyn Heights Promenade.** First developed in the mid-1800s as the business center of the then-independent city of Brooklyn, it boasts historic cobblestone streets of pristine brownstones.

In the early to mid-20th century, the Heights was a bohemian haven, home to writers like Arthur Miller, Truman Capote, Alfred Kazin, Marianne Moore, Norman Mailer, and W.E.B. DuBois. In the '80s a new generation of gentrifiers moved in, and today the borough's record-breaking home prices are almost all located in these few blocks.

Much of its early architecture has been preserved, thanks to its designation as New York's first historic district in the 1960s. Some 600 buildings built in the 19th century represent a wide range of American building styles. Many of the best line **Columbia Heights**, a residential

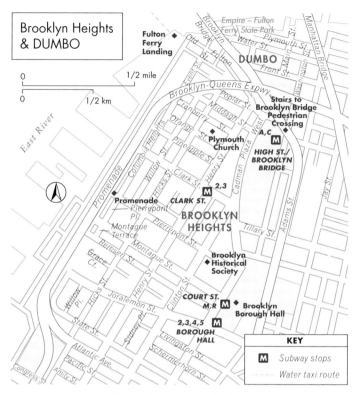

street that runs parallel to the promenade, but any of its adjoining streets are also worth strolling. On **Willow Street** be sure to note No. 22, Henry Ward Beecher's prim Greek Revival brownstone, and Nos. 155–159. These three brick Federal row houses were alleged stops on the Underground Railroad. The skylight in the pavement by the gate to No. 157 provided the light for an underground tunnel leading to an 1880 carriage house. And for those more interested in pop culture, head to the corner of Willow and Cranberry streets, where you may recognize the Federal-style town house from the movie *Moonstruck.*

Brooklyn Borough Hall. Built in 1848 as Brooklyn's City Hall, this Greek Revival landmark is one of Brooklyn's handsomest buildings. Adorned with Tuckahoe marble, the building features a hammered square rotunda and a two-story Beaux-Arts courtroom.Today it serves as the office of Brooklyn's borough president and the home of the **Brooklyn Tourism & Visitors Center** (☎718/802–3846), which has historical exhibits, a gift shop, and helpful information. It's open weekdays 10–6 and summer Saturdays from 10 to 4. On Tuesday and Saturday a greenmarket sets up on the flagstone plaza in front. ✉ *209 Joralemon St., between Court and Adams Sts.* ☎*718/802–3700* ⊕*www.visitbrooklyn.org* 🚇*Free* Ⓜ*2, 3, 4, 5 to Borough Hall; M, R to Court St.*

Fodor's Choice ★ ☺ **Brooklyn Heights Promenade.** Stretching from Orange Street in the to Remsen Street in the south, this esplanade provides enthralling vie of Manhattan. Find a bench and take in the skyline, the Statue of Liberty, and the Brooklyn Bridge—an impressive 1883 steel suspension bridge designed by John Augustus Roebling. To your left is Governors Island, a former Coast Guard base now partially a national park. Below you are the Brooklyn–Queens Expressway and Brooklyn's industrial waterfront of warehouses, piers, and parking lots. A greenway initiative is moving forward in a bid to replace all but the expressway. At the south end of the promenade, near Montague Street, is a small playground. Ⓜ *2, 3 to Clark St.; A, C to High St.*

Brooklyn Historical Society. Housed in an 1881 Queen Anne–style National Landmark building (one of the gems of the neighborhood), the Brooklyn Historical Society displays memorabilia, artifacts, art, and interactive exhibitions. Upstairs, an impressive library—which contains an original copy of the Emancipation Proclamation—is invaluable to researchers. ✉ *128 Pierrepont St., at Clinton St.* ☎ *718/222–4111* ⊕ *www.brooklyn history.org* 📷 *$6* ☽ *Wed.–Fri and Sun. noon–5, Sat. 10–5* Ⓜ *2, 3, 4, 5 to Borough Hall; A, C, F to Jay St.; M, R to Court St.*

☺ **Transit Museum.** Step down into a 1930's subway station where you'll find more than 60,000 square feet devoted to the history of public transportation. Interact with the collection of vintage trains and turnstiles, sit behind the wheel of city buses, and laugh over old advertisements and signs. The gift store is a treasure trove of NYC-theme souvenirs to bring home. ✉ *Boerum Pl. at Schermerhorn St.* ☎ *718/694–1600* ⊕ *www. mta.info/mta/museum/* 📷 *$5* ☽ *Tues.–Fri. 10–4, weekends noon–5.*

Plymouth Church of the Pilgrims. Built in 1849, this Protestant Congregational church was a center of abolitionist sentiment, thanks to the stirring oratory of Brooklyn's most eminent theologian and the church's first minister, Henry Ward Beecher (brother of Harriet Beecher Stowe, who wrote *Uncle Tom's Cabin*). Because it provided refuge to slaves, the church was known to some as the Grand Central Depot of the Underground Railroad. Though the architecture of this brick building may seem simple, it was enormously influential on subsequent American Protestant churches. Three Louis C. Tiffany stained-glass windows were added in the 1930s. In the gated garden beside the church, a statue of Beecher by Gutzon Borglum (who later sculpted Mount Rushmore) depicts one of the slave "auctions"—publicity stunts wherein church members purchased the slaves' freedom. A fragment of Plymouth Rock is in an adjoining arcade. ✉ *75 Hicks St. at Orange St.* ☎ *718/624–4743* ⊕ *www.plymouthchurch.org* ☽ *Service Sun. at 11; tours by appointment* Ⓜ *2, 3 to Clark St.; A, C to High St.*

WHERE TO EAT

$$ ✕ **Henry's End.** At this neighborhood favorite the casual decor belies the quality of the food and the extensive wine list you'll find here. Wild game such as elk, kangaroo, and ostrich take center stage during the winter months; seasonal seafood and foraged vegetables star in the springtime. ✉ *44 Henry St., near Cranberry St.* ☎ *718/834–1776* ⊟ *AE, D, DC, MC, V* ☽ *No lunch* Ⓜ *2, 3 to Clark St.; A, C to High St.*

$ ✕ **Noodle Pudding.** The name is bad, but the food is great at this cozy restaurant serving some of the best authentic regional Italian food in the city. Locals especially rave about the osso buco served with goat-cheese polenta. It does get crowded, but that means it's noisy enough that you can bring the kids. ✉ *38 Henry St. , near Middagh St.* ☎*718/625–3737* ⌖*Reservations not accepted* ▭ *No credit cards* ⊙*No lunch A, C to High St.*

$ ✕ **Teresa's.** This busy mom-and-pop coffee shop serves well-prepared Polish and American food, including breakfast all day. Fill up on delicate orange ricotta pancakes, pierogi, and juicy kielbasa. ✉*80 Montague St., near Hicks St.* ☎*718/797–3996* ▭ *AE, D, MC, V* Ⓜ*2, 3 to Clark St.; M, R to Court St.*

DUMBO

A downhill walk from Brooklyn Heights is the area called DUMBO (*Down Under the Manhattan Bridge Overpass*). It was once known as Fulton Landing, after the inventor and engineer Robert Fulton, who introduced steamboat ferry service from Brooklyn to Manhattan in 1814. Factories and dry-goods warehouses thrived here until the Manhattan Bridge was completed in 1909. The area then fell on hard times, but since the 1970s artists have been drawn by the historic warehouses for use as spacious studios. Today the area is full of luxury condos, art galleries, and small businesses.

The **Fulton Ferry Landing**'s view of Manhattan and the Brooklyn Bridge makes it a favorite site for wedding photos; the New York Water Taxi stops here as well. When all that sightseeing makes you hungry, walk uphill to the always excellent **Grimaldi's Pizzeria,** and the **Brooklyn Ice Cream Factory.** Wander the empty, old cobblestone streets for photo ops (try to frame the Empire State Building within the anchorage of the Manhattan Bridge) and visit the galleries and new boutiques.

☾ **Empire-Fulton Ferry State Park.** This charming 9-acre park is a great place for a riverside picnic, or just enjoying the view. The large playground includes a replica of a boat for make-believe voyages across the East River. From April to October the park is home to a wide range of arts performances, and on Thursday nights in July and August Movies with a View projects New York classic films on an outdoor screen with no cover charge. ✉ *New Dock St. at Water St.* ☎*718/858–4708* ⊕*nysparks.state.ny.us* ▱*Free* ⊙*Daily dawn–dusk* Ⓜ*A, C to High St.; F to York St.*

WHERE TO EAT

$$ ✕**Five Front.** Tucked into an old town house under the Brooklyn Bridge is this cozy "American bistro." Think French food with a gentle twist like mussels in curry sauce, although they also serve familiar fare like roast chicken and burgers. Be sure to get a table in the romantic back garden. ✉ *5 Front St., near Cadman Plaza W* ☎*718/625–5559* ▭*AE, DC, MC, V* ⊙*Closed Mon.* Ⓜ *A, C to High St.; 2, 3 to Clark St.; F to York St.*

12

$ ✕**Grimaldi's Pizzeria.** This classic New York–style parlor serves excellent pizza pies from its coal ovens. Although sometimes inconsistent, when they're good the thin crisp crust is slightly blackened, and the fresh mozzarella oozes satisfyingly. Grimaldi's popularity allows them to be picky: no slices, no reservations, no credit cards, and no empty tables (expect a wait). Impatient foodies have been known to phone in a to-go order, swoop past the lines, and then enjoy their pizza in the nearby Brooklyn Bridge Park. ⊠*19 Old Fulton St., between Front and Water Sts.* ☎*718/858–4300* ⚭*Reservations not accepted* ⊟*No credit cards* Ⓜ*A, C to High St.; 2, 3 to Clark St.; F to York St.*

$$$$ ✕**River Café.** The River Café's incredible views of the waterfront, lush flowers, and live piano music make it a favorite for romantic meals, marriage proposals, fancy birthdays and special celebrations. Though the food is good, the service is often poor, particularly in light of the high prices. Instead, skip the dining room and have a drink at the bar where you can still enjoy the amazing ambience. Gentlemen: Coat and tie are required after 5 PM. ⊠*1 Water St., near Old Fulton St., Brooklyn* ☎*718/522–5200* ⊕*www.rivercafe.com* Ⓜ*F to York St.; A, C to High St.*

GALLERIES

No trip to DUMBO would be complete without some gallery hopping—most are open afternoons Thursday through Sunday. On the first Thursday of every month hours are extended until 8:30 PM, and there are often receptions and live music. The **DUMBO Arts Center** *(DAC)* (⊠*30 Washington St., between Water and Plymouth Sts.* ☎*718/694–0831* ⊕*www. dumboartscenter.org*) exhibits contemporary art in a 3,000-square-foot gallery. Their popular fall Art Under the Bridge festival offers performances, special exhibits, and open studios throughout DUMBO. Inside a 6,000-square-foot restored boiler building, **Smack Mellon Studios** (⊠*92 Plymouth St., at Washington St.* ☎*718/834–8761* ⊕*www.smackmellon. org*) exhibits up-and-coming artists, and nurtures them with studio space and other support. At exhibition space and design shop **Spring** (⊠*126a Front St.* ☎*718/222–1054*) you can view contemporary art, then satisfy your shopping urges with quirky home goods.

NIGHTLIFE

Galapagos Art Space. Performances here could almost take a backseat to the unique architecture of supper-club red banquettes floating above a huge lagoon of water. Thankfully, the theater, music, and performance art is dynamic enough to grab your attention. ⊠*16 Main St.* ☎*718/222–8500* ⊕*www.galapagosartspace.com* ⚏*Ticket prices vary* ☉*Opening times vary.* Ⓜ*F to York St.; A, C to High St.*

Superfine. The huge orange pool table takes center stage for the young crowd at this sprawling restaurant and bar at the base of the Manhattan Bridge. Rotating artwork, exposed-brick walls lined with tall windows, sunken secondhand chairs, and mellow music (including a bluegrass brunch on Sunday) make for a distinctive scene. ⊠*126 Front St., between Jay and Pearl Sts.* ☎*718/243–9005* Ⓜ*F to York St.*

SHOPPING

At **Jacques Torres Chocolate** (⊠66 *Water St.* ☎718/875–9772 ⊕*www. mrchocolate.com*), feel like Charlie getting a peek at the Oompa Loompas as you peer into the small factory while munching on a few unusual-flavored chocolate bonbons and sipping a thick, rich cup of hot chocolate. (For the latter, try the "wicked" flavor, spiked with chilies and cinnamon.)

Forget the touristy "I Heart NY" shirts. Pick up souvenirs they'll actually wear at **Neighborhoodies** (⊠26 *Jay St.* ☎718/243–2265 ⊕*www. neighborhoodies.com* ⊙ *Weekdays 10–6, Sat. by appointment*),where locals swear allegiance by emblazoning sweatshirts and other clothing with their favorite nabe. The Brooklyn branch allows you to instantly create custom pieces.

WILLIAMSBURG

For much of the 20th century this industrial area on the East River was home to a mix of Latin Americans, Poles, Hasidic Jews, and factories. Then, as Manhattan rents rose in the 1990s, artists and indie rockers migrated across on the L train to transform the neighborhood into an artistic bohemian center.

Today, Williamsburg's main drag of Bedford Avenue is a veritable catwalk of fabulously dressed starving artists and wealthy hipsters, on their way from the L train to a range of stylish bars and clubs, artists' studios, vintage stores, and costly boutiques. Meanwhile, the area's young families and migrating Manhattanites head to one of the many posh restaurants near the Williamsburg Bridge. Note that the shops and attractions listed here are spread out, so be prepared to walk a few blocks on safe (though sometimes graffitied and abandoned) blocks filled with former factories.

WHERE TO EAT

$$$ ✕ **Dressler.** The critically acclaimed Dressler shares an owner and a chef with Dumont (*below*), but has a more upscale modern menu and wine list in a slightly more refined setting. The standout is the pork rib, served with pork belly and market-driven sides such as broccoli rabe and fresh mission figs. ⊠149 *Broadway, at S. 6th St.* ☎718/384–6343 ▭*AE, MC, V* Ⓜ*J, M, Z to Marcy Ave.*

$$ ✕ **Dumont.** Slide into a candlelit leather booth and order what is perhaps
Fodor'sChoice the best mac and cheese in the city, served bubbling hot and punctuated
★ with (optional) smoky bacon. The juicy burgers, which also have a large fan club, are best enjoyed at a table in the charming back garden. (Reservations only available online via opentable.com.) ⊠432 *Union Ave., between Metropolitan Ave. and Devoe St.* ☎718/486–7717 ▭*MC, V* Ⓜ *L to Lorimer St.*

$ ✕**Fette Sau.** It may surprise you to come to a former auto-body repair shop to eat meat, but the funky building and outside courtyard seem just right for some serious 'cue. Here a huge wood-and-gas smoker delivers well-smoked brisket, sausages, ribs, and even duck, ordered by the pound. Avoid the disappointing salads and sides, and instead

Where can I find...?

COFFEE IN PARK SLOPE	Gorilla Coffee 97 5th Ave. Grab an expertly pulled shot.	Red Horse Café 497 6th Ave. Sip some micro-roast.
A QUICK BITE NEAR THE BRIDGE	Brooklyn Ice Cream Factory 1 Water St. Superlative hot fudge.	Almondine Bakery 85 Water St. Awesome croissants and sandwiches are picnic-perfect.
COCKTAILS IN CARROLL GARDENS	Clover Club 210 Smith St. Swanky modern cocktails in a cozy atmosphere.	The Jake Walk 282 Smith St. Fifty wines, 130 whiskeys, and 40 artisanal cheeses.

order some of the more than 40 American whiskeys and 10 microbrews. Come early, as tables fill up, and even with 700 pounds of meat a night, the good stuff runs out by 9 PM. ⊠*354 Metropolitan Ave., near Havemeyer St.* ☎*718/963–3404* ⚠ *Reservations not accepted* ═*MC, V* Ⓜ *L to Lorimer St.*

$$$$ ✕ **Peter Luger Steak House.** Long before Brooklyn was chic, even the snobbiest Manhattanites flocked to Luger's. Other steak houses have more-elegant ambience, bigger wine lists, and less-brusque service, but the steak makes the trip to this 122-year-old temple of red meat worth it. You may not see a menu, but here's all you need to know: sizzling Canadian bacon, crisp German-fried potatoes, creamed spinach, and the main event—precision-chosen, dry-aged porterhouse steak, dripping in juices and melted butter. Three tips: bring a buddy (individual steaks are available, but porterhouse is only served for two, three, or four), make a reservation (prime slots fill up more than a month in advance), and bring lots of cash—Luger's doesn't take plastic. ⊠*178 Broadway, at Driggs Ave.* ☎*718/387–7400* ⚠*Reservations essential* ═*No credit cards* Ⓜ*J, M, Z to Marcy Ave.*

GALLERIES

Williamsburg's 70-plus galleries are distributed randomly, with no single main drag. Plan your trip ahead of time using the online **Williamsburg and Greenpoint Monthly Art Guide** at www.wagmag.org. (You can also pick up a copy at neighborhood galleries and some cafés.) Hours vary widely, but almost all are open weekends. Call ahead.

Although serendipitous poking is the best way to sample the art, two longtime galleries are must-sees. **Pierogi** (⊠*177 N. 9th St., between Bedford and Driggs Aves.* ☎*718/599–2144*) remains hip yet cheerfully accessible. Be sure to check out the famous "Flat Files," a collection of the portfolios of more than 700 young contemporary artists. At **Sideshow Gallery** (⊠*319 Bedford Ave., between S. 2nd and S. 3rd*

Sts. ☎718/486–8180) enjoy the diverse exhibitions as well as readings and concerts.

NIGHTLIFE

Barcade. Like Chuck E. Cheese for grown-ups, Barcade invites you to reminisce about your arcade-loving youth by playing one of more than 30 vintage arcade games for only a quarter. Casual players will love familiar favorites like "Ms. Pacman" while serious video gamers will gravitate toward rarities like "Rampage." But it's not just about the games; enjoy a full menu of small-label beers while you check out the hipster crowd. ✉*388 Union Ave. , near Ainslie* ☎718/302–6464 w*www.barcadenyc.com* Ⓜ*L to Lorimer St.*

Bembe. Attractive people of all kinds come here to dance to Latin DJs accompanied by live drummers. There's no velvet rope, and no bottle charge, just the sweaty passion of a packed dance floor. At Saturday-night salsa parties it gets incredibly crowded, and the ventless basement is exceedingly hot, but the crowd just seems to feed off the heat, building the energy ever stronger. ✉*81 S. 6th St., at corner of Berry St.* ☎ *718/387–5389* ⊕ *www.bembe.us* Ⓜ*J, M, Z to Marcy Ave.*

Brooklyn Brewery. Brooklyn was once known as America's brewing capital; at the turn of the 19th century Williamsburg alone was home to nearly 60 breweries. The originals are mostly gone, but this relative newcomer has been bringing back the hops since opening here in 1996. The Friday-evening happy hour means $3 beers—try the popular Brooklyn Lager, the Belgian-inspired Local 1, or one of the seasonal brews. Beer buffs can join a free guided tour on Saturday afternoons. ✉*79 N. 11th St., between Berry St. and Wythe Ave.* ☎718/486–7422 ⊕*www.brooklynbrewery.com* ⊗ *Fri. 6-11 PM, Sat. and Sun. noon-6 PM* Ⓜ*L to Bedford Ave.; G to Nassau Ave.*

Pete's Candy Store. Off Williamsburg's beaten path, this bar has a retro feel, a friendly crowd, and cheerful bartenders. The back room, smaller than a subway car, hosts intimate performances. Brainy hipsters come here on Monday nights for spelling bees and bingo, and on Wednesday nights for infamous trivia contests. Sorry, there's no actual candy here, so order a tasty sandwich instead. ✉*709 Lorimer St., between Frost and Richardson Sts.* ☎718/302–3770 ⊕*www.petescandystore.com* Ⓜ*L to Lorimer St.*

Spuyten Duyvil. Only the geekiest of beer geeks will recognize the names of the more than 100 imported microbrews available here. Fortunately for the rest of us, the friendly connoisseurs behind the bar are more than happy to offer detailed descriptions. ✉*359 Metropolitan Ave.,near Havermeyer St.* ☎718/963–4140 ⊕*www.spuytenduyvilnyc.com* Ⓜ*L to Lorimer St.; G to Metropolitan Ave.*

SHOPPING

Though the boutiques on Bedford Avenue are best for people-watching, you'll also find stores along Grand Street, and on many side streets, especially North 6th.

A good place to start is the **Girdle Building** (✉*218 Bedford Ave.*)—the closest thing Williamsburg has to a mall—pick up free newspapers and magazines that will help you get a read on the local scene. Attractions here include a small café, a new/used record store, achingly hip boutiques, and an art bookstore.

The small size of the **Bedford Cheese Shop** (⊠229 Bedford Ave., at N. 4th St. ☎718/599–7588) belies the fact that this is one of the city's best cheese stores, packed with an encyclopedic assortment of artisan cheeses as well as small-producer cured meats, gourmet imported oils, chocolates, and other dry goods. Don't miss the quirky and occasionally salacious descriptions of the cheeses ("looks like dirty scrimshaw but tastes like a peat-covered goat teat").

One of the standout boutiques on Bedford, **Catbird** (⊠219 Bedford Ave., near N. 5th St. ☎718/599–3457w www.catbirdnyc.com), is a dollhouse-size shop whose shelves are filled with handmade jewelry, home accessories, and whimsical hats.

Brooklyn's thriving home-design scene is often credited to the opening of **Future Perfect** (⊠115 N. 6th St.,at Berry St. ☎718/599–6278 ⊕www.thefutureperfect.com). Even if you're not planning on shipping home a Bone Chair made entirely of cow ribs, you'll have a great time browsing the playful and often ironic furnishings from better-known local Brooklyn designers and international exclusives. Two doors down, their sister store **A&G Merch** (⊠111 N. 6th St. ☎718/388–1779 ⊕ www.aandgmerch.com) sells more affordable home accessories.

Jumelle (⊠148 Bedford Ave., near N. 9th St. ☎718/388–9525 ⊕www. shopjumelle.com) is where you'll find trendy pieces by the latest talent, like shrunken cardigans by YMC.

CARROLL GARDENS/COBBLE HILL/BOERUM HILL

On Atlantic Avenue's south side, the three adjacent neighborhoods of Carroll Gardens, Cobble Hill, and Boerum Hill form a quiet residential area of leafy streets lined with 19th-century town houses. The action swirls around Smith Street, a famed restaurant row augmented by fresh, fashionable boutiques, as well as Court Street's restaurants, bookstores, and old-fashioned bakeries. Nearby on Atlantic Avenue between Court and Clinton is a rapidly gentrifying Middle Eastern enclave, which includes the emporium **Sahadi's,** great for purchasing a veritable bazaar of olives, baklava, and other treats. Get to this neighborhood by taking the F or G train to Bergen Street-Carroll Street.

WHERE TO EAT

$$$ ✕**Grocery.** This unpretentious favorite hasn't let outpourings of accolades go to its head. At just 30 seats, Grocery is small enough that chef-owners Sharon Pachter and Charles Kiely can stop by your table to chat about the food or advise you on a wine. Regulars recommend the slow-roasted duck breast, but as the short menu is well crafted, it's hard to go wrong with any of the dishes' flavor combos and inventive sauces. Small touches like a daily *amuse* help make the steep (for Brooklyn) prices worth it. ⊠288 Smith St. ☎718/596–3335 ⚫ Reservations essential ▭ MC, V ⊘ Closed Sun. and Mon. No lunch Ⓜ F, G to Carroll St.

Fodor's Choice
★

$$$ ✕ **Saul.** Owner Saul Bolton's experience as a cook at famed Le Bernar-
din shows; the dynamic menu of seasonal specials features first-rate
ingredients from the city's best purveyors. The food is so good that
patrons only wish the portions were larger. ✉ *140 Smith St.,near Ber-
gen* ☎*718/935–9844* ▭*AE, D, DC, MC, V* ☺ *No lunch.* Ⓜ*F, G to
Bergen St.*

FORT GREENE

One of Brooklyn's most diverse neighborhoods, Fort Greene has long
been a home to writers like Richard Wright, Marianne Moore, and
John Steinbeck, and many musicians such as Betty Carter, Branford
Marsalis, and even rapper Ol' Dirty Bastard. Architecture buffs will
see many great examples of Eastlake and Italianate styles, especially in
the facade of BAM, Brooklyn's performing arts jewel.

Today the city is attempting to build on the success of BAM by creating
a cultural district around it. Here, you can take a modern dance class at
the **Mark Morris Dance Center** *(3 Lafayette Ave., www.markmorrisdance-
group.org)*, see African diaspora performances at **651Arts** *(651 Fulton
St., www.651arts.org)*, catch avant-garde theater at the **Irondale Center**
(85 S. Oxford St., www.irondale.org), or spend a weekend learning to
blow glass at **UrbanGlass** *(647 Fulton St., www.urbanglass.org)*.

The Brooklyn Academy of Music. BAM is a comprehensive arts anchor for
the borough, with diverse and cutting-edge offerings in opera, theater,
dance, music, film, and more shown in a 1908 neo-Italianate showpiece.
Choreographer Pina Bausch, director Robert Wilson, and hip-hop art-
ist Mos Def have all recently presented work here. The movie theater
shows both art-house and mainstream films.

BAM also holds performances at the nearby **Harvey Theater** (✉*651
Fulton St.*), a 1904 vaudeville house whose renovation purposefully
retained some of its crumbling beauty. ✉*Peter Jay Sharp Bldg., 30
Lafayette Ave., between Ashland Pl. and St. Felix St.* ☎*718/636–4100*
⊕*www.bam.org* Ⓜ*G to Fulton St.; C to Lafayette Ave.; 2, 3, 4, 5, B,
Q to Atlantic Ave.; D, M, N, R to Atlantic Ave.-Pacific St.*

WHERE TO EAT

$$ ✕ **BAMcafé.** Starting two hours before opera-house performances, enjoy
casual fare on the mezzanine level, often with live music. On Friday
and Saturday when there is no opera-house performance, BAMcafé
opens at 8 PM with a limited menu. ✉*30 Lafayette Ave., at Ashland Pl.*
☎*718/623–7811* ▭*AE, D, DC, MC, V* Ⓜ*D, M, N, R to Pacific St.; 2,
3, 4, 5, B, Q to Atlantic Ave.; C to Lafayette Ave.; G to Fulton St.*

$ ✕ **Smoke Joint.** Up the hill from BAM, find in-house smoked "real New
York Barbecue," which translates to a mix of regional specialties like
incredibly moist chicken, spicy dry-rubbed beef short ribs, collard
greens, and meaty barbecued beans. Several kinds of sauces are served
on the side, and the counter service couldn't be friendlier. ✉*87 S. Elliot
Pl.* ☎*718/797–1011* ⚖*Reservations not accepted* ▭*AE, D, MC, V*
☺ *Closed Mon.* Ⓜ*G to Fulton St.; C to Lafayette Ave; 2, 3, 4, 5, B, Q
to Atlantic Ave.; D, M, N, R to Pacific St.*

$ ✕ **Thomas Beisl.** Fortify yourself before the theater with creative schnitzels and beef goulash as well as lighter roasted salmon. When ordering the wonderfully rich desserts, be sure to say "mit schlag," meaning "with whipped cream." Reservations are recommended on performance nights. ✉*25 Lafayette Ave.* ☎*718/222–5800* ⊟*AE* Ⓜ*D, M, N, R to Pacific St.; 2, 3, 4, 5, B, Q to Atlantic Ave.; C to Lafayette Ave.; G to Fulton St.*

12

PROSPECT PARK/ PROSPECT HEIGHTS/PARK SLOPE

Follow dog walkers and bicyclists to idyllic 526-acre **Prospect Park,** designed by the same landscapers as Central Park. Along with green lawns and shady trees, there are concerts, kids programs, and even a skating rink. Adjacent to the park are two of Brooklyn's main attractions: the **Brooklyn Botanic Garden,** a must-see during its springtime Cherry Blossom Festival, and the **Brooklyn Museum,** known for its Egyptian and feminist art collections.

The neighborhood that literally slopes down from the park, **Park Slope** is known affectionately as "Stroller Land." This family-friendly neighborhood is full of academics, writers, and late-blooming couples pushing Bugaboo strollers to its cafés and designer boutiques. One of Brooklyn's most comfortable places to live, Park Slope contains row after row of immaculate brownstones that date from its turn-of-the-20th-century heyday when Park Slope had the nation's highest per-capita income. To see some of the neighborhood's most beautiful houses, walk between 7th Avenue and Prospect Park along any of the streets between Sterling Place and 4th Street.

★ **Brooklyn Botanic Garden.** One of the finest botanic gardens in the country,
☺ the 52 acres are a must-see especially in spring and summer. A major attraction is the beguiling Japanese Hill-and-Pond Garden—complete with a 1-acre pond and blazing red *torii* gate, which signifies (accurately) that a shrine is nearby. Nearby, the Japanese cherry arbor turns into a breathtaking cloud of pink every spring, and the Cherry Blossom Festival is a hugely popular event.

Also be sure to wander through the Cranford Rose Garden (5,000 bushes, 1,200 varieties); the Fragrance Garden, designed especially for the blind; and the Shakespeare Garden, featuring more than 80 plants immortalized by the Bard. At the Steinhardt Conservatory, desert, tropical, temperate, and aquatic vegetation thrives. Don't miss the extraordinary C. V. Starr Bonsai Museum for close to 100 miniature Japanese specimens, some more than a century old. Near the conservatory are a café and a gift shop, with bulbs, plants, and gardening books as well as jewelry.

Entrances to the garden are on Eastern Parkway, next to the subway station; on Washington Avenue, behind the Brooklyn Museum; and on Flatbush Avenue at Empire Boulevard. Free garden tours meet at the front gate every weekend at 1 PM. ✉*900 Washington Ave., between Crown and Carroll Sts.* ☎*718/623–7200* ⊕*www.bbg.org* ✑*$5; free all day Tues. and Sat. before noon. Weekend combo ticket with Brooklyn Museum $11* ☉*Mar.–late Oct.: grounds Tues.–Fri. 8–6, weekends*

Park Slope &
Prospect Park

7TH AVE
B, Q
2, 3
GRAND ARMY PLAZA
Grand Army Plaza
Brooklyn Public Library
EASTERN PARKWAY
Botanic Garden Entrance 2, 3
Brooklyn Museum
Botanic Garden Entrance 2, 3, 4, 5, 5
7TH AVE.
Litchfield Villa
Botanic Garden
FRANKLIN AVE.
Picnic House (restrooms)
Zoo
15TH ST./ PROSPECT PARK
Bandshell
Prospect Park
Carousel
Botanic Garden Entrance
Audubon Center
B, Q, S
PROSPECT PARK
Tullwater Bridge
Wollman Rink
Empire Blvd.
Prospect Lake
Q
PARKSIDE AVE.

KEY
FORT HAMILTON PARKWAY

M Subway stops

0   1/4 mile
0   400 meters

10–6; *conservatory daily 10–5:30. Late Oct.–Mar.: grounds Tues.–Fri. 8–4:30, weekends 10–4:30; conservatory daily 10–4. Closed Mon. except holidays* ⓜ*2, 3 to Eastern Pkwy.; B, Q to Prospect Park.*

★ **Brooklyn Museum.** The Brooklyn Museum has long stood in the shadow of Manhattan's Metropolitan. Though it has more than 1 million pieces in its permanent collection, from Rodin sculptures to Andean textiles and Assyrian wall reliefs, Brooklyn is still only the second-largest art museum in the United States—the Met is larger. But, with a welcoming new design, more populist exhibitions, and neighborhood events, the city is finally starting to appreciate this hidden gem.

Along with changing exhibitions, highlights include Egyptian art, one of the best collections of its kind in the world; African and pre-Columbian art; and Native American art. Seek out the museum's works by Georgia O'Keeffe, Winslow Homer, John Singer Sargent, George Bellows, Thomas Eakins, and Milton Avery—all stunners. Also check out the Elizabeth A. Sackler Center for Feminist Art, which hosts traveling exhibits in addition to serving as the permanent home to Judy Chicago's installation *The Dinner Party* (1974–79). On the first Saturday of each month the museum throws an extremely popular free evening of art, music, dancing, film screenings, and readings, starting at 6 PM. ✉*200 Eastern Pkwy., at Washington Ave.* ☎*718/638–5000* ⊕*www.*

brooklynmuseum.org ⌨$8 suggested donation. Weekend combo ticket with Brooklyn Botanic Garden $11 ⊙ Wed.–Fri. 10–5, weekends 11–6; 1st Sat. every month 11–11; call for program schedule Ⓜ*2, 3 to Eastern Pkwy./Brooklyn Museum.*

Central Library. Across Grand Army Plaza from the park entrance is this sleek, modern temple of learning—the central location of the Brooklyn Public Library. The building resembles an open book, with the entrance at the book's spine; on the facade, gold-leaf figures celebrate art and science. Bright limestone walls and perfect proportions make this an impressive 20th-century New York building. Inside, more than 1.5 million books, public programs, and exhibitions in the lobby will keep you busy for at least a few hours. ✉*1 Grand Army Plaza* ☎*718/230–2100* ⊕*www.brooklynpubliclibrary.org* ⊙*Mon. and Fri. 9–6, Tues.–Thurs. 9–9, Sat. 10–6, Sun. closed* Ⓜ*2, 3 to Grand Army Plaza; Q to 7th Ave.*

☺ **Prospect Park.** Brooklyn residents are fiercely passionate about Prospect Park. Designed by Frederick Law Olmsted and Calvert Vaux, the park was completed in the late 1880s. Olmsted once said that he was prouder of it than any of his other works—including Manhattan's Central Park.

A good way to experience the park is to walk along its 3.5-mi circular drive and make detours off it as you wish. The drive is closed to cars at all times except weekday rush hours. Families with children should head straight for the eastern side, where most kids' attractions are clustered.

The park's north entrance is at **Grand Army Plaza**, where the Soldiers' and Sailors' Memorial Arch honors Civil War veterans. (Look familiar? It's patterned after the Arc de Triomphe in Paris.) Three heroic sculptural groupings adorn the arch: atop, a dynamic four-horse chariot; to either side, the victorious Union Army and Navy of the Civil War. The inner arch has bas-reliefs of presidents Abraham Lincoln and Ulysses S. Grant, sculpted by Thomas Eakins and William O'Donovan, respectively. To the northwest of the arch, Neptune and a passel of debauched Tritons leer over the edges of the **Bailey Fountain**. On Saturdays year-round a greenmarket at the plaza sells produce, flowers and plants, cheese, and baked goods to throngs of locals. Other days, you can find a few vendors selling snacks here and at the 9th Street entrance.

If you walk down the park's west drive from Grand Army Plaza, you'll first encounter **Litchfield Villa** (☎*718/965–8951* ⌨*Free* ⊙*Weekdays 9–5*), an Italianate mansion built in 1857 for a prominent railroad magnate. It has housed the park's headquarters since 1883; visitors are welcome to step inside and view the domed octagonal rotunda.

The **Prospect Park Band Shell** (☎*718/965–8999 park hotline, 718/855–7882 Celebrate Brooklyn Festival* ⊕*www.brooklynx.org/celebrate*) is the home of the annual Celebrate Brooklyn Festival, which from mid-June through the last weekend in August sponsors free films and concerts that have included Afro-Caribbean jazz, Nick Cave, and the Brooklyn Philharmonic.

A smaller cousin to Wollman Rink in Central Park, popular **Wollman Memorial Rink** offers skating in winter and pedal-boat rentals from spring through fall. ☎718/282–7789 ☞$5, skate rental $6.50; pedal boats $15 per hr ⊗Rink: Thanksgiving–mid-Mar.; hrs vary, call for specifics. Pedal boats: May and June, Thurs.–Sun. noon–5; July–Labor Day, Thurs.–Sun. noon–6; Sept.–mid-Oct., weekends noon–5.

Styled after Sansovino's 16th-century Library at St. Mark's in Venice, the **Prospect Park Audubon Center and Visitor Center at the Boathouse,** built in 1904, sits opposite the Lullwater Bridge, creating an idyllic spot for watching pedal boats and wildlife, or just taking a break at the café. Here, learn about nature through interactive exhibits, park tours, and educational programs especially for kids. On a nice day, take a ride on the electric boat to tour the Lullwater and Prospect Lake. You can also sign up for a bird-watching tour to see some of the 200 species spotted here. ☎718/287–3400 Prospect Park ⊕www.prospectparkaudubon. org ☞Audubon Center free; electric-boat tours $6 ⊗Audubon Center: Apr.–Nov., Thurs.–Sun. noon–5; Dec.–Mar., weekends noon–4; call for program and tour times. Electric-boat tours: Apr.–Oct., Thurs.–Sun. noon–4:30; Sept.–mid-Oct., weekends noon–4:30, every 30 mins.

Lefferts Historic House (☎718/789–2822 ☞Free ⊗Apr.–Nov., Thurs.–Sun. noon–5; Dec.–Mar., school holidays noon–5) is a Dutch Colonial farmhouse built in 1783 and moved to Prospect Park in 1918. Rooms of the historic house-museum are furnished with antiques and reproductions from the 1820s, when the house was last redecorated. The museum hosts all kinds of activities for kids; call for information.

Climb aboard a giraffe or sit inside a dragon-pulled chariot at the immaculately restored **Prospect Park Carousel,** handcrafted in 1912 by master carver Charles Carmel. ☎718/282–7789 ☞$1.50 per ride ⊗Apr.–June, Sept., and Oct., Thurs.–Sun. noon–5; July–Labor Day, Thurs.–Sun. noon–6.

Small and friendly, **Prospect Park Zoo** is perfect for those children who may be overwhelmed by the city's larger animal sanctuaries. Of the 400 inhabitants and 93 species, kids seem to be especially fond of the sea lions and the red pandas. An outdoor discovery trail has a simulated prairie-dog burrow, a duck pond, and kangaroos and wallabies in habitat. Be aware that there are no cafés, only vending machines. ✉450 Flatbush Ave. ☎718/399–7339 ⊕www.prospectparkzoo.com ☞$6 ⊗Apr.–Oct., weekdays 10–5, weekends 10–5:30; Nov.–Mar., daily 10–4:30; last ticket ½ hr prior to closing Ⓜ2, 3 to Eastern Pkwy.; B, Q to Prospect Park.

OFF THE BEATEN PATH

☼ **Brooklyn Children's Museum.** A mile east of Grand Army Plaza is the oldest children's museum in the country, now housed in a sparkling new Viñoly-designed "green" building. Here kids can become astronauts, run a bakery, create African-patterned fabric, and even become DJs, mixing the rhythms of the outdoors to make music. ✉145 Brooklyn Ave. ☎718/735–4400 ⊕ www.brooklynkids.org ☞$7.50 ⊗Weekends 10–6, Wed–Fri. 1–6 PM. Ⓜ C to Kingston-Throop Aves.; 3 to Kingston Ave.

WHERE TO EAT

$$ ✕**applewood.** Do the math: lavish devotion to seasonal ingredients + supporting local farmers + relaxed service in a pretty pale-yellow dining room + simple flavors layered in interesting ways = one thing—an amazing restaurant. The menu changes constantly; recent highlights have included a seared striped bass served with caramelized brussels sprouts, apples, and bacon lardons. ✉ *501 11th St., at 7th Ave.* ☎ *718/788–1810* ☰*D, MC, V* ⊙*Closed Mon. No lunch Tues.–Sat.* Ⓜ *F to 7th Ave.*

$$ ✕**al di là.** This northern Italian hot spot has been consistently packed since it first opened in 1988, and it's easy to understand why: affordable prices, a relaxed and charming environment, and simple yet soulfully comforting cuisine such as the red beet ravioli swimming in butter and poppy seeds. The no-reservations policy ensures that the place always has a buzz around it from waiting patrons. ✉ *248 5th Ave., at Carroll St.* ☎ *718/783–4565* ⚲*Reservations not accepted* ☰*MC, V* ⊙ *Closed Tues. No lunch* Ⓜ *F to 15th St.-Prospect Park; M, R to Union St.*

¢ ✕**Tom's Restaurant.** For friendly service and great diner fare like fluffy pumpkin-walnut pancakes served with homemade flavored butters, head three blocks north of the Brooklyn Museum to this family-owned, 70-year-old restaurant. On weekends lines are long, but your wait is eased by free coffee and orange slices. ✉ *782 Washington Ave., at Sterling Pl.* ☎ *718/636–9738* ⚲*Reservations not accepted* ☰*No credit cards* ⊙*Open 6 AM to 4 PM. Closed for dinner. Closed Sun.* Ⓜ*2, 3 to Grand Army Plaza.*

NIGHTLIFE

Barbès. It's not *quite* like stepping into the funky Parisian neighborhood of the same name, but this cozy bar does have French-accented bartenders, pressed-tin ceilings, and a red-tinted back room. There diverse events span from an energetic Slavic Soul Party to classical music concerts. ✉ *376 9th St., at 6th Ave.* ☎ *718/965–9177* ⊕*www.barbesbrooklyn.com* Ⓜ *F to 7th Ave.*

Farrell's. Those tired of pretension should head for this old-fashioned Irish bar that's been popular with firefighters since 1933; cheap beer and a big pool table keeps them coming back. It famously didn't admit unchaperoned women until Shirley MacLaine insisted on being served in the early '70's. ✉ *215 Prospect Park W., at 16th St.* ☎ *718/788–8779* Ⓜ *F to 15th St./Prospect Park.*

Southpaw. Folk, rock and pop for refined tastes are on the bill at this Park Slope hangout, recognized as one of Brooklyn's most popular music venues. The sprawling space is packed with glam twentysomethings on any given night, but country music showcases and the occasional kid-friendly family show on weekends keep everyone in the neighborhood happy. ✉ *125 5th Ave., between St. Johns Pl. and Sterling Pl.* ☎ *718/230–0236* ⊕*www.spsounds.com* Ⓜ*M, R to Union St.*

Union Hall. You'll feel immediately comfortable at this large, airy hangout. Grab a beer up front in the classy library, or, if you're up for a little sport, join friendly locals in a game of bocce ball. In the basement, check out some rising indie rock stars on stage. ⊠ *702 Union St., at 6th Ave.* ☎ *718/638–4400* ⊕ *www.unionhallny.com* Ⓜ *M, R to Union St.*

SHOPPING

Seventh Avenue is Park Slope's main shopping street, with long-established restaurants, bookstores, shops, cafés, bakeries, churches, and real-estate agents (one favorite neighborhood pastime is window-shopping for new apartments). More fun, however, are the newer restaurants and cute boutiques along 5th Avenue.

Start out with a snack from gourmet food store **Bierkraft** (⊠ *191 5th Ave., near Union St.* ☎ *718/230–7600*). In addition to nearly 1,000 craft beers (available by the bottle), they also sell cheeses, chocolates, olives, and other goodies you never knew you needed.

Just one of the many excellent women's clothing stores dotting the area, **Bird** (⊠ *316 5th Ave., between 2nd and 3rd Sts.,* ☎ *718/768–4940*) is one of the oldest and best. In addition to their many well-curated brands of women's clothing, like Mayle and 3.1 Phillip Lim, Bird now stocks both men's apparel and baby clothes.

At **Brooklyn Superhero Supply Co.** (⊠ *372 5th Ave. at 7th St.,* ☎ *718/499– 9884* ⊕ *www.superherosupplies.com*) young superheroes can purchase capes, grappling hooks, secret identity kits, and more from staff who never drop the game of pretend. Proceeds benefit the free drop-in tutoring center (run by nonprofit organization 826NYC) located in a "secret lair" behind a swinging bookcase.

CONEY ISLAND AND BRIGHTON BEACH

Fodor'sChoice
★ Experience the sounds, smells, and sights of a New York City summer: hot dogs and ice cream; suntan lotion; excited crowds; and weathered old men fishing.

Named Konijn Eiland (Rabbit Island) by the Dutch for its wild rabbit population, the Coney Island peninsula has a boardwalk, a 2.5-mi-long beach, amusement parks, and the **New York Aquarium.** Eating a Nathan's Famous hot dog (⊠ *1310 Surf Ave., Coney Island*) and strolling seaside has been a classic New York experience since 1916.

And then there are the freakish attractions at **Sideshows by the Seashore** and the **Coney Island Museum,** the heart-stopping plunge of the granddaddy of all roller coasters—the **Cyclone**—and the thwack of bats swung by the minor-league team, the Cyclones, at **Keyspan Park.** The area's banner day is the raucous Mermaid Parade, held in June. A fireworks display lights up the sky Friday nights from late June through Labor Day.

A pleasant stroll down the boardwalk is Brighton Beach, named after Britain's longstanding beach resort. In the early 1900s Brighton Beach was a resort in its own right, with seaside hotels that catered to rich Manhattan families visiting for the summer. Since the 1970s and '80s Brighton Beach has been known for its 100,000 Soviet émigrés.

To get to the heart of "Little Odessa" from Coney Island, walk about a mile east along the boardwalk to Brighton 1st Place, then head up to

Brighton Beach Avenue. To get here from Manhattan directly, take the B or Q train to the Brighton Beach stop; the trip takes about an hour.

12

Cyclone. One of the oldest roller coasters still operating, this world-famous, wood-and-steel colossus first roared around the tracks in 1927. Unfortunately, the adjacent, carnivalesque Astroland recently shut down, after pressure from developers. But fear not, thrill-seekers: the landmarked Cyclone will keep running, ensuring future generations of New Yorkers and visitors their most satisfying case of whiplash ever. ✉*1000 Surf Ave., at W. 10th St.* ☎*No phone* ☎*$5 per ride* ☉*Memorial Day–Labor Day, daily; call for seasonal hrs.* Ⓜ*D, F, N, Q to Coney Island Stillwell Ave.*

Deno's Wonder Wheel Park. You get a new perspective atop the 150-foot-tall Wonder Wheel, built in 1920. Though it appears tame, its swinging cars will quicken your heart rate. Fortunately, Deno's lease runs until 2020, so Coney-lovers still have time for the Spook-a-rama, the Thunderbolt, and bumper cars. ✉ *3059 Denos Vourderis Pl., at W. 12th St.* ☎*718/372–2592* ⊕*www.wonderwheel.com* ☎*$5 per ride, 5 rides for $20* ☉*Memorial Day–Labor Day, daily 11–midnight; Apr., May, Sept., and Oct., weekends noon–9* Ⓜ*D, F, N, Q to Coney Island Stillwell Ave.*

Keyspan Park. Rekindle your Brooklyn baseball memories (or make some new ones) at a Brooklyn Cyclones game. When this Mets-owned single-A farm team moved to Brooklyn it brought professional baseball to the borough for the first time since 1957. Now the intimate, bright park is especially great for introducing kids to the game. ✉*1904 Surf Ave., between 17th and 19th Sts.* ☎*718/449–849 7* ⊕*www.brooklyncyclones.com* ☎*$5–$8* ☉*Games June–Sept.; call for schedule* Ⓜ*D, F, N, Q to Coney Island Stillwell Ave.*

New York Aquarium. Home to more than 8,000 creatures of the ocean, New York City's only aquarium is also the nation's oldest. Tropical fish, sea horses, and jellyfish luxuriate in large tanks; otters, walruses, penguins, and seals lounge on a replicated Pacific coast; and a 90,000-gallon tank is home to several different types of sharks. ✉*W. 8th St. and Surf Ave.* ☎*718/265–3474* ⊕*www.nyaquarium.com* ☎*$13* ☉*Early Apr.–Memorial Day and Labor Day–Oct., weekdays 10–5, weekends 10–5:30; Memorial Day–Labor Day, weekdays 10–6, weekends 10–7; Nov.–early Apr., daily 10–4:30; last ticket sold 45 mins before closing* Ⓜ*F, Q to W. 8th St.*

Sideshows by the Seashore and the Coney Island Museum. Step right up for a lively circus sideshow, complete with a fire-eater, sword swallower, snake charmer, and contortionist. Upstairs, the small museum has Coney Island memorabilia and a great deal of tourist information. ✉*1208 Surf Ave., at W. 12th St.* ☎*718/372–5159* ⊕*www.coneyisland. com* ☎*Sideshow $5, museum 99¢* ☉*Sideshows: Memorial Day–Labor Day, Wed.–Fri. 2–8, weekends 1–11; Apr., May, and Sept., weekends 1–8. Museum: weekends noon–5. Hrs vary, so call ahead.* Ⓜ*D, F, N, Q to Coney Island Stillwell Ave.*

WHERE TO EAT

Nathan's Famous. No visit to Coney Island would be complete without a hot dog from this stand that first opened in 1916. On the Fourth of July thousands come to see their world-famous hot dog eating contest; the record stands at 66 in 10 minutes. ✉ *1310 Surf Ave. at Stillwell Ave.,* ☎ *718/946–2202* Ⓜ *D, F, N, Q to Coney Island Stillwell Ave.*

Queens, The Bronx, and Staten Island

WORD OF MOUTH

"I'm a big fan of the Bronx Zoo and the Botanic Gardens (both will
fill an entire day). If you go, get to Arthur Avenue nearby—it's the
Little Italy of the Bronx."

—Centralparkgirl

GETTING ORIENTED

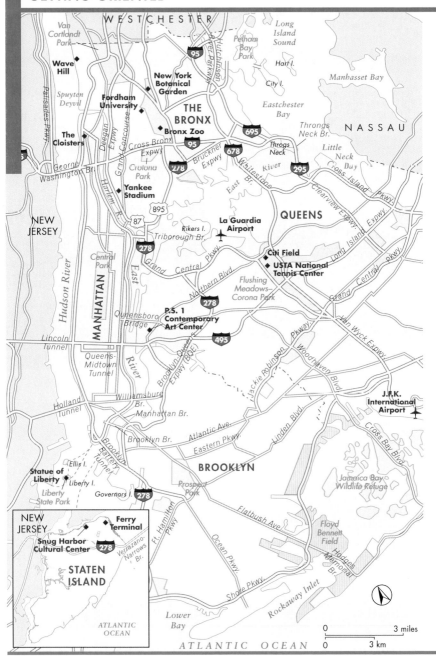

13

MAKING THE MOST OF YOUR TIME

Queens is rich with superb museums. An afternoon in Long Island City and Astoria will enable you to take in the P.S. 1 Contemporary Art Center, the American Museum of the Moving Image, and the Noguchi Museum. After that, jump on the 7 train and have dinner in Jackson Heights or Flushing at one of the borough's excellent restaurants.

It is easy to spend a full day at either of the Bronx's treasures: the New York Botanical Garden or the Bronx Zoo. To visit both, start early and plan on a late lunch or early dinner in the Arthur Avenue area. The garden and the zoo are less crowded on weekdays.

Many tourists' only sight of Staten Island is from a round-trip ride on the ferry, but the borough also holds unexpected offerings in its small museums and historic villages. Set aside the better part of a day for Historic Richmond Town, and add on a couple hours for the Tibetan Museum.

GETTING HERE

Queens is served by many subway lines. To get to Astoria, take the N or W train. For Long Island City, take the E, V, or 7 train. To get to Jackson Heights, take the 7 subway train to the 74th Street–Broadway stop. You can also take the E, F, R, or V train to Roosevelt Avenue.

The Bronx is serviced by the 2, 4, 5, 6, B, and D subway trains. The attractions in the Bronx are spread out across the borough, so you'll need to take different lines to get where you want to go, and it's not necessarily convenient to make connections across town. The B, D, and 4 trains all go to Yankee Stadium, and the B and D continue uptown to bring you to Arthur Avenue from the west. The 2 and 5 trains take you to the Bronx Zoo and to Arthur Avenue.

From the scenic and free Staten Island Ferry you can catch a local bus to attractions. Tell the driver where you're going, and ask about the return schedule.

Sightseeing
★★★

Nightlife
★★★

Dining
★★★★

Many tourists miss out on seeing these three boroughs, and that's a shame. They contain some of the city's best restaurants, museums, and attractions. They're closer than you think, and certainly worth the trip.

Lodging
★

Shopping
★★★★

Updated
by Nina
Callaway

Queens is a patchwork of diverse neighborhoods, each a small world with a distinct culture, all fascinating to explore. Thanks especially to the borough's strong immigrant population (almost 50%), you'll also find some of the city's most interesting cuisine here. Art lovers will definitely want to make the short trip for world-class museums such as P.S.1 Contemporary Art Center and the Noguchi Museum.

The **Bronx** is the city's most maligned and misunderstood borough. Its reputation as a gritty, down-and-out place is a little outdated, and more than a little incorrect. There's lots of beauty in the Bronx, including more parkland than any other borough, one of the world's finest botanical collections, and the largest metropolitan zoo in the country. Be aware that the borough covers a large area, and its attractions are spread out. However, on weekends from April through October the city operates the free Bronx Trolley, which departs from Manhattan in the morning, and offers hop on/hop off service to all major attractions. Whether you're relaxing at a ball game or scoping exotic species at the zoo, there's plenty of fun to be had here.

Staten Island is legally a part of New York City but in many ways it's a world apart. The "Forgotten Borough," as some locals refer to it, is geographically more separate, less populous, politically more conservative, and ethnically more homogeneous than the rest of the city. Along with suburban sprawl, there are wonderful small museums, walkable woodlands, and a historic village replicating New York's rural past. And for a view of the skyline and the Statue of Liberty, nothing beats the 25-minute free ferry trip to Staten Island.

WHAT IT COSTS				
¢	$	$$	$$$	$$$$
AT DINNER	under $10	$10–$17	$18–$24	$25–$35	over $35

Price per person for a median main course or equivalent combination of smaller dishes. Note: if a restaurant offers only prix-fixe (set-price) meals, it has been given the price category that reflects the full prix-fixe price.

13

QUEENS,

L.I.C. & ASTORIA

Just for the museums and restaurants alone, a short 15-minute trip on the 7 train to **Long Island City** and **Astoria** is truly worth it. Long Island City (L.I.C. for short) is the outer-borough art capital, boasting the MoMA-affiliated **P.S. 1 Contemporary Art Center,** which presents experimental and formally innovative work; the **Noguchi Museum,** showcasing the work of Japanese-American sculptor Isamu Noguchi in a large, peaceful garden and galleries; and **Socrates Sculpture Park.**

Nearby Astoria, nicknamed Little Athens, was the center of Greek immigrant life in New York City for over 60 years. An increase in Greek affluence has meant that many have left the borough, but they still return for authentic restaurants, grocery stores, and churches. Here you can buy kalamata olives and salty sheep's milk feta from storeowners who can tell you where to go for the best spinach pie. Today, substantial numbers of Asian, Eastern European, Irish, and Latino immigrants also live in Astoria. The heart of what remains of the Greek community is on Broadway, between 31st and Steinway streets. Thirtieth Avenue is another busy thoroughfare with almost every kind of food store imaginable. Astoria is also home to the nation's only museum devoted to the art, technology, and history of film, TV, and digital media. The **American Museum of the Moving Image** has a slew of hands-on exhibits that allow visitors to edit, direct, and step into favorite movies and television shows.

TOP ATTRACTIONS

Museum of the Moving Image. Step inside the world of movie- and television-making at this museum full of Hollywood memorabilia. Exhibitions range from the history of the film camera to the (literally) head-spinning special effects of *The Exorcist.* Try your hand at interactive stations that allow you to dub your voice into *Titanic,* create stop-action sequences, and more. Those wishing to improve their Space Invaders score should head to the darkened video arcade on the ground floor (games are moving images, too). Film buffs will love the film retrospectives, lectures, and other special programs. At press time, the Museum was undergoing an extensive renovation and expansion, expected to be complete in early 2010 when the temporary admission of $7.50 will be raised back to $10; call ahead to confirm access to certain galleries. ⊠*35th Ave. at 36th St., Astoria* ☎*718/784–0077* ⊕*www.*

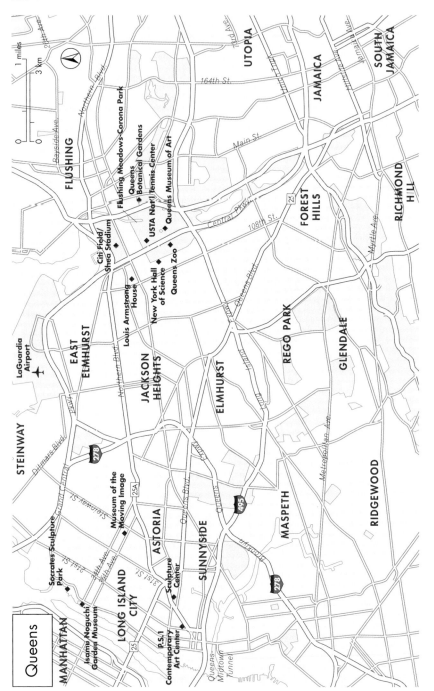

Queens

MANHATTAN

STEINWAY

LaGuardia Airport

EAST ELMHURST

FLUSHING

Socrates Sculpture Park

Isamu Noguchi Garden Museum

LONG ISLAND CITY

Museum of the Moving Image

ASTORIA

JACKSON HEIGHTS

Louis Armstrong House

Citi Field/ Shea Stadium

Flushing Meadows-Corona Park

Queens Botanical Gardens

USTA Nat'l Tennis Center

Queens Museum of Art

New York Hall of Science

Queens Zoo

Sculpture Center

P.S. 1 Contemporary Art Center

SUNNYSIDE

Queens-Midtown Tunnel

ELMHURST

REGO PARK

FOREST HILLS

UTOPIA

JAMAICA

SOUTH JAMAICA

RICHMOND HILL

MASPETH

GLENDALE

RIDGEWOOD

Central Pkwy.

Main St.

164th St.

108th St.

73rd Ave.

Jamaica Ave.

Myrtle Ave.

Metropolitan Ave.

Queens Blvd.

Northern Blvd.

Ditmars Blvd.

Bayside Ave.

25th Ave.

31st St.

21st St.

36th Ave.

Steinway St.

25A

25

278

495

278

25

1 miles

3 km

0

0

QUEENS BY THE NUMBERS

Addresses in Queens can seem confusing at first. Not only is there 30th Street and 30th Avenue, there's also 30th Place and 30th Road, all next to each other. Then there are those hyphenated building numbers. But the system is actually much more logical than you might think. Sequentially numbered avenues run east-to-west, and sequentially numbered streets run north-to-south. If there are any smaller roads between avenues, they have the same number as the nearest avenue, and are called roads or drives. Similarly, smaller side roads between streets are called places or lanes. Thus, 30th Place is one block east of 30th Street. Most buildings have two pairs of numbers, separated by a hyphen. The first pair indicates the nearest cross street, while the second gives the location on the block. So 47-10 30th Place is 10 houses away from the corner of 47th Avenue and 30th Place. Logical, right? If this all still seems confusing to you, there's good news: locals are used to giving directions to visitors.

13

movingimage.us ✉*$10; free after 4 on Fri.* ⊙ *Wed. and Thurs. 11–5, Fri. 11–8, weekends 11–6:30; screenings weekends and Fri. 7:30* Ⓜ*R, V to Steinway St.; N, W to 36th Ave.*

Noguchi Museum. In 1985, The Japanese-American sculptor Isamu Noguchi (1904–88) transformed this former photo-engraving plant into a place to display his modernist and earlier works. A peaceful central garden is surrounded by gallery buildings, providing room to show more than 250 pieces done in stone, metal, clay, and other materials. Temporary exhibits feature his collaborations with others, such as industrial designer Isamu Kenmochi. The museum is about a mile from subway stops; check the Web site for complete directions. On Sunday a shuttle bus leaves from the northwest corner of Park Avenue and 70th Street in Manhattan, hourly, beginning at 12:30; the round-trip costs $10. ✉*9–01 33rd Rd., at Vernon Blvd., Long Island City* ☎*718/204–7088* ⊕*www.noguchi.org* ✉*$10; 1st Fri. of month, pay what you wish* ⊙ *Wed.–Fri. 10–5, weekends 11–6* Ⓜ*N, W to Broadway.*

Fodor's Choice **P.S. 1 Contemporary Art Center.** A pioneer in the "alternative-space" move-
★ ment, P.S.1 rose from the ruins of an abandoned school in 1976 as a sort of community arts center for the future. Now a partner of MoMA, P.S.1 focuses on the work of currently active experimental and innovative artists. Long-term installations include work by James Turrell and William Kentridge. Every available corner of the enormous 100-room building is used; discover art not only in galleries but also on the rooftop, in the boiler room, and even in some bathrooms. Summer Saturdays from 3 to 9 pm, outdoor dance parties attract an art-school-like crowd. ✉*22–25 Jackson Ave., at 46th Ave., Long Island City* ☎*718/784–2084* ⊕*www.ps1.org* ✉*$5 suggested donation* ⊙*Thurs.–Mon. noon–6* Ⓜ*7 to 45th Rd.–Courthouse Sq.; E, V to 23rd St.–Ely Ave.; G to 21st St.*

CLOSE UP

Filmmaking in Astoria

Hollywood may be the king of movie-making now, but in the early days of sound Queens was where it was at. In the 1920s such stars as Gloria Swanson, Rudolph Valentino, and Claudette Colbert all acted in one of the more than 100 films made at Astoria Studios. Built in 1919 by the film company that would become Paramount, "the Big House" was the largest and most important filmmaking studio in the country.

Though Astoria's ideal location provided easy access to Broadway and vaudeville stars, Hollywood's weather soon lured away most studios. Astoria was able to hold its own for a while longer, creating such films as the Marx Brothers classics *The Cocoanuts* and *Animal Crackers.* But in 1942 the studio was sold to the U.S. Army. It became the Signal Corps Photographic Center, producing training films and documentaries including Frank's Capra's classic seven-film series *Why We Fight.* The Army retained the studio until the early '70s, when it began to fall into disrepair and was transferred to the government.

In 1982 the city leased the studio to real-estate developer George S. Kaufman, in partnership with Alan King and Johnny Carson. Kaufman-Astoria Studios, with six stages, is a thriving operation once again, used for television series (*Sesame Street, Law & Order*) as well as movies (*The Wiz, Hair,* and *The Pink Panther*). Although the studio is not open to the public, movie buffs can hope to spot stars at the Studio Café, and learn more about the craft next door at the fantastic Museum of the Moving Image.

ALSO WORTH SEEING

SculptureCenter. Founded by artists in 1928 to exhibit innovative contemporary work, SculptureCenter now occupies a former trolley repair shop renovated by artist Maya Lin and architect David Hotson, not far from P.S.1. Their indoor and outdoor exhibitions spaces sometimes close between shows; call ahead before visiting. ✉ *44–19 Purves St., at Jackson Ave., Long Island City* ☎ *718/361–1750* ⊕ *www.sculpture-center.org* ⊑ *$5 suggested donation* ⊘ *Thurs.–Mon. 11–6* Ⓜ *7 to 45th Rd.–Courthouse Sq.; E, V to 23rd St.–Ely Ave.; G to Court Sq.*

☾ **Socrates Sculpture Park.** In 1985 local artist Mark di Suvero and other residents rallied to transform what had been an abandoned landfill and illegal dump site into this 4.5-acre waterfront park devoted to public art. Today a superb view of the river and Manhattan frames changing exhibitions of contemporary sculptures and multimedia installations. Free public programs include art workshops and an annual outdoor film series (July and August, Wednesday evenings). ✉ *32–01 Vernon Blvd. , at Broadway, Long Island City* ☎ *718/956–1819* ⊕ *www.socratessculpturepark.org* ⊑ *Free* ⊘ *Daily 10–sunset* Ⓜ *N, W to Broadway, then walk 8 blocks west or take Q104 bus along Broadway to Vernon Blvd.*

WHERE TO EAT

After you're done with the sights, why head back to Manhattan? End your day with dinner at one of Astoria's legendary Greek restaurants (on or near Broadway) or venture to the Middle Eastern restaurants farther out on Steinway Street.

$ ✕**Bohemian Beer Garden.** If your favorite outdoor activities include drinking beer and eating kielbasa, you'll love this place. The last survivor of the more than 800 beer gardens that once graced New York, this popular spot offers imported Czech beers and Central-European eats like pierogi and schnitzel. Get there early to avoid long lines. Just drinking? Bring cash, as credit cards are reserved for orders from the kitchen. Weather bad? Don't worry, indoor seating is available. ✉*29–19 24th Ave., between 29th and 31st Sts., Astoria* ☎*718/274–4925* ▭*MC, V* ◔*Closed Tues.* Ⓜ *N, W to Astoria Blvd.*

$ ✕**Kabab Café.** Middle-Eastern restaurants are a dime a dozen in NYC, but Egyptian-Mediterranean spots are a rarer find. This charming yet eccentric 16-seat café, which excels at interesting home-style dishes, is a true hidden treasure. The menu changes nightly, but exceedingly tender lamb stuffed with pomegranate is always great. ✉*25–12 Steinway St., Astoria* ☎*718/728–9858* ◔*Reservations not accepted* ▭*No credit cards* ◔*Closed Mon.* Ⓜ *N, W to Astoria-Ditmars Blvd.*

$$ ✕**S'Agapo.** Astorians love to debate which Greek taverna is the best, but one thing's not debatable: this well-regarded spot is just two blocks away from the Museum of the Moving Image, making it convenient for a combo trip. Be sure to order any of the excellent dips like skordalia—a puree of potato and garlic. ✉*34–21 34th Ave., Astoria* ☎*718/626-0303* ▭*AE, MC, V* Ⓜ *36th Ave. to Broadway, Steinway St. to Crescent St.*

$ ✕**Uncle George's Greek Tavern.** This local 24-hour favorite serves simple preparations of Greek dishes, especially those involving fish. ✉*33–19 Broadway, Astoria* ☎*718/626–0593* ◔*Reservations not accepted* ▭*No credit cards* Ⓜ *N, W to Astoria-Ditmars Blvd.*

JACKSON HEIGHTS

Even in the diverse borough of Queens, Jackson Heights stands out for being a true polycultural neighborhood. In just a few blocks surrounding the three-way intersection of Roosevelt Avenue, 74th Street, and Broadway, you can find shops and restaurants catering to the area's strong Indian, Bangladeshi, Colombian, Mexican, and Ecuadorian communities. Built as a planned "garden community" in the 1920s, the area boasts many prewar apartments with elaborate block-long interior gardens as well as English-style homes. Celebs who grew up in the area include Lucy Liu and Gene Simmons. It's also the birthplace of the board game Scrabble.

WHERE TO EAT

$ ✕ **Delhi Palace.** Jackson Heights is full of Indian restaurants, but Delhi Palace, specializing in north Indian cuisine, stands out from the competition. Fans cite their varied daily $10 buffet, friendly service,

The 7 Train: A Food Lover's Favorite Subway Line

Manhattan may be known for its fine four-star restaurants, but food lovers know that there's one train line to take to some of the best eats in the city. The 7 train snakes its way through the middle of Queens, and conveniently also through some of the best eating neighborhoods in New York. Because the tracks are elevated, it's easy to get a handle on your surroundings—and to know where to find the train once your explorations are through.

Irish expats have long settled in the adjoining neighborhoods of Woodside and Sunnyside (near the 61st Street stop), the site of many great Gaelic bars and a few restaurants. Get a proper Irish breakfast, including black and white pudding, at the casual **Stop Inn** (✉ 60–22 Roosevelt Ave., Woodside ☎ 718/779–0290). At **Donovan's** (✉ Roosevelt Ave. and 58th St., Woodside ☎ 718/429–9339) ask for extra napkins and get one of the best burgers in New York City, nicely charred and served with home-cut steak fries.

But the main reason foodies flock to Woodside is for the Thai restaurant **Sripraphai** (✉ 64–13 39th Ave., Woodside ☎ 718/899–9599), pronounced See-PRA-pie, widely considered the best Thai restaurant in New York. Order spicy pork leg with chili and basil, or cooling papaya salad. It's closed Wednesday.

At either the 74th Street or 82nd Street stop, diverse Jackson Heights not only offers outstanding Indian restaurants but also many other Southeast Asian spots and fantastic eats from all over Latin America. Named after a town in Puebla, Mexico,

Taqueria Coatzingo (✉ 76–05 Roosevelt Ave., Jackson Heights ☎ 718/424–1977) has deeply flavorful mole poblano. Those in the know stick to daily handwritten specials like Pipian en Puerco Rojo—pork cooked in red pumpkin-seed sauce. **Chivito D'Oro III** (✉ 84–02 37th Ave., Jackson Heights ☎ 718/424–0600), a Uruguayan diner, serves up parades of grilled meats called parrilladas—easily enough for two. Since many Uraguayans are of Italian heritage, Chivito also serves delicate pastas.

The 7 train may save the best for last: at the end of the line is Flushing, home to the second-largest Chinatown in the United States. (First is San Francisco's.) Wide streets have few tourists and many interesting stores and restaurants, making the long trip worth it. The standout is **Spicy and Tasty** (✉ 39–07 Prince St., at 39th Ave., Flushing ☎ 718/359–1601), which lives up to its name with numbing Szechuan peppercorns and slicks of red chili oil. Tea-smoked duck has crispy skin and smoky, salty meat. Eggplant with garlic sauce tastes of ginger, tomatoes, and red chilies. Cool it all down with a Tsingtao beer.

A few tips: Bring cash, not many of these restaurants accept credit cards. Be prepared to encounter language difficulties, as English speakers are in the minority. In Manhattan, catch the 7 train at Times Square or Grand Central Terminal.

—Nina Callaway

and fewer crowds than the popular Jackson Diner down the street. Try the thin and crispy potato-filled crepes called masala dosa, made to order. ⊠*37–33 74th St., between Roosevelt and 37th Aves. Jackson Heights* ☎*718/507–0666* ⊟*AE, D, MC, V* Ⓜ*E, F, R, V to Jackson Hts.-Roosevelt Ave.; 7 to 74th St.-Broadway.*

13

$ ✕**Spicy Mina.** Since 2003, fans of Mina Azad's Bangladeshi food have eagerly followed her career. They mourned when her Sunnyside restaurant closed, and cheered when she briefly popped up again, cooking in Manhattan. Now they trek to the border of Jackson Heights and Woodside to wait patiently through spotty service while she prepares elaborately spiced feasts from scratch, an anomaly in a sea of steam-table buffet restaurants. ⊠*64–23 Broadway Woodside* ☎*718/205–2340* ⊟*MC, V* Ⓜ*G, R, V to 65th St.*

SHOPPING

At **Patel Brothers** (⊠*37–27 74th St., near 37th Ave.* ☎*718/898–3445*) let your nose lead your way through the aisles of this Indian grocery store minichain, inhaling the heady scents of rich spices, rare Kesar mangoes, and other exotic produce. Then follow your curiosity through dozens of varieties of lentils and an entire aisle devoted to rice, before stocking up on spicy fried snacks and cheap souvenirs for the folks back home.

For more special keepsakes, head to **Sahil Sari Palace** (⊠*37–39 74th St., between Roosevelt and 37th Aves.* ☎*718/426–9526*), filled with bolts of colorful silks and ready-to-wear sequined saris.

FLUSHING & CORONA

Before it became a part of New York City, Queens was once many small independent townships. So it makes sense that the historic town of Flushing is today a microcosm of a larger city, including a bustling downtown area, fantastic restaurants, and bucolic suburbanlike streets nearby.

Next door, quiet Corona could easily be overlooked, but that would be a mistake. Here are two huge legacies: the music of Satchmo and the cooling simplicity of an Italian ice.

TOP ATTRACTIONS

Citi Field. This is the sparkling new home of the New York Mets; catch them here from April through September. ⊠*Roosevelt Ave. off Grand Central Pkwy.* ☎*718/507–8499* ⊕*www.mets.com* Ⓜ*7 to Willets Point.*

☺ **Flushing Meadows–Corona Park.** Standing in the lush grass of this park, you'd never imagine that it was once a swamp and a dumping ground. But the gleaming Unisphere (an enormous 140-foot-high steel globe) might tip you off that this 1,255 acre-park was also the site of two World's Fairs.

Many New Yorkers head to a specific attraction, such as a Mets game or the science museum, not realizing the many discoveries to be made nearby. But savvy visitors can take advantage of "one-stop park shopping." Here are not only typical grassy knolls, barbecue pits, and sports fields, but also an art museum, a petting zoo, golf and minigolf, and even a model-plane field. It is too large to see everything in one day, so aim to hit a few primary spots. Though several destinations are clustered together on the northwest side of the park, be prepared for long peaceful walks in between. The flat grounds are ideal for family biking; rent bikes near the park entrance or Meadow Lake from March to October. ■ TIP➔ Although the park is great in daytime, avoid visiting once it gets dark; there has been some crime in this area.

At the northwestern edge of the park, the **New York Hall of Science** (☎ 718/699–0005 ⊕ *www.nyscience.org* ✉ *$11; free Fri. 2–5 and Sun. 10–11 Sept.–June* ⊘ *Sept.–June, Mon.–Thurs. 9:30–2, Fri. 9:30–5, weekends 10–6; July and Aug., weekdays 9:30–5, weekends 10–6)* has more than 400 hands-on exhibitions that make science a playground for inquisitive minds of all ages. Climb aboard a replica of John Glenn's space capsule, throw a fastball and investigate its speed, or explore Charles and Ray Eames's classic Mathematica exhibition.

Behind the Hall of Science lies the intimate **Queens Zoo** (☎ *718/271–1500* ⊕ *www.wcs.org* ✉ *$6* ⊘ *Early Apr.–late Oct., weekdays 10–5, weekends 10–5:30; late Oct.–early Apr., daily 10–4:30; last ticket sold 30 mins before closing),* whose small scale is especially well suited to easily tired young visitors. In only 11 acres you'll find North American animals such as bears, mountain lions, bald eagles, and pudu— the world's smallest deer. Buckminster Fuller's geodesic dome from the 1964 World's Fair is now the aviary. Across the street is a petting zoo.

Between the zoo and the Unisphere, you'll find the **Queens Museum of Art** (☎ *718/592–9700* ⊕ *www.queensmuseum.org* ✉ *$5 suggested donation* ⊘ *Sept.–June, Wed.–Fri. 10–5, weekends noon–5; call for extended hrs in July and Aug.).*Don't miss the astonishing Panorama, a nearly 900,000-building model of NYC made for the 1964 World's Fair. Many unsuspecting park visitors looking for a bathroom instead find themselves spending hours checking out the intricate structures that replicate every block in the city. There are also rotating exhibitions of contemporary art and a permanent collection of Louis Comfort Tiffany stained glass. ✉ *Between 111th St./Grand Central Pkwy and Van Wyck Expressway at 44th Ave., Flushing* Ⓜ *7 to 111th St. or Willets Point.*

USTA Billie Jean King National Tennis Center. Each August, 700,000 fans come here for the U.S. Open, which claims the title of highest-attended annual sporting event in the world. The rest of the year the 45 courts (33 outdoor and 12 indoor, all Deco Turf II) are open to the public for $20–$60 hourly. Make reservations up to two days in advance. ✉ *Flushing Meadows–Corona Park* ☎ *718/760–6200* ⊕ *www.usta. com* Ⓜ *7 to Willets Point.*

The Jungle habitat at the Bronx Zoo will make you forget the surrounding urban jungle.

ALSO WORTH SEEING

Louis Armstrong House Museum. For the last 28 years of his life the famed jazz musician lived in this modest three-story house in Corona with his wife, Lucille. Take a guided 40-minute tour and note the difference between the rooms vividly decorated by Lucille in charming mid-century style, and Louis's dark den, cluttered with phonographs and reel-to-reel tape recorders. Although photographs and family mementos throughout the house impart knowledge about Satchmo's life, it's in his den that you'll really understand his spirit. ✉ *34–56 107th St., at 37th Ave., Corona* ☎ *718/478–8274* ⊕ *www.satchmo.net* 💵 *$8* ⏱ *Tours hourly Tues.–Fri. 10–4, weekends noon–4* Ⓜ *7 to 103rd St.–Corona Plaza.*

Queens Botanical Garden. Adjacent to Flushing Meadows-Corona Park, these 39 acres include rose and herb gardens, an arboretum, and plantings especially designed to attract bees and birds. An environmentally friendly visitor center uses solar energy and recycles rainwater. ✉ *43–50 Main St., Flushing* ☎ *718/886–3800* ⊕ *www.queensbotanical.org* 💵 *Free* ⏱ *Apr.–Oct., Tues.–Fri. 8–6, weekends 8–7; Nov.–Mar., Tues.–Sun. 8–4:30* Ⓜ *7 to Main St.–Flushing.*

If you're looking for authentic Queens experiences, there are few as true as eating an Italian ice from the **Lemon Ice King of Corona** (✉ *52–02 108th St., at 52nd St., Corona* ☎ *718/699–5133*) while strolling by a nearby bocce court on a hot summer day. Though there aren't seats or friendly service, none of that will matter as soon as you taste one of the more than 30 flavors, homemade and fresh, from this 65-year-old institution.

THE BRONX

TOP ATTRACTIONS

FodorśChoice
★
☺

The Bronx Zoo. When it opened its gates in 1899, the Bronx Zoo only had 843 animals. But today, with 265 acres and more than 4,000 animals (of more than 600 species), it's the largest metropolitan zoo in the United States. Get up close and personal with exotic creatures in outdoor settings that re-create natural habitats; you're often separated from them by no more than

a moat or wall of glass. Don't miss the **Congo Gorilla Forest** (✉$3) a 6.5-acre re-creation of a lush African rain forest with two troops of lowland gorillas, as well as white-bearded DeBrazza's monkeys, okapis, and red river hogs. At **Tiger Mountain** an open viewing shelter lets you get incredibly close to Siberian tigers who frolic in a pool, lounge outside (even in cold weather), and enjoy daily "enrichment sessions" with keepers. As the big cats are often napping at midday, aim to visit in the morning or evening. In the new $62 million exhibit **Madagascar!**, the formality of the old Lion House has been replaced with a verdant re-creation of one of the most threatened natural habitats in the world. Here you'll see adorable lemurs and far-from-adorable hissing cockroaches.

Go on a minisafari via the **Wild Asia Monorail** (✉$4), open May–October, weather permitting. As you wind your way through the forest, see Asian elephants, Indo-Chinese tigers, Indian rhinoceroses, gaur (the world's largest cattle), Mongolian wild horses, and several deer and antelope species. ■TIP➔Try to visit the most popular exhibits, such as Congo Gorilla Forest, early to avoid lines later in the day. In winter the outdoor exhibitions have fewer animals on view, but there are also fewer crowds, and plenty of indoor exhibits to savor. From mid-November to January 1 the zoo is decorated with holiday lights and open until 9 pm. ✉*Bronx River Pkwy. and Fordham Rd., Fordham* ☎*718/367–1010* ⊕*www.bronxzoo.com* ✉*$15; extra charge for some exhibits; free Wed., donation suggested; parking $12* ☉*Apr.–Oct., weekdays 10–5, weekends 10–5:30; Nov.–Mar., daily 10–4:30; last ticket sold 30 mins before closing* Ⓜ*2, 5 to E. Tremont/West Farms, then walk 2 blocks up Boston Rd. to zoo's Asia entrance; Bx11 express bus to Bronx River entrance.*

FodorśChoice
★

New York Botanical Garden. Considered one of the leading botany centers of the world, this 250-acre garden is one of the best reasons to make a trip to the Bronx. Built around the dramatic gorge of the Bronx River, the Garden offers lush indoor and outdoor gardens, acres of natural forest, as well as classes, concerts, and special exhibits. Be astounded by the captivating fragrance of the Peggy Rockefeller Rose Garden's 2,700 plants of more than 250 varieties; see intricate orchids that look like the stuff of science fiction; relax in the quiet of the forest or the calm of the Conservatory; or take a jaunt through the Everett Children's Adventure

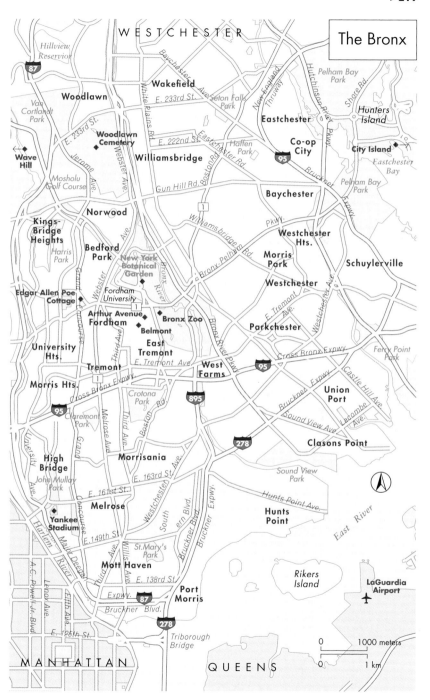

The Bronx

Garden: a 12-acre, indoor-outdoor museum with a boulder maze, giant animal topiaries, and a plant discovery center.

The Garden's roses bloom in June and September, but there's plenty to see year-round. The Victorian-style **Enid A. Haupt Conservatory** (⌨$5) houses re-creations of misty tropical rain forests and arid African and North American deserts as well as exhibitions, such as the annual Holiday Train Show and the Orchid Show. The **Combination Ticket** (⌨$13, off-peak days) gives you access to the Conservatory, Rock Garden, Native Plant Garden, Tram Tour, Everett Children's Adventure Garden, and exhibits in the library.

The most direct way to the Garden is via **Metro-North Railroad** (⊕www.mta.info/mnr) from Grand Central Terminal (Harlem Local Line, Botanical Garden stop). Round-trip tickets are $5 to $12.50, depending on time of day. A cheaper alternative is to take the D or 4 train to Bedford Park Boulevard, then walk east. ⊠200th St. at Kazimiroff Blvd., Bedford Park ☎718/817–8700 ⊕www.nybg.org ⌨Grounds only $6, free Sat. 10–noon and all day Wed.; All-Garden Pass $20; parking $12 ☉Tues.–Sun., 10 AM–6 PM. Ⓜ B, D, 4 to Bedford Park Blvd., then walk 8 blocks downhill to the garden; Metro-North to Botanical Garden.

Fodor'sChoice
★

Yankee Stadium. Fans are still mourning the original, legendary, Yankee Stadium, which saw its last season in 2008. But the gleaming new stadium, built adjacent to the old site, brings young and old to see the Bronx Bombers from April to September and—most-likely—during the playoffs as well. ⊠River Ave. at 161st St., South Bronx ☎718/293–4300 ⊕www.yankees.com Ⓜ B (weekdays only), D, or 4 to 161st St.-Yankee Stadium.

ALSO WORTH SEEING

Edgar Allan Poe Cottage. In hopes that the country air would help his sickly wife Virginia, the poet sought refuge at this tiny workman's cottage from 1846 until his death in 1849. The country air is gone, but visitors can see period furnishings, exhibits, and the spot where Poe wrote some of his most famous works. After Virginia's death in 1847 Poe sought solace in the church chimes at nearby St. John's College (now Fordham University); word has it that these haunting sounds inspired "The Bells." You may notice that the new visitor center has a winged roof, and featherlike shingles; it was inspired by "The Raven." ⊠E. Kingsbridge Rd. at Grand Concourse, Kingsbridge Heights ☎718/881–8900 ⊕www.bronxhistoricalsociety.org ⌨$3 ☉Sat. 10–4, Sun. 1–5 Ⓜ4, B, D to Kingsbridge Rd.

OFF THE BEATEN PATH

Wave Hill. Drawn by stunning views of the Hudson River and New Jersey's dramatic cliffs, 19th-century Manhattan millionaires built summer homes in the Bronx suburb of Riverdale. One of the most magnificent, Wave Hill, is now a 28-acre public garden and cultural center that attracts green thumbs from all over the world. Along with exquisite gardens, grand beech and oak trees adorn wide lawns, an elegant pergola overlooks the majestic river view, and benches on curving pathways provide quiet respite. Wave Hill House (1843) and

CLOSE UP

A New England Fishing Village in the Bronx

In the midst of the "Boogie Down Bronx" lies one of the city's best-kept and most surprising secrets: a picturesque fishing village. Just 1.5 mi long and 0.5 mi wide, City Island boasts marinas, antiques shops, and charming B&Bs. One spot is **Le Refuge Inn** (⊠ *586 City Island Ave., City Island* ☎ *718/885–2478*), with rates less than half of what a Manhattan hotel runs. Sure, the bathrooms are down the hall, but the generously sized rooms in an 1876 mansion are worth it. Be sure to make dinner or brunch reservations for Le Refuge's renowned French fare, or walk to the **Black Whale** (⊠ *279 City Island Ave., City Island* ☎ *718/885–3657*) for creative seafood.

Less than 2 mi away is "the Bronx Riviera"—the mile-long Orchard Beach where old Italian and Latino men sit for hours, sunscreen be damned. You can stroll the boardwalk listening to salsa music, play tennis or basketball on adjacent courts, catch a weekend concert at the band shell, or just bob in the gentle waves. It's part of the 2,700-acre Pelham Bay Park, which also offers an equestrian center, miniature golf, and miles of trails. Other attractions include the **City Island Museum** (⊠ *190 Fordham St., City Island* ☎ *718/885–0008*) for nautical history and memorabilia. The Bronx Zoo and the New York Botanical Garden are just 5 mi away.

You can catch a public bus to City Island (or take a quick taxi from the 6 train), but it's easier with a car. (Le Refuge has free parking for guests.) Though it's a bit of a commute from Manhattan, the quiet respite of City Island makes a great side trip. For those families where half want to see the city lights, and the other half want a relaxing small-town vacation, City Island offers a bit of both.

13

Glyndor House (1927) now house art exhibitions, Sunday concerts, and gardening workshops. ⊠*Independence Ave. at W. 249th St., Riverdale* ☎*718/549–3200* ⊕*www.wavehill.org* ☑*$6; free Tues. and Sat. mornings* ⊘*Mid-Apr.–mid-Oct., Tues.–Sun. 9–5:30; mid-Oct.–mid-Apr., Tues.–Sun. 9–4:30; closed Mon. except holidays. Free garden tours Sun. at 2:15* Ⓜ*1 to 231st St., then Bx7 or Bx10 bus to 252nd St. and Riverdale Ave. or free van service available hourly from station between 9:10* AM *and 3:10* PM*; Metro-North train: Hudson line to Riverdale then 15-min uphill walk.*

ARTHUR AVENUE (BELMONT)

Manhattan's Little Italy is sadly overrun with mediocre restaurants aimed at tourists, but Belmont, the Little Italy of the Bronx, is a real, thriving Italian-American community. Unless you have family in the area, the main reason to come here is for the food: eating it, buying it, looking at it fondly through windows. A secondary, but just as important, reason is chatting with shopkeepers so you can steal their recipes.

Nearly a century after pushcarts on Arthur Avenue catered to Italian-American workers constructing the zoo and Botanical Garden, the area teems with meat markets, bakeries, and cheese makers. There are long debates about which store or restaurant is the "best," but thanks to generations of Italian grandmothers, vendors here wouldn't dare offer anything less than superfresh, handmade foods.

Although the area is no longer solely Italian—many Latinos and Albanians share this neighborhood now—Italians dominate the food scene. Regulars mostly shop on Saturday afternoons; you'll find many stores shuttered on Sunday and after 6 PM. ⊠*Arthur Ave. between Crescent Ave./E. 184th St. and E. 188th Sts., and 187th St. from Lorillard Pl. to Hughes Ave. Belmont* ⊕*www.arthuravenue.com* Ⓜ*B, D, 4 to Fordham Rd., then Bx12 east; 2, 5 to Pelham Pkwy., then Bx12 west. On weekends and holidays Apr.–Oct., free Bronx Tour Trolley leaves from Fordham Plaza Metro-North and West Farms 2/5 stations.*

WHERE TO EAT

$$ ✕**Mario's.** Eat like Don Corleone at this 90-year-old restaurant that was memorialized by Mario Puzo in *The Godfather.* Tuxedoed waiters bring you typical red-sauce fare that regulars rave about, including giant antipasto platters and tangy eggplant Siciliana. ⊠*2342 Arthur Ave., Belmont* ☎*718/584–1100* ⊟*AE, MC, V* Ⓜ*B, D, 4 to Fordham Rd.*

$$ ✕**Roberto Restaurant.** Go early and brave long lines for huge portions of delicate handmade pastas and risottos at this stylishly casual space with long farmhouse tables, named by many as the best Italian restaurant in the city. ⊠*603 Crescent Ave., at Arthur Ave., Belmont* ☎*718/733–9503* ⊜*Reservations not accepted* ⊟*MC, V* ⊗*Closed Sun., no lunch Sat.* Ⓜ*B, D to 182–183 St.*

SHOPPING

The covered **Arthur Avenue Retail Market** (⊠*2344 Arthur Ave., at E. 187th St.Belmont* ☎*718/367–5686* ⊕*www.arthuravenue.com* Ⓜ*B, D, 4 to Fordham Rd., then 15 min. walk or Bx12 east*) , which houses more than a dozen vendors, was opened by Mayor Fiorello LaGuardia in an effort to get the pushcarts off the crowded streets. Inside you'll find great sandwiches and pizza, barrels of olives, a butcher specializing in offal, and lots of fresh pastas. Cigars are rolled by hand right at the building's entrance, alongside Italian gifts and kitchenware. It's open Monday through Saturday 7–6.

Let an Italian nonna (grandmother) sell you homemade fresh pastas of every kind, shape, and flavor at **Borgatti's Ravioli & Egg Noodles** (⊠*632 E. 187th St., between Belmont and Hughes Aves.,Belmont* ☎*718/367–3799*). It's closed all day Monday and Sunday afternoons, and frequently has shorter hours in summer.

Don't miss the porcine spectacle of **Calabria Pork Store** (⊠*2338 Arthur Ave., between 186th St. and Crescent Ave., Belmont* ☎*718/365–5145*), where a forest of house-aged salamis dangle thickly from the rafters. At **Calandra Cheese** (⊠*2314 Arthur Ave., between 186th St. and Crescent Ave., Belmont* ☎*718/365–7572*) bulbous spheres of freshly made cheese hang from the ceiling. Go for the cacciocavallo—a dry, salty mozzarella—or the clean-tasting ricotta.

The brick ovens at **Madonia Bros. Bakery** (⊠*2348 Arthur Ave., at 187th St., Belmont* ☎*718/295–5573*) have been turning out golden-brown

LIFE RING BUOY
WITH LINE

loaves since 1918, but the true stars are fresh, crispy cannoli, filled only when you order, with not-too-sweet ricotta cream.

At **Mike's Deli** (✉ *2344 Arthur Ave., inside the Arthur Avenue Retail Market, Belmont* ☎ *718/295–5033* Ⓜ *B, D, 4 to Fordham Rd., then 15 min. walk or Bx12 east)* prime cuts of meat and charcuterie, friendly service, a convenient location, and Italian sandwiches as big as your head keep customers satisfied. Pull up a seat near the deli counter and try the King David: sopressata, aged parmigiana, roasted peppers, and basil.

At **Teitel Bros.** (✉*2372 Arthur Ave., at E. 186th St.,Belmont* ☎*718/733–9400),* grab a number and stand elbow-to-elbow with locals buying pungent olives, hulking hunks of hard cheeses, pounds of dried beans, and gallons of olive oil.

STATEN ISLAND

Staten Island is full of surprises, from a premier collection of Tibetan art to a multifaceted historic village. To explore the borough, take the **Staten Island Ferry** from the southern tip of Manhattan. After you disembark, grab an S40 bus to the **Snug Harbor Cultural Center (about 10 minutes)** or take the S74 and combine visits to the **Tibetan Museum** and **Historic Richmond Town.**

TOP ATTRACTIONS

Fodor'sChoice
★
☺
Historic Richmond Town. Explore 27 vibrant historic buildings (15 of which are open to the public). This 100-acre village, constructed from 1695 to the 19th century, was the site of Staten Island's original county seat. Highlights include the Gothic Revival **Courthouse,** the one-room **General Store, and** the **Voorlezer's House,** one of the oldest buildings on the site. It served as a residence, a place of worship, and an elementary school. Also on-site is the **Staten Island Historical Society Museum,** built in 1848 as the second county clerk's and surrogate's office, which now houses Staten Island artifacts plus changing exhibitions about the island.

You may see staff in period dress demonstrate Early American crafts and trades such as tinsmithing or basket making. December brings a monthlong Christmas celebration. Take the S74–Richmond Road bus (30 minutes) or a car service (about $14) from the ferry terminal. ✉*441 Clarke Ave., Richmondtown* ☎*718/351–1611* ⊕*www.historicrichmondtown.org* ⊠*$5* ☼*July and Aug., Wed.–Fri. 11–5, weekends 1–5; Sept.–June, Wed.–Sun. 1–5* Ⓜ*S74 bus to St. Patrick's Pl.*

Jacques Marchais Museum of Tibetan Art. At the top of a hill sits this replica of a Tibetan monastery containing one of the largest collections of Tibetan and Himalayan sculpture, paintings, and artifacts outside Tibet. Meditate with visiting Buddhist monks, or just enjoy the peaceful views from the terraced garden. ✉*338 Lighthouse Ave., Richmondtown* ☎*718/987–3500* ⊕*www.tibetanmuseum.org* ⊠*$5* ☼*Wed.–Sun. 1–5* Ⓜ*S74 bus to Lighthouse Ave. and walk uphill 15 mins.*

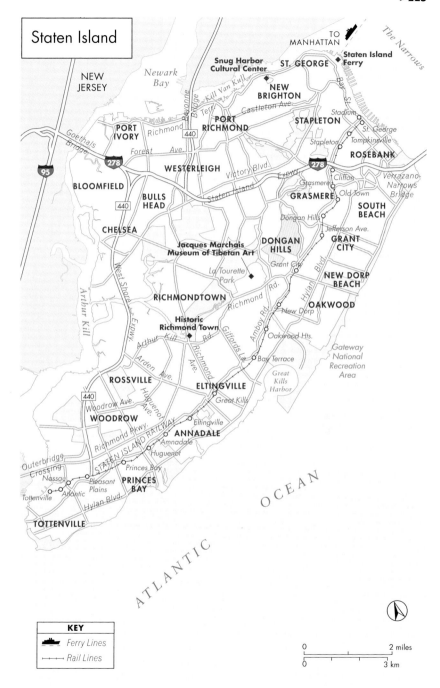

Staten Island

Staten Island Ferry. One of Staten Island's biggest attractions is free—the phenomenal view of Manhattan and the Statue of Liberty afforded by the 25-minute ferry ride across New York Harbor. From Whitehall Terminal at the southern tip of Manhattan, catch the ferry every half hour on weekdays and weekend afternoons. On weekend mornings until 11:30 AM, ferries run every hour on the half hour. From 11:30 AM until 7:30 PM, they run every half hour. Ⓜ *Runs between Manhattan's Whitehall Terminal, Whitehall and South Sts., and Staten Island's St. George Terminal ⊕ www.siferry.com* Ⓜ *4, 5 to Bowling Green; R, W to Whitehall St.; 1 to South Ferry.*

> ### SPLIT DECISION
>
> Staten Island joined New York City in 1898, and since then it is the only borough to talk seriously about a divorce. As recently as 1993 Staten Islanders voted to have the island become its own city. The State Assembly nixed the split.

ALSO WORTH SEEING

★ **Snug Harbor Cultural Center.** Once part of a sprawling farm, this 83-acre community is now a popular spot to see maritime art, frolic in the **Children's Museum**, or take a stroll through lush gardens.

Made up of 26 mostly restored historic buildings, Snug Harbor's center is a row of mid-19th-century Greek Revival temples. Main Hall—the oldest building on the property—is home to the **Eleanor Proske Visitors Center** (🎟️ *$3, including Newhouse Center*), which has exhibits on art and Snug Harbor's history. The adjacent **Newhouse Center for Contemporary Art** (☎ *718/448–2500* 🎟️ *$3, including visitor center*) shows multidisciplinary videos, mixed media, and performances. Next door at the **Noble Maritime Collection** (☎ *718/447–6490* ⊕ *www.noblemaritime.org* 🎟️ *$5*), an old seaman's dormitory is now a museum of ocean-inspired artwork.

Spread over the cultural center grounds is the **Staten Island Botanical Garden** (☎ *718/273–8200* ⊕ *www.sibg.org* 🎟️ *Free; $5 for Chinese Garden and Secret Garden* ⊙ *Daily dawn–dusk; Chinese Garden and Secret Garden Apr.–Sept., Tues.–Sun. 10–5; Oct.–Mar., Tues.–Sun. noon–4*), which includes an orchid collection, 9/11 memorial, 20-acre wetland, Chinese Scholar's Garden, and a sensory garden with fragrant, touchable flowers and a tinkling waterfall. Children love the Connie Gretz Secret Garden with its castle and maze among the flowers.

From the Staten Island Ferry terminal, take the S40 bus 2 mi (about 7 minutes) to the Snug Harbor Road stop. Or, grab a car service at the ferry terminal. (The ride should cost you about $5.) ✉ *1000 Richmond Terr., between Snug Harbor Rd. and Tyson Ave., Livingston* ☎ *718/448–2500* ⊕ *www.snug-harbor.org* 🎟️ *$3; gardens and galleries combined admission $6; Cultural Center grounds free* ⊙ *Tues.–Sun. 10–5; Noble Maritime Thurs.–Sun. 10–5; grounds dawn–dusk every day except major holidays.*

Museums

WORD OF MOUTH

"My sister and I...need to pick up something quick (sandwich, salad) sometime between galleries." —amyb

"Actually, the restaurant in the Neue Galerie, Cafe Sabarsky, is very good. Viennese food in a beautiful setting: light sandwiches, entrees, and divine desserts and coffees." —mp

MUSEUMS PLANNER

Underhyped

Frick Collection
Museum of the City of New York
New York City Police Museum
The Paley Center for Media
Whitney Museum of Modern Art

Best for Kids

Children's Museum of the Arts
Children's Museum of Manhattan
Lower East Side Tenement Museum
New York City Fire Museum
New York City Police Museum

Actually Free

Alexander Hamilton U.S. Custom House/National Museum of the American Indian
Asian American Arts Centre
Forbes Galleries
Goethe Institut
The Hispanic Society of America
Museum of American Illustration

Think Small

Manhattan could be called Museumpalooza—within just one 30-block area (the main stage, aka Museum Mile, 5th Avenue from 82nd Street to 105th Street)—there are nine world-class institutions, and, within that general vicinity, there are a dozen or so merely excellent ones. Trying to see all of this wonderfulness in a week or two is, unfortunately, impossible. Attempting to see all of even one or two of the big museums is equally futile; your feet will go on strike shortly before your brain shuts down with sensory overload.

So consider this your permission slip to think small. Pick one—at most, two—of the bigger museums—the Metropolitan Museum of Art and/or the American Museum of Natural History are the obvious choices, though the Museum of Modern Art is a definite contender—check out their Web sites, and choose just two exhibit halls in your selected museums to tour in depth. For a first visit to the Met perhaps choose the Egyptian gallery and the rather new Greek and Roman galleries; in Natural History, the Dinosaur and Ocean Life halls. See them, and then turn your attention to the city's smaller museums, where there are hidden treasures; elsewhere, many of them could be a city's cultural centerpiece.

Among our favorites are the Rubin Museum of Art on West 17th Street, the first museum in the Western world dedicated to the art of the Himalayas; the Museum of the City of New York on 5th Avenue at 103rd Street, which provides an outstanding overview of the city's origins; the American Folk Art Museum on West 53rd Street; the International Center of Photography on 6th Avenue and 43rd Street; and El Museo del Barrio at 104th Street and 5th Avenue, dedicated to Latino art and culture. (Bonus: all our picks also have outstanding gift shops.) But choose the museums that suit your interests—there are institutions dedicated to water, toys, money, film, television, transportation, assorted cultural heritages, fashion, gardening, and many more.

Updated by
Michelle Delio

14

People visiting New York often confess to being overwhelmed by the honking traffic, the masses of people on the move, the 24/7 energy of the place. We've learned to tune that static out, but no matter how long you live here you never cease to be amazed and somewhat besieged by the museums.

The word "besieged" may seem like an odd choice, but there are so many wonderful things to explore in our incredible cultural institutions—and not a chance that a mere mortal can ever experience it all. The entire island is home to such a wealth of cultural treasure that it is both a blessing and—to those who despair of ever really doing it justice—a curse. You'll likely see more of the museums in your visit to Manhattan than the locals do in a few years of living here full time. But to see even a little bit, you'll need a plan.

This chapter is front-loaded with the shouldn't-miss museums: MoMA, the Guggenheim, and the Whitney are famous but often overlooked and underhyped. The 800-pound gorillas, Natural History and the Metropolitan Museum of Art, are covered in depth in the following pages. Familiarizing yourself with their floor plans and permanent exhibits will help you make the most of your time.

Choose what museums you want to tour before you arrive. Then visit their Web sites to purchase tickets in advance when possible and peruse the information on special shows (almost always worth seeing) as well as daily events and tours. Most museum Web sites also do a great job of providing you with background on what you'll see, information that will definitely enrich your visit. And if you have kids, make sure to check the family or educator's sections of the sites for interesting activities—scavenger hunts, puzzles, doodling, etc.—that can make a trip to the museum more fun for younger visitors. And, hey, they'll liven up those long marble halls for parents, too.

Continued on page 245

INSECTS AND MYRIAPODS

SEGMENTED WORM

Theodore Roosevelt
Memorial Hall

AMERICAN MUSEUM OF NATURAL HISTORY

The largest natural history museum in the world is also one of the most impressive sights in New York. Four city blocks make up its 46 exhibition halls, which hold more than 30 million artifacts and wonders from the land, the sea, and outer space. With all those wonders, you won't be able to see everything on a single visit, but you can easily hit the highlights in half a day.

Before you begin, plan a route before setting out. Be sure to pick up a map when you pay your admission. The museum's four floors (and lower level) are mazelike.

To get the most from the museum's stunning riches, try to allow enough time to slow down and take advantage of the computer stations and the volunteer "Explainers," who are knowledgeable and able to point out their own favorite exhibits.

Getting into the museum can be time consuming. For the shortest lines, use the below-street-level entrance connected to the 81st Street subway station (look for the subway entrance to the left of the museum's steps). This entrance gives you quick access to bathrooms and the food court. The entrance on Central Park West, where the vast steps lead up into the impressive, barrel-ceilinged Theodore Roosevelt Rotunda, is the most impressive and memorable entrance at

the museum. Its central location makes a good starting place for exploring.

The Rose Center for Earth & Space, a must-visit, is attached to the museum. Enter from West 81st Street, where a path slopes down to the entrance, after which elevators and stairs descend to the ticket line on the lower level.

What to see? Check out the museum highlights on the following pages.

✉ Central Park West at W. 79th St., Upper West Side

Ⓜ Subway: B, C to 81st St.

☎ 212/769–5200

🌐 www.amnh.org

💲 $20 suggested donation, includes admission to Rose Center for Earth and Space

🕙 Daily 10–5:45. Rose Center until 8:45 on Fri.

Left, Spectrum of Life Wall

MUSEUM HIGHLIGHTS

Left, Tyrannosaurus rex
Above, Hadrosaurus

Dinosaurs and Mammals

An amazing assembly of dinosaur and mammal fossils covers the entire floor. The organization can be hard to grasp at first, so head to the **Wallace Orientation Center,** where a short film explains how each of the Fossil Halls lead into each other. You'll want to spend at least an hour here—the highlights include a *T. rex,* an *Apatosaurus* (formerly called a Brontosaurus), and the *Buettneria,* which resembles a modern-day crocodile.

The specimens are not in chronological order; they're put together based on their shared characteristics. Key branching-off points—a watertight egg, a grasping hand—are highlighted in the center of rooms and surrounded by related fossil groups. Check out the touch screens here; they make a complex topic more comprehensible.

Reptiles and Amphibians

Head for the Reptiles and Amphibians Hall to check out the Komodo dragon lizards and a 23-foot-long python skeleton. The weirdest display is the enlarged model of the Suriname toad *Pipa pipa,* whose young hatch from the female's back. The Primates hall carries brief but interesting comparisons between apes, monkeys, and humans. Also on the third floor is the upper gallery of the famed Akeley Hall of African Mammals.

SPECIAL SHOWS AND NEW EXHIBITS

Special exhibits, the IMAX theater, and the Space Show cost extra. The timed tickets are available in advance at the museum's Web site and are sold same day at the door. Between October and May, don't miss the warm, plant-filled Butterfly Conservatory, where blue morphos, monarchs, and other butterflies flit and feed. Ten minutes is probably enough time to enjoy it.

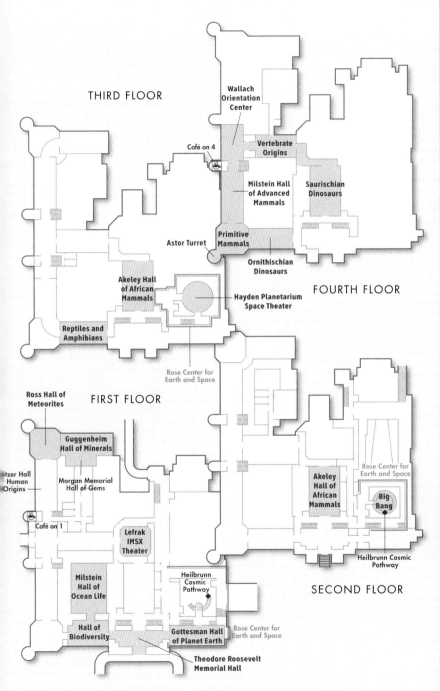

THIRD FLOOR

Wallach
Orientation
Center

Café on 4

Vertebrate
Origins

Saurischian
Dinosaurs

Milstein Hall
of Advanced
Mammals

Primitive
Mammals

Astor Turret

Ornithischian
Dinosaurs

Akeley Hall
of African
Mammals

Hayden Planetarium
Space Theater

FOURTH FLOOR

Reptiles and
Amphibians

Rose Center for
Earth and Space

Ross Hall of
Meteorites

FIRST FLOOR

Guggenheim
Hall of Minerals

Spitzer Hall
Human
Origins

Morgan Memorial
Hall of Gems

Café on 1

Lefrak
IMSX
Theater

Milstein
Hall of
Ocean Life

Heilbrunn
Cosmic
Pathway

Hall of
Biodiversity

Gottesman Hall
of Planet Earth

Theodore Roosevelt
Memorial Hall

Rose Center for
Earth and Space

Akeley
Hall of
African
Mammals

Rose Center for
Earth and Space

Big
Bang

Heilbrunn Cosmic
Pathway

SECOND FLOOR

Akeley Hall of African Mammals

Opened in 1936, this hall is one of the most beloved parts of the museum. Its 28 dramatically lighted dioramas may seem merely kitschy at first glance, but take a little time to let their beauty and technical brilliance shine through.

The hall was the life's work of the explorer Carl Akeley, who came up with the idea for the hall, raised the funds for the expeditions, gathered specimens, and sketched landscape studies for what would become the stunning backgrounds. (The backgrounds themselves were painted by James Perry Wilson, whose works can be found throughout the museum.)

Akeley died a decade before the hall opened on an expedition in what's now Rwanda. His grave site is near the landscape portrayed in the gorilla diorama, completed after his death as a memorial to him and his work. The dioramas make irresistible photo ops. If you want to snap one yourself, it's best to turn off your flash to prevent reflections off the glass.

Hall of Human Origins

The Spitzer Hall of Human Origins is a comprehensive exhibit that allows visitors to draw their own conclusions about human evolution by presenting both the scientific methods and the material evidence that goes into evolutionary theory. Visitors gain insight into the techniques and thinking of scientists and anthropologists.

The exhibit then traces the evolution of our species over six million years of fossil record and spells out our ancestors' physical and intellectual advancements. Highlights include casts of our famous hairy ancestor "Lucy," who walked the plains of Africa over 1.8 million years ago.

Hall of Biodiversity

The small **Hall of Biodiversity** includes a shady replica of a Central African Republic rain forest. Within a few yards are 160 species of flora and fauna—and also evidence of the forest's destruction. Nearby, the **Spectrum of Life Wall** showcases 1,500 specimens and models, helping show just how weird life can get. The wall opens into the gaping Milstein Hall of Ocean Life, designed to give it an underwater glow and to show off the 94-foot model of a **blue whale** that's suspended from the ceiling. The hall focuses on the vast array of life in the ocean that covers our planet.

AMNH ON FILM

Does the inside of AMNH look familiar? It should. The museum is a popular location for movies filming in New York. Here are a few of its recent close ups:

Spider-Man2: Peter Parker (Toby Maguire) has yet another bad day wrestling with his secret identity while in the Rose Planetarium.

Night at the Museum: Larry (Ben Stiller) is chased through the halls by a T. Rex and outsmarts a monkey in the Hall of African Mammals while working as a night security guard.

Blue Whale

The Squid & the Whale: Walt Berkman (Jesse Eisenberg) comes to a revelation that he is the squid and his father is the whale in front of the Hall of Ocean Life's famous diorama.

The Devil Wears Prada: Andrea (Anne Hathaway) wins over Miranda (Meryl Streep) by remembering the names of high society guests while attending a benefit here.

ROSE CENTER FOR EARTH & SPACE

The vast expanses of space and time involved in the creation of the universe can be hard to grasp even with the guiding hand of a museum, so visit the center when you're at your sharpest. The stunning glass building's centerpiece is the aluminum-clad Hayden Sphere, 87 feet in diameter. Enclosed within are the planetarium, called the Space Theater, and an audiovisual Big Bang presentation consisting of four minutes of narration by Maya Angelou, indistinct washes of color, and frightening bursts of sound. The rock-filled **Hall of Planet Earth** is particularly timely given the earthquakes and other natural disasters of recent years: one section uses a working earthquake monitor to help explain just what causes such seismic violence.

The Space Theater

At the Space Theater, the stage is the dome above you and the actors, heavenly projections. One of the world's largest virtual reality simulators, the theater uses surround sound and slight vibrations in the seats, to immerse you in scenes of planets, star clusters, and galaxies. The music of U2, Audioslave, and David Byrne among others inspire Sonic Vision, a digitally animated performance given every Friday and Saturday night.

TIME TO EAT?

Inside the Museum: The main food court on the lower level serves sandwiches for about $7.95; hamburgers cost $5.50. The animal- and planet-shaped cookies are draws for kids; adults should check out the barbecue station.

The small **Café on 4**, in a turret next to the fossil halls, sells pre-made sandwiches and salads, and yogurt and desserts, but nothing warm.

The über-white **Café on 1**, tucked away beside the Hall of Human Origins, sells warm sandwiches, soup, salads beer and wine at New York prices.

Outside the Museum: The nearest restaurants are expensive; to keep to a budget, head to a popular chain: **Uno Chicago Grill** (✉ Columbus Ave. and W. 81st St. ☎ 212/595–4700), where lunch specials run until 3 PM and kids' meals are $3.99 and up. For something special, try **Nice Matin** (Amsterdam Ave. and W. 79th St.), a French restaurant that specializes in food from the Nice region of France. They offer a brunch on the weekend from $7.50. Another option is a three course prix fixe dinner from 5:00–6:30 Monday–Friday that offers an array of selections from the menu for $32.50.

AMNH TALKS TO FODOR'S

Rose Center for Earth and Space

Interview with Ellen V. Futter, President of the American Museum of Natural History, conducted by Michelle Delio.

If You Only Have an Hour: The American Museum of Natural History has the world's finest collection of dinosaur fossils, so a visit to the fourth-floor's fossil halls, where more than 600 specimens are on display, is a must. An extraordinarily high percentage of the specimens on view—85%—are real fossilized bones as opposed to casts. At most museums those percentages are reversed, so here visitors have the chance to see the real thing including T. rex, velociraptor, and triceratops.

What to Hit Next? The museum also is renowned for its habitat dioramas, which are considered among the finest examples in the world. Visits to the Akeley Hall of African Mammals, the Hall of North American Mammals, and the Sanford Hall of North American Birds provide an overview of the diorama arts—pioneered and advanced at the museum—while allowing visitors to come face-to-face with some glorious and beautiful animals depicted in their natural habitats—habitats which in many cases no longer exist in such pristine conditions.

If You're Looking to Be Starstruck: Even if you don't have time to take in a space show in the Hayden Planetarium, the Rose Center for Earth and Space has lots of fascinating exhibits describing the vast range of sizes in the cosmos; the 13-billion-year history of the universe; the nature of galaxies, stars, and planets; and the dynamic features of our own unique planet Earth—all enclosed in a facility with spectacular award-winning architecture.

Hidden gems

The museum consists of 45 exhibition halls in 25 interconnected buildings so there are gems around every corner. Some lesser-known treasures include:

Star of India: The 563-carat Star of India, the largest and most famous star sapphire in the world, is displayed in the Morgan Memorial Hall of Gems.

WHERE'S PLUTO?

With all the controversy about what constitutes a planet, some visitors enjoy hunting for Pluto in the Cullman Hall of the Universe in the Rose Center for Earth and Space. We'll give you a hint: it's not with the other planets.

Black Smokers: These sulfide chimneys—collected during groundbreaking museum expeditions to the Pacific Ocean—are the only such specimens exhibited anywhere. Black smokers form around hot springs on the deep ocean floor and support a microbial community that does not live off sunlight but instead on the chemical energy of the Earth. Some of these microbes are considered the most ancient forms of life on Earth and may offer clues to the development of life here and the possibility of life elsewhere. See them in the Gottesman Hall of Planet Earth.

Star of India

Spectrum of Life: The Hall of Biodiversity aims to showcase the glorious diversity of life on Earth resulting from 3.5 billion years of evolution. The impressive "Spectrum of Life" display is a 100-foot-long installation of more than 1,500 specimens and models—microorganisms and mammals, bacteria and beetles, fungi and fish. Use the computer workstations to learn more about the species depicted in each area.

Dodo: One of the museum's rarest treasures is the skeleton of a dodo bird, displayed along with other endangered or extinct species in the "Endangered Case" in the Hall of Biodiversity.

Small Dioramas: Tucked along the sides of the Hall of North American Mammals are two easy-to-miss corridors displaying a number of exquisitely rendered dioramas. In these jewel-box-like displays, some a mere 3 feet deep, you will see the smaller animals such as wolves galloping through a snowy night, a Canada lynx stalking a snowshoe hare, and a spotted skunk standing on its hands, preparing to spray a cacomistle, to name just a few of the evocative scenes.

Dinosaur Eggs: In 1993 museum scientists working in the Gobi Desert of Mongolia were the first to unearth fossilized embryos in dinosaur eggs, as well as the fossil of an adult oviraptor in a brooding posture over its nest. This discovery provided invaluable information about dinosaur gestation and revolutionized thinking about dinosaur behavior. Look for the display in the museum's fossil halls on the fourth floor.

Ross Terrace: In warmer months the Ross Terrace, with its fountains and cosmic theme, offers a wonderful outdoor spot for resting and reflecting, while providing a spectacular view of the Rose Center for Earth and Space.

14

IN FOCUS AMERICAN MUSEUM OF NATURAL HISTORY

MOST INTERESTING OBJECT?

What's most interesting about the American Museum of Natural History is not any single object on exhibit, but the sheer range and scope of what you can experience here. Think of it is a field guide to the natural world, the universe, and the cultures of humanity—all under one roof. The experience of visiting the museum is ultimately about awakening a sense of discovery, wonder, awe, and stewardship of this Earth we call home.

THE METROPOLITAN MUSEUM OF ART

If the city held no other museum than the colossal Metropolitan Museum of Art, you could still occupy yourself for days roaming its labyrinthine corridors. Because the Metropolitan Museum has more than 2 million works of art representing 5,000 years of history, you're going to have to make tough choices. Looking at everything here could take a week.

Mesmerizing carvings in the ancient Egyptian Temple of Dendur.

Before you begin exploring the museum, check the museum's floor plan, available at all entrances, for location of the major wings and collections. Pick up the "Today's Events" flier at the desk where you buy your ticket. The museum offers gallery talks on a range of subjects; taking a tour with a staff curator can show you some of the collection's hidden secrets.

The posted adult admission, though only a suggestion, is one that's strongly encouraged. Whatever you choose to pay, admission includes all special exhibits and same-day entrance to the Cloisters (see page 231). The Met's audio guide costs an additional $7, and if you intend to stay more than an hour or so, it's worth it. The generally perceptive commentary covers museum highlights and directors' picks, with separate commentary tracks directed at kids.

If you want to avoid the crowds, visit weekday mornings. Also good are Friday and Saturday evenings, when live classical music plays from the Great Hall balcony. If the Great Hall (the main entrance) is mobbed, avoid the chaos by heading to the street-level entrance to the left of the main stairs, near 81st Street. Ticket lines and coat checks are much less ferocious here.

What to see? Check out the museum highlights on the following pages.

✉ 5th Ave. at 82nd St., Upper East Side

Ⓜ Subway: 4, 5, 6 to 86th St.

☎ 212/535-7710

🌐 www.metmuseum.org

💵 $20 suggested donation

🕒 Tues.–Thurs. and Sun. 9:30–5:30, Fri. and Sat. 9:30–9

Left, Great Hall

MUSEUM HIGHLIGHTS

Temple of Dendur

Egyptian Art

A major star is the **Temple of Dendur** (circa 15 BC), in a huge atrium to itself and with a moatlike pool of water to represent its original location near the Nile. The temple was commissioned by the Roman emperor Augustus to honor the goddess Isis and the sons of a Nubian chieftain. Look for the scratched-in graffiti from 19th-century Western explorers on the inside. Egypt gave the temple as a gift to the U.S. in 1964; it would have been submerged after the construction of the Aswan High Dam.

The Egyptian collections as a whole cover 4,000 years of history, with papyrus pages from the Egyptian Book of the Dead, stone coffins engraved with hieroglyphics, and tombs. The galleries should be walked through counterclockwise from the Ancient Kingdom (2650–2150 BC), to the period under Roman rule (30 BC–400 AD). In the latter, keep an eye out for the enormous, bulbous **Sarcophagus of Horkhebit,** hand-carved from basalt.

ART TO TAKE HOME

You don't have to pay admission to get to the mammoth gift shop on the first floor. One of the better souvenirs here is also one of the more reasonable: the Met's own **illustrated guide** to 858 of the best items in its collection ($19.95).

Greek and Roman Art

Today's tabloids have nothing on Ancient Greece and Rome. They had it all—sex, cults, drugs, unrelenting violence, and, of course, stunning art. The recently redone Greek and Roman galleries encompass 6,000 works of art that reveal aspects of everyday life in these influential cultures.

Englehard Court

The urnlike ceramic kraters were used by the Greeks for mixing wine and water at parties and other events. Given that, it's not surprising that most depict slightly racy scenes. Some of the most impressive can be found in the gallery covering 5th century BC.

On the mezzanine of the Roman galleries, the Etruscan bronze chariot from 650 BC depicts scenes from the life of Achilles. Notice how the simplistic Etruscan style in combination with the Greek influence evolved into the naturalistic Roman statues below.

The frescoes from a bedroom in the Villa of P. Fannius Synistor preserved by the explosion of Mt. Vesuvius in 79 AD give us a glimpse into the stylistic achievement of perspective in Roman painting.

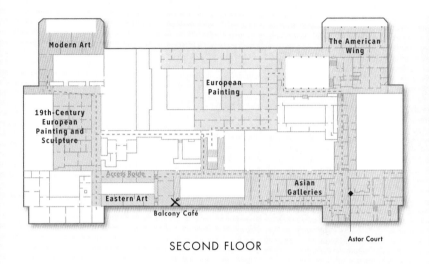

Modern Art

The American
Wing

European
Painting

19th-Century
European
Painting and
Sculpture

Access Route

Eastern Art

Asian
Galleries

Balcony Café

Astor Court

SECOND FLOOR

MEZZANINES

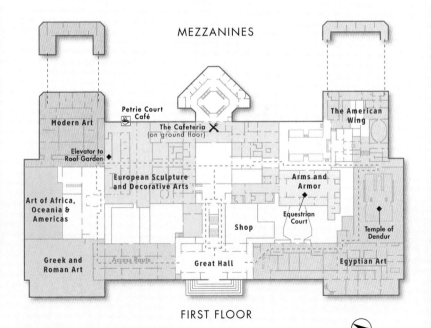

Petrie Court
Café

Modern Art

The American
Wing

The Cafeteria
(on ground floor)

Elevator to
Roof Garden

European Sculpture
and Decorative Arts

Arms and
Armor

Art of Africa,
Oceania &
Americas

Equestrian
Court

Temple of
Dendur

Shop

Greek and
Roman Art

Access Route

Great Hall

Egyptian Art

FIRST FLOOR

5th Avenue

Visitors ponder European paintings on the 2nd floor.

American Wing

The **Henry R. Luce Center for the Study of American Art,** on a mezzanine between the first and second floors, is a storage room open to the public. Row after row of multilevel glass enclosures hold furniture, decorative objects, and paintings that couldn't otherwise be on display due to space constraints. There are enough works here to make up a small museum of their own—the **Pennsylvania Dutch chests** in row 25 are especially cool.

Also on the mezzanine, near the stairs, is a group of five larger-than-life portraits by **John Singer Sargent.** One of them, *Madame X,* caused a scandal when it was first exhibited in Paris. The woman's pose, with one strap of her gown falling off her shoulder, seemed very suggestive to the onlookers of the time. Sargent later repainted the strap back up in its current, more proper position.

When you see it in person, Emanuel Leutze's *Washington Crossing the Delaware* (1851) is as powerful as it is familiar. For one thing, it's enormous—more than 12 by 21 feet. In the same room, on the opposite wall, is *The Last Moments of John Brown* (1882–84). With more than a little artistic license, the painting depicts the violent abolitionist kissing a black baby on the way to the gallows with a noose around his neck.

TIME TO EAT? INSIDE THE MUSEUM

The museum's restaurants are almost always full, and going to lunch at 2 PM doesn't mean there won't be a line. The **Petrie Café**, at the back of the 1st-floor European Sculpture Court, has waiter service, but aside from its wall of windows looking onto Central Park, it's very plain. Prices range from $12 for a sandwich to $21 for organic chicken salad. Tea, sweets, and savories are served from 2:30 PM to 4:30 PM during the week.

The **Balcony Café** located in the neo-classical Great Hall is a good place to people watch, enjoy a light meal or sip espresso. In the evenings, the café is transformed into a bar with live classical music.

The basement **cafeteria**, which has white tiles and a vaulted ceiling, has stations for pasta, main courses, antipasti, and sandwiches.

Tiffany

Arms and Armor

The **Equestrian Court**, where the knights are mounted on armored models of horses, is one of the most dramatic rooms in the museum. For a bird's-eye view, check it out again from the balconies in the Musical Instruments collection on the second floor.

European Sculpture and Decorative Arts

Among the many sculptures in the sun-filled Petrie Court, **Ugolino and His Sons** still stands out for the despairing poses of its subjects. Ugolino, a nobleman whose family's tragic story is told in Dante's *Inferno*, was punished for treason by being left to starve to death with his grandsons and sons in a locked tower. (It's not clear if putting such a sculpture so near the Petrie Court's café is some curator's idea of a joke or not.) By the way, the redbrick and granite wall on the court's north side is the museum's original entrance.

The newly renovated Wrightsman Galleries for French Decorative Arts on the first floor displays the opulence that caused Louis the XVI to lose his head. The blindingly golden Boiserie from the Hotel de Cabris, a remnant of French 18th century Neo-classical interiors, represents the finest collection of French decorative arts in the country.

Modern Art

The museum's most famous Picasso is probably his 1906 portrait **Gertrude Stein** in which the writer's face is stern and masklike. The portrait was bequeathed to the museum by Stein herself.

Of the Georgia O'Keeffes on view, 1931's **Red, White, and Blue** painting of a cow skull is a standout. The color, composition, and natural motif work together to create a work with religious as well as nationalist overtones.

European Paintings

On the second floor, the 13th- to 18th-century paintings are in one block, at the top of the Great Hall's stairs. To get to the 19th-century paintings and sculptures, walk through the the narrow corridor of Drawings, Prints, and Photographs. Both sections can be hard to navigate quickly, with a masterpiece around every corner.

Recently, the Met spent about $45 million to buy Duccio di Buoninsegna's **Madonna and Child**, painted circa 1300. The last remaining Duccio in private hands,

TIME TO EAT?
OUTSIDE THE MUSEUM

Because museum admission is good all day, you can always leave for lunch and come back later. The deli-style **City Market Café** (1100 Madison Ave., between. 82nd and 83rd Sts., 212/535–2070) with 10 small tables, serves pizzas, sandwiches, and make-your-own salad. At the fairly inexpensive sit-down eatery **Le Pain Quotidien** (1131 Madison Ave., at 84th St., 212/327–4900), the hungry dine at long communal tables for sandwiches (around $9), salads, and pastries high in both calories and quality. If you'd rather try for a typical New York diner, head for the **Amity Restaurant** (1134 Madison Ave, between 84th and 85th Sts.). A burger with fries cost under $10.

14

IN FOCUS THE METROPOLITAN MUSEUM OF ART

Equestrian Court (1930)

this painting, the size of a piece of typewriter paper, is unimpressive at first glance. The work, though rigid, represents a revolution in Byzantine art. The humanity reflected in the baby Jesus grabbing his mother's veil changed European painting.

The Triumph of Fame, a round, double-sided "commemorative birth tray" by Scheggia, shows a crowd of mounted knights saluting winged Fame, who holds both a cupid and a sword (they symbolize two timeless ways to get famous). The tray heralds the arrival of Lorenzo de' Medici (1449–92), who did indeed become a famed figure of the Italian Renaissance.

Vincent van Gogh,
Wheatfield with Cypresses

Rembrandt's masterful *Aristotle with a Bust of Homer* (1653) shows a philosopher contemplating worldly gains versus values through its play of light and use of symbols. Around Aristotle is a gold medal of Alexander the Great, one of the philosopher's students.

In the room dedicated to **Monet** you can get to all his greatest hits—poplar trees, haystacks, water lilies, and the Rouen Cathedral. The muted tones of Pissaro are followed by a room full of bright and garish colors announcing works by Gauguin, Matisse, and Van Gogh.

Asian Galleries

The serene **Astor Court,** which has its own skylight and pond of real-life koi (goldfish), is a model of a scholar's court garden in Soochow, China.

The Han dynasty (206 BC–220 AD) introduced the practice of sending the dead on to the afterlife with small objects to help them there. Keep an eye out for these **small clay figures,** which include farm animals (enclosed in barnyards) and dancing entertainers.

On display in a glass case in the center of an early-Chinese gallery is a complete set of 14 **bronze altar vessels.** Dating 1100 BC—800 AD, these green and slightly crusty pieces were used for worshipping ancestors. The Met displays some of its finest **Asian stoneware and porcelain** along the balcony overlooking the Great Hall.

The teak dome and balconies from a **Jain meeting hall** in western India were carved in western India around 1500. Just about the entire surface is covered with musicians, animals, gods, and servants.

GREAT VIEWS

Looking for one of the best views in town? The Roof Garden (open May–October) exhibits contemporary sculptures, but most people take the elevator here to have a drink or snack while checking out Central Park and the skyline.

SOLOMON R. GUGGENHEIM MUSEUM

✉ 1071 5th Ave., between E. 88th and E. 89th Sts., Upper East Side

☎ 212/423–3500

🌐 www.guggenheim.org

💲 $18

🕑 Sun.–Wed. 9–5:45, Fri. and Sat. 9–8. Closed Thurs.

Ⓜ 4, 5, 6 to 86th St.

14

TIPS

■ Gallery talks provide richer understanding of the masterpieces in front of you. The museum offers tours at a terrific price: free!

■ Eat before trekking over to 5th Avenue; restaurants on Lexington offer more varied fare than the museum's cafeteria.

■ The museum is pay what you wish on Friday after 5:45. Lines can be long, so go early. The last tickets are handed out at 7:15.

Frank Lloyd Wright's landmark museum building is visited as much for its famous architecture as it is for its superlative art. Opened in 1959, shortly after Wright's death, the Guggenheim is acclaimed as one of the greatest buildings of the 20th century. After a three-year restoration project completed at the end of October 2008, the Guggenheim building is once again a glorious vision. Eleven coats of paint were removed, exterior cracks were fixed, and supporting structures were reinforced. Inside, under a 92-foot-high glass dome, a seemingly endless ramp spirals down past changing exhibitions. The museum has strong holdings of Wassily Kandinsky, Paul Klee, Marc Chagall, Pablo Picasso, and Robert Mapplethorpe.

HIGHLIGHTS

Wright's design was criticized by some who believed that the distinctive building detracted from the art within, but the interior nautilus design allows artworks to be viewed from several different angles and distances. Be sure to notice not only what's in front of you but also what's across the spiral from you.

On permanent display, the museum's Thannhauser Collection is made up primarily of works by French impressionists and Postimpressionists Matisse, van Gogh, Toulouse-Lautrec, and Cézanne. Perhaps more than any other 20th-century painter, Wassily Kandinsky, one of the first "pure" abstract artists, has been closely linked to the museum's history. Beginning with the acquisition of his masterpiece *Composition 8* (1923) in 1930, the collection has grown to encompass more than 150 works.

MUSEUM OF MODERN ART (MOMA)

✉ 11 W. 53rd St., between 5th and 6th Aves., Midtown East

☎ 212/708–9400

🌐 www.moma.org

🎫 $20

🕐 Sat.–Mon., Wed., and Thurs. 10:30–5:30, Fri. 10:30–8. Closed Tues.

Ⓜ E, V to 5th Ave./53rd St.; B, D, F, V to 47th–50th Sts./ Rockefeller Center

TIPS

■ MoMA is a popular destination for locals and tourists, and that translates into lines that sometimes snake down the block. Weekdays tend to be less crowded. Come without bags or backpack to avoid the wait for the checkroom.

■ Consider lining up for the free audio guide, especially if the scribbled and rather ambiguous nature of modern art occasionally confounds you.

■ Entrance between 4 and 8 PM on Friday is free, but come expecting to wait in line.

Novices and reluctant art enthusiasts are often awestruck by the masterpieces before them here, including Monet's *Water Lilies*, Picasso's *Les Demoiselles d'Avignon*, and van Gogh's *Starry Night*. The museum's somewhat recent $425 million face-lift by Yoshio Taniguchi increased exhibition space by nearly 50%, including space to accommodate large-scale contemporary installations. Its current building gave the museum an opportunity to shift focus from modern to contemporary art, evident in the recent creation of a media department. The museum continues to collect: most recently it obtained important works by Martin Kippenberger, David Wojnarowicz, Jasper Johns, Kara Walker, and Neo Rauch. One of the top research facilities in modern and contemporary art is housed inside the museum's eight-story "Education and Research" building.

HIGHLIGHTS

In addition to the artwork, one of the main draws of MoMA is the building itself. A maze of glass walkways permits art viewing from many angles.

The 110-foot atrium entrance (accessed from either 53rd or 54th Street) leads to the movie theater and the main floor restaurant, "Modern," with the Alsatian-inspired cuisine of Chef Gabriel Kreuther.

The museum has other worthy food options: Café 2 on the second floor serves rustic Italian cooking; Terrace 5, adjacent to the Painting and Sculpture Galleries, has sophisticated American food, specialty cocktails, and microbrewed beers along with spectacular views.

A favorite area in which to take a break is the Abby Aldrich Rockefeller Sculpture Garden. Designed by Philip Johnson, it features Barnett Newman's *Broken Obelisk* (1962–69). The glass wall lets visitors look directly into the surrounding galleries from the garden.

Contemporary art (1970 to the present) from the museum's six curatorial departments shares the second floor of the six-story building, and the skylighted top floor showcases an impressive lineup of changing exhibits.

MODERN ART FOR THE MASSES

MoMA works hard to make modern art accessible and enjoyable, including a variety of audio tours for both adults and kids. You can grab a portable player free of charge at the museum, or download podcasts onto your own handheld device from the museum's Web site. Check out the free wireless service within the museum to listen to audio tours as you wander through MoMA (log onto www.moma.org/wifi with your HTML browser-enabled device).

Interactive kiosks in the museum help you navigate the massive space and let you relate works you've seen with those not on display.

MOVIES & THE MOMA

With so much art on display, it's hard to remember that the MoMA has a movie theater. Film passes to the day's screenings are included with the price of admission. Film-only tickets are $10 and must be purchased in person at specific locations and times; check MoMA's Web site for details. Hang onto the ticket stub, the cost will be deducted from your admission fee if you return to the museum within 30 days.

TWO FOR THE PRICE OF ONE

Tickets to MoMA include free admission to another museum—the avant-garde P.S. 1 in Queens. Don't worry; you won't need to trek out to Queen on the same day. Save your ticket and you can go in for free any time within 30 days of your original purchase. Also check MoMA's Web site (where you can prepurchase tickets) for special deals and packages that include admission to other NYC venues.

Interview with Peter Reed, Senior Deputy Director for Curatorial Affairs, the Museum of Modern Art.

For visitors planning to see highlights of the collection, I recommend they begin in the Painting and Sculpture Galleries on the fifth floor. Here the stories of modern art unfold, from the late 19th century up to World War II. Renowned paintings such as Vincent van Gogh's *Starry Night* (1889), Pablo Picasso's *Les Demoiselles d'Avignon* (1907), Henri Matisse's *Dance* (1909), and Joan Miró's *The Birth of the World* (1925) are installed in the context of other extraordinary works. In the fourth-floor galleries I enjoy showing visitors the diverse works by abstract expressionists, such as Jackson Pollock's *One* (1950), a masterpiece of the "drip" technique.

To best understand the richness and complexity of MoMA's collection, try to visit the galleries devoted to contemporary art, architecture and design, drawings, photography, prints, media, as well as the international film program in the museum's Titus theaters.

Don't miss: One of my favorite places at MoMA is the Abby Aldrich Rockefeller Sculpture Garden, designed by Philip Johnson in 1953. The garden lies at the heart of the museum and is a spectacular urban oasis with its reflecting pools, seasonal plantings, and masterworks of modern sculpture.

14

WHITNEY MUSEUM OF AMERICAN ART

✉ 945 Madison Ave., at E. 75th St., Upper East Side

☎ 800/WHITNEY

⊕ www.whitney.org

🎫 $15

🕙 Wed., Thurs., and weekends 11–6; Fri. 1–9

Ⓜ 6 to 77th St.

TIPS

■ After 6 PM on Friday the price of admission is pay-what-you-wish. On some of those nights, the Whitney Live series presents new artists and reinterpretations of American classics. Be fore-warned that this combination may result in long lines.

■ Sarabeth's at the Whitney serves a tasty selection of sandwiches, pastries, and soups.

With its bold collection of 20th-centuy and contemporary American art, this museum presents an eclectic mix of more than 16,000 works in its permanent collection. The museum was originally a gallery in the studio of sculptor and collector Gertrude Vanderbilt Whitney, whose talent and taste were accompanied by the money of two wealthy families. In 1930, after the Met turned down Whitney's offer to donate her collection of 20th-century American art, she established an independent museum in Greenwich Village. Now uptown, the minimalist gray-granite building opened in 1966 and was designed by Marcel Breuer and Hamilton Smith.

HIGHLIGHTS

Start your visit on the fifth floor, where the eight sparse galleries house rotating exhibitions of postwar and contemporary works from the permanent collection by artists such as Jackson Pollock, Jim Dine, Jasper Johns, Mark Rothko, Chuck Close, Cindy Sherman, and Roy Lichtenstein.

Notable pieces include Hopper's *Early Sunday Morning* (1930), Bellows's *Dempsey and Firpo* (1924), Alexander Calder's beloved *Circus*, and several of Georgia O'Keeffe's dazzling flower paintings.

The lower floors feature exhibitions of contemporary artists such as Kara Walker and Gordon Matta-Clark as well as retrospective exhibitions that focus on movements and themes in American art.

The often-controversial Whitney Biennial, which showcases the most important developments in American art over the previous two years, takes place in the spring of even-numbered years.

TOP MUSEUMS

American Folk Art Museum. Weather vanes, quilts, pottery, scrimshaw, sculpture, and paintings give an excellent overview of the freewheeling folk-art genre, but the exterior is a work of art as well: the eight-story building was designed in 2001 by husband-and-wife-team Tod Williams and Billie Tsein, and the facade, consisting of 63 hand-cast panels of alloyed bronze, reveals individual textures, sizes, and plays of light. The museum's award-winning gift shop has an outstanding collection of handcrafted items. ⊠*45 W. 53rd St., between 5th and 6th Aves., Midtown West* ☎*212/265–1040* ⊕*www.folkartmuseum.org* ✉*$9; free Fri. 5:30 PM–7:30 PM* ⊙*Tues.–Thurs. and weekends 10:30–5:30, Fri. 10:30–7:30* Ⓜ*E, V to 5th Ave./53rd St.; B, D, E to 7th Ave.; B, D, F, V to 47th–50th Sts./Rockefeller Center.*

The Cloisters. Perched on a wooded hill in Fort Tryon Park, near Manhattan's northern tip, the Cloisters, which shelters the medieval collection of the Metropolitan Museum of Art, is a scenic destination on its own. Colonnaded walks connect authentic French and Spanish monastic cloisters, a French Romanesque chapel, a 12th-century chapter house, and a Romanesque apse. One room is devoted to the 15th- and 16th-century Unicorn Tapestries—a must-see masterpiece of medieval mythology. The tomb effigies are another highlight. Three gardens shelter more than 250 species of plants similar to those grown during the Middle Ages, including herbs and medicinals; the Unicorn Garden blooms with flowers and plants depicted in the tapestries. Concerts of medieval music are held here regularly (concert tickets include same-day admission to the museum) and an outdoor café decorated with 15th-century carvings serves biscotti and espresso from May through October. ⊠*Fort Tryon Park, Inwood* ☎*212/923–3700* ⊕*www.metmuseum.org* ✉*$20 suggested donation* ⊙*Mar.–Oct., Tues.–Sun. 9:30–5:15; Nov.–Feb., Tues.–Sun. 9:30–4:45* Ⓜ*A to 190th St.*

Cooper-Hewitt National Design Museum. More than 2,000 years of international design is on display inside the 64-room mansion, formerly home to industrialist Andrew Carnegie. The 250,000-plus objects here include drawings, textiles, furniture, metalwork, ceramics, glass, and woodwork. Changing exhibitions are drawn from the permanent collection, highlighting everything from antique cutlery and Japanese sword fittings to robotics and animation. The museum's shows are invariably enlightening and often amusing. In summer some exhibits are displayed in the museum's lush garden. ⊠*2 E. 91st St., at 5th Ave., Upper East Side* ☎*212/849–8400* ⊕*www.cooperhewitt.org* ✉*$10* ⊙*Tues.–Fri. 10–5, Sat. 10–6, Sun. noon–6* Ⓜ*4, 5, 6 to 86th St.*

★ **Frick Collection.** Henry Clay Frick made his fortune amid the soot and smoke of Pittsburgh, where he was a coke (a coal fuel derivative) and steel baron. Decidedly removed from soot is this facility, once Frick's private New York residence. Édouard Manet's *The Bullfight* (1864) hangs in the East Gallery, which also exhibits the Chinard portrait bust (1809; bought in 2004 and the museum's first purchase in eight years). Two of the Frick's three Vermeers—*Officer and Laughing Girl* (circa 1658) and *Girl Interrupted at Her Music* (1660–61)—hang by

14

the front staircase. Nearly 50 additional paintings, as well as sculpture, decorative arts, and furniture, are in the West and East galleries. Three Rembrandts, including *The Polish Rider* (circa 1655) and *Self-Portrait* (1658), as well as a third Vermeer, *Mistress and Maid* (circa 1665–70), hang in the former; paintings by Whistler, Goya, Van Dyck, Lorrain, and David in the latter. An audio guide, available in several languages, is included with admission, as are the year-round temporary exhibits. The tranquil indoor garden court is a great spot for a rest. Children under 10 are not admitted, 10–16 with adult only. ✉ *1 E. 70th St., at 5th Ave., Upper East Side* ☎ *212/288–0700* ⊕ *www.frick.org* 🖃 *$15* ⊙ *Tues.–Sat. 10–6, Sun. 11–5* Ⓜ *6 to 68th St./Hunter College.*

☺ *Intrepid* **Sea-Air-Space Museum.** Formerly the USS *Intrepid*, this 900-foot aircraft carrier is serving out its retirement as the centerpiece of Manhattan's only floating museum. The carrier's most trying moment of service, the day it was attacked in World War II by kamikaze pilots, is recounted in a multimedia presentation. Aircraft on deck include an A-12 Blackbird spy plane, a Concorde, helicopters, and two dozen other aircraft. Docked alongside, and also part of the museum, is the *Growler,* a strategic-missile submarine. Children can explore the ships' skinny hallways and winding staircases, as well as manipulate countless knobs, buttons, and wheels. For an extra thrill (and an extra $8), kids can try the Navy flight simulator and "land" an aircraft on board. The original Iwo Jima sculpture upon which the memorial in Washington, D.C., is based, is one of the museum's most photographed objects. ✉ *Hudson River, Pier 86, 12th Ave. at W. 46th St., Midtown West* ☎ *212/245–0072 or 877/957–7447* ⊕ *www.intrepidmuseum.org* 🖃 *$19.50; free to active and retired U.S. military personnel* ⊙ *Apr.–Sept., weekdays 10–5, weekends 10–6; Oct.–Mar., Tues.–Sun. 10–5; last admission 1 hr before closing* Ⓜ *A, C, E to 42nd St.; M42 bus to pier.*

Madame Tussaud's New York. Join Captain Jack Sparrow's pirate crew, sing along with an American Idol, mix your own R&B hit alongside Usher, or forecast tomorrow's weather with Al Roker. Much of the fun here comes from the photo opportunities—you're encouraged to pose with and touch the nearly 200 realistic replicas of the famous and infamous (disposable cameras are for sale). But there's more to do here than just pal around with the waxworks. Interactive options include a karaoke café, a celebrity walk down the red carpet, and a haunted town, the latter populated with both wax figures and real people. ✉ *234 W. 42nd St., between 7th and 8th Aves., Midtown West* ☎ *212/512–9600* ⊕ *www.madame-tussauds.com* 🖃 *$29* ⊙ *Weekdays 10–9, weekends 10–10* Ⓜ *1, 2, 3, 7, A, C, E, N, Q, R, W, S to 42nd St.*

★ ☺ **Museum of the City of New York.** Within a Colonial Revival building designed for the museum in the 1930s, the city's history and many quirks are revealed through engaging exhibits. Permanent collections detail firefighting, theater, and New York's role as a port. Period rooms include several that John D. Rockefeller Sr. acquired when he bought a fully furnished New York mansion in the 1880s. The historic toys on view include the beloved Stettheimer Dollhouse, a miniature mansion outfitted down to postage-stamp-size artworks imitating 20th-century masters. Don't miss *Timescapes,* a 25-minute media projection that innovatively illustrates New York's physical expansion and population changes. The museum hosts New York–centric lectures, films, and walking tours. ■TIP➔ When you're finished touring the museum, cross the street and stroll through the Vanderbilt Gates to enter the Conservatory Garden, one of Central Park's hidden gems. ⊠*1220 5th Ave., at E. 103rd St., Upper East Side* ☎*212/534–1672* ⊕*www.mcny.org* ⊠*$9 suggested donation* ⊙*Tues.–Sun. 10–5* Ⓜ *6 to 103rd St.*

Museum of Jewish Heritage—A Living Memorial to the Holocaust. In a granite 85-foot hexagon at the southern end of Battery Park City, this museum pays tribute to the 6 million Jews who perished in the Holocaust. Architects Kevin Roche and John Dinkeloo built the museum in the shape of a Star of David, with three floors of exhibits demonstrating the dynamism of 20th-century Jewish culture. Visitors enter through a gallery that provides a context for the early-20th-century artifacts on the first floor: an elaborate screen hand-painted for the fall harvest festival of Sukkoth, wedding invitations, and tools used by Jewish tradesmen. Original documentary films play throughout the museum. The second floor details the rise of Nazism and anti-Semitism, and the ravages of the Holocaust. A gallery covers the doomed voyage of the SS *St. Louis*, a ship of German Jewish refugees that crossed the Atlantic twice in 1939 in search of a safe haven. Signs of hope are also on display, including a trumpet that Louis Bannet (the "Dutch Louis Armstrong") played for three years in the Auschwitz-Birkenau inmate orchestra. The third floor covers postwar Jewish life. The east wing contains a theater, memorial garden by artist Andy Goldsworthy, resource center, library, more galleries, classrooms, and a café. ⊠*36 Battery Pl., Battery Park City, Lower Manhattan* ☎*646/437–4200* ⊕*www.mjhnyc.org* ⊠*$10* ⊙*Thurs. and Sun.–Tues. 10–5:45, Wed. 10–8, Fri. and eve of Jewish holidays 10–3* Ⓜ*4, 5 to Bowling Green.*

Fodor'sChoice
★
Ⓒ
The Paley Center for Media. Three galleries of photographs and artifacts document the history of broadcasting in this 1989 limestone building by Philip Johnson and John Burgee. But the main draw here is the computerized catalog of more than 100,000 television and radio programs. If you want to see a performance of "Turkey Lurkey Time" from the 1969 Tony Awards, for example, type the name of the song, show, or performer into a computer terminal. You can then proceed to a semi-private screening area to watch your selection. People nearby might be watching classic comedies from the '50s, miniseries from the '70s, or news broadcasts from the '90s. Adding to the delight of screening TV shows from yesteryear is that the original commercials are still embedded in many of the programs; if ads are your thing you can also skip the programming altogether and watch different compilations of classic commercials. ⊠*25 W. 52nd St., between 5th and 6th Aves., Midtown West* ☎*212/621–6800* ⊕*www.paleycenter.org* ⊠*$10* ⊙*Tues., Wed., and Fri.–Sun. noon–6; Thurs. noon–8* Ⓜ*E, V to 5th Ave./53rd St.; B, D, F, V to 47th–50th Sts./Rockefeller Center.*

14

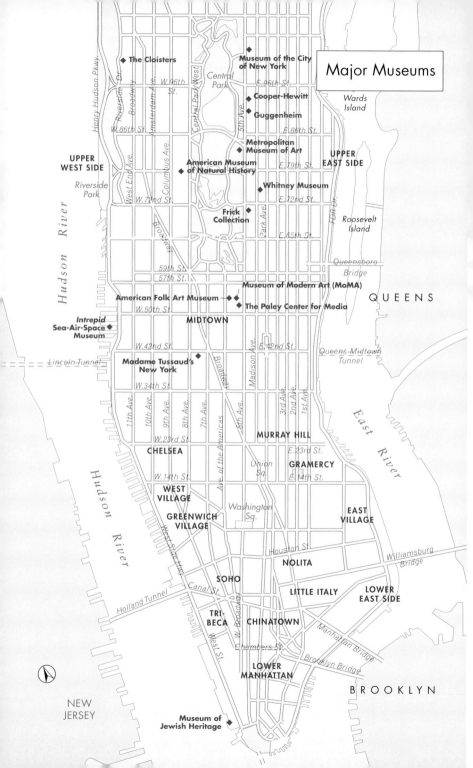

Major Museums

The Cloisters ◆

Museum of the City ◆
of New York

*Central
Park*

Cooper-Hewitt ◆

Guggenheim ◆

Metropolitan ◆
Museum of Art

American Museum ◆
of Natural History

Whitney Museum ◆

Frick ◆
Collection

Museum of Modern Art (MoMA) ◆

American Folk Art Museum ◆ ◆
◆ The Paley Center for Media

Intrepid
Sea-Air-Space ◆
Museum

MIDTOWN

Madame Tussaud's ◆
New York

MURRAY HILL

CHELSEA

GRAMERCY

WEST
VILLAGE

GREENWICH
VILLAGE

*Washington
Sq.*

EAST
VILLAGE

NOLITA

SOHO

LITTLE ITALY

LOWER
EAST SIDE

TRI-
BECA

CHINATOWN

LOWER
MANHATTAN

NEW
JERSEY

BROOKLYN

Museum of ◆
Jewish Heritage

UPPER
WEST SIDE

UPPER
EAST SIDE

*Riverside
Park*

Wards
Island

Roosevelt
Island

QUEENS

Hudson River

East River

*Union
Sq.*

Henry Hudson Pkwy

Riverside Dr.

Broadway

Amsterdam Ave.

Central Park West

5th Ave.

Columbus Ave.

West End Ave.

Park Ave.

FDR Dr.

Broadway

11th Ave.

10th Ave.

9th Ave.

8th Ave.

7th Ave.

Ave. of the Americas

5th Ave.

Madison Ave.

3rd Ave.

2nd Ave.

1st Ave.

Broadway

West St.

West Side Hwy.

W. Broadway

West St.

W. 96th St.

E. 96th St.

E. 86th St.

W. 86th St.

E. 79th St.

E. 72nd St.

W. 72nd St.

E. 65th St.

59th St.

57th St.

W. 50th St.

W. 42nd St.

E. 42nd St.

W. 34th St.

W. 23rd St.

E. 23rd St.

W. 14th St.

E. 14th St.

Houston St.

Canal St.

Chambers St.

Lincoln Tunnel

Holland Tunnel

Queens-Midtown
Tunnel

Queensboro
Bridge

Williamsburg
Bridge

Manhattan Bridge

Brooklyn Bridge

MUSEUMS ALSO WORTH SEEING

Alexander Hamilton U.S. Custom House/National Museum of the American Indian. The Beaux-Arts Alexander Hamilton U.S. Custom House (1907) is one of Lower Manhattan's finest buildings. Massive granite columns rise to a pediment topped by a double row of statues. Inside, the egg-shape stairwell and rotunda embellished with shipping-theme murals (completed in the 1930s) are incredibly impressive. Changing presentations drawn from the National Museum of the American Indian, a branch of the Smithsonian, are exhibited here with modern stylishness. You can see everything without being overwhelmed. The Diker Pavilion provides a venue for dance, music, and storytelling programs. Videos and films made by indigenous people from around the world are shown here regularly. ⊠ *1 Bowling Green, between State and Whitehall Sts., Lower Manhattan* ☎ *212/514–3700* ⊕ *www.americanindian. si.edu* ☛ *Free* ☼ *Mon.–Wed. and Fri.–Sun. 10–5, Thurs. 10–8* Ⓜ *4, 5 to Bowling Green.*

American Folk Art Museum: Eva and Morris Feld Gallery. Across from Lincoln Center, this branch of the American Folk Art Museum on West 53rd Street has a small selection of art and decorative objects culled from all over the Americas. You might see painted store signs, outsider art, weather vanes, or carousel mounts. On permanent display is *The National Tribute Quilt,* made up of 3,466 blocks for each person who died on 9/11. The gift shop is worth a browse. ⊠ *2 Lincoln Sq., Columbus Ave. between W. 65th and W. 66th Sts., Upper West Side* ☎ *212/595–9533* ⊕ *www.folkartmuseum.org* ☛ *$3 suggested admission* ☼ *Tues.–Sat. noon–7:30, Sun. noon–5* Ⓜ *1 to 66th St./ Lincoln Center.*

Asia Society and Museum. The Asian art collection of Mr. and Mrs. John D. Rockefeller III forms the museum's major holdings, which include South Asian stone and bronze sculptures; art from India, Nepal, Pakistan, and Afghanistan; bronze vessels, ceramics, sculpture, and paintings from China; Korean ceramics; and paintings, wooden sculptures, and ceramics from Japan. Founded in 1956, the society has a regular program of lectures, films, and performances, in addition to changing exhibitions. Trees grow in the Garden café, which serves an eclectically Asian menu for lunch and dinner. ⊠ *725 Park Ave., at 70th St., Upper East Side* ☎ *212/288–6400* ⊕ *www.asiasociety.org* ☛ *$10; free Fri. 6–9* ☼ *Tues.–Sun. 11–6; open until 9 pm on Fri. from the day after Labor Day–July 3* Ⓜ *6 to 68th St./Hunter College.*

Asian American Arts Centre. This space holds impressive contemporary works by Asian-American artists, annual folk-art exhibitions during the Chinese New Year, Asian-American dance performances, and videos of Asian-American art and events. The center also sells unique art objects from all over Asia. The inconspicuous entrance doesn't have a permanent sign, but the address is posted on a doorway to the right of the entrance to a McDonald's. A steep flight of stairs leads to the third-floor gallery. ⊠ *26 Bowery, between Bayard and Pell Sts., Chinatown* ☎ *212/233–2154* ⊕ *www.artspiral.org* ☛ *Free* ☼ *Mon.–Wed.*

14

and Fri. 12:30–6:30, Thurs. 12:30–7:30 Ⓜ*6, J, M, N, Q, R, W, Z to Canal St.*

Chelsea Art Museum. In a former Christmas ornament factory, this contemporary art museum was created to display a collection of postwar European art and to host traveling exhibitions from European museums. Exhibits examine relatively unexplored dimensions of 20th- and 21st-century art, as well as display the work of French abstract painter Jean Miotte. ✉*556 W. 22nd St., at 11th Ave., Chelsea* ☎*212/255–0719* ⊕*www.chelseaartmuseum.org* 🎫*$6* ☉*Tues., Wed., Fri., and Sat. noon–6; Thurs. noon–8* Ⓜ*C, E to 23rd St.*

☺ **Children's Museum of the Arts.** In this bi-level space a few blocks from Broadway, children ages 1 to 10 can amuse and educate themselves with various activities, including diving into a pool of colorful balls; playacting in costume; music making with real instruments; and art making, from computer art to old-fashioned painting, sculpting, and collage. ✉*182 Lafayette St., between Grand and Broome Sts., SoHo* ☎*212/941–9198* ⊕*www.cmany.org* 🎫*$8* ☉*Wed. and Fri.–Sun. noon–5, Thurs. noon–6* Ⓜ*6 to Spring St.*

☺ **Children's Museum of Manhattan.** In this five-story exploratorium, children ages 1 to 10 are invited to paint their own masterpieces, float boats down a "stream," and put on shows at a puppet theater. Art workshops, science programs, and storytelling sessions are held daily. ✉*212 W. 83rd St., between Broadway and Amsterdam Ave., Upper West Side* ☎*212/721–1234* ⊕*www.cmom.org* 🎫*$9* ☉*Tues.–Sun. 10–5* Ⓜ*1 to 86th St.*

China Institute Gallery. A pair of stone lions guards the doorway of this pleasant redbrick town house. The institute's gallery is open for two exhibitions each year (September–November and March–June). Recent exhibitions include a collection of Chinese shadow puppets. The gallery is closed on holidays and between exhibits. ✉*125 E. 65th St., between Lexington and Park Aves., Upper East Side* ☎*212/744–8181* ⊕*www. chinainstitute.org* 🎫*Gallery $5; free Tues. and Thurs. 6–8* ☉*Mon., Wed., Fri., and Sat. 10–5; Tues. and Thurs. 10–8* Ⓜ*6 to 68th St./Hunter College; F to 63rd St.-Lexington Ave.*

Dahesh Museum of Art. On view from the street is the chic, bazaarlike gift store, but downstairs are the elegant galleries filled with Orientalist and classicist works of 19th-century and early-20th-century European academic art. The vivid paintings idealize the human figure and are usually of historical, mythological, or religious subjects. The evolving collection features mostly French and British artists, including works by such painters as Bonheur, Bouguereau, and Gérôme, and sculptor Barye. The pricey Opaline café on the second floor has a great view over the avenue. ✉*580 Madison Ave., between E. 56th and E. 57th Sts., Midtown East* ☎*212/759–0606* ⊕*www.daheshmuseum.org* 🎫*$10* ☉*Tues.–Sun. 11–6* Ⓜ*N, R, W to 5th Ave-59th S.*

El Museo del Barrio. *El barrio* is Spanish for "the neighborhood" and the nickname for East Harlem, a largely Spanish-speaking Puerto Rican and Dominican community. The museum, on the edge of this neighborhood, focuses on Latin American and Caribbean art. The 8,000-object

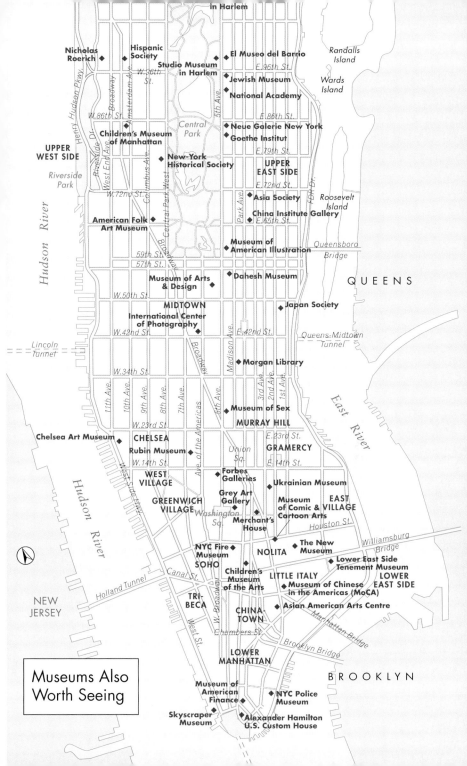

Museums Also Worth Seeing

permanent collection includes numerous pre-Columbian artifacts, sculpture, photography, film and video, and traditional art from all over Latin America. The collection of 360 *santos,* carved wooden folk-art figures from Puerto Rico, is a popular attraction. ⊠*1230 5th Ave., between E. 104th and E. 105th Sts., Upper East Side* ☎*212/831–7272* ⊕*www.elmuseo.org* ⬚*$6* ☉*Wed.–Sun. 11–5* Ⓜ*6 to 103rd St.*

☾ **Forbes Galleries.** Marvel at the idiosyncratic personal collection of the late publisher Malcolm Forbes, on view in the limestone Forbes Magazine Building. Those who like toys and flea-market finds (see the Trophies room), should definitely take a look at this small, personal museum. Military music is piped into the displays of warships and ocean liners. A tiny, dramatic diorama captures the adrenaline of the men on the gun deck of the HMS *Victory* during the Battle of Trafalgar. Of the 10,000 toy soldiers depicted in action, you'll see Aztecs resisting Cortez in 1521, Mussolini marching into Ethiopia in 1935, and a skirmish between "cowboys and Indians." ⊠*62 5th Ave., at E. 12th St., Greenwich Village* ☎*212/206–5548* ⊕*www.forbesgalleries. com* ⬚*Free* ☉*Tues.–Sat. 10–4* Ⓜ*L, N, Q, R, W, 4, 5, 6 to 14th St./ Union Sq.*

Goethe Institut. In a 1907 Beaux-Arts town house across from the Met, this German cultural center hosts lectures, films, and concerts; its extensive library includes German newspapers and periodicals. Look for work by young, cutting-edge German photographers and other artists in the gallery space. ⊠*1014 5th Ave., between E. 82nd and E. 83rd Sts., Upper East Side* ☎*212/439–8700* ⊕*www.goethe.de/newyork* ⬚*Exhibitions free* ☉*Library Tues. and Thurs. noon–7; Wed., Fri., and Sat. noon–5. Gallery weekdays 10–5* Ⓜ*4, 5, 6 to 86th St.*

Hispanic Society of America. This is the best collection of Spanish art outside the Prado in Madrid, with (primarily 15th- and 16th-century) paintings, sculptures, textiles, and decorative arts from Spain, Portugal, Italy, and South America. There are notable pieces by Goya, El Greco, and Velázquez. An entire room is filled with a collection of antique brass knockers. ⊠*Audubon Terr., Broadway, between W. 155th and W. 156th Sts., entrance up steps to left, Harlem* ☎*212/926–2234* ⊕*www. hispanicsociety.org* ⬚*Free* ☉*Sept.–July, Tues.–Sat. 10–4:30, Sun. 1–4* Ⓜ*1 to 157th St.*

International Center of Photography (ICP). Founded in 1974 by photojournalist Cornell Capa (photographer Robert Capa's brother), this leading photography museum and school has a permanent collection focused on American and European documentary photography of the 1930s to the 1990s. Changing exhibits display work by famous and should-be-famous photographers and theme group shows on topics such as ecology, health, religion, science, war, and candid street shots. The gift shop offers amazing imagery on postcards, posters, and prints, and outstanding photography books. ⊠*1133 6th Ave., at W. 43rd St., Midtown West* ☎*212/857–0000* ⊕*www.icp.org* ⬚*$12* ☉*Tues.–Thurs. and weekends 10–6, Fri. 10–8* Ⓜ*B, D, F, V to 42nd St.*

Japan Society. The stylish and serene lobby of the Japan Society has interior bamboo gardens linked by a second-floor waterfall. Works by well-known Japanese artists are exhibited in the second-floor gallery—past shows have included the first-ever retrospective of Yoko Ono's works and "Hiroshi Sugimoto: History of History." ✉️ *333 E. 47th St., between 1st and 2nd Aves., Midtown East* ☎️ *212/832–1155* ⊕ *www.japansociety.org* 💲*$12* ⊗ *Building weekdays 9:30–5:30. Gallery Tues.–Thurs. 11–6, Fri. 11–9, weekends 11–5* Ⓜ️ *6 to 51st St./Lexington Ave.; E, V to Lexington–3rd Aves./53rd St.*

Jewish Museum. Within a Gothic-style 1908 mansion, the museum draws on a large collection of art and ceremonial objects to explore Jewish identity and culture. The two-floor permanent exhibition, "Culture and Continuity: The Jewish Journey" displays nearly 800 objects. The wide-ranging collection includes a 3rd-century Roman burial plaque, 20th-century sculpture by Elie Nadelman, and contemporary art. ✉️ *1109 5th Ave., at E. 92nd St., Upper East Side* ☎️ *212/423–3200* ⊕ *www.jewishmuseum.org* 💲*$12; Sat. free all day* ⊗ *Sat.–Wed. 11–5:45, Thurs. 11–8* Ⓜ️ *6 to 96th St.*

🕙 **Lower East Side Tenement Museum.** Step back in time and into the partially restored 1863 tenement building at 97 Orchard Street, where you can squeeze through the preserved apartments of immigrants on one of five one-hour tours. This is America's first urban living-history museum dedicated to the life of immigrants—and one of the city's most underrated and overlooked. "Getting By" visits the homes of Natalie Gumpertz, a German-Jewish dressmaker (dating from 1878) and Adolph and Rosaria Baldizzi, Catholic immigrants from Sicily (1935). "Piecing it Together" visits the Levines' garment shop/apartment and the Rogarshevsky family from Eastern Europe (1918). The tour through the Confino family apartment is designed for children, who are greeted by a costumed interpreter playing Victoria Confino. Her family of Sephardic Jews came from Kastoria, Turkey, which is now part of Greece (1916). Another tour explores the life of the Moores, an Irish American family in the 1800s. Building tours are limited to 15 people so consider buying tickets in advance. Select tours are followed by free one-hour discussions with snacks provided. Walking tours of the neighborhood are also held regularly. The visitor information center and excellent gift shop displays a video with interviews of Lower East Side residents past and present. An antiques shop at 90 Orchard Street further benefits the museum. ✉️ *108 Orchard St., between Delancey and Broome Sts., Lower East Side* ☎️ *212/431–0233* ⊕ *www.tenement.org* 💲*Tenement and walking tours $17* ⊗ *Tenement tours leave in 40-min intervals, Tues.–Fri. 1–4:45, weekends 11–5; check Web site for full details. Confino apartment tour weekends, hourly noon–3. Walking tours Apr.–Dec., weekends 1 and 3. Visitor center and gift shop Mon. 11–5:30, Tues.–Fri. 11–6, weekends 10:45–6* Ⓜ️ *B, D to Grand St.; F to Delancey St.; J, M, Z to Essex St.*

🕙 **Merchant's House Museum.** Built in 1832, this redbrick house, combining Federal and Greek Revival styles, provides a glimpse into the family life of that era. Retired merchant Seabury Tredwell and his descendants lived here from 1835 until it became a museum in 1933. The original furnishings and architectural features remain intact; family memorabilia are also on display. Self-guided tour brochures are always available, and guided tours are given on weekends. Kids under 12 get in free. ✉ *29 E. 4th St., between Bowery and Lafayette St., East Village* ☎ *212/777–1089* ⊕ *www.merchantshouse.org* 💲 *$8* ⊙ *Thurs.–Mon. noon–5* Ⓜ *6 to Astor Pl. or Bleecker St.; B, D, F, V to Broadway– Lafayette St.; R, W to 8th St.*

Morgan Library. The treasures inside this museum, gathered by John Pierpont Morgan (1837–1913), one of New York's wealthiest financiers, are exceptional: medieval and Renaissance illuminated manuscripts, old-master drawings and prints, rare books, and autographed literary and musical manuscripts. Architect Renzo Piano's redesign of the museum was unveiled in April 2006. The original Renaissance-style building (1906) by Charles McKim of McKim, Mead & White has been preserved, but now there's twice the gallery space, an enlarged auditorium, and two cafés. Crowning achievements produced on paper, from the Middle Ages to the 20th century, are on view here: letters penned by John Keats and Thomas Jefferson; a summary of the theory of relativity in Einstein's own elegant handwriting; three Gutenberg Bibles; drawings by Dürer, Leonardo da Vinci, Rubens, Blake, and Rembrandt; the only known manuscript fragment of Milton's *Paradise Lost;* Thoreau's journals; and original manuscripts and letters by Charlotte Brontë, Jane Austen, Thomas Pynchon, and many others.

The library shop is within an 1852 Italianate brownstone, once the home of Morgan's son, J. P. Morgan Jr. Outside on East 36th Street, the sphinx in the right-hand sculptured panel of the original library's facade was rumored to wear the face of architect Charles McKim. ✉ *225 Madison Ave., at 36th St., Murray Hill* ☎ *212/685–0610* ⊕ *www.morganlibrary.org* 💲 *$12* ⊙ *Tues.–Fri. 10:30–5, weekends 11–6* Ⓜ *B, D, F, N, Q, R, V, W to 34th St./Herald Sq.; 6 to 33rd St.*

Museum of American Finance. This Smithsonian Institution affiliate has made it big on Wall Street: in early 2006 it moved from a room in the Standard Oil Building on Broadway to the grandiose former banking hall of the Bank of New York. On view are artifacts of the financial market's history, a replica ticker-tape machine that will print out your name, and well-executed temporary exhibits. ✉ *48 Wall St., at William St., Lower Manhattan* ☎ *212/908–4110* ⊕ *www.financialhistory.org* 💲 *$2* ⊙ *Tues.–Sat. 10–4* Ⓜ *2, 3 to Wall St.*

Museum of American Illustration. Founded in 1901, the museum of the Society of Illustrators presents its annual "Oscars," a juried, international competition, from February to May. The best in children's book illustrations is featured every November. In between are eclectic exhibitions on everything from cartoons to Norman Rockwell paintings. ✉ *128 E. 63rd St., between Lexington and Park Aves., Upper East Side* ☎ *212/838–2560* ⊕ *www.societyillustrators.org* 💲 *Free* ⊙ *Tues. 10–8, Wed.–Fri. 10–5, Sat. noon–4* Ⓜ *F to 63rd St.; 4, 5, 6, N, R, W to 59th St./Lexington Ave.*

Museum of Arts and Design. In a whimsical building right next door to the Time-Warner center, the Museum of Art and Design celebrates joyful quirkiness and personal, sometimes even obsessive, artistic visions. The art is human-scale here, much of it neatly housed in display cases rather than on the walls, with a strong focus on contemporary jewelry, glass, ceramic, fiber, wood, and mixed-media works. Recent exhibits included "Second Lives: Remixing the Ordinary," which showcased 50 contemporary artists' works made with found objects such as telephone books, gun triggers, coins, tires, and spools of thread and "Elegant Armor: The Art of Jewelry," which showed pieces made with virtually everything and anything—from precious metals to pig intestines. Thursday is a good time to drop by; the admission is pay-what-you-wish. ⊠*2 Columbus Circle , 59th St. at 8th Ave., Midtown* ☎*212/299–7777* ⊕ *www.madmuseum.org* ✉*$15* ⊘ *Wed.–Sun. 11 AM–6 PM, Thurs. 11–9* Ⓜ*A, B, C, D, 1 to Columbus Circle/59th St.; N, Q, R, W to 57th St./7th Ave.; F to 57th St. /6th Ave.*

Museum of Chinese in the Americas (MoCA). The only East Coast museum dedicated to the history of the Chinese people, MoCA moved in early 2009 to its new home on Centre street. The current 14,000-square-foot gallery space increased the size of the museum by more than five times. Designed by Maya Lin, architect of the Vietnam Veterans Memorial in Washington, D.C. MoCa features a permanent exhibit on Chinese-American history, "The Chinese American Experience," which includes artworks, personal and domestic artifacts, and historical documentation. Slippers for binding feet, Chinese musical instruments, a reversible silk gown worn at a Cantonese opera performance, and antique business signs are some of the unique objects on display. Rotating shows such as The Chinatown Film Project, which presented short Chinatown-focused films by 10 New York City filmmakers, are on display in the second gallery. MoCA sponsors workshops, walking tours, lectures, and family events. ⊠ *211–215 Centre St. , between Grand and Howard Sts.,Chinatown* ☎*212/619–4785* ⊕*www.moca-nyc.org* ✉*$3* ⊘*Tues.–Thurs. and weekends noon–6, Fri. noon–7* Ⓜ*6, J, M, N, Q, R, W, Z to Canal St.*

Museum of Comic and Cartoon Art. Don't be put off by the uninspiring and small space, the Museum of Comic and Cartoon Art features smartly curated artist spotlights (such as Will Eisner, Todd McFarlane, and Kim Deitch) and genre exhibits. Recent shows included a retrospective of Saturday Morning Cartoons, which included a Smurf village along with the more predictable (but still swell) sketches, animation cells, videos, a horror-theme "Things That Go Bump…" review, modern fairy tales, and a comprehensive look at the history and future of independent comics. New shows are mounted frequently, but MOCCA's Web site tends to list only coming-very-soon shows, so don't worry if nothing seems to be happening while you're planning your trip; check the site a week or so before you arrive in the city to see what's scheduled. And stay on the lookout for MOCCA's annual Art Festival, a comic and cartoon bonanza typically in June. ⊠*594 Broadway, Suite 401, between W. Houston and Broome Sts., SoHo* ☎*212/254–3511* ⊕*www. moccany.org* ✉*$5* ⊘*Tues.–Sat. noon–5 (Thurs. noon–6).* Ⓜ*B, D, F, G to Broadway/Layfayette St.; N, R to Prince St.*

Museum of Sex. Ponder the profound history and cultural significance of sex while staring at vintage pornographic photos, Playboy bunny costumes, S&M paraphernalia, and silent movies. The subject matter is given serious curatorial treatment, though an alternative museum like this has to credit sex-product companies rather than foundations for sponsorship, and the gift shop preceding the galleries is full of fun sexual kitsch. On two floors, special exhibits and the permanent collection probe topics such as Japanese pornographic art from the 1700s or classic American pinup art. Evenings bring readings by cutting-edge authors and performance artists. No one under 18 is admitted, unless accompanied by an adult. ✉ *233 5th Ave., entrance on 27th St., Flatiron District* ☎ *212/689–6337* ⊕ *www.museumofsex.com* 💲 *$14.50* ⊗ *Sun.–Fri. 11–6:30, Sat. 11–8* Ⓜ *R, W to 28th St.*

National Academy. Since its founding in 1825, the academy has required each member elected to its museum and School of Fine Arts (the oldest art school in New York) to donate a representative work of art. This criterion produced a strong collection of 19th- and 20th-century American art, as members have included Mary Cassatt, Samuel F. B. Morse, Winslow Homer, Frank Lloyd Wright, Jacob Lawrence, I. M. Pei, Robert Rauschenberg, Maya Lin, Frank Gehry, and Red Grooms. The collection's home is a 19th-century mansion donated in 1940 by sculptor and academy member Anna Hyatt Huntington. Huntington's bronze, *Diana of the Chase* (1922), is in the academy's foyer. ✉ *1083 5th Ave., between E. 89th and E. 90th Sts., Upper East Side* ☎ *212/369–4880* ⊕ *www.nationalacademy.org* 💲 *$10* ⊗ *Wed. and Thurs. noon–5, Fri.–Sun. 11–6* Ⓜ *4, 5, 6 to 86th St.*

Neue Galerie New York. Early-20th-century German and Austrian art and design are the focus here, with Gustav Klimt, Wassily Kandinsky, Paul Klee, Egon Schiele, Josef Hoffman, and other designers from the Wiener Werkstätte. The Neue Galerie was founded by the late art dealer Serge Sabarsky and cosmetics heir and art collector Ronald S. Lauder. The two-floor gallery, Viennese-style café, and design shop are in a 1914 wood- and marble-floored mansion designed by Carrère and Hastings, which was home to Mrs. Cornelius Vanderbilt III. An audio guide is included with admission. Note that children under 12 are not admitted and teens 12–16 must be accompanied by an adult.

In an elegant, high-ceiling space below the Neue Galerie, **Café Sabarsky** serves Viennese coffee, cakes, strudels, and Sacher tortes (Monday and Wednesday 9–6, Thursday–Sunday 9–9). If you seek something more than a sugar fix, the savory menu includes trout crepes and Hungarian goulash. ✉ *1048 5th Ave., at E. 86th St., Upper East Side* ☎ *212/628–6200* ⊕ *www.neuegalerie.org* 💲 *$15* ☞ *Children under 12 not admitted* ⊗ *Sat.–Mon. and Thurs. 11–6, Fri. 11–9* Ⓜ *4, 5, 6 to 86th St.*

The New Museum. Focused on contemporary art, the New Museum moved to 235 Bowery in late 2007, marking the first time in its 30 years of existence that the institution has had its very own building. It's also the first building in downtown Manhattan constructed from the ground up with the purpose of being a museum. The seven-story, 60,000-square-foot structure—a glimmering metal mesh-clad assemblage of off-centered squares—was designed by avant-garde architects Kazuyo Sejima and Ryue Nishizawa. Previous exhibits include the annual "Altoids Curiously Strong Collection," a yearly survey of emerging artists, and shows on computer hacking and life inside "the grid" of modern society. Be sure to run up to the seventh-floor "sky room" for a twirl around the panoramic balcony above Lower Manhattan. ✉*235 Bowery, at Prince St., Lower Manhattan* ☎*212/219–1222* ⊕*www.newmuseum.org* 🎫*$12* ⊙ *Wed., Sat., and Sun. noon–6; Thurs. and Fri. noon–10* Ⓜ*6 to Spring St.; F, V to 2nd Ave.*

New York City Fire Museum. In the former headquarters of Engine 30, a handsome Beaux-Arts building dating from 1904, retired firefighters volunteer their time to answer visitors' questions. The collection of fire-fighting tools from the 18th century to the present includes hand-pulled and horse-drawn engines, pumps, and uniforms. A memorial exhibit with photos, paintings, children's artwork, and found objects relating to the September 11 attacks is also on view. On 9/11, the city's fire department lost 343 members at the World Trade Center. The museum is two subway stops (via the E train) north of the Ground Zero site. ✉*278 Spring St., near Varick St., SoHo* ☎*212/691–1303* ⊕*www. nycfiremuseum.org* 🎫*$5 suggested donation* ⊙*Tues.–Sat. 10–5, Sun. 10–4* Ⓜ*C, E to Spring St.*

New York City Police Museum. Why are police called cops? Why does a police badge have eight points? When was fingerprinting first used to solve a crime? Find the answers at this museum dedicated to New York's finest. The force's history from colonial times through the present is covered through permanent and rotating exhibits. A permanent exhibit, "9/11 Remembered," includes a video with interviews with those who were first responders to the attack. The Hall of Heroes honors police officers who have fallen in the line of duty. Special events include a vintage police car show the first weekend in June, and the first Saturday in October, when kids get to meet police officers and events take place. ✉*100 Old Slip, near South St., Lower Manhattan* ☎*212/480–3100* ⊕*www.nycpolicemuseum.org* 🎫*$5 suggested donation* ⊙*Mon.–Sat. 10–5* Ⓜ*2, 3 to Wall St.*

New-York Historical Society. Manhattan's oldest museum, founded in 1804, has one of the city's finest research libraries and a collection of 6 million pieces of art, literature, and memorabilia. Special exhibitions shed light on New York's—and America's—history, art, and architecture. Major exhibits have included Hudson River School landscapes and an examination of New York City's role in the slavery debate and the Civil War. Unlike other museums that keep much of their collections in storage, virtually all of the museum's huge and eclectic permanent collection—ranging from 19th-century cockroach traps to the armchair that George Washington sat in during his inaugural ceremony—are displayed in glass shelves in the museum's Henry Luce III Center for the Study of American Culture. It's a bit of a jumble but you're bound to stumble across many wonderful things. ✉*2 W. 77th St., at Central Park W, Upper West Side* ☎*212/873–3400* ⊕*www.nyhistory.org* 🎫*$10* ⊙*Tues.–Thurs. and weekends 10–6, Fri. 10–8* Ⓜ*B, C to 81st St.*

Nicholas Roerich Museum. An 1898 Upper West Side town house contains this small, eccentric museum dedicated to the work of Russian artist Nicholas Roerich, who immigrated to New York in the 1920s and quickly developed an ardent following. Some 200 of his paintings hang here—notably some vast canvases of the Himalayas. Free chamber music concerts are held here most Sunday afternoons at 5, except in summer. ⊠ *319 W. 107th St., between Broadway and Riverside Dr., Morningside Heights* ☎*212/864–7752* ⊕*www.roerich.org* ✉*By donation* ۞ *Tues.–Sun. 2–5* Ⓜ*1 to 110th St./Cathedral Pkwy.*

Rubin Museum of Art. Opened in 2004, this sleek and serene museum is the first in the western hemisphere dedicated to art of the Himalayas. It provides a great deal of the explanation for the colorful works, which are religious and rich with symbols. Six floors contain paintings on cloth, metal sculptures, and textiles dating from the 12th century onward. The works from areas such as Tibet, Nepal, southwest China, and India are all related to Buddhism, Hinduism, or the Bon religions. A pleasant café and gift shop are on the ground floor. ⊠ *150 W. 17th St., near 7th Ave., Chelsea* ☎*212/620–5000* ⊕*www.rmanyc.org* ✉*$10* ۞ *Mon. and Thurs. 11–5, Wed. 11–7, Fri. 11–10, weekends 11–6* Ⓜ*1 to 18th St.*

Skyscraper Museum. This small museum will either delight or disappoint skyscraper fans. To evoke space, the stainless-steel floor and ceiling are polished to mirror quality, but the open room with column partitions does not include a comprehensive overview of the rise of the skyscraper. Focused exhibits change every few months; on permanent view is the daily photo journal a contractor kept during the Empire State Building's construction. Models of current or future buildings; short videos; and exhibits that reveal the influence of history, real estate, and individuals on architecture are regular features. ⊠ *39 Battery Pl., Battery Park City, Lower Manhattan* ☎*212/968–1961* ⊕*www.skyscraper.org* ✉*$5* ۞ *Wed.–Sun. noon–6* Ⓜ*4, 5 to Bowling Green.*

Studio Museum in Harlem. Contemporary art by African-American, Caribbean, and African artists is the focus of this small museum with a light-filled sculpture garden. Its changing exhibits have included "Black Artists and Abstraction" and "Africa Comics." Three artists in residence present their works each year. ⊠ *144 W. 125th St., between Lenox Ave. and Adam Clayton Powell Jr. Blvd., Harlem* ☎*212/864–4500* ⊕*www.studiomuseuminharlem.org* ✉*$7 suggested donation* ۞ *Wed.–Fri. and Sun. noon–6, Sat. 10–6* Ⓜ*2, 3 to 125th St.*

Ukrainian Museum. Folk art, fine art, and documentary materials addressing the life of Ukrainians in the Americas make up the permanent collection. Ceramics, jewelry, hundreds of brilliantly colored Easter eggs, and an extensive collection of Ukrainian costumes and textiles are the highlights. ⊠ *222 E. 6th St., between 2nd and 3rd Aves., East Village* ☎*212/228–0110* ⊕*www.ukrainianmuseum.org* ✉*$8* ۞ *Wed.–Sun. 11:30–5* Ⓜ*6 to Astor Pl.*

The Performing Arts

WORD OF MOUTH

"We would like to see at least 1 Broadway show anytime throughout our stay...Can anyone provide more specific details of good
seating?"
—invinciblesummer

"I'm a big believer that front row mezzanine is the best row for most
musicals in most theaters."
—NeoPatrick

Updated by
Lynne Arany

"Which restaurant?" is the legendary cruel question you might ask a New Yorker if he identifies himself to you as an actor. The beauty of that scenario is that most of our actors are tough enough to tell you which one they wait at without missing a beat. And if you're a performer here, you had better be tough, and competitive: thousands of actors, singers, dancers, musicians, and other artists infuse the city and its cultural scene with unparalleled crackling energy. Just as tough are the audiences, many out-of-towners, many discerning local patrons who help drive the arts scene as they strive to keep up with the latest—from flocking to a concert hall to hear a world-class soprano deliver a flawless performance to crowding into a cramped café to support young writers floundering through their own prose.

New York has somewhere between 200 and 250 legitimate (aka, with theatrical performances, not movies or pornography) theaters, and many more ad hoc venues—parks, churches, lofts, galleries, rooftops, even parking lots. The city is also a revolving door of special events: summer jazz, one-act-play marathons, film festivals, and music and dance celebrations from the classical to the avant-garde, to name just a few. It's this unrivaled wealth of culture and art that many New Yorkers cite as the reason why they're here and the reason why many millions more say they're visiting here.

TICKETS 101

What do tickets sell for, anyway? Not counting the limited "premium seat" category (or discount deals), the top ticket price for Broadway musicals is now hovering at $130; the low end for musicals is in the $70 range. Nonmusical comedies and dramas start at about $60 and top out at about $120. Off-Broadway show tickets average $35–$70, while off-off-Broadway shows can run as low as $15–$20. Tickets to an opera start at about $25 for nosebleed seats and can soar to well over $300 for prime locations. Classical music concerts go for $25 to $100, depending on the venue. Dance performances are usually in the $15 to $60 range, but expect seats for the ballet to go higher.

Scoring tickets is fairly easy, especially if you have some flexibility. But if timing or cost is critical, the only way to ensure you'll get the seats you want is to make your purchase in advance—and that might be months ahead for a hit show. In general, tickets for Saturday evenings and for weekend matinees are the toughest to secure.

For opera, classical music, and dance performances, go to the box office or order tickets through the venue's Web site. For smaller performing-arts companies, including dance, music, and off-Broadway shows, also try **Ticket Central** (☎212/279–4200 ⊕*www.ticketcentral. com*). For Broadway (and some other big-hall events), sure bets are the box office or either **Telecharge** (☎212/239–6200, 800/432–7250 outside NYC ⊕*www.telecharge.com*) or **Ticketmaster** (☎212/307–4100, 866/448–7849 *automated service, 212/220–0500 premium tickets* ⊕*www.ticketmaster.com*). Virtually all larger shows are listed with one service or the other, but never both; specifying "premium" will help you get elusive—and expensive (upwards of $200–$300)—seats. A broker or your hotel concierge should be able to procure last-minute tickets, but prices may even exceed "premium" rates. Be prepared to pay add-on fees (per ticket *and* per order) for all ticketing services.

■TIP➜Although most online ticket services provide seating maps to help you choose, the advantage of going to the box office is twofold: there are no add-on service fees, and a ticket seller can personally advise you about sight lines for the seat location you are considering.

If you're in Midtown, inside the Times Square Visitors Center is the League of American Theatres and Producers' **Broadway Ticket Center** (✉*1560 Broadway, between W. 46th and W. 47th Sts. Midtown West* ☎*888/BROADWAY* ⊕*www.livebroadway.com* Ⓜ*1, 2, 3, 7, N, Q, R, W, S to 42nd St./Times Sq.; N, R, W to 49th St.*). Ticket hours are Monday–Saturday 10–7, Sunday 11–6. You can find a selection of discount vouchers here; it also serves as a one-stop shopping place for full-price tickets for most Broadway shows.

BROADWAY (AND OFF) AT A DISCOUNT

The cheapest—though chanciest—ticket opportunities are found at participating theater box offices on the day of the performance. These tickets, usually about $25, may be distributed by lottery and are usually for front-row (possibly neck-craning) seats. Check the box office or the *Times*'s theater directory to discover current shows offering this kind of deal, or similarly priced "rush" offers. Obstructed-view seats or those in the very rear balcony are sometimes available for advance purchasing; the price point on these is usually in the $35–40 range.

What's Playing Where

New York is rich with easily accessible and comprehensive listings resources in both print and online formats. The *New York Times*'s (*www.nytimes.com*) listings are concentrated in its Thursday, Friday, and Sunday papers, as well as online. *The New Yorker* (*www.newyorker.com*) is highly selective, but calls attention to performances with its succinct reviews. It hits the stands on Monday. In *New York* magazine (*www.nymag.com*), also on newsstands on Monday, see "The Week" section for hot-ticket events. The freebie tabloid the *Village Voice* (*www.villagevoice.com*), comes out on Wednesday; it has extensive listings—especially for theater, music, and dance—as well.

Online-only venues *www.nytheatre.com*, *www.nyconstage.org*, *www.tdf.org*, *indietheater.org*, and *offoffonline.com* provide synopses, schedules when theaters are dark, accessibility info, run times, seating charts, and links to ticket purchases. (Tip: most of these also cover nontheater performances, but they do Broadway and independent theater programming best.)

But for advanced discount purchases, the best seating is likely available by using an discount "code"—procure these 20%–50%-off codes online (you will need to register on each Web site). The ⊕*www.broadwaybox.com* site provides a compilation of all discount codes available; ⊕*bestofoffbroadway.com* does the same, but concentrates on the smaller shows off the Great White Way. In some cases, as with all discount codes offered through the online subscriber services **TheaterMania** (⊕*www.theatermania.com*) and **Playbill** (⊕*www.playbill.com*), you must bring a printout of the offer to the box office, and make your purchase there.

For seats at 25%–50% off the usual price go to one of the **TKTS booths** (✉*Duffy Sq. at W. 47th St. and Broadway, Midtown West* Ⓜ*1, 2, 3, 7, N, Q, R, S, W to 42nd St./Times Sq.; N, R, W to 49th St.; 1 to 50th St.* ✉*South St. Seaport at Front and John Sts., Lower Manhattan* Ⓜ*2, 3, 4, 5, A, C, E, J, M, Z to Fulton St./Broadway-Nassau* ✉*Downtown Brooklyn, at the Myrtle St. Promenade and Jay St., Brooklyn* Ⓜ*A, C, F to Jay St.-Borough Hall; M, R, 2, 3, 4, 5 to Court St.-Borough Hall* ⊕*www.tdf.org*). Although they do tack on a $4 per ticket service charge, and not all shows are predictably available, the broad choices and ease of selection—and of course, the solid discount—make TKTS the go-to source for the flexible theatergoer. Check the electronic listings board near the ticket windows to mull over your options while you're on line. At the snazzily updated Duffy Square location (look for the bright red glass staircase), there is a separate *play only* window to further simplify, and speed, things. Duffy hours are Monday–Saturday 3–8 (for evening performances); for Wednesday and Saturday matinees 10–2; for Sunday matinees 11–3; Sunday evening shows, from 3 until a half hour before curtain. Seaport hours are Monday–Saturday 11–6, Sunday 11–4. Brooklyn hours are weekdays 11–6. With the exception of matinees at the Seaport and Brooklyn locations (they sell these for next-day performances only), all shows offered are for that same day. Credit cards, cash, or traveler's checks are accepted *at all locations.* ■TIP➜Planning ahead? Their Web site lists what was available at the booths in the previous week to give you an idea of what shows you'll find; and for all current shows, it notes whether they are "frequently," "occasionally," "rarely," or "never" available at their booths.

THEATER

Broadway—not the Statue of Liberty or even the Empire State Building—is the city's number-one tourist attraction. Sure there's blaring neon, but it is the fabulously restored historic theaters—and the popular productions within them—that draw most folks to the bedazzling showtime nexus at Times Square and 42nd Street. And to fully experience theater in New York, you'll also want to consider the many offerings outside this area. From a splashy musical to an austere performance piece, from the Battery to the Bronx, New York has shows for every taste and budget—on just about any night (or day) of the week.

15

BROADWAY

Even if you're just a legend in your own mind, there's nothing quite like making your own grand entrance at a show on the Great White Way. As you find your seat, the anticipation starts to rise; you sit, the houselights dim, and the orchestra strikes up the first notes of the overture, filling the theater with excitement. There is no other experience like it and no visit to the city—at least your first or second visit—is really complete if you haven't seen a Broadway show (or three). So secure your tickets, settle in, and prepare to be transported.

Some of the 39 Broadway theaters are just as interesting for their history as for their current productions. The onetime Selwyn—the venerable home to the works of Coward, Kaufman, and Porter in their heyday—is now known as the **American Airlines Theatre** (⊠227 W. 42nd St., between 7th and 8th Aves., Midtown West ☎212/719–1300 ⊕www.round-abouttheatre.org Ⓜ1, 2, 3, 7, N, Q, R, W, S to 42nd St./Times Sq.; A, C, E to 42nd St./Port Authority). After incarnations as a burlesque hall and pornographic movie house, this splendidly restored 1918 Venetian-style playhouse is now home to the Roundabout Theatre Company, which is acclaimed for its revivals of classic musicals and plays, such as a Doug Hughes–directed production of *A Man for All Seasons.* The **Ethel Barrymore Theatre** (⊠243 W. 47th St., between Broadway and 8th Ave., Midtown West ☎212/239–6200 ⊕www.shubertorganization. com Ⓜ1, 2, 3, 7, N, Q, R, W, S to 42nd St./Times Sq.; C, E to 50th St.) was that rare Broadway house that stayed legit throughout the Depression and still honors its original namesake. The 1928 Elizabethan wonder greets theatergoers with two stone archways. Shows within have included David Rabe's original *Hurly Burly* in 1984, and the innovative revival of Sondheim's *Company* in 2006. Disney refurbished the elaborate 1903 art nouveau **New Amsterdam Theater** (⊠214 W. 42nd St., between 7th and 8th Aves., Midtown West☎212/282–2907 Ⓜ1, 2, 3,

7, N, Q, R, W, S to 42nd St./Times Sq.; A, C, E to 42nd St./Port Authority), where Eddie Cantor, Will Rogers, Fanny Brice, and the Ziegfeld Follies once drew crowds. *The Lion King* ruled here for the first nine years of its run. Moorish Revival in style, the **St. James** (⌧*246 W. 44th St., between Broadway and 8th Ave., Midtown West* ☎*212/269–6300* Ⓜ*1, 2, 3, 7, N, Q, R, W, S to 42nd St./Times Sq.; A, C, E to 42nd St./Port Authority*) went up in 1927, and has been running legit at least since the late 1930s. Home of Mel Brooks's juggernaut *The Producers* in its heyday, and where a Tony-laden revival of *Gypsy* held sway late in the first decade of the 21st century, the St. James is where Lauren Bacall was an usherette in the '40s and where a little show called *Oklahoma!* premiered, and, with its rousing score and choreography, changed the musical forever.

OFF-BROADWAY THEATERS

Off-Broadway houses—defined by seat count, not the theater's proximity to Broadway's Times Square nexus—are where you can find showcases for emerging playwrights, unexpected stagings of classic plays, and perennial crowd-pleasers like *Blue Man Group*. The venues themselves are found throughout the city—clustering below 14th Street, these shows indeed play in the Times Square area as well as in parts of Brooklyn.

At the cozy 178-seat theater belonging to the **Classic Stage Company** (⌧*136 E. 13th St., between 3rd and 4th Aves., East Village* ☎*212/677–4210* ⊕*www.classicstage.org* Ⓜ*4, 5, 6, L, N, Q, R, W to Union Sq.*) you can see revivals—such as Chekhov's *Three Sisters* or Shakespeare's *The Tempest*—perhaps with a modern spin, and often with reigning theatrical stars.

The **New York Theater Workshop (NYTW)** (⌧*79 E. 4th St., between Bowery and 2nd Ave., East Village* ☎*212/460–5475* ⊕*www.nytw.org* Ⓜ*F, V to 2nd Ave.; B, D, F, V to Broadway–Lafayette St.; 6 to Bleecker St.*) produces work by new and established playwrights. Tony Kushner's *Homebody Kabul* premiered at NYTW, and Jonathan Larson's *Rent* got its pre-Broadway start here. Hit the box office for Sunday night "CheapTix"; those seats are $20, as available.

Playwrights Horizons (⌧*416 W. 42nd St., between 9th and 10th Aves., Midtown West* ☎*212/564–1235, 212/279–4200 tickets* ⊕*www.playwrightshorizons.org* Ⓜ*A, C, E to 42nd St./Port Authority*) shows productions ranging from the debut of the acclaimed Broadway musical *Grey Gardens* to Pulitzer Prize winners such as Wendy Wasserstein's *The Heidi Chronicles* and the latest work from Craig Lucas. The **Public Theater** (⌧*425 Lafayette St., south of Astor Pl., East Village* ☎*212/260–2400* ⊕*www.publictheater.org* Ⓜ*6 to Astor Pl.; R, W to 8th St.*) presents fresh theater like the work of Suzan-Lori Parks, a 2008 Stephen Sondheim debut, *Road Show,* and monologuist Mike Daisey's *If You See Something Say Something*. Many noted productions that began here (*Hair, A Chorus Line*) went on to Broadway. In summer you won't want to miss their incomparable—and free—Shakespeare in the Park performances.

Signature Theatre Company (✉*Peter Norton Space, 555 W. 42nd St., between 10th and 11th Aves., Midtown West* ☎*212/244–7529* ⊕*www.signaturetheatre.org* Ⓜ*A, C, E to 42nd St./Port Authority*) devotes each season to works by a single playwright (August Wilson, Lanford Wilson, and Sam Shepard among them), or an entire tradition, such as—in 2008–09—the seminal works of the Negro Ensemble Company. Twenty-dollar tickets are the norm. In 2005 a revival of *Hurly Burly* inaugurated the **37 Arts** (✉*450 W. 37th St., between 9th and 10th Aves., Garment District* ☎*212/560–8912* ⊕*www.37arts.net* Ⓜ*A, C, E to 34th St./Penn Station*) complex. Encompassing the **Baryshnikov Arts Center (BAC)**, the stages in development here are expected to be put to good use by the genre-stretching Elizabeth LeCompte-directed collective the Wooster Group, for a regular segment of their annual season, starting as early as 2009.

OFF-OFF BROADWAY AND PERFORMANCE ART

15

The following theaters are all small—even tiny—but host works that are often startling in their originality; expect their shows to stretch the boundaries of what's found on Broadway *and* off-Broadway.

HERE Arts Center (✉*145 6th Ave., between Spring and Broome Sts., SoHo* ☎*212/352–3101* ⊕*www.here.org* Ⓜ*C, E to Spring St.*), the original home to Eve Ensler's 1997 Obie winner *The Vagina Monologues*, 2007's lauded *Removable Parts*, and all manner of genre-bending productions, also has an art gallery and café. **The Kitchen** (✉*512 W. 19th St., between 10th and 11th Aves., Chelsea* ☎*212/255–5793* ⊕*www.thekitchen.org* Ⓜ*C, E to 23rd St.*) is *the* place for multimedia performance art. Ellen Stewart, also known as La Mama, founded **La Mama E.T.C.** (✉*74A E. 4th St., between Bowery and 2nd Ave., East Village* ☎*212/475–7710* ⊕*www.lamama.org* Ⓜ*F, V to 2nd Ave.; B, D, F, V to Broadway–Lafayette St.; 6 to Bleecker St.*) in a tiny basement space in 1961. It's grown now, and her influential "Experimental Theater Club" continues to support new works that cross cultures and performance disciplines.

★ **Performance Space 122 (P.S. 122)** (✉*150 1st Ave., at E. 9th St., East Village* ☎*212/477–5288, 212/352–3101 tickets* ⊕*www.ps122.org* Ⓜ*6 to Astor Pl.*), housed in a former public school, has nurtured talent like Karen Finley, Spalding Gray, and Eric Bogosian, and offers a dazzling repertoire of performance from the fringe.

Fodor'sChoice ★ **St. Ann's Warehouse** (✉*38 Water St., between Main and Dock Sts., DUMBO, Brooklyn* ☎*718/254–8779* ⊕*stannswarehouse.org* Ⓜ*A, C to High St.; F to York St.*) hosts everything from the National Theatre of Scotland's evisceration of war, *Black Watch*, to the Tiger Lillies, and is also a regular home for the Wooster Group's larger productions—such as their 2009 opera, *La Didone*.

A four-theater cultural complex, **Theater for the New City** (✉*155 1st Ave., between E. 9th and E. 10th Sts., East Village* ☎*212/254–1109* ⊕*www.theaterforthenewcity.net* Ⓜ*6 to Astor Pl.*) puts on 30–40 new American plays each year, including works by Moises Kaufman and Mabou Mines. Housed in a onetime factory, the **Zipper Theater** (✉*336 W. 37th*

Three Tips for Doing Broadway Better

Whether you're handing over a hundred bucks for a top ticket or shoestringing it in a nosebleed seat, seeing one show or seven, you'll have better Broadway experiences to brag about if you take our advice.

Reserve ahead. The TKTS booth is great when you're up for what the fates make available, but for must-sees, we recommend booking early. While you're at it, don't forget to ask whether the regular cast is expected (an in-person stop at the box office is the most reliable way to score this information ahead, but don't hold them to it unless it's the day-of-performance. If there is a change then—and the replacement cast is not acceptable to you—you may get a refund). For musicals, live music will always add a special zing; confirm when ticketing to avoid surprises on the rare occasion when recorded music is used.

Know your seats. Know that Front Mezzanine is a great option; with seats that overhang the stage, they can be better than many Orchestra locations. Always book with a seating chart at hand (available online and at the box office); although even the priciest seats might be tight, it is always worth splurging for the best sight lines. Check accessibility, especially at older theaters with multiple flights of stairs and scarce elevators.

Know when to go. Surprisingly, Friday evening is a good option; Saturday night and weekday matinees are the most difficult. Do like the locals and go on weeknights. Tuesday is especially promising, and typically an earlier curtain—7 or 7:30 instead of the usual 8 PM—helps ensure you'll get a good night's sleep for your next day of touring.

St, between 8th and 9th Aves., Garment District ☎212/352–3101 ⊕ www.zippertheater.com Ⓜ A, C, E to 34th St./Penn Station) is a congenial space given over to theater and performance events from searing monologues to burlesque.

THEATER FOR CHILDREN

★ **Just Kidding at Symphony Space** (✉ 2537 Broadway, at W. 95th St., Upper West Side ☎212/864–5400 ⊕ www.symphonyspace.org Ⓜ 1, 2, 3 to 96th St.) is a family series that has it all—musicals especially, but a nonstop parade of plays, sing-alongs, and puppets as well.

Fodor's Choice **The New Victory Theater** (✉ 209 W. 42nd St., between 7th and 8th ★ Aves., Midtown West ☎212/239–6200 ⊕ www.newvictory.org Ⓜ 1, 2, 3, 7, A, C, E, N, Q, R, W, S to 42nd St./Times Sq.) presents plays, music, and dance performances, and even minicircuses in a magnificently restored century-old theater. On weekends **the Paper Bag Players** (☎212/663–0390 ⊕ www.thepaperbagplayers.org), the country's oldest children's theater group, stage original—and exuberant—plays for youngsters under 10 at venues throughout the city. Finely detailed wooden marionettes and hand puppets are on the bill at **Puppetworks** (✉ 338 6th Ave., at 4th St., Park Slope, Brooklyn ☎718/965–3391 ⊕ www.puppetworks.org Ⓜ F to 7th Ave.). Familiar childhood tales like *Little Red Riding Hood* and *Peter and the Wolf* come to life in this 75-seat neighborhood theater.

The **Swedish Cottage Marionette Theater** (✉ *Swedish Cottage, W. Park Dr., north of W. 79th St., Central Park* ☎ *212/988–9093* ⊕ *www.cityparks-foundation.org or www.centralparknyc.org* Ⓜ *B, C to 81st St.*) was originally part of Sweden's exhibit at the 1876 Centennial Exposition in Philadelphia (park designer Frederick Law Olmsted had it moved here the following year). The charming wooden 100-seat (and now state-of-the-art) playhouse presents classics like *Hansel and Gretel* and *Cinderella.* **TADA!** (✉ *15 W. 28th St., between Broadway and 5th Ave., Chelsea* ☎ *212/252–1619* ⊕ *www.tadatheater.com* Ⓜ *1, 6, R, W to 28th St.*) presents vibrant musical theater pieces performed by children. Latino arts and culture are celebrated with a sly sense of humor at the **Teatro SEA @ Los Kabayitos Puppet & Children's Theater** (✉ *Clemente Soto Vélez Cultural & Educational Center, 107 Suffolk St., between Delancey and Rivington Sts., Lower East Side* ☎ *212/529–1545* ⊕ *www.sea-ny.org* Ⓜ *F to Delancey St.; J, M, Z to Essex St.*). All shows are presented in English and Spanish, and you may even see the *Three Little Pigs* dancing to salsa music.

Theatreworks/USA (✉ *Lucille Lortel Theatre, 121 Christopher St., between Hudson and Bleecker Sts., West Village* ☎ *800/497–5007, 212/279–4200 Ticket Central* ⊕ *www.theatreworksusa.org* Ⓜ *1 to Christopher St.*) offers a Family Series for ages four and over. Its original productions are based on popular children's books like *Henry and Mudge* and *Junie B. Jones.*

MUSIC

"Gentlemen," conductor Serge Koussevitzky once told the assembled Boston Symphony Orchestra, "maybe it's good enough for Cleveland or Cincinnati, but it's not good enough for New York." In a nutshell he described New York's central position in the musical world. New York has the country's oldest symphony orchestra (the New York Philharmonic) as well as three renowned conservatories (the Juilliard School, the Manhattan School of Music, and Mannes College of Music). For more than a century, the best orchestras have made this a principal stop on their tours. The city is also a mecca for an astonishing variety of musicians playing everything from early music to minimalism, klezmer to Senegalese percussion. In summer the city comes fully alive with the best music it has to offer—performed outdoors from river to river and throughout the five boroughs—often for free.

CONCERT HALLS

The **Brooklyn Academy of Music (BAM)** (✉ *Howard Gilman Opera House, Peter Jay Sharp Bldg., 30 Lafayette Ave., between Ashland Pl. and St. Felix St., Fort Greene, Brooklyn* ☎ *718/636–4100* ⊕ *www.bam.org* Ⓜ *2, 3, 4, 5, B, Q to Atlantic Ave.*) is the performing home of the **Brooklyn Philharmonic** (☎ *718/488–5700* ⊕ *www.brooklynphil harmonic.org*), which, under the direction of Michael Christie, has some of the most adventurous symphonic programming to be found in the city. The impressive acoustics here perfectly complement the Philharmonic and the wide selection of nontraditional musical programming featured here throughout the year.

Fodor'sChoice ★ ☺ **Carnegie Hall** (⊠ *881 7th Ave., at W. 57th St., Midtown West* ☎*212/247–7800* ⊕*www.carnegiehall.org* Ⓜ*N, Q, R, W to 57th St.; B, D, E to 7th Ave.*) is one of the best venues—anywhere—to hear classical music. The world's top orchestras sound so good because of the incomparable acoustics of the fabulously steep Stern Auditorium. So do smaller ensembles and soloists such as sopranos Renée Fleming and Deborah Voight. A noted roster of Family Concerts are also part of Carnegie's programming. The subterranean **Zankel Hall,** with equally excellent acoustics, attracts performers such as the Kronos Quartet, Nick Lowe, and Youssou N'Dour. Many young talents make their New York debuts in the **Weill Recital Hall.**

★ **Lincoln Center for the Performing Arts** (⊠ *W. 62nd to W. 66th Sts., Broadway to Amsterdam Ave., Upper West Side* ☎*212/546–2656* ⊕*www.lincolncenter.org* Ⓜ*1 to 66th St./Lincoln Center*) is the city's musical nerve center, especially when it comes to classical music. Formal and U-shape, the massive Avery Fisher Hall presents the world's great musicians, and is home to the **New York Philharmonic** (☎*212/875–5656* ⊕*newyorkphilharmonic.org*), one of the finest symphony orchestras. Lorin Maazel conducts from late September to early June. Bargain-price weeknight "rush hour" performances at 6:45 PM and Saturday matinee concerts at 2 PM are occasionally offered; orchestra rehearsals at 9:45 AM are open to the public on selected weekday mornings (usually Wednesday or Thursday) for $15. The **Chamber Music Society of Lincoln Center** (☎*212/875–5788* ⊕*www.chambermusicsociety.org*) performs in Alice Tully Hall, which is considered to be as acoustically perfect as a concert hall can get. In August Lincoln Center's longest-running classical series, the **Mostly Mozart Festival** (☎*212/875–5399*), captures the crowds.

15

OTHER VENUES

In Brooklyn, **Bargemusic** (⊠ *Fulton Ferry Landing, at Old Fulton and Furman Sts., Brooklyn Heights* ☎*718/624–2083* ⊕*www.bargemusic.org* Ⓜ*A, C to High St.; 2, 3 to Clark St.*) keeps chamber music groups busy year-round on a reoutfitted old barge with a fabulous view of the Manhattan skyline. Anything you come to hear at the **Cathedral of Saint John the Divine** (⊠ *Amsterdam Ave., at W. 112th St., Upper West Side* ☎ *212/280–0330 Early Music concerts, 212/316–7540 performances* ⊕*www.stjohndivine.org* Ⓜ*1, B, C to 110th St./Cathedral Pkwy.*) may be considered an unforgettable experience, but the programming of the resident **Early Music New York** (☎*212/749–6600* ⊕*www.earlymusicny.org)* ensemble is essential. **The Gatehouse** (⊠ *Harlem Stage, 150 Convent Ave. at W. 135th St., Hamilton Heights* ☎*212/281–9240* ⊕*www.harlemstage.org* Ⓜ*1 to 137th St.*) is an uptown venue for jazz, world music, and dance. The intimate 196-seater complements Harlem Stage's **Aaron Davis Hall** across the street.

Merkin Concert Hall (✉ *Kaufman Center, 129 W. 67th St., between Broadway and Amsterdam Ave., Upper West Side* ☎ *212/501–3330* ⊕ *www.kaufman-center.org* Ⓜ *1 to 66th St./Lincoln Center*), which was freshly refurbished for the 2008/09 season with the artful touch of architect Robert A.M. Stern, is a lovely, acoustically advanced 450-seater that presents chamber pieces; it's also a fine spot for jazz, world, and new music. In its Grace Rainey Rogers Auditorium (and occasionally in the Medieval Sculpture Hall and the Temple of Dendur) the **Metropolitan Museum of Art** (✉ *1000 5th Ave., at E. 82nd St., Upper East Side* ☎ *212/570–3949* ⊕ *www.metmuseum.org* Ⓜ *4, 5, 6 to 86th St.*) offers a rich seasonal music program with concerts by leading classical and jazz musicians. Also part of the Met, and well worth the trip farther uptown, is **The Cloisters** (✉ *Fort Tryon Park, Morningside Heights* ☎ *212/650–2290* Ⓜ *A to 190th St.*), which has matinee performances of sacred and secular music from the Middle Ages. It all take places within a 12th-century Spanish chapel. Well-known soloists and chamber music groups perform in **Kaufmann Concert Hall** (✉ *Tisch Center for the Arts, 92nd St. Y, 1395 Lexington Ave., at E. 92nd St., Upper East Side* ☎ *212/996–1100* ⊕ *www.92y.org* Ⓜ *6 to 96th St.*).

★ The **Miller Theatre** (✉ *Columbia University, 2960 Broadway, at W. 116th St., Morningside Heights* ☎ *212/854–1633, 212/854–7799 box office* ⊕ *www.millertheatre.com* Ⓜ *1 to 116th St.*), where the wizardly programming legacy of former director George Steel lives on, presents an adventurous program of jazz, classical, early and modern music, and dance. A well-designed 688-seater, this is a hall that rewards serious listeners. **Symphony Space** (✉ *2537 Broadway, at W. 95th St., Upper West Side* ☎ *212/864–5400* ⊕ *www.symphonyspace.org* Ⓜ *1, 2, 3 to 96th St.*) presents an energetic roster of music (including its famed Wall to Wall composer programs), and is a regular host to **World Music Institute** (☎ *212/545–7536* ⊕ *www.worldmusicinstitute.org*) events. Historic **Town Hall** (✉ *123 W. 43rd St., between 6th and 7th Aves., Midtown West* ☎ *212/840–2824* ⊕ *www.the-townhall-nyc.org* Ⓜ *1, 2, 3, 7, N, Q, R, W, S to 42nd St./Times Sq.*) hosts programs of jazz, cabaret, rock, and world music. The **Tribeca Performing Arts Center** (✉ *199 Chambers St., at Greenwich St., TriBeCa* ☎ *212/220–1460* ⊕ *www.tribecapac.org* Ⓜ *1, 2, 3 to Chambers St.*) celebrates jazz in all its forms; "Highlights in Jazz" and "Lost Jazz Shrines" are two of its special series. Count on the **Winter Garden** (✉ *World Financial Center, West St., between Vesey and Liberty Sts., Lower Manhattan* ☎ *212/945–2600* ⊕ *www.worldfinancialcenter.com* Ⓜ *E to World Trade Center; 1 to Rector St.*) for an array of free musical events from gospel to site-specific sonic installations…and a little dance as well.

OPERA

The greatest singers in the world clamor to test their mettle at the Metropolitan Opera, where they can work alongside internationally admired directors and designers. But there's plenty of talent to go around, and the city has no dearth of venues in which to appreciate masters of this grand art.

MAJOR COMPANIES

FodorsChoice ★ The titan of American opera companies, the **Metropolitan Opera** (✉ W. 62nd to W. 66th Sts., Broadway to Amsterdam Ave., Upper West Side ☎212/362–6000 ⊕www.metopera.org Ⓜ1 to 66th St./Lincoln Center) brings the world's leading singers to its vast stage at Lincoln Center from October to April. The company's music director and principal conductor, James Levine, ensures that the orchestra rivals the world's finest symphonies. Ranging from the traditional to a growing emphasis on the modern (Doctor Atomic in 2008), all performances, including those sung in English, are unobtrusively subtitled on small screens on the back of the seat in front of you. ■TIP➔ For programs Monday–Thursday, a limited number of same-day $20 Rush orchestra-seat tickets are available for seniors (by phone or online beginning at noon); they are released two hours prior to that day's performance to the general public at the box office only. Standing-room tickets go on sale at 10 AM on the day of the performance (buy them online, by phone, or at the Met box office); they are $20 for the orchestra level and $15 for the family circle.

Perhaps not as famous as its next-door neighbor, the **New York City Opera** (✉ W. 62nd to W. 66th Sts., Broadway to Amsterdam Ave., Upper West Side ☎212/870–5570 ⊕www.nycopera.com Ⓜ1 to 66th St./Lincoln Center) draws a crowd to its performances at the David H. Koch Theater (formerly the New York State Theater). Founded in 1943, the company is known for its innovative and diverse repertory, and its soft spot for American composers. Artistic director Gèrard Mortier resigned in late 2008, shaking up the 2009/10 season that would have included new pieces by Philip Glass. But you can still expect to find a commitment to the fresh, and rarely seen baroque operas such as Acis and Galatea and Rinaldo. Placido Domingo and Beverly Sills began their careers at City Opera; generations of great voices follow in their footsteps. City Opera performs September to November and March and April. All performances of foreign-language operas have supertitles—line-by-line English translations—displayed above the stage. ■TIP➔For all performances, $16 same-day standing room tickets may be purchased during City Opera box office hours.

SMALLER COMPANIES

Dicapo Opera Theatre (✉184 E. 76th St., between Lexington and 3rd Aves. Upper East Side ☎212/288–9438 ⊕www.dicapo.com Ⓜ6 to 77th St.) may be in a church basement (St. Jean Baptiste), but the 204-seater's boffo reputation—and its thoroughly modern facility—belie its humble-sounding setting. Productions range from Puccini to Robert Ward's The Crucible. The **Gotham Chamber Opera** (✉Harry de Jur Playhouse, Abrons Arts Center, 466 Grand St., at Pitt St., Lower East Side ☎212/868–4460 ⊕www.gothamchamberopera.org Ⓜ F to Delancey St.; J, M, Z to Essex St.) presents American premieres of little-known chamber works such as Handel's Arianna in Creta. A 350-seat Georgian Revival theater, this is a fine home for pieces from the baroque era to the present. The **New York Gilbert & Sullivan Players** (☎212/769–1000 ⊕www.nygasp.org) stages lively productions of such G&S favorites as The Pirates of Penzance and

The Mikado, plus rarities like Sullivan's last completed work, *The Rose of Persia*. Their New York performance season—usually throughout January—is spent primarily at City Center.

DANCE

Bodies in motion tend to stay in motion here in New York City. Ballet aficionados are spoiled with options at New York's landmark performing arts centers, and those in search of something less classical will find it in all corners of the city, including downtown venues that veer toward experimental fare.

BALLET

The **American Ballet Theatre (ABT)** (☎212/477–3030 ⊕*www.abt*.org) is renowned for its gorgeous renditions of the 19th-century classics (*Swan Lake, Giselle, La Bayardère*) as well as its modern repertoire, including works by such 20th-century masters as George Balanchine, Jerome Robbins, and Agnes de Mille. Since its founding in 1940, the company has nurtured a stellar array of dancers, including Mikhail Baryshnikov, Natalia Makarova, Rudolf Nureyev, Gelsey Kirkland, and Cynthia Gregory. ABT has two New York seasons—eight weeks beginning in May at its home in the Metropolitan Opera House and two weeks in fall (usually October) at City Center.

☾ With more than 90 dancers, the **New York City Ballet** (☎212/870–5570 ⊕*www.nycballet.com*) has an unmatched repertoire of 20th-century works. Its fall season, which runs from mid-November through December, includes the beloved annual production of George Balanchine's *The Nutcracker*. Its spring season runs from April through June; an eight-week Winter Repertory program runs in January and February. The company continues to stress the works themselves rather than individual performers, although that hasn't stopped a number of principal dancers (such as Jock Soto, Kyra Nichols, Darci Kistler, Damian Woetzel, and Wendy Whelan) from earning kudos. The company performs in Lincoln Center's David H. Koch Theater along with City Opera. Family-friendly Saturday matinees are offered throughout the regular season.

MODERN DANCE

The world's most innovative dance companies perform in New York throughout the year, especially in fall and spring, showcasing the works of such legendary and endlessly creative choreographers as Twyla Tharp, Lar Lubovitch, Bill T. Jones, Karole Armitage, Doug Varone, Trisha Brown, Mark Morris, Martha Graham, and Merce Cunningham.

World-renowned dance troupes **Alvin Ailey American Dance Theater** (⊕ *www.alvinailey.org*) and **Paul Taylor Dance Company** (⊕ *www.ptdc. org*) present their primary New York seasons at **City Center** (⊠*131 W. 55th St., between 6th and 7th Aves., Midtown West* ☎212/581–1212 ⊕*www.nycitycenter.org* Ⓜ*N, Q, R, W to 57th St./7th Ave.; F to 57th*
★ ☾ *St./6th Ave.*). Its annual "Fall for Dance" showcase is a must. **Dance**

Theater Workshop (✉ *219 W. 19th St., between 7th and 8th Aves., Chelsea* ☎ *212/924–0077* ⊕ *www.dtw.org* Ⓜ *1 to 18th St.; A, C, E, L to 14th St.-8th Ave.*) serves as a laboratory for new choreographers. They are also known for their multimedia and kid-friendly "Family Matters" series. **Danspace Project** (✉ *St. Mark's Church-in-the-Bowery, 131 E. 10th St., at 2nd Ave., East Village* ☎ *212/674–8112,866/811–4111 reservations* ⊕ *www.danspaceproject.org* Ⓜ *6 to Astor Pl.*), founded to foster the work of independent choreographers such as **Lucinda Childs and David Gordon**, sponsors performances that are as fresh— and idiosyncratic—as this space.

Fodor's Choice
★
☺
In a former art-deco movie house in Chelsea, the 500-seat **JoyceTheater** (✉ *175 8th Ave., at W. 19th St., Chelsea* ☎ *212/242–0800* ⊕ *www. joyce.org* Ⓜ *A, C, E to 14th St.; L to 8th Ave.*) has superb sight lines and presents a full spectrum of contemporary dance. The buoyant **Pilobolus** (⊕ *www.pilobolus.org*), **Ballet Hispanico** (⊕ *www.ballethispanico. org*), and **Parsons Dance Company** (⊕ *www.parsonsdance.org*) as well as the unforgettable cross-dressing **Les Ballets Trockadero de Monte Carlo** (⊕ *www.trockadero.org*) are regulars on the lineup. Their **Joyce SoHo** location (✉ *155 Mercer St., between Houston and Prince Sts., SoHo* ☎ *212/431–9233* ⊕ *www.joyce.org* Ⓜ *R, W to Prince St.; B, D, F, V to Broadway/Lafayette St.*) showcases more experimental work.

PERFORMING ARTS CENTERS

Fodor's Choice
★
America's oldest performing arts center, the **Brooklyn Academy of Music (BAM)** (✉ *Peter Jay Sharp Bldg., 30 Lafayette Ave., between Ashland Pl. and St. Felix St., Fort Greene, Brooklyn* ☎ *718/636–4100* ⊕ *www. bam.org* Ⓜ *2, 3, 4, 5, B, Q to Atlantic Ave.*), opened in 1859. BAM has a much-deserved reputation for daring—and spectacular—dance, music, opera, and theatrical productions, and its film programming. The main performance spaces are the sublime 2,100-seat **Howard Gilman Opera House,** a restored Renaissance Revival palace built in 1908, and the 874-seat **Harvey Theater,** an updated 1904 theater a block away at 651 Fulton Street. Every fall BAM's multimedia Next Wave Festival fills the house with a global audience. Year-round you can catch other live performances (including the **Brooklyn Philharmonic** ⊕ *www.brooklyn- philharmonic.org*), a movie at the **BAM Rose Cinemas,** or hit the glam BAMcafé (☎ *718/623–4139 reservations*), which becomes a cabaret venue on Friday and Saturday nights. For a fare of $7 each way, **BAM- bus** (✉ *120 Park Ave., between E. 41st and E. 42nd Sts.,* Ⓜ *4, 5, 6 to 42nd St.*) provides round-trip transportation from Manhattan one hour prior to certain live performances. Pickup is in Midtown East, on the west side of Park Avenue; drop-offs are at multiple locations around the city. Call BAM's main number 24 hours ahead to make reservations.

Carnegie Hall (✉ *881 7th Ave., at W. 57th St., Midtown West* ☎ *212/247–7800* ⊕ *www.carnegiehall.org* Ⓜ *N, Q, R, W to 57th St.; B, D, E to 7th Ave.*) is, of course, one of the world's most famous concert halls. Virtually every important musician of the 20th century performed in this century-old Italian Renaissance–style building, often at the peak of his or her creative powers. Tchaikovsky conducted the opening-night concert on May 5, 1891, Leonard Bernstein had his debut here, and Vladimir Horowitz made his historic return to the concert stage here. Performances are given in the grand 2,804-seat **Isaac Stern Auditorium,** the 268-seat **Weill Recital Hall,** and the modern and stylish 644-seat **Judy and Arthur Zankel Hall** on the lower level. Although the emphasis is on classical music, Carnegie Hall also hosts jazz, pop, cabaret, and folk music concerts.

★ **City Center** (✉ *131 W. 55th St., between 6th and 7th Aves., Midtown West* ☎ *212/581–1212 CityTix* ⊕ *www.nycitycenter.org* Ⓜ *N, Q, R, W to 57th St./7th Ave.; F to 57th St./6th Ave.*) has a neo-Moorish look (it was built in 1923 for the Ancient and Accepted Order of the Mystic Shrine). Pause as you enter to admire the beautifully ornate tile work that plasters the lobby. The 2,750-seat main stage is perfectly suited for its role as a showplace for world-class dance troupes (including American Ballet Theatre and Alvin Ailey) and special theatrical events. The popular Encores! musicals-in-concert series is staged here, as are—on the smaller **City Center Stages I** and **II**—a number of productions and programs of the Manhattan Theatre Club.

Lincoln Center for the Performing Arts (✉ *W. 62nd to W. 66th Sts., Broadway to Amsterdam Ave., Upper West Side* ☎ *212/546–2656 (LIN-COLN) or 212/875–5456, 212/875–5375 for accessibility information, 212/721–6500 CenterCharge* ⊕ *www.lincolncenter.org* Ⓜ *1 to 66th St./Lincoln Center*) is a 16-acre complex. As of this writing, construction geared to improving access, updating, and enhancing the stately facility was at various stages of completion, but all is expected to be revealed throughout the 2009–2010 season, in time for its 50th anniversary. Among the cultural lights comprising Lincoln Center's main campus are the **Metropolitan Opera House** (☎ *212/362–6000),* which also presents American Ballet Theatre); **New York State Theater** (☎ *212/870–5570),* home to New York City Opera and New York City Ballet and renamed the David H. Koch Theater in 2008; **Avery Fisher Hall** (☎ *212/875–5030),* where the New York Philharmonic performs; **Alice Tully Hall** (☎ *212/875–5050);* the **Vivian Beaumont and Mitzi E. Newhouse theaters** (☎ *212/362–7600);* the **New York Public Library for the Performing Arts** (☎ *212/870–1630);* and the **Walter Reade Theater** (☎ *212/875–5600).* The predominantly travertine-clad buildings were designed by multiple architects, all of whom applied a classical aesthetic to their cleanly modern structures. Avery Fisher, designed by Max Abramovitz, broke ground first. Opened in 1962, it was then known as Philharmonic Hall. The 2,738-seater's original acoustics were greatly improved with a 1976 renovation by Philip Johnson and John Burgee. Philip Johnson also designed the State (now Koch) Theater, which opened in 1964; a spruced-up interior is part of the Center's 50th-anniversary refurb. In 1965 came Eero Saarinen's finely scaled theaters, the 1,047-seat Beaumont and the 334-seat Newhouse. The 3,800-seat Met, with its Austrian-crystal chandeliers and Marc Chagall paintings, premiered in 1966. Alice Tully Hall, designed by Pietro Belluschi for a music and film audience of 1,100, followed in 1969; when it reopened for the spring 2009 season, concertgoers were greeted by an aesthetic

15

transformation by Diller Scofidio + Renfro (in collaboration with FX Fowle Architects).

🕓 An outpost a few blocks south of the main campus was dedicated to **Jazz at Lincoln Center** (☎*212/258–9800* ⊕*www.jalc.org*) in 2004. Stages in Rafael Viñoly's crisply modern **Frederick P. Rose Hall** feature the 1,100-seat **Rose Theater** (where a worthy Jazz for Young People series joins the buoyant adult programming a few times each year). Also here is the **Allen Room,** an elegant and intimate 310–460 seater, and the even more intimate 140-seat Dizzy's Club Coca-Cola. Back on the main campus, seasonal festivals—music, theater, dance, film, and more—abound, and often take place in the grand plaza surrounding the famous fountain, and in adjacent Damrosch Park.

🕓 **Radio City Music Hall** (✉*1260 6th Ave., between W. 50th and W. 51st Sts. Midtown West* ☎*212/247–4777* ⊕*www.radiocity.com* Ⓜ*B, D, F to 47th-50th/Rockefeller Center*) is the famed home of the scissor-kicking Rockettes and the Radio City Christmas Spectacular, but this stunning art-deco showplace also packs its some 6,000 seats for musical events, kids entertainment like *Dora the Explorer Live!* and the occasional film. More kids programming is held at its affiliates, the Beacon Theatre and the theater at Madison Square Garden.

FILM

On any given week New York City theaters screen all the major new releases, classics renowned and obscure, foreign films, small independent flicks, hard-to-find documentaries, and experimental video. The theaters themselves run the gamut from sleek multiplexes with large screens and stadium seating to shoe-box-size screening rooms with room for fewer than a hundred people.

GETTING TICKETS

New Yorkers have such a ravenous appetite for celluloid that even barely publicized independent projects can expect a full house, as can revivals of obscure movies and foreign film. Sold-out shows are common, so it's a good idea to purchase tickets in advance. Tickets to most theaters in New York are $12, and edging higher. Although there are no bargain matinees in Manhattan, discounts for senior citizens and children are usually available. For quick access to showtimes and locations, try the ticket services listed below or the *New York Times* (⊕*www.nytimes.com*). For print listings, Friday's *New York Times* is comprehensive.

Oddly enough, no one phone or online ticket service handles advance ticket purchase for all of the city's screens. Although the occasional indie house allows purchases directly through its own Web site, for chains and most independents you'll need to contact one of the following to charge tickets ahead. There's usually a service fee of $1 to $2 for phone or online orders. **Fandango** (☎*800/326–3264 [FANDANGO]* ⊕*www. fandango.com*) handles AMC Loews, City Cinemas, and Regal theaters. **Moviefone** (☎*212/777–3456 [777–FILM]* ⊕*www.moviefone.com*) covers the remaining chains, including Landmark and Clearview.

If you prefer to get your tickets the old-fashioned way, a good rule of thumb is to try get to the box office three hours ahead of showtime; this is especially true for evening performances and most new releases. If you're seeing a blockbuster, you'll need even more lead time. Save last-minute arrivals for smaller films, or something that has been out awhile; in those cases you may still have to hunt for the few remaining seats.

FIRST-RUN MOVIES

Wherever you are in New York City, you usually don't have to walk far to find a movie theater showing recent releases; nationwide chains and cookie-cutter multiplexes abound. But noting that "first-run" in New York is as much about independent ventures, documentaries, and foreign films as it is about commercial blockbusters, we list below the one-of-a-kind venues that make catching a movie a unique New York City experience.

15

Foreign, independent, and, on occasion, mainstream films are screened at the **Angelika Film Center** (⊠ *18 W. Houston St., at Mercer St., Greenwich Village* ☎*212/995–2000* ⊕*www.angelikafilmcenter.com* Ⓜ*B, D, F, V to Broadway–Lafayette St.; 6 to Bleecker St.*). Despite its (six) tunnel-like theaters, it's usually packed. **Cinema Village** (⊠*22 E. 12th St., between University Pl. and 5th Ave., Greenwich Village* ☎*212/924–3363* ⊕*www.cinemavillage.com* Ⓜ*4, 5, 6, L, N, Q, R, W to 14th St./Union Sq.*) has three tiny screening rooms (with surprisingly good sight lines) that show a smart selection of hard-to-find first-run domestic and foreign films.

A comfortable subterranean multiplex with four good-size screens, **Lincoln Plaza Cinemas** (⊠*1886 Broadway, at 62nd St., Upper West Side* ☎*212/757–2280* ⊕*www.lincolnplazacinema.com* Ⓜ*1 to 66th St./Lincoln Center*) is especially big on foreign-language film. Adjacent to the Plaza Hotel sits the **Paris** (⊠*4 W. 58th St., between 5th and 6th Aves., Midtown West* ☎*212/688–3800* Ⓜ*N, R, W to 5th Ave./59th St.; F to 57th St.*)—a rare stately remnant of the single-screen era. Opened in 1948, it retains its wide screen (and its balcony) and is a fine showcase for new movies, often foreign and with a limited release.

Movie lovers adore the **Quad Cinema** (⊠*34 W. 13th St., between 5th and 6th Aves., Greenwich Village* ☎*212/255–8800* ⊕*www.quadcinema. com* Ⓜ*1, 2, 3, F, V to 14th St.; L to 6th Ave.*), probably because the four tiny theaters feel so much like a private screening room. First-run art and foreign films are the fare here. Within a sleekly renovated space that was once a vaudeville theater, the **Sunshine Cinema** (⊠*143 E. Houston St., between 1st and 2nd Aves., Lower East Side* ☎*212/330–8182* ⊕*www. landmarktheatres.com* Ⓜ*F, V to 2nd Ave.*) has five decent-size screens showing a mix of art-house and smaller-release mainstream films.

The **Village East Cinemas** (⊠*181–189 2nd Ave., at E. 12th St., East Village* ☎*212/529–6799* Ⓜ*6 to Astor Pl.; L to 1st Ave.*) is housed in a former Yiddish theater that was restored and converted to a six-screen multiplex. Catch a film that's screening upstairs (you can call ahead to find out); sit in the balcony to best appreciate the Moorish-style decor and domed ceiling.

★ Its vintage is late 1960s, but the **Ziegfeld** (⊠ *141 W. 54th St., between 6th and 7th Aves., Midtown West* ☏ *212/307–1862* Ⓜ *F to 57th St./6th Ave.; N, Q, R, W to 57th St./7th Ave.*) is as close as you'll come to a movie-palace experience in New York today. Wide screen, chandeliers and crimson decor, good sight lines, and solid sound system make the Ziegfeld a special place to view the latest blockbusters as well as classics; grand-opening red-carpet galas often take place here as well.

SERIES AND REVIVALS

Although many of the screens listed here also show first-run releases, old favorites and rarities are the heart of their programming. These gems—which include every genre from noir to the most au courant experimental work—frequently screen at museums, cultural societies, and other public spaces, such as the **French Institute** (☏ *212/355– 6100* ⊕ *www.fiaf.org*), **Scandinavia House** (☏ *212/879–9779* ⊕ *www. scandinaviahouse.org*), **Instituto Cervantes** (☏ *212/308–7720* ⊕ *www. cervantes.org*), and even branches of the **New York Public Library** (⊕ *www.nypl.org*).

Dedicated to preserving and exhibiting independent and avant-garde film, **Anthology Film Archives** (⊠ *32 2nd Ave., at E. 2nd St., East Village* ☏ *212/505–5181* ⊕ *www.anthologyfilmarchives.org* Ⓜ *F, V to 2nd Ave.*) consists of two small screening rooms in a renovated courthouse. This is a good place for hard-to-find films and videos. The Essential Cinema series delves into the works of filmmakers like Stan Brakhage, Robert Bresson, and more. The four-screen **BAM Rose Cinemas** (⊠ *Brooklyn Academy of Music, Peter Jay Sharp Bldg., 30 Lafayette Ave., between Ashland Pl. and St. Felix St., Fort Greene, Brooklyn* ☏ *718/636–4100* ⊕ *www.bam.org* Ⓜ *2, 3, 4, 5, B, Q to Atlantic Ave.*) includes BAMcinématek, an impressively eclectic repertory series, as well as the latest from Sundance plus first-run foreign-language and popular independent films.

Fodor's Choice In addition to premiering new releases, **Film Forum** (⊠ *209 W. Houston* ★ *St., between 6th Ave. and Varick St., Greenwich Village* ☏ *212/727– 8110* ⊕ *www.filmforum.org* Ⓜ *1 to Houston St.*), a very special nonprofit theater with three small screening rooms, hosts movies by directors from Hitchcock to Bertolucci; genre series with themes from pre-Code to samurai; and newly restored prints of classic works. The small café serves tasty cakes and fresh-popped popcorn. Tickets are available online.

The **Museum of Modern Art (MoMA)** (⊠ *11 W. 53rd St., between 5th and 6th Aves., Midtown West* ☏ *212/708–9400* ⊕ *www.moma.org* Ⓜ *E, V to 5th Ave./53rd St.; B, D, F, V to 47th–50th Sts./Rockefeller Center*) has some of the most engaging international repertory you'll find anywhere; it's shown in the state-of-the-art Roy and Niuta Titus theaters 1 and 2. Movie tickets are available at the museum for same-day screenings (a limited number are released up to one week in advance for an extra fee); they're free if you have purchased museum admission.

The film programs at **92YTribeca** (⊠ *200 Hudson St., at Canal St., TriBeCa* ☏ *212/601–1000* ⊕ *www.92y.org/92yTribeca* Ⓜ *1, E to Canal St.*)

emphasize participation, with directors often on hand, and a Q&A afterwards is the norm. View a fresh and eclectic take on series concepts, with the likes of the Found Footage Festival, Vintage Mexican Sci-Fi Festival, Camp Nostalgia, and Desi Diaspora (South Asian) films to the latest by documentarians Chris Hegedus and D.A. Pennebaker.

The Silent Clowns Film Series (⊠ *The New-York Historical Society, 170 Central Park West, at W. 77th St., Upper West Side* ☎ *212/712–7237 [212/712–SCFS] reservations* ⊕ *www.silentclowns.com* Ⓜ *B, C to 81st St.*). Newbies and serious buffs enjoy the rarely seen prints of the silent era's comedy masters; a film historian Q&A follows.

★ The comfy 268-seat auditorium of the **Walter Reade Theater** (⊠ *Lincoln Center, 165 W. 65th St., between Broadway and Amsterdam Ave., Upper West Side* ☎ *212/875–5600* ⊕ *www.filmlinc.com* Ⓜ *1 to 66th St./Lincoln Center*) has what may be the best sight lines in town. It presents series devoted to "the best in world cinema" that run the gamut from silents (with occasional live organ accompaniment) and documentaries to retrospectives and recent releases, often on the same theme or from the same country. Purchase tickets at the box office, by phone, or online.

15

FESTIVALS, INDOORS AND OUT

New York's preeminent film event is the annual **New York Film Festival** (☎ *212/875–5050* ⊕ *www.filmlinc.com* Ⓜ *1 to 66th St./Lincoln Center*), sponsored by the Film Society of Lincoln Center every September and October. Screenings—which feature many U.S. premieres—are announced more than a month in advance and sell out rapidly. Venues are usually Lincoln Center's Alice Tully Hall (with opening- and closing-night extravaganzas in Avery Fisher Hall) and the Walter Reade Theater. Each March the Film Society joins forces with MoMA to produce **New Directors–New Films** (☎ *212/875–5050* ⊕ *www.filmlinc.com*). Fans also flock to annual events like the **Asian American International Film Festival** (⊕ *www.asiancinevision.org*) in July, **DocFest** (⊕ *paleycenter.org*) in late October.

★ The latest entry to the New York film-o-philic scene, the **Tribeca Film Festival** (⊕ *www.tribecafilmfestival.org)* takes place in late April and May.

Summer in New York sees a bonanza of alfresco film. Even better, it's usually free (but arrive early to secure a space; screenings begin at dusk). You'll want to check out lovely **Bryant Park** (⊠ *42nd St., between 5th and 6th Aves., Midtown West* ☎ *212/512–5700* ⊕ *www.bryantpark. org* Ⓜ *B, D, F, V to 42nd St./Bryant Park; 7 to 5th Ave.*) for its Monday night festival, June–August.

☺ **Hudson River Park** (⊠ *Pier 54, at W. 13th St., Greenwich Village* ⊕ *www. hudsonriverpark.org* Ⓜ *A, C, E to 14th St.; L to 8th* Ave.) runs its "RiverFlicks" series in July and August. Movies for "grown-ups" are on Wednesday evenings; RiverFlicks for kids are shown on Pier 46, on Friday. And a venture to **Socrates Sculpture Park** (⊠ *Broadway at Vernon Blvd., Long Island City, Queens* ☎ *718/956–1819* ⊕ *www.socrates sculpturepark.org* Ⓜ *N, W to Broadway*) is in order for their inspired "Outdoor Cinema" program on Wednesday July–September.

FILM FOR CHILDREN

Several museums—notably the Museum of Modern Art and the American Museum of Natural History (don't miss their IMAX Theater)—sponsor special programs aimed at families and children.

Each March the **New York International Children's Film Festival (NYICFF)** (☎212/349–0330 ⊕*www.gkids.com*) screens 60 new films and videos for ages 3–18 at venues around the city. The **Tribeca Family Film Festival** is a perennially popular feature of the Tribeca Film Fest in late April and May (☎866/941–3378 ⊕*www.tribecafilmfestival.org*).

SonyWonder Technology Lab (✉*550 Madison Ave., between E. 55th and E. 56th Sts., Midtown East* ☎*212/833–7858 weekdays* ⊕*www.sonywondertechlab.com* Ⓜ*E, V to 5th Ave.–53rd St.*), the kid-oriented hands-on extravaganza of high-tech how-to for moviemaking and more, also shows free films. Children under 18 must be accompanied by an adult. You may call ahead to reserve tickets. **Symphony Space**'s "Just Kidding" series is once again at the fore, with its fun Saturday film program (☎*212/864–5400* ⊕*www.symphonyspace.org*).

READINGS AND LECTURES

Literary figures great and small share their work at dozens of readings held each week in the city. From formal venues like the New School where you might hear well-known panelists comment on local architecture to the spontaneous scene at the Nuyorican Poets Café, you'll find New Yorkers speaking out.

The Web site ⊕*Poetz.com* has the best roundup of poetry and spoken-word events. Admission to most of these events is usually under $15, and often free—although certain luminaries might command as much as $25 or $35.

SERIES AND SPECIAL EVENTS

The **Center for Architecture** (✉*536 LaGuardia Pl., between W. 3rd and Bleecker Sts., Greenwich Village* ☎ *212/683–0023* ⊕ *www.aiany.org* Ⓜ*A, B, C, D, E, F, V to W. 4th St./Washington Sq.*), a glass-faced gallery, hosts lively discussions (which may be accompanied by films or other visuals) on topics like radical architecture in Mexico City or visionary American architects of the 1930s. The **Lesbian, Gay, Bisexual & Transgender Community Center** (✉*208 W. 13th St., between 6th and 7th Aves., West Village* ☎*212/620–7310* ⊕*www.gaycenter.org* Ⓜ*1, 2, 3, F, V to 14th St.; L to 6th Ave.*) sponsors "Center Voices," a series of engaging and topical talks (and occasional films or musical events), with themes ranging from out lawyers to Elaine Stritch.In the historic Villard Houses, the nonprofit **Municipal Art Society** (✉*Urban Center, 457 Madison Ave., at E. 51st St., Midtown East* ☎*212/935–3960* ⊕*www.mas.org* Ⓜ*6 to 51st St.; E, V to 5th Ave./53rd St.*) is dedicated to preserving New York's architectural treasures. It presents a free lecture series at noon on Thursday, with well-known authors addressing topics from subway ornamentation to houses of worship; their walking tours are also good. At the **New School** (✉ *66 W. 12th St., between 5th and 6th Aves., Greenwich Village* ☎ *212/229–5488* ⊕ *www.newschool.ed* Ⓜ *1, 2, 3, F, V to 14th St.*) topical panels predominate; expect incisive and thought-provoking results whether the subject is economics or design. The **New York Public Library** (✉ *Celeste Bartos Forum W. 42nd St., at 5th Ave. , Midtown West* ☎ *212/868–4444* ⊕ *www.nypl.org/live* Ⓜ *B, D, F, V to 42nd St.*) presents "LIVE from the NYPL," a rich program of lectures and reading events at the famous main library and its branches elsewhere in the city. **New York Studio School** (✉ *8 W. 8th St., between 5th and 6th Aves., Greenwich Village* ☎ *212/673–6466* ⊕ *www.nyss. org* Ⓜ *A, B, C, D, E, F to W. 4th St./Washington Sq.*) hosts two evening lecture series on contemporary issues in art. Hear from both emerging and established artists, and from some of the biggest names in art history and criticism. Authors, poets, and playwrights, as well as political pundits, industry leaders, and media bigwigs, take the stage at the **92nd Street Y** (✉ *1395 Lexington Ave., at E. 92nd St., Upper East Side* ☎ *212/415–5500* ⊕ *www.92y.org* Ⓜ *6 to 96th St.*). The intent at **92YTribeca** (✉ *200 Hudson St., at Canal St., Tribeca* ☎ *212/601–1000* ⊕ *www.92y.org* Ⓜ *1, E to Canal St.*) is to appeal to a twenty- to thirty-ish set, but just about anyone should find something to their liking in their extensive daytime and evening lineups. Try talks on American Media & the Green Movement to JewBu: Exploring Jewish Dharma, and themes from the arts, food, and technology. **Symphony Space** (✉ *2537 Broadway, at W. 95th St., Upper West Side* ☎ *212/864–5400* ⊕ *www.symphonyspace.org* Ⓜ *1, 2, 3 to 96th St.*) hosts a celebrated roster of literary events, including Bloomsday and the famed "Selected Shorts" series of stories read by prominent actors and broadcast live on National Public Radio.

★ Insight into the creative process is what the superb **Works & Process** (✉ *Guggenheim Museum, 1071 5th Ave., at E. 89th St., Upper East Side* ☎ *212/423–3587* ⊕ *www.worksandprocess.org* Ⓜ *4, 5, 6 to 86th St.*) program is all about. Often drawing on dance and theater works-in-progress, live performances are complemented with illuminating discussions with their (always top-notch) choreographers, playwrights, and directors.

FICTION AND POETRY READINGS

"Poetry Czar" Bob Holman's **Bowery Poetry Club** (✉ *308 Bowery, at Bleecker St., Lower East Side* ☎ *212/614–0505* ⊕ *www.bowerypoetry. com* Ⓜ *B, D, F, V to Broadway–Lafayette St.; 6 to Bleecker St.*) serves up coffee and comestibles along with its ingenious poetry events. Expect every permutation of the spoken word—and art and music, too.

★ The **Cornelia Street Café** (✉ *29 Cornelia St., between W. 4th and Bleecker Sts., Greenwich Village* ☎ *212/989–9319* ⊕ *www.corneliastreetcafe. com* Ⓜ *A, B, C, D, E, F, V to W. 4th St./Washington Sq.*) is a good bet for original poetry—the Pink Pony West open-mike series takes place here—and fiction readings, live jazz, and a good meal as well.

Amid its collection of 45,000 titles for sale, the **Housing Works Used Book Café** (✉ *126 Crosby St., between E. Houston and Prince Sts.,*

SoHo ☎212/334–3324 ⊕*www.housingworksbookstore.com* Ⓜ*R, W to Prince St.; B, D, F, V to Broadway–Lafayette St.; 6 to Bleecker St.*) sponsors readings—often by breakout local authors or from books on social issues—and a monthly acoustic music series. Events at this cozy nonprofit benefit homeless people with HIV/AIDS. At **KGB Bar** (✉*85 E. 4th St., between Bowery and 2nd Ave., East Village* ☎212/505–3360 ⊕*www.kgbbar.com* Ⓜ*F, V to 2nd Ave.; B, D, F, V to Broadway– Lafayette St.*) the series never stop: start with "Sunday Night Fiction" or "Monday Night Poetry," then there's "Fantastic Sci-fi" on Wednesday night, and more.

The **Nuyorican Poets Café** (✉*236 E. 3rd St., between Aves. B and C, East Village* ☎212/505–8183 ⊕*www.nuyorican.org* Ⓜ*F, V to 2nd Ave.*) schedules daily readings, open-mike events, and screenplay readings, and hosts the granddaddy of the current spoken word scene, the "Friday Night Poetry Slam."

Having settled into its new home directly on the Hudson in 2009, **Poets House** (✉*10 River Terr., at Murray St., Battery Park City* ☎212/431–7920 ⊕*www.poetshouse.org* Ⓜ*E to Fulton St.; 1, 2, 3 to Chambers St.*) finally has a setting that rises to its theme: it is an open resource for all ages, one that offers a huge library and readings and events that exalt the art of poetry.

The Poetry Project (✉*At St. Mark's Church in-the-Bowery, 131 E. 10th St., at 2nd Ave., East Village* ☎212/674–0910 ⊕*www.poetryproject. com* Ⓜ*6 to Astor Pl.*) had its start in 1966, and has been a source of sustenance for poets (and their audiences) ever since. This is where Allen Ginsberg, Amiri Baraka, and Sam Shepard first found their voices, and where you're likely to find folks of the same caliber today.

☼ The famed **Strand Bookstore** (✉*828 Broadway, at E. 12th St., East Village* ☎212/473–1452 ⊕*www.strandbooks.com* Ⓜ*L, N, Q, R, W, 4, 5, 6 to 14th St./Union Sq.*) hosts the occasional nonfiction panel and special Family Hour events, but its primary fare is current fiction readings with authors like Marisha Pessl, Colson Whitehead, Calvin Trillin, and Mark Kurlansky.

Nightlife

WORD OF MOUTH

"I've always wanted to visit a little dark atmosphere bar with a jazz or blues band playing . . . Do you know of any nice places?"
—schnookies

"Bemelman's bar in the Carlyle Hotel—this place is a CLASSIC NYC establishment with famous Bemelmans murals and great cocktails."
—mclaurie

Updated by
Alia Akkam

"Everybody's working for the weekend?" Please. New Yorkers seldom wait for the actual weekend to party—in fact, many prefer to do it during the week (Thursday's particularly popular) when there's not a thicket of hormone-drenched singles prowling the floorboards. If word gets out that a hot band is playing in a bar on a Tuesday, or if a well-known DJ takes over a dance club on a Wednesday, you can be assured these places will be packed like it's a Saturday night.

The nightlife scene is still largely downtown—in drab-by-day dives in the East Village and Lower East Side, classic jazz joints in the West Village, and the Meatpacking District's and Chelsea's see-and-be-seen clubs—but you don't have to go below 14th Street to have a good time. Midtown, especially around Hell's Kitchen, has developed quite the vibrant scene, too, and there are still plenty of preppy hangouts on the Upper East and Upper West sides. Across the East River, Brooklyn's Williamsburg neighborhood has become a haven for artists, hipsters, and rock-and-rollers *(For venues in Brooklyn see Chapter 12)*.

There are enough committed club crawlers to support venues for almost every idiosyncratic taste. But keep in mind that *when* you go is just as important as *where* you go. A spot is only hot when it's hopping—a club that is packed at 11 might empty out by midnight, and a bar that raged last night may be completely empty tonight. These days, night prowlers are more loyal to floating parties, DJs, and club promoters than to any specific addresses.

For the totally hip, *Paper* magazine has a good list of the roving parties and the best of the fashionable crowd's hangouts. You can check their online nightlife guide, PM (NYC), via their Web site, ⊕*www.papermag. com*. Another streetwise mag, *The L Magazine* (⊕*www.thelmagazine. com*), lists what's happening day by day at many of the city's lounges and clubs, as well as dance and comedy performances. The *Village*

Voice, a free weekly newspaper, probably has more club ads than any other rag in the world. Also check out the *New York Press,* which has pages and pages of nightlife listings. The *New York Times* has listings of cabaret and jazz shows. You may also get good tips from an in-the-know hotel concierge. Keep in mind that events change almost weekly, and venue life spans are often measured in months, not years. Phone ahead to make sure your target hasn't closed or turned into a trendy polka hall (although that might be fun, too).

CLUBS AND ENTERTAINMENT

CLASSIC NEW YORK

If you want quintessential New York City, these social venues are distinguished by an unbeatable location, a unique style, a rich history, or a combination of the three. Reservations are essential, and many places' dress codes require jackets or prohibit jeans, so call ahead to make sure your threads are up to snuff. Admission to the performance venues can be steep—cover charges for big-name acts go as high as $100—but in many cases you can snag a less pricey spot at the bar if you show up several hours before showtime.

16

Fodor'sChoice
★

The Carlyle. The hotel's discreetly sophisticated Café Carlyle hosts such top cabaret and jazz performers as Christine Ebersole, John Pizzarelli, and Steve Tyrell. Stop by on a Monday night and take in Woody Allen, who swings on the clarinet with the Eddy Davis New Orleans Jazz Band. **Bemelmans Bar,** with a mural by the author of the *Madeline* books, features a rotating cast of pianist-singers. ⊠*35 E. 76th St., between Madison and Park Aves., Upper East Side* ☎*212/744–1600* ⊕*www.thecarlyle.com* Ⓜ*6 to 77th St.*

Four Seasons. New York City (and American) history is made here in Philip Johnson's landmark temple of modern design. Watch for politicos and media moguls in the Grill Room, or enjoy the changing foliage in the romantic Pool Room. ⊠*99 E. 52nd St., between Park and Lexington Aves., Midtown East* ☎*212/754–9494* ⊕*www.fourseasonsrestaurant. com* Ⓜ*E, V to Lexington Ave./53rd St.; 6 to 51st St.*

Lever House. This spot on the garden level of one of the city's most stylish office buildings (built in 1952), draws a younger and faster crowd than its closest competition, the Four Seasons. People flock here to see and be seen in a futuristic, honeycomb setting where just about everybody looks like they're somebody. ⊠*390 Park Ave., at 53rd St., entrance on 53rd St., Midtown East* ☎*212/888–2700* ⊕*www.leverhouse.com* Ⓜ*E, V to Lexington Ave./53rd St.; 6 to 51st St.*

Oak Room. One of the great classic cabaret venues, the Oak Room is formal (jackets are mandatory; ties are the norm). You might find the hopelessly romantic singer Andrea Marcovicci, among other top-notch performers, crooning here. ⊠*Algonquin Hotel, 59 W. 44th St., between 5th and 6th Aves., Midtown West* ☎*212/840–6800* Ⓜ*B, D, F, V to 42nd St.; 7 to 5th Ave.*

Rainbow Room. On select Friday and Saturday evenings, this romantic institution on the NBC building's 65th floor opens its doors to the public for a dinner dance, where a revolving dance floor and big band orchestra delight those who like to swing-dance and tango. Call ahead for the dance schedule and be aware that this venue is changing hands and may be closed in the process of reopening under new owners. The dress code is good news for those who like to put on the ritz: tuxedoes or suits for men, and cocktail dresses or evening gowns for women. ⊠*30 Rockefeller Plaza, between 5th and 6th Aves., Midtown West* ☎*212/632–5100* ⊕*www.rainbowroom.com* Ⓜ*B, D, F, V to 47th–50th Sts./Rockefeller Center.*

Rise. Ensconced on the 14th floor of the Ritz-Carlton Battery Park, this swank lounge has stunning views of the harbor and the Statue of Liberty. In summer you can sit outside and watch the sun set over that American icon. ⊠*2 West St., at Battery Pl., Lower Manhattan* ☎*917/790–2626* Ⓜ*1 to Rector St.; 4, 5 to Bowling Green.*

★ **'21' Club.** A row of lawn jockeys welcomes you to this former speakeasy, celebrated for attracting famous writers and movie stars through most of the past century. Privilege and whimsy are mixed together here: the well-dressed order excellent American cuisine in the lively Bar Room and enjoy drinks next to a roaring fire in the cozy front lounge. ⊠*21 W. 52nd St., between 5th and 6th Aves., Midtown West* ☎*212/582–7200* ⊕*www.21club.com* Ⓜ*B, D, F, V to 47–50th Sts./Rockefeller Center.*

DANCE CLUBS AND DJ VENUES

Gossiping, drinking, posing, prowling: dancing isn't quite incidental at dance clubs, but it's not always the most compelling draw. Some clubs are cavernous spaces filled with a churning sea of bodies. Others are like small get-togethers in a basement belonging to a friend of a friend of a friend. Parties—dance and otherwise—with DJs, salsa bands, and themes ranging from '60s bossa nova nights to soul-and-drag galas often crop up at different hot spots. A few places host parties only on weekends, so call ahead, or come up with an alternate plan. Also be aware that weeknight parties don't make allowances for early-morning risers: the crowd often doesn't arrive until well after midnight.

Apt. Music is the priority at this polished club, where some of the world's top DJs—those who elevate record spinning to a high art—ply their trade in a tiny, luminous basement room. At the restaurant upstairs you can partake of a few nibbles or sip a cocktail. ⊠*419 W. 13th St., between 9th Ave. and Washington St., Meatpacking District* ☎*212/414–4245* Ⓜ*A, C, E to 14th St.; L to 8th Ave.*

Canal Room. Polished wood floors, elegant potted palms, and stylish chairs give this intimate club—known for its Artist You Should Know series—an air of glamour. Musicians perform here several times a month but they also come just to enjoy themselves. The owners' record-business connections, a spectacular speaker system, and DJs who keep the crowds moving have drawn the likes of Mariah Carey, Missy Elliott, and Diddy. ⊠*285 West Broadway, at Canal St., TriBeCa* ☎*212/941–8100* ⊕*www.canalroom.com* Ⓜ*A, C, E to Canal St.*

Cielo. A relatively mature crowd gravitates to this small, superfashionable Meatpacking District destination to sip cocktails and groove to soulful Latin beats and techno on the sunken dance floor. ⊠*18 Little W. 12th St., between 9th Ave. and Washington St., Meatpacking District* ☎*212/645–5700* ⊕*www.cieloclub.com* Ⓜ*A, C, E to 14th St.; L to 8th Ave.*

Club Shelter. This bi-level space is home to some of the best dancing in the city, with frequent parties and a stellar sound system. ⊠*150 Varick St., at Vandam St., SoHo* ☎*646/862–6117* ⊕*www.clubshelter.com* Ⓜ*1 to Houston St.*

Sapphire Lounge. The party gets started late at this lively Lower East Side hangout, but the well-known DJs keep a diverse crowd going with deep house, hip-hop, soul, funk, and Latin music, and ultrafriendly patrons might just drag you onto the floor to strut your stuff. Early birds can partake of $4 happy hours Monday–Friday. ⊠*249 Eldridge St., between E. Houston and Stanton Sts., Lower East Side* ☎*212/777–5153* ⊕*www.sapphirenyc.com* Ⓜ*F, V to 2nd Ave.*

JAZZ CLUBS

16

Greenwich Village is still New York's jazz mecca packed with jazz nightclubs, but many more venues are strewn around town. Cover charges can be steep, and it's common for a venue to present multiple sets each evening.

Bar Next Door. It doesn't get more intimate than this dark, inviting music den downstairs from the Italian café La Lanterna. On Wednesday night the stage is dedicated to the Jonathan Kreisberg Trio, while Thursday attracts an ever-changing roster of musicians. Get there early to grab a seat and tuck into a thin-crust Margherita pizza. In summer, hang out in the lovely garden for a prelude. ⊠*129 MacDougal St., between W. 3rd St. and W. 4th Sts., Greenwich Village* ☎*212/529–5945* ⊕ *www. lalanternacaffe.com* Ⓜ*A, B, C, D, E, F, V to W. 4th St.*

Birdland. This place gets its name from saxophone great Charlie Parker, so expect serious musicians such as John Pizzarelli, the Dave Holland Sextet, and Chico O'Farrill's Afro-Cuban Jazz Orchestra. The dining room serves moderately priced American fare with a Cajun accent. If you sit at the bar your cover charge includes a drink. ⊠*315 W. 44th St., between 8th and 9th Aves., Midtown West* ☎*212/581–3080* ⊕*www. birdlandjazz.com* Ⓜ*A, C, E to 42nd St./Port Authority.*

★ **Blue Note.** Considered by many to be the jazz capital of the world, the Blue Note hosts a varied repertoire from Chris Botti to the Count Basie Orchestra to Boz Scaggs. Expect a steep cover charge except for late shows on weekends, when the music is less jazzy and more funky. ⊠*131 W. 3rd St., near 6th Ave., Greenwich Village* ☎*212/475–8592* ⊕*www.bluenote.net/newyork* Ⓜ*A, B, C, D, E, F, V to W. 4th St.*

Garage Restaurant & Café. There's no cover *and* no minimum at this Village hot spot, where two bands perform live jazz seven nights a week and a fireplace sets the mood upstairs. ⊠*99 7th Ave. S, between Bleecker and Christopher Sts., Greenwich Village* ☎*212/645–0600* ⊕*www.garagerest.com* Ⓜ*1 to Christopher St./Sheridan Sq.*

Continued on page 300

⌐ YORK NIGHTS by Sarah Gold

New York is the city that never sleeps—and when you come to visit, you might not, either. It doesn't matter if you're a disco dolly, a lounge lizard, a class act, or a rock n' roll headbanger; the nightlife options here will give you your fix. So pop some No-Doz, take a late-afternoon nap, do whatever it is you have to do to get ready. You can catch up on your sleep next time you're in Cleveland.

A NIGHT OF JAZZ
GREENWICH VILLAGE

It's no surprise that the Village, a legendary haunt for Beat poets, avant-garde performance artists, and countercultural politicos, is also a hotbed of jazz. This neighborhood's vibe is all about experimentation and free expression . . . so put on your dark glasses and your artfully distressed leather jacket, grab your Gauloises (for the sidewalk, anyhow), and get ready to improvise.

Making advance reservations may not entirely jibe with jazz's spontaneous sensibility, but it's not a bad idea, especially if you want to get into some of the Village's best-known venues. Booking weeks ahead for a table at the **Blue Note** will only ensure that you have

a memorable night; you'll be able to see jazz greats like Herbie Hancock, McCoy Tyner, Cassandra Wilson, and Taj Mahal right up close from one of the cramped 40-or-so tables. This is also a great place to have dinner; the Note serves up some notable barbecue.

Another spot that's worth pre-booking for is the nearby "Carnegie Hall of Cool," the **Village Vanguard**. John Coltrane and Sonny Rollins used to jam here regularly, and modern-day jazz giants like Wynton Marsalis make rare appearances. When the headline act's not huge, though, you can sometimes wander in at 8 (when the doors open) and still get a seat.

OUTSIDE THE BOX

Although the Village has the highest concentration of jazz clubs in the city, there are a few fabulous venues that are worth the cab fare uptown. **Smoke**, way up near Columbia University, is a true jazz-lover's haven; Sunday nights, when the scatting and vocal acrobatics of top

vocalists fill the tiny space, are not to be missed. A less arduous trip to Midtown will bring you to **Iridium**, where guitar great Les Paul plays on Monday nights. A bit farther south near Times Square is the famous **Birdland**, named for the late great Charlie Parker; the cover charge here includes a drink.

With smaller, less famous Village venues, you can afford to extemporize a bit; these places are almost always packed with nodding jazz fans, but you can show up without a reservation (often without paying a cover charge) and still catch some top-quality music. The **Garage Restaurant & Café** is one such spot; you can have a steak dinner in front of the giant fireplace while listening to great local trios and quartets (or, on Monday, big-band swing). The **Knickerbocker Bar & Grill** is another place where you can satisfy both your gastronomic and musical appetites; on Friday and Saturday nights live ensembles play while diners dig in to St. Louis ribs or slow baked salmon.

Arthur's Tavern is another no-cover venue, with a coolly grotty dark-wood (or, more accurately, dark wood–veneer) ambience; you can chill out in the piano

bar or catch a jazz trio from one of the dining room tables. **Sweet Rhythm**, also a great choice, is even greater if you're a starving student; on Monday nights, a jazz ensemble from the nearby New School University's music program takes the stage, and anyone with student ID gets in free.

For addresses and phone numbers of these venues, see the main Nightlife listings in this chapter.

A NIGHT OF CLUBBING
THE MEATPACKING DISTRICT & CHELSEA

Ever since Studio 54 hung its first mirrored ball and ignited a citywide disco inferno, New York has been a playground for the young late-night club set. The '70s may be over; the multilevel megaclubs of the '80s and pulsing raves of the '90s are now largely in the past. But if DJ-spun grooves and packed dance floors are what you love, there's still plenty of New York spots where you can party like it's 1999 (or 1989, or 1979).

It's best to start your long evening with some sustenance, so your first stop—no earlier than 9 PM—should be one of the Meatpacking District's super-hip eateries. **Spice Market** and **Pastis** serve excellent food (Southeast Asian and French bistro, respectively), and will also ease you into the clubland vibe; they both have killer cocktails, a see-and-be-seen crowd, and sometimes even lines of people waiting to get inside (advance reservations are highly recommended).

Once you've lingered until a more respectable hour (11 PM or so), meander over to one of the neighborhood's more civilized clubs. **APT's** basement room, where funk and soul are in heavy rotation, has just a narrow slice of dance floor between the bar and a seating area; it's a safe place to do some preliminary head-bobbing. **Cielo**, where deep-house DJs reign, is another relatively chill and

OUTSIDE THE BOX

Although the Meatpacking and Chelsea neighborhoods are Clubland Central, a couple of New York's best clubs are a bit off the beaten path. **Club Shelter**, in SoHo, has been luring the flamboyantly fabulous since 2002 (forever, in club years). For clubbing with a touch of elegance, try TriBeCa's posh Canal Room.

HOW TO GET IN

Unless you're a model, movie star, or recording artist, there's no surefire way to make sure you'll get past the velvet ropes at top New York clubs. But there are some things you can do to increase your chances.

■ **Arranging for bottle service** is an expensive proposition, but one of the only ways to reserve a table for you and your friends inside a club. Bottle service means you agree to purchase an entire bottle (or several) of, say, vodka or champagne, which is then used to serve your group. You won't be paying liquor-store prices, though; a bottle of Grey Goose with mixers can easily set you back a couple hundred dollars.

intimate place to dance. The smaller size, though, means exclusivity; you'll need to impress the door staff to get in.

When the wee hours arrive, it's time to get serious; New York's biggest and wildest clubs only really come alive around 1 AM. Many of these are in Chelsea, the next neighborhood over and just a short cab ride away from the Meatpacking District. **Marquee** (289 10th Ave., 646/473–0202) is similarly fabulous and similarly hard to get into; the DJs aren't as major here but the beautiful-people ratio is high.

No matter where your night of clubbing takes you, have at least $150 on you. Many places don't take plastic, and if they do, you'll only exasperate the people behind you if you whip it out. Most clubs charge a cover ranging from $5 to $25, depending on the night and venue. Have another $40–$50 socked away for round-trip cab fare: it's a relatively small price to pay for the convenience and the designated driver.

■ **Surrounding yourself with good-looking, sexily dressed females** is always a good bet when you're trying to catch the doorman's eye (if he's straight, that is). Club owners and managers want to keep their venues packed with eye candy—so if you're a girl, pour yourself into tight jeans, stiletto heels, and some sort of dressy top, and get your friends together. If you're a guy, do your best to cobble together an entourage, and steer clear of sports jerseys, baseball hats, sneakers...in general, wear something that would make your mom feel proud.

■ **Showing up early** may make you feel like a loser—nothing's more dismal than a cavernous, empty dance floor—but it's easier to get in when the door staff is simply trying to get bodies inside.

■ **Cash** has been known to part even the most stubborn velvet ropes like the Red Sea. So if you're not famous, good-looking, or rich enough for bottle service, you can always try slipping the doorman a $20 (just do it discreetly, and don't consider it a guarantee).

For addresses and phone numbers of these venues, see the main Nightlife listings in this chapter.

16

IN FOCUS NEW YORK NIGHTS

A NIGHT OF ELEGANCE
MIDTOWN, THE UPPER EAST & UPPER WEST SIDES

I like the city air
I like to drink of it
The more I know New York
The more I think of it

It hardly matters that these Cole Porter lyrics (from "I Happen to Like New York") are decades old. The nighttime Manhattan that Porter knew—of moonlit walks in Central Park, swanky piano bars, chandeliered dining rooms, and dancing check to cheek—is still alive and kicking. Some of the city's classiest nightspots have been around since Porter himself was a regular, and some are more newly minted—but all of them share a sense of old-world, uniquely New York style.

Begin your evening by dining among the swirling murals (or just sipping a cocktail in the cozy bar) at **Café des Artistes.** The dining room, with its well-heeled clientele (Katie Couric and Natalie Portman have been spotted here), gleaming crystal, and impeccable waitstaff, is the embodiment of old-school opulence; accordingly, you'll need reservations to beat the upper-crusty regulars to a table. If you prefer a clubbier, less formal but still elegant meal, try the **'21' Club,** where you can enjoy one of the city's best, and most expensive, hamburgers ($30) in front of a roaring fire. (Jackets are required for men at both of these restaurants at dinnertime.)

For post-dinner drinks, head east to the gorgeously wood-paneled **Campbell Apartment**—a small warren of rooms inside Grand Central that was once the private residence of a New York tycoon. Cocktails with Fitzgerald-esque names will literally help get you in the spirit.

CLASSIC CHAMPAGNE COCKTAILS

If sipping bubbly while gazing at the New York skyline sounds like the epitome of class, you're in luck; many of the elegant nightspots listed here serve up signature Champagne cocktails. Here are a few you can try:

The Fountain of Youth, at Café des Artistes: Poire Williams-scented Champagne with spiced pear

The Flapper's Delight, at the Campbell Apartment: Champagne with papaya juice and amaretto

The ChamPino, at Bemelmans Bar: A concoction made with Champagne, Campari, and sweet vermouth

The Kir Royale, at the Rainbow Room: An oldie but goodie, made with Champagne and crème de cassis

BACK IN THE DAY

Or, head north to the posh Carlyle Hotel, where you can slip into one of the leather banquettes and listen to live piano music at **Bemelmans Bar.** The Carlyle is also home to the famed **Café Carlyle,** where big-name entertainers like Judy Collins dazzle in an intimate setting (you'll need to buy tickets well in advance for these shows). Another nearby spot for live music (except in the summertime, when it's closed) is **Feinstein's** at the Regency Hotel (540 Park Ave., 212/759–4100). Featured performers here have included Florence Henderson.

A whirl around the dance floor is just the thing to cap off a night of romantic about-towning, and the obvious place to do it is the **Rainbow Room,** way up on the 65th floor of the NBC building in Rockefeller Center. Call ahead before you go (The venue is changing hands and could be closed during the transition), but once you're there, the view of twinkling city lights, the revolving dance floor, and the swinging live big band will transport you back in time.

Although Café des Artistes and the '21' Club are among the city's classiest restaurants today, both have wildly bohemian pasts. Café des Artistes, so named because its adjoining hotel was home to dozens of painters, sculptors, and performers back in the 1930s, started out as a sort of community kitchen. Because the hotel apartments were so small, residents would routinely buy their own groceries, then have them sent down to the café with instructions for how they should be cooked. Dishes, once they were prepared, were sent back up to the artists' rooms via dumbwaiter. One of the most famous inhabitants of the hotel was illustrator Howard Chandler Christy; rumor has it that he painted the restaurant's sweeping wood-nymph murals to pay off his bar tab.

The '21' Club, founded during Prohibition, began its life as a speakeasy. The club was raided several times, but it never closed, largely because of the ingenious preventive measures set up by its owners, Jack Kreindler and Charlie Berns. One of these was a mechanical system of pulleys that, when activated, immediately swept all the alcohol bottles off the bar shelves and down a chute, away from the prying eyes of police.

For addresses and phone numbers of these venues, see the main Nightlife listings in this chapter.

A NIGHT OF ROCK N' ROLL
THE LOWER EAST SIDE

The Ramones, the New York Dolls, the Velvet Underground, Television, Blondie . . . easily half the bands that are today considered rock and punk legends cut their teeth in the gritty grottoes of the Lower East Side. Now that the neighborhood's undergone a revival—it's now home base for a new generation of jaded, creative young things—new live-music venues have been popping up around the old dives like weeds in a junkyard. Some of these are full-blown performance spaces, others just bars with a guitarist, an amp, and a drummer crammed into a corner; but the good news is, if you don't like the band playing in one place, you'll have to walk only a block or two to get to the next one. And hey—now that smoking's been banned, you can actually see what's happening on stage.

The venerable **Bowery Ballroom**, a staple of the downtown music scene, is the perfect place to start your a rock n' roll pilgrimage. You'll need advance tickets to see the bands that play here, especially ultra-hip headliners like Patti Smith and the Yeah Yeah Yeahs. But the relatively small size of the auditorium, the great acoustics, and the beer-sloshing enthusiasm of the crowd make it worth the Ticketmaster prices. On your way out, you may find yourself passing 315 Bowery, the address of the legendary and now defunct CBGB. A battle-scarred, stinking pit even in its 1970s heyday—when bands like The Ramones, Talking Heads, and Blondie launched their careers here—the club finally closed its doors in October of 2006.

The nearby intersection of Ludlow and Stanton streets is a zenith of sorts; small but rocking clubs seem to radiate in every direction for several blocks. This is the part of the LES that can get as crowded as a suburban mall late at night; between around 11 and 3 or 4 AM., the sidewalks are awash in young hipsters smoking Luckies and parading their thrift-store best. (If you want to blend in here, think scruffy retro-chic; no logos, no Manolos, no bling.) A favorite of this crowd is **Pianos,** once a piano shop (the new owners didn't bother to change the sign) and now an intimate performance space for acoustic and rock bands. **Arlene's Grocery,** just a block away, has been pulling in alternative music acts for more than a decade; The Strokes played here before anyone else had heard of them. If you need to channel your own inner Julian Casablancas, come on Monday night and join in the super-popular Rock n' Roll Karaoke party.

Heading less than a block east on Stanton will bring you to the deceptively un-rocklike **Cake Shop,** which looks like a record store crossed with a bakery. It is—at least on the first floor—but downstairs is a whole other story. Here, up-and-coming punk and garage bands play for a crowd of too-cool twenty-somethings (who also like to tank up on Fridays with the two-for-one happy hour, 5–8). Following Ludlow up to Houston, though, will take you right to **Mercury Lounge,** whose back room is famous for hosting big names before they were big. The White Stripes played here in their early days; more recent performers, like Cold War Kids and Voxtrot are already starting to hit the mainstream.

IF YOUR EARS ARE RINGING...

Hopping from one LES music bar to another is a blast—until the killer headache sets in. If you need a place to chill out between venues and wait for the Tylenol to take effect, try one of these lower-key neighborhood lounges:

■ **Local 138.** This unpretentious pub, with neon signs and sports on the television, has a back room with low lighting and couches—perfect for nursing a $3 draft.

■ **The Pink Pony.** A book-lined eatery with good café au lait and a sort-of-French menu, the Pony is one of the more relaxing places on the sceney Ludlow strip.

■ **Teany.** It's open only until 11 during the week (1 AM during the weekend), and you'll find lots of teas, juices, and vegetarian fare. But if you decide early on that going out on a bender was a mistake, you can start doing your penance here.

For addresses and phone numbers of these venues, see the main Nightlife listings in this chapter.

CLOSE UP

Drinks with a Panoramic Punch

In New York you can take in the sights without leaving your bar stool. The pot of gold at the **Rainbow Room** (⊠ *30 Rockefeller Plaza, between 5th and 6th Aves., Midtown West* ☎ *212/632–5000*) is the view from the 65th floor of Rockefeller Center. Within the Ritz-Carlton Battery Park, **Rise** (⊠ *2 West St., at Battery Pl., Lower Manhattan* ☎ *917/790–2626*) has clear sight lines to the Statue of Liberty.

The **River Café** (⊠ *1 Water St., near Old Fulton St., DUMBO, Brooklyn* ☎ *718/522–5200*) under the Brooklyn Bridge, has unobstructed views of the city skyline. *(See chapter 12.)* From the 23rd floor of the Peninsula Hotel you can nearly touch the sky at the **Salon de Ning** (⊠ *700 5th Ave., at W. 55th St., Midtown West* ☎ *212/956–2888*). The only sight more beautiful than the skyline is its reflection in the East River at the **Water Club** (⊠ *500 E. 30th St., at FDR Dr., Midtown East* ☎ *212/683–3333*).

Iridium. This cozy, top-notch club is a sure bet for big-name talent like the David Murray Black Saint Quartet and Michael Wolff. The sight lines are good, and the sound system was designed with the help of Les Paul, the inventor of the solid-body electric guitar, who takes the stage on Monday night. The rest of the week sees a mix of artists like Chuck Mangione and the Eddie Daniels Band. ⊠ *1650 Broadway, at W. 51st St., Midtown West* ☎ *212/582–2121* ⊕ *www.iridiumjazzclub.com* Ⓜ *1 to 50th St.; N, R, W to 49th St.*

Jazz at Lincoln Center. This branch of Lincoln Center at Columbus Circle, located several blocks south of the iconic music complex, is devoted to jazz. Check out performances at either the Frederick P. Rose Hall or the more intimate Dizzy's Club Coca-Cola, known for its late-night After Hours concerts. ⊠ *Time Warner Center, Broadway at W. 60th St., Midtown West* ☎ *212/258–9800* ⊕ *www.jalc.org* Ⓜ *A, B, C, D, 1 to 59th St.*

Ⓒ **Jazz Standard.** This sizable underground room draws the top names in the business. Part of Danny Meyer's Southern-food restaurant Blue Smoke, it's one of the few spots where you can get dry-rubbed ribs to go with your bebop. Bring the kids for the Jazz Standard Youth Orchestra concerts every Sunday afternoon. ⊠ *116 E. 27th St., between Park and Lexington Aves., Murray Hill* ☎ *212/576–2232* ⊕ *www.jazzstandard.net* Ⓜ *6 to 28th St.*

Knickerbocker Bar and Grill. Jazz acts are on the menu on Friday and Saturday nights at this old-fashioned steak house, a longtime staple of the city's more intimate music scene. ⊠ *33 University Pl., at E. 9th St., Greenwich Village* ☎ *212/228–8490* ⊕ *www.knickerbockerbarandgrill.com* Ⓜ *R, W to 8th St.*

Lenox Lounge. This art-deco lounge opened in the 1930s and currently hosts jazz ensembles, blues acts, and jam sessions in the Zebra Room. The restaurant in back serves great food to go with the soulful music.

✉ *288 Lenox Ave., between W. 124th and W. 125th Sts., Harlem* ☎ *212/427–0253* ⊕ *www.lenoxlounge.com* Ⓜ *2, 3 to 125th St.*

Smoke. If you can't wait until after dark to get your riffs on, head uptown to this lounge near Columbia University, where the music starts as early as 6 PM. Performers include some of the top names in the business, including turban-wearing organist Dr. Lonnie Smith and the drummer Jimmy Cobb (who laid down the beat on Miles Davis's seminal album *Kind of Blue*). ✉ *2751 Broadway, between W. 105th and W. 106th Sts., Upper West Side* ☎ *212/864–6662* ⊕ *www.smokejazz.com* Ⓜ *1 to 103rd St.*

Sweet Rhythm. Every Monday at this sleek West Village nightspot an ensemble from the New School University's famed jazz and contemporary music program takes the stage. On those nights college students with ID get in for just a $5 drink minimum. Tuesday nights are devoted to vocals. ✉ *88 7th Ave. S, between Bleecker and Grove Sts., Greenwich Village* ☎ *212/255–3626* ⊕ *www.sweetrhythmny.com* Ⓜ *1 to Christopher St./Sheridan Sq.*

Fodor'sChoice
★ **Village Vanguard.** This prototypical jazz club, tucked into a cellar in Greenwich Village, has been the haunt of legends like Thelonious Monk. Today you might hear jams from the likes of Bill Charlap and Ravi Coltrane, among other jazz personalities. Go on a Monday night for a performance by the resident Vanguard Jazz Orchestra. ✉ *178 7th Ave. S, between W. 11th and Perry Sts., Greenwich Village* ☎ *212/255–4037* ⊕ *www.villagevanguard.com* Ⓜ *1, 2, 3 to 14th St.*

16

ROCK CLUBS

New York continues to birth rock stars, but the majority of bands—and there are many—struggle day and night to make it out of the city. You can try to catch a star on the rise at one of the small clubs on the Lower East Side (and in Brooklyn, ⇨ Chapter 12) or check out the stellar schedules at the city's midsize venues, where more established groups deliver the goods night after night. Buy tickets in advance whenever possible; bands that are obscure to the rest of the country frequently play here to sold-out crowds.

Arlene's Grocery. On Monday nights crowds pack into this converted convenience store for Rock and Roll Karaoke, where they live out their rock-star dreams by singing favorite punk anthems onstage with a live band. The other six nights of the week are hit-or-miss. ✉ *95 Stanton St., between Ludlow and Orchard Sts., Lower East Side* ☎ *212/995–1652* ⊕ *www.arlenesgrocery.net* Ⓜ *F, V to 2nd Ave.*

Bitter End. This Greenwich Village standby has served up its share of talent since 1961; Billy Joel, David Crosby, and Dr. John are among the stars who have played here. These days you're more likely to find lesser-known musicians playing blues, rock, funk, and jazz. ✉ *147 Bleecker St., between Thompson St. and LaGuardia Pl., Greenwich Village* ☎ *212/673–7030* ⊕ *www.bitterend.com* Ⓜ *A, B, C, D, E, F, V to W. 4th St.*

Fodor'sChoice
★ **Bowery Ballroom.** This theater with art-deco accents is the city's top midsize concert venue. Packing in the crowds here is a rite of passage for musicians on their way to stardom, including Nada Surf, Clap Your

Hands Say Yeah!, and The Go! Team. You can grab one of the tables on the balcony or stand on the main floor. There's a comfortable bar in the basement. ⊠*6 Delancey St., between the Bowery and Chrystie St., Lower East Side* ☎*212/533–2111* ⊕*www.boweryballroom.com* Ⓜ*J, M, Z to Bowery St.*

The Delancey. From the palm-studded rooftop deck (heated in wintertime, hosting barbecues in summertime) down to the basement where noisy rock and punk bands hold court, this multifaceted bar at the foot of the Williamsburg Bridge strikes an invigorating balance between classy and trashy. ⊠*168 Delancey St., between Clinton and Attorney Sts., Lower East Side* ☎*212/254–9920* ⊕*www.thedelancey.com* Ⓜ*F, J, M, Z to Delancey St.–Essex St.*

Fodor'sChoice
★
The Fillmore New York @ Irving Plaza. This two-story venue, now affiliated with San Francisco's legendary club of the same name, is known for its solid indie rock performances (DJ Shadow and Sleater-Kinney have kicked out the jams here), even if they can get a little pricey. Red walls and chandeliers add a Gothic touch. ⊠*17 Irving Pl., at E. 15th St., Gramercy* ☎*212/777–6800* ⊕*www.irvingplaza.com* Ⓜ*4, 5, 6, L, N, Q, R, W to 14th St./Union Sq.*

Mercury Lounge. You'll have to squeeze past all the sardine-packed hipsters in the front bar to reach the stage, but it's worth it. This top-quality venue specializes in bands big on the indie scene like Holly Golightly & The Broke-Offs and Apostle of Hustle. ⊠*217 E. Houston St., at Ave. A, Lower East Side* ☎*212/260–4700* ⊕*www.mercuryloungenyc.com* Ⓜ*F, V to 2nd Ave.*

WORLD MUSIC VENUES

Former New York City Mayor David N. Dinkins once referred to our rich ethnic mix of inhabitants as a "gorgeous mosaic," and the same holds true for our music scene. At the clubs listed here, you'll find musical traditions and innovations that mirror the energy of the city's diverse communities as well as those of farther-flung locales.

Connolly's. This *Cheers*-like tri-level Irish pub often hosts the Irish rock-and-roots hybrid Black 47 on Saturday night. Really get into the spirit with one of their shepherd's pies. ⊠*121 W. 45th St., between Broadway and 6th Ave., Midtown West* ☎*212/597–5126* ⊕*www.connollys pubandrestaurant.com* Ⓜ*B, D, F, V to 42nd St.*

★ **S.O.B.'s.** The initials stand for Sounds of Brazil and it's *the* place for reggae, African, and Latin music—don't miss the monthly Southeast Asian party Basement Bhangra. Or, if you prefer, head over for one of the Haitian dance parties or Bossa Nova brunches. Dinner is served as well. ⊠*204 Varick St., at W. Houston St., SoHo* ☎*212/243–4940* ⊕*www.sobs.com* Ⓜ*1 to Houston St.*

ACOUSTIC AND BLUES VENUES

B.B. King Blues Club & Grill. This lavish Times Square club is vast and shiny and host to a range of musicians from the Harlem Gospel Choir to George Clinton and the P-Funk All-Stars. Every so often the relentlessly touring owner stops by as well. ⊠*237 W. 42nd St., between 7th* *and 8th Aves., Midtown West* ☎*212/997–4144* ⊕*www.bbkingblues. com* Ⓜ*1, 2, 3, 7, A, C, E, N, Q, R, W, S to 42nd St./Times Sq.*

FodorśChoice **Living Room.** Singer-songwriters—some solo, some with their bands—are
★ what you'll find at this casually classy club. If you're craving a more intimate experience, head upstairs to Googie's Lounge, their acoustic space with just a piano. ✉*154 Ludlow St., between Stanton and Rivington Sts., Lower East Side* ☎*212/533–7235* ⊕*www.livingroomny. com* Ⓜ*F, V to 2nd Ave.*

Terra Blues. A second-story haven for blues lovers, this cozy Greenwich Village club is surprisingly short on NYU students and rowdy folk. Great national and local acts grace the stage year-round. ✉*149 Bleecker St., between Thompson St. and LaGuardia Pl., Greenwich Village* ☎*212/777–7776* ⊕*www.terrablues.com* Ⓜ*B, D, F, V to Broadway–Lafayette St.; 6 to Bleecker St.*

COMEDY CLUBS

Sitting in the front row of a comedy club is not necessarily a rite of passage for New Yorkers, because if the club is small enough (and some are) and you're distracting enough, the performers will find you. At the bigger venues, expect to pay upwards of $30 for big-name acts, sometimes topped off by a nonnegotiable drink minimum and/or tipping minimum for parties of a certain size (inquire in advance about policies). Although, sometimes you can find a good show for as little as $15. Reservations are recommended and usually necessary.

Caroline's on Broadway. This high-gloss club presents established names as well as comedians on the edge of stardom. Janeane Garofalo, David Alan Grier, Colin Quinn, and Gilbert Gottfried have headlined. ✉*1626 Broadway, between W. 49th and W. 50th Sts., Midtown West* ☎*212/757–4100* ⊕*www.carolines.com* Ⓜ*N, R, W to 49th St.; 1 to 50th St.*

FodorśChoice **Chicago City Limits.** This crew touts itself as performing in the longest-
★ running improv show in the city. The shows, heavy on audience participation, take place Wednesday through Saturday and seldom fail to whip visitors into a laughing frenzy. ✉*318 W. 53rd St., between 8th and 9th Aves., Midtown West* ☎*212/888–5233* ⊕*www.chicagocitylimits.com* Ⓜ*C, E to 50th St.*

Comedy Cellar. Laughter fills this space beneath the Olive Tree Café. The bill features hilarious television personalities like Colin Quinn and Godfrey. ✉*117 MacDougal St., between W. 3rd St. and Minetta La., Greenwich Village* ☎*212/254–3480* ⊕*www.comedycellar.com* Ⓜ*A, B, C, D, E, F, V to W. 4th St.*

Comic Strip Live. The atmosphere here is strictly corner bar belying its storied history. For example, Eddie Murphy is said to have discovered Chris Rock here. The famous stage also helped launch the careers of funnymen Paul Reiser and Jerry Seinfeld. ✉*1568 2nd Ave., between E. 81st and 82nd Sts., Upper East Side* ☎*212/861–9386* ⊕*www.comicstriplive.com* Ⓜ*4, 5, 6 to 86th St.*

Dangerfield's. Since 1969 this has been an important showcase for prime comic talent like Jay Leno and Jim Carrey. Prices are reasonable ($15 during the week and $20 on the weekends, with no drink minimum). ✉*1118 1st Ave., between E. 61st and E. 62nd Sts., Upper East Side*

☎212/593-1650 ⊕*www.dangerfields.com* Ⓜ*4, 5, 6, N, R, W to 59th St.–Lexington Ave.*

Gotham Comedy Club. This 10,000-square-foot club—complete with a chandelier and roomy downstairs lounge—showcases popular head-liners such as Johnny Walker and Kate Clinton. ⊠*208 W. 23rd St., between 7th and 8th Aves., Chelsea* ☎212/367–9000 ⊕*www.gotham comedyclub.com* Ⓜ*1 to 23rd St.*

Fodor's Choice   **Upright Citizens Brigade Theatre.** Raucous sketch comedy, audience-ini-
★   tiated improv, and stand-up take turns onstage here at the city's go-to place for alternative comedy. There are even classes available; the Upright Citizens bill their program as the world's largest improv school. Catch indie comic darlings like SNL's Amy Poehler or Human Giant's Rob Huebel. ⊠*307 W. 26th St., between 8th and 9th Aves., Chelsea* ☎212/366–9176 ⊕*www.uprightcitizens.org* Ⓜ*C, E to 23rd St.*

CABARET AND PERFORMANCE SPACES

From a lone crooner at the piano to a full-fledged song-and-dance revue, cabaret takes many forms in New York. Some nightspots have stages; almost all have a cover and a minimum food and/or drink charge. In addition to the Carlyle and the Oak Room (⇨ *Classic New York)*, here are some of the best venues.

Don't Tell Mama. Composer-lyricist hopefuls and established talents show their stuff until 4 AM, seven nights a week, at this convivial Theater District cabaret. Extroverts will be tempted by the piano bar's open-mike policy. In the club's two rooms you might find singers, comedi-ans, or drag acts. Take a break from the music in the exposed brick lounge. ⊠*343 W. 46th St., between 8th and 9th Aves., Midtown West* ☎212/757–0788 ⊕*www.donttellmamanyc.com* Ⓜ*A, C, E to 42nd St./Port Authority.*

The Duplex. No matter who's performing, the largely gay audience hoots and hollers in support at this music-scene veteran on busy Sheridan Square that's been around since 1951. Singers, songwriters, and come-dians gather in the cabaret theater, while those who want to take their shot at open-mike night head downstairs to the lively piano bar. ⊠*61 Christopher St., at 7th Ave. S, Greenwich Village* ☎212/255–5438 ⊕*www.theduplex.com* Ⓜ*1 to Christopher St.*

Feinstein's at the Regency. That the world-touring Michael Feinstein per-forms here only once a year (usually in winter) and still gets a venue named after him speaks volumes about the charismatic cabaret star. This space presents some of the top names in the business. ⊠*540 Park Ave., at E. 61st St., Upper East Side* ☎212/339–4095 ⊕*www.feinsteins attheregency.com* Ⓜ*4, 5, 6, N, R, W to 59th St.–Lexington Ave.*

★   **Joe's Pub.** Wood paneling, red-velvet walls, and comfy sofas make a lush setting for top-notch performers and the A-list celebrities who come to see them. There's not a bad seat in the house, but if you want to sit, arrive at least a half hour early for the Italian-inspired dinner menu. ⊠*425 Lafayette St., between E. 4th St. and Astor Pl., East Village* ☎212/539–8770 ⊕*www.joespub.com* Ⓜ*6 to Astor Pl.*

Exquisite Mixes

What good is atmosphere if the beverages aren't up to par? At **Flatiron Lounge** (✉ *37 W. 19th St., between 5th and 6th Aves., Chelsea* ☎ *212/727–7741*), resident mixologist Julie Reiner relies on the freshest ingredients available, so the cocktail menu changes frequently. Eleven different martinis, nine bourbons, and 13 single-malt Scotches are just the beginning of the extensive drink menu at **MercBar** (✉ *151 Mercer St.,* *between Prince and W. Houston Sts., SoHo* ☎ *212/966–2727*). The Russian retreat of **Pravda** (✉ *281 Lafayette St., between Prince and W. Houston Sts., SoHo* ☎ *212/226–4944*) has more than 70 brands of vodka, including 10 house-infused flavored vodkas, which means your choice of martinis is nearly endless.

BARS

16

A convenient truth about the city is that if velvet ropes or shoulder-to-shoulder crowds ever rub you the wrong way, you can easily find a more comfortable spot, because there's always another one nearby. You'll find a glut of mahogany-panel taverns in Greenwich Village; chic lounges in SoHo and TriBeCa; yuppie hangouts on the Upper West and Upper East sides; and hipster bars in the East Village or Lower East Side (or Brooklyn, ⇨ Chapter 12). Most pubs and taverns have a wide draft selection, and bars and lounges often have special drink menus with concoctions no one would ever think up (or perhaps even drink) on their own. A single martini of the increasingly creative variety can send your tab into double digits. Note that under city liquor laws, bars can stay open until 4 AM.

LOWER MANHATTAN, SOHO, AND TRIBECA

Brandy Library. The only book in this classy, wood-panel room is the leather-bound menu listing hundreds of brandies and single-malt Scotches. Many of the bottles are on gorgeous backlighted "bookshelves." Learn what makes each of them special by chatting with the spirit sommelier. ✉ *25 N. Moore St., between Varick and Hudson Sts., TriBeCa* ☎ *212/226–5545* ⊕ *www.brandylibrary.com* Ⓜ *1 to Franklin St.*

Bridge Café. A hop away from South Street Seaport, this busy little restaurant flanking the Brooklyn Bridge is a world apart from the surrounding touristy district. The bar, dating from 1794, is one of the oldest in Manhattan. Though the space is small, the selection is huge: choose from more than 100 domestic wines and 85 single-malt Scotches. ✉ *279 Water St., at Dover St., Lower Manhattan* ☎ *212/227–3344* ⊕ *www.eatgoodinny.com* Ⓜ *2, 3, 4, 5, A, C, J, M, Z to Fulton St./ Broadway–Nassau.*

Broome Street Bar. A local hangout since 1972, this casual corner still feels like the old SoHo, before trendy boutiques replaced artists' lofts. There's a fine selection of draft beers and a full menu of hefty burgers and other pub food. ⊠*363 West Broadway, at Broome St., SoHo* ☎*212/925–2086* Ⓜ*C, E to Spring St.*

Fanelli's. Linger over the *New York Times* at this down-to-earth neighborhood bar and restaurant known for its burgers, which harks back to 1847. ⊠*94 Prince St., at Mercer St., SoHo* ☎*212/226–9412* Ⓜ*R, W to Prince St.*

Lucky Strike. The supermodels party elsewhere, but this ultracool bistro is still the domain of hipsters who pose at the cozy back tables. DJs play reggae, R&B, and hip-hop on crowded weekend nights. ⊠*59 Grand St., between West Broadway and Wooster St., SoHo* ☎*212/941–0772* ⊕*www.luckystrikeny.com* Ⓜ*A, C, E, R, W, 1 to Canal St.*

★ **MercBar.** A chic local crowd and Europeans in the know come to this dark, nondescript bar for the wonderful martinis. Its street number is barely visible—look for the French doors, which stay open in summer. ⊠*151 Mercer St., between Prince and W. Houston Sts., SoHo* ☎*212/966–2727* ⊕*www.mercbar.com* Ⓜ*R, W to Prince St.*

Pegu Club. Modeled after an officers' club in what's now Myanmar, the Pegu Club manages to feel expansive and calm even when packed. The well dressed and flirtatious come here partly for the beautiful surroundings, but primarily for the elegant cocktails, which are pricey, creative, and prepared with top-notch ingredients. ⊠*77 W. Houston St., between West Broadway and Wooster St., SoHo* ☎*212/473–7348* ⊕*www.peguclub.com* Ⓜ*B, D, F, V to Broadway–Lafayette St.; 6 to Bleecker St.*

Fodor's Choice **Pravda.** Cocktails rule at this Eastern European–style bar. Choose from
★ more than 70 brands of vodka, including house infusions, or opt for a house martini. The cellarlike space, with an atmospheric vaulted ceiling, is illuminated with candles. Reserve a table for the Russian-inspired fare, especially on weekends. ⊠*281 Lafayette St., between Prince and E. Houston Sts., SoHo* ☎*212/226–4944* ⊕*www.pravdany.com* Ⓜ*B, D, F, V to Broadway–Lafayette St.; 6 to Bleecker St.*

Raoul's. One of the first trendy spots in SoHo, this arty French restaurant has yet to lose its touch. Expect a chic bar scene filled with polished PYTs, and an intriguing fortune-teller upstairs. ⊠*180 Prince St., between Sullivan and Thompson Sts., SoHo* ☎*212/966–3518* ⊕*www.raouls.com* Ⓜ*C, E to Spring St.*

The Room. The vibe's so relaxed it's like squeezing into someone's living room (be prepared to share couch space) at this minimalist spot, where the great selection of 70 bottled beers draws a friendly mix of locals and international visitors. Alternative rock music is actually played low enough to have a conversation. ⊠*144 Sullivan St., between W. Houston and Prince Sts., SoHo* ☎*212/477–2102* Ⓜ*C, E to Spring St.*

Thom Bar. This lounge inside the 60 Thompson boutique hotel is the perfect place to perch on a banquette and splurge on a Thom martini. Pick a weeknight if you want to have a relaxed drink among the other elegant patrons. ⊠*60 Thompson St., between Spring and Broome Sts., SoHo* ☎*212/219–3200* ⊕*www.60thompson.com* Ⓜ*C, E to Spring St.*

CHELSEA, THE MEATPACKING DISTRICT, AND GREENWICH VILLAGE

Fodor'sChoice
★ **Cornelia Street Café.** Share a bottle of merlot at a street-side table on a quaint West Village lane. Downstairs you can catch live jazz or a poetry reading, or take in the monthly "Entertaining Science" evenings hosted by the Nobel laureate chemist Roald Hoffmann. ⊠*29 Cornelia St., between W. 4th and Bleecker Sts., Greenwich Village* 🕾*212/989–9319* ⊕*www.corneliastreetcafe.com* Ⓜ*A, B, C, D, E, F, V to W. 4th St./ Washington Sq.*

Corner Bistro. Opened in 1961, this neighborhood saloon serves what many think are the best hamburgers in town. Once you actually get a seat, the space feels nice and cozy, but until then, be prepared to drink a beer amid loud and hungry patrons. ⊠*331 W. 4th St., at 8th Ave., Greenwich Village* 🕾*212/242–9502* Ⓜ*A, C, E to 14th St.; L to 8th Ave.*

★ **Flatiron Lounge.** Soft lighting and smart leather banquettes distinguish this art-deco hideout, where guest mixologists, a seasonal drink menu, and owner Julie Reiner's daily "flights" of fanciful mini-martinis elevate bartending to an art form. ⊠*37 W. 19th St., between 5th and 6th Aves., Chelsea* 🕾*212/727–7741* ⊕*www.flatironlounge.com* Ⓜ*F, R, V, W to 23rd St.*

Half King. Writer Sebastian Junger (*The Perfect Storm*) is one of the owners of this mellow pub, which draws a friendly crowd of media types and stragglers from nearby Chelsea galleries for its Monday night readings, gallery exhibits, and Irish-American menu. ⊠*505 W. 23rd St., between 10th and 11th Aves., Chelsea* 🕾*212/462–4300* ⊕*www. thehalfking.com* Ⓜ*C, E to 23rd St.*

Hogs & Heifers. This raucous place is all about the saucy barkeeps berating men over their megaphones and baiting women to get up on the bar and dance (and add their bras to the collection on the wall). Celebrities still drop in from time to time to get their names in the gossip columns. ⊠*859 Washington St., at W. 13th St., Meatpacking District* 🕾*212/929–0655* ⊕*www.hogsandheifers.com* Ⓜ*A, C, E to 14th St.; L to 8th Ave.*

La Bottega. Vintage Italian posters, international magazines, and a huge Italian oven set the stage at the Maritime Hotel's European-style restaurant and bar. In winter bring your drink out to the lobby and nestle in front of the fireplace. ⊠*363 W. 16th St., at 9th Ave., Chelsea* 🕾*212/242–4300* ⊕*www.maritimehotel.com* Ⓜ*A, C, E to 14th St.; L to 8th Ave.*

Little Branch. The owners of the secretive, hard-to-access lounge Milk & Honey have created this open-to-all cousin with the same simple yet quality cocktails. The dim lighting and snug booths make it the ideal romantic lair for a date. ⊠*20 7th Ave., at Leroy St., Greenwich Village* 🕾*212/929–4360* Ⓜ*1 to Houston St.*

Madame X. This blood-red hangout is big on a bordello atmosphere, attracting a stylish crowd without the attitude. The garden in the back is open year-round, thanks to outdoor heaters. ⊠*94 W. Houston St., between LaGuardia Pl. and Thompson St., Greenwich Village* 🕾*212/539–0808* ⊕*www.madamex.com* Ⓜ*1 to Houston St.*

16

★ **Ono.** The O Bar at Ono, Hotel Gansevoort's trendy Japanese restaurant, must be seen to be believed. Designed by Jeffrey Beers International, it has elegant touches that include gold-leaf brick walls and a fiber-optic "waterfall" chandelier. Sip on sake in the lounge or the stylish outdoor garden. ✉*18 9th Ave., at W. 13th St., Meatpacking District* ☎*212/660–6766* ⊕*www.hotelgansevoort.com* Ⓜ*A, C, E to 14th St.; L to 8th Ave.*

Fodor'sChoice
★ **Spice Market.** Asian street fare served with a twist accompanies Spice Market's equally exotic cocktails like the ginger margarita or the kumquat mojito in season. A multilevel open space with slowly rotating fans, intricately carved woodwork, and sheer flowing curtains lends an aura of calm to this hangout for the posh at play. ✉*403 W. 13th St., at 9th Ave., Meatpacking District* ☎*212/675–2322* Ⓜ*A, C, E to 14th St.; L to 8th Ave.*

Tortilla Flats. The back room is a tribute to the stars of Las Vegas, from Martin and Lewis to Siegfried and Roy, but the real action is in the main room, where a rambunctious crowd packs the tight quarters for games (bingo on Monday and Tuesday, hula-hooping on Wednesday, trivia on Sunday), tequila, and Mexican food. The Flats is a prime bachelorette-party destination. ✉*767 Washington St., at W. 12th St., Greenwich Village* ☎*212/243–1053* ⊕*www.tortillaflatsnyc.com* Ⓜ*A, C, E to 14th St.; L to 8th Ave.*

Velour. Gallerygoers winding down the day and nightclubbers just revving up both stop by this West Chelsea watering hole (formerly known as Brite Bar) for signature drinks made with energy-infused vodka. The welcoming vibe, with red drapes and a candlelit lounge, is casual compared with the more sceney places nearby. ✉*297 10th Ave., at W. 27th St., Chelsea* ☎*212/279–9706* ⊕*www.britebar.com* Ⓜ*1 to 28th St.*

Vol de Nuit. The Belgian Beer Bar (as everybody calls it) is tucked away from the street. A European-style, enclosed outdoor courtyard and a cozy dark interior draw NYU grad-student types. The selection of beers on tap is superb, as are the fries, which are served with a Belgian flair, in a paper cone with an array of sauces on the side. ✉*148 W. 4th St., between MacDougal St. and 6th Ave., Greenwich Village* ☎*212/982–3388* ⊕*www.voldenuitbar.com* Ⓜ*A, B, C, D, E, F, V to W. 4th St./Washington Sq.*

White Horse Tavern. According to (dubious) New York legend, Dylan Thomas drank himself to death in this historic tavern founded in 1880 that seems perpetually popular with literary types. When the weather's nice, try to snag a seat at one of the sidewalk tables for great people-watching to go along with your pint. ✉*567 Hudson St., at W. 11th St., Greenwich Village* ☎*212/989–3956* Ⓜ*1 to Christopher St./Sheridan Sq.*

LOWER EAST SIDE AND EAST VILLAGE THROUGH EAST 20S

B Bar. Long lines of people peer through Venetian blinds at the stylish downtown crowd within this long-running but still fairly trendy bar and grill. If the bouncer says there's a private party going on, more likely than not it's his way of turning you away nicely. Dress your best if you want a seat in the covered outdoor space, a far cry from this spot's former gas station days. ⊠*358 Bowery, at E. 4th St., East Village* ☎*212/475–2220* ⊕*www.bbarandgrill.com* Ⓜ*6 to Astor Pl.*

Back Room. The Prohibition-era atmospheric touches here don't stop at the hidden entrance. Drinks come in old-fashioned teacups or wrapped in paper bags. This speakeasy's vintage quirks attract a slightly older clientele than many of its rowdy neighbors. ⊠*102 Norfolk St., between Delancey St. and Rivington St., Lower East Side* ☎*212/228–5098* Ⓜ*F to Delancey St.; J, M, Z to Essex St.*

Beauty Bar. Grab a seat in a barber chair or under a dryer at this made-over hair salon where, during happy hour, the manicurist will do your nails for a fee that includes a drink. The DJ spins everything from Britpop to rock. ⊠*231 E. 14th St., between 2nd and 3rd Aves., East Village* ☎*212/539–1389* ⊕*www.beautybar.com* Ⓜ*4, 5, 6, L, N, Q, R, W to 14th St./Union Sq.*

Cibar. Descend into the warm pink-and-peach basement to find this candlelight martini lounge. Nightly DJs play an eclectic mix of music. The bamboo garden provides a party sanctuary. ⊠*56 Irving Pl., between E. 17th and E. 18th Sts., Gramercy* ☎*212/460–5656* ⊕*www.cibarlounge. com* Ⓜ*4, 5, 6, L, N, Q, R, W to 14th St./Union Sq.*

Decibel. Red paper lanterns dimly illuminate cool couples sipping sake from small wooden boxes at this underground Japanese bar. Polite servers can help navigate the impressive but reasonably priced list, as well as the menu of Japanese bar food. The entrance is easy to miss: look for a small wooden sign at the top of a sidewalk staircase; walk down and ring the buzzer to get in. ⊠*240 E. 9th St., between 2nd and 3rd Aves., East Village* ☎*212/979–2731* ⊕*www.sakebardecibel.com* Ⓜ*6 to Astor Pl.*

Good World Bar & Grill. On an isolated street in Chinatown is this glass-fronted bar full of artists, writers, and their subjects, as well as a catwalk-ready staff. Expect cool music and—believe it or not—tasty Swedish specialties like gravlax, herring, and meatballs. ⊠*3 Orchard St., between Canal and Division Sts., Lower East Side* ☎*212/925–9975* ⊕*www.goodworldbar.com* Ⓜ*F to East Broadway.*

Louis 649. At this warmly lighted nook the major draw is the free nightly jazz, with a range of performers from Brazilian to traditional quartets. Choose a drink from the extensive selection of single-malt Scotches and Kentucky bourbons. ⊠*649 E. 9th St., between Aves. B and C, East Village* ☎*212/673–1190* ⊕*www.louis649.com* Ⓜ*L to 1st Ave.*

Lucky Cheng's. Although locals deride its subpar Asian fare, Lucky Cheng's is famous for its stunning drag queens who cavort and kick up their heels with the tourists and bachelorettes singing karaoke in the lounge downstairs. ⊠*24 1st Ave., between E. 1st and E. 2nd Sts., East Village* ☎*212/473–0516* ⊕*www.planetluckychengs.com* Ⓜ*F, V to 2nd Ave.*

Max Fish. This crowded, kitschy palace on a gentrified Lower East Side strip has one of the most eclectic jukeboxes in town, a pool table and pinball machine in the back, and a crowd of young rocker types that comes for the live music. ⊠*178 Ludlow St., between E. Houston and Stanton Sts., Lower East Side* ☎*212/529–3959* ⊕*www.maxfish.com* Ⓜ*F, V to 2nd Ave.*

16

Burlesque Is More

Since the mid-1990s a not-so-new activity has returned to the New York City nightlife scene—burlesque. The phenomenon is something more (as well as something less) than the elaborate Ziegfeld and Minsky Brothers revues of the '20s and '30s and the stripped-down striptease acts of the '50s, which eventually gave way to go-go dancers and strippers of the '60s and '70s and lap dancers of the '80s and '90s. The latter are still around, of course, but the new burlesque stands apart.

Although not exactly family-friendly, many of today's shows are self-consciously feminist, organized and run by women. What's missing, though, are the bright lights and the glamour. There'll probably never be another performer as big as Sally Rand or Gypsy Rose Lee, but the movement's stars carry on with their own

underground following. Some of the scene's finest performers include the heavily touring World Famous Pontani Sisters, classy diva Dirty Martini, the coed Dazzle Dancers (who usually end their shows wearing nothing but glitter and smiles), and Ixion, a troupe that takes its plots straight from Greek mythology, turning epic tales into erotic adventures. Check out the following Web sites for events and locations: www.starshineburlesque.com, www.vavavoomroom.com, or www. thisisburlesque.com.

If your trip is timed right, the **New York Burlesque Festival** (⊕ www. thenewyorkburlesquefestival.com) is a must for fans of this adult art form. This four-day event attracts more than 40 performers from all around the world to several snazzy rooms throughout the city.

McSorley's Old Ale House. One of New York's oldest saloons (it claims to have opened in 1854) and immortalized by *New Yorker* writer Joseph Mitchell, this is a must-see for beer lovers, even if only two kinds of brew are served: McSorley's light and McSorley's dark. Go early to avoid the down-the-block lines on Friday and Saturday night. ⊠ *15 E. 7th St., between 2nd and 3rd Aves., East Village* ☎ *212/473–9148* ⊕ *www.mcsorleysnewyork.com* Ⓜ *6 to Astor Pl.*

Old Town Bar & Restaurant. This proudly unpretentious bi-level watering hole is heavy on the mahogany and redolent of old New York—it's been around since 1892. Tavern-style grub keeps you afloat through the evening. ⊠ *45 E. 18th St., between Broadway and Park Ave. S, Gramercy* ☎ *212/529–6732* ⊕ *www.oldtownbar.com* Ⓜ *4, 5, 6, L, N, Q, R, W to 14th St./Union Sq.*

Otto's Shrunken Head. A bamboo bar with fish lamps floating overhead sets the mood at this tiki bar with a tattooed, punk crowd. Otto's sells beef jerky to chew on as you play the pinball machine, pose inside the photo booth, or jive to the DJ or band playing anything from '50s to surf rock. ⊠ *538 E. 14th St., between Aves. A and B, East Village* ☎ *212/228–2240* ⊕ *www.ottosshrunkenhead.com* Ⓜ *L to 1st Ave.*

PDT. For those who like their cocktails with a little cloak-and-dagger, the bar PDT (standing for Please Don't Tell) doesn't disappoint. Housed below the unassuming hot-dog joint Crif Dogs, this pseudo-speakeasy can only be reached through a phone booth on the main floor. Patrons with phoned-in reservations are escorted through the phone booth's false back into the building's underbelly, which is decorated with warm wooden beams and tongue-in-cheek taxidermy. ⊠*113 St. Marks Pl., at Ave. A, East Village* ☎*212/614–0386* ⊕*www.pdtnyc.com* Ⓜ*6 to Astor Pl.*

Pete's Tavern. This saloon is famous as the place where (allegedly) O. Henry wrote *The Gift of the Magi* (in the booth up front). These days it's crowded with locals enjoying a beer or a burger. ⊠*129 E. 18th St., at Irving Pl., Gramercy* ☎*212/473–7676* ⊕*www.petestavern.com* Ⓜ*4, 5, 6, L, N, Q, R, W to 14th St./Union Sq.*

★ **The Pink Pony.** Maintaining a bohemian feel on trendy Ludlow Street, this shabby-chic bar-café draws young writers, filmmakers, and designers who come to escape the cacophony from nearby music venues and make conversation over bottles of cheap wine and cup after cup of coffee. ⊠*176 Ludlow St., between E. Houston and Stanton Sts., Lower East Side* ☎*212/253–1922* Ⓜ*F, V to 2nd Ave.*

Temple Bar. This unmarked haunt is famous for its classic cocktails and romantic atmosphere. Walk past the elegant bar to the back where, swathed in almost complete darkness, you can lounge on a comfy banquette and, as its vibe suggests, sip an old-fashioned. ⊠*332 Lafayette St., between Bleecker and E. Houston Sts., East Village* ☎*212/925–4242* ⊕*www.templebarnyc.com* Ⓜ*B, D, F, V to Broadway–Lafayette St.; 6 to Bleecker St.*

16

MIDTOWN AND THE THEATER DISTRICT

Algonquin Hotel. This venerable bar plays up its history as the home of the Algonquin Roundtable, a literary clique that included sharp-tongued Dorothy Parker. The clubby, oak-panel lobby and comfortable sofas encourage lolling over cocktails and conversation. ⊠*59 W. 44th St., between 5th and 6th Aves., Midtown West* ☎*212/840–6800* ⊕*www.algonquinhotel.com* Ⓜ*B, D, F, V to 42nd St.*

Fodor'sChoice **Campbell Apartment.** Commuting professionals pack into this Grand
★ Central Terminal bar on their way to catch trains home during the evening rush. One of Manhattan's more beautiful rooms, the restored space dates to the 1920s, when it was the private office of an executive named John W. Campbell. He knew how to live, and you can enjoy his good taste sipping a well-made cocktail from an overstuffed chair—if you avoid the evening rush. ⊠*15 Vanderbilt Ave. entrance, Grand Central Station, Midtown East* ☎*212/953–0409* ⊕*www.hospitality holdings.com* Ⓜ*4, 5, 6, 7, S to 42nd St./Grand Central.*

Cellar Bar. This stylish spot inside the Bryant Park Hotel is distinguished by a tiled, arched ceiling. One of the more spectacular spaces in Midtown, it lures an attractive crowd from the fashion industry. A DJ with a taste for classic R&B keeps the crowd on its toes. ⊠*40 W. 40th St., between 5th and 6th Aves., Midtown West* ☎*212/642–2260* ⊕*www. bryantparkhotel.com* Ⓜ*B, D, F, V to 42nd St.; 7 to 5th Ave.*

Fodor'sChoice **Hudson Bar.** This swank establishment combines the exclusive feeling of
★ a hot club with the excellent taste of a top hotel. Slip in between the beautiful people mingling under the hand-painted ceiling. The room is illuminated by lights in the glass floor. ⊠*356 W. 58th St., between 8th*

and 9th Aves., Midtown West ☎*212/554–6303* ⊕*www.hudsonhotel. com* Ⓜ*1, A, B, C, D to 59th St.*

Joe Allen. At this old reliable on Restaurant Row, celebrated in the musical version of *All About Eve*, everybody's en route to or from a show. The posters that adorn the "flop wall" are from Broadway musicals that bombed. ✉*326 W. 46th St., between 8th and 9th Aves., Midtown West* ☎*212/581–6464* ⊕*www.joeallenrestaurant.com* Ⓜ*A, C, E to 42nd St.*

Keens Steakhouse. Single-malt Scotch aficionados will appreciate the selection of more than 200 varieties at this 120-year-old restaurant just around the corner from Madison Square Garden. Take a look at the ceilings, which are lined with thousands of clay pipes that once belonged to patrons. ✉*72 W. 36th St., between 5th and 6th Aves., Midtown West* ☎*212/947–3636* ⊕*www.keens.com* Ⓜ*B, D, F, N, Q, R, V, W to 34th St./Herald Sq.*

King Cole Bar. A famed Maxfield Parrish mural is a welcome sight at this classic Midtown meeting place, where the Bloody Mary was introduced to American drinkers. ✉*St. Regis Hotel, 2 E. 55th St., between 5th and Madison Aves., Midtown East* ☎*212/753–4500* Ⓜ*E, V to 5th Ave./53rd St.*

Morgans Bar. Willowy supermodels and their kin frequent this dark, perpetually hip lounge in the basement of Ian Schrager's namesake boutique hotel. The after-work crowd of trendy Manhattanites can be overwhelming, and later at night DJs turn up the volume. ✉*237 Madison Ave., between E. 37th and E. 38th Sts., Midtown East* ☎*212/726–7600* ⊕*www.morganshotel.com* Ⓜ*4, 5, 6, 7, S to 42nd St./Grand Central.*

Morrell Wine Bar and Café. This vibrant bar takes its wine very seriously, with one of the city's best selections of wine by the glass and an epic array of bottles. In summer you can sip at outdoor tables in the heart of Rockefeller Center. ✉*1 Rockefeller Plaza, W. 49th St. between 5th and 6th Aves., Midtown West* ☎*212/262–7700* ⊕*www.morrellwinebar. com* Ⓜ*B, D, F, V to 47th–50th Sts./Rockefeller Center.*

P.J. Clarke's. Mirrors and polished wood adorn New York's most famous Irish bar, where scenes from the 1945 movie *Lost Weekend* were shot. The after-work crowd that unwinds here, drinking beer and eating juicy burgers, seems to appreciate the old-fashioned flair. ✉*915 3rd Ave., at E. 55th St., Midtown East* ☎*212/317–1616* ⊕*www.pjclarkes.com* Ⓜ*4, 5, 6, N, R, W to 59th St–Lexington Ave.*

Fodor's Choice ★ **Royalton.** At this chic hotel, a mainstay among the fashion crowd, wander into Bar 44 for a cocktail against a leather tufted wall before a Broadway show or have your dinner at the hotel's Brasserie 44. ✉*44 W. 44th St., between 5th and 6th Aves., Midtown West* ☎*212/869–4400* ⊕*www.royaltonhotel.com* Ⓜ*B, D, F, V to 42nd St.; 7 to 5th Ave.*

Salon de Ning. Take a break from 5th Avenue shopping at this glass-lined penthouse bar on the 23rd floor. Drinks are pricey but the views are impressive, especially from the rooftop terraces. ✉*Peninsula Hotel, 700 5th Ave., at W. 55th St., Midtown West* ☎*212/956–2888* Ⓜ*E, V to 5th Ave./53rd St.*

Sardi's. "The theater is certainly not what it was," said a forlorn feline in the musical *Cats,* and the same could be said for this Broadway institution. Still, theater fans should make time for a drink in one of the red-leather booths, which are surrounded by caricatures of stars past and present. ✉ *234 W. 44th St., between Broadway and 8th Ave., Midtown West* ☎*212/221–8440* ⊕*www.sardis.com* Ⓜ*A, C, E to 42nd St.*

Top of the Tower. There are lounges at higher altitudes, but this one on the 26th floor feels halfway to heaven. The atmosphere is elegant and subdued. There's live piano music Wednesday–Sunday nights. ✉ *Beekman Tower, 3 Mitchell Pl., near 1st Ave. at E. 49th St., Midtown East* ☎*212/980–4796* ⊕*www.thebeekmanhotel.com* Ⓜ*6 to 51st St./Lexington Ave.; E, V to Lexington Ave./53rd St.*

Water Club. You're not sailing on the East River, although you might feel as if you are, when you step onto the pleasing outdoor deck at the Water Club. This is a special-occasion place—especially for those who've already been to all the landlocked ones in town. A fireplace warms the downstairs bar, and there's piano music every night except Sunday. ✉ *500 E. 30th St., at FDR Dr., Midtown East* ☎*212/683–3333* ⊕*www.thewaterclub.com* Ⓜ*6 to 28th St.*

UPPER EAST SIDE

American Trash. Bicycle tires, golf clubs, and other castoffs cover the walls and ceiling, ensuring that this bar merits its descriptive name. Eight plasma TVs, three video games, a rock-and-roll jukebox, and a pool table keep the neighborhood crowd busy. Some nights local bands play classic rock. ✉ *1471 1st Ave., between E. 76th and E. 77th Sts., Upper East Side* ☎*212/988–9008* ⊕*www.americantrashnyc.com* Ⓜ*6 to 77th St.*

Auction House. This Victorian lounge brings a touch of downtown chic to the sometimes suburban-feeling Upper East Side with its candlelight, high ceilings, and velvet couches. Rap and hip-hop fans should look elsewhere; the only tunes coming out of this joint are alternative and rock. Leave your baseball caps, sneakers, and fur at home. The dress code here forbids them. ✉ *300 E. 89th St., between 1st and 2nd Aves., Upper East Side* ☎*212/427–4458* Ⓜ*4, 5, 6 to 86th St.*

Session 73. Live music sets this sizable restaurant and bar apart from others in the neighborhood. Young locals groove to the nightly mix of funk, jazz, and blues. If the songs don't set your heart racing, there's always the generous assortment of tequilas and beers on tap. ✉ *1359 1st Ave., at E. 73rd St., Upper East Side* ☎*212/517–4445* ⊕*www.session73.com* Ⓜ*6 to 77th St.*

UPPER WEST SIDE

Café des Artistes. At this restaurant known for its glorious art nouveau murals and old-school, upper-crust clientele, the small, warm bar is one of the city's special hideaways. Here interesting strangers tell their life stories. The house drink is a pear-flavor champagne. ✉ *1 W. 67th St., between Central Park W and Columbus Ave., Upper West Side* ☎*212/877–3500* ⊕*www.cafenyc.com* Ⓜ*1 to 66th St.*

Emerald Inn. Hailed by Upper West Siders and visitors from across the five boroughs as the ideal neighborhood bar, this welcoming Irish pub offers friendly staff and a perfect locale to meet a friend for a beer.

16

✉*205 Columbus Ave., between 69th and 70th Sts., Upper West Side* ☎*212/874–8840* Ⓜ*1 to 66th St.*

Gabriel's. It can be hard to find a good grappa in New York, but this highly regarded northern Italian restaurant has a stupendous selection of the strong grape-based elixir, and a 35-foot curved mahogany bar to boot. The atmosphere couldn't be warmer. ✉*11 W. 60th St., between Broadway and Columbus Ave., Upper West Side* ☎*212/956–4600* ⊕*www.gabrielsbarandrest.com* Ⓜ*A, B, C, D, 1 to 59th St.*

Hi-Life. Padded black walls, large round mirrors, and an L-shape bar give this spot the look of a 1940s movie. Settle into a banquette and watch the budding neighborhood bons vivants in action. ✉*477 Amsterdam Ave., at W. 83rd St., Upper West Side* ☎*212/787–7199* ⊕*www.hi-life. com* Ⓜ*1 to 86th St.*

Peter's. A staple of the Upper West Side scene since the early 1980s, this vast, noisy establishment, adorned with copies of the frescoes at Pompeii, hosts a pretheater crowd. Patrons range from their late twenties to their early forties. ✉*182 Columbus Ave., between W. 68th and W. 69th Sts., Upper West Side* ☎*212/877–4747* Ⓜ*B, C to 72nd St.*

Shark Bar. The classy bar at this soul-food (and soul-music) restaurant fills with eye candy every night. Rapper LL Cool J has been known to stop by, and it's very popular among young black executives, music industry bigwigs, and professional athletes. ✉*307 Amsterdam Ave., between W. 74th and W. 75th Sts., Upper West Side* ☎*212/874–8500* Ⓜ*1, 2, 3 to 72nd St.*

GAY AND LESBIAN

Any night of the week, gay men and lesbians can find plenty to keep them occupied. For the latest listings of nightlife options, check out gay publications such as *HX (www.hx.com)*, *Next (www.next magazine.net)*, *MetroSource (www.metrosource.com)*, the *New York Blade (www.nyblade.com)*, and *Paper (www.papermag.com)*. *GO Magazine (www.gomag.com)* is a good source for lesbian happenings.

Some venues always have a mixed crowd, whereas others are exclusively for gay men or lesbians. Some clubs have one night a week where they roll out the red carpet for one group or the other. We sort it out for you below.

DANCE CLUBS AND PARTIES

Beige. Gay men in fashion and advertising predominate at this long-running Tuesday get-together. An occasional celebrity or two keeps it lively. Dress up, or look as if you don't have to. ✉ *B Bar, 358 Bowery, at E. 4th St., East Village* ☎*212/475–2220* Ⓜ*6 to Astor Pl.*

Big Apple Ranch. Country-western and other dance styles are in full swing on Saturday nights at this venue, with half-hour two-step lessons at 8 PM, line dancing at 8:30 PM, and then a down-home dance party. ✉*Dance Manhattan, 39 W. 19th St., 5th fl., between 5th and 6th Aves., Chelsea* ☎*212/358–5752* ⊕*www.bigappleranch.com* Ⓜ*F, R, V, W to 23rd St., 1 to 18th St.*

Easternbloc. Sweaty guys pack into this small, dingy hot spot to dance in red light beneath the hammer-and-sickle-theme decor. The go-go boys swinging around a pole at the center of the room show off the latest fashionable sneakers, and the clientele ranges from East Village hipsters to muscled Chelsea boys in tight black tank tops. ⊠*505 E. 6th St., between Aves. A and B, East Village* ☎*212/777–2555* ⊕*www. easternblocnyc.com* Ⓜ*F, V to 2nd Ave.*

Splash Bar New York. At this large, perennially crowded Chelsea bar-club, beefy go-go boys vie for attention with equally buff bartenders who are frequently clad in their underwear. The daily happy hour, with campy music videos on three huge screens, is a hit. Late-night covers can be high. ⊠*50 W. 17th St., between 5th and 6th Aves., Chelsea* ☎*212/691–0073* ⊕*www.splashbar.com* Ⓜ*6 to Astor Pl.*

LOUNGES

Barracuda. The drag shows are what lures in a mostly male crowd to this comfortable neighborhood hangout. ⊠*275 W. 22nd St., between 7th and 8th Aves., Chelsea* ☎*212/645–8613* Ⓜ*C, E to 23rd St.*

★ **Therapy.** With slate floors, wood-panel walls, and a small stone-filled pond, the decor at this spacious lounge in Hell's Kitchen is as upscale as its mostly male clientele, which includes older uptown profession-als as well as some twentysomething hipsters. An appetizing menu of small dishes is available. ⊠*348 W. 52nd. St., between 8th and 9th Aves., Midtown West* ☎*212/397–1700* ⊕*www.therapy-nyc.com* Ⓜ*C, E to 50th St.*

NEIGHBORHOOD BARS

The Cubby Hole. Early in the evening the crowd is mixed at this neighbor-hood institution, where the DJs and $2 margaritas are popular. Later on, the room belongs to the women. ⊠*281 W. 12th St., at W. 4th St., Greenwich Village* ☎*212/243–9041* ⊕*www.cubbyholebar.com* Ⓜ*A, C, E to 14th St.; L to 8th Ave.*

Gym Sports Bar. At New York's first gay sports bar, the plentiful flat-screen TVs and lots of cheap Bud draw sports enthusiasts of every stripe, from athlete to armchair. The bar sponsors—and frequently hosts parties for—a number of local gay sports teams. ⊠*167 8th Ave., at W. 18th St., Chelsea* ☎*212/337–2439* ⊕*www.gymsportsbar.com* Ⓜ*A, C, E to 14th St.; L to 8th Ave.*

Henrietta Hudson. The nightly parties at this laid-back bar attract young professional women, out-of-towners, and longtime regulars. But be warned that the DJ and the pool table can quickly pack a crowd. ⊠*438 Hudson St., at Morton St., Greenwich Village* ☎*212/924–3347* ⊕*www.henriettahudson.com* Ⓜ*1 to Christopher St./ Sheridan Sq.*

PIANO BARS

Brandy's Piano Bar. A singing waitstaff warms up the mixed crowd at this classy lounge, getting everyone in the mood to belt out their favorite tunes. ⊠*235 E. 84th St., between 2nd and 3rd Aves., Upper East Side* ☎*212/744-4949* ⊕*www.brandysnyc.com* Ⓜ*4, 5, 6 to 86th St.*

16

Marie's Crisis. Everyone seems to know all the words to show tunes you've never even heard of, but after a few drinks you'll be singing along with lots of new friends. ✉ *59 Grove St., at 7th Ave., Greenwich Village* ☎ *212/243–9323* Ⓜ *1 to Christopher St./ Sheridan Sq.*

The Monster. A longtime meeting place in the West Village, the Monster has a piano bar upstairs and a disco downstairs. It's mostly men, but women won't feel out of place. ✉ *80 Grove St., between W. 4th St. and 7th Ave. S, Greenwich Village* ☎ *212/924–3558* ⊕ *www.manhattan-moster.com* Ⓜ *1 to Christopher St./Sheridan Sq.*

The Townhouse. Older, well-off men from the Upper East Side as well as their admirers congregate at this gentlemen's club, which sometimes has a piano player. ✉ *236 E. 58th St., between 2nd and 3rd Aves., Midtown East* ☎ *212/754–4649* ⊕ *www.townhouseny.com* Ⓜ *4, 5, 6, N, R, W to 59th St.–Lexington Ave.*

Shopping

WORD OF MOUTH

"I realize you probably have a Macy's at home, but this one is huge (one whole square block, nine sales floors). I had a friend who was there recently who was totally entranced with the wood escalators. . . . Sounds like she spent 30 minutes just going up and down them!"

—Liz5959

By Jennifer
Paull

Updated by
Nicole Crane
and Sandra
Ramani

New York shopping is a nonstop eye-opener, from the pristine couture houses flanking Madison Avenue to quirkier shops downtown. No matter which threshold you cross, shopping here is an event. For every bursting department store there's an echoing, minimalist boutique; for every familiar national brand there's a secret local favorite. The foremost American and international companies stake their flagships here; meanwhile, small neighborhood shops guarantee unexpected pleasures. National chains often make their New York branches something special, with unique sales environments and exclusive merchandise.

For most New Yorkers, window shopping is almost unavoidable. Midtown workers are constantly passing tempting displays while running to the office or dashing out for coffee. The must-hit shopping neighborhoods concentrate their temptations, sometimes with boutiques in nearly every address on a block, so you can easily spend a couple of hours just browsing.

Special neighborhood profiles throughout this chapter will point you to the best areas and give you expert navigating tips. The individual reviews in this chapter are organized by type of merchandise, in alphabetical order by category. Many specialty stores have several branches in the city; in these cases we have listed the locations in the busier shopping neighborhoods. Happy hunting!

ANTIQUES AND VINTAGE FURNITURE

Antiquing is a fine art in Manhattan. Goods include everything from rarefied museum-quality pieces to wacky and affordable bric-a-brac. Premier shopping areas are on Madison Avenue north of 57th Street, and East 60th Street between 2nd and 3rd avenues, where more than

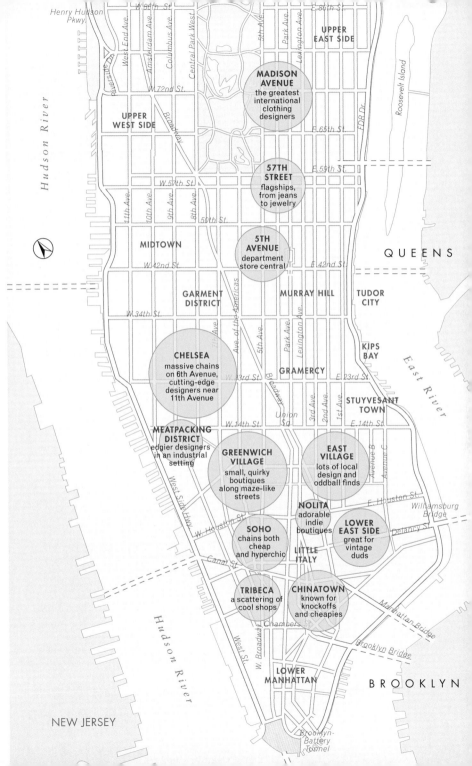

20 shops, dealing in everything from 18th-century French furniture to art-deco lighting fixtures, cluster on one block. Around West 11th and 12th streets between University Place and Broadway, a tantalizing array can be seen in the windows of about two dozen dealers, many of whom have TO THE TRADE signs on their doors; a card from your architect or decorator, however, may get you inside.

AMERICAN AND ENGLISH

Florian Papp. The shine of gilt—on ormolu clocks, chaise lounges, and marble-top tables—lures casual customers in, but this store has an unassailed reputation among knowledgeable collectors. ✉ *962 Madison Ave., between E. 75th and E. 76th Sts., Upper East Side* ☎ *212/288–6770* Ⓜ *6 to 77th St.*

Kentshire Galleries. Pristine furniture is displayed in room settings on seven floors here, with an emphasis on formal English pieces from the 18th and 19th centuries, particularly the Georgian and Regency periods. The collection of period and estate jewelry is a showstopper, from Edwardian pearl earrings to art-deco diamond brooches. ✉ *37 E. 12th St., between University Pl. and Broadway, Greenwich Village* ☎ *212/673–6644* Ⓜ *4, 5, 6, L, N, Q, R, W to 14th St./Union Sq.* ✉ *700 Madison Ave., between E. 62nd and E. 63rd Sts., Upper East Side* ☎ *212/421–1100* Ⓜ *6 to 68th St./Hunter College.*

Leigh Keno American Antiques. Twins Leigh and Leslie Keno set an auction record in the American antiques field by paying $2.75 million for a hairy paw–foot Philadelphia wing chair. They have a good eye and an interesting inventory; gaze up at a tall case clock or down at the delicate legs of a tea table. It's best to make an appointment. ✉ *127 E. 69th St., between Park and Lexington Aves., Upper East Side* ☎ *212/734–2381* Ⓜ *6 to 77th St.*

Newel Art Galleries. Near the East Side's interior-design district, this huge collection spans from the Renaissance through the 20th century. The nonfurniture finds, from figureheads to bell jars, make for prime conversation pieces. ✉ *425 E. 53rd St., between 1st Ave. and Sutton Pl., Midtown East* ☎ *212/758–1970* Ⓜ *6 to 51st St./Lexington Ave.; E, V to Lexington–3rd Aves./53rd St.*

ASIAN

Chinese Porcelain Company. Though the name of this prestigious shop indicates one of its specialties, its stock covers more ground, ranging from lacquerware to Khmer sculpture to 18th-century French furniture. ✉ *475 Park Ave., at E. 58th St., Midtown East* ☎ *212/838–7744* Ⓜ *N, R, W to 5th Ave.*

Flying Cranes Antiques. Here you can find a well-regarded collection of rare, museum-quality pieces from the Meiji period, the time known as Japan's Golden Age. Items include ceramics, cloisonné, metalwork, carvings, ikebana baskets, and samurai swords and fittings. ✉ *Manhattan Art and Antiques Center, 1050 2nd Ave., between E. 55th and E. 56th Sts., Midtown East* ☎ *212/223–4600* Ⓜ *N, R, W, 4, 5, 6 to 59th St./Lexington Ave.*

Jacques Carcangues, Inc. Carrying goods from Japan to India, this SoHo gallery offers an eclectic array of objects, from pillboxes to 18th-century

Burmese Buddhas. ✉*21 Greene St., between Grand and Canal Sts., SoHo* ☎*212/925–8110* Ⓜ*4, 5, 6, R, W to Canal St.*

EUROPEAN

Newel Art Galleries and Florian Papp, covered under American and English antiques, and the Chinese Porcelain Company, listed under Asian antiques, also carry European pieces.

L'Antiquaire & The Connoisseur, Inc. Proprietor Helen Fioratti has written a guide to French antiques, but she's equally knowledgeable about her Italian and Spanish furniture and decorative objects from the 15th through the 18th century, as well as about the medieval arts. ✉*36 E. 73rd St., between Madison and Park Aves., Upper East Side* ☎*212/517–9176* Ⓜ*6 to 77th St.*

Leo Kaplan Ltd. The impeccable items here include art nouveau glass and pottery, porcelain from 18th-century England, antique and modern paperweights, and Russian artwork. ✉*114 E. 57th St., between Park and Lexington Aves., Upper East Side* ☎*212/249–6766* Ⓜ*N, R, W, 4, 5, 6 to 59th St./Lexington Ave.*

Les Pierre Antiques. Pierre Deux popularized French Provincial through reproductions; come here for a strong selection of the real thing, from etchings to sconces to armoires. Inside one of the period birdcages flutters a pet dove. ✉*369 Bleecker St., at Charles St., Greenwich Village* ☎*212/243–7740* Ⓜ*1 to Christopher St./Sheridan Sq.*

20TH-CENTURY FURNITURE AND MEMORABILIA

17

Las Venus. Step into this kitsch palace and you may feel as though a time machine has zapped you back to the '50s, '60s, or groovy '70s—depending on which vintage pieces are in stock. Look for bubble lamps, lots of brocade, and Knoll knockoffs; a second location around the corner catches the overflow. ✉*163 Ludlow St., between E. Houston and Stanton Sts., Lower East Side* ☎*212/982–0608* Ⓜ*F, V to 2nd Ave.*

Lost City Arts. In addition to mod furniture, like pod and Eames chairs, and industrial memorabilia, such as neon gas-station clocks, Lost City can help you relive the Machine Age with an in-house, retro-modern line of furniture. ✉*18 Cooper Sq., at E. 5th St., East Village* ☎*212/375–0500* Ⓜ*6 to Astor Pl.*

BEAUTY

FRAGRANCE

★ **Aedes De Venustas.** Swathed in red velvet, this jewel-box-size store stocks a well-edited selection of hard-to-find skin-care lines like Annick Goutal and Duchess Marden; fragrance from Creed, Les Bains du Marais, Costes, and Heeley; and pricey candles from Diptyque and Mariage Freres. Their signature gift wrap is as beautiful as what's inside the box. ✉*9 Christopher St., between 6th and 7th Aves., Greenwich Village* ☎*212/206–8674* Ⓜ*1 to Christopher St./Sheridan Sq.*

★ **Bond No. 9.** Created by the same fragrance team as Creed, this line of scents is intended to evoke the New York City experience. Perfumes are named after neighborhoods: Central Park, a men's fragrance, is woodsy and "green"; the feminine Park Avenue is regal and sophisticated,

Continued on page 324

SOHO

Somehow, everything looks a bit more beautiful here. Maybe it's because of the way sunlight filters down the cast-iron facades, glinting off the shop windows. Maybe it's because the uneven cobblestone streets prompt you to slow down, giving you time to notice details.

Jaded locals call this neighborhood a touristy outdoor mall. True, you'll see plenty of familiar company names, and several common, less expensive chains, like Banana Republic and Sephora, have made land grabs on Broadway. There's also a certain amount of luxury one-upmanship, as stores like Prada, Chanel, and Louis Vuitton have planted themselves here for downtown cred. But you can still hit a few clothing and housewares boutiques you won't find elsewhere in this country. The hottest shopping area runs west from Broadway over to 6th Avenue, between West Houston and Grand streets. Don't overlook a couple of streets east of Broadway: Crosby and Lafayette each have a handful of intriguing shops.
—by Jennifer Paull

BEST TIME TO GO

Wednesday through Friday afternoons, when all the stores are open and the people-watching is prime, but the streets aren't hideously crowded. On weekends, Broadway and Prince Street can feel like a cattle drive.

BEST SOUVENIR FOR YOUR IN-LAWS

If they're caffeine fiends, consider the house-blend coffees and teas at **Dean & Deluca** (560 Broadway at Prince St.), which you can pair with sophisticated snacks in a D&D tote or metal lunch box.

IN FOCUS SOHO

KEY

Ⓜ Subway stops

Ⓜ A,C,E

BEST FOR

WHAT TO WEAR

Prada: the high-concept, Rem Koolhaas–designed store steals the spotlight from the clothes.

Kirna Zabête: uncommon, sought-after women's clothing in a cheerful, unpretentious space.

Kate Spade: the mother lode for clever handbags, plus retro-ish shoes and a few baubles.

HOUSEWARES

Moss: exquisite, innovative design for everything from wineglasses to bathtubs.

Clio: low-key vibe but high-scoring selection of unique tableware.

Jonathan Adler: a loving spin on mid-century mod (and kitsch) in ceramics and furniture.

De Vera: eclectic selection of antiques and new objets d'art, from Murano glass to Japanese lacquer.

REFUELING

For something on the fly, drop by **Balthazar Bakery** (✉ *80 Spring St., between Broadway and Crosby St.* ☎ *212/965–1785*) for a scone, madeleine, or walnut-studded brownie with a potent cup of coffee. If you'd rather have a seat, make your way to the tearoom hidden in the back of Marie Belle for a cup of their excellent hot chocolate.

with hints of iris and rose. The Bond Street shop, with its airy space and wood-panel Tea Library, is a lovely place to linger. ⊠ *9 Bond St., between Lafayette St. and Broadway, East Village* ☎*212/228–1940* Ⓜ *6 to Bleecker St. 897 Madison Ave., between E. 72nd and E. 73rd Sts., Upper East Side* ☎*212/794–4480* Ⓜ *6 to 68th St/Hunter College 680 Madison Ave., between E. 61st and E. 62nd Sts., Upper East Side* ☎*212/838–2780* Ⓜ*N, R, W, 4, 5, 6 to 59th St./Lexington Ave. 399 Bleecker St., between Perry and W. 11 Sts., Greenwich Village* ☎*212/633–1641* Ⓜ*1 to Christopher St.; A, C, E to 14th St.*

Jo Malone. Consider this extra incentive to visit the landmark Flatiron Building. Unisex scents such as lime blossom and vetiver can be worn alone or, in the Malone style, layered. Since Malone uses colognes, not perfumes, it's not overpowering. You can also book one of the famed massage-based facials. (The uptown branch offers all the scents, but not the facial.) ⊠ *949 Broadway, at 5th Ave., Flatiron District* ☎*212/673–2220* Ⓜ*R, W to 23rd St. 946 Madison Ave., between E. 74th and E. 75th Sts., Upper East Side* ☎*212/472–0074* Ⓜ*6 to 77th St.*

L'Artisan Parfumeur. These tiny shops may look unassuming, but the line of gorgeous, limited-edition scents sold here is nothing to sneeze at. Some fragrances, like the myrrh-and-vetiver-infused Timbuktu, conjure faraway locales. Others, like the rosy, feminine La Chasse aux Papillons ("Chasing the Butterflies"), evoke nostalgic whimsy. ⊠ *68 Thompson St., between Spring and Broome Sts., SoHo* ☎*212/334–1500* Ⓜ*R, W to Prince St. 1100 Madison Ave., between E. 82nd and E. 83rd Sts., Upper East Side* ☎*212/794–3600* Ⓜ*6 to 68th St./Hunter College.*

MAKEUP AND SKIN CARE

Fresh. It sounds good enough to eat: a brown-sugar skin-care line, pomegranate hair conditioner, pear-cassis cologne. The 3rd Avenue location offers decadent skin and body treatments—many of which are free with the purchase of product—in a back spa room. ⊠ *57 Spring St., between Lafayette and Mulberry Sts., SoHo* ☎*212/925–0099* Ⓜ*6 to Spring St.* ⊠*1367 3rd Ave., at E. 78th St., Upper East Side* ☎*212/585–3400* Ⓜ*6 to 77th St.* ⊠*159 Columbus Ave., between W. 67th and W. 68th Sts., Upper West Side* ☎*212/396–4545* Ⓜ*1 to 66th St.* ⊠*388 Bleecker St., between Perry and W. 11th Sts., Greenwich Village* ☎*917/408–1850* Ⓜ*1, 2, 3 to 14th St.* ⊠*872 Broadway, at 18th St., Flatiron District* ☎*212/477–1100* Ⓜ*N, R to 23rd St.*

Fodor'sChoice
★

Kiehl's Since 1851. At this favored haunt of top models and stylists, white-smocked assistants can help you choose between the lotions and potions, all of which are packaged in deceptively simple-looking bottles and jars. Some of the products, such as the pineapple-papaya facial scrub, Silk Groom hair-styling aid, and the superrich Creme de Corps, have attained near-cult status among beautyphiles. ■ TIP➔Kiehl's is also known for being generous with samples, so be sure to ask for your own bag of take-home testers. ⊠*109 3rd Ave., at E. 13th St., East Village* ☎*212/677–3171* Ⓜ*4, 5, 6, L, N, Q, R, W to 14th St./Union Sq.* ⊠*154 Columbus Ave., at W. 67th St., Upper West Side* ☎*212/799–3438* Ⓜ*1 to 66th St./Lincoln Center*

CLOSE UP

Deals & Steals

Even a temporary New Yorker loves a bargain. Scoring a good deal is a rite of passage for everyone, economic bracket be darned. The city offers everything from low-cost department stores like Century 21 to hawkers of pseudo Rolex watches and Kate Spade bags stationed at street corners and in Canal Street stalls. And then there are the sample sales.

If a seasonal sale makes New Yorkers' eyes gleam, a sample sale throws shoppers into a frenzy. With so many designer flagships and corporate headquarters in town, merchandise fallout periodically leads to tremendous deals. Although, technically, the phrase "sample sale" refers to stock that's a sample design, show model, leftover, or is already discounted, the term is now also used for sales of current season goods. Location adds a bit of an illicit thrill to the event: sales are held in hotels, warehouses, offices, or loft spaces, where items both incredible and unfortunate jam a motley assortment of racks, tables, and bins. Generally, there is a makeshift communal dressing room but mirrors are scarce, so veteran sample-sale shoppers come prepared for wriggling in the aisles; some wear skirts, tights, and tank tops for modest quick-changes. Two rules of thumb: grab first and inspect later, and call in advance to find out what methods of payment are accepted. One of the ultimate experiences is the Barneys Warehouse Sale, held in February and August in Chelsea. Other luscious sales range from the Vera Wang bridal-gown sale (early winter) to TSE cashmere (spring and late fall).

How to find out about these events? The level of publicity and regularity of sales vary. The print and online versions of *New York* magazine are always worth checking for sample sale tip-offs, as are regular bulletins on Racked (*http://racked.com*) and Daily Candy (*www.dailycandy.com*). If you're interested in specific designers, call their shops and inquire—you may get lucky.

17

Korres. Greece's oldest homeopathic pharmacy rolls out its line of herb- and flower-based skin treatments. Best sellers like wild-rose moisturizer and thyme-honey cream line the modular shelves of the gallerylike store. ✉*110 Wooster St., between Prince and Spring Sts., SoHo* ☎*212/219–0683* Ⓜ*N, R to Prince St.*

★ **Santa Maria Novella.** A heavy, iron-barred door leads to a hushed, scented inner sanctum of products from this medieval Florentine pharmacy. Many of the colognes, creams, and soaps are intriguingly archaic, such as the iris toothpaste and the Vinegar of the Seven Thieves (a variant on smelling salts). Everything is packaged in bottles and jars with antique-style apothecary labels. ✉*285 Lafayette St., between E. Houston and Prince Sts., SoHo* ☎*212/925–0001* Ⓜ*N, R to Prince St.*

BOOKS

CHILDREN'S BOOKS

Books of Wonder. The friendly, knowledgeable staff can help select gifts for all reading levels from the extensive, beautiful selection of children's books. Oziana is a specialty. An outpost of the Cupcake Café gives little browsers a second wind. ⊠*18 W. 18th St., between 5th and 6th Aves., Chelsea* 🕾*212/989–3270* Ⓜ*F, V to 14th St.*

Scholastic Store. An 11-foot orange dinosaur—with a cushioned tail doubling as a reading sofa—and a life-size Magic School Bus welcome kids to this truly fun emporium. With games, toys, DVDs, computers, arts and crafts workshops, and above all, books, this downtown spot is so family friendly, it has a separate entrance just for strollers (at 130 Mercer Street). ⊠*557 Broadway, at Prince St., SoHo* 🕾*212/343–6166* Ⓜ*R, W to Prince St.*

FOREIGN LANGUAGE

Librairie de France/Libreria Hispanica. This store offers one of the country's largest selections of foreign-language books, videos, and periodicals, mostly in French and Spanish. You can also find dozens of dictionaries, phrase books, and other learning materials. ⊠*610 5th Ave., Rockefeller Center Promenade, Midtown West* 🕾*212/581–8810* Ⓜ*B, D, F, V to 47th–50th Sts./Rockefeller Center.*

GENERAL INTEREST

Barnes & Noble. Without argument, this is the biggest bookstore presence in the city. ⊠*1972 Broadway, at W. 66th St., Upper West Side* 🕾*212/595–6859* Ⓜ*1 to 66th St./Lincoln Center* ⊠*33 E. 17th St., at Union Sq., Flatiron District* 🕾*212/253–0810* Ⓜ*4, 5, 6, N, Q, R, W to 14th St./Union Sq.*

Biography Bookshop. Published diaries, letters, biographies, and autobiographies fill this neighborly store. There's also a thoughtful selection of general nonfiction, fiction, guidebooks, and children's books. The sale tables outside have deals on everything from Graham Greene to Chuck Palahniuk. ⊠*400 Bleecker St., at W. 11th St., Greenwich Village* 🕾*212/807–8655* Ⓜ*1 to Christopher St./Sheridan Sq.*

Borders. The smart, cheery flagship Columbus Circle branch of this second-biggest bookstore chain in the city is worth a browse. ⊠*461 Park Ave., at E. 57th St., Midtown East* 🕾*212/980–6785* Ⓜ*N, R, W, 4, 5, 6 to 59th St./Lexington Ave.* ⊠*10 Columbus Circle, at 59th St., Upper West Side* 🕾*212/823–9775* Ⓜ*1, A, B, C, D to Columbus Circle.*

The Complete Traveller Antiquarian Bookstore. Founded in the '80s by two former travel writers, this store specializes in rare and antique voyage-related books, and promises the country's largest selection of out-of-print Baedeker travel guides. They stock surprisingly affordable vintage maps, unusual tomes with New York City themes, and a full spectrum of books—from history and geography to poetry and fiction—that emphasize travel. ✉ *199 Madison Ave., at 35th St., Murray Hill* ☎ *212/685–9007* Ⓜ *6 to 33rd St.*

★ **Crawford Doyle Booksellers.** You're as likely to see an old edition of Wodehouse as a best seller in the window of this shop. You'll find a quality selection of fiction, nonfiction, and biographies, plus some rare books on the balcony. Salespeople offer their opinions *and* ask for yours. ✉ *1082 Madison Ave., between E. 81st and E. 82nd Sts., Upper East Side* ☎ *212/288–6300* Ⓜ *4, 5, 6 to 86th St.*

Idlewild. Named for the pre-1960s JFK Airport, this travel-inspired bookstore groups its goods by destination. It has much more than guidebooks, though; novels, histories, cookbooks, and children's books share each segment, giving you a fascinating look at any given locale. If those chairs look familiar, you may have spent a layover in one of them, once upon a time in the American Airlines terminal. ✉ *12 W. 19th St., 2nd fl., at 5th Ave., West Village* ☎ *212/414–8888* Ⓜ *4, 5, 6, L, Q, R, W to 14th St./Union Sq.*

★ **McNally Jackson.** McNally makes a happy counterpart to the nearby Housing Works bookstore; both places have that welcoming vibe. Check the tables up front for hot-off-the-press novels, nonfiction, and manifestos. Upstairs you'll find fiction arranged by the authors' region of origin, a great way to learn more about, say, Asian or South American writing. (Salman Rushdie gets grouped with the Global Nomads.) The staff are by and large literary themselves, so ask for recommendations if you're browsing. ✉ *52 Prince St., between Lafayette and Mulberry Sts., SoHo* ☎ *212/274–1160* Ⓜ *R, W to Prince St.*

Partners & Crime. Imported British paperbacks, helpful staff, a rental library, and whodunits galore—new, out-of-print, and first editions—make this a must-browse for fans. Revered mystery writers give readings here. ✉ *44 Greenwich Ave., between 6th and 7th Aves., Greenwich Village* ☎ *212/243–0440* Ⓜ *F, V, 1, 2, 3 to 14th St.*

★ **St. Mark's Bookshop.** Downtown residents, NYU students, and intellectuals in general love this store, spending hours poking through popular and oddball fiction and nonfiction. You'll find a truly eclectic, attitudinal collection of books here, not unlike the salespeople. On the main floor, books on critical theory are right up front, across from new fiction titles—this is perhaps the only place where you can find Jacques Derrida facing off against T. C. Boyle. Cultural and art books are up front as well; literature and literary journals fill the back of the store. ■ TIP➔ It's open daily until midnight. ✉ *31 3rd Ave., at 9th St., East Village* ☎ *212/260–7853* Ⓜ *6 to Astor Pl.*

Shakespeare & Co. Booksellers. The stock here represents what's happening in just about every field of publishing today: students can grab a last-minute Gertrude Stein for class, then rummage through the homages to cult pop-culture figures. Late hours at the Broadway location (until 11 PM Monday through Saturday; 9 PM on Sunday) are a plus. ✉ *939 Lexington Ave., between E. 68th and E. 69th Sts., Upper East Side* ☎ *212/570–0201* Ⓜ *6 to 68th St./Hunter College* ✉ *137 E. 23rd St., at Lexington Ave., Gramercy* ☎ *212/505–2021* Ⓜ *6 to 23rd St.* ✉ *716*

17

Broadway, at Washington Pl., Greenwich Village ☎*212/529–1330* Ⓜ*R, W to 8th St.*

FodorśChoice   **The Strand.** The Broadway branch—a downtown hangout—proudly
★   claims to have "18 miles of books." Craning your neck among the
tall-as-trees stacks will likely net you something from the mix of new
and old. Rare books are next door, at 826 Broadway, on the third floor.
(The buildings are connected inside.) ⊠*828 Broadway, at E. 12th St.,
East Village* ☎*212/473–1452* Ⓜ*L, N, Q, R, W, 4, 5, 6 to 14th St./
Union Sq.*

★   **Three Lives & Co.** Three Lives has one of the city's best book selections.
The display tables and counters highlight the latest literary fiction and
serious nonfiction, classics, quirky gift books, and gorgeously illustrated
tomes. The staff members' literary knowledge is formidable, and they
can help you find most any book—even if it's not carried in the store.
⊠*154 W. 10th St., at Waverly Pl., Greenwich Village* ☎*212/741–2069*
Ⓜ*1 to Christopher St./Sheridan Sq.*

MUSIC AND THEATER

Colony Music. Siphoning energy from Times Square, this place keeps its
neon blinking until 1 AM Monday through Saturday, and midnight on
Sunday. Inspired by the Broadway musical or concert you've just seen?
Snap up the sheet music, CD, or karaoke set here. ⊠*1619 Broadway,
at W. 49th St., Midtown West* ☎*212/265–2050* Ⓜ*R, W to 49th St.*

Drama Book Shop. If you're looking for a script, be it a lesser-known Russian translation or a Broadway hit, chances are you can find it here. The
range of books spans film, music, dance, TV, and biographies. ⊠*250 W.
40th St., between 7th and 8th Aves., Midtown West* ☎*212/944–0595*
Ⓜ*A, C, E to 42nd St./Port Authority.*

Joseph Patelson Music House. A huge collection of scores (some 47,000
pieces of sheet music for piano, organ, strings, woodwind, and brass,
and chambers and ensembles) has long made this a hub for music lovers. Fittingly, it's right by Carnegie Hall. ⊠*160 W. 56th St., between
6th and 7th Aves., Midtown West* ☎*212/582–5840* Ⓜ*F, N, Q, R, W
to 57th St.*

RARE AND USED BOOKS

Crawford Doyle Booksellers, Complete Traveller, and the Strand, covered under General Interest, also carry rare and used titles.

Argosy Bookstore. This sedate landmark, established in 1921, keeps a
scholarly stock of books and autographs. It's also a great place to look
for low-price maps and prints. ⊠*116 E. 59th St., between Park and
Lexington Aves., Midtown East* ☎*212/753–4455* Ⓜ*N, R, W, 4, 5, 6
to 59th St./Lexington Ave.*

★   **Housing Works Used Book Café.** If the jostling sidewalks of SoHo have
you on edge, head one block east of Broadway to this sanctuary of a
used-book store. There's lots of room to browse, and plenty of chairs
where you can relax and flip through your finds (for hefty art books,
you might want to grab a table at the café in back). ⊠*126 Crosby St.,
between E. Houston and Prince Sts., NoLita* ☎*212/334–3324* Ⓜ*R,
W to Prince St.*

Skyline Books. An endearingly scruffy, small, old-school space makes this the Woody Allen of used-book stores. Come here for out-of-print books in all categories, a large Beat Generation selection, and literary first editions. ✉*13 W. 18th St., between 5th and 6th Aves., Chelsea* ☎*212/675–4773* Ⓜ*4, 5, 6, N, Q, R, W to 14th St./Union Sq.*

Westsider Rare & Used Books. This wonderfully crammed space is a lifesaver on the otherwise sparse Upper West Side. Squeeze in among the stacks of art books and fiction; clamber up the steep stairway and you'll find all sorts of rare books. ✉*2246 Broadway, between W. 80th and W. 81st Sts., Upper West Side* ☎*212/362–0706* Ⓜ*1 to 79th St.*

CAMERAS AND ELECTRONICS

Apple Store. After Apple's first store, in a former SoHo post office, hooked the e-mail generation, the brand took things a step further. The 5th Avenue location, topped by a giant translucent cube, is open 24 hours a day, every day, to satisfy those wee-hours computer cravings. ■TIP➔In-store events include Midnight Mixes spun by top DJs. At all stores you'll have to elbow through a crowd, but they're the best places to check out the latest equipment, software, demos, and troubleshooting Genius Bars. ✉*103 Prince St., at Greene St., SoHo* ☎*212/226–3126* Ⓜ*R, W to Prince St* ✉*767 5th Ave., between E. 58th and E. 59th Sts., Midtown East* ☎*212/336–1440* Ⓜ*R, W to 60th St.* ✉*401 W. 14th St., at 9th Ave., Meatpacking District* ☎*212/444–3400* Ⓜ*A, C, E to 14th St.*

Fodor's Choice
★ **B&H Photo Video and Pro Audio.** As baskets of purchases trundle along on tracks overhead, you can plunge into the excellent selection of imaging, audio, video, and lighting equipment. The staff are generous with advice and will happily compare merchandise. Low prices, good customer service, and a liberal returns policy make this a favorite with pros and amateurs alike. ■TIP➔Be sure to leave a few extra minutes for the checkout procedure; also, keep in mind that the store is closed Friday evening through Saturday. ✉*420 9th Ave., between W. 33rd and W. 34th Sts., Midtown West* ☎*212/444–5000* Ⓜ*A, C, E, 1, 2, 3 to 34th St./Penn Station.*

J&R Music World. Just south of City Hall, J&R has emerged as the city's most competitively priced one-stop electronics outlet, with an enormous selection of video equipment, computers, stereos, and cameras. The staff is hands-on and super knowledgeable; many of them are A/V wizards who've worked here since the early 1990s. Home-office supplies are at No. 1, computers at No. 15, small appliances at No. 27. ✉*23 Park Row, between Beekman and Ann Sts., Lower Manhattan* ☎*212/238–9000* Ⓜ*4, 5, 6 to Brooklyn Bridge/City Hall.*

SONY Style. This equipment and music store comes in a glossy package, with imaginative window displays and a downstairs demonstration area for the integrated systems. You'll find all the latest stereo and entertainment systems, digital cameras, and MP3 players on the shelves. ✉*550 Madison Ave., at E. 55th St., Midtown East* ☎*212/833–8800* Ⓜ*E, V, 6 to 51st St./Lexington Ave.*

17

Continued on page 332

NOLITA

The Nabokovian nickname, shorthand for "North of Little Italy," covers a neighborhood that has taken the commercial baton from SoHo and run with it.

Like SoHo, NoLita has gone from a locals-only, understated area to a crowded weekend magnet, as much about people-watching as it is about shopping. Still, unlike those of its SoHo neighbor, these stores remain largely one-of-a-kind. Running along the parallel north–south spines of Elizabeth, Mott, and Mulberry streets, between East Houston and Kenmare streets, NoLita's boutiques tend to be small and, as real estate dictates, somewhat pricey. —J.P.

BEST TIME TO GO

Wednesday through Friday afternoons if you're keen to shop without too many distractions, weekends for more people to scope out. Shops stay open latest (usually until 8 PM) Thursday through Saturday.

BEST SOUVENIR FOR YOUR BABYSITTER

Beautifully packaged, petal-topped candles exclusive to **Red Flower** (✉ *13 Prince St., at Elizabeth St.* ☎ *212/966–5301*) in dreamy scents like jasmine and Japanese peony. Or perhaps some calming chamomile or lavender bath products from the ancient Italian perfumer-pharmacist **Santa Maria Novella**.

BEST FOR

TOO-COOL-FOR-SCHOOL CLOTHES

Mayle: ladylike looks with two dashes of retro flair and a pinch of eccentricity.

Seize sur Vingt: whether customized or off the rack, these button-downs and suits are perfectly cut.

Resurrection: mint-condition vintage Pucci and Courrèges make this a stylist's gold mine.

Calypso: a half dozen boutiques in NoLita alone for softly exotic clothes and housewares.

FOXY SHOES

Sigerson Morrison: this strappy-sandal success has the biggest footprint in the 'hood.

...AND OTHER ACCESSORIES

Jamin Puech: run-away-bohemian-heiress handbags dripping with embroidery and fringe.

Me + Ro: Indian-inspired gold and silver jewelry, from shoulder-duster ear-rings to tiny lotus-petal pendants.

REFUELING

Hit the takeout window of **Café Gitane** (✉ *242 Mott St., at Prince St.* ☎ *212/334–9552*) for the best espresso; it comes with a little square of dark chocolate for an extra boost. Or, if you don't mind getting your fingers messy, stop by **Café Habana to Go** (✉ *17 Prince St., at Elizabeth St.* ☎ *212/625–2002*) for an addictively salty, cheese-topped ear of grilled corn.

Cool Spots for Souvenirs

What to get from the city that has everything? Major tourist attractions keep their gift shops well stocked with all the standard souvenirs, and dozens of gift shops dot the Times Square area. If you're looking for grungier souvenirs of downtown (T-shirts with salty messages, tattoos), troll St. Marks Place between 2nd and 3rd avenues in the East Village. But for more unique mementos of the city, see this chapter's neighborhood spotlights for ideas and try the sources below.

City Store. Discover all kinds of books and pamphlets that explain New York City's government, from pocket maps, NYPD T-shirts, and cocktail napkins printed with subway routes to manhole-cover coasters and a New York City–scented candle (don't worry, it smells like apple pie, not exhaust). The store shuts at 4:30 on weekdays and is closed weekends. ✉ *1 Centre St., at Chambers St., Lower Manhattan* ☎ *212/669–8246* Ⓜ *4, 5, 6 to City Hall/Brooklyn Bridge.*

Eleni's. Take a bite out of the Big Apple—in cookie form—with these perfectly decorated treats. The "I'll Take Manhattan" tin includes sugar cookies that mimic local icons like yellow cabs and the Statue of Liberty. ✉ *Chelsea Market, 75 9th Ave., between W. 15th and W. 16th Sts., Chelsea* ☎ *212/255–6804* Ⓜ *A, C, E to 14th St., L to 8th Ave.*

H&H Bagels. Looking for a taste of the city? Although a slice of pizza may not travel so well, bagels are another story. H&H can pack its bagels to withstand any plane ride—and in true New York spirit, the store is open 24 hours a day. ✉ *2239 Broadway, at W. 80th St., Upper West Side* ☎ *212/595–8003* Ⓜ *1 to 79th St.*

New York City Transit Museum Gift Shop. In the symbolic heart of New York City's transit system, all the store's merchandise is somehow linked to the MTA, from straphanger ties to skateboards decorated with subway-line logos. ✉ *Grand Central Terminal, Vanderbilt Pl. and E. 42nd St., Midtown East* ☎ *212/878–0106* Ⓜ *4, 5, 6, 7 to 42nd St./Grand Central Terminal.*

CHILDREN'S CLOTHING

PLAY CLOTHES

Oilily. Stylized flowers, stripes, and animal shapes splash across these brightly colored play and school clothes from the trippy Dutch brand. Note that the SoHo location doesn't stock the boys' line. ✉ *820 Madison Ave., between E. 68th and E. 69th Sts., Upper East Side* ☎ *212/772–8686* Ⓜ *6 to 68th St./Hunter College* ✉ *465 West Broadway, between Prince and Houston Sts., SoHo* ☎ *212/871–0201* Ⓜ *6 to Spring St.*

Petit Bateau. Fine cotton is spun into comfortable underwear, play clothes, and pajamas; T-shirts come in dozens of colors and to every specification, with V-necks, round necks, snap-fronts, and more. ✉ *1094 Madison Ave., at E. 82nd St., Upper East Side* ☎ *212/988–8884* Ⓜ *4, 5, 6 to 86th St.*

Shoofly. Children's shoes and accessories are the name of the game here; you can choose from Mary Janes, wing tips, and Dolce & Gabbana fur-lined booties along with pom-pom hats, brightly patterned socks, and jewelry. ⊠*42 Hudson St., between Thomas and Duane Sts., TriBeCa* ☎*212/406–3270* Ⓜ*1 to Franklin St.*

★ **Space Kiddets.** The funky (Elvis-print rompers, onesies made from old concert tees) mixes with the old-school (retro cowboy-print pants, brightly colored clogs, New York borough-pride gear) and the high-end (Lilli Gaufrette, Kenzo, Boo Foo Woo from Japan) at this casual, trendsetting store. The original space around the corner, at 46 East 21st Street, now stocks toys only. ⊠*26 E. 22nd St., between Broadway and Park Ave., Flatiron District* ☎*212/420–9878* Ⓜ*6 to 23rd St.*

PRECIOUS

Bonpoint. The sophistication here lies in the beautiful designs and impeccable workmanship—velvet-tipped coats with matching caps and hand-embroidered jumpers and blouses. ⊠*1269 Madison Ave., at E. 91st St., Upper East Side* ☎*212/722–7720* Ⓜ*4, 5, 6 to 86th St.* ⊠*810 Madison Ave., at 68th St., Upper East Side* ☎*212/879–0900* Ⓜ*6 to 68th St./Hunter College* ⊠*392 Bleecker St., at 68th St., Upper East Side* ☎*212/647–1700* Ⓜ*1 to Christopher St./Sheridan Sq.*

Bu and the Duck. Vintage-inspired children's clothing, shoes, and toys distinguish this shop. The Italian-made spectator boots might make you wish your own feet were tiny again. ⊠*106 Franklin St., at Church St., TriBeCa* ☎*212/431–9226* Ⓜ*1 to Franklin St.*

Flora and Henri. The padded twill coats, slate-blue pleated skirts, and pin-dot cotton dresses here are cute but not overly so. They'll stand up to wear and tear; witness the sturdy Italian-made shoes. ⊠*1023 Lexington Ave., between E. 73rd and E. 74th Sts., Upper East Side* ☎*212/249–1695* Ⓜ*6 to 77th St.*

Infinity. Mothers gossip near the dressing rooms as their daughters try on slinky Les Tout Petits dresses, Miss Sixty Jeans, and cheeky tees with slogans like "chicks ahoy." The aggressively trendy and the rather sweet meet in a welter of preteen accessories. ⊠*1116 Madison Ave., at E. 83rd St., Upper East Side* ☎*212/517–4232* Ⓜ*4, 5, 6 to 86th St.*

Les Petits Chapelais. Designed and made in France, these kids' clothes are adorable but also practical. Corduroy outfits have details like embroidered flowers and contrasting cuffs; soft fleecy jackets are reversible, and sweaters have easy-zip-up fronts and hoodies. ⊠*86 Thompson St., between Spring and Prince Sts., SoHo* ☎*212/625–1023* Ⓜ*C, E to Spring St.*

Lilliput. At both locations, which face each other across the street, kids can up their coolness quotient with Paul Smith sweaters, sequined party dresses, and denim wear by Diesel. The difference is that the shop at No. 265 carries it all up to size 8, whereas the original shop goes up to teens. ⊠*240 Lafayette St., between Prince and Spring Sts., SoHo* ☎*212/965–9201* Ⓜ*R, W to Prince St.* ⊠*265 Lafayette St., between Prince and Spring Sts., SoHo* ☎*212/965–9567* Ⓜ*6 to Spring St.*

17

CHOCOLATE

Chocolate Bar. Along with this shop's signature and retro chocolate bars (the latter include such flavors as caramel apple and coconut cream pie) is an array of filled chocolate bonbons. At the café counter you can get a steaming cup of cocoa. The bar is open until 10 PM nightly. ⊠*127 E. 7th St ., between 1st Ave. and Ave. A, East Village* ☎*212/366–1541* Ⓜ*6 to Astor Pl.*

★ **Jacques Torres Chocolate Haven.** Visit the café and shop here and you'll literally be surrounded by chocolate. The glass-walled space is in the heart of Torres's chocolate factory, so you can watch the goodies being made while you sip a richly spiced cocoa. ■TIP→Signature taste: the

"wicked" chocolate, laced with cinnamon and chili pepper. ⊠*350 Hudson St., at King St., SoHo* ☎*212/414–2462* Ⓜ*1 to Houston St.*

Kee's Chocolates. Walking into this small store, you might get a whiff of warm chocolate or spy a few smeared spatulas in the back, attesting to the candy's homemade origin. Yet what's in the case looks preternaturally perfect: dark chocolates filled with *yuzu* (a Japanese citrus), covered with freshly crushed pistachios, or flavored with lemon and basil. ⊠*80 Thompson St., between Spring and Broome Sts., SoHo* ☎*212/334–3284* Ⓜ*A, C to Spring St.*

★ **La Maison du Chocolat.** Stop in at this chocolatier's small tea salon to dive into a cup of thick, heavenly hot chocolate. The Paris-based outfit sells handmade truffles, chocolates, and pastries that could lull you into a chocolate stupor. ⊠*1018 Madison Ave., between E. 78th and 79th Sts., Upper East Side* ☎*212/744–7117* Ⓜ*6 to 77th St.* ⊠*30 Rockefeller Center, between 5th and 6th Aves., Midtown West* ☎*212/265–9404* Ⓜ*B, D, F, V to 47th–50th St./Rockefeller Center*

Li-Lac Chocolates. They've been feeding the Village's sweet tooth since 1923. You can buy dark-chocolate-dipped marzipan acorns here by the pound, as well as such specialty items as chocolate-molded Statues of Liberty. ⊠*40 8th Ave., at Jane St., Greenwich Village* ☎*212/242–7374* Ⓜ*A, C, E to 14th St.*

★ **MarieBelle.** The handmade chocolates here are nothing less than works of art. Square truffles and bonbons—which come in such flavors as Earl Grey tea, cappuccino, passion fruit, and saffron—are painted with edible dyes so each resembles a miniature painting. Tins of aromatic tea leaves and Aztec hot chocolate are also available. ⊠*484 Broome St., between West Broadway and Wooster St., SoHo* ☎*212/925–6999* Ⓜ*R, W to Prince St.* ⊠*762 Madsion Ave., between 65th and 66th Sts. Upper East Side* ☎*212/249–4588* Ⓜ*6 to 68th St.*

Max Brenner: Chocolate by the Bald Man. This isn't the place to make a fuss about cocoa percentages or impeccable handcrafted bonbons; instead, this Aussie arrival is all about a Wonka-ish sense of entertainment. The cafés encourage the messy enjoyment of gooey treats like chocolate fondues. Take-away treats include pralines and "The Magnet," a chocolate egg meant to be shared by couples in a "melting kiss ceremony." ⊠*841 Broadway, between E. 13th and E. 14th Sts., East Village* ☎*212/388–0030* Ⓜ*L, N, Q, R, W, 4, 5, 6 to 14th St./Union*

Sq. ✉*142 2nd Ave., at E. 9th St., East Village* ☎*212/388–0030* Ⓜ*6 to Astor Pl.*

Fodor'sChoice **Vosges Haut Chocolat.** This chandeliered salon takes chocolate couture
★ to a new level. The creations are internationally themed: the Budapest
bonbons combine dark chocolate and Hungarian paprika, the Black
Pearls contain wasabi, and the Aboriginal collection uses such esoteric
ingredients as wattle seed and rye berry. ✉*132 Spring St., between
Greene and Wooster Sts., SoHo* ☎*212/625–2929* Ⓜ*R, W to Prince St.*
✉*1100 Madison Ave., at 83rd St., Upper East Side* ☎*212/717–2929*
Ⓜ*6 to 86th St.*

CLOTHING: DISCOUNT

Besides the following standby, don't overlook the discount department
stores, especially Century 21.

Loehmann's. Label searchers can turn up $40 Polo/Ralph Lauren chinos
and Donna Karan and Yves Saint Laurent suits in the men's department
here on a regular basis. Head up to the "back room" on the top floor
for the best women's designers, but you may need to make a repeat
visit or two before emerging victorious. ✉*101 7th Ave., at W. 16th St.,
Chelsea* ☎*212/352–0856* Ⓜ*1, 2, 3 to 14th St.*

CLOTHING: JUST FOR MEN

17

Duncan Quinn. Shooting for nothing less than sartorial splendor, this
designer provides everything from chalk-stripe suits to cuff links in a
shop not much bigger than its silk pocket squares. Only a few of each
style of shirt are made, so the odds are slim that you will see someone
else in your blue, violet, or orange button-down with contrast-color
under cuffs. ✉*8 Spring St., between Elizabeth and Bowery Sts., NoLita*
☎*212/226–7030* Ⓜ*6 to Spring St.*

Dunhill. Corporate brass come here for finely tailored clothing, both
ready- and custom-made, and smoking accessories; the walk-in humidor
stores top-quality tobacco and cigars. ✉*545 Madison Ave., at E. 55th
St., Midtown East* ☎*212/753–9292* Ⓜ*F to 57th St.*

John Varvatos. Over the past few years Varvatos has amplified his rock
and roll ties, with rock-star photos in his stores and ad campaigns starring Perry Farrell and Cheap Trick. He may have overstepped himself,
though, by taking over the CBGB club space to use as another boutique for hawking expensive, soft-shouldered suits, cotton crewnecks,
and jeans in leather, velvet, or denim. ✉*122 Spring St., at Greene St.,
SoHo* ☎*212/965–0700* Ⓜ*6 to Spring St.* ✉*315 Bowery, between E.
1st and E. 2nd Sts., East Village* ☎*212/358–0315* Ⓜ*F, V to Lower
East Side-2nd Ave.*

Nom de Guerre. Brave the narrow staircase at this basement-level hipster
hideaway to find racks filled mainly with the house men's line, plus a
selection of items by A.P.C., Comme de Garçons, and others. There's
an Army-Navyish vibe, with camo-green dressing room curtains and a
concrete floor, but the staff is militant only about style and fit. ✉*640*

Broadway, at Bleecker St., Greenwich Village ☏*212/253–2891* Ⓜ*F, V to Broadway–Lafayette.*

★ **Sean.** These snug shops carry low-key, well-priced, and comfortable apparel from France—wool and cotton painter's coats, very-narrow-wale corduroy pants, and a respectable collection of suits and dress shirts. ✉*199 Prince St., between Sullivan and MacDougal Sts., SoHo* ☏*212/598–5980* Ⓜ*R, W to Prince St.* ✉*224 Columbus Ave., between W. 70th and W. 71st Sts., Upper West Side* ☏*212/769–1489* Ⓜ*B, C to 72nd St.*

Tom Ford. After making his name sexing up the Gucci women's lines, Ford lasers in on the XY set for his next major retail effort. The suits are relatively traditional (and impeccably made) but the shirts are more interesting, as they come in literally hundreds of colors. Glide up the ebony staircase for the made-to-measure services, which will customize anything from suits to pajamas. ✉*845 Madison Ave., at E. 70th St., Upper East Side* ☏*212/359–0300* Ⓜ*6 to 68th St./Hunter College*

Vilebrequin. Allow St-Tropez to influence your swimsuit; these striped, floral, and solid-color French-made trunks come in sunny hues. Waterproof pocket inserts keep your essentials safe from beachcombers. Many styles come in boys' sizes, too. ✉*1070 Madison Ave., at E. 81st St., Upper East Side* ☏*212/650–0353* Ⓜ*6 to 77th St.* ✉*436 West Broadway, between Prince and Spring Sts., SoHo* ☏*212/431–0673* Ⓜ*R, W to Prince St.*

CLOTHING: MEN'S AND WOMEN'S

CASUAL AND COOL

Agnès b. With this quintessentially French line, women can look like Parisienne schoolgirls—in snap-front tops, slender pants, sweet floral prints—or like a chic *maman* in tailored dark suits and leather jackets. For men, the designer's love for the movies makes it easy to come out looking a little Godard around the edges: turtleneck sweaters, lean black suits, and black leather porkpie hats demand the sangfroid of Belmondo. The Flatiron and Upper East Side stores are women's only. ✉*103 Greene St., between Prince and Spring Sts., SoHo* ☏*212/925–4649* Ⓜ*6 to Spring St.* ✉*13 E. 16th St., between 5th Ave. and Union Sq. W, Flatiron District* ☏*212/741–2585* Ⓜ*N, Q, R, W, 4, 5, 6 to 14th St./Union Sq.* ✉*1063 Madison Ave., between E. 80th and E. 81st Sts., Upper East Side* ☏*212/570–9333* Ⓜ*6 to 77th St.*

A.P.C. This hip French boutique proves to be deceptively simple. Watch your step on the uneven wooden floorboards while choosing narrow gabardine and corduroy suits or dark denim jeans and jackets, some with a hint of military. ✉*131 Mercer St., between Prince and Spring Sts., SoHo* ☏*212/966–9685* Ⓜ*6 to Spring St.; R, W to Prince St.*

Christopher Fischer. Featherweight cashmere sweaters, wraps, and throws in Easter-egg colors have made Fischer the darling of Hamptonites. His shop also carries leather accessories and such home wares as flokati pillows and wooden bowls from South Africa. ✉*80 Wooster St., between Spring and Broome Sts., SoHo* ☏*212/965–9009* Ⓜ*R, W to Prince St.*

Destination. The model pigs guarding this store fit right in with the Meat-packing District. Inside are clothes and accessories that telegraph "south of 14th Street": hard-to-find, roomy Jacques le Corre bags, skull jewelry, bright floral tunics from Hartford, cult sunglasses. ✉*32–36 Little W. 12th St., between Greenwich and Washington Sts., Meatpacking District* ☎*212/727–2031* Ⓜ*1 to Christopher St./Sheridan Sq.*

DKNY. Cocktail-party ensembles, chunky-knit sweaters, and knock-around denim vie for notice; the "pure" line is reserved for all-natural fibers. A scattering of vintage pieces, such as leather bomber jackets and 1930s jewelry, ensures that you can have something no one else has. Scout out the nonwearables, too; the candles and home accessories are unfailingly cool. Then you can belly up to the juice bar or listen to a featured CD. ✉*655 Madison Ave., at E. 60th St., Upper East Side* ☎*212/223–3569* Ⓜ*N, R, W, 4, 5, 6 to 59th St./Lexington Ave.* ✉*420 West Broadway, between Prince and Spring Sts., SoHo* ☎*646/613–1100* Ⓜ*C, E to Spring St.*

H By Hilfiger. With their patriotic red, white, and blue logos, bright colors, and casual, outdoorsy look, these clothes have a recognizably American style. The West Broadway store takes a more upscale tack, with tailored suits for men, smart sweater sets and pencil skirts for women, and broadcloth shirts for both; Bleecker Street is just womenswear, and Broadway stocks men's and women's denim. ✉*372 West Broadway, at Broome St., SoHo* ☎*917/237–0774* Ⓜ*R, W to Prince St.* ✉*375 Bleecker St., at Broome St.,* ☎*646/638–4812* Ⓜ*1 to Christopher St-Sheridan Sq.* ✉*500 Broadway, between Spring and Broome Sts., Greenwich Village* ☎*212/334–0042* Ⓜ*6 to Spring St.*

Írma. This unprepossessing nook with its squeaky plank floors is actually home to some of the most hard-to-find designers in the city. Besides carrying a good selection of Vivienne Westwood, the store stockpiles whisper-light cashmere by Kristesen du Nord, ready-to-wear from Canadian brand Ports 1961, and Belstaff motorcycle boots and jackets. ✉*378 Bleecker St., between Charles and Perry Sts., Greenwich Village* ☎*212/206–7475* Ⓜ*A, C, E, F, V to W. 4th St./Washington Sq.*

J. Crew. The preppy-chic brand has opened a couple of special store-fronts in New York, in addition to the many standard branches around town. A selection of menswear has taken over an old-time TriBeCa tavern, keeping the original wood bar and adding vintage photos and a fitting room that doubles as an art gallery. Some of the best finds are accessories: Borsalino hats and Selima Optique sunglasses (both in exclusive designs), vintage tie bars, money clips, and books. Uptown, there's a posh, one-off Women's Collection shop, where whitewashed walls set off color-coded rows of calfskin jackets, cashmere sweaters, and snakeskin handbags. Both specialty stores also carry some staples like denim and corduroy. ✉*235 West Broadway, at White St., TriBeCa* ☎*212/226–5476* Ⓜ*1 to Franklin St.* ✉*1035 Madison Ave., at 79th St., Upper East Side* ☎*212/249–3869* Ⓜ*6 to 77th St./Lexington Ave.*

Paul Frank. The flat visage of Julius the monkey, the original Paul Frank character, plasters vinyl wallets, flannel PJs, skateboards, and, of course, T-shirts. Also look for tees evoking such formative elements of '80s youth as corn dogs and break dancing. A selection of monkey-free

17

Continued on page 341

FIFTH AVENUE & 57TH STREET

Fifth Avenue from Rockefeller Center to Central Park South pogos between landmark department stores, glossy international designer boutiques, and casual national chains. What they all have in common: massive flagship spaces.

The intersection of 5th Avenue with 57th Street distills this mix of old and new, exclusive and accessible. From these corners you'll see blue-chip New York classics (jeweler Tiffany & Co., the Bergdorf Goodman department stores), luxury giants (Gucci and the glass box of Louis Vuitton), a high-tech wonderland (another glass box for Apple), and show-off digs for informal brands (Nike-Town, Abercrombie & Fitch). Capping this shopping stretch at East 58th Street is the colossal, exceptional toy store F.A.O. Schwarz. If you're keen to shop the high end or to see the impressive flagships, it's worth coming to this neighborhood—but if large-scale doesn't do it for you, you're better off heading downtown.   —J.P.

BEST TIME TO GO

Wednesday through Friday if you're trying to avoid crowds. Weekends before the winter holidays get extremely hectic and can spark "sidewalk rage" in even the most patient shopper—try to come earlier in the week, especially if you want to see the fantastic department store window displays.

BEST SOUVENIR FOR KIDS

An incredibly lifelike stuffed animal from F.A.O. Schwarz. They've got exclusive Steiff "purebred" dogs, for instance, that come with authenticity certificates from the American Kennel Club.

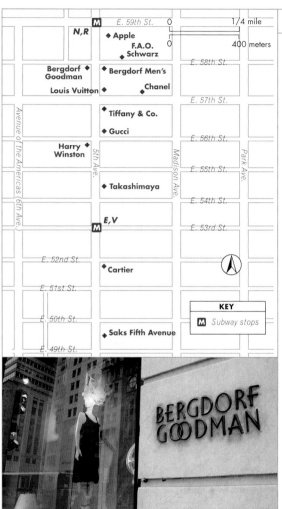

BEST FOR

DEPARTMENT STORES

Saks Fifth Avenue: fashion and nothing but.

Bergdorf Goodman: these partner stores (one for women, the other for men; guess which has the housewares) are both genteelly tasteful.

Takashimaya New York: a cool and collected Japanese emporium with a gorgeous florist on the top floor.

FLAGSHIP STORES

Louis Vuitton: every permutation of the signature handbags and leather goods, plus the jet-set clothing line upstairs.

Chanel: all the hallmarks, from little black dresses to double-C jewelry.

Apple: all sorts of chip-driven devices, 24 hours a day.

Gucci: check out classic designs and goodies exclusive to this store.

SERIOUS JEWELRY

Tiffany & Co.: hum "Moon River," check out the dazzling gems and pearls, then head upstairs for all sorts of silver ornaments.

Cartier: both classic and slinky new designs glitter in a turn-of-the-20th-century mansion.

Harry Winston: the ultimate for diamonds (just ask Marilyn Monroe).

REFUELING

Soothe frazzled nerves with a stop at **Fika** (⌗ *41 W. 58th St., between 5th and 6th Aves.* ☎ *212/832–0022*), a calm, friendly Swedish café. Settle in for a gravlax salad, a bracing cup of coffee, and an airy-yet-buttery *drömmar* cookie. If you'd rather stay in the energetic current of 5th Avenue, nab a table, or a seat with a fold-down tray, at the time-warped **Prime Burger** (⌗ *5 E. 51st St., between 5th and Madison Aves.* ☎ *212/759–4729*). You'll find all the diner standbys; if you order a burger, you'll have to specify all the toppings you'd like with it.

CLOSE UP

Cool Local Chains

Following are the best of the local chain stores, the places New Yorkers head to in a fashion pinch.

Calypso. An island-vacation vibe swept the city in the form of Calypso's colorful silk women's wear, dangly jewelry, and boho housewares. The flagship's now on Madison Avenue; several themed branches, including an outlet and one dedicated to sample sales, cluster downtown. ⊠ *815 Madison Ave., between E. 68th and E. 69th Sts., Upper East Side* ☎ *212/585-0310* Ⓜ *6 to 68th St./Hunter College* ⊠ *Sample Sale, 424 Broome St., at Crosby St., SoHo* ☎ *212/274-0449* Ⓜ *6 to Spring St.* ⊠ *280 Mott St., between E. Houston and Prince Sts., NoLita* ☎ *212/965-0990* Ⓜ *6 to Bleecker St.* ⊠ *Outlet 407 Broome St., between Lafayette and Centre Sts., NoLita* ☎ *212/941-9700* Ⓜ *6 to Spring St.* ⊠ *Home, 199 Lafayette St., at Broome St., NoLita* ☎ *212/925-6200* Ⓜ *6 to Spring St.* ⊠ *654 Hudson St., at Gansevoort St., Meatpacking District* ☎ *646/638-3000* Ⓜ *A, C, E to 14th St.* ⊠ ⊠ *191 Lafayette St., at Broome St., NoLita* ☎ *212/941-6512* Ⓜ *6 to Spring St. 137 West Broadway, between Thomas and Duane Sts., TriBeCa* ☎ *212/608-2222* Ⓜ *1, 2, 3 to Chambers St.*

Ricky's. The loud and fun drugstores attract an eclectic, mostly young crowd who come just as often for the crazy-color wigs or fishnet stockings as they do for the body glitter and Neutrogena soap. Every fall the stores turn into Halloween central, with a huge assortment of feather boas, masks, and spray-on hair color. ⊠ *590 Broadway, at Prince St., SoHo* ☎ *212/226-5552* ⊠ *7 E. 14th St., Union Sq.* ☎ *212/691-7930* ⊠ *466 6th Ave., at W. 12th St., Greenwich Village* ☎ *212/924-3401* ⊠ *44 E. 8th St., between Broadway and University Pl., Greenwich Village* ☎ *212/254-5247* ⊠ *267 W. 23rd St., between 7th and 8th Aves., Chelsea* ☎ *212/206-0234* ⊠ *509 5th Ave., at 42nd St., Midtown East* ☎ *212/949-7230.*

Scoop. These clothes help you fit in with the too-cool-to-dress-up crowd. They have lots of jeans (limited-edition Levi's, Chip & Pepper), slinky tops, vintage-looking tees, and rugby shirts. The SoHo branch is for women only. ⊠ *1273–1277 3rd Ave., between E. 73rd and E. 74th Sts., Upper East Side* ☎ *212/535-5577* ⊠ *430 W. 14th St., at Washington St., Meatpacking District* ☎ *212/929-1244 men's shop, 212/691-1905 women's, 212/691-1926 kids, 212/633-6535* ⊠ *473-475 Broadway, between Broome and Grand Sts., SoHo* ☎ *212/925-3539.*

Searle. Mostly strung along the East Side, these stores have a devoted following for their coats, and there are plenty of other designer items to layer, from cowl-neck sweaters to fitted tees. ⊠ *1051 3rd Ave., at E. 62nd St., Upper East Side* ☎ *212/838-5990* ⊠ *635 Madison Ave., between E. 59th and E. 60th Sts., Midtown East* ☎ *212/753-9021* ⊠ *805 Madison Ave., between E. 67th and E. 68th Sts., Upper East Side* ☎ *212/628-6665* ⊠ *1296 3rd Ave., between E. 74th and E. 75th Sts., Upper East Side* ☎ *212/717-5200* ⊠ *1035 Madison Ave., at E. 79th St., Upper East Side* ☎ *212/717-4022* ⊠ *1124 Madison Ave., at E. 84th St., Upper East Side* ☎ *212/988-7318* ⊠ *156 5th Ave., between W. 20th and W. 21st Sts., Flatiron District* ☎ *212/924-4330.*

accessories, including perfect weekender bags, is more stylish than sassy. ✉ *195 Mulberry St., at Kenmare St., NoLita* ☎ *212/965–5079* Ⓜ *6 to Spring St.*

R by 45rpm. Japanese interpretations of Western styles, from peacoats to bandannas, are marked by their attention to detail. Look for hand-stressed denim. ✉ *169 Mercer St., between W. Houston and Prince Sts., SoHo* ☎ *917/237–0045* Ⓜ *R, W to Prince St.*

Reiss. These casual-but-tailored clothes have sleek details and a relatively gentle price. Women's blouses and skirts have delicate pleats and contrast-stitched embroidery; halter dresses have swirly, summery prints. Men's slouchy pants are complemented by shrunken blazers, military-cut shirts, and trim leather jackets. ✉ *387 West Broadway, between Spring and Broome Sts., SoHo* ☎ *212/925–5707* Ⓜ *R, W to Prince St.* ✉ *309-313 Bleecker St., between 7th Ave. and Grove St., Greenwich Village* ☎ *212/488–2411* Ⓜ *1 to Christopher St./Sheridan Sq.*

Fodor's Choice
★
UNIQLO. Past the 30-foot wall of seasonal staples near the entrance of this Japanese retail giant, a tri-level space bursts with affordable, well-tailored basics. Cashmere crew- and V-necks (most under $100), slim-fit denims, and casual coats share space with edgier tees designed by Japanese graphic artists. Most of the clothing has been tweaked or made specifically for the American market. ■TIP➜Weekday mornings are the best time to avoid long lines for the dressing rooms. ✉ *546 Broadway, between Prince and Spring Sts., SoHo* ☎ *917/237–8800* Ⓜ *R, W to Prince St.*

HIGH DESIGN

Burberry. The signature plaid is hardly square these days, as bikinis, leather pants, and messenger-style bags join the traditional gabardine trench coats. The flagship store on East 57th Street is the mother lode; the SoHo branch has an abbreviated assortment. ✉ *9 E. 57th St., between 5th and Madison Aves., Midtown East* ☎ *212/407–7100* Ⓜ *N, R, W to 5th Ave./59th St.* ✉ *131 Spring St., between Greene and Wooster Sts., SoHo* ☎ *212/925–9300* Ⓜ *R, W to Prince St.*

Calvin Klein. Though the namesake designer has bowed out, the label keeps channeling his particular style. This stark flagship store emphasizes the luxe end of the clothing line. Men's suits tend to be soft around the edges; women's evening gowns are often a fluid pouring of silk. There are also shoes, accessories, housewares, and makeup. ✉ *654 Madison Ave., at E. 60th St., Upper East Side* ☎ *212/292–9000* Ⓜ *N, R, W, 4, 5, 6 to 59th St./Lexington Ave.*

Christian Dior. The New York outpost of one of France's most venerable fashion houses makes its home in the dazzlingly modern LVMH tower. The designs bring elements of everything from raceways to skate punks to haute couture. If you're not in the market for an investment gown, peruse the glam accessories, like the latest status bag. The Dior menswear boutique is next door; the rocking cigarette-thin suits are often pilfered by women. ✉ *21 E. 57th St., at Madison Ave., Midtown East* ☎ *212/931–2950* Ⓜ *E, V to 5th Ave./53rd St.* ✉ *Men's store, 17 E. 57th St., between 5th and Madison Aves., Midtown East* ☎ *212/421–6009* Ⓜ *E, V to 5th Ave./53rd St.*

17

Comme des Garçons. The designs in this stark, white, swoopy space consistently push the fashion envelope with brash patterns, unlikely juxtapositions (tulle and neoprene), and cuts that are meant to be thought-provoking, not flattering. Architecture students come just for the interior design. ✉520 W. 22nd St., between 10th and 11th Aves., Chelsea ☎212/604–9200 Ⓜ C, E to 23rd St.

Costume National. Although entering this chrome-lined shop may seem intimidating (all those hard, shiny surfaces), the sexy, slim-cut leather coats and sheer black shirts for both men and women are chic and beautifully made. ✉160 Mercer St., between Prince and W. Houston Sts., SoHo ☎212/431–1530 Ⓜ C, E to Spring St.

Dolce & Gabbana. It's easy to feel like an Italian movie star amid these extravagant (in every sense) clothes. Pinstripes are a favorite; for women, they could be paired with something sheer, furred, or leopard-print, and for men they elongate the sharp suits. ✉825 Madison Ave., between E. 68th and E. 69th Sts., Upper East Side ☎212/249–4100 Ⓜ6 to 68th St./Hunter College.

Emporio Armani. At this middle child of the Armani trio, the clothes are dressy without quite being formal, and are frequently offered in cream, muted blues, and ever-cool shades of soot. ✉601 Madison Ave., between E. 57th and E. 58th Sts., Midtown East ☎212/317–0800 Ⓜ N, R, W, 4, 5, 6 to 59th St./Lexington Ave. ✉410 West Broadway, at Spring St., SoHo ☎646/613–8099 Ⓜ C, E to Spring St.

Etro. Echoes of 19th-century luxury pervade Etro's clothing. Trademark paisleys sprawl over richly covered suits, dresses, and lustrous pillows, while juicy colors and cool details (metallic embroidery, origami-esque appliqués) keep things modern. ✉720 Madison Ave., between E. 63rd and E. 64th Sts., Upper East Side ☎212/317–9096 Ⓜ6 to 68th St./Hunter College.

Gianni Versace. Filling a five-story flagship store, the sometimes outrageous designs and colors of Versace clothes might not be to everyone's taste (or budget), but they're never boring. ✉647 5th Ave., near E. 51st St., Midtown East ☎212/317–0224 Ⓜ E, V to 5th Ave./53rd St.

★ **Gucci.** The 5th Avenue flagship store sets a new standard for giantism. This incarnation has a special "heritage" department, plus goods exclusive to the store. With a female designer in place, the clothing is less aggressively sexy than it was in the Tom Ford era. Skintight pants might be paired with a blousey jacket; lace tops leave a little more to the imagination. The accessories, like wraparound shades and studded or snakeskin shoes, continue to spark consumer frenzies. ✉725 5th Ave., at 56th St., Midtown East ☎212/826–2600 Ⓜ N, R, W to 5th Ave./59th St. ✉840 Madison Ave., between E. 69th and E. 70th Sts., Upper East Side ☎212/717–2619 Ⓜ6 to 68th St./Hunter College.

Hermès. Sweep up and down the curving stairway in this contemporary flagship while on the prowl for the classic, distinctively patterned silk scarves and neckties, the coveted Kelly and Birkin handbags, or the beautifully simple separates. True to its roots, Hermès still stocks saddles and other equestrian items. ⊠691 Madison Ave., at E. 62nd St., Upper East Side ☎212/751–3181 ⓂN, R, W, 4, 5, 6 to 59th St./ Lexington Ave.

Issey Miyake. Pleats of a Fortuny-like tightness are the Miyake signature—but instead of Fortuny's silks, these clothes are in polyester or ultra-high-tech textiles, often forming sculptural shapes. **Pleats Please** carries a line with simpler silhouettes, from tunics to long dresses. ⊠802 Madison Ave., between 67th and 68th Sts., Upper East Side ☎212/439–7822 Ⓜ6 to 68th St./Hunter College ⊠119 Hudson St., at N. Moore St., TriBeCa ☎212/226–0100 Ⓜ1 to Franklin St. ⊠Pleats Please, 128 Wooster St., at Prince St., SoHo ☎212/226–3600 ⓂR, W to Prince St.

Jeffrey. The Meatpacking District really arrived when this Atlanta-based mini-Barneys opened its doors. You can find an incredible array of designer shoes—Valentino, Lanvin, and red-soled Christian Louboutin are some of the best sellers—plus überlabels like Marni and Gucci. ⊠449 W. 14th St., between 9th and 10th Aves., Meatpacking District ☎212/206–1272 ⓂA, C, E, L to 14th St./8th Ave.

FodorśChoice
★ **Marc Jacobs.** The West Village is getting steadily infiltrated with boutiques carrying the more casual lines of the Jacobs juggernaut. The saturation zone teems with tongue-in-cheek tees, downplayed duds in plaids and stripes, and the eternally popular shoes and bags. In SoHo a former garage is filled with ladylike designs made with luxurious fabrics: silk, cashmere, wool bouclé, and tweeds ranging from the demure to the flamboyant. The details, though—oversize buttons, circular patch pockets, and military-style grommet belts—add a sartorial wink. ⊠163 Mercer St., between W. Houston and Prince Sts., SoHo ☎212/343–1490 ⓂR, W to Prince St. ⊠Accessories boutique: 385 Bleecker St., at Perry St., Greenwich Village ☎212/924–6126 Ⓜ1 to Christopher St./Sheridan Sq. ⊠403–405 Bleecker St., at W. 11th St., Greenwich Village ☎212/924–0026 Ⓜ1 to Christopher St./ Sheridan Sq.

★ **Polo/Ralph Lauren.** One of New York's most distinctive shopping experiences, Lauren's flagship store graces the turn-of-the-20th-century Rhinelander mansion. Clothes range from summer-in-the-Hamptons madras to exquisite silk gowns and Purple Label men's suits. **Polo Sport** (⊠1055 Madison Ave., at 80th St., Upper East Side ☎212/434–8000 Ⓜ6 to 68th St./Hunter College) carries casual clothes and sports gear, from puffy anoraks to wick-away tanks. The Village branches of **Ralph Lauren,** on the other hand, are small, tightly packed boutiques. They pull together sequin-slicked skirts, sturdy cable knits and tweeds, western and denim, and the odd bit of vintage. ⊠867 Madison Ave., at E. 72nd St., Upper East Side ☎212/606–2100 Ⓜ6 to 68th St./Hunter College ⊠379 West Broadway, between Spring and Broome Sts., SoHo ☎212/625–1660 ⓂC, E to Spring St. ⊠380–383 and 390 Bleecker St., at Perry St., Greenwich Village ☎212/645–5513 Ⓜ1 to Christopher St./Sheridan Sq.

17

Street Vendors

If you're looking for original or repro-duced artwork, the two areas to visit for street vendors are the stretch of 5th Avenue in front of the Metropoli-tan Museum of Art (roughly between 81st and 82nd streets) and the SoHo area of West Broadway, between Houston and Broome streets. In both areas, you'll find dozens of artists sell-ing original paintings, drawings, and photographs (some lovely, some lurid), as well as photo reproductions of famous New York scenes (the Chrysler building, South Street Seaport). Prices can start as low as $10.

The east–west streets in SoHo are an excellent place to look for handmade crafts: Spring and Prince streets, especially, are jammed with tables full of beaded jewelry, tooled leather belts, and homemade hats and purses. These streets are also a great place to find deals on art books; several vendors have titles featuring the work of artists from Diego Rivera to Annie Leibovitz, all for about 20% less than you'd pay at a chain. It's best to know which books you want ahead of time, though; street vendors wrap theirs in clear plastic, and can get testy if you unwrap them but don't wind up buying.

Faux-designer handbags, sunglasses, wallets, and watches are some of the most popular street buys in town—but crackdowns on knockoffs have made them harder to find. The hub used to be Canal Street, roughly between Greene and Lafayette streets, but many vendors there have swept their booths clean of fake Vuitton, Prada, Gucci, and Fendi merchandise. You might have better luck finding a Faux-lex near Herald Square or Madison Square Garden; and good old-fashioned fake handbags are still sold by isolated vendors around such shopping areas as Rockefeller Center and Lexington Avenue near Bloom-ingdale's. The one thing Canal Street is still good for, though, is cheap lug-gage: for $30–$40 (be sure to haggle), you can walk away with a giant roll-ing suitcase to lug home all your loot.

Prada. The design shop's gossamer silks, slick black suits, and luxe shoes and leather goods are among the all-time great Italian fashion coups. The uptown stores pulse with pale green walls (remember this if you start questioning your skin tone). The 57th Street branch carries just the shoes, bags, and other accessories. The SoHo location, an ultramodern space designed by Rem Koolhaas, incorporates so many technological innovations that it was written up in *Popular Science*. The dressing-room gadgets alone include liquid crystal displays, changeable lighting, and scanners that link you to the store's database. ⊠*724 5th Ave., between W. 56th and W. 57th Sts., Midtown West* ☎*212/664–0010* Ⓜ*Q, W to 5th Ave./60th St.* ⊠*45 E. 57th St., between Madison and Park Aves., Midtown East* ☎*212/308–2332* Ⓜ*E, V to 5th Ave./53rd St.* ⊠*841 Madison Ave., at E. 70th St., Upper East Side* ☎*212/327–4200* Ⓜ*6 to 68th St./Hunter College* ⊠*575 Broadway, at Prince St., SoHo* ☎*212/334–8888* Ⓜ*R, W to Prince St.*

Roberto Cavalli. Rock-star style (at rock-star prices) delivers denim decked with fur, feathers, prints, and even shredded silk overlays. ⊠*711*

Madison Ave., at E. 63rd St., Upper East Side ☎*212/755–7722* Ⓜ*N, R, W to 5th Ave./59th St.*

Valentino. The mix here is at once audacious and beautifully cut; the fur or feather trimmings, low necklines, and opulent fabrics are about as close as you can get to celluloid glamour. No one does a better red. ✉*747 Madison Ave., at E. 65th St., Upper East Side* ☎*212/772–6969* Ⓜ*6 to 68th St./Hunter College.*

Yohji Yamamoto. Although almost entirely black and white, these clothes aren't as severe as they seem. Whimsical details, like giant polka dots, shirts with drawstring hems, and slouchy, rolled trouser cuffs, add a dash of levity. ✉*103 Grand St., at Mercer St., SoHo* ☎*212/966–9066* Ⓜ*J, M, N, Q, R, W, Z, 6 to Canal St.* ✉*1 Gansevoort St., at W. 13th St., Meatpacking District* ☎*212/966–3615* Ⓜ*A, C, E to 14th St.*

Yves Saint Laurent Rive Gauche. Tom Ford's successor, Stephano Pilati, is lightening up the fabled French house; think seduction instead of sexpot, with ruffles, wide belts, and safari-style jackets. ✉*855 Madison Ave., between E. 70th and E. 71st Sts., Upper East Side* ☎*212/988–3821* Ⓜ*6 to 68th St./Hunter College* ✉*3 E. 57th St., between 5th and Madison Aves., Midtown East* ☎*212/980–2970* Ⓜ*N, R, W to 5th Ave./59th St.*

TAILORED

Barbour. The company's waxed jackets are built to withstand raw British weather. The tweeds, moleskin pants, lamb's-wool sweaters, and tattersall shirts invariably call up images of country rambles. Trusty hunting dog is not included. ✉*1047 Madison Ave., at E. 80th St., Upper East Side* ☎*212/570–2600* Ⓜ*6 to 77th St.*

Brooks Brothers. The clothes at this classic American haberdasher are, as ever, traditional, comfortable, and fairly priced. Summer seersucker, navy blue blazers, and the peerless oxford shirts have been staples for generations. The women's selection has variations thereof. ■**TIP➔**At the Madison Avenue store you can step into a computer scanner to get precisely measured for a custom shirt or suit; appointments are recommended. ✉*666 5th Ave., at W. 53rd St., Midtown West* ☎*212/261–9440* Ⓜ*E, V to 5th Ave./53rd St.* ✉*346 Madison Ave., at E. 44th St., Midtown East* ☎*212/682–8800* Ⓜ*4, 5, 6, 7, S to 42nd St./Grand Central* ✉*1 Church St., at Liberty St., Lower Manhattan* ☎*212/267–2400* Ⓜ*R, W to Cortlandt St.*

Paul Smith. Victorian mahogany cases complement the dandyish British styles they hold. Embroidered vests, brightly striped socks, scarves, and shirts, and tongue-in-cheek cuff links leaven the classic, double-back-vent suits for men. Women head for the tailored suits and separates, classic outerwear, and plush knits. The SoHo flagship also carries furniture and a selection of ashtrays, photography books, cordial glasses, and other such oddments that beg for a cultured bachelor pad. The 5th Avenue store carries menswear only. ✉*142 Greene St., between Prince and W. Houston Sts., SoHo* ☎*646/613–3060* Ⓜ*R, W to Prince St.* ✉*108 5th Ave., at E. 16th St., Flatiron District* ☎*212/627–9770* Ⓜ*F, V to 14th St.*

Seize sur Vingt. In bringing a contemporary sensibility to custom tailoring, this store realized an ideal fusion. Brighten a suit or cotton moleskin flat-front pants with a checked or striped shirt; all can be made to order.

Continued on page 348

MADISON AVENUE

If you're craving a couture fix, cab it straight to Madison Avenue between East 57th and East 79th streets. Here the greatest Italian, French, and American fashion houses form a platinum-card corridor for ladies who lunch. (If you're going to be pointedly overlooked by a salesperson, odds are it will happen here.)

Most occupy large, glass-facade spaces but there are some exceptions, from intimate boutiques in old brownstones to the imposing turn-of-the-20th-century mansion now home to Ralph Lauren. Barneys, a full-fledged if very select department store, fits right in with the avenue's recherché roll call. But Madison isn't just a fashion funnel. A couple of marvelous booksellers and several outstanding antiques dealers and art galleries share this address as well.　　　　　　　　—J.P.

BEST TIME TO GO

Saturday is the busiest day and thus better for people-watching. Perhaps because of the European influence, the pace is calmer here, especially on weekdays. Avoid coming on a Sunday, since several stores close, especially in summer when they figure their main clientele is out in the Hamptons.

BEST SOUVENIR FOR AN EX-MANHATTANITE

Take a whiff of the Manhattan-inspired perfumes like Chelsea Flowers and Park Avenue at **Bond No. 9**. Can't decide? Snap up the sampler box with travel-size spray scents wrapped like bonbons.

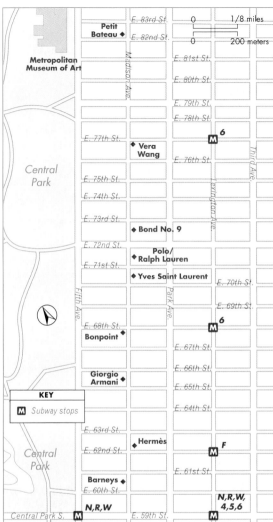

IN FOCUS MADISON AVENUE

17

BEST FOR

INTERNATIONAL MEGA-DESIGNERS

Barneys: dozens of the most cutting-edge names.

Polo/Ralph Lauren: haute-WASP style in a Rhinelander mansion.

Hermès: those divine silk scarves and handbags are waiting....

Giorgio Armani: a sleek setting for perfectly cut suits and dramatic evening wear.

Yves Saint Laurent Rive Gauche: Left Bank chic, *fabuleux* accessories.

Vera Wang: Big Occasion gowns, bridal and beyond.

FANCY CHILDREN'S CLOTHES

Bonpoint: precious European designs with hand-embroidering, velvet ribbons, you get the picture.

Petit Bateau: all superfine, hypoallergenic, colorful cotton, all the time.

REFUELING

Join the Upper East Side yummy mummies and their trilingual children at the local branch of **Le Pain Quotidien** (✉ *1131 Madison Ave. , between E. 84th and E. 85th Sts.* ☎ *212/327–4900*) for a fruit tart, vegetarian soup, or steaming bowl of cocoa. If you're willing to pull yourself away from Madison Avenue, the front room of **Payard** (✉ *1032 Lexington Ave., between E. 73rd and E. 74th Sts.* ☎ *212/717–5252*) has a handful of small tables where you can order a decadent, glossy pastry.

Department Store Discounts

At a few major department stores visitors from out of town can ring up a special discount as a shopping incentive. If you show identification to prove you live outside New York State, you're eligible for a markdown. Score one for the tourist team!

Bloomingdale's: go to the visitor center on the balcony level between the ground and second floors. With your out-of-town ID you'll get a card for an 11% discount on all purchases bought that day. You can apply for this card on any given visit.

Lord & Taylor: hit the ground-floor information desk to pick up a coupon for 15% off that day's purchases.

Macy's: stop by the visitor center on the balcony level between the ground and second floors for an out-of-state 11% discount voucher. The coupon is valid for five days for U.S. visitors and one month for international visitors.

Women are also the beneficiaries of the store's crisp button-downs and single-pleat trousers. ⊠ *243 Elizabeth St., between Prince and E. Houston Sts., NoLita* ☎ *212/343–0476* Ⓜ *R, W to Prince St.*

WITH AN EDGE

A Bathing Ape. Known simply as BAPE to devotees, this exclusive label has a cult following in its native Tokyo. At first it may be hard to see what the fuss is about. A small selection of camouflage gear and limited-edition T-shirts are placed throughout the minimalist space; the real scene-stealers are the flashy retro-style sneakers in neon colors. ⊠ *91 Greene St., between Prince and Spring Sts., SoHo* ☎ *212/925–0222* Ⓜ *R, W to Prince St.*

DDC Lab. The superhip street-wear offerings include bomber jackets and pleated skirts in the brand's signature paper-thin, washable Lycra-leather, plus brazenly colored PF Flyers sneakers for men. The overdyed denim comes in black and navy, along with some supersaturated seasonal hues. ⊠ *427 W. 14th St., at Washington St., Meatpacking District* ☎ *212/414–5801* Ⓜ *A, C, E to 14th St.*

Patricia Field. If you loved Carrie Bradshaw's wild outfits on *Sex and the City,* this is the place for you. As well as designing costumes for the show, Field has been a longtime purveyor of flamboyant club-kid gear. Her East Village emporium is chockablock with teeny kilts, lamé, marabou, pleather, and vinyl, as well as wigs in every color and stiletto heels in some very large sizes. ⊠ *302 Bowery, between Bleecker and Houston Sts., East Village* ☎ *212/966–4066* Ⓜ *6 to Bleecker St.*

Seven New York. Björk-worthy levels of experimental fashion are achieved at this boutique; check out the designs of such cutting-edge designers as Cosmic Wonder, Preen, Henrik Vibscob, and Obesity and Speed. ⊠ *110 Mercer St., between Prince and Spring Sts., SoHo* ☎ *646/654–0156* Ⓜ *N, R to Prince St.*

Trash and Vaudeville. Goths, punks, and other nightcrawlers have favored this standby for years. You might hear the Ramones on the sound system while you browse through bondage-inspired pants and skirts covered in straps, buckles, and other hardware. You'll also find striped stovepipe pants, vinyl corsets, and crinolines painted with flames. ⊠*4 St. Marks Pl., between 2nd and 3rd Aves., East Village* ☎*212/982–3590* Ⓜ*6 to Astor Pl.*

Triple 5 Soul. Headquarters for urban, hip-hop gear, this Brooklyn-based label's shop has graffiti murals on the walls and experimental beats playing on the stereo. The label's signature cargo pants, parkas, shoulder bags, and hoodies—many incorporating camo and high-tech fabrics—fill the racks. ⊠*290 Lafayette St., between Prince and Houston Sts., Greenwich Village* ☎*212/431–2404* Ⓜ*B, D, F, V to Broadway–Lafayette St.*

CLOTHES: VINTAGE AND RESALE

Allan & Suzi. The proprietors, whom you'll no doubt find behind the counter, are the godparents of fashion collecting. Their wacky shop preserves 1980s shoulder pads and 1940s gowns for posterity (or sale). ⊠*416 Amsterdam Ave., between W. 79th and W. 80th Sts., Upper West Side* ☎*212/724–7445* Ⓜ*1, 2, 3 to 72nd St.*

Cheap Jack's. Jack's two-floor space may be 12,000 square feet, but it's still jammed with interesting, not-too-expensive duds. There's almost everything you could wish for: track suits, bomber jackets, early 1980s madras shirts, old prom dresses, and fur-trimmed wool ladies' suits with the eau-de-mothball stamp of authenticity. ⊠*303 5th Ave., at 31st St., Midtown West* ☎*212/777–9564* Ⓜ*N, Q, R, W to 34th St./ Herald Sq.*

Fisch for the Hip. These resale racks are evenly split between men's and women's clothes, with a well-edited selection throughout. You may find last season's Catherine Malandrino chiffon dress with its tags intact, or a Zegna jacket for under $300. Look for multiple discounts on such wardrobe warhorses as little black dresses. ⊠*153 W. 18th St., between 6th and 7th Aves., Chelsea* ☎*212/633–9053* Ⓜ*F, V, 1, 2, 3 to 14th St.*

Frock. Models and stylists frequent this tiny shop for vintage women's wear from the 1960s, '70s, and '80s. The store carries pieces from such new-wave, mid-'80s designers as Thierry Mugler, Stephen Sprouse, and Claude Montana, not to mention pumps and lizard clutch purses from Ferragamo, Bruno Magli, and Charles Jourdan. ⊠*148 Orchard St., between Stanton and Rivington Sts., Lower East Side* ☎*212/594–5380* Ⓜ*F, J, M, Z to Delancey St./Essex St.*

INA. Although you may spot something vintage, like a 1960s Yves Saint Laurent velvet bolero, most clothing at these small boutiques harks back only a few seasons, and in some cases, the item has never been worn. The Mott Street and flagship Bleecker Street locations rack up menswear; the other stores carry women's resale. The Spring Street location has a consistently good spread of womens' shoes, but also consistently surly service. ⊠*101 Thompson St., between Prince and Spring Sts., SoHo* ☎*212/941–4757* Ⓜ*6 to Spring St.* ⊠*21 Prince St., between Elizabeth and Mott Sts., NoLita* ☎*212/334–9048* Ⓜ*6 to Spring St.* ⊠*262 Mott St., between Prince and E. Houston Sts., NoLita* ☎*212/334–2210* Ⓜ*6 to Spring St.* ⊠*15 Bleecker St., at Elizabeth*

17

St., NoHo ☎212/228–8511 Ⓜ6 to Bleecker St. Ⓜ 208 E. 73rd St., between 2nd and 3rd Aves., Upper East Side ☎212/249–0014 Ⓜ6 to 77th St.

New York Vintage. No patience to search through flea markets? Ransack the racks of women's wear in this narrow Chelsea space, where the prime picks have been winnowed for you. The 1930s chiffon blouses, '50s circle skirts, and '60s cocktail dresses are well kept; there's a good selection of handbags and pumps, too. ✉ 117 W. 25th St., between 6th and 7th Aves., Chelsea ☎212/647–1107 Ⓜ1 to 28th St.

★ **Resurrection.** With original Chanels, Puccis, and foxy boots, this store is a retro-chic gold mine. Prices, however, are decidedly 21st century. Designers like Marc Jacobs and Anna Sui have sought inspiration among the racks, and the store returns the love by presenting occasional in-store designer exhibits, often with pieces from an honoree's personal collection. ✉217 Mott St., between Prince and Spring Sts., NoLita ☎212/625–1374 Ⓜ6 to Spring St.

Screaming Mimi's. Vintage 1960s and '70s clothes and retro-wear include everything from djellabas to soccer shirts to prom dresses. You can also find a selection of huge tinted sunglasses, in case you feel like channeling Yoko Ono or one of the Olsen twins. ✉382 Lafayette St., between 4th and Great Jones Sts., East Village ☎212/677–6464 ⓂF, V to Broadway–Lafayette St.

What Comes Around Goes Around. Thanks to the staff's sharp eyes, the denim and leather racks here are reliably choice. You can also find such hip-again items as rabbit-fur jackets, decorative belt buckles, and some terrific vintage rock concert T-shirts. If the idea of forking out $100 for an Alice Cooper number pains you, just remember: unlike the copies everyone else is wearing, you'll be sporting the real deal. ✉351 West Broadway, between Grand and Broome Sts., SoHo ☎212/343–9303 ⓂJ, M, N, Q, R, W, Z, 6 to Canal St.

CLOTHES: WOMEN ONLY

CASUAL AND COOL

Butik. Supermodel Helena Christensen and flower artist Leif Sigersen stock their small shop with eclectic goodies picked up on their global-nomad travels. Most of the clothes hail from the owners' native Denmark, including the billowing silk dresses and tight black pants of Baum und Pferdgarten, and Mads Noergaard's striped tees. Vintage accessories and furniture are culled from flea markets, while the odd bracelet gets whipped up in-store. ✉605 Hudson St., at W. 12th St., Greenwich Village ☎212/367–8014 ⓂA, C, E to 14th St.

Comptoir des Cotonniers. The "cotton counter" angles for multigenerational shopping, lining up stylish, comfortable basics for babies, twentysomethings, ladies of a certain age, and everyone in between. There's a subtle Parisian vibe to the understated tunics, dresses, and separates; colors tend to be earthy. The brand's first U.S. branch has a nature-friendly minimalist look, with pale wood floors and lots of natural light. ✉155 Spring St. , at West Broadway, SoHo ☎ 212/274–0830 ⓂC, E to Spring St.

Foley & Corinna. Images of flowers and butterflies waft along the walls, while the racks divulge both vintage finds, like embroidered leather jackets, and Foley's own line of new clothes. Many looks are lingerie-inspired, with flounces and lace. ✉*114 Stanton St., between Ludlow and Essex Sts., Lower East Side* ☎*212/529–2338* Ⓜ*F to 2nd Ave. or Delancey St.*

Intermix. Aimed at those who like to pair denim with silk, chiffon, or just plain revealing tops, this boutique gathers together a solid mid- to high-range lineup, plus a just-enough layout of shoes and accessories. ✉*210 Columbus Ave., between W. 69th and W. 70th Sts., Upper West Side* ☎*212/769–9116* Ⓜ*1, 2, 3 to 72nd St.* ✉*1003 Madison Ave., between E. 77th and E. 78th Sts., Upper East Side* ☎*212/249–7858* Ⓜ*6 to 77th St.* ✉*125 5th Ave., between 19th and 20th Sts., Flatiron* ☎*212/533–9720* Ⓜ*R, W to 23rd St.* ✉*98 Prince St., SoHo* ☎*212/966–5303* Ⓜ*R, W to Prince St.* ✉*365 Bleecker St. , at Charles St., Greenwich Village* ☎*212/929–7180* Ⓜ*1 to Christopher St./Sheridan Sq.*

TG-170. Chiffon Jill Stuart camisoles, peacoats, and a terrific assortment of one-of-a-kind Swiss Freitag messenger bags (made from colorful reused trucking tarps) can be found at this downtown store. ✉*170 Ludlow St., between E. Houston and Stanton Sts., Lower East Side* ☎*212/995–8660* Ⓜ*F, J, M, Z to Delancey St./Essex St.*

CHIC (BUT NOT CHEAP)

Anna Sui. The violet-and-black salon, hung with Beardsley prints and alterna-rock posters, is the ideal setting for Sui's bohemian, flapper- and rocker-influenced designs and colorful beauty products. ✉*113 Greene St., between Prince and Spring Sts., SoHo* ☎*212/941–8406* Ⓜ*R, W to Prince St.*

Castor & Pollux. The store's interior signals a finely tuned balance of high taste (vintage Bergdorf Goodman display cases) and quirkiness (grass-cloth wall coverings and small horse sculptures). Hard-to-find brands like the Swedish Rodebjer are mixed with better-known names like Sonia by Sonia Rykiel and 3.1 Philip Lim. There's also an eye-catching in-house line of jewelry and clutches. ✉*1238 W. 10th St. , at Hudson St. West Village* ☎ *212/645–6572* Ⓜ*1 to Christopher St./ Sheridan Sq.*

Charles Nolan. Formerly an exclusive designer for Saks, Nolan's craftsmanship is impeccable: colorful quilted jackets have decorative stitching; body-skimming skirts are beautifully cut; and silken trousers have a creamy drape. There are also a few whimsical styles, such as the black wool coat covered in puli-like cords. ✉*30 Gansevoort St., at Hudson St., Meatpacking District* ☎*212/924–4888* Ⓜ*A, C, E to 14th St.*

WORD OF MOUTH

"That night, we went to bed early, dreaming of Century 21. True to our word, we arrived there at 7:45 AM. It was the best time to go. There were few people roaming through the racks and I even overheard one gal say, 'we should come here more often in the mornings—this is way more organized than we usually see it.' "

—gigglepots

17

Ludivine. If it's being worn in Paris, it's being sold here, from the floaty tops of Les Prairies de Paris to the draped tunics and nonchalant bags by Vanessa Bruno. Notify denim tosses off a Gallic-rocker look. Most of the lines are French designed and made, though a few like-minded Italians have slipped in. ✉ *172 W. 4th St., between Jones and Leroy Sts., Greenwich Village* ☎ *646/336–6576* Ⓜ *1 to Christopher St.*

Lyell. Browse the racks for enticing, vintage-inspired finds like draped silk dresses that would do well for dancing to Benny Goodman. Don't miss the vintage shoe selection, ranged in rows on the floor. ✉ *173 Elizabeth St., between Spring and Kenmare Sts., NoLita* ☎ *212/966–8484* Ⓜ *6 to Spring St.*

★ **Malia Mills.** Fit fanatics have met their match here. Bikini tops and bottoms are sold separately: halters, bandeaus, and triangle tops, plus boy-cut, side-tie, and low-ride bottoms. There are a few one-pieces, too. If you've got a warm-weather honeymoon coming up, you may want the bikini with "Just Married" across your bum. ✉ *199 Mulberry St., between Spring and Kenmare Sts., NoLita* ☎ *212/625–2311* Ⓜ *6 to Spring St.* ✉ *1031 Lexington Ave., at E. 74th St., Upper East Side* ☎ *212/517–7485* Ⓜ *6 to 77th St.* ✉ *220 Columbus Ave., at 70th St., Upper West Side* ☎ *212/874–7200* Ⓜ *B, C to 72nd St.*

Marina Rinaldi. These plus-size tailored suits, hip-slung belts, and sweeping coats know just how to flatter. ✉ *800 Madison Ave., between E. 67th and E. 68th Sts., Upper East Side* ☎ *212/734–4333* Ⓜ *6 to 68th St./Hunter College.*

Marni. Weaving among the suspended garments in Marni's first U.S. store, you may fall prey to a hemp-cloth duster jacket, brightly striped cotton trousers, or a coyly creased floral blouse. ✉ *161 Mercer St., between W. Houston and Prince Sts., SoHo* ☎ *212/343–3912* Ⓜ *R, W to Prince St.*

Max Mara. Think subtle colors and plush fabrics—straight skirts in cashmere or heathered wool, tuxedo-style evening jackets, and several choices of wool and cashmere camel overcoats. The SoHo location just carries the Sport Max collection. ✉ *813 Madison Ave., at E. 68th St., Upper East Side* ☎ *212/879–6100* Ⓜ *6 to 68th St./Hunter College* ✉ *450 West Broadway, between W. Houston and Prince Sts., SoHo* ☎ *212/674–1817* Ⓜ *C, E to Spring St.*

Mayle. This boutique basks in the ineffable vapor of cool. Designer Jane Mayle whips up close-fitting knit tops, lanky pants, and retro-inflected dresses that always look effortless, never overdone. ✉ *242 Elizabeth St., between E. Houston and Prince Sts., NoLita* ☎ *212/625–0406* Ⓜ *6 to Bleecker St.*

Michael Kors. In his deft reworkings of American classics, *Project Runway* judge Kors gives sportswear the luxury treatment, as with sorbet-color cashmere pullovers. A haute-hippie element is creeping in, too, with keyhole necks, hobo bags, and floppy hats. ✉ *974 Madison Ave., at E. 76th St., Upper East Side* ☎ *212/452–4685* Ⓜ *6 to 77th St.*

Miu Miu. Prada front woman Miuccia Prada established a secondary line (bearing her childhood nickname, Miu Miu) to showcase her more experimental ideas. Look for Prada-esque styles in more daring colors and cuts, such as high-waisted skirts with scalloped edges, Peter Pan–collar dresses in trippy patterns, and patent-leather pumps. ⊠*100 Prince St., between Mercer and Greene Sts., SoHo* Ⓜ*212/334–5156* Ⓜ*R, W to Prince St.* ⊠*831 Madison Ave., at E. 69th St., Upper East Side* ☎*212/249–9660* Ⓜ*6 to 68th St./ Hunter College.*

Tory Burch. Bright-orange lacquer zings through this space, which, in a reversal of the usual flow, brings

WORD OF MOUTH

"Chinatown—what an experience! The madness of all of the vendors was something to see. Very crowded (on Saturday) but very fun. Still can't get over all the knockoff stuff, never knew how much existed!"   —monalua

uptown downtown. Orange joins navy, flamingo pink, and mossy green on espadrilles, printed cotton blouses, and signature side-split tunics, available in bold prints or with embellished necklines. ⊠*257 Elizabeth St., between E. Houston and Prince Sts., NoLita* ☎*212/334–3000* Ⓜ*R, W to Prince St.*

FLIRTY

BCBG/Max Azria. If flirtation's your sport, you'll find your sportswear here: fluttering skirts, beaded camisoles, chiffon dresses, and leather pants fill the racks. ⊠*120 Wooster St., between Prince and Spring Sts., SoHo* ☎*212/625–2723* Ⓜ*R, W to Prince St.* ⊠*770 Madison Ave., at E. 66th St., Upper East Side* ☎*212/717–4225* Ⓜ*6 to 68th St./Hunter College*

Betsey Johnson. The SoHo store departs from the traditional (if such a word can be applied) hot-pink interior; instead its walls are sunny yellow with painted roses, and there's a bordello-red lounge area in back. Besides the quirkily printed dresses, available in all stores, there's a slinky upscale line. This is not the place for natural fibers—it's ruled by rayon, stretch, and the occasional faux fur. ⊠*138 Wooster St., between Prince and W. Houston Sts., SoHo* ☎*212/995–5048* Ⓜ*R, W to Prince St.* ⊠*251 E. 60th St., between 2nd and 3rd Aves., Upper East Side* ☎*212/319–7699* Ⓜ*N, R, W, 4, 5, 6 to 59th St./Lexington Ave.* ⊠*248 Columbus Ave., between W. 71st and W. 72nd Sts., Upper West Side* ☎*212/362–3364* Ⓜ*1, 2, 3 to 72nd St.* ⊠*1060 Madison Ave., between E. 80th and E. 81st Sts., Upper East Side* ☎*212/734–1257* Ⓜ*6 to 77th St.*

Catherine Malandrino. Designs here evoke the flapper era: frothy chiffon dresses with embroidered Empire waists, beaded necklines, and tiny matching fur stoles let you pretend you're Daisy Buchanan. ⊠*468 Broome St., at Greene St., SoHo* ☎*212/925–6765* Ⓜ*6 to Spring St.* ⊠*652 Hudson St., at W. 13th St., Meatpacking District* ☎*212/929–8710* Ⓜ*A, C, E to 14th St.*

Cynthia Rowley. As one half of the *Swell* team, you can expect this designer to be a party-outfit pro. She delivers with such flirty picks as bow-top pumps, swingy, swirly halter dresses with heart-shape appliqués, and handbags with small inset mirrors, ideal for checking your lipstick. The *Swell* books are on hand, too, natch. ⊠*376 Bleecker St., between Charles and Perry Sts., Greenwich Village* ☎*212/242–3803* Ⓜ*1 to Christopher St./Sheridan Sq.*

Continued on page 356

THE MEATPACKING DISTRICT

BEST TIME TO GO

Wednesday through Friday afternoons. Most stores are open daily but a few are closed Monday and Tuesday. A plus if you're here in the late afternoon: a cinematic glow as the light coming off the river burnishes the area's rough edges. On weekends some stores stay open until 7 or 8 PM, overlapping with the overeager nightlife crowd.

For nearly a century, this industrial western edge of downtown Manhattan was defined by slaughterhouses and meatpacking plants, blood-splattered cobblestoned streets, and men lugging carcasses into warehouses way before dawn.

But in the late 1990s the area between West 14th Street, Gansevoort Street, Hudson Street, and 11th Avenue speedily transformed into another kind of meat market. Many of the old warehouses now house ultrachic shops, nightclubs, and restaurants packed with angular fashionistas. Jeffrey, a pint-size department store, was an early arrival, followed by edgy but established designers like Stella McCartney and a few lofty furniture stores. Despite the influx of a few chains—albeit stylish ones like Scoop— eclectic boutiques keep popping up. The one thing it's hard to find here is a bargain.   —J.P.

BEST SOUVENIR FOR YOUR GIRLFRIEND (OR BOHO AUNT)

Candy-color Pyrex rings or quirky dangling earrings from **Auto** (✉ *803 and 805 Washington St., at Horatio St.* ☎ *212/229-2292*), a boutique focusing on New York–based jewelry designers.

17

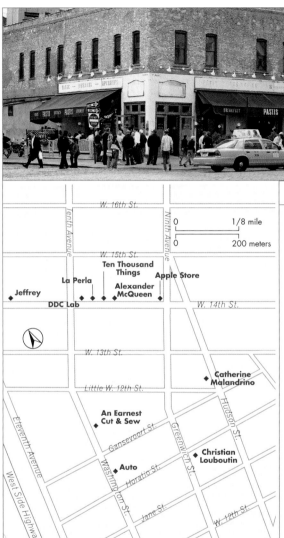

BEST FOR

FABULOUS FROCKS
Jeffrey: culls the coolest outfits from high-end labels.

Alexander McQueen: impeccably tailored, take-no-prisoners style.

Catherine Malandrino: romantic chiffon and swingy layers, at more-reasonable prices.

DENIM
Earnest Sewn (⊠ *821 Washington St.* ☎ *212/242–3414*): customize the cut, buttons, and pockets of your cult jeans.

DDC Lab: high-tech yet earthy, with vegetable indigo dyes, hand-scratching, and sometimes a dash of Lycra.

KILLER ACCESSORIES
Ten Thousand Things: unusual stones in delicate, handwrought settings.

La Perla: the most minxy outpost for this brand's lace lingerie.

Christian Louboutin: vampy heels with telltale crimson soles.

REFUELING

Hit the buzzing bistro **Pastis** (⊠ *9 9th Ave., at Little W. 12th St.* ☎ *212/929–4844*) for a croque monsieur, a bracing coffee, or a cocktail with the namesake hooch. For a quicker stop, follow the smell of grilled meat to **Pop Burger** (⊠ *58-60 9th Ave., between 14th and 15th Sts.* ☎ *212/414–8686*). The mini burgers are tempting, but locals swear by the sides: crispy fries and thick-as-cement milkshakes.

Diane von Furstenberg. Flit through the perennial wrap dresses or tops with a deep-V neckline, some with ruffles along the edge to accentuate the plunge. The space has just a hint of disco, with flecks of mirrors spangling the ceiling. ⊠, *at 14th St., Meatpacking District* ☎*646/486–4800* Ⓜ*A, C, E to 14th St.*

Morgane Le Fay. The clothes here used to have a sort of billowy, Stevie Nicks quality, but though they're still Renaissance-inspired, the designs are more streamlined. Silk organza gowns have Empire waists and crinkly skirts; fitted velvet jackets have covered buttons. ⊠*746 Madison Ave., between E. 64th and E. 65th Sts., Upper East Side* ☎*212/879–9700* Ⓜ*6 to 68th St./Hunter College* ⊠*67 Wooster St., between Broome and Spring Sts., SoHo* ☎*212/219–7672* Ⓜ*C, E to Spring St.*

Nanette Lepore. "Girly" may well be the description that comes to mind as you browse through this cheerful shop; skirts are pleated and adorned with bows, jackets are enhanced by embroidery and floral appliqués, fur shrugs have tiny sleeves. ⊠*423 Broome St., between Lafayette and Crosby Sts., NoLita* ☎*212/219–8265* Ⓜ*6 to Spring St.*

Rebecca Taylor. Follow the dandelion fluff painted on the walls around racks of lace-overlay dresses and silk-piped trousers. Appliqués and embroideries add fillips of craftiness. ⊠*260 Mott St., between Prince and W. Houston Sts., NoLita* ☎*212/966–0406* Ⓜ*6 to Spring St.*

★ **Saja.** From flirty sundresses to black chiffon numbers, this boutique has got your party dress needs covered. Less-expensive frocks and separates—many vintage-inspired—start around $200, a bargain considering the quality. ⊠*250 Elizabeth St., between Prince and W. Houston Sts., NoLita* ☎*212/226–7570* Ⓜ*6 to Spring St.*

Tracy Feith. *Mr.* Feith makes the most of feminine curves by creating vibrant dresses and separates. Necklines on tees scoop wide and low, skirts flirt with flounces and yokes, and the sexy printed silk dresses are light as a feather. ⊠*1318 Madison Ave., between 92nd and 93rd Sts., Upper East Side* ☎*212/334–3097* Ⓜ*6 to 96th St.*

★ **Tracy Reese.** Unabashedly girly garb is Reese's specialty, as she plays with lush fabrics (silk chiffon is a favorite), quirky color combos, and notice-me embellishments like rhinestones and ruffles. The cuts flatter all sorts of figures, often emphasizing the waist. This flagship carries both the ladylike Tracy Reese line and the funkier, lower-price Plenty label. ⊠*641 Hudson St., between Horatio and Gansevoort Sts., Meatpacking District* ☎*212/807–0505* Ⓜ*A, C, E to 14th St.*

Vivienne Tam. Tam is known for her playful "China chic" take on familiar Asian images. Cold-weather creations in emerald-and-ruby–color silk are embroidered with dragons and flowers; the warm-weather clothes are pale and floaty. ⊠*40 Mercer St., at Grand St., SoHo* ☎*212/966–2398* Ⓜ*R, W to Prince St.*

HAUTE DESIGN

Alexander McQueen. No matter how flouncy McQueen's ensembles become, they retain idiosyncratic, unsettling elements. Delicate, floaty dresses might be printed with eagles; fitted pantsuits could be juxtaposed with stiff leather corsets or Victorian lace. ⊠*417 W. 14th St.,*

between 9th and 10th Aves., Meatpacking District ☎*212/645–1797*
Ⓜ*A, C, E to 14th St.*

Balenciaga. Nicolas Ghesquière, a current *amour fou* in the fashion
world, took a page from the neighboring galleries for the first U.S. store.
His clothing's not always the most wearable, but it's always stimulating.
You might luck onto a reissue from the (Cristobal) Balenciaga archives,
made up in modern fabrics. The stash of more accessible handbags and
shoes is worth a browse. ✉*542 W. 22nd St., between 10th and 11th
Aves., Chelsea* ☎*212/206–0872* Ⓜ*C, E to 23rd St.*

Carolina Herrera. This couture deserves a truly outstanding occasion; the
beading and sequin work are stunning. Expect anything from demure,
shimmering bands of decoration to knockout swaths of beaded lace.
✉*954 Madison Ave., at E. 75th St., Upper East Side* ☎*212/249–6552*
Ⓜ*6 to 77th St.*

Chanel. The Midtown flagship has often been compared to a Chanel
suit—slim, elegant, and timeless. Inside wait the famed suits themselves,
along with other pillars of Chanel style: chic little black dresses and
evening gowns, chain-handled bags, and yards of pearls. Downtown's
branch concentrates on morecontemporary forays, including ski gear,
while Madison's boutique is dedicated to shoes, handbags, and other
accessories. The jewelry outpost gleams with showstopper pieces based
on Chanel's own jewels, as well as stars and comets sparkling with
diamonds and gold worked into a quilted design. ✉*139 Spring St., at
Wooster St., SoHo* ☎*212/334–0055* Ⓜ*C, E to Spring St.* ✉*15 E. 57th
St., between 5th and Madison Aves., Midtown East* ☎*212/355–5050*
Ⓜ*N, R, W to 5th Ave./59th St.* ✉*737 Madison Ave., at E. 64th St.,
Upper East Side* ☎*212/535–5505* Ⓜ*6 to 68th St./Hunter College*
✉*Chanel Fine Jewelry, 733 Madison Ave., at E. 64th St., Upper East
Side* ☎*212/535–5828* Ⓜ*6 to 68th St./Hunter College.*

★ **Kirna Zabête.** A heavy-hitting lineup of prestigious designers—Balenciaga, Chloé, Jean Paul Gaultier, Proenza Schouler—is managed with
an exceptionally cheerful flair. Step downstairs for Ella Dish dog hoodies, French Bowl home accessories, and hip infant gear. ✉*96 Greene
St., between Spring and Prince Sts., SoHo* ☎*212/941–9656* Ⓜ*R, W
to Prince St.*

O.M.O. Norma Kamali. A fashion fixture from the 1980s has a newly modern, though still '80s-influenced, line. Her luminously white store carries
bold black-and-white-patterned bathing suits, slinky separates in velvet
and jersey, and poofy "sleeping-bag coats." You can also choose from
a selection of skin-care products, olive oils, and fragrances. ✉*11 W.
56th St., between 5th and 6th Aves., Midtown West* ☎*212/957–9797*
Ⓜ*E, V to 5th Ave./53rd St.*

Oscar de la Renta. The ladylike yet lighthearted runway designs of this
upper-crust favorite got their first U.S. store here. Skirts swing, ruffles
billow, embroidery brightens up tweed, and even a tennis dress looks like
something you could go dancing in. ✉*772 Madison Ave., at E. 66th St.,
Upper East Side* ☎*212/288–5810* Ⓜ*6 to 68th St./Hunter College.*

Philosophy di Alberta Ferretti. The designer's eye for delicate detailing is
evident in the perforated hemlines, embroidered stitching, and sprin-
kling of beads across gauzy fabrics or soft knits. ✉*452 West Broadway,*

Holiday Markets

Between Thanksgiving and Christmas, holiday markets—rows of wooden stalls, many with red-and-white-stripe awnings—spring up around town. The gifts and goods vary from year to year, but there are some perennial offerings: colorful handmade knitwear and jewelry; sweet-smelling soaps, candles, and lotions with hand-lettered labels; glittery Christmas ornaments of every stripe; and New York–theme gift items (a group called Gritty City offers T-shirts, coin purses, and undies printed with pictures of taxicabs and manhole covers).

Though the holiday market in **Grand Central Terminal's Vanderbilt Hall** is indoors, most vendors set up outside. There's one every year at **Columbus Circle**, near the southwest entrance to Central Park, and another at **Bryant Park**, behind the New York City Public Library. The largest and most popular, however, is at the south end of **Union Square**, where you can go from the greenmarket to the stalls like the downtowners who meet in the afternoon or after work to look for unique or last-minute gifts.

between W. Houston and Prince Sts., SoHo ☎*212/460–5500* Ⓜ*F, V to Broadway–Lafayette St.*

★ **Stella McCartney.** A devout vegetarian setting up shop in the Meatpacking District may seem odd, but it's further proof that chic trumps many other considerations. You could put together an outfit of head-to-toe satin or chiffon, but it's more in keeping to mix it with shredded denim or a pair of knee-high Ultrasuede cowboy boots (since leather is verboten, shoes and accessories come in satin, canvas, and synthetics). The dressing rooms are so beautiful you might just want to move in. ✉*429 W. 14th St., at Washington St., Meatpacking District* ☎*212/255–1556* Ⓜ*A, C, E to 14th St.*

Vera Wang. Though practically synonymous with made-to-order, modern-princess bridal gowns, Wang's also a star at evening wear. Her gowns manage to pull off vintage-inspired shapes (mermaid sheaths, portrait necklines) and lots of satin, beading, and embroidery while still looking elegantly streamlined. Periodic prêt-à-porter sales offer the dresses for a (relative) song. A second store in SoHo, at 158 Mercer Street has also recently opened; it stocks the ready-to-wear lines. ✉*991 Madison Ave., at E. 77th St., Upper East Side* ☎*212/628–3400* Ⓜ*6 to 77th St.*

DEPARTMENT STORES

Most department stores keep regular hours on weekdays and are open late (until 8 or 9) at least one night a week. Many have personal shoppers who can walk you through the store at no charge, as well as concierges who will answer all manner of questions. Some have restaurants or cafés that offer decent meals and pick-me-up snacks.

Fodor's Choice   **Barneys New York.** Barneys continues to provide fashion-conscious and
★   big-budget shoppers with irresistible, must-have items at its uptown

flagship store. The extensive menswear selection has a handful of edgier designers, though made-to-measure is always available. The women's department showcases posh designers of all stripes, from the subdued lines of Armani and Jil Sander to the irrepressible Alaïa and Zac Posen. The shoe selection trots out Prada boots and strappy Blahniks; the cosmetics department will keep you in Kiehl's, Sue Devitt, and Frederic Malle; jewelry runs from the whimsical (Kazuko) to the classic (Ileana Makri). Expanded versions of the less expensive **Co-op** department occupy the old Barneys' warehouse space on West 18th Street and a niche on Wooster Street. ⊠*660 Madison Ave., between E. 60th and E. 61st Sts., Upper East Side* ☎*212/826–8900* Ⓜ*N, R, W, 4, 5, 6 to 59th St./Lexington Ave.* ⊠*Barneys Co-op, 236 W. 18th St., between 7th and 8th Aves., Chelsea* ☎*212/593–7800* Ⓜ*A, C, E to 14th St.* ⊠*116 Wooster St., between Prince and Spring Sts., SoHo* ☎*212/965–9964* Ⓜ*R, W to Prince St.*

Bergdorf Goodman. Good taste reigns in an elegant and understated setting, but remember that elegant doesn't necessarily mean sedate. Bergdorf's carries some brilliant lines, such as Marchesa, Narciso Rodriguez, and Carmen Marc Valvo. In the basement Level of Beauty, find a seat in the manicure–pedicure lounge (no appointments) for a bit of impromptu pampering. The home department has rooms full of magnificent linens, tableware, and gifts. Across the street is another entire store devoted to menswear: made-to-measure shirts, custom suits, designer lines by the likes of Ralph Lauren and Gucci, and scads of accessories, from hip flasks to silk scarves. ⊠*754 5th Ave., between W. 57th and W. 58th Sts., Midtown West* ⊠*Men's store, 745 5th Ave., at 58th St., Midtown East* ☎*212/753–7300* Ⓜ*N, R, W to 5th Ave./59th St.*

Bloomingdale's. Only a few stores in New York occupy an entire city block; the uptown branch of this New York institution is one of them. The main floor is a crazy, glittery maze of mirrored cosmetic counters and perfume-spraying

> ### WORD OF MOUTH
>
> "Century 21 carries much, much more than designer clothes. The designer section is just one part of the store, which is massive. I go there for everything from gym socks to wineglasses." —lizziea06

salespeople. Once you get past this dizzying scene, you can find good buys on designer clothes, bedding, and housewares. The downtown location is smaller, and has a well-edited, higher-end selection of merchandise, so you can focus your search for that Michael Kors handbag or pricey pair of stilettos. ⊠*1000 3rd Ave., main entrance at E. 59th St. and Lexington Ave., Midtown East* ☎*212/705–2000* Ⓜ*N, R, W, 4, 5, 6 to 59th St./Lexington Ave.* ⊠*504 Broadway, between Spring and Broome Sts., SoHo* ☎*212/729–5900* Ⓜ*R, W to Prince St.*

Fodor's Choice ★ **Century 21.** For many New Yorkers this downtown fixture—right across the street from the former World Trade Center site—remains the mother lode of discount shopping. Four floors are crammed with everything from Gucci sunglasses and half-price cashmere sweaters to Ralph Lauren towels, though you'll have to weed through racks of less fabulous stuff to find that gem. The best bets in the men's department are shoes and the designer briefs; the full floor of designer women's wear can yield some dazzling finds, such as a Calvin Klein leather trench coat for less than $600 or a sweeping crinoline skirt from Jean Paul Gaultier. ■TIP→Since lines for the communal dressing rooms can be prohibitively long, you might want to wear a bodysuit under your clothes for quick, between-the-racks try-ons. ✉*22 Cortlandt St., between Broadway and Church St., Lower Manhattan* ☎*212/227–9092* Ⓜ*R, W to Cortlandt St.*

Henri Bendel. Behind the graceful Lalique windows you can discover more than the usual fashion suspects. Bendel's dedication to the unusual begins in the ground-floor cosmetics area and percolates through the floors of women's clothing and accessories. Designers such as Alice + Olivia, Michael Kors, Catherine Malandrino, and Diane von Furstenberg have room to breathe here. Bendel's in-house lines, which include the signature cashmeres and brown-and-white dopp kits, are displayed throughout. This isn't a fully comprehensive store, though; for instance, there are no true shoe or lingerie departments. ✉*712 5th Ave., between W. 55th and W. 56th Sts., Midtown West* ☎*212/247–1100* Ⓜ*E, V to 5th Ave./53rd St.*

Lord & Taylor. Comfortably conservative and never overwhelming, Lord & Taylor is a stronghold of classic American designer clothes. Instead of unpronounceable labels, you can find Dana Buchman, Jones New York, and a lot of casual wear. The store tends to attract an older, decidedly untrendy crowd. It also has a large selection of reasonably priced full-length gowns. ✉*424 5th Ave., between W. 38th and W. 39th Sts., Midtown West* ☎*212/391–3344* Ⓜ*B, D, F, N, Q, R, V, W to 34th St./Herald Sq.*

Macy's. Macy's headquarters store claims to be the largest retail store in America; expect to lose your bearings at least once. Fashion-wise, there's a concentration on the mainstream rather than on the luxe. One strong suit is denim, with everything from Hilfiger and Calvin Klein to Earl Jeans and Paper Denim & Cloth. There's also a reliably good selection of American designs from Ralph Lauren, Tommy Hilfiger, and Nautica. For cooking gear and housewares, the Cellar nearly outdoes Zabar's. ✉*Herald Sq., 151 W. 34th St., between 6th and 7th Aves., Midtown West* ☎*212/695–4400* Ⓜ*B, D, F, N, Q, R, V, W to 34th St./Herald Sq.*

★ **Pearl River Mart.** If you want to redecorate your entire apartment with a Chinese theme for less than $1,000, this is the place to do it. Every Asian-style furnishing, houseware, and trinket can be found here, from bamboo rice steamers and ceramic tea sets to paper lanterns and grinning wooden Buddha statues. On the main floor, under a ceiling festooned with dragon kites and rice-paper parasols, you can buy kimono-style robes, pajamas, and embroidered satin slippers for the whole family. There's also a dry-goods section, where you can load up on packages of ginger candy, jasmine tea, and cellophane noodles. ✉*477 Broadway, between Broome and Grand Sts., SoHo* ☎*212/431–4770* Ⓜ*N, R, Q, W to Canal St.*

Saks Fifth Avenue. A fashion- and beauty-only department store, Saks sells an astonishing array of clothing. The choice of American and

European designers is impressive without being esoteric—the women's selection includes Gucci, Narciso Rodriguez, and Marc Jacobs, plus devastating ball gowns galore. The footwear collections are gratifyingly broad, from Ferragamo to Juicy. In the men's department, sportswear stars such as John Varvatos counterbalance formal wear and current trends. The ground-floor beauty department stocks everything from the classic (Sisley, Lancôme, La Prairie) to the fun and edgy (Nars, M.A.C.). ⊠*611 5th Ave., between E. 49th and E. 50th Sts., Midtown East* ☎*212/753–4000* Ⓜ*E, V to 5th Ave./53rd St.*

Takashimaya New York. This pristine branch of Japan's largest department store carries stylish accessories and fine household items, all of which reflect a combination of Eastern and Western designs. There's also a lovely basement-level tearoom, top-floor floral section, and an expanded children's department store anchored by a merry-go-round and a high-design playhouse. ⊠*693 5th Ave., between E. 54th and E. 55th Sts., Midtown East* ☎*212/350–0100* Ⓜ*E, V to 5th Ave./53rd St.*

HOME DECOR

Fodor'sChoice
★
ABC Carpet & Home. ABC seems to cover most of the furnishings alphabet; over several floors it encompasses everything from rustic furniture to 19th-century repros, refinished Chinese chests, and Vitra chairs, not to mention that loose category, "country French." The ground floor teems with a treasure-attic's worth of accessories. Three restaurants offer places to refuel. Rugs and carpets are unrolled across the street at 881 Broadway. ⊠*888 Broadway, at E. 19th St., Flatiron District* ☎*212/473–3000* Ⓜ*L, N, Q, R, W, 4, 5, 6 to 14th St./Union Sq.*

Armani Casa. In keeping with the Armani aesthetic, the minimalist furniture and home wares have a subdued color scheme (cream, black, a crimson accent here and there). You might find lacquered ebony-stain boxes, square-cut porcelain bowls and plates, or silky linens and pillows. ⊠*97 Greene St., between Prince and Spring Sts., SoHo* ☎*212/334–1271* Ⓜ*R, W to Prince St.*

★ **Bellora.** Fine linens for bath and bedroom have been the trademark of this Italian family business since the late 19th century. High-thread-count sheets, duvets, and pillowcases come in soothing color combinations: beachy stripes in pale blue and cream; springtime checks in celadon and rose. There are baffled cotton towels and robes, too, and a line of linen sprays and body lotions to keep everything (including you) smelling lovely. ⊠*156 Wooster St., at W. Houston St., SoHo* ☎*212/228–6651* Ⓜ*R, W to Prince St.; B, D, F, V to Broadway–Lafayette.*

Clio. Take a shortcut to find the accessories you've seen in the shelter mags. This boutique sets its table with delicate Czech glass vases, bone china with raised dots, and colorful handblown glass bottles. ⊠*92 Thompson St., between Prince and Spring Sts., SoHo* ☎*212/966–8991* Ⓜ*C, E to Spring St.*

★ **De Vera.** The objets d'art here all seem to have stories behind them. Many are antique and hint of colonial travels: Indian carvings, Japanese lacquer boxes, 19th-century British garnet earrings. Others exemplify modern forms of traditional workmanship, such as the Murano glass

Continued on page 364

LOWER EAST SIDE

Once home to multitudes of Jewish immigrants from Russia and Eastern Europe, the Lower East Side has traditionally been New Yorkers' bargain beat. The center of it all is Orchard Street, where vendors still holler, "Lady, have I got a deal for you!"

Here tiny, no-nonsense clothing stores and scrappy stalls hang on to the past, while funky local designers gradually claim more turf. A few cool vintage clothing and furniture spots bridge the two camps. Ludlow Street, one block east of Orchard, has become the main drag for twentysomethings with attitude, its boutiques wedged in between bars and low-key restaurants. Anything too polished is looked on with suspicion—and that goes for you, too. For the full scope of this area, prowl from Allen to Essex streets, south of East Houston Street down to Broome Street. A tip: wear closed shoes to stay clear of broken glass and other crud on the sidewalks. —J.P.

BEST TIME TO GO

Come on a Sunday afternoon, when Orchard Street between East Houston and Delancey streets becomes a vehicle-free pedestrian zone. On Saturday the old-school stores close for the Jewish Sabbath.

BEST SOUVENIR FOR YOUR FAVE KITCHEN AIDE

Raid the **Lower East Side Tenement Museum** gift shop (✉ *108 Orchard St., between Delancey and Broome Sts.* ☎ *212/431–0233*) for a cheery reproduction 1950 Empire State souvenir kitchen towel and some retro fridge magnets with skyscrapers trumpeting "New York the Wonder City." Bonus point: wrapping paper with a 1930s NYC map design.

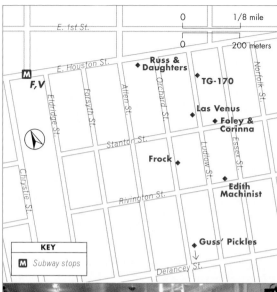

KEY

Ⓜ *Subway stops*

BEST FOR

VINTAGE
Frock: big names from the 1970s and '80s, whopping shoulder pads, and often hefty price tags.

Las Venus: Danish modern furniture, princess phones, boomerang ashtrays in punchy colors.

CLOTHES WITH BITE
TG-170: rock-chick wardrobe staples like superdark, tight jeans and tough Freitag bags.

Foley & Corinna: mixes vintage-y new clothes with the truly vintage.

OLD-WORLD FOOD
Russ & Daughters (⊠*179 E. Houston St. at 1st Ave.*): smoked salmon, pickled herring, and babka, oh my.

Guss' Pickles (⊠*85 Orchard St.* ☎*No phone*): move beyond the half-sours to the zingy full-sour and spicy pickle spears.

REFUELING

Get your calcium with a stop at **il laboratorio del gelato** (⊠*95 Orchard St., between Delancey and Broome Sts.* ☎*212/343–9922*) for creamy scoops in unusual flavors like nutmeg, ricotta, or ginger. Cake with your gelato? Zip to **Sugar Sweet Sunshine** (⊠*126 Rivington St. , between Essex and Norfolk Sts.* ☎*212/995–1960*), a homey little bakery where you can nibble on a cupcake with chocolate-almond frosting or a slice of red velvet cake. For something healthier, get a table at the **teany café** (⊠*90 Rivington St. , between Orchard and Ludlow Sts.* ☎*212/475–9190*), a vegetarian spot with light meals, sweets, and more than 90 teas to try.

IN FOCUS LOWER EAST SIDE

17

vases or incredibly lifelike glass insects. ⊠ *1 Crosby St., at Howard St., SoHo* ☎ *212/625–0838* Ⓜ *N, Q, R, W, 6 to Canal St.*

Design Within Reach. "An interesting plainness is the most difficult and precious thing to achieve" reads one of the quotes discreetly placed on the walls here. You can get a lot closer to Mies van der Rohe's ideal with these tasteful mid-20th-century pieces, such as Noguchi's paper column lamps and Le Cor-

busier's steel-frame sofa, plus contemporary furnishings in the same spirit, such as Jesús Gasca's beech "globus" chair. ⊠ *408 W. 14th St., at 9th Ave., Meatpacking District* ☎ *212/242–9449* Ⓜ *A, C, E to 14th St.* ⊠ *142 Wooster St., between Prince and spring W. Houston Sts., SoHo* ☎ *212/471–0280* Ⓜ *F, V to Broadway–Lafayette* ⊠ *110 Greene St., between Prince and Spring Sts., SoHo* ☎ *212/475–0001* Ⓜ *F, V to Broadway–Lafayette* ⊠ *27 E. 62nd St., between Park and Madison Aves., Upper East Side* ☎ *212/888–4539* Ⓜ *N, R, W, 4, 5, 6 to 59th St./Lexington Ave.* ⊠ *124 Hudson St., between Beach and N. Moore Sts., TriBeCa* ☎ *212/219–2217* Ⓜ *1 to Franklin St.* ⊠ *341 Columbus Ave., at W. 76th St., Upper West Side* ☎ *212/799–5900* Ⓜ *1, 2, 3 to 72nd St.* ⊠ *903 Broadway, at 20th St., Flatiron* ☎ *212/477–1155* Ⓜ *N, R, W to 23rd St.*

Fishs Eddy. The dishes, china, and glassware for resale come from all walks of crockery life, from corporate dining rooms to failed restaurants. New wares often look retro, such as a service with a ticker-tape border. They also stock lots of oddball pieces, such as finger bowls. ⊠ *889 Broadway, at E. 19th St., Flatiron District* ☎ *212/420–9020* Ⓜ *L, N, Q, R, W, 4, 5, 6 to 14th St./Union Sq.*

Hable Construction. Vivid colors and graphic shapes (stripes, dots, leaves) give these wool-felt and cotton-linen pillows all-around warmth. Cotton canvas hats and beach totes come out in spring; appliquéd felt stockings are hung up for the holidays. ⊠ *117 Perry St., between Hudson and Greenwich Sts., Greenwich Village* ☎ *212/989–2375* Ⓜ *A, C, E to 14th St.*

Jonathan Adler. Adler gets mid-20th-century-modern and Scandinavian styles to lighten up with his striped, striated, or curvy handmade pottery (ranging from a $30 vase to a chunky $400 lamp) as well as the hand-loomed wool pillow covers, rugs, and throws with blunt graphics (stripes, crosses, circles). ⊠ *47 Greene St., between Broome and Grand Sts., SoHo* ☎ *212/941–8950* Ⓜ *N, Q, R, W, 6 to Canal St.* ⊠ *37 Greenwich Ave., at Charles St., Greenwich Village* ☎ *212/488–2803* Ⓜ *1 to Christopher St./Sheridan Sq.*

Kiosk. Is it a gallery or a boutique? Duck under the neon arrow sign, head up the stairway, and you'll come upon this novelty shop-cum-art installation. The owners travel the globe in search of locally unique, interestingly designed or packaged items, then sell their gleanings at this outpost. A new destination is highlighted every few months. You might find wooden rattles from Vermont, beeswax crayons from Finland, or incense from Hong Kong. ⊠*95 Spring St., 2nd fl., at Broadway, SoHo* ☎ *212/226–8601* Ⓜ*R, W to Prince St.*

Moss. International designers put a fantastic spin on even the most utilitarian objects, which are carefully brought together by Murray Moss at his store–cum–design museum. The latest innovations from Jasper Morrison, Ted Muehling, and Philippe Starck are interspersed with vintage Baccarat crystal and classic chair designs from Frank Gehry. The neighboring Moss Gallery spotlights work that's even more arty. ⊠*150–152 Greene St., between W. Houston and Prince Sts., SoHo* ☎*212/204–7100* Ⓜ*R, W to Prince St.*

★ **Muji.** If you're into simple, chic, cheap style, Muji will be your trifecta. The name of this Japanese import translates to "no brand" and indeed, you won't find a logo plastered on the housewares or clothes. Instead, their hallmark is streamlined, often monochrome design. The whole range of goods, from milky porcelain teapots to wooden toys, is invariably user-friendly. At the Midtown branch you can glimpse the lobby of the *New York Times*. ⊠*455 Broadway, at Grand St., SoHo* ☎*212/334–2002* Ⓜ*N, Q, R, W to Canal St.* ⊠*620 8th Ave., at W. 40th St., Midtown West* ☎*212/382–2300* Ⓜ*A, C, E to 42nd St./Port Authority.*

Mxyplyzyk. Hard to pronounce (*mixy plit sick*) and hard to resist, this is a trove of impulse buys—creative riffs on household standbys such as dishes (covered in psychedelic patterns or made from old vinyl LPs), handbags (made to look like boccie balls), and toothbrush holders (shaped like giant teeth). ⊠*125 Greenwich Ave., at W. 13th St., Greenwich Village* ☎*212/989–4300* Ⓜ*A, C, E, L to 14th St./8th Ave.*

Nina Griscom. Another socialite has joined the commercial fray, allowing those of us without a boldface name to sample the rarified style. The objets d'art, furniture, and jewelry here have an exotic–organic appeal, with natural materials like ivory, sandalwood, and coral turning up as candlesticks, decorative boxes, and chunky cuff bracelets. ⊠*958 Lexington Ave., at E. 70th St., Upper East Side* ☎*212/717–7373* Ⓜ*6 to 68th St./Hunter College.*

★ **Olatz.** The wife and muse of painter Julian, Olatz Schnabel modeled her linen shop on a historic Havana pharmacy after the couple visited Cuba. The black-and white checkerboard floors and mint-green walls breathe a sort of lazy, faded elegance, a spot-on backdrop to her collection of luxurious sheets, blankets, and pajama sets, all of which have sky-high thread counts and are bordered with bold stripes or intricate damask embroidery. ⊠*43 Clarkson St., between Hudson and Greenwich Sts., Greenwich Village* ☎*212/255–8627* Ⓜ*1 to Houston St.*

Pylones. Even the most utilitarian items get a goofy, colorful makeover from this French company. Toasters and thermoses are coated in stripes or flowers, hairbrushes have pictures of frogs or ladybugs on their backs, and whisks are reimagined as squid. ■TIP➔There are plenty of fun gifts for less than $20, such as old-fashioned robot toys and candy-color boxes. ⊠*69 Spring St., between Crosby and Lafayette Sts., SoHo* ☎*212/431–3244* Ⓜ*6 to Spring St.*

17

★ **Terence Conran Shop.** The small glass pavilion beneath the 59th Street Bridge caps this British stylemonger's vast underground showroom of kitchen and garden implements, fabrics, furniture, and glassware. Even the shower curtains are cool. ⊠407 E. 59th St., at 1st Ave., Midtown East ☎212/755–9079 Ⓜ N, R, W to 59th St./Lexington Ave.

Troy. In this spare space the clean lines of Lucite, leather, cedar, and resin furniture and home accessories may well wreak havoc with your credit card. In addition to the seriously sleek furnishings, you can also find slightly less imposing items like stone-shape lamps in Murano glass, teakwood serving trays, and creative ceramic tableware. ⊠99 Madison Ave., between 29th and 30th Sts., Murray Hill ☎212/941–4777 Ⓜ6 to 28th St.

William-Wayne & Co. Silver julep cups, Viennese playing cards, butler's trays, candelabras made from coral, and other whimsical decorative items all vie for your attention at this shop. ⊠40 University Pl., at E. 9th St., Greenwich Village ☎212/533–4711 Ⓜ6 to Astor Pl. ⊠846 Lexington Ave., at E. 64th St., Upper East Side ☎212/737–8934 Ⓜ6 to 68th St./Hunter College ⊠850 Lexington Ave., at E. 64th St., Upper East Side ☎212/288–9243 Ⓜ6 to 68th St./Hunter College

JEWELRY

FOR EVERY DAY

Alexis Bittar. Bittar began selling his first jewelry line, made from Depression-era glass, on a corner in SoHo. Now the Brooklyn-born designer has multiple Manhattan stores showcasing his hand-sculpted and hand-painted treasures. He makes clean-lined, big-statement jewelry from vermeil, colored Lucite, pearls, and vintage glass. The stores mirror this aesthetic with a mix of old and new, like antiqued white Victorian-era lion's claw tables and Plexiglass walls. ⊠465 Broome St., between Mercer and Greene Sts., SoHo ☎ 212/625–8340 Ⓜ R, W to Prince St. ⊠353 Bleecker St., between E. 65th and E. 66th Sts., West Village ☎212/727–1093 Ⓜ1 to Christopher St./Sheridan Sq.

Beads of Paradise. Browse a rich selection of African trade-bead necklaces, earrings, and rare artifacts. You can also create your own designs. ⊠16 E. 17th St., between 5th Ave. and Broadway, Flatiron District ☎212/620–0642 Ⓜ4, 5, 6, N, Q, R, W to 14th St./Union Sq.

Dinosaur Designs. Translucent and colorful, this antipodean work uses an untraditional medium: resin. Some resins look like semiprecious stone, such as onyx or jade; the rest delve into stronger colors like aqua or crimson. Cruise the stacks of chunky bangles and cuffs or rows of rings; prices start at less than $50. There's some striking tableware, too. ⊠250 Mott St., between Prince and E. Houston Sts., NoLita ☎212/680–3523 Ⓜ R, W to Prince St.

★ **Fragments.** This spot glitters with pieces by nimble new jewelry designers, many of them local. Most use semiprecious stones—you could try on turquoise-bead shoulder-duster earrings, an oversize opal ring, or a tourmaline pendant—but a few bust out the sapphires and rubies. ⊠116 Prince St., between Greene and Wooster Sts., SoHo ☎212/334–9588

Ⓜ*R, W to Prince St.* ✉*997 Madison Ave., between E. 77th and E. 78th Sts., Upper East Side* ☎*212/537–5000* Ⓜ*6 to 77th St.*

Me + Ro. Eastern styling has gained these designers a cult following. The Indian-inspired, hand-finished gold bangles and earrings covered with tiny dangling rubies or sapphires may look bohemian, but the prices target the trust-fund set. ✉*241 Elizabeth St., between Prince and E. Houston Sts., NoLita* ☎*917/237–9215* Ⓜ*R, W to Prince St.*

Robert Lee Morris. Gold and silver take on bold, sculptural shapes here: cuff bracelets are chunky but fluidly curved, and necklaces and earrings have dangling hammered disks for a "wind chime" effect. Some pieces incorporate diamonds; others have semiprecious stones like turquoise or citrine. ✉*400 West Broadway, between Broome and Spring Sts., SoHo* ☎*212/431–9405* Ⓜ*C, E to Spring St.*

Stuart Moore. Many of the Teutonic designs are minimalist, almost industrial-seeming: diamonds are set in brushed platinum, and some rings and cuff links have a geometric, architectural aesthetic. Pieces here tend to be modest in scale. ✉*128 Prince St., at Wooster St., SoHo* ☎*212/941–1023* Ⓜ*R, W to Prince St.*

Fodor's Choice ★ **Ten Thousand Things.** You might find yourself wishing for 10,000 things from the showcases in this gallerylike space. Designs run from thin gold and silver chains to bold resin pieces. Many shapes are abstract reflections of natural forms, like buttercups or seedpods. Unusual stones beckon from the glass cases, such as the pendants of purple rubies or labradorites. ✉*423 W. 14th St., between 9th and 10th Aves., Meatpacking District* ☎*212/352–1333* Ⓜ*A, C, E to 14th St.*

Versani. Silver teams up with all kinds of materials here: leather, denim, and snakeskin, as well as semiprecious stones. There's a good selection of silver rings and pendants under $50. ✉*152 Mercer St., between Prince and W. Houston Sts., SoHo* ☎*212/941–9919* Ⓜ*R, W to Prince St.* ✉*227 Mulberry St., between Prince and Spring Sts., NoLita* ☎*212/431–4944* Ⓜ*6 to Spring St.*

MONEY'S NO OBJECT

A La Vieille Russie. Stop here to behold bibelots by Fabergé and others, enameled or encrusted with jewels. ✉*781 5th Ave., at E. 59th St., Midtown East* ☎*212/752–1727* Ⓜ*N, R, W to 5th Ave./59th St.*

Asprey. Its net spreads to cater to all kinds of luxury tastes, from leather goods and rare books to polo equipment and cashmere sweaters. Asprey's claim to fame, though, is jewelry; its own eponymous diamond cut has A-shape facets. ✉*853 Madison Ave., between 70th and 71st Sts., Upper East Side* ☎*212/688–1811* Ⓜ*6 to 68th St./Hunter College.*

Bulgari. This Italian company is certainly not shy about its name, which encircles gems, watch faces, even lighters. There are beautiful, weighty rings, pieces mixing gold with stainless steel or porcelain, and the latest Astrale line, which incorporates delicate motifs, like concentric circles of small diamonds, into drop earrings and necklaces. ✉*730 5th Ave., at W. 57th St., Midtown West* ☎*212/315–9000* Ⓜ*N, R, W to 5th Ave.* ✉*783 Madison Ave., between E. 66th and E. 67th Sts., Upper East Side* ☎*212/717–2300* Ⓜ*6 to 68th St./Hunter College.*

Fred Leighton. If you're in the market for vintage diamonds, this is the place, whether your taste is for tiaras, art-deco settings, or sparklers

17

once worn by a Vanderbilt. ⊠773 Madison Ave., at E. 66th St., Upper East Side ☎212/288–1872 Ⓜ6 to 68th St./Hunter College.

H. Stern. Sleek designs pose in an equally modern 5th Avenue setting; smooth cabochon-cut stones, most from South America, glow in pale wooden display cases. The designers make notable use of semiprecious stones such as citrine, tourmaline, and topaz. ⊠645 5th Ave., between E. 51st and E. 52nd Sts., Midtown East ☎212/688–0300 Ⓜ E, V to 5th Ave./53rd St.

Ivanka Trump. Compared to the style of Trump père, this small jewelry boutique is quite discreet. All things being relative, though, The Donald's daughter would like to see you dripping with her diamonds. Drop earrings, briolette tassels, and lots of icy rings are shown in an unstuffy yet glam salon. ⊠685 Madison Ave., between E. 61st and E. 62nd Sts., Midtown East ☎212/756–9912 Ⓜ N, R, W, 4, 5, 6 to 59th St./Lexington Ave.

Mikimoto. The Japanese originator of the cultured pearl, Mikimoto presents a glowing display of high luster pearls. Besides the creamy strands from their own pearl farms, check out the dazzlingly colored South Sea pearls, dramatic black-lip and silver-lip varieties, and rare conch pearls. ⊠730 5th Ave., between W. 56th and W. 57th Sts., Midtown West ☎212/457–4600 Ⓜ F to 57th St.

NEW YORK CLASSICS

Cartier. Pierre Cartier allegedly won the 5th Avenue mansion location by trading two strands of perfectly matched natural pearls with Mrs. Morton Plant. The jewelry is still incredibly persuasive, from such established favorites as the interlocking rings to the more recent additions such as the handcufflike Menotte bracelets. ⊠653 5th Ave., at E. 52nd St., Midtown East ☎212/753–0111 Ⓜ E, V to 5th Ave./53rd St. ⊠828 Madison Ave., at E. 69th St., Upper East Side ☎212/472–6400 Ⓜ6 to 68th St./Hunter College.

Harry Winston. Ice-clear diamonds of impeccable quality sparkle in Harry Winston's inner sanctum. They're set in everything from emerald-cut solitaire rings to wreath necklaces resembling strings of flowers. No wonder the jeweler was immortalized in the song "Diamonds Are a Girl's Best Friend." ⊠718 5th Ave., at W. 56th St., Midtown West ☎212/245–2001 Ⓜ F to 57th St.

Fodor'sChoice
★ **Tiffany & Co.** The display windows can be soigné, funny, or just plain breathtaking. Alongside the $80,000 platinum-and-diamond bracelets, a lot here is affordable on a whim (check out the sterling silver floor)—and everything comes wrapped in that unmistakable Tiffany blue. ⊠727 5th Ave., at E. 57th St., Midtown East ☎212/755–8000 Ⓜ N, R, W to 5th Ave./59th St.

LINGERIE

Agent Provocateur. The bustiest mannequins in Manhattan vamp in the front window of this British underpinnings phenom. Showpieces include boned corsets, lace sets with contrast-color trim, bottoms tied with satin ribbons, and a few fetish-type leather ensembles. A great selection of stockings is complemented by the garter belts to secure them. ✉*133 Mercer St., between Prince and Spring Sts., SoHo* ☎*212/965–0229* Ⓜ*R, W to Prince St.*

★ **Bra Smyth.** Chic and sweetly sexy French and Canadian underthings in soft cottons and silks line the shelves of this East Side staple. In addition to the selection of bridal-ready white bustiers and custom-fit swimsuits (made, cleverly, in bra-cup sizes), the store is best known for its knowledgeable staff, many of whom can offer tips on proper fit and size you up on sight. Cup sizes run from AA to H. ✉*905 Madison Ave., at 73rd St., Upper East Side* ☎*212/772–9400* Ⓜ*6 to 68th St./ Hunter College.*

La Perla. From the Leavers lace, soutache, and embroidery to unadorned tulle, these underthings are so gorgeous they've inspired a trilogy of books. Look for the sets of sheer underwear embroidered with the days of the week in Italian—a grown-up alternative to Bloomie's classic bloomers. ✉*803 Madison Ave., between E. 67th and E. 68th Sts., 3rd fl., Upper East Side* ☎*212/459–2775* Ⓜ*6 to 68th St./Hunter College* ✉*93 Greene St., between Prince and Spring Sts., SoHo* ☎*212/219–0999* Ⓜ*R, W to Prince St.-* ✉*425 W. 14th St., between 9th and 10th Aves., Meatpacking District* ☎*212/242–6662* Ⓜ*A, C, E to 14th St.*

La Petite Coquette. Among the signed photos on the walls is one of ultimate authority—from Frederique, longtime Victoria's Secret model. The store's own line of silk slips, camisoles, and other underpinnings comes in a range of colors, and as befits the name, they have special petite cuts. ✉*51 University Pl., between E. 9th and E. 10th Sts., Greenwich Village* ☎*212/473–2478* Ⓜ*R, W to 8th St.*

Mixona. The minx-at-heart will have a field day among the lace and mesh bras of Huit and the flirty, lower-cut bras by Mimi Holliday. Some lines trace back to such major design houses as Blumarine and D&G. There's also a house line of silk sleepwear and a small selection of indie label ready-to-wear clothing. ■TIP➜There are usually good finds on the sales racks in back. ✉*262 Mott St., between Prince and E. Houston Sts., NoLita* ☎*646/613–0100* Ⓜ*R, W to Prince St.*

LUGGAGE, LEATHER GOODS, AND HANDBAGS

Altman Luggage. Great bargains—a Samsonite Pullman for a little more than $100—are the thing at this discount store, which also stocks tough Timberland and Swiss Army backpacks. ✉*135 Orchard St., between Delancey and Rivington Sts., Lower East Side* ☎*212/254–7275* Ⓜ*F, J, M, Z to Delancey St./Essex St.*

Anya Hindmarch. Although some of these divine British handbags in calf, satin, or velvet are ready for a very proper occasion, others cut loose with funny silk-screened photos or sequined designs of candy or painkillers. ✉*29 E. 60th St., between Madison and Park Aves., Upper East Side* ☎*212/750–3974* Ⓜ*N, R, W to 5th Ave./59th St.* ✉*115 Greene St., between Prince and Spring Sts., SoHo* ☎*212/343–8147* Ⓜ*R, W to Prince St.*

Bottega Veneta. The signature crosshatch weave graces leather handbags, slouchy satchels, and shoes; the especially satisfying brown shades

Continued on page 372

WEST VILLAGE

It's easy to feel like a local, not a tourist, while shopping in the West Village. Unlike 5th Avenue or SoHo, the pace is slower, the streets relatively quiet, and the scale small. This is the place to come for unusual finds rather than global-brand goods (well, if you don't count Marc Jacobs).

Bleecker Street is a particularly good place to indulge all sorts of shopping appetites. Foodies love the blocks between 6th and 7th avenues for the specialty purveyors like Murray's Cheese (254 Bleecker St.). Fashion foragers prowl the stretch between West 10th Street and 8th Avenue, while avid readers lose themselves in the Biography Bookshop. Hudson Street and Greenwich Avenue are also prime boutique-browsing territory. Christopher Street, true to its connection with the lesbian and gay community, has a handful of rainbow-flag stops. High rents mean there are fewer student-oriented shops around NYU than you might expect.

BEST TIME TO GO

Tuesday through Friday afternoons for a focused shopping stint, Saturday afternoon if you get a buzz from people-watching or the competitive aspect of busier boutiques. (Keep in mind that most stores here are small, so even a half dozen fellow browsers can make a shop feel crowded.) On Sunday the area's a bit bogged down by brunchers, and stores have shorter hours.

BEST SOUVENIR FOR A SWEET TOOTH

Invest in real estate at **Li-Lac Chocolates**: a chocolate townhouse or Empire State Building.

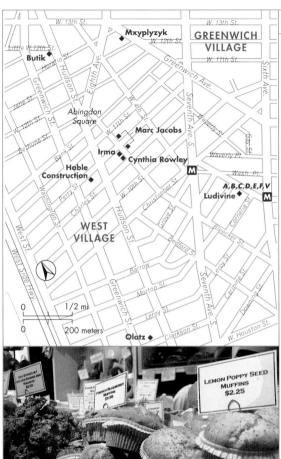

BEST FOR

NONCHALANT-CHIC CLOTHES

Marc Jacobs: the casual (but not cheap) line with seemingly unstoppable downtown street cred.

Butik: rare Danish designs collected by a supermodel.

Írma: the place to pair cult jeans, motorcycle boots, and a revealing top.

Ludivine: a direct feed to the Parisian femme's fashion scene.

Cynthia Rowley: party-friendly outfits for when a girl needs a halter top or a filmy dress.

HOME DECOR

Mxyplyzyk: household necessities and accessories get a jolt of saucy humor.

Olatz: divine bedding and pajamas in a Havana-inspired setting.

Hable Construction: a down-home aesthetic of bold patterns and sturdy fabrics, for everything from pillows to garden gloves.

17

REFUELING

Skip Magnolia Bakery; there's always a line, and besides, there's a vast number of other great places for a pick-me-up in this neighborhood. The house-made sweets at **Amy's Bread** (✉ *250 Bleecker St. , at Leroy St.* ☎ *212/675–7802*), like the layer-cake slices and "kitchen sink" cookies, are both homey and delicious. Try an Irish soda roll or a sandwich on raisin-and-fennel bread. A few doors away at **Cones** (✉ *272 Bleecker St., between Morton and Jones Sts.* ☎ *212/414–1795*), you can lap up a rich ginger or banana ice cream. For something more sophisticated, slide into a table at **Sant Ambroeus** (✉ *259 W. 4th St., at Perry St.* ☎ *212/604-9254*). This gracious Italian spot is perfect for a light meal, gelato, or espresso.

extend from fawn to deep choco-late. ⊠*699 5th Ave., between E. 54th and E. 55th Sts., Midtown East* ☎*212/371–5511* Ⓜ*N, R, W, 4, 5, 6 to 59th St./Lexington Ave.*

Crouch & Fitzgerald. Since 1839 this store has offered an unimpeachable selection of hard- and soft-sided luggage, as well as a huge number of attaché cases. ⊠*400 Madison Ave., at E. 48th St., Midtown East* ☎*212/755–5888* Ⓜ*B, D, F, V to 47th–50th St./Rockefeller Center.*

Fendi. Once known for its furs, Fendi is now synonymous with deca-dent handbags. The purses are beaded, embroidered, and fantastically embellished within an inch of their lives, resulting in prices that sky-rocket over $1,000. Fancy leathers, furs, and other accessories are also available. ⊠*677 5th Ave., between E. 53rd and E. 54th Sts., Midtown East* ☎*212/759–4646* Ⓜ*E, F to 5th Ave./53rd St.*

★ **Flight 001.** Frequent flyers can one-stop-shop at this travel-theme store. Carry-on bags, passport holders, and personal-size down pillows share shelf space with mini–alarm clocks, satin sleep masks, and mel-low music CDs for soothing frazzled nerves. ⊠*96 Greenwich Ave., between W. 12th and Jane Sts., Greenwich Village* ☎*212/989–0001* Ⓜ*A, C, E to 14th St.*

Furla. Shoulder bags, oblong clutches, and roomy totes can be quite proper or attention-getting, from a cocoa-brown, croc-embossed zipper-top to a patent leather, cherry-red purse. ⊠*598 Madison Ave., at E. 57th St., Midtown East* ☎*212/980–3208* Ⓜ*N, R, 4, 5, 6 to 59th St.* ⊠*727 Madison Ave., between E. 63rd and E. 64th Sts., Upper East Side* ☎*212/755–8986* Ⓜ*N, R, W, 4, 5, 6 to 59th St./Lexington Ave.*

Henry Beguelin. The aroma of leather pervades this boutique on the ground floor of the Hotel Gansevoort, and it's no wonder: everything here, even the floor, is made from it. Many of the pieces have an ethnic-bohemian look, with fringe and beading on jackets and swingy skirts. ⊠*18 9th Ave., at W. 13th St., Meatpacking District* ☎*212/647–8415* Ⓜ*A, C, E to 14th St.*

High Way. Some of these breezy, colorful handbags come trimmed with grosgrain ribbon or with a coin-purse-like snapping closure. Others open like minigarment bags to disclose a wealth of inner pockets. ⊠*238 Mott St., between Prince and Spring Sts., NoLita* ☎*212/966–4388* Ⓜ*6 to Bleecker St.*

Jamin Puech. Wanderlust is evident in many of these bags; the colors, embroideries, fringes, and fabrics may suggest Morocco and Polyne-sia, and the bags can cost as much as an off-season plane ticket to the Continent. ⊠*14 Prince St., at Elizabeth St., NoLita* ☎*212/431–5200* Ⓜ*R, W to Prince St.*

Fodor'sChoice **Kate Spade.** These eminently desirable (and oft-copied) handbags in
★ lush-color leather, tweed, and canvas have a classic but kicky retro style. Totes and shoulder bags are lined in fun fabrics; wicker baskets

for summer are jazzed up with bright leather accents or shaped like birdhouses. The Broome Street shop also carries shoes, hats, scarves, linens, sunglasses, and baby and travel accessories. Around the corner at **Jack Spade** (✉ *56 Greene St., between Broome and Spring Sts., SoHo* ☎ *212/625–1820* Ⓜ *C, E to Prince St.*), you'll find bags, dopp kits, and other men's accessories in a nostalgic setting. ✉ *454 Broome St., between Mercer and Greene Sts., SoHo* ☎ *212/274–1991* Ⓜ *C, E to Spring St.* ✉ *135 5th Ave., at 20th St., Flatiron District* ☎ *212/358–0420* Ⓜ *N, R, W to 23rd St.*

Leiber. A door handle twinkling with Swarovski crystals signals the entrance to the Kingdom of Sparkle. Instantly recognizable handbags are completely frosted in crystals, from simple, colorful rectangles to minaudières shaped like animals or flowers. Crystals also spangle the heels of satin pumps and the bows of oversize (to cut the glare?) sunglasses. ✉ *680 Madison Ave., at E. 61st St., Upper East Side* ☎ *212/223–2999* Ⓜ *4, 5, 6 to E. 59th St.*

Longchamp. Its nylon bags have become an Upper East Side staple and can be spotted everywhere in the Hamptons. The store carries the entire line of luggage, wallets, and totes in a rainbow of colors. ✉ *713 Madison Ave., between E. 63rd and E. 64th Sts., Upper East Side* ☎ *212/223–1500* Ⓜ *N, R, W, 4, 5, 6 to 59th St./Lexington Ave.*

Fodor'sChoice ★ **Louis Vuitton.** In the mammoth 57th Street store vintage examples of Vuitton's famous monogrammed trunks float above the fray on the ground floor, where shoppers angle for the latest accessories. Joining the initials are the Damier check pattern and colorful striated leathers, plus devastatingly chic clothes and shoes designed by Marc Jacobs. ✉ *1 E. 57th St., at 5th Ave., Midtown East* ☎ *212/758–8877* Ⓜ *E, V to 5th Ave./53rd St.* ✉ *116 Greene St., between Prince and Spring Sts., SoHo* ☎ *212/274–9090* Ⓜ *R, W to Prince St.*

Lulu Guinness. Hit this lavender-upholstered salon for such whimsically retro accessories as handbags adorned with appliqué, beads, and bows; polka-dot scarves; and umbrellas patterned with poodles. ✉ *394 Bleecker St., between W. 11th and Perry Sts., Greenwich Village* ☎ *212/367–2120* Ⓜ *1 to Christopher St.*

Fodor'sChoice ★ **Belle by Sigerson Morrison.** Ready to seduce your shoulder as well as your feet, this outpost stocks Sigerson Morrison's Belle line of shoes and bags, the latter in calfskin, pigskin, suede, and the occasional fabric, and often equipped with zippered exterior pockets for cell phones and other things you need close at hand. ✉ *242 Mott St., between Prince and E. Houston Sts., NoLita* ☎ *212/941–5404* Ⓜ *R, W to Prince St.*

Token Store. You know you want one, so visit the source of the Manhattan Portage messenger-bag fad. Although they're a dime a dozen around these parts, these sturdy nylon and canvas numbers cost real money—$20 to $100—and will impress the folks back home. The store also carries Manhattan Portage's newer, more-high-end line of leather carryalls, totes, and travel bags for those who grew up carting the messenger style, but now need something a bit more professional. ✉ *258 Elizabeth St., between E. Houston and Prince Sts., NoLita* ☎ *212/226–9655* Ⓜ *R, W to Prince St.*

17

MUSEUM STORES

Cooper-Hewitt National Design Museum. Prowl the shelves here for intriguing urban oddments and ornaments, like sculptural tableware, rare design books, rose corsages made from bulletproof material, and ceramic versions of New York deli coffee cups. ⊠ *2 E. 91st St., at 5th Ave., Upper East Side* ☎ *212/849–8400* Ⓜ *4, 5, 6 to 86th St.*

Metropolitan Museum of Art Shop. Of the three locations, the store in the museum has a phenomenal book selection, as well as posters, art videos, and computer programs. Reproductions of jewelry, statuettes, and other *objets* fill the gleaming cases in every branch. ⊠ *1000 5th Ave., at E. 82nd St., Upper East Side* ☎ *212/879–5500* Ⓜ *4, 5, 6 to 86th St.* ⊠ *14 Fulton St., between Front and South Sts., Lower Manhattan* ☎ *212/248–0954* Ⓜ *4, 5, A, C to Fulton St./Broadway–Nassau* ⊠ *15 W. 49th St., between 5th and 6th Aves., Rockefeller Center, Midtown West* ☎ *212/332–1360* Ⓜ *B, D, F, V to 47th–50th Sts./ Rockefeller Center.*

Museum of Arts and Design. In this museum's new home, the gift shop stocks beautiful handmade tableware, unusual jewelry, and other adornments, often tied in to ongoing exhibits. ⊠ *2 Columbus Circle, at 8th Ave., Midtown West* ☎ *212/299–7777* Ⓜ *1, A, B, C, D to 59th St./ Columbus Circle*

★ **Museum of Modern Art Design and Book Store.** The redesigned MoMA expanded its in-house shop with a huge selection of art posters and more than 2,000 titles on painting, sculpture, film, and photography. Across the street is the **MoMA Design Store** (⊠ *44 W. 53rd St., between 5th and 6th Aves., Midtown West* ☎ *212/767–1050* Ⓜ *E, V to 5th Ave./53rd St.*), where you can find Frank Lloyd Wright furniture reproductions, vases designed by Alvar Aalto, and lots of clever trinkets. The SoHo branch combines most of the virtues of the first two, although its book selection is smaller. ⊠ *11 W. 53rd St., between 5th and 6th Aves., Midtown West* ☎ *212/708–9700* Ⓜ *E, V to 5th Ave./53rd St.* ⊠ *81 Spring St., between Broadway and Crosby St., SoHo* ☎ *646/613–1367* Ⓜ *6 to Spring St.*

Museum of the City of New York. Satisfy your curiosity about New York City's past, present, or future with the terrific selection of books, cards, toys, and photography posters. If you've something classic in mind, look for the Tin Pan Alley tunes and stickball sets. ⊠ *1220 5th Ave., at E. 103rd St., Upper East Side* ☎ *212/534–1672* Ⓜ *6 to 103rd St.*

Neue Galerie. Like the museum, this bookshop focuses on German, Austrian, and Central European art. The solid selection includes catalogs, literature, and decorative items, including lovely wrapping papers. ⊠ *1048 5th Ave., between E. 85th and E. 86th Sts., Upper East Side* ☎ *212/628–6200* Ⓜ *4, 5, 6 to 86th St.*

MUSIC AND VIDEO

The city's best record stores provide browsers with a window to New York's cooler subcultures. The East Village is especially good for dance tracks and used music.

Bleecker Bob's Golden Oldies Record Shop. One of the oldest independent record stores in town, this pleasingly shabby-looking shop with its old-fashioned neon sign sells punk, jazz, metal, and reggae, plus good old rock on vinyl, until the wee hours. ⊠*118 W. 3rd St., at MacDougal St., Greenwich Village* ☎*212/475–9677* Ⓜ*A, C, E, F, V to W. 4th St./ Washington Sq.*

Jazz Record Center. Long-lost Ellingtons and other rare pressings come to light here; the jazz-record specialist also stocks collectibles, DVDs, videos, posters, and LPs. ⊠*236 W. 26th St., between 7th and 8th Aves., 8th fl., Chelsea* ☎*212/675–4480* Ⓜ*1 to 28th St.*

Fodor's Choice ★ **Other Music.** The antidote to music megastores, this niche spot carries hard-to-find genres on CD and vinyl, from Japanese electronica and Krautrock to acid folk and Americana. ■**TIP➔**There's also a great selection of used CDs, including seminal punk classics from the Clash and the Stooges. ⊠*15 E. 4th St., between Lafayette St. and Broadway, East Village* ☎*212/477–8150* Ⓜ*6 to Astor Pl.*

PAPER, GREETING CARDS, AND STATIONERY

Fodor's Choice ★ **Kate's Paperie.** Avid correspondents and gift givers adore Kate's, which rustles with fabulous wrapping papers, ribbons, blank books, writing implements of all kinds, and more. ⊠*72 Spring St., between Crosby and Lafayette Sts., SoHo* ☎*212/941–9816* Ⓜ*6 to Spring St.* ⊠*8 W. 13th St., between 5th and 6th Aves., Greenwich Village* ☎*212/633–0570* Ⓜ*F, V to 14th St.* ⊠*1282 3rd Ave., between E. 73rd and E. 74th Sts., Upper East Side* ☎*212/396–3670* Ⓜ*6 to 77th St.* ⊠*140 W. 57th St., between 6th and 7th Aves., Midtown West* ☎*212/459–0700* Ⓜ*F to 57th St.*

Smythson of Bond Street. Stationery fit for a queen— literally—check out the royal warrant from England's HRH. But keepsakes here are far from stuffy: make notes on your purchases, deepest thoughts, or conquests in softbound leather diaries with appropriate gilded titles, such as Passions & Pleasures and Juicy Gossip. They also carry an array of elegant formal stationery, address books, and buttery leather travel accessories. ⊠*4 W. 57th St., between 5th and 6th Aves., Midtown West* ☎*212/265–4573* Ⓜ*F to 57th St.*

17

PERFORMING ARTS MEMORABILIA

Drama Book Shop. The comprehensive stock here includes scripts, scores, and librettos. ⊠*250 W. 40th St., between 7th and 8th Aves., Midtown West* ☎*212/944–0595* Ⓜ*A, C, E to 42nd St./Port Authority.*

Movie Star News. As you flip through images from blockbusters, cult faves, and memorable bombs, it's hard to doubt their claim that they have the world's largest variety of movie photos and posters. Behind the counter are signed photos of many of the stars seen on the posters. ■**TIP➔**A poster of a New York film such as *Manhattan, The Royal Tenenbaums,* or *Taxi Driver* makes for a good souvenir for less than $20. ⊠*134 W. 18th St., between 6th and 7th Aves., Chelsea* ☎*212/620–8160* Ⓜ*1, 2, 3 to 14th St.*

One Shubert Alley. Souvenir posters, tees, and other knickknacks memorializing past and present Broadway hits reign at this Theater District shop. ✉*1 Shubert Alley, between W. 44th and W. 45th Sts., Midtown West* ☎*212/944–4133* Ⓜ*N, Q, R, S, W, 1, 2, 3 to 42nd St./Times Sq.*

Triton Gallery. Theatrical posters large and small are available, and the selection is democratic, with everything from Marlene Dietrich's *Blue Angel* to recent Broadway shows represented. ✉*630 9th Ave., between W. 44th and W. 45th Sts., Suite. 808, Midtown West* ☎*212/765–2472* Ⓜ*A, E to 42nd St./Port Authority.*

SHOES

MEN'S AND WOMEN'S SHOES

Bally. A few curveballs, like olive-green or slate-blue wing tips, liven up the mainly conservative selection. Carry-ons and clothing, such as deerskin or lamb jackets, join the shoe leather. ✉*628 Madison Ave., at E. 59th St., Midtown East* ☎*212/751–9082* Ⓜ*N, R, W, 4, 5, 6 to 59th St./Lexington Ave.*

Camper. These Euro-fave walking shoes, with their sturdy leather uppers and nubby rubber soles, have also proved popular on the cobblestone streets of SoHo. Comfort is a priority; all the slip-ons and lace-ups here have generously rounded toes and a springy feel. ✉*125 Prince St., at Wooster St., SoHo* ☎*212/358–1841* Ⓜ*R, W to Prince St.*

Cole-Haan. No longer wedded to staid moccasin styles, Cole-Haan has of late broken into stylish territory. Shoes for both sexes now come in exotic skins like python and crocodile; for warm weather, check out the orange suede thongs for men and metallic stiletto sandals for women. The handbag line is much more playful, too. ✉*620 5th Ave., at Rockefeller Center, Midtown West* ☎*212/765–9747* Ⓜ*E, V to 5th Ave./53rd St.* ✉*667 Madison Ave., at E. 61st St., Upper East Side* ☎*212/421–8440* Ⓜ*N, R, W, 4, 5, 6 to 59th St./Lexington Ave.* ✉*10 Columbus Circle, at W. 59th St., Midtown West* ☎*212/823–9420* Ⓜ*1, A, B, C, D to Columbus Circle.*

J. M. Weston. Specially treated calfskin for the soles and handcrafted construction have made these a French favorite; they could also double the price of your outfit. Red suede sneakers stand out among the shining leather oxfords and moccasins. ✉*812 Madison Ave., at E. 68th St., Upper East Side* ☎*212/535–2100* Ⓜ*6 to 68th St./Hunter College.*

John Fluevog Shoes. The inventor of the Angelic sole (protects against water, acid… "and Satan"), Fluevog designs chunky, funky shoes and boots. ✉*250 Mulberry St., at Prince St., NoLita* ☎*212/431–4484* Ⓜ*R, W to Prince St.*

Salvatore Ferragamo. Elegance typifies these designs, from black-tie patent to weekender ankle boots. The company reworks some of their women's styles from previous decades, like the girlish Audrey (as in Hepburn) ballet flat, released seasonally for limited runs. ✉*655 5th Ave., at E. 52nd St., Midtown East* ☎*212/759–3822* Ⓜ*E, V to 53rd St.*

Fodor'sChoice
★ **Sigerson Morrison.** The details—just-right T-straps, small buckles, metallic leathers—make the women's shoes irresistible. Prices rise well above $300, so the sales are big events. ✉*28 Prince St., between*

Mott and Elizabeth Sts., NoLita ☎212/219–3893 Ⓜ*F, V to Broadway–Lafayette St.* ☒*987 Madison Ave., between E. 76th and E. 77th Sts., Upper East Side* ☎212/734–2100 Ⓜ*6 to 77th St.*

Stuart Weitzman. The broad range of styles, from wing tips to strappy sandals, is enhanced by an even wider range of sizes and widths. ☒*625 Madison Ave., between*

E. 58th and E. 59th Sts., Midtown East ☎212/750–2555 Ⓜ*N, R, W, 4, 5, 6 to 59th St./Lexington Ave.* ☒*10 Columbus Circle, at W. 59th St., Midtown West* ☎212/823–9560 Ⓜ*1, A, B, C, D to Columbus Circle.*

Tod's. Diego Della Valle's coveted driving moccasins, casual loafers, and boots in colorful leather, suede, and pony skin are right at home on Madison Avenue. Though most of the women's selection is made up of low-heeled or flat styles, an increasing number of high heels are bent on driving sales, rather than cars. Men's choices stay low to the track with rubber-sole loafers, sneakers, and oxfords. ☒*650 Madison Ave., near E. 60th St., Upper East Side* ☎212/644–5945 Ⓜ*N, R, W to 5th Ave./59th St.*

MEN'S SHOES

Billy Martin's. Quality hand-tooled and custom-made boots for the urban cowboy are carried here. To complete the look, you can add a suede shirt or a turquoise-and-silver belt. ☒*1034 3rd Ave., between 61st and 62nd Sts., Upper East Side* ☎212/861–3100 Ⓜ*N, R, 4, 5, 6 to 59th St.*

Church's English Shoes. The high quality of these shoes is indisputable; you could choose something highly polished for an embassy dinner, a loafer or a crepe-sole suede ankle boot for a weekend, or even a black-and-white spectator style worthy of Fred Astaire. ☒*689 Madison Ave., at E. 62nd St., Upper East Side* ☎212/758–5200 Ⓜ*N, R, 4, 5, 6 to 59th St.*

John Lobb. These British shoes often use waxed leather, the better to contend with London levels of dampness. Ankle boots with padded collars or zips join the traditional oxfords and derbies; some shoes have elegantly tapered toes. ☒*680 Madison Ave., between E. 61st and E. 62nd Sts., Upper East Side* ☎212/888–9797 Ⓜ*N, R, 4, 5, 6 to 59th St.*

WOMEN'S SHOES

Christian Louboutin. Lipstick-red soles are the signature of Louboutin's delicately sexy couture slippers and stilettos, and his latest, larger downtown store has carpeting to match. The pointy-toe creations come trimmed with brocade, tassels, buttons, or satin ribbons. ☒*965 Madison Ave., between E. 75th and E. 76th Sts., Upper East Side* ☎212/396–1884 Ⓜ*6 to 77th St.* ☒*59 Horatio St., between Hudson*

17

and Greenwich Sts., Meatpacking District ☎*212/255–1910* Ⓜ*A, C, E to 14th St.*

Iris. As the Italian shoe manufacturers for splashy brands like Galliano, Viktor & Rolf, Marc Jacobs and Chloé, Iris's sole U.S. store is able to carry every style from those lines, including pieces not previously available on our shores. ✉*827 Washington St., at Little W. 12th St., Meatpacking District* ☎*212/645–0950* Ⓜ *A, C, E, L to 14th St.*

Jimmy Choo. Pointy toes, low vamps, narrow heels, ankle-wrapping straps—these British-made shoes are undeniably vampy, and sometimes more comfortable than they look. ✉*716 Madison Ave., between E. 63rd and E. 64th Sts., Upper East Side* ☎*212/759–7078* Ⓜ*6 to 68th St./Hunter College* ✉*645 5th Ave., at E. 51st St., Midtown East* ☎*212/593–0800* Ⓜ*B, D, F, V to 47th–50th Sts./Rockefeller Center.*

Manolo Blahnik. These are, notoriously, some of the most expensive shoes money can buy. They're also devastatingly sexy, with pointed toes, low-cut vamps, and spindly heels. Mercifully, the summer stock includes flat (but still exquisite) sandals; look for gladiator styles with ankle laces, or thongs embellished with sparkly beads. Pray for a sale. ✉*31 W. 54th St., between 5th and 6th Aves., Midtown West* ☎*212/582–3007* Ⓜ*E, V to 5th Ave./53rd St.*

Robert Clergerie. Not without its sense of fun, this place is often best in summer, when the sandal selection includes curvaceous soles and beaded starfish shapes. ✉*19 E. 62nd St., between 5th and Madison Aves., Upper East Side* ☎*212/207–8600* Ⓜ*R, W to 5th Ave.*

TOYS AND GAMES

Most of these stores are geared to children, but a few shops that cater to grown-up toy-lovers are mixed in. In addition to the stores listed below, *see* Pylones *in* Home Decor.

American Girl Place. No toy pink convertibles here; instead, the namesake dolls are historically themed, from Felicity of colonial Virginia to Kit of Depression-era Cincinnati. Each character has her own affiliated books, furniture, clothes, and accessories. There's a doll hairdressing station, a café, and even a theater showing a musical based on the dolls' stories. ✉*609 5th Ave., at E. 49th St., Midtown East* ☎*212/371–2220* Ⓜ*B, D, F, V to 47th–50th Sts./Rockefeller Center.*

Compleat Strategist. This store puts on a great spread—from board games and classic soldier sets to fantasy games. ✉*11 E. 33rd St., between 5th and Madison Aves., Murray Hill* ☎*212/685–3880* Ⓜ*6 to 33rd St.*

Dinosaur Hill. These toys leave the run-of-the-mill far behind, with mini–bongo drums, craft kits, jack-in-the-boxes, and a throng of marionettes and hand puppets, from mermaids to farmers to demons. ✉*306 E. 9th*

St., between 1st and 2nd Aves., East Village ☎*212/473–5850* Ⓜ*R, W to 8th St.; 6 to Astor Pl.*

Fodor'sChoice ★ **F.A.O. Schwarz.** A New York classic that's better than ever, this children's paradise more than lives up to the hype. The ground floor is a zoo of extraordinary stuffed animals, from cuddly $20 teddies to towering, life-size elephants and giraffes (with larger-than-life prices to match). F.A.O. Schweets stocks M&Ms in every color of the rainbow; upstairs, you can dance on the giant musical floor keyboard, browse through Barbies wearing Armani and Juicy Couture, and design your own customized Hot Wheels car. ☒*767 5th Ave., at E. 58th St., Midtown East* ☎*212/644–9400* Ⓜ*4, 5, 6 to E. 59th St.*

Kid Robot. Even if you've never heard of Urban Vinyl Toys, which, in quainter times, were simply referred to as "action figures," you can get a kick out of this shop, where adult and kid collectors flock to stock up on the latest toys from Asian designers. This is a far cry from Mattel—the artist-driven figures are more likely to represent smoking cupcakes. ☒*118 Prince St., between Greene and Wooster Sts., SoHo* ☎*212/966–6688* Ⓜ*N, R to Prince St.*

Kidding Around. This unpretentious shop is piled high with old-fashioned wooden toys, Playmobil and Brio sets, and a fun selection of hand puppets. The costume racks are rich with dress-up potential. ☒*60 W. 15th St., between 5th and 6th Aves., Flatiron District* ☎*212/645–6337* Ⓜ*L, N, Q, R, W, 4, 5, 6 to 14th St./Union Sq.*

Toys "R" Us. The Times Square megastore is so big that a three-story Ferris wheel revolves inside. With all the movie tie-in merchandise, video games, pogo sticks, stuffed animals, and what seems to be the entire Mattel oeuvre, this store has a lock on sheer volume. ☒*1514 Broadway, at W. 44th St., Midtown West* ☎*646/366–8800* Ⓜ*1, N, Q, R, W to 42nd St./Times Sq.*

World of Disney New York. Expect to be flooded with merchandise relating to Disney films and characters—pajamas, toys, figurines, you name it. There's also the largest collection of Disney animation art in the country. ☒*711 5th Ave., between E. 55th and E. 56th Sts., Midtown East* ☎*212/702–0702* Ⓜ*F to 57th St.*

17

WINE

Acker Merrall & Condit. Known for its selection of red burgundies, this store has knowledgeable, helpful personnel. ☒*160 W. 72nd St., between Amsterdam and Columbus Aves., Upper West Side* ☎*212/787–1700* Ⓜ*1, 2, 3 to 72nd St.*

Astor Wines & Spirits. This is a key spot for everything from well-priced champagne to Poire Williams to Riesling, in a beautiful location with a wine library and an organic wines area. ■TIP➜A selection of house favorites is discounted 15% every Tuesday. ☒*399 Lafayette St., at E. 4th St., East Village* ☎*212/674–7500* Ⓜ*6 to Astor Pl.*

Best Cellars. In a novel move, the stock here is organized by the wine's characteristics (sweet, fruity) rather than by region. Even better, the prices are amazingly low—between $10 and $14 a bottle. ☒*1291*

Lexington Ave., between E. 86th and E. 87th Sts., Upper East Side ☎*212/426–4200* Ⓜ*4, 5, 6 to 86th St.*

★ **Bottle Rocket.** Bright and approachable, this shop puts a new spin on wine shopping. Vintages are organized by quirky factors like their compatibility with local take-out menus and who they'd best suit as gifts (ranging from "Someone You Barely Know" to "The Boss"). A reference library, kids' play nook, and doggie area make the space extra welcoming. ✉*5 W. 19th St., between 5th and 6th Aves., Chelsea* ☎*212/929–2323* Ⓜ*R, W to 23rd St.*

Morrell & Company. Peter Morrell is a well-regarded and very colorful figure in the wine business, and his store reflects his expertise. Free wine tastings are held several times a month (for serious oenophiles, ask about the rare vintage auctions). Next door is his café, where dozens of fine wines are available by the glass. ✉*1 Rockefeller Plaza, at W. 49th St., Midtown West* ☎*212/688–9370* Ⓜ*B, D, F, V to 47th–50th Sts./Rockefeller Center.*

Union Square Wine & Spirits. Tastings are easy at this well-stocked store, thanks to Enomatic machines. These card-operated contraptions let you sample dozens of wines. ✉*140 4th Ave., at 13th St., East Village* ☎*212/675–8100* Ⓜ*L, N, Q, R, W, 4, 5, 6 to 14th St./Union Sq.*

Where to Eat

WORD OF MOUTH

"For lunch we went to Tía Pol. The food was nothing short of fabulous. The menu is basically tapas with a few concessions. . . . We had red peppers stuffed with potato salad and topped with a dollop of tuna. The red peppers tasted as if they were picked right on 10th Avenue."

—Aduchamp1

Updated by
Jen Laskey

Taking a bite out of the Big Apple is like taking a tasting trip around the world. At every meal you can dash off to a new country and dip your fork and spoon into the local cuisine without the international jet lag. People from all corners of the globe have opened restaurants here, and Manhattan's hungry masses, urban gourmands, and food critics have welcomed their diverse dishes and asked for seconds.

Whether you love Italian pasta, Thai noodle soups, or French pastries or you're looking to try something new, like Ethiopian *kifto* (spiced ground steak), a Scandinavian herring sampler, Lebanese pita bread, or Japanese desserts, just seek and you shall find. Your food journey may lead you to Chinatown for Cantonese, Cambodian, or Malaysian, to East 6th Street for Indian, to Harlem for Soul Food, or to Little Italy and Koreatown.

And New Yorkers aren't only infatuated with "foreign" food. We love our delis and diners, our American comfort food and regional cuisines. You'll find plenty of great burgers, bagels, seafood, steak houses, Texas BBQ, and New York pizza, the best kind (take that, Chicago). For elegant American fare, visit Gramercy Tavern, Hundred Acres, Dovetail, Apiary, or Per Se. For something a little spicier, try Elettaria, a Greenwich Village restaurant that serves contemporary American cuisine with Indian and South Asian influences. For adventurous food where cooking and alchemy meet, make reservations at Wylie Dufresne's wd~50, P*ong, or Eleven Madison Park.

New food trends hit the NYC dining scene all the time. Currently, restaurants are big on the *locavore* movement. More and more chefs—like those at Blue Hill and Eighty One—are seeking local, all-natural, market-to-table ingredients, and putting an emphasis on seasonal menus. We've also seen an insurgence of mobile gourmet food trucks doling out everything from desserts, dumplings, and waffles to tacos, pizza, and BBQ, a moveable feast indeed.

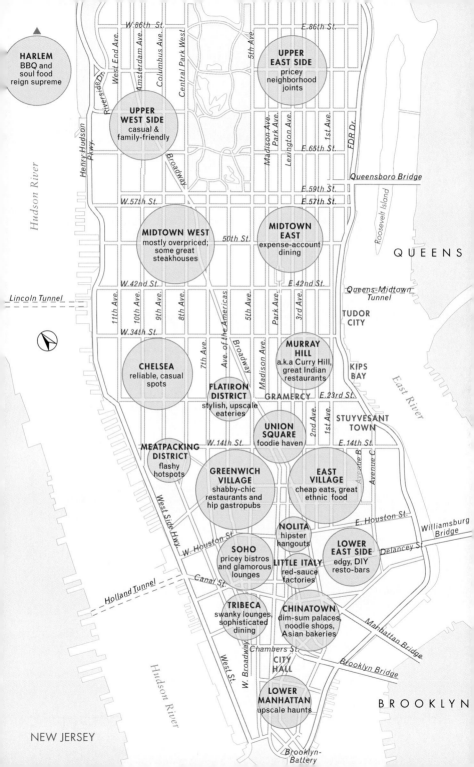

WHERE TO EAT PLANNER

Eating Out Strategy

Where should we eat? With thousands of Manhattan eateries competing for your attention, it may seem like a daunting question. But fret not—our expert writers and editors have done most of the legwork. The 160-plus selections here represent the best this city has to offer—from hot dogs to haute cuisine. Search "Best Bets" for top recommendations by price, cuisine, and experience. Sample local flavor in the neighborhood features. Or find a review quickly in the alphabetical listings. Dive in, and enjoy! For restaurants in the Outer Boroughs, see the Brooklyn chapter, and the Queens, Bronx, and Staten Island chapter.

Children

Though it's unusual to see children in the dining rooms of Manhattan's most elite restaurants, dining with youngsters in New York does not have to mean culinary exile. Many of the restaurants reviewed in this chapter are excellent choices for families, and are marked with a ☕ symbol.

Reservations

You'll be happy to hear it's getting easier to snag a desired reservation, but it's still a good idea to plan ahead. Some renowned restaurants are booked weeks or even months in advance. If that's the case, you can get lucky at the last minute if you're flexible—and friendly. Most restaurants keep a few tables open for walk-ins and VIPs. Show up for dinner early (5:30 pm) or late (after 10 pm) and politely inquire about any last-minute vacancies or cancellations. Occasionally, an eatery may ask you to call the day before your scheduled meal to reconfirm: don't forget or you could lose out.

What to Wear

When in the nation's style capital, do as the natives do: dress up to eat out. Whatever your style, dial it up a notch. Have some fun while you're at it. Pull out the clothes you've been saving for a special occasion and get glamorous. Unfair as it is, the way you look can influence how you're treated—and where you're seated. Generally speaking, jeans and a button-down shirt will suffice at most table-service restaurants in the $ to $$ range. Moving up from there, many pricier restaurants require jackets, and some insist on ties. In reviews, we note dress only when a jacket or jacket and tie is required. If you have doubts, call the restaurant and ask.

Tipping and Taxes

In most restaurants, tip the waiter 15%–20%. (To figure out a 20% tip quickly, just move the decimal point one place to the left on your total and double that amount.) Bills for parties of six or more sometimes include the tip already. Tip at least $1 per drink at the bar, and $1 for each coat checked. Never tip the maître d' unless you're out to impress your guests or expect to pay another visit soon.

Smoking

Smoking is prohibited in all enclosed public spaces in New York City, including restaurants and bars.

Hours

New Yorkers seem ready to eat at any hour. Many restaurants stay open between lunch and dinner, some offer late-night seating, and still others serve around-the-clock. Restaurants that serve breakfast often do so until noon. Restaurants in the East Village, the Lower East Side, SoHo, TriBeCa, and Greenwich Village are likely to remain open late, while Midtown spots and those in the Theater and Financial districts generally close earlier. Unless otherwise noted, the restaurants listed in this guide are open daily for lunch and dinner.

Prices

If you're watching your budget, be sure to ask the price of daily specials recited by the waiter. The charge for specials at some restaurants is noticeably out of line with the other prices on the menu. Beware of the $10 bottle of water; ask for tap water instead. And always review your bill.

If you eat early or late you may be able to take advantage of a prix-fixe deal not offered at peak hours. Most upscale restaurants offer great lunch deals with special menus at cut-rate prices designed to give customers a true taste of the place.

Credit cards are widely accepted, but many restaurants (particularly smaller ones downtown) accept only cash. If you plan to use a credit card it's a good idea to double-check its acceptability when making reservations or before sitting down to eat.

Some restaurants are marked with a price range ($$–$$$, for example). This indicates one of two things: either the average cost straddles two categories, or if you order strategically, you can get out for less than most diners spend.

WHAT IT COSTS AT DINNER

¢	$	$$	$$$	$$$$
Under $10	$10–$17	$18–$24	$25–$35	over $35

Price per person for a median main course or equivalent combination of smaller dishes. Note: if a restaurant offers only prix-fixe (set-price) meals, it has been given the price category that reflects the full prix-fixe price.

In This Chapter

Orientation

Throughout the chapter, you'll see mapping symbols and coordinates (⊕ 3:F2) after property names or reviews. To locate the property on a map, turn to the New York City Dining and Lodging Atlas at the end of this chapter. The first number after the ⊕ symbol indicates the map number. Following that is the property's coordinate on the map grid.

18

Double Check

The nature of the restaurant industry means places open and close in a New York minute—and in this economy make that more like 30 NY seconds. It's always a good idea to phone ahead and make sure your restaurant is still turning over tables.

BEST BETS FOR NEW YORK CITY DINING

With thousands of restaurants to choose from, how will you decide where to eat? Fodor's writers and editors have selected their favorite restaurants by price, cuisine, and experience in the Best Bets lists below. In the first column, Fodor's Choice properties represent the "best of the best" in every price category. You can also search by neighborhood for excellent eats—just peruse the following pages. Or find specific details about a restaurant in the full reviews, listed later in the chapter.

Fodor'sChoice ★

A Voce, $$$
Adour Alain Ducasse, $$$$
Bar Boulud, $$
Elettaria, $$
Eleven Madison Park, $$$$
Fatty Crab, $
Hundred Acres, $$
Kampuchea, $
Katz's Delicatessen, $
L'Atelier de Joël Robuchon, $$$$
Momofuku Ko, $$$$
Nha Trang, ¢
Per Se, $$$$
Shake Shack ¢
Tía Pol, $$

By Price

¢
Burger Joint
Financier Patisserie
Gray's Papaya
Nha Trang
Shake Shack
Veniero's Pasticceria

$
Back Forty
Bubby's
City Bakery
Fatty Crab
Kampuchea
Katz's Delicatessen
Mexicana Mama
Momofuku Noodle Bar

$$
Arturo's
Balthazar
Bar Boulud
Elettaria
Hill Country
'inoteca
Tía Pol

$$$
A Voce
Babbo
Bagatelle
BLT Steak
Craft
Matsugen
The Modern (Bar Room)
Scarpetta

$$$$
Adour Alain Ducasse
Del Posto
Eleven Madison Park
Jean Georges
L'Atelier de Joël Robuchon
Le Bernardin
Per Se

By Cuisine

AMERICAN
Back Forty, $
Gramercy Tavern, $$$$
Hundred Acres, $$
Park Avenue, $$$
Per Se, $$$$

BARBECUE
Blue Smoke, $$
Dinosaur Bar-B-Que, $
Hill Country, $$
R.U.B. BBQ, $
Wildwood Barbecue, $$

BISTRO
Bagatelle, $$$
Blue Ribbon Bakery, $$
Payard Pâtisserie & Bistro, $$$
Schiller's Liquor Bar, $

BRASSERIE
Artisanal, $$
Balthazar, $$
Paris Commune, $$
Pastis $$$

CAFÉ

Bouchon Bakery $
City Bakery $
Le Pain Quotidien $

CHINESE

Chinatown Brasserie, $$
Grand Sichuan International, $
Great New York Noodletown ¢
Joe's Shanghai, $
Shun Lee Palace, $$$

FRENCH

Adour Alain Ducasse,, $$$$
Bar Boulud, $$
Daniel, $$$$
Jean Georges, $$$$
Le Bernardin, $$$$
The Modern and Bar Room, $$$$/$$$

INDIAN

Tabla, $$$$
Tamarind, $$

ITALIAN

Alloro, $$$
Babbo, $$$
Del Posto, $$$$
'inoteca, $$
Lupa, $$
Scarpetta, $$$

JAPANESE

Bar Q, $$$
Kuruma Zushi, $$$$
Matsugen, $$$
Sushi of Gari, $$
Sushi Yasuda, $$

MEDITERRANEAN

August, $$
Il Buco, $$$
Mia Dona, $$
Picholine, $$$$

MEXICAN

Maya, $$$
Mexicana Mama, $
Toloache, $$

NEW AMERICAN

Blue Ribbon Brasserie$$
Craft, $$$
Elettaria, $$
Eleven Madison Park, $$$$
Hundred Acres, $$

PIZZA

Arturo's, $$
Lombardi's, $
Piola, $
Una Pizza Napoletana, $

SEAFOOD

BLT Fish, $$$
Esca, $$$

SPANISH

Boqueria, $$
Tía Pol, $$

STEAK HOUSE

BLT Prime, $$$$
BLT Steak, $$$
Porter House, $$$$
Sparks Steakhouse, $$$$

VIETNAMESE

Mai House, $$
Nha Trang ¢

By Experience

BRUNCH

Aquavit, $$$$
Balthazar, $$
Bubby's, $
Hundred Acres, $$
Sarabeth's, $$

BUSINESS DINING

BLT Steak, $$$
DB Bistro Moderne, $$$
Four Seasons, $$$$
Gotham Bar & Grill, $$$$
Jean Georges, $$$$

CELEB-SPOTTING

Balthazar, $$
Café Boulud, $$$$
Four Seasons, $$$$
Nobu, $$$
'21' Club, $$$$

CHILD-FRIENDLY

Bubby's, $
Carmine's, $$
City Bakery, $
Joe's Shanghai, $
Lombardi's, $
Odeon, $$$
Serafina, $$
Veniero's Pasticceria, ¢

GOOD FOR GROUPS

Buddakan, $$$
Carmine's, $$
Churrascaria Plataforma, $$$$
Hundred Acres, $$
Nobu, $$$
Vento, $$

GREAT VIEW

Asiate, $$$$
Michael Jordan's The Steakhouse NYC, $$$
Per Se, $$$$
Porter House, $$$$

LATE-NIGHT DINING

Balthazar, $$
Blue Ribbon Brasserie, $$
Fatty Crab, $
Pastis, $$$

WINE LIST

Babbo, $$$
Del Posto, $$$$
The Modern and Bar Room, $$$$/$$$
'21' Club, $$$$
Veritas, $$$$

18

LOWER MANHATTAN

BELOW CANAL STREET, INCLUDING CHINATOWN & TRIBECA

Since 9/11 thousands of new residents have moved to Lower Manhattan, fueling an up-and-coming neighborhood scene.

The most visible changes? Restaurants in and around the Financial District no longer adhere to banker's hours, and formal dining rooms have been outnumbered by casual cafés and wine bars. On the pedestrian-only Stone Street, throngs of young professionals gather for after-work drinks and dinner at nearby bistros, oyster bars, and steak houses.

To the north, Chinatown beckons adventurous diners, with restaurants representing numerous regional cuisines of China, including Cantonese, Szechuan, Hunan, Fujian, Shanghai, and Hong Kong–style cooking. Malaysian and Vietnamese restaurants also have taken root here, and the neighborhood continues to grow rapidly, encroaching into what was Little Italy.

To the west, TriBeCa still holds an air of exclusivity, with glamorous dining rooms in converted warehouses and some of the city's best French cuisine.

TRIBECA BRUNCH

Local loft dwellers descend on **Bubby's** (120 Hudson St., at N. Moore St., 212/219–0666 ⊕ 2:C5) for Southern-accented comfort fare like buttermilk biscuits, house-made pork sausage, and cheese grits. But save room for dessert: the restaurant started in 1990 as a pie company. The whiskey apple pie with pecan crumble is a crowd favorite. If you're looking for a more elegant atmosphere, try **Capsouto Frères** (451 Washington St., near Watts St., 212/966–4900 ⊕ 2:C5), a landmark French bistro that makes the city's best sweet and savory soufflés. We love the praline soufflé with hazelnut crème anglaise, and the three-cheese savory soufflé.

CHINATOWN CHOWDOWN

With more than 200 restaurants in just under 2 square mi, deciding where to dine may take longer than the actual meal. Here are our favorite places to enjoy Chinatown's diverse bounty.

Cantonese: For Hong Kong–style dim sum, head to **Ping's Seafood** (22 Mott St., near Worth St., 212/602–9988 ✛ *2:F6*) or **HSF** (46 Bowery, near Canal St., 212/374–1319 ✛ *2:F5*). Both spots are crowded but offer addictive fare like turnip cakes, steamed pork buns, and fried sesame-seed balls.

One of the best deals in Chinatown is at **Dumpling House** (118 Eldridge St., near Broome St., 212/625–8008 ✛ *2:G4*), where sizzling pork-and-chive dumplings are five for a buck.

Malaysian: There's something for everyone at **New Malaysia** (48 Bowery, near Canal St., 212/964–0284 ✛ *2:G5*)—great tofu dishes, sweet and spicy prawns, pepper beef, and delicious red-bean and coconut-milk drinks.

Shanghainese: The city's best soup dumplings—doughy pouches filled with ground pork and meaty broth—are ripe for the slurping at **Joe's Shanghai** (9 Pell St., near Bowery, 212/233–8888 ✛ *2:F5*).

Szechuan: Foodies go ga-ga for the twice-cooked pork in bean sauce and scallion pancakes at **Grand Sichuan** (125 Canal St., at Chrystie St., 212/625–9212 ✛ *2:G5*). At the **Peking Duck House** (28 Mott St., near Mosco St., 212/227–1810 ✛ *2:F5*), don't miss the stunning signature dish. Crispy-skinned Peking duck comes with pancakes, scallions, cucumbers, and hoisin sauce.

FINANCIAL DISTRICT'S RESTO ROW

Nestled alongside skyscrapers and the towering New York Stock Exchange, Stone Street is a two-block restaurant oasis that feels more like a village than the center of the financial universe. After the market closes, Wall Streeters head to **Ulysses'** (95 Pearl St., near Hanover Sq., 212/482–0400 ✛ *1:E4*), a popular pub with 50 beers on tap.

Clerks might stop in for a broccoli rabe–and–sausage slice at **Adrienne's Pizza Bar** (54 Stone St., near Hanover Sq., 212/248–3838 ✛ *1:E4*), while high-rolling brokers continue down the block to **Harry's Steak** (1 Hanover Sq., at Stone St., 212/785–9200 ✛ *1:E4*), for a dry-aged porterhouse and a reserve-collection cabernet. Those with a sweet tooth end up at **Financier Patisserie** (62 Stone St., between Mill La. and Hanover Sq., 212/344–5600), pictured below.

AND FOR DESSERT...

Bouley Bakery (120 West Broadway, near Duane St., 212/964–2525 ✛ 2:D6)
Renowned chef David Bouley's bustling TriBeCa bakery is both a downtown dessert haven and the entryway to Bouley's three-floor bakery/café, market, and upstairs dining complex. But you won't need to go farther than the first floor to satisfy your sweet tooth. The breads and pastries here represent many classic French favorites, including poppy-seed and fig loaves, brioche, croissants, and pains au chocolat. If you're looking for something more decadent, try the eclairs, meringues, Napoleons, fruit tarts, or one of Bouley's artisanal cakes. The colorful macaroons will make your mouth water with flavors like passion fruit filled with milk chocolate, raspberry with dark chocolate filling, and pistacio. One very special macaroon—and possibly the prettiest tasting dessert you'll ever try—is called the Ispahna. It's filled with a buttercream, rosewater, raspberry, and lychee mixture.

SOHO, NOLITA & LITTLE ITALY

In this high-rent neighborhood dining options are somewhat limited, resulting in crowded restaurants with steep prices. But snacking is a great strategy for experiencing the local flavor without buyer's remorse.

Longtime New Yorkers lament that SoHo has evolved from a red-hot art district into a big-brand outdoor mall. Shoppers engulf the neighborhood on weekends like angry bees, turning Lafayette Street into a buzzing hive of commerce. As a result, popular spots can be tough to get into during prime times.

In NoLita, the trendy next-door neighborhood of indie boutiques and restaurants, the spirit of old SoHo prevails. Modest eateries are squeezed between boutiques featuring products from up-and-coming designers.

If you want authentic Italian food, don't head south to Little Italy: most of the pasta factories along the main strip of Mulberry Street have developed reputations as tourist traps. As with SoHo, it's a better bet to snack your way through this area.

FRESH-BAKED

Follow the beguiling scent of fresh-baked bread to **Balthazar Bakery** (80 Spring St., near Crosby St., 212/965–9590 ✦ 2:E4), where you'll find baguettes, boules, batards, brioche, and at least six other different breads. The bakery—an extension of Keith McNally's well-loved Balthazar restaurant—boasts an extensive menu of paninis, sandwiches, quiches, and homemade soups. The pastry chefs also turn out custom-made pastries, cakes, and cookies. Try the chocolate pignon tart, passion-fruit soufflé, or coconut cake, or keep it simple with a few of Balthazar Bakery's buttery lemon, chocolate, or pistachio madeleines.

SOHO SIPS AND SNACKS

3 QUICK BITES
Relax and refuel at one of these neighborhood haunts.

Cuban sandwich at Café Habana (17 Prince St., at Elizabeth St., 212/625–2002 ✣ *2:F3*): This popular pan-Latin dive also boasts excellent Mexican-style grilled corn and café con leche. The Cuban sandwich features roasted pork, ham, Swiss cheese, pickles, and chipotle mayo.

Tacos at La Esquina (106 Kenmare St., 646/613–7100 ✣ *2:F4*): Order tasty pulled chicken or char-grilled steak tacos and tortas to go from the counter-service taqueria, or squeeze into the small café around the corner for a bigger sit-down meal.

Antipasti at Ama (48 MacDougal St., near King St., 212/358–1707 ✣ *2:D3*): Visit this stylish Italian restaurant at happy hour, weekdays 5:30 PM to 7:30 PM, when cocktails come with free snacks. The daily selection may include fried olives, spinach flan, arancini, cheeses, and hot and cold crostini.

ELEVATE YOUR COCKTAIL CONSCIOUSNESS

The American cocktail renaissance is underway at **Pegu Club** (77 W. Houston St., near West Broadway, 212/473–7348 ✣ *2:D3*), where renowned mixologist Audrey Saunders crafts impeccable modern cocktails steeped in pre-Prohibition tradition.

Inspired by a 19th-century British officer's club in Burma, the intimate second-floor lounge has a colonial aura, outfitted with palm trees, dark woods, and low-slung brown velvet couches.

But libations command the starring role, with fresh-squeezed juices and house infusions in every cocktail. Saunders's Earl Grey Martini uses tea-infused gin, and her Jamaican Firefly features fresh ginger beer with rum and lime.

"You have to look at well-crafted cocktails as fine cuisine with elements of sweet, sour, bitter, and spicy," Saunders says. "With well-crafted cocktails, you have parallel complexities, not just fruit and booze. You need spices and herbs and other ingredients to add complexity."

AND FOR DESSERT...

MarieBelle
(484 Broome St., between Wooster St. and West Broadway, 212/925–6999 ✣ *2:D4*)
Slip into MarieBelle to experience chocolate nirvana in an opulent Parisian-style café setting. At the front of the shop you'll find a decadent assortment of artisanal chocolates filled with velvety ganache in flavors like passion fruit, cardamom, saffron, hazelnut, and lavender. But real chocoholics head to the Cacao Bar at the back of the store for MarieBelle's überrich hot chocolate, crafted from ground cacao beans instead of cocoa powder, then mixed with boiling water (European style) or steamed milk (American style). For an unusual treat, try the spicy hot chocolate—it has a real kick to it. Tea lovers will be delighted by MarieBelle's diverse hand-blended selection from around the world. Not to worry if you're visiting during the late spring or summer, skip the hot chocolate and cool off with MarieBelle's Aztec iced chocolate—the warm-weather version of her decadent cacao elixir.

EAST VILLAGE & LOWER EAST SIDE

With luxury condos on Avenue C, the East Village—once Manhattan's edgiest enclave—has become yet another high-rent neighborhood. Nearby, the Lower East Side, home to generations of immigrant newcomers, is undergoing a similar transformation.

Both neighborhoods still offer some of the best meal deals in the city, and the influx of flush new residents has steadily raised the bar on quality eats. Dirt-cheap legends like **Katz's**, the all-night Jewish deli, coexist these days with high-end destinations featuring tasting menus and hard-to-score tables. There's something for every budget and craving, from yakitori parlors and German beer halls to kitschy diners and mid-price trattorias. St. Mark's Place is the center of New York's downtown Little Tokyo, while 6th Street is its Indian row. On the Lower East Side, meanwhile, cute little bistros have been inching into new gentrified stretches south of Delancey Street. And the neighborhoods have even given birth to their own homegrown star chefs, wildly creative young renegades with cultish followings like **Momofuku**'s David Chang and **wd~50**'s Wylie Dufresne.

NYC'S BEST DELI

Since 1888, **Katz's Delicatessen** (205 E. Houston St., at Ludlow St., 212/254–2246 ⊕ *2:G2*), pictured, has been serving up pastrami and corned beef on rye to an adoring public of locals and travelers alike. Katz's was the site of Meg Ryan's fake orgasm scene ("I'll have what she's having") in the 1989 film *When Harry Met Sally*—and it now serves 1,000 sandwiches per day, with pastrami ordered at a rate of 2-to-1 over corned beef. Other menu items include tongue, brisket, turkey, and Reuben sandwiches. Be sure to take a ticket at the door, and order at the counter for quickest service.

CHEAP ETHNIC EATS

You can find entrées for under $10 at most of these neighborhood favorites.

CAMBODIAN

With exposed brick and tall, communal tables, **Kampuchea Restaurant** (78 Rivington St., at Allen St., 212/529–3901 ⊹ *2:G3*) looks more like a wine bar than the city's best Cambodian eatery. Come here for adventure on a plate: pulled oxtail sandwich topped with tamarind and green papaya sauce and savory crepes stuffed with shrimp. The rich Phom Peng Katiev soup is perfect for sharing. The huge bowl is filled with rice noodles, ground pork, duck and chicken breast, and grilled shrimp.

JAPANESE

It's all about the broth at **Rai Rai Ken** (214 E. 10th St., near 2nd Ave., 212/477–7030 ⊹ *3:H5*), where Tokyo expats go for authentic ramen made three ways: in soy broth, seafood broth, or miso broth. Adventurous diners should try *takoyaki*, or fried octopus fritters.

MIDDLE EASTERN

The shawafel—a combination of falafel and shawarma—sandwich is a favorite at **Chickpea** (23 3rd Ave., near St. Marks Pl., 212/254–9500 ⊹ *3:G5*), though purists may opt to order these items separately. At **Hummus Place** (109 St. Marks Pl., near 1st Ave., 212/529–9198 ⊹ *3:H5*) around the corner, connoisseurs will be pleased to find a menu devoted to tahini-infused chickpea dip, which is served in three variations with pickles and warm pita.

UKRAINIAN

In a part of town known for Ukrainian food, **Veselka** (144 2nd Ave., at 9th St., 212/228–9682 ⊹ *3:H5*) stands out for its fantastic pierogi, borscht, and blintzes. The 24-hour eatery, located near pubs and bars, is a favorite for late-night dining.

AND FOR DESSERT...

ChikaLicious (203 E. 10th St., near 2nd Ave., 212/995–9511 ⊹ *3:H5*)

Throngs of dessert lovers descend on this chic 20-seat dessert bar for Chika Tillman's innovative creations, including her Fromage Blanc Island "cheesecake," her warm chocolate tart with pink peppercorn ice cream and red wine sauce, and her signature 3-course prix-fixe menu, which Chika describes as "American desserts, French presentation, and Japanese tasting portions." For $12, the prix-fixe includes a small amuse bouche, a dessert of your choice from the ChikaLicious menu, and assorted petit fours, which may include coconut marshmallows, cream puffs, or chocolate mousse drops. Chika's husband Tom, the general manager and sommelier, also suggests wine pairings for each of the desserts. Keep in mind that ChikaLicious has a 4-guests-per-party maximum; there's usually a line after 8 p.m. Chika and her husband also run the Dessert Club across the street with takeout "puddin," cupcakes, cookies, and other sweet specialties.

GREENWICH VILLAGE WITH WEST VILLAGE & MEATPACKING DISTRICT

Dining styles collide on the West Side, with quaint, chef-driven eateries in Greenwich Village facing off against the Meatpacking District's massive, celebrity-fueled hot spots.

Francophiles and fashionistas flock to Pastis, a brasserie in the Meatpacking District, for its stylish scene and standout seared tuna niçoise.

Greenwich Village's bohemian days may have faded with the Beatnik era, but the romantic allure of its tiny bistros, bars, and cafés remains. Around New York University, shabby-chic eateries and takeout joints line the streets and are patronized by a student clientele. Avoid heavily trafficked thoroughfares like Bleecker Street, as most of the Village's culinary gems lie tucked away on side streets and alleyways, especially west of 7th Avenue, in the West Village. The vibe here is low-key and friendly, with patrons squeezed together at tiny tables in matchbox-size eateries.

For a glitzier scene, head to the Meatpacking District, which has transformed in recent years from a gritty commercial warehouse area to the celebrity-chef–driven epicenter of the city's dining scene. The vibe is flashy, favored by actors, models, and their suitors.

DOSA TO GO

Snap up a savory snack from Thiru Kumar's cart perched at West 4th and Sullivan streets. Also known as the **Dosa Man** (✛ *2:D2)* of Washington Square Park, Kumar serves traditional South Indian fare like *masala dosa* (crepes stuffed with potato and onion), *idlis* (steamed lentil flour cakes), and *samosas* (savory potato-stuffed dumplings), all served with spicy vegetable soup and coconut chutney for about $5.

THE MEATPACKING DISTRICT 2 WAYS

	SAVE	SPLURGE
Creative Asian tapas	Rising star Zak Pelaccio's affordable cantina **Fatty Crab** (643 Hudson St., bet. Gansevoort and Horatio Sts., 212/352–3590 ✛3:C5) doubles as a late-night chef hangout. Stop in for chili-spiced crab and hard-to-find Japanese beer.	Celebrities and scene-seekers frequent **Spice Market** (403 W. 13th St., at 9th Ave., 212/675–2322 ✛3:B4), chef Jean-Georges Vongerichten's sprawling hot spot. Try the pineapple mojitos and spicy black-pepper shrimp.
Molto Italian flavor	Meet up with friends at **Vento** (675 Hudson St., at 14th St., 212/699–2400 ✛3:B4), where affordable small plates and wood-fired pizzas are served in a lively atmosphere.	Mario Batali's fine-dining flagship, **Del Posto** (85 10th Ave., bet. 15th and 16th Sts., 212/497–8090 ✛3:A4), features luxe touches like live piano, stools for ladies' purses, and $60 risotto for two.
Red-blooded cravings	Order itty-bitty burgers (two for $5) from the futuristic front counter at **Pop Burger** (58-60 9th Ave., bet. 14th and 15th Sts., 212/414–8686 ✛3:C4), then shoot pool with locals in the hipster lounge.	Excess is on the menu at Top Chef judge Tom Colicchio's latest venture, **Craftsteak** (85 10th Ave., at 15th St., 212/400-6699 ✛3:A4), where big spenders gravitate to the $110 strip steak.

ITALIAN FLAVOR IN THE VILLAGE

Pocket-size wine bar **'ino** (21 Bedford St., between 6th Ave. and Downing St., 212/989–5769 ✛2:C3) pours generous glasses from Italian winemakers. Pair an earthy Nebbiolo with 'ino's signature truffled egg toast. Italian expatriates craving a perfect cappuccino sidle up to the marble espresso bar at **Sant Ambroeus** (259 W. 4th St., near Perry St., 212/604–9254 ✛2:B1). The *pollo al forno* (roasted chicken) at **Barbuto** (775 Washington St., between Jane and W. 12th Sts., 212/924–9700 ✛3:B5) is fired in a brick oven and served with Chef Jonathan Waxman's rich citrus salsa verde—mamma mia!

AND FOR DESSERT…

Batch
(150B W. 10th St., at Waverly Pl., 212/929–0250 ✛3:D5)
Batch "bakery, dessert shop, and everything sweet" is the brainchild of Pichet Ong, internationally acclaimed pastry chef and chef/owner of P*ong restaurant next door. Batch's interior is a striking explosion of color punctuated by seductive displays of Ong's cookies, cakes, cupcakes, puddings, and other sweets. Before making your selection, tease yourself a little by reading Ong's tantalizing descriptions: Frangelico-soaked chocolate cake with hazelnut Bavarian and Valrhona chocolate buttercream; Vietnamese coffee cake with condensed milk glaze; strawberry rhubarb cupcake with coconut cake, rhubarb compote filling, strawberry buttercream, and candied violet. Check out the striking results of mixing savory with sweet; check out the green tea-iced chocolate cupcakes, lime cream cheese–filled carrot cupcakes with salted caramel frosting, sweet and salty peanut butter cookies, or the basil truffles.

18

UNION SQUARE, WITH GRAMERCY, MURRAY HILL & FLATIRON DISTRICT

The blocks around Union Square and its open-air greenmarket are filled with upscale foodie havens featuring market-driven menus. But fancy seasonal fare isn't all the area offers: Curry Hill and Koreatown are just blocks away.

Some of the city's most popular restaurants, including **Craft** and **Union Square Cafe**, are located in the area northwest of Union Square, called the Flatiron District. The neighborhood is also a hot shopping destination, with plenty of refueling spots like City Bakery, a gourmet deli that's a standby for many New Yorkers. Heading up from Union Square, Park Avenue South and streets nearby are packed with crowd-pleasers like Blue Smoke, Dos Caminos, and Les Halles.

Lexington Avenue between 27th and 29th streets is known as Curry Hill (it borders Murray Hill) for its wall-to-wall Indian restaurants, spice shops, and takeout joints. The area near Koreatown, on West 32nd Street, between 5th and 6th avenues, may look deserted, as eateries often lack visible signage—it's best to go with a specific spot in mind than to try your luck window-shopping.

BURGER BLISS

Just off Union Square, get your burger any way you like it. **Stand** (24 E. 12th St., near University Pl., 212/488–5900 ✥ *3:F4*) offers upscale fast fare in a sleek, cafeterialike setting. We recommend the odd-sounding bacon-and-egg cheeseburger, topped with cheddar and hard-boiled egg mayo. For an old–New York feel, try the classic burgers at the **Old Town Bar** (45 E. 18th St., near Park Ave. S, 212/529–6732 ✥ *3:F3*), where they've been serving 'em up for over 100 years. Or, if the weather is nice, head up to Madison Square Park, where burger lovers are always queued up at **Shake Shack** (23rd St. near Madison Ave., 212/889–6600 ✥ *3:F2*) for juicy burgers and frozen custard to go (pictured at upper right).

TASTE OF THE CITY

Adam Roberts
*Food Blogger, Author,
Playwright*

Food lover Adam Roberts is best known for his hilarious and informative blog, AmateurGourmet.com, where he champions his favorite places to eat, writes and performs songs about food, and recounts tales of cooking adventures. He's also the author of the book *The Amateur Gourmet: How to Shop, Chop, and Table Hop like a Pro (Almost)*, and is working on several projects with the Food Network.

Q: How would you recommend that out-of-towners approach eating in New York?
A: Try to do things you can only experience here. Go to Chinatown. Go to a great Jewish Deli like Katz's for pastrami sandwiches, or the 2nd Avenue Deli (162 E. 33rd, 212/689-9000) for matzoh-ball soup. You have to get a bagel while you're here—I always go to Murray's (500 6th Ave., 212/462-5054). Explore the places that are deeply rooted in the fabric of the city.

Q: What's your favorite restaurant to recommend to visitors?
A: It's hard to choose just one, but I do love Prune, which is one of the most welcoming, happy places in the city. Their food is top-notch and interesting but also familiar. It arouses

the intellect but still feels like Mom's cooking. If you can get to Blue Hill at Stone Barns (630 Bedford Rd., Pocantico Hills, 914/366-9600), just 35 minutes outside the city on the MetroNorth train, it's one of the most beautiful restaurants and is set on a working farm. Dan Barber is a brilliant chef who walks the line between surprising yet familiar food.

Q: As an avid theatergoer, where do you go for pretheater meals?
A: We often go to the Burger Joint—it's like an episode of *Happy Days*. For a splurge, the Mario Batali–owned Esca is phenomenal but expensive. To see Broadway stars, go after the show to Joe Allen, where I've seen Chita Rivera and Angela Lansbury.

Q: Speaking of splurges, where do you go when you're feeling flush, and conversely, when you're on a budget?
A: Jean Georges and Le Bernardin both do incredible 4-star food. JG is more playful, and Le Bernardin is impeccable. On the other end, Grand Sichuan on St. Marks serves some of the best Chinese food anywhere. You have to get the pork soup dumplings and the dry sautéed string beans.

—Nina Callaway

AND FOR DESSERT...

Max Brenner: Chocolate by the Bald Man (841 Broadway, near 13th St., 212/388-0030 ✛ 3:F4) Sure, it's an international chain, but if you're looking for a major chocolate fix, you can count on this place to provide your poison—in at least a hundred different ways. Max Brenner: Chocolate by the Bald Man is a Willy Wonka–esque chocolate emporium filled with college kids, families, and tourists—chocolate lovers, one and all. The extensive chocoholic menu boasts flavored chocolate beverages in custom-made sipping "hug mugs," chocolate fondues, cookies, cakes, brownies, ice creams, and spreads...even chocolate pizzas, and of course, boxes and bars of chocolate. Finally, the hot and cold chocolate cocktails may not be the most refined happy hour concoctions in NYC, but they are tasty. If the Max Brenner scene isn't for you, check out the more-sophisticated **City Bakery** (3 W. 18th St., between 5th and 6th Aves., 212/366-1414 ✛ 3:E3) a few blocks to the north and west where you can sip gourmet cocoa as thick as mud and nosh on crème brulée tartlettes with chocolate crusts.

18

MIDTOWN WEST & CHELSEA

Big is the buzz in Times Square and neighboring hoods, where neon-lighted billboards, towering skyscrapers, and Broadway theaters play starring roles. Watch out for restaurant rip-offs in this urban-theme-park environment.

Some say it's the stratospheric rents that cause restaurants here to skimp on ingredients and rush customers through their meals. It's true that tourist traps abound on the Great White Way, but fortunately you needn't head far from Times Square to score a stellar meal. Just move away from the bright lights and unrelenting foot traffic that clogs the area. On calmer side streets there are excellent dining options for budget travelers and expense-account diners alike. Some of the best steak houses and Italian restaurants are located here, and many eateries offer budget pretheater dinners and prix-fixe lunch menus to draw in new business.

But if the constant hustle-and-bustle unsettles your stomach, head south to Chelsea, a calmer neighborhood filled with art galleries and casual eateries. Chelsea may not be a white-hot dining destination, but you can eat well if you know where to go.

STEAK WITH STYLE

The design at **Quality Meats** (57 W. 58th St., near 6th Ave., 212/371–7777 ✛ *4:D1*), pictured above, is inspired by classic New York City butcher shops in its use of warm wood, stainless steel, and white marble. Sit at the bar to peruse the extensive menu of wines and single-malt Scotches. Then retire to the dining room for sophisticated riffs on steak-house classics like beef Wellington. Steak aficionados should know that Midtown has quality meats on every block. Here are more sure bets: **Ben Benson's** (123 W. 52nd St., near 6th Ave., 212/581–8888 ✛ *4:D2*) and **Uncle Jack's** (440 9th Ave., at 35th St., 212/244–0005 ✛ *4:B6*).

DINING IN TIMES SQUARE

There are plenty of chain eateries here that charge a premium for a substandard, rushed meal. But we've narrowed the field, selecting the best spots for a range of experiences and prices—from fun family dining to pretheater favorites.

For family-style fun, you can't miss the retro, 1950s-style **Ellen's Stardust Diner** (1650 Broadway, at 51st St., 212/956–5151 ⊹ *4:C3*), complete with a singing waitstaff. Enjoy all-American classics such as meat loaf and chicken potpie while your waiters and waitresses serenade you with Broadway tunes.

Unlike the mostly kitschy, theme restaurants that occupy Times Square, the sleek **Blue Fin** (1567 Broadway, near 47th St., 212/918–1400 ⊹ *4:C3*) seafood restaurant is a refreshing departure. Watch the crowds go by from the corner glass bar or head upstairs.

Toloache (251 W. 50th St., between Broadway and 8th Ave., 212/581–1818 ⊹ *4:B3*), a festive Mexican cantina, is a top foodie destination for its fresh ceviches, guacamoles, and standout dishes like the Negra Modelo–braised brisket taco or the quesadilla with black truffle and *huitlacoche* (corn fungus).

A mixed crowd of tourists, theatergoers, and thespians frequent **Joe Allen Restaurant** (326 W. 46th St., between 8th and 9th Aves., 212/581–6464 ⊹ *4:B3*), a pretheater favorite. This casual yet classy restaurant serves reliable American cuisine. Don't fret about missing the show—the Broadway-knowledgeable staff will make sure you get to the theater in time for the opening number.

Plates of fresh antipasti are displayed right as you walk into **Bond 45 (154 W. 45th St., between 6th and 7th Aves.,** 212/869–4545 ⊹ *4:C4*). This Italian eatery, with a dark-wood bar and leather-backed booths, serves a variety of pizzas, pastas, and steaks. With a separate pretheater menu, this Theater District hot spot is an ideal option for dining and then dashing to your show of choice.

AND FOR DESSERT...

Kyotofu
(705 9th Ave., near 48th St., 212/974–6012 ⊹ 4:A3) Even if you're not crazy about tofu, the soy-based delights at this Japanese dessert bar will make you reconsider the merits (and versatility) of the soybean. Kyotofu's signature sweet tofu with Kuromitsu black sugar syrup is so creamy and delicious you won't believe it's not a traditional panna cotta. The strawberry shortcake with strawberry sake sorbet and the warm miso chocolate cake with chocolate soybean ganache and green tea cream are two more totally compelling favorites. Kyotofu's menu is full of intriguing options, so your best bet, on your first visit, is to go for the Kaiseki prix fixe, a tantalizing three-course tasting menu that enables you to try six different mini-desserts. Kyotofu uses all-natural, healthful ingredients, including their artisanal tofu, which is made fresh daily. Their menu changes seasonally and it also includes savory brunch, lunch, and dinner options as well as an extensive sake and shochu cocktail list.

18

MIDTOWN EAST/UPPER EAST SIDE

Power brokers like to seal their deals over lunch on the East Side, so that means more than a few suits and ties at the restaurants during the day.

At night Midtown's streets are relatively quiet, but the restaurants are filled with expense-account diners celebrating their successes. Some of the most formal dining rooms and most expensive meals in town can be found here, at restaurants like the landmark **Four Seasons** and newcomer **L'Atelier de Joël Robuchon** or the **Modern**.

Farther uptown, the Upper East Side is jam-packed with pricey neighborhood eateries that cater to the area's well-heeled residents. Long viewed as an enclave of the privileged, these neighborhoods have plenty of elegant restaurants that serve the society "ladies who lunch," and bankers looking forward to a steak and single-malt Scotch at the end of the day. However, visitors to Museum Mile and 5th Avenue shopping areas need not be put off. Whether you're looking to celebrate a special occasion or just want to grab a quick bite, you're sure to find something here for almost any budget.

URBAN PICNIC

For a uniquely New York experience, take a picnic lunch to one of the outdoor plazas that line Park Avenue from 51st to 53rd streets, and seat yourself alongside scores of local office workers. (For architecture buffs, the Mies van der Rohe-designed Seagram Building is at 375 Park Avenue, at 52nd Street). First, pick up your wares at the **Market at Grand Central Terminal** (Main Concourse, East), a trusted resource for gourmet goods on-the-go. Your menu could include fresh-baked bread from **Corrado Bread & Pastry**; olives, roasted red peppers, and prosciutto from **Ceriello Fine Foods**; and fresh mozzarella or Parmigiano-Reggiano from **Murray's Cheese**.

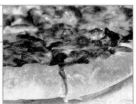

MUSEUM MUNCHING

	SAVE	SPLURGE
Museum of Modern Art	The **La Bonne Soupe** (48 W. 55th St., bet. 5th and 6th Aves., 212/586–7650 ✣4:E2) special includes a bowl of soup with bread, salad, a glass of wine, and dessert for $17.25.	The Modern's **Bar Room** (9 W. 53rd St., nr. 5th Ave., 212/333–1220 ✣4:D2) offers Alsatian-inspired fare—don't miss the sinful tarte flambé, charred flat bread topped with bacon, onion, and crème fraîche.
Neue Galerie	**Pintaile's** (26 E. 91st St., at Madison Ave., 212/722–1967 ✣6:F5) pizza offers delicious slices with a thin whole-wheat crust and gourmet toppings like roasted eggplant, wild mushrooms, and chorizo.	**Café Sabarsky** (1048 5th Ave., nr. 86th St., 212/288–0665 ✣6:E6) entices museumgoers with hearty sandwiches and entrées like sausage and goulash. Rich pastries complete the caloric spree.
Metropolitan Museum of Art	Grab a bite at Belgian chain **Le Pain Quotidien** (1131 Madison Ave., bet. 84th and 85th Sts., 212/327–4900 ✣5:F1), which offers an array of light fare, like cheese boards and gourmet salads.	**E.A.T.** (1064 Madison Ave., bet. 80th and 81st Sts., 212/772–0022 ✣5:F2), Eli Zabar's upscale American diner, may have high prices, but devotees return for excellent soups, sandwiches, and salads.

AND FOR DESSERT…

Little Pie Company (107 E. 42nd St., Grand Central Terminal's Lower Dining Concourse, 212/983–3538 ✣4:F4) The Grand Central Dining Concourse is not your typical food court—it contains outposts for some of the city's most popular restaurants and food shops, including a pie-lover favorite: the Little Pie Company. The flakey crusts here are baked from scratch with fresh, all-natural ingredients. And they don't skimp on the fillings either. The big pies, as well as the little ones, get filled right up to the top with fresh fruit, chocolate, or custard. Little Pie Company favorites include the Sour Cream Apple Walnut Pie, which is topped with a brown sugar, cinnamon, and walnut streusel, the Three Berry Pie (1. strawberry, 2. blueberry, and 3. raspberry), the Key Lime Pie (yep, made with real key lime juice) and the decadent triple chocolate Mississippi Mud Pie. You'll also find seasonal pies, such as a 100% pure pumpkin pie and their Southern Pecan pie with Texas pecans.

18

FORAGING IN CENTRAL PARK

There are plenty of pushcarts offering hot dogs and sodas, but if you're looking to soak up Central Park's magical ambience in an elegant setting, head for the **Central Park Boathouse Restaurant** (E. 72nd St. at Park Dr. N, 212/517–2233 ✣5:E3), which overlooks the gondola lake. There you can relax on the outdoor deck with a glass of wine and a cheese plate, or go for a more formal meal inside the restaurant. In warmer months, the restaurant can get crowded: go for a late lunch or early-evening cocktail.

UPPER WEST SIDE/HARLEM

Anchoring this mostly residential section of town—in terms of dining experiences—are the high-end restaurants at the Time Warner Center, which some like to call a "fine-dining food court." Head farther uptown for cheaper eats.

Dining room at Per Se in the Time Warner building.

With Lincoln Center theatergoers, hungry shoppers, and visitors to Central Park nearby, one might expect the Upper West Side to be jammed with fantastic eateries catering to all tastes and budgets. The main avenues are indeed lined with restaurants, but many of them are mediocre; they survive by catering to a local population that has neither the time nor the inclination to cook at home. Sure, there are a few notable destination-dining spots beyond the Time Warner Center. The best are **Jean Georges**, **Picholine**, and **Telepan**—but family-friendly Italian spots and grab-and-go delis have a tight grasp on the turf here. Without question, the best meal to eat in this neighborhood is brunch. There are flaky scones and fluffy omelets at **Sarabeth's**, and blintzes and bagels at **Barney Greengrass**. For a more adventurous eating experience, head up to Harlem for the city's best Southern cooking.

BRUNCH FAVES

If you haven't yet sorted out the city's obsession for smoked fish on a bagel, now's your chance to find out. **Barney Greengrass** (541 Amsterdam Ave., near 86th St., 212/724–4707 ✛*6:B6*) is the Upper West Side's best-loved brunch institution. Try succulent sable, pickled lox in cream sauce, and the famed sturgeon. Caveats: reservations are not accepted, and the bill can hit $30-plus per person.

WHAT'S HOT IN HARLEM?

Visitors in decades past may remember Harlem as an area scarred by crime and poverty. But times have changed: the Harlem of today is a vibrant community with excellent restaurants of all stripes. Those unfamiliar with the area may consider catching a cab late in the evening. But don't be scared off: Harlem's ethnic eats are worth the trip.

Here are our top picks for savoring the multicultural flavor of the neighborhood:

Amy Ruth's (113 W. 116th St., near Lenox Ave., 212/280–8779 ⊹6:C1) doesn't serve wine or beer, but offers a favorite childhood quencher: "Kool-Aid of the Day." Each of the Southern-accented dishes is named for a famous African-American personality. The title of the signature entrée, waffles and chicken, belongs to the Rev. Al Sharpton.

Miss Mamie's Spoonbread Too (366 W. 110th St., near Manhattan Ave., 212/865–6744 ⊹6:B2) is a much-loved Southern spot that's known for its friendly staff as well as its fried chicken, grits, and corn bread. Local politicians are sometimes seen rubbing elbows with the Columbia University students who gather here.

Native (161 Lenox Ave., at 118th St., 212/665–2525 ⊹6:C1) is a mildly Caribbean restaurant serving flavorful rice bowls and entrées that span a broad range of cuisines. Boasting a curry chicken, a seafood dish called the "The Bahamian Cobble," and catfish with chili sauce and cheese grits, this eatery manages to be all over the map and still find its way.

Sylvia's (328 Lenox Ave., near 127th St., 212/996–0660 ⊹ 6:D1): This Harlem mainstay has been serving soul food favorites like smothered chicken, barbecue ribs, collard greens, and mashed potatoes to a dedicated crowd of locals, tourists, and college students since 1962. The food is so popular, owner Sylvia Woods bottled her signature sauces and spices for the masses, available for purchase at the restaurant and online.

AND FOR DESSERT...

Levain Bakery
(167 W. 74th St., near Amsterdam Ave., 212/874–6080 ⊹5:B3)
A big cookie for the big city. Completely unpretentious and utterly delicious, Levain's cookies are rich…and hefty. In fact, they clock in at 6 ounces each! Choose from the chocolate chip walnut, dark chocolate chocolate chip, dark chocolate peanut butter chip, or oatmeal raisin. Batches are baked fresh daily and they taste best when they're warm and melty right out of the oven, so it's definitely worth seeking out this small basement bakery for a cookie craving. Levain's also bakes artisanal breads, including banana chocolate chip and pumpkin ginger spice, sour cream coffee cake, chocolate chip and cinnamon brioche, sourdough rolls stuffed with Valerhona chocolate, blueberry muffins, a variety of scones, and bombolincini—their unique jelly doughnuts.

18

RESTAURANT REVIEWS

Listed alphabetically within neighborhoods

LOWER MANHATTAN

CHINATOWN

¢
CHINESE
☺

✕**Great New York Noodletown.** Although the soups and noodles are unbeatable at this no-frills restaurant, what you should order are the window decorations—the hanging lacquered ducks and roasted pork, which are superb served with pungent garlic-and-ginger sauce on the side. Seasonal specialties like duck with flowering chives and salt-baked soft-shell crabs are excellent. So is the *congee*, or rice porridge, available with any number of garnishes. Solo diners may end up at a communal table. ⊠*28 Bowery, at Bayard St.Chinatown* ☎*212/349–0923* ⊟*No credit cards* Ⓜ *6, J, M, Z to Canal St.; B, D to Grand St.* ✛*2:F*

$
CHINESE
☺

✕**Jing Fong.** Come to this dim sum palace for a jolting taste of Hong Kong. On weekend mornings people pour into the escalator to Jing Fong's carnivalesque third-floor dining room. Servers push carts of steamed dumplings, barbecue pork buns, and shrimp balls. For adventurous eaters, there's chicken feet, tripe, and snails. Arrive early for the best selection, and save room for mango pudding. ⊠*20 Elizabeth St. , 2nd fl., between Bayard and Canal Sts.,Chinatown* ☎*212/964–5256* ⊟*AE, MC, V* Ⓜ *6, J, M, N, Q, R, W, Z to Canal St.* ✛*2:F5*

$
CHINESE
Multiple
Locations
☺

✕**Joe's Shanghai.** Joe opened his first Shanghai restaurant in Queens in 1995, but buoyed by the accolades accorded his steamed soup dumplings—filled with a rich, fragrant broth and ground pork or pork-crab-meat mixture—he saw fit to open in Manhattan's Chinatown. There's always a wait, but the line moves fast. Try the crisp turnip shortcakes to start, homemade Shanghai noodles, and rich pork meatballs braised in brown sauce. Other, more familiar Chinese dishes are also excellent. ⊠*9 Pell St., between the Bowery and Mott St.,Chinatown* ☎*212/233–8888* ⊕*www.joeshanghairestaurants.com* ☝*Reservations not accepted* ⊟*No credit cards* Ⓜ *6, J, M, N, Q, R, W, Z to Canal St.* ✛*2:F5* ⊠*24 W. 56th St., between 5th and 6th Aves.* ☎*212/333–3868* ☝*Reservations not accepted* ⊟*AE, MC, V* Ⓜ *F to 57th St.; E, V to 5th Ave./53rd St.* ✛*4:E2*

¢
VIETNAMESE
Multiple
Locations
Fodor$Choice
★

✕**Nha Trang.** You can get a great meal for under $10 at this low-atmosphere Vietnamese restaurant in Chinatown. Start with crispy spring rolls, sweet-and-sour seafood soup, or shrimp grilled on sugarcane. For a follow-up, don't miss the thin pork chops, which are marinated in a sweet vinegary sauce and grilled until charred. Another favorite is deep-fried squid on shredded lettuce with a tangy dipping sauce. If the line is long, which it usually is, even with a second location around the corner, you may be asked to sit at a table with strangers. ⊠*87 Baxter St., between Bayard and Canal Sts.,Chinatown* ☎*212/233–5948* ⊟*No credit cards* Ⓜ *6, J, M, N, Q, R, W, Z to Canal St.* ✛*2:F5* ⊠*148 Centre St., at Walker and White Sts.* ☎*212/941–9292* ⊟*No credit cards* Ⓜ *6, J, M, N, Q, R, W, Z to Canal St.* ✛*2:E5*

$$ ✕**Peking Duck House.** This Chinatown institution is the place to go in
CHINESE New York for authentic Peking Duck. Although the restaurant offers
Multiple a full Chinese menu, everyone—and we mean everyone—orders the
Locations duck. Begin, as most tables do, with an order of Shanghai soup dump-
lings, then move onto the bird. It's carved up table-side with plenty of
fanfare—crisp burnished skin separated from moist flesh. Roll up the
duck, with hoisin and scallions, in tender steamed pancakes. ⊠*28 Mott
St., at Mosco St., Chinatown* ☏*212/227–1810* ⊕*www.pekingduck
housenyc.com* ⊟ *AE, MC, V* Ⓜ *6, J, M, N, Q, R, W, Z to Canal St.*
✛*2:F5* ⊠*236 E. 53rd St.between 2nd and 3rd Aves.* ☏*212/759–8260*
⊕*www.pekingduckhousenyc.com* ⊟ *AE, MC, V* Ⓜ *6 to 53rd St.-
Lexington Ave.* ✛*4:G2*

$$ ✕**Ping's Seafood.** Although the original location in Queens still has the
CHINESE most elaborate menu with the most extensive selection of live seafood,
☾ the Manhattan location is more accessible both geographically and
gastronomically. Helpful menus have pictures of most of the specialties. Among them are Dungeness crab in black bean sauce, crisp fried
tofu, silken braised *e-fu* noodles, and crisp Peking duck. Pricier than
some other Chinatown haunts, Ping's is also a notch above in setting
and service. ⊠*22 Mott St., near Pell St.Chinatown* ☏*212/602–9988*
⌂*Reservations essential* ⊟*AE, MC, V* Ⓜ *6, J, M, N, Q, R, W, Z to
Canal St.* ✛*2:F6*

¢ ✕**XO Kitchen.** Chinese students throng this Hong Kong–style eatery. The
CHINESE walls resemble bulletin boards—they're tacked with dozens of sheets
☾ announcing a mind-boggling variety of foods, from dim sum to Thai
(there is also a menu). The food is some of Chinatown's finest. Try the
delicate shrimp wonton soup, or the refreshingly light Hong Kong–style
lo mein. ⊠*148 Hester St., between Elizabeth St. and Bowery, Chinatown* ☏*212/965–8645* ⊟*No credit cards* Ⓜ *B, D to Grand St.; 6, J,
M, Z to Canal St.* ✛*2:F5*

FINANCIAL DISTRICT

$$$$ ✕**Delmonico's.** As the oldest continually operating restaurant in New
STEAKHOUSE York City, opened in 1837, austere Delmonico's is steeped in cultural,
political, and culinary history. Lobster Newburg and Baked Alaska were
invented here—and are still served. Inside the stately mahogany-panel
dining room, tuck into the classic Delmonico's steak, a 20-ounce bone-
less rib eye smothered with frizzled onions, and don't forget to order
creamed spinach on the side. ⊠*56 Beaver St., at William St.,Lower
Manhattan* ☏*212/509–1144* ⊕*www.delmonicosny.com* ⌂*Reservations essential* ⊟*AE, D, DC, MC, V* ⊘ *Closed Sun. No lunch weekends* Ⓜ *2, 3 to Wall St.; R, W to Whitehall St./South Ferry; 4, 5 to
Bowling Green.* ✛*1:D4*

¢ ✕**Financier Patisserie.** On the cobblestone pedestrian street that has
CAFÉ become the Financial District's restaurant row, this quaint patisserie
Multiple serves up excellent pastries and delicious savory foods, like paninis,
Locations soup, salad, and quiches. After lunch, relax with a cappuccino and a
financier, an almond tea cake, or an elegant French pastry. In warm
weather, perch at an outdoor table and watch Manhattanites buzz by.
⊠*62 Stone St., between Mill La. and Hanover Sq.,Lower Manhattan*
☏*212/344–5600* ⊕*www.financierpastries.com* ⌂*Reservations not*

18

accepted ▭*AE, DC, MC, V* ◷*Closed Sun. No dinner* Ⓜ *2, 3 to Wall St.; 4, 5 to Bowling Green.* ⊕ *1:E4* ✉*35 Cedar St.between Pearl and William Sts.* ☎*212/952–3838* 🌐*www.financierpastries.com* ✍*Reservations not accepted* ▭*AE, DC, MC, V* ◷ *No dinner* Ⓜ *2, 3, 4, 5 to Wall St.; J, M, Z to Broad St.* ⊕ *1:E4* ✉*3-4 World Financial Center, in Battery Park City* ☎*212/786–3220* 🌐*www.financierpastries.com* ✍*Reservations not accepted* ▭*AE, DC, MC, V* ◷*No dinner* Ⓜ *E to World Trade Center; 4, 5 to Fulton St.* ⊕ *1:C3*

$$ STEAKHOUSE

✕**Harry's Steak and Harry's Café.** Its noise-dampening acoustics and maze of underground nooks combine to make Harry's Steak—the fine-dining half of the resurrected Harry's of Hanover—the city's most intimate steak house. Request the grotto for a stealthy rendezvous, or the long dozen-seater for a raucous night out with the boys. Begin with savory baked clams buried in smoked bacon and bread crumbs or the lively tomato trio, starring thick beefsteak slices topped with bacon and blue cheese, mozzarella and basil, and shaved onion with ranch dressing. The star attraction—prime aged porterhouse for two—is nicely encrusted with sea salt and a good match for buttery mashed potatoes infused with sweet roasted shallots and thick steak sauce spooned from mason jars. ✉*1 Hanover Sq., between Stone and Pearl Sts., Financial District* ☎*212/785–9200* 🌐*www.harrysnyc.com* ✍*Reservations essential for Harry's Steak* ▭*AE, D, MC, V* ◷*Closed Sun.* Ⓜ *4, 5 to Bowling Green; 2, 3 to Wall St.* ⊕*1:E4*

$$ AMERICAN

Multiple Locations

✕**P.J. Clarke's.** This East Side institution has been dispensing burgers and beer for more than a century. Despite a physical upgrade under new owners in 2002, the original P. J. Clarke's (there's now another offshoot way downtown) maintains the beveled-glass and scuffed-wood look of an old-time saloon. Many of the bartenders and patrons are as much of a fixture as the decor. More civilized at lunchtime, weekday evenings the bar area heaves with an after-work mob. Pull up a stool if you can for superlative bar food like fried oysters, shepherd's pie, or the signature burger smothered in creamy béarnaise. ✉*250 Vesey St. at World Financial Center,Financial District* ☎*212/285–1500* Ⓜ*A, C, E, 1, 2, 3, 9 to Chambers St.* ⊕*1:B3* ✉*915 3rd Ave., at 55th St.* ☎*212/317–1616* ✍ ▭*AE, MC, V* Ⓜ*E, V, 6 to 51st St.* ⊕*4:G2* ✉*205 E. 55th St. between 2nd and 3rd Aves.* ☎*212/317–2044* ◷*Closed Sun. No lunch weekends* Ⓜ*E, V, 6 to 51st St./Lexington Ave.; 4, 5, 6 to Lexington Ave./59th St.* ⊕*4:G2* ✉*44 W. 63rd St. near Columbus Ave.* ☎*212/957–9700* Ⓜ *A, C, B, D, 1 to 59th St./Columbus Circle* ⊕*5:C5*

TRIBECA

$$ ITALIAN

✕**Ago Ristorante.** Chef Agostino Sciandri's Italian New York City hot spot adds a bit of pizzazz to restaurant-starved TriBeCa. Judging by the see-and-be-seen crowd packing the tables, he is well poised to develop a following in New York City after his previous successes in Los Angeles and South Beach. The large, airy space, attached to Robert DeNiro's Greenwich Hotel, has exposed brick walls, wood paneling, and an open kitchen. The latter allows diners to get a glimpse of the nonstop action involved in turning out Italian classics such as antipasti, thin pizzas, pastas, and seafood. Meat lovers shouldn't miss their signature *bistecca alla fiorentina*, a 22-ounce Tuscan-style T-bone steak cooked in a wood-burning oven. As a sweet ending to every meal, patrons are sent home with mini biscotti. ✉*377 Greenwich St., between N. Moore and Franklin Sts., TriBeCa* ☎ *212/925–3797* ⊕*www.agorestaurant.com* ⊟*AE, D, MC, V* Ⓜ*1 to Franklin St.; A, C, E to Canal St.* ✛*1:B1*

$
AMERICAN
☺

✕**Bubby's.** Crowds clamoring for coffee and freshly squeezed juice line up for brunch at this TriBeCa mainstay, but the restaurant serves fine lunches and dinners as well. The dining room is homey and comfortable with big windows; in summer, neighbors sit at tables outside with their dogs. For brunch you can order almost anything, including homemade granola, sour-cream pancakes with bananas and strawberries, and *huevos rancheros* with guacamole and grits. Eclectic comfort food—macaroni 'n cheese, fried chicken—make up the lunch and dinner menus. ✉*120 Hudson St., at N. Moore St.,TriBeCa* ☎*212/219–0666* ⊕*www. bubbys.com* ⊟*D, DC, MC, V* Ⓜ*1 to Franklin St.* ✛*2:C5*

$$$$
FRENCH

✕**Chanterelle.** Soft peach walls, luxuriously spaced tables, and towering floral arrangements set the stage for what is the most understated of New York's top French restaurants. Chef David Waltuck's simple, elegant creations include delicious signature grilled seafood sausage that will always be available, but the bulk of the prix-fixe menu is dictated by the season. Roger Dagorn, the restaurant's exceptional sommelier, can help find value in the discriminating, well-chosen wine list. You can fully expect to be enthralled. ✉*2 Harrison St.,, at Hudson St.TriBeCa* ☎*212/966–6960* ⊕*www.chanterellenyc.com* ⌖*Reservations essential* ⊟*AE, D, DC, MC, V* ☾ *No lunch Sun.–Wed.* Ⓜ*1 to Franklin St.* ✛*2:C6*

$$$
AMERICAN

✕**The Harrison.** Jimmy Bradley's formula for the perfect neighborhood eatery, which they mastered at the Red Cat in Chelsea, works like a charm in TriBeCa. The warm, woody room serves as a relaxed backdrop for the seasonal American food, like biscuits and gravy with clams and chorizo, and meaty Long Island duck breast with quark spaetzle and date-turnip puree. Desserts, including a not-too-sweet chocolate cake with mint ice cream and chocolate espresso flan, are at once accessible and sophisticated. ✉*355 Greenwich St., at Harrison St.,TriBeCa* ☎*212/274–9310* ⊕*www.theharrison.com* ⌖*Reservations essential* ⊟*AE, D, DC, MC, V* ☾*No lunch* Ⓜ*1 to Franklin St.* ✛*2:C6*

$
AMERICAN
Multiple
Locations
☺

✕**Kitchenette.** This small, comfy restaurant lives up to its name with tables so close together you're likely to make new friends. The dining room feels like a breakfast nook, and the food tastes like your mom made it—provided she's a great cook. There are no frills, just solid cooking, friendly service, and a long line at peak times. For brunch don't miss the blackberry-cherry pancakes or the pear streusel French toast. Seafood potpie with shrimp, cod, and scallops is a heavenly dinner. ✉*156 Chambers St., near Greenwich St.,TriBeCa* ☎*212/267–6740* ⊕*www. kitchenetterestaurant.com* ⊟*AE, MC, V* Ⓜ*1, 2, 3, A, C to Chambers St.* ✛*1:C2* ✉*1272 Amsterdam Ave., near 123rd St.* ☎*212/531–7600* ⊟*AE, MC, V* Ⓜ*1 to 125th St.* ✛*6:A1*

$$
VIETNAMESE

✕**Mai House.** With his latest overnight sensation, restaurateur Drew Nieporent adds the food of Vietnam to his international TriBeCa stable (he has Mexican, French, and Japanese spots nearby). The restaurant offers some of the city's most inventive Vietnamese food, which is

18

delivered in a sultry dining room featuring lamps and silk panels on a lotus motif. From a kitchen visible through a wood lattice wall come playful riffs on Vietnamese classics—crispy mushroom spring rolls, sizzling lemongrass shortribs, and sweet-and-sour spicy whole red snapper with mouthwatering tomatoes, pineapple, and Chinese celery. ⊠*186 Franklin St., between Greenwich and Hudson Sts.TriBeCa* ☎*212/431–0606* ⊕*www.myriadrestaurantgroup.com/maihouse* ⊟*AE, MC, V* ⊗*Closed Sun. No lunch* Ⓜ*1 to Franklin St.* ✛*2:C6*

$$ ✗ **Matsugen.** Situated in the former space of the upscale Chinese res-
JAPANESE   taurant 66, Matsugen is Jean-Georges's latest venture, offering authentic Japanese cuisine. The contemporary design, long communal dining table, and fish tank filled with unusual crustaceans is essentially the same as the restaurant's former incarnation, but the menu has a new life. Classic Japanese dishes are offered, such as sushi, sashimi, Wagyu beef, and shabu-shabu (where diners try their own hand at cooking lobster and pork loin in a pot of boiling water at their table). The real stars here, however, are the more than dozen takes on soba noodles, which are made from buckwheat flour—served hot, chilled, and with additions such as tofu, duck, yams, and prawns. The extensive sake menu makes for a nice accompaniment to the meal. If you're not in the mood to sit in the main dining room, the large bar area in the front of the restaurant has comfortable chairs and is ideal for lingering. ⊠*241 Church St., at Leonard St., TriBeCa* ☎*212/952–0202* ⊕*www. jean-georges.com* ⊟*D, DC, MC, V* Ⓜ*1 to Franklin St.* ✛*2:D5*

$$$ ✗**Nobu.** At this huge, bustling TriBeCa dining room (or its sister loca-
JAPANESE   tion uptown), you may just spot a celeb or two. New York's most
Multiple   famous Japanese restaurant has gained a lot of competition in recent
Locations   years, but this is still the destination for the innovative Japanese cuisine Nobu Matsuhisa made famous, like fresh yellowtail sashimi with jalapeño, creamy spicy crab, or miso-marinated Chilean sea bass. Put yourself in the hands of the chef by ordering the tasting menu, the *omakase*, specify how much you want to spend, and let the kitchen do the rest. Can't get reservations? Try your luck at the first-come, first-served **Nobu Next Door,** with a similar menu plus a sushi bar. ⊠*105 Hudson St., at Franklin St., TriBeCa* ☎*212/219–0500* ⊕*www. myriadrestaurantgroup.com* ✍*Reservations essential* ⊟*AE, D, DC, MC, V* ⊗*No lunch weekends* Ⓜ*1 to Franklin St.* ✛*1:B1* ⊠ *Nobu Next Door, 105 Hudson St., at Franklin St.* ☎*212/334–4445* ⊟*AE, D, DC, MC, V* ⊗*No lunch* Ⓜ*1 to Franklin St* ✛*1:B1* ⊠*40 W. 57th St., between 5th and 6th Aves.* ☎*212/757–3000* ⊟*AE, D, DC, MC, V* ⊗*No lunch weekends* Ⓜ*F to 57th St.* ✛*4:D1*

$$$ ✗**Odeon.** New Yorkers change hangouts faster than they can press
BISTRO   speed-dial, but this spot has managed to maintain its quality and flair
☾   for more than 25 years. The neo-art-deco room is still packed nightly with revelers. Now children are also welcome. The pleasant service and well-chosen wine list are always in style. The bistro-menu highlights include *frisée aux lardons* with truffled poached egg, grilled sirloin steak, and pan-roasted cod with vegetable orzo and sorrel sauce. ⊠*145 West Broadway, between Duane and Thomas Sts.,TriBeCa* ☎*212/233–0507* ⊕*www.theodeonrestaurant.com* ⊟*AE, D, DC, MC, V* Ⓜ*1, 2, 3, A, C to Chambers St.* ✛*2:D6*

SOHO WITH NOLITA AND LITTLE ITALY

SOHO

$$$
SEAFOOD

✕**Aquagrill.** Owned by a husband-and-wife team, Aquagrill is a popular SoHo standard. The lively neighborhood eatery makes its own pastries and baked goods—including the bread for its challah French toast with cinnamon apples and pecan butter. Fans rave about the lunchtime $20.50 prix-fixe Shucker Special—a half dozen oysters, with homemade soup or chowder and a salad. Dinner specialties include roasted Dungeness crab cake napoleon with sun-dried tomato oil, and falafel-crusted salmon. Try the knockout chocolate tasting plate with handmade chocolates, warm chocolate cake, white chocolate mousse, and milk chocolate ice cream. ✉*210 Spring St., at 6th Ave.,SoHo* ☎*212/274–0505* ⊕*www.aquagrill.com* ⌚*Reservations essential* ▭*AE, D, DC, MC, V* Ⓜ*C, E to Spring St.* ✛*2:D4*

$$
BRASSERIE

✕**Balthazar.** Even with long waits and excruciating noise levels, most out-of-towners agree that it's worth making reservations to experience restaurateur Keith McNally's flagship, a painstakingly accurate reproduction of a Parisian brasserie. Like the decor, entrées re-create French classics: Gruyère-topped onion soup; steak-frites; and icy tiers of crab, oysters, and other pristine shellfish. Brunch is one of the best in town—if you can get a table. The best strategy is to go at off-hours, or on weekdays for breakfast, to miss the crush of hungry New Yorkers. ✉*80 Spring St., between Broadway and Crosby St.,SoHo* ☎*212/965–1414* ⊕*www.balthazarny.com* ⌚*Reservations essential* ▭*AE, MC, V* Ⓜ*6 to Spring St.; N, R, W to Prince St.; B, D, F, V to Broadway–Lafayette.* ✛*2:E4*

$$
NEW AMERICAN

✕**Blue Ribbon Brasserie.** After more than a decade, Blue Ribbon remains *the* late-night foodie hangout. Join the genial hubbub for midnight noshing, namely the beef marrow with oxtail marmalade and the renowned raw-bar platters. Trust funders, literary types, chefs, designers—a good-looking gang—fill this dark box of a room until 4 AM. The menu appears standard at first blush, but it's not. Instead of the usual fried calamari, try exceptionally tender squid lightly sautéed with garlic. ✉*97 Sullivan St., between Prince and Spring Sts., SoHo* ☎*212/274–0404* ⊕*www.blueribbonrestaurants.com* ⌚*Reservations not accepted* ▭*AE, D, DC, MC, V* ⊘*No lunch* Ⓜ*C, E to Spring St.; R, W to Prince St.* ✛*2:D3*

$$
JAPANESE

✕**Blue Ribbon Sushi.** Sushi, like pizza, attracts plenty of opinionated fanatics. Stick to the excellent raw fish and specials here if you're a purist. Others might want to try one of the experimental rolls: the Blue Ribbon—lobster, shiso, and black caviar—is popular. The dark, intimate nooks, minimalist design, and servers with downtown attitude attract a stylish crowd that doesn't mind waiting for a table or for chilled sake served in traditional wooden boxes. ✉*119 Sullivan St., between Prince and Spring Sts., SoHo* ☎*212/343–0404* ⊕*www.blueribbonrestaurants.com* ⌚*Reservations not accepted* ▭*AE, D, DC, MC, V* Ⓜ*C, E to Spring St.; R, W to Prince St.* ✛*2:D3*

$$
NEW AMERICAN
Fodor'sChoice
★

✕**Hundred Acres.** The owners of Cookshop and Five Points have set up new digs on MacDougal Street. Their latest restaurant, Hundred Acres, has a rustic, country feel and offers simple yet sophisticated cooking á la Marc Meyer and Cookshop chef Joel Hough. Don't count on a big

18

menu: the daily choices are limited to seven main dishes and one special entrée. The steamed littleneck clams appetizer served with garlic-oregano butter, pickled corn, cilantro, and garlic toasts is particularly delicious. For the mains, try the seared Wreckfish with bicolored corn, lima beans, and pearl onion succotash, or the grilled Hampshire pork chop with smoky mustard greens and spicy peach catsup. The classic burger made from pasture-raised beef, topped with Goot Essa cheddar and served with fries and Vidalia onion mayonnaise, should not to be missed. ⊠*38 MacDougal St., between Houston and Prince Sts., Soho* ☎*212/475–7500* ⊕*hundredacresnyc.com* ═*AE, DC, MC, V* Ⓜ*1 to Houston; C, E to Spring St.; N, R, W to Prince St.* ✛*2:D3*

$ ✕**La Esquina.** Anchoring a downtown corner under a bright neon sign,
MEXICAN   La Esquina looks nothing more than a fast-food taqueria. But beyond the top-notch, dirt-cheap tacos sold to-go until 5 in the morning lurks an entire restaurant complex. Just around the corner you'll find a modestly priced sit-down café featuring those same tacos along with more ambitious fare like fine chiles rellenos (stuffed peppers) and carne asada (grilled meat). Meanwhile, the real hipster draw remains completely hidden from sight. La Esquina's basement brasserie, like a Mexican speakeasy, is accessible by reservation only, through an unmarked door just inside the ground-floor taqueria. Once inside you'll discover a buzzy subterranean scene along with potent margaritas and robust upscale fare. Though prices downstairs are high, portions are huge. ⊠ *106 Kenmare St., between Cleveland Pl. and Lafayette St., SoHo* ☎*212/613–7100* ═ *AE, MC, V* Ⓜ*6 to Spring St.* ✛*2:F4*

$$$ ✕**Lure.** Outfitted like the interior of a sleek luxury liner, Lure offers oce-
SEAFOOD   anic fare prepared in multiple culinary styles. From the sushi bar, feast on Lure House Rolls, shrimp tempura rolls crowned with spicy tuna and Japanese tartar sauce. From the kitchen, order creative dishes like steamed branzino with oyster mushrooms, scallions, and ponzu sauce, or Manila clams over pancetta-studded linguine. For an all-American treat, you can't go wrong with a classic lobster roll on brioche. ⊠*142 Mercer St., at Prince St., SoHo* ☎*212/431–7676* ⊕*www.lurefishbar. com* ═*AE, MC, V* ◷*No lunch weekends* Ⓜ*6 to Bleecker St.; B, D, F, V to Broadway-Lafayette St.; N, R, W to Prince St.* ✛*2:E3*

$ ✕**MarieBelle.** Practically invisible from the front of the chocolate empo-
CAFÉ   rium, the back entry to the Cacao Bar opens into a sweet, high-ceiling,
Multiple   12-table hot-chocolate shop. Most people order the Aztec, Europe-
Locations an-style (that's 60% Colombian chocolate mixed with hot water—no
ↄ   cocoa powder here!). The first sip is startlingly rich but not too dense. American-style, made with milk, is sweeter. Preface it with a salad or sandwich from the dainty lunch menu, or request one of the expensive but ravishing flavored chocolates sold out front, like passion fruit, or *dulce de leche.* ⊠*484 Broome St., between West Broadway and Wooster St. SoHo* ☎*212/925–6999* ⊕*www.mariebelle.com* ⊱*Reservations not accepted* ═*AE, D, MC, V* ◷ *No dinner* Ⓜ*6 to Spring St.; A, C, E to Canal St.* ✛*2:D4* ⊠*762 Madison Ave., between 65th and 66th Sts.* ☎*212/249–4584* ⊕*www.mariebelle.com* ⊱*Reservations not accepted* ═*AE, D, MC, V* ◷ *No dinner* Ⓜ*6 to 68th St./ Hunter College* ✛*5:F5*

$$$ ✕**Savoy.** Chef-owner Peter Hoffman's two-story restaurant has the coziAMERICAN ness of a country inn, with blazing fireplaces upstairs and downstairs, soft wood accents, and windows looking onto the cobblestone street. Hoffman is one of the city's strongest proponents of using local, seasonal ingredients, which shows in disarmingly simple dishes like a suckling pig roulade with apple polenta and bacon-apple marmalade, and salt-crusted baked duck with parsley root, caramelized sweet potatoes, and jalapeño-parsley salad. The winter prix-fixe menu includes a dish grilled in the dining-room hearth. The wine list emphasizes small producers. ⊠ *70 Prince St., at Crosby St., SoHo* ☎ *212/219–8570* ⊕ *www. savoynyc.com* ⊟ *AE, MC, V* ⊘ *No lunch Sun.* Ⓜ *R, W to Prince St.; 6 to Spring St.; F, V to Broadway–Lafayette St.* ✢ *2:E3*

$$ ✕**Woo Lae Oak.** Not so much an authentic Korean eatery, Woo Lae Oak KOREAN uses traditional Korean flavors to create an elevated cuisine in a tony SoHo setting. The food is spicy and flavorful: kimchi burns the lips and prepares the palate for such dishes as *ke sal mari* (Dungeness crab and leek wrapped in spinach crepes), and *o ree mari* (duck slices wrapped in miso blini sweetened with plum sauce). But fans of tabletop grilling will still be able to get their tender sliced beef *bul go gi*. Since this is SoHo, the tables are dark marble slabs and the lighting is low. ⊠ *148 Mercer St., between Prince and W. Houston Sts.SoHo* ☎ *212/925–8200* ⊕ *www.woolaeoaksoho.com* ⊟ *AE, DC, MC, V* Ⓜ *R, W to Prince St.; 6 to Spring St.; B, D, F, V to Broadway–Lafayette St.* ✢ *2:E3*

NOLITA

$$$ ✕**Peasant.** The crowd at this rustic restaurant is stylishly urban. Inspired ITALIAN by the proverbial "peasant" cuisine where meals were prepared in the kitchen hearth, chef-owner Frank DeCarlo cooks all of his wonderful food in a bank of wood- or charcoal-burning ovens, from which the heady aroma of garlic perfumes the room. Don't fill up on the crusty bread and fresh ricotta, though, or you'll miss out on other flavorful Italian fare like sizzling sardines that arrive in terra-cotta pots, or rotisserie lamb that's redolent of fresh herbs. ⊠ *194 Elizabeth St., between Spring and Prince Sts., NoLita* ☎ *212/965–9511* ⊕ *www.peasantnyc. com* ⌕ *Reservations essential* ⊟ *AE, MC, V* ⊘ *Closed Mon. No lunch* Ⓜ *6 to Spring St.; R, W to Prince St.* ✢ *2:F3*

$$ ✕**Public.** Public's space is complex and sophisticated, with soaring ceilECLECTIC ings and whitewashed brick walls, skylights, fireplaces, three dining areas, a vast bar, and even the occasional elegant bookcase. The menu flaunts its nonconformity. A terrine of rabbit confit has coils of flavor, gracefully incorporating foie gras and Tahitian vanilla, with quinceglazed grapes and mild radishes nearby for pungent contrast. Giant ravioli are stuffed with minced oxtail and snail meat, plated with pickled sautéed shiitake mushrooms and oven-dried tomatoes, all dribbled with smoked paprika oil. New Zealand venison loin is roasted perfectly and served with sweet-potato dauphinoise and sour-cherry compote. Cinnamon-and-orange-blossom rice pudding is not at all sweet, so that the scoop of pistachio-saffron ice cream can make a better contrast. You will not soon forget your meal at Public. ⊠ *210 Elizabeth St. between Prince and Spring Sts., NoLita* ☎ *212/343–7011* ⊕ *www.public-nyc.com*

18

⊟*AE, D, MC, V* ⊘*No lunch weekdays* Ⓜ*6 to Spring St.; N, R to Prince St.; J, M to Bowery* ✛*2:F3*

$$ ✕**Tasting Room.** The menu changes daily at this earnest greenmarket spot
NEW AMERICAN   run by husband-and-wife-team Colin and Renee Alevras. The restaurant
raised its prices considerably following a move to spacious new NoLita
digs (their original East Village location is now a thriving, more casual
hangout). Despite the new sticker shock, the Tasting Room's home-
spun food and decor—and the focus on seasonality and local farmers—
continue to inspire an almost cultish following. The menu is designed
to encourage grazing, with every dish available in "taste" and "share"
portions. The fresh produce offered nightly is among the most varied
and offbeat in New York. A meal—five or six "shares" make dinner
for two—might include olive-oil cured trout with mizuna, hen of the
woods mushrooms with baby carrots and ramps, or seared Montauk
tilefish with crosnes, salsify, and dandelion greens. ⊠*264 Elizabeth St.
between Prince and Houston Sts., NoLita* ☎*212/358–7831* ⊕*www.
thetastingroomnyc.com* ⊟*AE, DC, MC, V* ⊘*Closed Mon. No lunch
weekdays* Ⓜ*6 to Bleecker St.; B, D, F to Broadway-Lafayette St.; R,
W to Prince St.* ✛*2:F3*

LITTLE ITALY

$ ✕**Lombardi's.** Brick walls, red-and-white checkered tablecloths, and the
PIZZA   aroma of thin-crust pies emerging from the coal oven set the mood for
ↄ   some of the best pizza in Manhattan. Lombardi's has served pizza since
1905 (though not in the same location), and business has not died down
a bit. The mozzarella is always fresh, resulting in an almost grease-
less slice, and the toppings, such as meatballs, pancetta, or imported
anchovies, are also top quality. Lombardi's is perhaps best known for
its toothsome clam pizza, which features freshly shucked clams, garlic
oil, pecorino-Romano cheese, and parsley. ⊠*32 Spring St., at Mott St.,
Little Italy* ☎*212/941–7994* ⊕*www.firstpizza.com* ⊟*No credit cards*
Ⓜ*6 to Spring St.; B, D, F, V to Broadway–Lafayette St.* ✛*2:F4*

EAST VILLAGE AND LOWER EAST SIDE

EAST VILLAGE

$$$ ✕**Apiary.** After working as chef de cuisine for 16 years at Bobby Flay's
NEW AMERICAN Mesa Grill, Bolo, and Bar Americain, Neil Manacle ventures out on
his own with this smart New American spot in the heart of the East
Village. The restaurant is partly owned by furniture design company
Ligne Roset, and the contemporary space is furnished sleekly by the
brand. The menu isn't huge, but is devoted to seasonal—and whenever
possible, local—produce, poultry, and seafood. Current picks include
light creations such as crispy soft-shell crab with lime custard, and
chilled golden tomato soup. Heartier options are the New York State
rabbit served with wild mushrooms, and a spice crusted lamb. The
extensive wine list has 30 picks from New York State alone, and the
beer list has 24 domestic options. ⊠*60 3rd Ave., at 11th St.,East Village* ☎*212/254–0888* ⊕*www.apiarynyc.com* ⊟*AE, D, DC, MC, V*
⊘*No lunch weekdays* Ⓜ*6 to Astor Place; R, W to 8th St.; L to 3rd
Ave.* ✛*3:G5*

$ · AMERICAN · ✕**Back Forty.** Pioneering chef Peter Hoffman, a longtime leader in promoting local, sustainable food, attracts a devoted crowd at this casual restaurant that feels like a neighborhood joint. Despite Hoffman's pedigree, Back Forty displays plenty of humility. Prices on the short, rustic, greenmarket menu are low and the homey decor features a pastoral mural behind the bar and rusty farm tools on the walls. Begin with bar snack bacon and shrimp beignets washed down with a fine house cocktail like the rum and Concord grape fizz. The simple family-style dinner selections include a perfect grilled trout; a moist, shareable whole rotisserie chicken; and a wide array of seasonal sides including the cauliflower gratin and roasted brussels sprouts with dried cherries. ⊠*190 Ave. B, at 12th St.,East Village* ☎*212/388–1990* ⊕ *www.backfortynyc. com* ⊟*AE, MC, V* ⊘*No lunch Mon.–Sat.* Ⓜ *L to 1st Ave.* ⊹*3:H4*

$$ · CHINESE · ✕**Chinatown Brasserie.** This large, bi-level 175-seat dining room is thrillingly vibrant, featuring dark cherry banquettes and 10 stunning crimson pagoda silk lanterns suspended from two central columns. Chicken and pine nuts are wrapped in Bibb lettuce. Crispy Peking duck is roasted in a special barbecuing oven, then sliced and presented on a long platter with the crackling skin still attached to the succulent flesh. Fresh Mandarin pancakes, julienned scallions, and sweet, pungent hoisin sauce are on hand. Dark-chocolate fortune cookies contain salient quotes from Albert Einstein and Ronald Reagan. ⊠*380 Lafayette St., at Great Jones St., East Village* ☎*212/533–7000* ⊕*www.chinatownbrasserie. com* ⊟*AE, MC, V* Ⓜ*6 to Bleecker St.; B, D, F, V to Broadway and Lafayette St.* ⊹*2:E2*

$$ · ITALIAN · ✕**Gnocco.** Owners Pierluigi Palazzo and Rossella Tedesco named the place not after gnocchi but after a regional specialty—deep-fried dough bites served alongside salami and prosciutto. Head to the roomy canopied garden out back for savory salads, house-made pastas like orecchiette with tomato sauce and tiny meatballs, pizza, and hearty entrées like pork tenderloin in a balsamic emulsion with flakes of grana padano cheese. ⊠*337 E. 10th St., between Aves. A and B, East Village* ☎*212/677–1913* ⊕*www.gnocco.com* ⊟*AE* Ⓜ*L to 1st Ave.; 6 to Astor Pl.* ⊹*3:H5*

$ · CHINESE · Multiple · Locations · ✕**Grand Sichuan International.** This regional Chinese chainlet may be low on ambience, but it serves delicious Szechuan specialties like fiery *dan dan* noodles, shredded potatoes in vinegar sauce, crab soup dumplings, minced pork with cellophane noodles, and sautéed loofah, a gourd. ⊠*19-23 St. Marks Pl., near 3rd Ave.,East Village* ☎*212/529–4800* ⊟*AE, MC, V* Ⓜ*6 to Astor Pl.* ⊹*2:F1* ⊠*229 9th Ave., at W. 24th St.* ☎*212/620–5200* ⊟*AE, D, MC, V* Ⓜ*C, E to 23rd St.* ⊹*3:B2* ⊠*15 7th Ave. S, between Leroy and Carmine Sts.* ☎*212/645–0222* ⊟*AE, MC, V* Ⓜ*1 to Houston St.; A, B, C, D, E, F, V to W. 4th St.* ⊹*2:C3*

$$$ · MEDITERRANEAN · ✕**Il Buco.** The unabashed clutter of vintage kitchen gadgets and tableware harks back to Il Buco's past as an antiques store. The tables, two of which are communal, are each unique—the effect is a festive, almost romantic country-house atmosphere. The restaurant features meats and produce from local farms for the daily entrées and Mediterranean tapaslike appetizers. Book the inspirational wine cellar (with more than 450 varieties) for dinner. ⊠*47 Bond St., between Bowery*

18

and Lafayette St., East Village ☎*212/533–1932* ⊕*www.ilbuco.com* ▭*AE, MC, V* ⊘*No lunch Sun. and Mon.* Ⓜ*6 to Bleecker St.; B, D, F, V to Broadway–Lafayette St.* ✛*2:F2*

$$$$ ✕ **Jewel Bako.** In a minefield of cheap, often inferior sushi houses gleams
JAPANESE tiny Jewel Bako. In one of the best sushi restaurants in the East Village, the futuristic bamboo tunnel of a dining room is gorgeous, but try to nab a place at the sushi bar and put yourself in the hands of Masato Shimizu. His *omakase*, or chef's menu, starts at $85. He will serve you only what's freshest and best. ✉ *239 E. 5th St., between 2nd and 3rd Aves., East Village* ☎*212/979–1012* ◈*Reservations essential* ▭*AE, MC, V* ⊘*Closed Sun. No lunch* Ⓜ*6 to Astor Pl.* ✛*3:G6*

$$$$ ✕ **Momofuku Ko.** A seasonal tasting menu full of clever combinations
ASIAN and esoteric ingredients explains the deafening buzz for James Beard award-winning chef David Chang's latest venture. Ko's small, intimate space is sparsely furnished with a counter of blond wood and only a dozen stools. Diners get to see Ko's chefs in action as they prepare all manner of inventive dishes: they garnish soft-boiled eggs and caviar with potato chips, grate foie gras over lychee, and set cereal milk panna cotta on avocado-painted plates. Reservations can only be made online, no more than seven days ahead, and are extremely difficult to get. Log on at 10 AM (credit card number needed just to get in the system), when new reservations are available, and keep hitting reload. ✉*163 1st Ave., at E. 10th St., East Village* ☎*212/228–0031 or 212/475–7899* ⊕*www. momofuku.com* ◈*Reservations essential* ▭*AE, MC, V* ⊘*No lunch* Ⓜ*L to 1st Ave.; 6 to Astor Place* ✛*3:H5*

$ ✕ **Momofuku Noodle Bar.** Chef-owner David Chang has created a shrine
ASIAN to ramen with this stylish 20-seat restaurant. His riff on the Japanese classic features *haute* ingredients like Berkshire pork, free-range chicken, and organic produce. His modern take on pork buns with cucumber and scallions is phenomenal—worth the trip alone. Go early or late— the tiny restaurant is packed during regular mealtimes. ✉*171 1st Ave., between E. 10th and E. 11 Sts., East Village* ☎*212/777–7773* ⊕*www. momofuku.com/noodle* ◈*Reservations not accepted* ▭*AE, MC, V* Ⓜ*L to 1st Ave.* ✛*3:H5*

$$ ✕ **Momofuku Ssäm Bar.** New York foodies have been salivating over chef
ASIAN David Chang's Asian-influenced fare since he opened his first restaurant, a Japanese noodle shop, in 2004. Momofuku Ssäm Bar, the wunderkind's much larger follow-up, is packed nightly with downtown diners cut from the same cloth as the pierced and tattooed waitstaff and cooks. The no-reservation policy means you'll likely have to wait for a chance to perch at the communal food bar and nibble on Chang's truly original small-plate cuisine. Dishes from the seasonally changing menu arrive like tapas for sharing. Although the chef works mostly with Asian flavors, his food is impossible to pigeonhole. Chang's not-to-bemissed riff on a classic Chinese pork bun helped build his cult following. ✉*207 2nd Ave., at 13th St., East Village* ☎*212/254–3500* ⊕*www. momofuku.com/ssam* ◈*Reservations not accepted* ▭*AE, MC, V* Ⓜ*L to 1st Ave.* ✛*3:H4*

$ ✕ **Piola.** Festive rainbow lighting fills the spacious dining room of Piola,
PIZZA which has 20 restaurants around the world. But it couldn't feel less like

a chain, as it bursts with character and Italian-Brazilian bonhomie. The entire kitchen staff was trained in Treviso, and the menu lists 60 thin-crust pizzas, from a simple tomato-mozzarella-Parmesan-arugula to the Brooklyn, which features broccoli, chicken, and Gorgonzola cheese. There are some fine pastas and salads as well, and delicious profiteroles for dessert. It's the perfect place to slake those late-night hunger pangs: Piola is open until 1 AM Friday and Saturday and open until midnight all other nights. ⊠*48 E. 12th St., between Broadway and University Pl., East Village* ☎*212/777–7781* ⊕*www.piola.it* ⊟*AE, D, DC, MC, V* Ⓜ*4, 5, 6, N, Q, R, W to Union Sq./14th St.* ✛*3:F4*

$$
NEW AMERICAN

✕**Prune.** There's just something very right-on about the food at Prune, a cozy treasure of a restaurant serving eclectic, well-executed American food. The choices change with the season, but you might find roasted suckling pig with pickled tomatoes, lamb shank braised in parchment, or a pasta "kerchief" with poached egg, French ham, and brown butter. There's usually a wait, and the quarters are very cramped, so don't expect to feel comfortable lingering at your table. ⊠*54 E. 1st St., between 1st and 2nd Aves., East Village* ☎*212/677–6221* ⊕*www. prunerestaurant.com* ♨*Reservations essential* ⊟*AE, MC, V* Ⓜ*F, V to 2nd Ave.* ✛*2:F2*

$
PIZZA

✕**Una Pizza Napoletana.** Owner Anthony Mangieri raises pizza to an art. Only San Marzano or cherry tomatoes touch his crust. The cheese: fresh buffalo mozzarella. His pizzas need only two minutes in the wood-burning oven. You'll find no slices here; the crisp 12-inch pies are relatively costly but well worth it. An important point: the restaurant is open only Thursday through Sunday, from 5 PM until they run out of dough, so it's best to get there early. Beer and Italian wine are also served. ⊠*349 E. 12th St., near 1st Ave., East Village* ☎*212/477–9950* ⊕*www.unapizza.com* ♨*Reservations not accepted* ⊟*No credit cards* ☾*Closed Mon.–Wed.* Ⓜ*L to 1st Ave.* ✛*3:H4*

¢
CAFÉ

✕**Veniero's Pasticceria.** More than a century old, this bustling bakery-café sells every kind of Italian *dolci* (sweet), from cherry-topped cookies to creamy cannoli and flaky *sfogliatelle*. A liquor license means you can top off an evening with a nightcap. ⊠*342 E. 11th St., near 1st Ave., East Village* ☎*212/674–7070* ⊕*www.venierospastry.com* ♨*Reservations not accepted* ⊟*AE, D, DC, MC, V* Ⓜ*6 to Astor Pl.; L to 1st Ave.* ✛*3:H5*

LOWER EAST SIDE

$$
NEW AMERICAN

✕**Allen & Delancey.** Opening your own restaurant in a culinary hot spot like New York City sounds daunting, but not for Neil Ferguson. The original chef de cuisine at Gordon Ramsay's The London NYC, Ferguson now brings his own brand of British flair to the Lower East Side. The interior of this charming restaurant is a cross between a cozy old London pub and a speakeasy. The exposed-brick walls of the small dining rooms flicker with the light of dozens of candles and the old-fashioned paintings and timeworn books seem to call you back to another time and place. The comforting menu, a nod to the neighborhood's vast cultural past, is an epicure's salve. Ribbons of prosciutto are paired with truffled fingerling potatoes and leek vinaigrette. A dish like cabbage, beef, and onion flaunts its own artistic twist—a ball of cabbage stuffed with beef and a delicate onion stuffed with cabbage. ⊠ *115 Allen St.,*

18

at Delancey St., Lower East Side ☎ *212/253–5400* ⊕*www.allenand delancey.com* ▭ *AE, D, DC, MC, V* ⊘ *No lunch* Ⓜ *F to Delancey St.; J, M, Z to Essex St.* ✛*2:G4*

$$ ✕**'inoteca.** The Italian terms on the menu may be a little daunting, ITALIAN but the food is not. An Italian small-plates concept with an excellent by-the-glass wine list, this rustic eatery is perpetually packed. (Reservations are accepted for parties of 6 or more.) Come for cheese and charcuterie plates, the famous truffled egg toast, and delicious panini sandwiches filled with cured meat, runny cheeses, and hot peppers. Fresh salads and creative entrées like polenta with braised escarole and pancetta, and braised chicken in a mushroom-chickpea sauce play supporting roles. ⊠*98 Rivington St., at Ludlow St.,Lower East Side* ☎*212/614–0473* ⊕*www.inotecanyc.com* ▭*AE, MC, V* Ⓜ*F, J, M, Z to Delancey St.* ✛*2:G3*

$ ✕**Kampuchea Restaurant.** Cambodian-born Ratha Chau is the drivCAMBODIAN ing force at this sophisticated Southeast Asian street-food spot. With **Fodor's**Choice exposed-brick walls, elevated bar-style seating, and a well-planned wine ★ list, it's the most stylish noodle bar we've ever encountered. Kampuchea's menu changes often, according to both the bounty of the season and chef-owner Chau's culinary desires. Diners are encouraged to dabble different section of the menu, moving from the small plates onto the sandwiches and crepes, and then to the big-bowl noodle soups and stews. Start with grilled corn lathered in coconut mayo, coconut flakes, and chili powder. Follow it up with the spicy house-cured pickles or the melt-in-your-mouth crispy pork belly. Next, go for the savory catfish Cambodian crepe or the Shiitake mushroom crepe with soybeans and butternut squash. For sandwiches, the sweet pulled oxtail with spicy tamarind is a fantastic combo. Finally, the Phnom Penh Katiev noodle soup with ground pork, duck confit, chicken, and tiger shrimp and the bountiful Bwah Moun with jasmine rice, chicken, and tiger shrimp are both delicious and each one is definitely big enough to share. Just remember, with all those chilis, Kampuchea's dishes are often spicy, so let your server know if you need to take a walk on the "mild" side, or just cool off with a refreshing glass of Riesling while reveling in the knowledge that you found one of New York's best hidden eats. ⊠*78 Rivington St., at Allen St., Lower East Side* ☎*212/529–3901* ⊕*www. kampucheanyc.com* ▭*D, DC, MC, V* Ⓜ*F to Delancey St.; J, M, Z to Essex St.* ✛*2:G3*

$ ✕**Katz's Delicatessen.** Everything and nothing has changed at Katz's since DELI it first opened in 1888, when the neighborhood was dominated by Jewish **Fodor's**Choice immigrants. The rows of Formica tables, the long self-service counter, and ★ such signs as "Send a salami to your boy in the army" are all completely authentic. What's different are the area's demographics, but all types still flock here for succulent hand-carved corned beef and pastrami sandwiches, soul-warming soups, juicy hot dogs, and crisp half-sour pickles. ⊠*205 E. Houston St., at Ludlow St.,Lower East Side* ☎*212/254–2246* ⊕*www.katzdeli.com* ▭*AE, MC, V* Ⓜ*F, V to 2nd Ave.* ✛*2:G2*

$$$ ✕**Rayuela.** The young and sexy frequent this vibrant Lower East Side LATIN restaurant to sample Latin cuisine courtesy of Máximo Tejada, the chef who built his reputation cooking at New York City's popular Pipa and

Lucy Latin Kitchen. This bi-level eatery has a dining area, a ceviche bar, and—growing in the center of the restaurant—an olive tree. The menu features small plates with nearly three dozen ceviches and tapas, including the must-have lobster with Uruguayan caviar. If you'd like a predinner drink, arrive early to grab a stool at the first-floor bar and enjoy a standout cocktail, like the pisco made with fresh quince and aloe vera juice. ⊠ *165 Allen St., between Rivington and Stanton Sts.,Lower East Side* ☎ *212/253–8840* ⊕ *www.rayuelanyc.com* ▤ *AE, D, DC, MC, V* ⊗*No lunch* Ⓜ*F, V to 2nd Ave.; J, M, Z to Essex and Delancey Sts.* ✥*2:G3*

$ | BISTRO | ☾ ✕**Schiller's Liquor Bar.** It's the kind of hip Lower East Side hangout where you'd be equally comfortable as a celebrity or a parent with a stroller. The folks at Schiller's work hard to make it feel as if it's decades old. Vintage mirrored panels, forever-in-style subway tiles, a tin ceiling, and a checkered floor lend a Parisian feel. Cuban sandwiches and steak-frites reveal a steady hand in the kitchen. Dollar doughnuts, baguettes with sweet or savory fillings, and a standard bar menu fill out the list. ⊠*131 Rivington St., at Norfolk St.,Lower East Side* ☎*212/260–4555* ⊕*www.schillersny.com* ▤*AE, MC, V* Ⓜ*F, J, M, Z to Delancey St.* ✥*2:G3*

$ | AMERICAN ✕**Spitzer's Corner.** In warm weather this sprawling Lower East Side gastropub throws open its windows and doors, and the party inside seems to consume the whole block. After you see the crowd at the bar tasting the 40 beers on tap, you'll likely be tempted to pop in for a pint. Once inside, seated at one of the long wooden communal tables, you may be inclined to stick around for dinner or snacks. The upscale pub grub includes a full raw bar selection (briny just-shucked oysters) and bar snacks like extra-sinful popcorn cooked in pork fat and topped off with bacon. ⊠*101 Rivington St., at Ludlow St.,Lower East Side* ☎*212/228–0027* ⊕*www.spitzerscorner.com*▤*MC, V* Ⓜ*F to Delancey St.; J, M, Z to Essex St.* ✥*2:G3*

$$$ | NEW AMERICAN ✕**wd~50.** The chef has been called a mad genius. Chef Wylie Dufresne mixes colors, flavors, and textures with a master hand. His staff encourages people to feel at ease trying things like fried quail with banana tartar and nasturtium or a parsnip tart with quinoa, hazelnuts, and bok choy. Desserts follow suit: soft white chocolate with potato, malt, and white beer ice cream, anyone? ⊠*50 Clinton St., between Rivington and Stanton Sts., Lower East Side* ☎*212/477–2900* ⊕*www.wd-50.com* ▤*AE, D, DC, MC, V* ⊗*No lunch Sat.–Tues.* Ⓜ*F to Delancey St.; J, M, Z to Essex St.* ✥*2:H3*

18

GREENWICH VILLAGE WITH MEATPACKING DISTRICT AND WEST VILLAGE

GREENWICH VILLAGE

$$ | PIZZA | ☾ ✕**Arturo's.** Few guidebooks list this classic New York pizzeria, but the jam-packed room and pleasantly smoky scent foreshadow a satisfying meal. There's a full menu of Italian classics, but don't be fooled: pizza is the main event. The thin-crust beauties are cooked in a coal oven, emerging sizzling with simple toppings like pepperoni, sausage, and eggplant. Monday to Thursday you can call ahead to reserve a table;

weekends, be prepared to wait and salivate. ✉ *106 W. Houston St., near Thompson St.,Greenwich Village* ☎ *212/677–3820* ▭ *AE, DC, MC, V* ⊘ *No lunch* Ⓜ *1 to Houston St.; B, D, F, V to Broadway–Lafayette St.* ✛ *2:D3*

$$$
ITALIAN

✕ **Babbo.** After one bite of the ethereal homemade pasta or tender barbecued squab, you'll understand why it's so hard to get reservations at Mario Batali's casually elegant restaurant. The complex and satisfying menu hits numerous high points, such as "mint love letters," ravioli filled with pureed peas, ricotta, and fresh mint, finished with spicy lamb sausage ragout; and rabbit with brussels sprouts, house-made pancetta, and carrot vinaigrette. Babbo is the perfect spot for a raucous celebratory dinner with flowing wine and festive banter. But be forewarned: if anyone in your party is hard of hearing, or bothered by loud rock music, choose someplace more sedate. ✉ *110 Waverly Pl., between MacDougal St. and 6th Ave., Greenwich Village* ☎ *212/777–0303* ⊕ *www.babbonyc.com* ⊜ *Reservations essential* ▭ *AE, MC, V* ⊘ *No lunch* Ⓜ *A, B, C, D, E, F, V to W. 4th St.* ✛ *2:C1*

> **WORD OF MOUTH**
>
> "The food we had at Babbo was wonderful. However if I was going again I would definitely do the tasting menu for one simple reason. The entire menu is in Italian and unless you have traveled to Italy or know about real Italian food you are not going to recognize a thing on the menu. I think it would be wonderful to go with someone who knows the menu and can guide you, or do the tasting menu." —artman

$$$
NEW AMERICAN

✕ **Blue Hill.** This tasteful, sophisticated chocolate-brown den of a restaurant—formerly a speakeasy—on a quiet, quaint side street maintains an impeccable reputation for excellence and consistency under the leadership of Dan Barber. Part of the "slow food," sustainable agriculture movement, Blue Hill mostly uses ingredients grown or raised within 200 mi, including the Four Season Farm at Stone Barns Center for Food and Agriculture, Barber's second culinary project, in nearby Westchester County. The chefs produce precisely cooked and elegantly constructed food such as Chatham cod with curried zucchini and Marcona almonds in a shellfish broth. ✉ *75 Washington Pl., between Washington Sq. W and 6th Ave.,Greenwich Village* ☎ *212/539–1776* ⊕ *www.bluehillnyc.com* ⊜ *Reservations essential* ▭ *AE, D, DC, MC, V* ⊘ *No lunch* Ⓜ *A, B, C, D, E, F, V to W. 4th St.* ✛ *2:C1*

$$
BISTRO

✕ **Blue Ribbon Bakery.** When the owners renovated this space, they uncovered a 100-year-old wood-burning oven. They relined it with volcanic brick and let it dictate the destiny of their restaurant. The bakery/restaurant has an eclectic menu featuring substantial sandwiches on homemade bread (from the oven, of course), small plates, a legendary bread pudding, and entrées that span the globe, from hummus to grilled catfish with chorizo, bacon-studded collards, and sweet potatoes. The basement dining room is dark and intimate; upstairs is a Parisian-style café. ✉ *35 Downing St., at Bedford St.,Greenwich Village* ☎ *212/337–0404* ⊕ *www.blueribbonrestaurants.com* ▭ *AE, D, DC, MC, V* Ⓜ *1 to Houston St.; A, B, C, D, E, F, V to W. 4th St.* ✛ *2:C2*

$$$ ✕**Centro Vinoteca.** Top Chef contestant and Eleven Madison Park alum
ITALIAN Leah Cohen is now presiding over the cucina at this bi-level Italian hot
spot decked out in gleaming white tiles and a wall of windows look-
ing out onto 7th Avenue. Cohen's menu retains a dedication to serving
"creative authentic" interpretations of dishes from the motherland. If
you want to go Italiano yourself, precede your meal with an aperitivo—
a glass of Prosecco and some nibbles from the piccolini menu: olives,
truffled deviled eggs, or perhaps the white marinated anchovies. When
you're ready to move on, the octopus antipasto is tender and grilled to
perfection. Deciding between the primis will be tough, but the Kabocha
squash ravioli with walnuts, brown butter, and vincotto and the far-
rotto (a barley-like risotto) with lobster and wild mushrooms are both
excellent choices. As for your secondo, if you're into lamb, the grilled
rack of lamb is the way to go. Cohen serves it with seared lamb belly,
braised lamb shank, Swiss chard, and plump black mission figs. And in
true Italian form, the kitchen stays open till midnight. ✉ *74 7th Ave.
S., at Barrow St., Greenwich Village* ☎*212/367–7470* ⊕*www.centro
vinoteca.com* ▱*AE, MC, V* Ⓜ*1 to Christopher St./Sheridan Sq.; A,
B, C, D, E, F, V to W. 4th St.-Washington Sq.* ✛*2:B2*

$$ ✕**Elettaria.** It's hard to imagine that in a past life this space was a rock
NEW AMERICAN club where a young Jimi Hendrix played. Now the vibe is warm, almost
Fodor'sChoice rustic space with a reclaimed barn-wood ceiling, exposed brick walls,
★ lush velvet curtains, and white-powder steel bar. The former stage is an
elegant open kitchen where chef Akthar Nawab and his culinary staff
prepare inventive contemporary American dishes infused with Indian
and South Asian flavors, ingredients, and spices. The restaurant is a joint
venture between two former Craftbar colleagues, Nawab from India
and his partner, Noel Cruz, who is from the Philippines. They offer their
diners inspired dishes, such as lightly beer-battered quail over frisée with
bacon, mango, and a small fried egg; the succulent duck keema with
nettles and cardamom; and the day-boat cod with corn milk, avocado,
and star anise vinaigrette—all at reasonable prices. Cocktail connoisseurs will also appreciate the mixology contingent at the bar, serving
up intriguing beverages, including one that honors 33 West 8th Street's
former rock club, the 8th Wonder, a cardamom chai-infused Buffalo
Trace bourbon with lemon, sweet vermouth, and soda. ✉ *33 W. 8th
St., at MacDougal St., Greenwich Village* ☎*212/677–3833* ⊕*www.
elettarianyc.com* ▱*AE, D, DC, MC, V* ☾*No lunch weekdays* Ⓜ*A, B,
C, D, E, F, V to W. 4th St./Washington Sq.* ✛*2:D1*

$$ ✕**Five Points.** This cheerful restaurant is a refreshing oasis, with a
AMERICAN rushing stream of water running through a hollowed-out log for the
entire length of the dining room. Chef-owner Marc Meyer's menus
are seasonal and market-driven. Expect plump chilled oysters, exem-
plary Caesar salad, and splendid house-made pasta, followed by the
likes of pan-seared day-boat halibut with cucumber gazpacho and
chopped tomato salsa; and grilled baby lamb chops with rosemary
potatoes, mint-yogurt sauce, and black-olive-stuffed tomato. Sunday
brunch is one of the very best in the city, and prices are quite friendly.
✉*31 Great Jones St., between Lafayette St. and Bowery, Greenwich Vil-
lage* ☎*212/253–5700* ⊕*www.fivepointsrestaurant.com* ✍*Reservations*

18

essential ⊟*AE, MC, V* Ⓜ*6 to Bleecker St.; B, D, F, V to Broadway-Lafayette St.* ✛*3:G6*

$$
ITALIAN
✕**Gonzo.** Once you're seated in the cathedral-ceiling dining room, you'll swear you're in Florence. The restaurant is usually packed and can be noisy, but that's part of the scene. Start with Venetian bar snacks called *cicchetti*—fried stuffed olives, marinated roasted peppers, and a salad of fava beans, pecorino, and walnuts are just a few of the selections. Then try one of the cracker-thin grilled pizzas topped with wild mushrooms and Taleggio cheese, or eggplant caponata and cumin-scented ricotta. If you've still got room, the entrées include inventive pairings like fennel-crusted pork tenderloin with raspberry-onion marmalade, and fried cornmeal-crusted soft-shell crabs with sweet relish and spicy aioli. The praline ice-cream sandwich with Tahitian vanilla gelato is even better than it sounds. ⊠*140 W. 13th St., between 6th and 7th Aves., Greenwich Village* ☏*212/645–4606* ✍*Reservations essential* ⊟*AE, MC, V* ☾*No lunch* Ⓜ*1, 2, 3 to 14th St.; L, F, V to 6th Ave.* ✛*3:D4*

$$$$
AMERICAN
✕**Gotham Bar & Grill.** A culinary landmark, Gotham Bar & Grill is every bit as thrilling as it was when it opened in 1984. Celebrated chef Alfred Portale, who made the blueprint for "architectural food," that is, towers of stacked ingredients, builds on a foundation of simple, clean flavors. People come for Portale's transcendent preparations: no rack of lamb is more tender, no seafood salad sweeter. A stellar 20,000-bottle cellar provides the perfect accompaniments—at a price. There's also a fantastic three-course $27 prix-fixe lunch from noon to 2:30 weekdays. ⊠*12 E. 12th St., between 5th Ave. and University Pl., Greenwich Village* ☏*212/620–4020* ⊕*www.gothambarandgrill.com* ⊟*AE, D, DC, MC, V* ☾*No lunch weekends* Ⓜ*L, N, Q, R, W, 4, 5, 6 to 14th St./Union Sq.* ✛*3:E4*

¢
FAST FOOD
Multiple
Locations
☺
✕**Gray's Papaya.** It's a stand-up, takeout dive. And, yes, limos do sometimes stop here for the legendary hot dogs. More often than not, though, it's neighbors or commuters who know how good the slim, traditional, juicy all-beef dogs are. Fresh-squeezed orange juice, a strangely tasty creamy banana drink, and the much-touted, healthful papaya juice are available along with more standard drinks, served up 24/7. You'll find other Gray's Papaya outposts around the city, but this one's our favorite. ⊠*402 6th Ave., at W. 8th St.,Greenwich Village* ☏*212/260–3532* ✍*Reservations not accepted* ⊟*No credit cards* Ⓜ*A, B, C, D, E, F, V to W. 4th St.* ✛*3:D5* ⊠*539 8th Ave., at 37th St.* ☏*212/904–1588* ✍*Reservations not accepted* ⊟*No credit cards* Ⓜ*A, C, E to 34th St./Penn Station* ✛*4:B5* ⊠*2090 Broadway, at 72nd St.* ☏*212/799–0243* ✍*Reservations not accepted* ⊟*No credit cards* Ⓜ*1, 2, 3 to 72nd St.* ✛*5:B4*

$$
ITALIAN
✕**Lupa.** Even the most hard-to-please connoisseurs have a soft spot for Lupa, Mario Batali and Joseph Bastianich's "downscale" Roman trattoria. Rough-hewn wood, great Italian wines, and simple preparations with top-quality ingredients define the restaurant. People come repeatedly for dishes such as ricotta gnocchi with sweet-sausage ragout, house-made salumi, and sardines with fennel and cracked wheat. The front of the restaurant is seated on a first-come, first-served basis; reservations are taken for the back. ⊠*170 Thompson St., between Bleecker*

and W. Houston Sts., Greenwich Village ☎*212/982–5089* ⊕*www. luparestaurant.com* ▭*AE, MC, V* Ⓜ*A, B, C, D, E, F, V to W. 4th St.* ✛*2:D3*

¢   ✗**Moustache.** There's typically a
MIDDLE EASTERN   crowd waiting outside for one of the copper-topped tables at this appealing Middle Eastern neighborhood restaurant. The focal point is the perfect pita that accompanies tasty salads like lemony chickpea and spinach, and hearty lentil and bulgur. Also delicious is *lahambajin,* spicy ground lamb on a crispy flat crust. For entrées, try the leg of lamb or merguez sausage sandwiches. Service is slow but friendly. ✉*90 Bedford St., between Barrow and Grove Sts.,Greenwich Village* ☎*212/229–2220* ⌧*Reservations not accepted* ▭*No credit cards* Ⓜ*1 to Christopher St./Sheridan Sq.* ✛*2:B2*

$ ✗**P*ONG.** Lately New York pastry chefs have been migrating en masse
DESSERT   from their usual supporting roles into the restaurant spotlight. Pichet Ong, who previously worked for top chef Jean-Georges Vongerichten, was one of the first to open his own stand-alone restaurant. The Asian-inflected menu at this cozy West Village spot—filled with cushions in bright pop-art colors—blurs the line between entrée and dessert. His beautifully constructed small-plate cuisine includes dishes that purposefully straddle the sweet-savory divide, including a foie gras–dark-chocolate truffle, and lamb with green curry and cardamom ice cream. Desserts, like pineapple tiramisu and jasmine rice pudding, remain, thankfully, pure sugary indulgences. ✉*150 W. 10th St., at Waverly Pl.,Greenwich Village* ☎*212/929–0898* ⊕*www.p-ong.com* ▭*AE, MC, V* ⊘*No lunch* Ⓜ*1 to Christopher St./Sheridan Sq.; A, B, C, D, E, F, V to W. 4th St./Washington Sq.* ✛*3:D5*

$$ ✗**Paris Commune.** Wraparound floor-to-ceiling windows, dark cher-
BRASSERIE   ry banquettes, and papered-and-clothed tables characterize this old favorite's new space, along with a certain self-assurance. Begin with an extraordinarily tender crab cake, carefully seasoned and given a certain edge by an apple-horseradish rémoulade. Grilled ostrich steak isn't something you run across too often; it's surprisingly rich in flavor for such a lean meat. Herbed polenta and a dried-fruit compote make the perfect partners for the ostrich. Finish with a wedge of flourless chocolate cake topped with bourbon-infused crème anglaise and mixed-berry coulis. ✉*99 Bank St., at Greenwich St.,Greenwich Village* ☎*212/929–0509* ⊕*www.pariscommune.net* ▭*AE, MC, V* Ⓜ*1 to Chrisopher St./Sheridan Sq.; A, C, E to 14th Sts.; L to 8th Ave.* ✛*2:A1*

$$$ ✗**Wallsé.** Kurt Gutenbrunner's modern Austrian menu at this neighbor-
AUSTRIAN   hood restaurant with a quasi–Wiener Werkstätte look is soulful and satisfying, with a strong emphasis on Austrian tradition and urban New York attitude. It's hard to argue with such dishes as Wiener schnitzel with potato-cucumber salad and lingonberries or venison goulash with bacon, mushrooms, and fresh-herbed spaetzle. Desserts do Vienna

18

proud: apple-walnut strudel is served with apple sorbet. ⊠*344 W. 11th St., at Washington St.,Greenwich Village* ☎*212/352–2300* ⊕*www. wallse.com* ⌕*Reservations essential* ▭*AE, DC, MC, V* ⊗*No lunch weekdays* Ⓜ*1 to Christopher St./Sheridan Sq.; A, C, E to 14th St.; L to 8th Ave.* ✛*3:B6*

MEATPACKING DISTRICT

$$$ ✕**Bagatelle.** Situate yourself at a table in Bagatelle's elegant and spacious
FRENCH white dining room, sip on a cocktail like La Poire Royale (pear vodka, pear brandy, pear purée, Cointreau, and champagne), and watch the Meatpacking District's beautiful people strut by and coo at the bar. Executive chef Nicolas Cantrel's appealing menu of Provençal bistro classics includes some excellent appetizers: buttery elbow pasta with veal juice, ham, and Swiss cheese, and a tartine with goat cheese and tomato confit are highbrow, addictive comfort food. There are still a few kinks to work out though. Filet mignon was nicely cooked and seasoned but accompanied by unmemorable frites, and the flavorful bouillabaisse—a Provençal fish stew with rouille and croutons—suffered from rather bland seafood. Leave room for dessert, especially "le Paris Brest"—choux pastry, praline cream, and almonds. The wine list includes many French varietals; only a few are offered by the glass. ⊠*409 W. 13th St., between 9th Ave. and Washington St., Meatpacking District* ☎*212/675–2400* ▭*AE, D, MC, V* ⊗*No lunch weekdays* Ⓜ *A, C, E to 14th St.; L to 8th Ave.* ✛*3:B4*

$$$ ✕**Del Posto.** Mario Batali's high-profile stab at four-star immortality
ITALIAN helped kick off the big-box restaurant boom in the Meatpacking District. Much more formal than his still hugely popular Babbo, the restaurant initially struck many as too grown-up for a big kid like Batali. The dining room—with its sweeping staircase, formal decor, and live tinkling from a baby grand—has the feel of an opulent hotel lobby. But Del Posto prevailed and is now regarded as one of the most consistently dazzling special-occasion spots in a neighborhood overrun with overpriced eateries. A partnership with TV chef Lidia Bastianich, the restaurant offers pitch-perfect risotto made fresh to order for two persons or more (and served in the oversize pan), big shareable roast hunks of meat (veal chops), as well as ethereal pastas. For a little taste of the experience, come for a cocktail and sample the bargain bar menu. ⊠*85 10th Ave., between 15th and 16th Sts.,Meatpacking District* ☎*212/497–8090* ⊕*www.delposto.com* ⌕*Reservations essential* ▭*AE, MC, V* ⊗ *No lunch Tues.–Sat.* Ⓜ*A, C, E to 14th St.; L to 8th Ave.* ✛*3:A4*

$$$ ✕**Pastis.** A trendy spin-off of Balthazar in SoHo, Pastis looks like it was
BRASSERIE shipped in, tile by nicotine-stained tile, from Pigalle. At night throngs of whippet-thin cell-phone-slinging boys and girls gather at the bar up front to sip martinis and be seen. French favorites are front and center, including toothsome steak-frites with béarnaise, mussels steamed in Pernod, and tasty apple tartlet with phyllo crust. ⊠*9 9th Ave., at Little W. 12th St.,Meatpacking District* ☎*212/929–4844* ⊕*www.pastisny. com* ⌕*Reservations essential* ▭*AE, MC, V* Ⓜ*A, C, E to 14th St.; L to 8th Ave.* ✛*3:B4*

$$$ ✕**Scarpetta.** When Scott Conant left L'Impero and Alto, New Yorkers
ITALIAN wondered when they'd get their next fix of seasonal Italian cooking

from this popular chef. The waiting game is now over with the opening of Scarpetta, located adjacent to the glitz of the Meatpacking District. Walk past the bar into the polished dining room, where orange belts loop around mirrors and a retractable roof ushers in natural light. For a refreshing start, try the chilled summer pea soup, poured over a mound of crab before enjoying one of the house-made pastas, like the al dente tagliatelle laced with strands of tender lamb ragout. Save room for dessert: the honey-caramel gelato that accompanies the polenta-crust apple "pie" brings à la mode to a whole new level. . ⊠ *355 W. 14th St., at 9th Ave., Meatpacking District* ☎ *212/691–0555* ⊕ *www.scarpettanyc.com* ⊟ *AE, D, DC, MC, V* ⊘ *No lunch* Ⓜ *A, C, E to 14th St.; L to 8th Ave.* ✛ *3:B4.*

$$$
ASIAN
✗ **Spice Market.** This playground for New York's elite is set in a cavernous space amid embroidered curtains and artifacts from Burma, India, and Malaysia. Chef Jean-Georges Vongerichten's playful takes on Southeast Asian street food will keep you asking the waiters for information: what exactly was in that? Sometimes the playfulness works, sometimes it doesn't, but don't miss the steamed lobster with garlic, ginger, and dried chili, or the squid salad with papaya and cashews. ⊠ *403 W. 13th St., at 9th Ave.,Meatpacking District* ☎ *212/675–2322* ⊕ *www.jean-georges.com* ⌁ *Reservations essential* ⊟ *AE, D, DC, MC, V* Ⓜ *A, C, E to 14th St.; L to 8th Ave.* ✛ *3:B4*

$
ITALIAN
✗ **Vento.** The pan-Italian menu here features small plates as well as pizzas and full-size entrées at friendly prices. You can make a meal of small tastes, from a full array of sliced Italian meats to chilled artichokes with pecorino cheese, or opt for full portions of dishes like extra-virgin-olive-oil-poached salmon with pink grapefruit and arugula salad, or slow-roasted veal breast in a morel mushroom sauce. For dessert, chewy zeppole are dusted with cinnamon sugar. ⊠ *675 Hudson St., at W. 14th St., Meatpacking District* ☎ *212/699–2400* ⊕ *www.brguestrestaurants.com* ⊟ *AE, MC, V* Ⓜ *A, C, E to 14th St.; L to 8th Ave.* ✛ *3:B4*

WEST VILLAGE

$$
MEDITERRANEAN
✗ **August.** Rustic simplicity is the unifying theme at this bustling West Village eatery helmed by Terrence Gallivan (The Modern and Gordon Ramsay's in the London Hotel). A wood-burning oven in the dining room turns out regional European dishes like tarte flambé; an Alsatian flat bread topped with onion, bacon, and crème fraîche; and Sicilian orata, a meaty white fish grilled whole and doused with citrus, olive oil, and fresh herbs. Wood-planed floors and an arched cork ceiling envelop the busy 40-seat dining room. For a quieter meal, ask for a table in the glass-enclosed 15-seat atrium in back. ⊠ *359 Bleecker St., at Charles St., West Village* ☎ *212/929–8727* ⊕ *www.augustny.com* ⌁ *Reservations essential* ⊟ *AE, MC, V* Ⓜ *1 to Christopher St./Sheridan Sq.; A, B, C, D, E, F, V to W. 4th St.* ✛ *3:C6*

$$$
ASIAN
✗ **Bar Q.** Anita Lo, the chef behind New York City's perennially popular contemporary American spot Annisa and the casual Rickshaw Dumpling Bar, has expanded her empire with this hip Asian bar. The space has minimalist decor in the main room and also features a greenhouse atrium. Bar Q's menu subtly twists upscale finger food, offering and small plates such as the grilled tuna ribs with yuzu and green chili;

18

grilled short rib with Korean flavors; and spareribs stuffed with lemongrass barbecue sauce, peanuts and Thai basil. Instead of cornbread and collard greens, tasty sides such as steamed buns and sticky rice with Chinese sausage round out the meal. There is also a playful cocktail menu with creations such as the "Margaret Lo," a kaffir lime margarita with a chili salt rim. ⊠ *308 Bleecker St., at 7th Ave. S., West Village* ☎*212/206–7817* ⊕*www.barqrestaurant.com* ▭*AE, D, DC, MC, V* ⊘*Closed Sun. No lunch* Ⓜ*1 to Christopher St.-Sheridan Sq.; A, B, C, D, E, F, V to W. 4th St.* ⊹*2:B2*

$$ ✕**Barbuto.** In this structural, airy space you'll be facing either the kitchen
ITALIAN or the quiet street outside. The Italian bistro food depends deeply on fresh seasonal ingredients, so the menu changes daily. Chef Jonathan Waxman specializes in rustic preparations like house-made duck sausage with creamy polenta, red-wine-braised short ribs, and pasta carbonara. Waxman's acclaimed roasted chicken is usually on the menu in one form or another. ⊠ *775 Washington St., between Jane and W. 12th Sts., West Village* ☎*212/924–9700* ⊕*www.barbutonyc.com* ▭*AE, MC, V* Ⓜ*A, C, E, to 14th St.; L to 8th Ave.; 1 to Christopher St./ Sheridan Sq.* ⊹*3:B5*

$$$ ✕**Commerce.** This former speakeasy harkens back to days gone by with
NEW AMERICAN its Diego Rivera–style murals, vintage sconces, and restored subway tiles. The young crowd comes not only for the decor, but to taste Chef Harold Moore's seasonal cuisine. Appetizers range from truffle-flecked asparagus and morels with poached egg to yuzu-marinated hamachi ceviche. The entrées are just as vibrant: bright, sweet peas offset pristine halibut, and the shareable roast chicken, presented table-side, is served with foie gras bread stuffing. The smart, nimble waitstaff constantly replenishes your bread basket with warm baguettes and brioche, and steers you toward the dainty pineapple cheesecake with cilantro sorbet for a sweet ending. For a quieter meal, choose one of the booths near the bar. ⊠ *50 Commerce St., West Village* ☎*212/524–2301* ⊕*www. commercerestaurant.com* ▭*AE, MC, V* ⊘*No lunch* Ⓜ*1 to Christopher St.-Sheridan Sq.; A, B, C, D, E, F, V to W. 4th St.* ⊹*2:B2*

$$ ✕**dell'anima.** Lines snake out the door of this neighborhood favorite.
ITALIAN Check out the open kitchen, where the stylish crowd converges to watch chefs prepare authentic Italian dishes like simple arugula salad or a bowl of pizzocheri pasta with fontina and potatoes. The lamb shank with polenta is the ultimate cold-weather comfort food, especially when paired with one of the restaurant's 100 wines. If you can't get a table, head to the 10-seat bar and drown your sorrows in a glass of homemade limoncello. ⊠ *38 8th Ave., at Jane St., West Village* ☎ *212/366–6633* ⊕*www.dellanima.com* ▭ *AE, MC, V* ⊘ *No lunch weekdays* Ⓜ*A, C, E to 14th St.; L to 8th Ave.* ⊹*3:C5*

$$ ✕**Do Hwa.** If anyone in New York is responsible for making Korean
KOREAN food cool and user-friendly, it is the mother-daughter team behind this perennially popular restaurant and its East Village sister, Dok Suni's. Jenny Kwak and her mother, Myung Ja, serve home cooking in the form of *kalbi jim* (braised short ribs), *bibimbop* (a spicy, mix-it-yourself vegetable-and-rice dish), and other favorites that may not be as pungent as they are in Little Korea, but they're satisfying nevertheless.

✉ *55 Carmine St., between Bedford St. and 7th Ave., West Village* ☎ *212/414–1224* ⊕ *www.dohwanyc.com* ▭ AE, D, MC, V ⊗ *No lunch weekends* Ⓜ *1 to Houston St.; A, B, C, D, E, F, V to W. 4th St.* ✛ *2:C2*

$ ✕ **Fatty Crab.** This rustic Malaysian cantina showcases the exciting cuisine of chef Zak Pelaccio, who spent years cooking at famous French restaurants before escaping to Southeast Asia, where he fell in love with the flavors of the region. Start with the addictive pickled watermelon and crispy pork salad, an improbable combination that is refreshing and decadent. The can't-miss signature dish is chili crab—cracked Dungeness crab in a pool of rich, spicy chili sauce, served with bread for dipping. It's messy for sure, but worth rolling up your sleeves for. The restaurant stays open until 4 AM Thursday through Saturday, making it a late-night hangout for chefs and other folks in the restaurant industry. ✉ *643 Hudson St., between Gansevoort and Horatio Sts., West Village* ☎ *212/352–3590* ⊕ *www.fattycrab.com* ⊜ *Reservations not accepted* ▭ *AE, D, MC, V* Ⓜ *A, C, E to 14th St.; L to 8th Ave.* ✛ *3:C5*

MALAYSIAN
Fodor's Choice
★

$$ ✕ **The Little Owl.** This tiny neighborhood joint, with seating for 28 people, is exceptionally eager to please. The menu is congruently small, which actually makes it easier to decide what you want. And what you want are the pork-veal-beef-pecorino-cheese meatball "sliders" or miniburgers. The unusually juicy pork loin chop is gigantic, and hugely satisfying. Raspberry-filled beignets, served with a ramekin of warm Nutella, are otherworldly. ✉ *90 Bedford St. at Grove St., West Village* ☎ *212/741–4695* ⊕ *www.thelittleowlnyc.com* ⊜ *Reservations essential* ▭ *AE, MC, V* ⊗ *No lunch Mon.* Ⓜ *1 to Christopher St.; A, B, C, D, E, F, V to W. 4th St.* ✛ *3:D6*

NEW AMERICAN

$ ✕ **Mexicana Mama.** This quaint and colorful—and very popular—space serves vividly flavored fare. The kitchen is serious enough to create a dozen different salsas daily, and several dishes come with your choice of salsa and filling. The tomato-habanero salsa is simply unforgettable; cream tames the habaneros, but only slightly. Three chili-roasted pork tacos are also filled with piquant chihuahua cheese and black beans, and served over Mexican rice and avocado cubes. Quesadillas are made with fresh corn tortillas (for a change!), filled with that melted chihuahua cheese and your choice of chicken, barbacoa beef, chicken mole, or a daily special vegetable filling. For dessert, look no further than the eggy flan topped with caramel. ✉ *525 Hudson St., near Charles St., West Village* ☎ *212/924–4119* ▭ *No credit cards* Ⓜ *1 to Christopher St./Sheridan Sq.; A, B, C, D, E, F, V to W. 4th St./Washington Sq.* ✛ *3:C6*

MEXICAN

$$$ ✕ **Perry St.** The clean lines of this austere dining room with its gauze-swaddled wraparound windows and straight-backed cream banquettes get you to focus on the main event: master chef Jean-Georges Vongerichten's marvelous food. Black-pepper crab dumplings are plated with delicate snow peas. Rack of lamb is vivified by chili crumbs, and calmed down again by braised artichoke. A rare rabbit roulade has a clarity of flavors punctuated by citrus-chili seasoning. Goat cheesecake comes with Concord grapes and honeyed cashews. ✉ *176 Perry St. at West St. West Village* ☎ *212/352–1900* ⊕ *www.jean-georges.com* ▭ *AE, D, MC, V* Ⓜ *1 to Christopher St./Sheridan Sq.* ✛ *2:A2*

NEW AMERICAN

18

UNION SQUARE WITH FLATIRON DISTRICT, GRAMERCY PARK, AND MURRAY HILL

FLATIRON DISTRICT

$$$ ✕**A Voce.** Executive chef Missy Robbins has a passion for Italian cuisine,
ITALIAN and it shows. The American-born Robbins honed her Italian chops in
Fodor'sChoice northern Italy at the highly acclaimed Agli Amici restaurant in Friuli.
★ For five years prior to joining A Voce, she was the executive chef at
Chicago's Spiaggia. Her menu is inspired, and represents regional dishes
from all over Italy, including melt-in-your-mouth swiss chard and cre-
senza cheese-stuffed cassoncini pockets with prosciutto from Puglia,
spaghetti alla chitarra from Abruzzo, and Venetian grilled foie gras. The
pasta is prepared fresh every day and Robbins's fish and meat dishes are
exceptional. The agnello in due modi entrée is especially well prepared
with tender lamb chops and a flavorful vegetable soffrito. For des-
sert, try the Tuscan bomboloni doughnuts with dark chocolate dipping
sauce. The attentive staff also help to make the dining experience here
a real pleasure. A Voce's atmosphere is warm, and the 90-seat dining
room has a retro Italian feel to it—walnut floors, pale green leather-top
tables, and Eames chairs. There's also additional seating on the patio
when weather permits. ⊠*41 Madison Ave., between 25th and 26th
Sts., Flatiron District* ☎*212/545–8555* ⊕*www.avocerestaurant.com*
🖃*AE, MC, V* Ⓜ*N, R to 23rd St.* ✛*3:F2*

$$$ ✕**BLT Fish.** Two stories above the less formal Fish Shack, BLT Fish is
SEAFOOD an elegantly appointed dining room set under a spectacular skylight.
"BLT" stands for Bistro Laurent Tourondel, and he proves once again,
as at BLT Steak uptown, that he embellishes his dishes more success-
fully than nearly anyone. "Buffalo rock shrimp" are beer-battered
shrimp sauced in the manner of Buffalo wings, with surprisingly delicious results. Tourondel's signature roasted Alaskan black cod is simply
marinated overnight, then roasted. The piping-hot result is among the
best seafood dishes in town. Whole fish is sold by the pound, with most
fish averaging 1–3 pounds each. At about $32 per pound, that can really
add up. ⊠ *21 W. 17th St., between 5th and 6th Aves., Flatiron District*
☎*212/691–8888* ⊕*www.bltfish.com* ◈*Reservations essential* 🖃*AE,
D, DC, MC, V* ⊗*Closed Sun. No lunch* Ⓜ*4, 5, 6, L, N, Q, R, W to
Union Sq./14th St.; F, V, L to 6th Ave./14th St.* ✛*3:E3*

$$ ✕**Boqueria.** This warm, buzzy restaurant features comfortable wheat-
SPANISH color leather banquettes and, if you want to make friends, a communal
table running down the center of the dining room. Chef Seamus Mullen
spent two years tromping around Spanish kitchens, and he came to New
York armed with dozens of ideas for classic tapas and even better mid-
size dishes and entrées. Fried quail eggs and chorizo on roasted bread
are even better than they sound. Salt cod, suckling pig, and mushroom
croquettes are perched on dabs of flavored aioli. *Garbanzos al Pinotxo*
is a luscious mix of chickpeas, morcilla, a steamed hen's egg, and toasted
pine nuts. Traditional churros come with a thick hot chocolate for dip-
ping. ⊠*53 W. 19th St., between 5th and 6th Aves., Flatiron District*
☎*212/255–4160* ⊕*www.boquerianyc.com* 🖃*AE, D, MC, V* Ⓜ*6, F,
R, V, W to 23rd St.* ✛*3:E3*

$
CAFÉ
☺

✗ **City Bakery.** This self-service bakery-restaurant has the urban aesthetic to match its name. Chef-owner Maury Rubin's baked goods—giant cookies, flaky croissants, elegant tarts—are unfailingly rich. A major draw is the salad bar that's worth every penny—a large selection of impeccably fresh food, including whole sides of baked salmon, roasted vegetables, and several Asian-accented dishes. Much of the produce comes from the nearby farmers' market. In winter the bakery hosts a hot-chocolate festival; in summer it's lemonade time. Weekend brunch includes limited table-side service. ⊠ *3 W. 18th St., between 5th and 6th Aves., Flatiron District* ☎ *212/366–1414* ⊕ *www.thecitybakery.com* ⌂ *Reservations not accepted* ═ *AE, MC, V* ⊘ *No dinner* Ⓜ *L, N, Q, R, W, 4, 5, 6 to 14th St./Union Sq.; F, V to 14th St.* ✛ *3:E3*

$$–$$$$
AMERICAN

✗ **Country and The Café at Country.** Don't let the name fool you; Jeffrey Zakarian's upstairs-downstairs urban canteen is neither pastoral nor rustic. The chef's sophomore restaurant has a split personality. Up a translucent staircase you'll find a fine-dining aerie with beautifully executed—and pricey—highbrow cuisine. The much more accessible downstairs Café, in dark masculine leather and wood, offers three meals a day including an exceptional brunch (don't miss the buttery take on shrimp and grits). Zakarian updates comfort food with refined ingenuity, delivering a Caesar salad with crisped prosciutto and a coddled egg cradled in cubed brioche toast. His "roast chicken" features succulent off-the-bone meat cut into angular shapes, rich cranberry relish, grilled red onion, grilled cornbread, and pitch-perfect al dente green beans. ⊠ *90 Madison Ave., at 29th St., Flatiron District* ☎ *212/889–7100* ⊕ *www.countryinnnewyork. com* ═ *AE, D, DC, MC, V* Ⓜ *6 to 28th St.* ✛ *3:F1*

$$
NEW AMERICAN

✗ **Craftbar.** The casual sibling to Tom Colicchio's Craft is a spacious and inviting bargain. The menu features similarly assertive seasonal cooking as you can find at the upscale flagship just around the corner. The "snacks" category on the menu elevates tiny nibbles to sausage-stuffed fried sage leaves or addictive fluffy salt cod croquettes tempting you to forget the main course entirely. The rest of the menu is eclectic enough to satisfy just about every comfort-food craving, from orecchiette with cauliflower and sausage to braised fork-tender short ribs with celery. ⊠ *900 Broadway, between 19th and 20th Sts., Flatiron District* ☎ *212/461–4300* ⊕ *www.craftrestaurant.com/craftbar.html* ⌂ *Reservations essential* ═ *AE, D, DC, MC, V* Ⓜ *L, N, Q, R, W, 4, 5, 6 to 14th St.–Union Sq.* ✛ *3:F3*

$$
MEXICAN
Multiple
Locations
☺

✗ **Dos Caminos.** Stephen Hanson, the visionary behind a dozen New York restaurants, has created a hit with the Dos Caminos brand. Start with guacamole, served in a granite mortar called a *molcajete*, and peruse the selection of 150 tequilas. Beef tacos studded with chilies, and slow-roasted pork ribs in chipotle barbecue sauce are solid choices. On weekend nights at both locations, the noise level can get out of control. ⊠ *373 Park Ave. S, between E. 26th and E. 27th Sts., Flatiron District* ☎ *212/294–1000* ⊕ *www.brguestrestaurants.com* ⌂ *Reservations essential* ═ *AE, DC, MC, V* Ⓜ *6 to 28th St.* ✛ *3:F2* ⊠ *475 West Broadway, at W. Houston St.* ☎ *212/277–4300* ═ *AE, DC, MC, V* Ⓜ *R, W to Prince St.; C, E to Spring St.* ✛ *2:D3* ⊠ *825 3rd Ave., at 50th St.* ☎ *212/336–5400* ═ *AE, DC, MC, V* Ⓜ *6 to 51st St.* ✛ *4:G3*

18

¢ ✕**Eisenberg's Sandwich Shop.** Since 1929 this narrow coffee shop with
CAFÉ its timeworn counter and cramped tables has provided the city with
some of the best tuna-, chicken-, and egg-salad sandwiches. On chilly
days Eisenberg's classic matzoh-ball soup also really hits the spot. The
lively and friendly staff use the cryptic language of soda jerks, in which
"whiskey down" means rye toast and "Adam and Eve on a raft" means
two eggs on toast. Considering the mayhem in the place, it's a pleasant surprise that you always get your meal, quickly and precisely as
ordered. ⊠*174 5th Ave., between E. 22nd and E. 23rd Sts., Flatiron
District* 📞*212/675–5096* ⊕*www.eisenbergsnyc.com* ✍*Reservations
not accepted* ⊟*AE, D, MC, V* ⊘*No dinner* Ⓜ*R, W, 6 to 23rd St.*
✛*3:E2*

$$$$ ✕**Eleven Madison Park.** Under Swiss-born chef Daniel Humm, who was
NEW AMERICAN lured from San Francisco's Campton Place by restaurateur Danny Mey-
Fodor's Choice er, this art nouveau jewel overlooking Madison Park has become one of
★ the city's most consistently exciting places to dine. Humm announces
his lofty intentions with dishes like foie gras with golden raisin brioche and African kili pepper, butter-poached Scottish langoustines with
carrot-orange nage, and Jamison Farm herb roasted lamb with tomato confit and niçoise olives. Don't forget your breakfast cake—a gift
from the chef—as you walk out the door. ⊠*11 Madison Ave., at 24th
St.,Flatiron District* 📞*212/889–0905* ⊕*www.elevenmadisonpark.com*
✍*Reservations essential* ⊟*AE, D, DC, MC, V* ⊘ *Closed Sun. No
lunch weekends* Ⓜ*N, R, W, 6 to 23rd St.* ✛*3:E2*

$$$$ ✕**Gramercy Tavern.** Danny Meyer's intensely popular restaurant tops
AMERICAN many a New Yorker's favorite restaurant list. In front, the first-come,
first-served tavern presents a lighter menu. The more formal dining
room has a prix-fixe American menu; three courses at dinner is $86.
Choose from seasonal dishes such as lightly smoked Spanish mackerel,
grilled sturgeon with lemon fennel sauce, or stuffed meatball with fon-
tina cheese. Meyer's restaurants—he owns several well-regarded eateries
in the city—are renowned for their food and hospitality, and Gramercy
Tavern sets the standard. ⊠*42 E. 20th St., between Broadway and Park
Ave. S, Flatiron District* 📞*212/477–0777* ⊕*www.gramercytavern.
com* ✍*Reservations essential for main dining room; reservations not
accepted for the Tavern* ⊟*AE, D, DC, MC, V* Ⓜ*6, R, W to 23rd St.*
✛*3:F3*

$$ ✕**Hill Country.** This enormous barbecue joint is perfect for big groups
BARBECUE and carnivorous appetites. The pit master from Queens has a champi-
onship knack for real Texas barbecue. The beef-centric menu features
meaty ribs and exceptionally succulent slow-smoked brisket (check your
diet at the door and go for the moist, fatty option). Plump pork sau-
sages, in regular and jalapeño cheese versions, are flown in direct from
Kreuz Market in Lockhart, Texas. The market-style setup can mean
long lines for meat, sold by the pound, or ribs at cutter-manned stations.
Bring your tray downstairs for a fine bourbon selection and nightly live
music. ⊠*30 W. 26th St., between Broadway and 6th Ave., Flatiron
District* 📞*212/255–4544* ⊕*www.hillcountryny.com* ⊟*AE, MC, V*
Ⓜ*N, R, W to 28th St.; 6 to 28th St.; F, V to 23rd St.* ✛*3:E2*

$ ✕**Ilili.** Famed Washington, D.C., restaurateur and chef Philippe Mas-
MIDDLE EASTERN soud brings his culinary talents to New York City with this bi-level, 400-seat eatery that showcases cuisine from his native Lebanon. The menu includes standard Middle Eastern fare but also unexpected dishes like Wagyu beef kebab and black cod with pomegranate molasses. Wait-ers never fail to refresh the basket of hot, fluffy, baked-in-house pita bread. A glass of Lebanese or French wine is a nice accompaniment to the cuisine. Late-night entertainment includes belly dancing. ✉ *236 5th Ave., between 27th and 28th Sts., Flatiron District* ☎*212/683–2929* ⊕*www.ililinyc.com* ▭*AE, D, DC, MC, V* ⊘*No lunch weekends* Ⓜ*N, R, W to 28th St.* ✛*3:E2*

$$$$ ✕**Primehouse New York.** This sleek steak house comes from the reliable
STEAKHOUSE group that operates Dos Caminos, Vento, and several other perpetu-ally mobbed New York restaurants. Here you'll find classic presen-tations like Caesar salad and steak tartare prepared table-side, and respectable dry-aged prime cuts, ranging from hanger steak ($24) to porterhouse for two ($86). For something lighter, try skate sautéed in lemon–brown-butter sauce, or the Berkshire pork chop with fig glaze and apple compote. The mod space has a cream-and-black motif that recalls The Jetsons' futuristic 1960s feel, interspersed with geometric M.C. Escher–like patterns. Given the popularity of other B.R. Guest restaurants, expect a see-and-be-seen scene, and be sure to call ahead for reservations. ✉ *381 Park Ave. S, at 27th St., Flatiron District* ☎ *212/824–2600* ⊕ *www.brguestrestaurants.com/restaurants/prime-house_new_york* ▭ *AE, MC, V* Ⓜ*6, R, W to 28th St.* ✛*3:F2*

$$$$ ✕**Tabla.** In concert with restaurant guru Danny Meyer, chef Floyd Car-
INDIAN doz creates exciting cuisine based on the tastes of his native India, fil-tered through his European training. Indian ingredients garnish familiar fish and meats like striped bass, chicken, and lamb. At the casual Bread Bar you can get in and out faster and for less money while watching naan emerge from the tandoori ovens. ✉*11 Madison Ave., at E. 25th St.,Flatiron District* ☎*212/889–0667* ⊕*www.tablany.com* ✐*Reser-vations essential* ▭*AE, D, DC, MC, V* ⊘*No lunch Sun.* Ⓜ*R, W, 6 to 23rd St.* ✛*3:F2*

$$ ✕**Tamarind.** Many consider Tamarind Manhattan's best Indian restau-
INDIAN rant. Forsaking the usual brass, beads, sitar, and darkness, you'll find a lustrous skylighted dining room awash in soothing neutral colors and awaft with tantalizing fragrances. Your welcoming hosts, owner Avtar Walia and his nephew, general manager Gary, practically reinvent charm. The busy kitchen offers multiregional dishes, some familiar (tandoori chicken, a searing lamb vindaloo), some unique (succulent venison chops in a vigorously spiced cranberry sauce, she-crab soup with saf-fron, nutmeg, and ginger juice). The more intriguing a dish sounds, the better it turns out to be. Next door is a quaint teahouse–café–takeout shop. ✉*41–43 E. 22nd St., between Broadway and Park Ave. SFlatiron District* ☎*212/674–7400* ⊕*www.tamarinde22.com* ✐*Reservations essential* ▭*AE, DC, MC, V* Ⓜ*N, R, 6 to 23rd St.* ✛*3:F2*

$$$$ ✕**Veritas.** What do you do when you own more wine than you can
AMERICAN drink—as in 150,000 bottles? Veritas's wine-collecting owners decid-ed to open a restaurant. Chef Grégory Pugin's prix-fixe contemporary

18

menu runs from such rich, earthy dishes as short ribs braised in Barolo wine with parsnip puree to porcini-crusted cod with lobster emulsion, mashed potatoes, mushrooms, and sweet corn. A glass of Tokaj and a black-pepper shortcake positively sing together. The dignified dining room is distinguished by clean, natural lines, with one wall of Italian tile and another flaunting a backlighted collection of handblown vases. ✉ *43 E. 20th St., between Broadway and Park Ave. S, Flatiron District* ☎ *212/353–3700* ⊕ *www.veritas-nyc.com* ✍ *Reservations essential* ⊟ *AE, DC, MC, V* ⊘ *No lunch* Ⓜ *R, W, 6 to 23rd St.* ✛ *3:F3*

$$ ✕ **Wildwood Barbecue.** Prolific restaurateur Steve Hanson's latest venture
BARBECUE has been smokin' since day one, appeasing rabid barbecue aficionados. Pit master (and former Queens cop) "Big Lou" Elrose deserves credit for excellent ribs: succulent lamb and saucy baby back. Dine at the bar or at adjacent high tables where the animated scene is fueled by whiskey and potent mint juleps. Families should settle in the dining room for fiery fried jalapeño slices called "bottle caps," shareable platters of apricot-glazed chicken and pulled pork, and towering carrot and chocolate layer cakes. A crafty combination of reclaimed wood, distressed garage doors, recycled paper, blackboards, and bell jars has made a trendy Manhattan block feel kitschy and comfortable. ✉ *225 Park Ave. S, at 18th St., Flatiron District* ☎ *212/533–2500* ⊕ *www.brguestrestaurants. com/restaurants/wildwood_bbq* ⊟ *AE, D, DC, MC, V* Ⓜ *4, 5, 6, L, N, Q, R, W to 14th St./Union Sq.* ✛ *3:F3*

GRAMERCY PARK

$$$$ ✕ **BLT Prime.** A masculine, vivacious space is the showcase for Lau-
STEAKHOUSE rent Tourondel's third "BLT" restaurant featuring Franco-American cuisine. Menu specials are scrawled on a blackboard. Everything is served à la carte, and prices are high, but so is the quality of every dish. Tourondel has brought his signature steaming-hot Gruyère popovers downtown from BLT Steak. They're light and buttery with an addictive texture. Although there are poultry, veal, and lamb dishes on the menu, from lemon-rosemary chicken to a lamb T-bone, steaks are the main event. The dry-aged USDA prime steaks are broiled at 1,700°, some spread lightly with herb butter and offered with a choice of sauce (the béarnaise is perfection). ✉ *111 E. 22nd St., between Lexington and Park Aves., Gramercy Park* ☎ *212/995–8500* ⊕ *www.bltprime. com* ✍ *Reservations essential* ⊟ *AE, DC, MC, V* ⊘ *No lunch* Ⓜ *6, R, W to 23rd St.* ✛ *3:F3*

$$ ✕ **Blue Smoke.** Ever the pioneer, Danny Meyer led the way for barbe-
BARBECUE cue in Manhattan with a United Nations–like approach representing regional 'cue styles. The menu features Texas salt-and-pepper beef ribs, saucy Kansas City–style ribs, and tangy North Carolina pulled pork on brioche buns. If mac and cheese is a weakness, many insist there's none better than Blue Smoke's. Or for something lighter, start with deviled eggs and a blue cheese–topped iceberg wedge. After dinner, waddle downstairs to Jazz Standard, one of the best jazz clubs in New York. ✉ *116 E. 27th St., between Lexington and Park Aves., Gramercy Park* ☎ *212/447–7733* ⊕ *www.bluesmoke.com* ⊟ *AE, D, DC, MC, V* Ⓜ *6, R, W to 28th St.* ✛ *3:F2*

$$ ✗**Casa Mono.** Andy Nusser put in his time cooking Italian under Mario
SPANISH Batali at Babbo before an obsession with Spain landed him his own
acclaimed Iberian niche. The perennially cramped and crowded Casa
Mono sends its overflow to Bar Jamon, the annex wine-and-ham bar
next door. Pick at plates of *jamon* serrano while awaiting the call
for a prime seat at the counter overlooking the chef's open kitchen.
Though everything is delectably shareable, of particular note are all
things seared *à la plancha* (on the hot top), including blistered peppers
and garlic-kissed mushrooms. Like his renowned mentor, Nusser has a
weakness for the most neglected cuts of meat. Check your food fears at
the door and order up the blood sausage, cockscombs, and tripe. ✉*52
Irving Pl., at E. 17th St.,Gramercy Park* ☎*212/253–2773* ⊕*www.
casamononyc.com* ▭*AE, DC, MC, V* Ⓜ*4, 5, 6, L, N, Q, R, W to
Union Sq.* ✛*3:G3*

$$$ ✗**Irving Mill.** This seasonal American hot spot, run by former Gramercy
AMERICAN Tavern chef John Schaefer, is shaping up to be one of the city's hottest
restaurants. The large dining room has a homey feel, with beige accents
and traditional wood walls. The waitstaff is eager to please with warm,
unobtrusive service. The menu isn't huge, but the choices incorporate
the freshest produce and meat. The winter selection includes celery-
root chowder and baby beet salad as starters, and braised rabbit and
roasted arctic char as mains. If you can't snag a reservation in the main
dining room, try the Front Tap Room, which accepts walk-ins. ✉ *116
E/ 16th St., between Union Square E and Irving Pl., Gramercy Park*
☎*212/254–1600* ⊕ *www.irvingmill.com* ▭ *AE, D, DC, MC, V* Ⓜ*4,
5, 6, L, N, Q, R, W to 14th St./Union Sq.* ✛*3:F4*

MURRAY HILL

$$ ✗**Artisanal.** This spacious brasserie is a beloved shrine to cheese, the
BRASSERIE passion of chef-owner Terrance Brennan. Gastronomes flock here for
the more than 150 cheeses—available for on-site sampling or retail
sale—then stay to enjoy their selections with one of 160 wines by the
glass. Hot *fromage*-imbued fare also is satisfying, with preparations like
addictive gougères, onion soup gratiné, and several types of fondue. For
curd-adverse customers, chicken paillard, steak-frites, or selections from
the raw bar should satisfy. ✉*2 Park Ave., at E. 32nd St., Murray Hill*
☎*212/725–8585* ⊕*www.artisanalbistro.com* ◿*Reservations essential*
▭*AE, D, DC, MC, V* Ⓜ*6 to 33rd St.* ✛*3:F1*

$ ✗**Gahm Mi Oak.** The deconstructed industrial design, inexpensive
KOREAN 24-hour menu, and late-night hours attract a young and stylish crowd
here. Every item on the limited menu goes well with *soju*, a Korean
spirit, or beer. There are even photos on the menu to help bleary-eyed
revelers order. Korean-style fried mung bean pancakes with scallions,
onions, carrots, and ground pork make for addictive stomach-lining
fare. The kimchi is renowned, as is the *sul long tang*, a milky ox-
bone soup with thin slices of beef, rice, and noodles that is reputed
to be an effective hangover cure. ✉*43 W. 32nd St., between 5th Ave.
and Broadway, Murray Hill* ☎*212/695–4113* ◿*Reservations not
accepted* ▭*AE, D, DC, MC, V* Ⓜ*B, D, F, N, Q, R, V, W to 34th St./
Herald Sq.* ✛*3:E1*

18

$$ ✕**Les Halles.** This local hangout, owned by Philippe Lajaunie since 1990,

BRASSERIE

Multiple

Locations

is boisterous and unpretentious—just like a true French brasserie. A good bet is steak-frites—with fries regarded by some as the best in New York. Other prime choices include crispy duck-leg confit with frisée salad, blood sausage with caramelized apples, and steak tartare, prepared table-side. ⊠*411 Park Ave. S, between E. 28th and E. 29th Sts., Murray Hill* ☏*212/679–4111* ⊕*www.leshalles.net* ⌲*Reservations essential* ⊟*AE, DC, MC, V* Ⓜ*6 to 33rd St.* ✛*3:F1* ⊠*15 John St., between Broadway and Nassau St.* ☏*212/285–8585* Ⓜ*A, C to Broadway/Nassau St.; 4, 5, J, M, Z to Fulton St.* ✛*1:D3*

$ ✕**Turkish Kitchen.** This striking multilevel room with crimson walls,

TURKISH

chairs with red skirted slipcovers, and colorful kilims is Manhattan's busiest and best Turkish restaurant. For appetizers, choose from the likes of velvety char-grilled eggplant or tender octopus salad, creamy hummus, or poached beef dumplings. The luscious stuffed cabbage is downright irresistible. The restaurant also hosts one of the most alluring Sunday brunch buffets in town, featuring 90 items, Turkish and American—all house-made, including a dozen breads. ⊠*386 3rd Ave., between E. 27th and E. 28th Sts., Murray Hill* ☏*212/679–6633* ⊕*www.turkishkitchen.com* ⊟*AE, D, DC, MC, V* ⊘*No lunch Sat.* Ⓜ*6 to 28th St.* ✛*3:G2*

UNION SQUARE

$$$ ✕**Craft.** Dining here is like a choose-your-own-adventure game in the

NEW AMERICAN

pantry of the gods. Every delectable dish comes à la carte, including sides for your roasted guinea hen or braised monkfish. Craft is Tom Colicchio's flagship in a mini-empire of excellent restaurants around the country, including the upscale Craftbar and Craftsteak brands, as well as grab-and-go sandwich bars called 'wichcraft.Just about everything here is exceptionally prepared with little fuss, from simple yet intriguing starters (grilled French sardines) and sides (sautéed sugar-snap peas) to desserts (lemon steamed pudding with rhubarb jelly and vanilla ice cream). The serene dining room features burnished dark wood, custom tables, a curved leather wall, and a succession of dangling radiant bulbs. ⊠*43 E. 19th St., between Broadway and Park Ave. S, Union Square* ☏*212/780–0880* ⊕*www.craftrestaurant.com* ⌲*Reservations essential* ⊟*AE, D, DC, MC, V* ⊘*No lunch* Ⓜ*L, N, Q, R, W, 4, 5, 6 to 14th St.-Union Sq.* ✛*3:F3*

¢ ✕**Republic.** Epicureans on a budget flock to this Asian noodle emporium

ASIAN

that looks like a cross between a downtown art gallery and a Japanese school cafeteria. The young waitstaff dressed in black T-shirts and jeans hold remote-control ordering devices to accelerate the already speedy service. Sit at the long, bluestone bar or at the picnic-style tables and order appetizers such as smoky grilled eggplant and luscious fried wontons. Entrées are all based on noodles or rice. Spicy coconut chicken soup and Vietnamese-style barbecued pork are particularly delicious. ⊠*37 Union Sq. W, between E. 16th and E. 17th Sts., Union Square* ☏*212/627–7172* ⊕ *www.thinknoodles.com* ⌲*Reservations not accepted* ⊟*AE, D, MC, V* Ⓜ*L, N, Q, R, W, 4, 5, 6 to 14th St./Union Sq.* ✛*3:F4*

$$$
NEW AMERICAN

✕**Tocqueville.** Hidden just steps from busy Union Square, Tocqueville is a refined dining oasis that's a secret even to many New York foodies. Guests enter through an austere reception area that gives no indication of the luxury appointments inside. Pushing past heavy curtains and a six-seat bar, the dining area is an intimate, modern room lined with warm gold- and sand-toned fabrics. Chef-owner Marco Moreira's signature starter is the unctuous sea urchin and angel hair carbonara. Main courses are steeped in French tradition, but with international flavors, like pan-roasted turbot with mushroom fondue and kohlrabi- and sea bean-confit, and lemon verbena–scented tofu with lily-bulb puree. The three-course, $24 prix-fixe lunch is a steal. ✉ *1 E. 15th St., between 5th Ave. and Union Sq. W, Union Square* ☎ *212/647–1515* ⊕ *www.tocquevillerestaurant.com* ⌕ *Reservations essential* ▭ *AE, MC, V* Ⓜ *L, N, Q, R, W, 4, 5, 6 to 14th St./Union Sq.* ✛ *3:F4*

$$$
AMERICAN

✕**Union Square Cafe.** When he opened Union Square Cafe in 1985, Danny Meyer changed the American restaurant landscape. The combination of upscale food and unpretentious but focused service sparked a revolution. Today chef Carmen Quagliata still draws devotees with his crowd-pleasing menu. Wood paneling and white walls are hung with splashy modern paintings; in addition to the three dining areas, there's a long bar ideal for solo diners. The cuisine is American with a thick Italian accent: for example, the grilled, marinated filet mignon of tuna can land on the same table as creamy polenta with mascarpone. ✉ *21 E. 16th St., between 5th Ave. and Union Sq. W, Union Square* ☎ *212/243–4020* ⊕ *www.unionsquarecafe.com* ⌕ *Reservations essential* ▭ *AE, D, DC, MC, V* Ⓜ *L, N, Q, R, W, 4, 5, 6 to 14th St./Union Sq.* ✛ *3:F4*

18

MIDTOWN WEST AND CHELSEA

CHELSEA

$$$
ASIAN

✕**Buddakan.** Few—if any—restaurants in Manhattan can rival the 16,000-square-foot Buddakan in terms of sheer magnitude and buoyant theatricality. Restaurateur Steven Starr created a New York edition of his Philadelphia original. The feeling of the vast downstairs space is like a dining hall in a medieval castle. Highly pedigreed chef Lon Symensma has cooked at Spice Market in New York City. His toothsome tuna spring rolls are narrow flutes of ruby tuna tartare in a crisp contrapuntal fried shell. Crisp-tender sizzling short ribs are served with tender wide noodles and highly comforting results. "Crying Chocolate" is a warm white-chocolate ganache finished with coffee ice cream and milk. Truly a transporting experience. ✉ *75 9th Ave., between 15th and 16th Sts.,Chelsea* ☎ *212/989–6699* ⊕ *www.buddakannyc.com* ⌕ *Reservations essential* ▭ *AE, D, MC, V* ⊘ *No lunch* Ⓜ *A, C, E to 14th St.; L to 8th Ave.* ✛ *3:B4*

$
BARBECUE

✕**R.U.B. BBQ.** Among the American barbecue capitals, Kansas City's smoked fare stands out as perhaps the most versatile, characterized by dry rubs with sauces strictly on the side. Executive chef Paul Kirk is from Kansas City, and is a legend on the growing New York City barbecue competition circuit. This is not a restaurant for the timid of appetite. Platters are so bountiful that even the side dishes come in overwhelming quantities. The shameless menu promises everything from beef, pork, ham, pastrami, and turkey to chicken, sausage, and of course ribs. Burned ends— delicious charred-crisp, rich edges of beef brisket—are legendary, and they sell out every night. In fact, many items on the menu sell out by 8 PM, so it's wise to arrive fairly early. ✉ *208 W. 23rd St., between 7th and 8th Aves., Chelsea* ☎*212/524–4300* ⊕ *www.rubbbq. net* ☆*Reservations not accepted* ▭*AE, DC, MC, V* Ⓜ*1, C, E, F, V to 23rd St.* ✛*3:D2*

$$ ╳**Tía Pol.** This tiny, dark, out-of-the-way, but highly popular tapas bar is
SPANISH usually packed, but there are good reasons for that: it's the best in town.
Fodor's Choice The tables and stools are small and high, but the flavors are enormous.
★ One highly original tapa that everyone was talking about is a signature here: bittersweet chocolate smeared on a baguette disc and topped with salty Spanish chorizo. Rough-cut potatoes are deep-fried and served with a dollop of spicy aioli. You won't want to share them. The pork loin, piquillo pepper, and mild tetilla cheese sandwich is scrumptious, and so is the Galician octopus terrine. In fact, everything on the menu is transporting and delicious. ✉*205 10th Ave. between 22nd and 23rd Sts., Chelsea* ☎*212/675–8805* ⊕*www.tiapol.com* ☆*Reservations essential for groups of 6-8* ▭*AE, D, MC, V* ☾*No lunch Mon.* Ⓜ*C, E to 23rd St.* ✛*3:A2*

MIDTOWN WEST

$$$ ╳**Abboccato.** Making an attempt to convey the vast regional styles of
ITALIAN Italian cooking, Abboccato is an ambitious restaurant in a cozy space adjacent to the Blakely Hotel. The name, which means "pleasing to the mouth," lives up to that assertion with rich dishes like braised veal cheeks with Belgian endive and white polenta. Another favorite is spaghettini with razor clams, toasted bread crumbs, and orange zest. ✉*136 W. 55th St., between 6th and 7th Aves., Midtown West* ☎*212/265–4000* ⊕*www.abboccato.com* ☆*Reservations essential* ▭*AE, DC, MC, V* Ⓜ*N, R to 57th St.* ✛*4:C2*

$$$ ╳**Bar Americain.** Chef Bobby Flay's largest Manhattan restaurant is the
BRASSERIE soaring Bar Americain. The 200-seat two-story space looks like a dining room on a luxury liner. Southern-inflected brasserie fare includes Dungeness crab griddle cakes, smoked chicken with hatch-green chili spoon bread and black-pepper vinegar sauce, and roasted duck breast surrounded by dirty wild rice with bourbon-soaked pecans. Slightly naughtier are the éclairs piped with whiskey-infused pastry cream and burnished with a burnt-sugar glaze. Prices are fairly high, but you get what you pay for. ✉*152 W. 52nd St. between 6th and 7th Aves., Midtown West* ☎*212/265–9700* ⊕ *www.baramericain.com* ☆*Reservations essential* ▭*AE, D, DC, MC, V* Ⓜ*B, D, E to 7th Ave.; 1, C, E to 50th St.; N, R, W to 49th St.* ✛*4:C2*

$$$ ╳**Becco.** An ingenious concept makes Becco a prime Restaurant
ITALIAN Row choice for time-constrained theatergoers. There are two pricing

scenarios: one includes an all-you-can-eat selection of antipasti and three pastas served hot out of pans that waiters circulate around the dining room; the other adds a generous entrée to the mix. The pasta selection changes daily but often includes gnocchi, fresh ravioli, and fettuccine in a cream sauce. The entrées include braised veal shank, grilled double-cut pork chop, and rack of lamb, among other selections. ⊠*355 W. 46th St., between 8th and 9th Aves., Midtown West* ☎*212/397–7597* ⊕*www.becco-nyc.com* ⩘*Reservations essential* ⊟*AE, D, DC, MC, V* Ⓜ*A, C, E to 42nd St.* ✛*4:B3*

$$$$
STEAKHOUSE

✕**Ben Benson's Steakhouse.** Among the most venerable steak houses around, Ben Benson's feels like a clubby hunting lodge. The gracefully choreographed, intensely focused staff will bring you only the finest dry-aged prime meats and only the freshest seafood, all classically prepared, teeming with familiar and beloved flavors. The trimmings are ravishing, too: comforting creamed spinach, sizzling onion rings, and decadent hash browns are essential. Power lunches were practically invented here; just being in the place makes you feel important. ⊠*123 W. 52nd St., between 6th and 7th Aves., Midtown West* ☎*212/581–8888* ⊕*www.benbensons.com* ⩘*Reservations essential* ⊟*AE, D, DC, MC, V* ⊘*No lunch weekends* Ⓜ*B, D, E to 7th Ave.; 1 to 50th St.; N, R, W to 49th St.* ✛*4:D2*

$$$
BRASSERIE

✕**Brasserie Ruhlmann.** In a plush 120-seat dining room with just enough art-deco touches to harmonize with its Rockefeller Center setting, the sublime French cookery of Laurent Tourondel is on display. There is a decorous countenance to the room, but the staff is so friendly that the place could never be stuffy. Nineteen excellent French wines are available by the glass. Perfect oysters Rockefeller must be on the menu, naturally, and the oysters and cooked spinach are napped with béchamel just before roasting with results soothing and rich enough to comprise a lunch entrée. If it's on the menu, order braised rabbit nestled in mustard cream on a bed of fresh pappardelle, sprinkled with pitted cherries. Desserts like Floating Island—delicately baked meringue floating on a pond of crème anglaise—are embellished by a tangled flurry of spun sugar. ⊠*45 Rockefeller Plaza, 50th St. between 5th and 6th Aves., Midtown West* ☎*212/974–2020* ⊕*www.brasserieruhlmann. com* ⩘*Reservations essential* ⊟*AE, MC, V.* Ⓜ*B, D, F, V to 47th–50th Sts./Rockefeller Center* ✛*4:D3*

¢
BURGER
Fodor's Choice
★

✕**Burger Joint.** What's a college burger bar, done up in particleboard and rec-room decor, doing hidden inside of a five-star Midtown hotel? This tongue-in-cheek lunch spot buried in the Parker Meridien does such boisterous midweek business that lines often snake through the lobby. Stepping behind the beige curtain you can find baseball cap–wearing grease-spattered cooks dispensing paper-wrapped cheeseburgers and crisp thin fries. Forget Kobe beef or foie gras—these burgers are straightforward, cheap, and delicious. ⊠*118 W. 57th St., between 6th and 7th Aves., Midtown West* ☎*212/245–5000* ⊕*www.parkermeridien.com* ⊟*No credit cards* Ⓜ*F, N, Q, R, W to 57th St.* ✛*4:D1*

$$$$
BRAZILIAN

✕**Churrascaria Plataforma.** This sprawling, boisterous shrine to meat, with its all-you-can-eat prix-fixe menu, is best experienced with a group of ravenous friends. A *caipirinha*, featuring sugarcane liquor, sugar, and

18

lime, will kick things off nicely. Follow up with a trip to the salad bar piled with vegetables, meats, and cheeses. But restrain yourself—there's a parade of all manner of grilled meats and poultry, from pork ribs to chicken hearts, delivered to the table on long skewers until you beg for mercy. ✉ *316 W. 49th St., between 8th and 9th Aves., Midtown West* ☎ *212/245–0505* ⊕ *www.churrascariaplataforma.com* ⌖ *Reservations essential* ▭ *AE, D, DC, MC, V* Ⓜ *C, E to 50th St.* ✛ *4:B3*

$$$ ✗ **DB Bistro Moderne.** Daniel Boulud's "casual bistro" (it's neither, actual-
FRENCH   ly) consists of two elegantly appointed dining rooms. The menu is orga-
nized by the French names of seasonal ingredients—lobster (*homard*), tuna (*thon*), and mushroom (*champignon*), for example. Within each category, appetizers and main courses are listed. There was quite a fuss made over the $32 hamburger, available at lunch and dinner. But considering it's gloriously stuffed with braised short ribs, foie gras, and black truffles, it's almost a bargain. Almost. ✉ *55 W. 44th St., between 5th and 6th Aves., Midtown West* ☎ *212/391–2400* ⊕ *www. danielnyc.com/dbbistro* ⌖ *Reservations essential* ▭ *AE, DC, MC, V* ⊗ *No lunch Sun.* Ⓜ *B, D, F, V to 42nd St./Bryant Park; 7 to 5th Ave./ Bryant Park* ✛ *4:D4*

$$$ ✗ **Esca.** Mario Batali's Esca, Italian for "bait," lures diners in with
SEAFOOD   delectable raw preparations called *crudo*—such as tilefish with orange and Sardinian oil or pink snapper with a sprinkle of crunchy red clay salt—and hooks them with such entrées as whole, salt-crusted *branzino*, sea bass for two, or *bucatini* pasta with spicy baby octopus. The menu changes daily. If you're a low-sodium diner, you should probably cast your net elsewhere. Batali's partner, Joe Bastianich, is in charge of the wine cellar, so expect an adventurous list of Italian bottles. ✉ *402 W. 43rd St., at 9th Ave.,Midtown West* ☎ *212/564–7272* ⊕ *www. esca-nyc.com* ⌖ *Reservations essential* ▭ *AE, DC, MC, V* ⊗ *No lunch Sun.* Ⓜ *A, C, E to 42nd St.* ✛ *4:A4*

$$–$$$$ ✗ **Gordon Ramsay at The London and Maze.** With more than a dozen res-
FRENCH   taurants around the world—and an ever-busy TV schedule—you're not likely to find British chef Gordon Ramsay at his eponymous Mid-town restaurant. What you will find, however, are Ramsay's trembling acolytes producing flawless facsimiles of his classically muted haute cuisine. The flagship fine-dining restaurant is an exorbitant time com-mitment, with menus that start at $110 for three courses. It is hidden behind opaque glass doors just beyond the comparatively casual, and much more reasonably priced, Maze. The lower-key annex, in a silver-gray dining room, specializes in elegant small-plate cuisine (often very small). Although dinner is a mix-and-match affair, the $45 prix-fixe three-course lunch is one of the top bargains in Midtown. ✉ *151 W. 54th St. between 6th and 7th Aves., Midtown West* ☎ *212/468–8888* ⊕ *www.thelondonnyc.com/gordon_ramsay.com* ▭ *AE, D, DC, MC, V* ⊗ *No lunch Sat.–Wed.* Ⓜ *B, D, E to 7th Ave.; N, Q, R, W to 57th St.* ✛ *4:D2*

$$$$ ✗ **Le Bernardin.** Owner Maguy LeCoze presides over the teak-panel din-
FRENCH   ing room at this trendsetting French seafood restaurant, and chef-partner Eric Ripert works magic with anything that swims—preferring at times not to cook it at all. Deceptively simple dishes such as poached lobster

in rich coconut-ginger soup or crispy spiced black bass in a Peking duck bouillon are typical of his style. It is widely agreed that there's no beating Le Bernardin for thrilling cuisine, seafood or otherwise, coupled with some of the finest desserts in town. ⊠*155 W. 51st St., between 6th and 7th Aves., Midtown West* ☎*212/554–1515* ⊕*www. le-bernardin.com* △*Reservations essential, jacket required* ▭*AE, DC, MC, V* ⊙*Closed Sun. No lunch Sat.* Ⓜ*1 to 50th St.; R, W to 49th St.; B, D, F, V to 47th–50th Sts./Rockefeller Center.* ✛*4:C2*

$$
MEDITERRANEAN

✕**Marseille.** With great food and a convenient location near several Broadway theaters, Marseille is perpetually packed. Executive Chef and partner Andy d'Amico's Mediterranean creations are continually impressive. The daube is classic: a hunk of beef is slowly braised into submission in red wine, then plated on a crispy square of fried polenta with diced sautéed root vegetables. Leave room for the spongy beignets with chocolate and raspberry dipping sauces. ⊠*630 9th Ave., at W. 44th St., Midtown West* ☎*212/333–2323* ⊕*www.marseillenyc. com* △*Reservations essential* ▭*AE, MC, V* Ⓜ*A, C, E to 42nd St./ Port Authority Bus Terminal.* ✛*4:B4*

$
ETHIOPIAN

✕**Meskerem.** The tasty Ethiopian delicacies offered in this Hell's Kitchen storefront include *kitfo,* spiced ground steak, which you can order raw, rare, or well done, and *yebeg alecha,* tender pieces of lamb marinated in Ethiopian butter flavored with curry, rosemary, and an herb called *kosart,* and then sautéed with fresh ginger and more curry. The vegetarian combination, served on injera, a yeasty and slightly porous flat bread used as a utensil to sop up the food, is a great deal. ⊠*468 W. 47th St., near 10th Ave.,Midtown West* ☎*212/664–0520* ▭*AE, D, DC, MC, V* Ⓜ*C, E to 50th St.* ✛*4:A3*

$$$–$$$$
FRENCH

✕**The Modern and Bar Room.** Both spots competing for the title of the country's best museum restaurant sit side by side on the ground floor of the New York MoMA. The Modern, run by restaurateur Danny Meyer, is two restaurants in one. Both offer the dazzling food of Alsatian chef Gabriel Kreuther. The formal dining room features a view of the museum's sculpture garden and an ambitious, pricey, prix-fixe menu. The far more accessible and popular Bar Room lies just beyond a partition. Here you can find a dizzying collection of shareable plates like the refreshing arctic char tartare and oysters with leeks and caviar. Two or three make a fine if extravagant afternoon snack—double that number and you have a full meal. ⊠*9 W. 53rd St., between 5th and 6th Aves., Midtown West* ☎*212/333–1220* ⊕*www.themodernnyc.com* ▭*AE, D, DC, MC, V* ⊙*Closed Sun.* Ⓜ*E, V to 5th Ave./53rd St.* ✛*4:D2*

$$
PIZZA
Multiple
Locations
↺

✕**Serafina.** Mediterranean-hue friezes, a most inviting upstairs terrace, and a steady stream of models and celebrities grace this very Italian café. Scene aside, the real draw here is some authentic Neopolitan pizza—they even filter the water for the pizza dough to make it more closely resemble the water in Naples. Beyond the designer pizzas (Nutella, mascarpone, and robiola cheese; mozzarella, smoked salmon, and dill) are antipasti, salads, pastas including a number of ravioli dishes, and second courses like bass fillet pinot grigio. ⊠*210 W. 55th St. at Broadway, Midtown West* ☎*212/315–1700* Ⓜ*N, Q, R, W to 57th St.–7th Ave.* ✛*4:C2* ⊠*29 E. 61st St., between Madison and*

18

Park Aves. ☎*212/702–9898* Ⓜ*N, R, W, 4, 5, 6 to 59th St.–Lexington Ave.* ✦*5:F6* ✉*1022 Madison Ave., at E. 79th St.* ☎*212/734–2676* ⊕*www.serafinarestaurant.com* ⊟*AE, DC, MC, V* Ⓜ*6 to 77th St.* ✦*5:F2* ✉*38 E. 58th St. near Madison Ave.* ☎*212/832–8888* Ⓜ*N, R, W to 5th Ave.* ✦*5:F6* ✉*393 Lafayette St., at 4th St.* ☎*212/995–9595* Ⓜ*6 to Astor Pl.* ✦*2:E2*

$$ ╳**Sosa Borella.** This is one of the Theater District's top spots for reli-
ITALIAN   able food at a reasonable cost. This bi-level, casual Italian eatery is an inviting and friendly space where diners choose from a wide range of options. The lunch menu features staples like warm sandwiches and entrée-size salads, while the dinner menu is slightly gussied up with meat, fish, and pasta dishes (the rich agnolotti with lamb Bolognese sauce, topped with a wedge of grilled pecorino cheese is a must-try). The warm bread served at the beginning of the meal with pesto dipping sauce is a nice touch as you wait for your meal. The service, at times, can be slow, so leave yourself plenty of time before the show. ✉ *832 8th Ave., between 50th and 51st Sts.,Midtown West* ☎*212/262–8282* ⊕*www. sosaborella.com* ⊟*AE, MC, V* Ⓜ *C, E, 1 to 50th St.* ✦*4:B3*

$$ ╳**Toloache.** Make a quick detour off heavily trafficked Broadway into
MEXICAN   this pleasantly bustling Mexican cantina that's one of the best dining options around Times Square. The bi-level eatery has a festive, celebra-tory vibe, with several seating options (bar, balcony, main dining room, and ceviche bar), oversize bronze chandeliers, and gold and terra-cotta tones throughout. Foodies flock here for the Mexico City–style tacos with Negro Modelo–braised brisket, quesadillas studded with black truffle and *huitlacoche* (a corn fungus), and the extensive tequila selec-tion—upwards of 100 brands. Adventurous palates will be drawn to tacos featuring chili-studded dried grasshoppers, lobes of seared foie gras, and caramelized veal sweetbreads. ✉ *251 W. 50th St., near 8th Ave., Midtown West* ☎ *212/581–1818* ⊕*www.toloachenyc.com* ⊟ *AE, D, MC, V* Ⓜ*1, C, E to 50th St.; N, R, W to 49th St.* ✦*4:B3*

$$$$ ╳**′21′ Club.** It's undeniably exciting to hobnob with celebrities at this
AMERICAN   town-house landmark, a former speakeasy that opened in 1929. Chef John Greeley tries to satisfy everyone with standards like the famous '21' burger and '21' Caesar salad, and sophisticated modern dishes, such as risotto of squab and wild mushrooms with butternut squash, Parmesan foam, and black truffles. Service is seamless. And yes, fellas, a jacket is required, but thanks to a new more relaxed dress code you can leave your tie at home. ✉*21 W. 52nd St., between 5th and 6th Aves., Midtown West* ☎*212/582–7200* ⊕*www.21club.com* ⌂*Jacket required* ⊟*AE, D, DC, MC, V* ◷*Closed Sun. No lunch Sat.* Ⓜ*E, V to 53rd St./5th Ave.; B, D, F, V to 47th–50th Sts./Rockefeller Center.* ✦*4:D2*

$$$$ ╳**Uncle Jack's Steakhouse.** Surpassing even its celebrated flagship restau-
STEAKHOUSE   rant in Bayside, Queens, Uncle Jack's soars directly into the pantheon of the best steak houses in Manhattan. As in most great steak houses, you can feel the testosterone throbbing all through the place. The space is vast and gorgeously appointed, and service is swift and focused. USDA Prime steaks are dry-aged for 21 days. Australian lobster tails are so enormous they have to be served carved, yet the flesh is meltingly

tender. ✉*440 9th Ave., between W. 34th and W. 35th Sts., Midtown West* ☎*212/244–0005* ⊕*www.unclejacks.com* ✍*Reservations essential* ▭*AE, MC, V* ⊘*No lunch weekends* Ⓜ*A, C, E to 34th St./Penn Station* ✛*4:B6*

$$ ✗**Virgil's Real BBQ.** Neon, wood, and Formica set the scene at this
BARBECUE   massive roadhouse in the Theater District. Start with stuffed jalape-
☺   ños or—especially—unbelievably succulent barbecued chicken wings. Then, what the hell: go for the "Pig Out"—a rack of pork ribs, Texas hot links, pulled pork, rack of lamb, chicken, and, of course, more. It's that kind of place. There are also five domestic microbrews on tap and a good list of top beers from around the world. The place is absolutely mobbed pretheater, so if that's when you're going, arrive by 6 PM or you'll miss your curtain. ✉*152 W. 44th St., between 6th Ave. and Broadway, Midtown West* ☎*212/921–9494* ⊕*www.virgilsbbq.com* ✍*Reservations essential* ▭*AE, MC, V* Ⓜ*N, Q, R, W, S, 1, 2, 3, 7 to 42nd St./Times Sq.* ✛*4:C4*

MIDTOWN EAST AND UPPER EAST SIDE

MIDTOWN EAST

$$$$ ✗**Adour Alain Ducasse.** Master chef Alain Ducasse adds to his grow-
MODERN FRENCH   ing empire with the upscale and elegant Adour, located in the equally
Fodor'sChoice   sophisticated St. Regis Hotel. Celebratory couples of all ages gravitate
★   to the Left and Right Bank rooms, while a mix of tourists, shoppers, and businessmen settle on plush burgundy chairs and banquettes in the regal but relaxed main dining room. Beautifully baked baguettes and fragrant olive and sourdough rolls are flown in from Paris. Deep pockets splurge on artfully arranged dishes, such as foie gras ravioli with black truffles, and lobster Thermidor. Sommeliers help decipher an international wine list (displayed on interactive computer screens at the bar) with bottles that range from $35 to $19,000. ✉*2 E. 55th St., near 5th Ave., Midtown East* ☎*212/710–2277* ⊕*www.adour-stregis. com* ✍*Reservations essential* ▭*AE, D, DC, MC, V* ⊘*No lunch* Ⓜ*E, V to 5th Ave./53rd St.; F to 57th St.* ✛*4:E2*

$$$$ ✗**Aquavit and Aquavit Café.** Celebrity chef Marcus Samuelsson may not
SCANDINAVIAN   be in the kitchen every night, but you'd never know it from the impec-
cable cuisine and service at this fine-dining restaurant and upscale café. The elegant atmosphere features warm woods and modern decor from a Scandinavian design team. In the café, try a two-course dinner of daily "Swedish home cooking" specials, or order à la carte to try the herring sampler, with boldly flavored selections like curry and apple, and vodka-lime. Hot-smoked salmon, served with celeriac purée, asparagus salad, and apple-horseradish broth, is a standout. The main dining room is prix-fixe only, with a three-course dinner for $82. ✉*65 E. 55th St., between Madison and Park Aves., Midtown East* ☎*212/307–7311* ⊕*www.aquavit.org* ✍*Reservations essential* ▭*AE, DC, MC, V* ⊘*No lunch Sat., except in café* Ⓜ*E, V to 5th Ave./53rd St.* ✛*4:F2*

$$$ ✗**BLT Steak.** Chef Laurent Tourondel sets a new steak-house standard
STEAKHOUSE   in this classy space decked out in beige and suede and resin-topped black tables. The no-muss, no-fuss menu is nonetheless large, and so

18

are the portions of supple crab cakes with celery-infused mayonnaise and luscious ruby tuna tartare with avocado, ramped up with soy-lime dressing. As soon as you're settled, puffy Parmesan popovers arrive still steaming. A veal chop is crusted with rosemary and Parmesan, which imbue the veal with more flavor than veal ever has. At lunch the quintessential BLT includes Kobe beef, foie gras, bacon, and tomato in a split ciabatta. Sides and desserts are all superior. ⊠*106 E. 57th St., between Lexington and Park Aves., Midtown East* ☎*212/752–7470* ⊕*www.bltsteak.com* ✍*Reservations essential* ▭*AE, DC, MC, V* ☾*Closed Sun. No lunch Sat.* Ⓜ*4, 5, 6, N, R, W to 59th St./Lexington Ave.* ✛*4:F1*

$$
ITALIAN

✕**Convivio.** Formerly L'Impero, this renamed but still trendy restaurant has a bold new menu under the helm of chef Michael White. The orange-and-white room has 110 seats, all filled with locals and tourists who come for the chic ambience, polished service, and even better food. Tasty *sfizi*, or nibbles—such as baby eggplant with basil, vinegar, and chili—foreshadow well-prepared basics such as buffalo mozzarella with tomatoes and grilled lamb chops with white beans and escarole. Eclectic and flavorsome offerings like grilled quail skewers and suckling pig are also available. The spot has several outdoor tables for alfresco dining and a spacious bar area to drink from the all-Italian beer list, or from the 550-bottle wine list with many Sicilian selections. ⊠*45 Tudor City Pl., between 42nd and 43rd Sts.,Midtown East* ☎*212/599–5045* ⊕*www.convivionyc.com* ▭*AE, D, DC, MC, V* ☾*Closed Sun. No lunch Sat.* Ⓜ*4, 5, 6, 7, S to Grand Central* ✛*4:H4*

$$$$
AMERICAN

✕**Four Seasons.** The landmark Seagram Building houses one of America's most famous restaurants, truly an only–in–New York experience. The stark Grill Room, birthplace of the power lunch, has one of the best bars in New York. Illuminated trees and a gurgling Carrara marble pool characterize the more romantic Pool Room. The menu changes seasonally; there's a $65 prix-fixe pretheater dinner—a delicious indulgence. You can't go wrong with classic dishes like Dover sole, filet mignon, or crispy duck. Finish with pear William, Grand Marnier, or chocolate soufflé. ⊠*99 E. 52nd St., between Park and Lexington Aves., Midtown East* ☎*212/754–9494* ⊕*www.fourseasonsrestaurant.com* ✍*Reservations essential, jacket required* ▭*AE, D, DC, MC, V* ☾*Closed Sun. No lunch Sat.* Ⓜ*E, V to Lexington Ave./53rd St.; 6 to 51st St.* ✛*4:F2*

$$$$
JAPANESE

✕**Kuruma Zushi.** Only a small sign in Japanese indicates the location of this extraordinary restaurant that serves only sushi and sashimi. Bypass the tables, sit at the sushi bar, and put yourself in the hands of Toshihiro Uezu, the chef-owner. Among the selections are hard-to-find fish that Uezu imports directly from Japan. The most attentive, pampering service staff in the city completes the wildly expensive experience. ⊠ *7 E. 47th St., 2nd fl., between 5th and Madison Aves., Midtown East* ☎*212/317–2802* ✍*Reservations essential* ▭*AE, MC, V* ☾*Closed Sun.* Ⓜ*4, 5, 6, 7 to 42nd St./Grand Central.* ✛*4:E3*

$$$$
FRENCH
Fodor's Choice
★

✕**L'Atelier de Joël Robuchon.** The New York branch of Joël Robuchon's superluxurious tapas bar, inside the Four Seasons Hotel, features essentially the same food (with a more natural-hue decor) as the Paris original. And that, it turns out, is a very good thing. The perfectionist chef installed a longtime Japanese protégé to uphold the standards that can make a Robuchon meal a life-changing experience. Skip the regular-size appetizers and entrées. Instead, secure a seat at the pear-wood counter and cobble together your own small-plate feast. But be warned; with heady ingredients like Scottish langoustines (tempura fried), steak tartare (with hand-cut french fries) and foie gras (paired with caramelized eel), Robuchon's little bites come at a steep price. ✉*57 E. 57th St., between Madison and Park Aves., Midtown East* ☎*212/350–6658* ⊕*www.fourseasons.com/newyorkfs/dining.html* ⌕*Reservations essential* ⊟*AE, MC, V* ◷*No lunch* Ⓜ*4, 5, 6 to 59th St.* ✛*4:F1*

$$$$
FRENCH

✕**Le Cirque.** Impresario-owner Sirio Maccioni still presides over a dining room filled nightly with a who's who of political, business, and society circles—regulars who've table-hopped from Le Cirque's first incarnation to its latest, in a glass-enclosed aerie on the ground floor of the Bloomberg headquarters. Billowing silk, tall gauzy shades, and porcelain monkeys in a display-case pillar create a playful big-top effect. The menu strikes a balance between the creative and classic. Dover sole, filleted table-side, gives way to more avant-garde preparations like a duo of seared foie gras and sushi-grade tuna. Desserts, too, have a split personality, with the menu divided into the "classic" and "new." The foot-tall napoleon that seems to arrive at every second table is an old favorite, but newer creations like the rich, peanut-butter "candy bar" also satisfy high-society sweet tooths. ✉*151 E. 58th St., at Lexington Ave., Midtown East* ☎*212/644–0202* ⊕*www.lecirque.com* ⌕*Reservations essential* ⊟*AE, D, DC, MC, V* ◷*Closed Sun. No lunch Sat.* Ⓜ*4, 5, 6, N, R, W to Lexington Ave./59th* St. ✛*4:F1*

$$
MEDITERRANEAN

✕**Mia Dona.** When Dona abruptly closed in 2007, disappointing thousands of fans, restaurateur Donatella Arpaia and chef Michael Psilakis vowed a comeback. This warm Italian joint with a distinctive menu proves they've returned in full force. The long and narrow space has three dining rooms: one with a zebra theme, another with a library theme, and a third with banquettes and exposed brick. The menu includes all the dishes one would expect in a typical Italian restaurant, but they're presented in Psilakis's unique style. Instead of standard buffalo mozzarella, for example, he serves up a Burrata, a version of the cheese so soft it melts in your mouth. Meat lovers shouldn't miss the crispy rabbit with salt and vinegar chips or the Florentine meat loaf. Pasta fans will enjoy comforting options like bucatini carbonara with smoked chicken legs and radicchio. The wine list is heavy on Italian varietals, but there are French and American vintages, too. ✉*206 E. 58th St., at 3rd Ave., Midtown East* ☎*212/750–8170* ⊕*www.mia dona.com* ⊟*AE, D, DC, MC, V* Ⓜ*4, 5, 6, N, R, W to Lexington Ave./59th St.* ✛*4:G1*

$$$
STEAKHOUSE

✕**Michael Jordan's The Steakhouse NYC.** Don't be dissuaded by the fact that this place is technically part of a chain: there's nowhere remotely like it. The handsomely appointed space in Grand Central Terminal overlooks one of the most famous interiors in America. Start with toasted bread and hot Gorgonzola fondue. Follow with pristine oysters, then lunge for a prime dry-aged rib eye or a 2½-pound lobster, grilled, steamed, sautéed, or broiled. Finish with the luscious 5-inch-tall chocolate cake.

18

✉*Grand Central Terminal, West Balcony, 23 Vanderbilt Ave., between E. 43rd and E. 44th Sts., Midtown East* ☎*212/655–2300* ⊕*www. theglaziergroup.com/restaurants/michaeljordan* ☙*Reservations essential* ▭*AE, D, DC, MC, V* Ⓜ*4, 5, 6, 7 to 42nd St./Grand Central.* ✛*4:F4*

$$ ✕**Mint.** With a delightful dining room splashed with bright colors and
INDIAN flattering lighting, and executive chef and owner Gary Sikka's brightly seasoned dishes, this newcomer has joined the ranks of the best Indian restaurants in town. The large menu includes rarely encountered specialties from Goa and Sikkim. Freshly grilled moist ground lamb kebabs deliver a slow burn to the palate. Chili heat punctuates other spices in the lamb vindaloo, resulting in a well-rounded array of savory flavors. Finish with carrot pudding with saffron and coconut flakes. ✉*150 E. 50th St., between Lexington and 3rd Aves., Midtown East* ☎*212/644–8888* ▭*AE, D, DC, MC, V* Ⓜ*6, E, V to 51st St./Lexington Ave.* ✛*4:G3*

$$$ ✕**Oyster Bar.** Nestled deep in the belly of Grand Central Station, the
SEAFOOD Oyster Bar has been a worthy seafood destination for over nine decades. Sit at the counter and slurp an assortment of bracingly fresh oysters, or a steaming bowl of clam chowder washed down with an ice-cold brew. Or experience the forgotten pleasure of fresh, unadorned seafood such as lobster with drawn butter or grilled herring in season. Avoid anything that sounds too complicated, like cream-smothered seafood pan roasts. ✉*Grand Central Station, dining concourse, E. 42nd St. at Vanderbilt Ave., Midtown East* ☎*212/490–6650* ⊕*www.oysterbarny. com* ☙*Reservations essential* ▭*AE, D, MC, V* ⊙*Closed Sun.* Ⓜ*4, 5, 6, 7, S to 42nd St./Grand Central.* ✛*4:F4*

$$$ ✕**Palm.** They may have added tablecloths, but it would take more than
STEAKHOUSE that to hide the brusque, no-nonsense nature of this West Side branch of
Multiple the legendary steak house. The steak is always impeccable, and the Nova
Locations Scotia lobsters are so big—4 pounds and up—there may not be room at the table for such classic side dishes as rich creamed spinach, served family-style for two or more. The "half-and-half" side combination of cottage-fried potatoes and fried onions is particularly addictive. ✉*837 2nd Ave.between 44th and 45th Sts.,Midtown East* ☎*212/687–2953* ⊕*www.thepalm.com* ☙*Reservations essential* ▭*AE, D, DC, MC, V* ⊙*Closed Sun. No lunch Sat.* Ⓜ*4, 5, 6, 7, S to Grand Central* ✛*4:G4* ✉*250 W. 50th St., between Broadway and 8th Ave.* ☎*212/333–7256* ⊕*www.thepalm.com* ☙*Reservations essential* ▭*AE, D, DC, MC, V* ⊙*No lunch Sun.* Ⓜ*F, N, Q, R, W to 57th St.* ✛*4:B3* ✉*840 2nd Ave. between 44th and 45th Sts.* ☎*212/697–5198* ⊕*www.thepalm.com* ☙*Reservations essential* ▭*AE, D, DC, MC, V* ⊙*No lunch weekends* Ⓜ*4, 5, 6, 7, S to Grand Central* ✛*4:G4* ✉*206 West St.at Chambers St.* ☎*646/395–6393* ⊕*www.thepalm.com* ☙*Reservations essential* ▭*AE, D, DC, MC, V* ⊙*No lunch weekends* Ⓜ*1, 2, 3 to Chambers St.* ✛*1:B2*

$$$ ✕**Shun Lee Palace.** If you want inexpensive Cantonese food without pre-
CHINESE tensions, head to Chinatown; but if you prefer to be pampered and don't mind spending a lot of money, this is the place. The cuisine is absolutely classic Chinese. Beijing panfried dumplings make a good starter, and

rack of lamb Szechuan style, grilled with scallions and garlic, is a popular entrée. Beijing duck is sure to please. ✉ *155 E. 55th St., between Lexington and 3rd Aves., Midtown East* ☎ *212/371–8844* ⊕ *www.shunlee palace.lanteck.net/index2.htm* ⚸ *Reservations essential* ☰ *AE, DC, MC, V* Ⓜ *N, R, W, 4, 5, 6 to 59th St./Lexington Ave.* ✛ *4:G2*

$$$$　✕ **Sparks Steakhouse.** Magnums of wines that cost more than most
STEAKHOUSE　people earn in a week festoon the large dining rooms of this classic New York steak house. Although seafood is given more than fair play on the menu, Sparks is really about dry-aged steak. The extra-thick lamb and veal chops are also noteworthy. Classic sides of hash browns, creamed spinach, sautéed mushrooms, and grilled onions are all you need to complete the experience. ✉ *210 E. 46th St., between 2nd and 3rd Aves., Midtown East* ☎ *212/687–4855* ⊕ *www.sparkssteakhouse. com* ⚸ *Reservations essential* ☰ *AE, D, DC, MC, V* ⊙ *Closed Sun. No lunch Sat.* Ⓜ *4, 5, 6, 7, S to 42nd St.–Grand Central.* ✛ *4:G3*

$$　✕ **Sushi Yasuda.** The sleek bamboo-lined space in which chef Naomichi
JAPANESE　Yasuda works his aquatic sorcery is as elegant as his food. Whether he's using fish flown in daily from Japan or the creamiest sea urchin, Yasuda makes sushi so fresh and delicate it melts in your mouth. A number of special appetizers change daily (crispy fried eel backbone is a surprising treat), and a fine selection of sake and beer complements the lovely food. ✉ *204 E. 43rd St., between 2nd and 3rd Aves., Midtown East* ☎ *212/972–1001* ⊕ *www.sushiyasuda.com* ☰ *AE, D, MC, V* ⊙ *Closed Sun. No lunch Sat.* Ⓜ *4, 5, 6, 7 to 42nd St./Grand Central.* ✛ *4:G4*

UPPER EAST SIDE

$$$　✕ **Alloro.** Italian chef Salvatore Corea and his wife Gina, a native New
ITALIAN　Yorker, are living their dream of opening an old-fashioned family-run restaurant here on the Upper East Side just a block away from the apartment they share with their two young daughters. It's not Corea's first New York restaurant endeavor—he's opened three other successful venues in the city (Cacio e Pepe, Spiga, and Bocca), but Alloro is his first venture with his wife, and judging by the friendly vibe and the delicious dishes coming out of Corea's *cucina,* it's off to a great start. Chef Corea's creative take on traditional, regional Italian cuisines leads the way for delicious dishes, like *paccheri,* a wide tube-shape pasta, with a white ragout of quail, porcini mushrooms, black truffles, and fresh blueberries. Both the filet mignon with the potato pie and wild mushrooms and the duck breast served with polenta cake are fantastic. ✉ *307 E. 77th St., near 2nd Ave., Upper East Side* ☎ *212/535–2866* ⊕ *www.alloronyc.com* ☰ *AE, MC, V* Ⓜ *6 to 77th St.* ✛ *5:H2*

$$$$　✕ **Café Boulud.** The food and service are top-notch at Daniel Boulud's
FRENCH　conservative (but not stuffy) bistro in the Surrey Hotel. The menu is divided in four parts: under La Tradition you can find classic French dishes such as roasted duck breast "Montmorency" with cherry chutney, green Swiss chard, and baby turnips; Le Potager tempts with lemon ricotta ravioli; La Saison follows the rhythms of the season; and Le Voyage reinterprets cuisines of the world. ✉ *20 E. 76th St., between 5th and Madison Aves., Upper East Side* ☎ *212/772–2600* ⊕ *www.*

18

danielnyc.com/cafeboulud ⚠*Reservations essential* ⊟*AE, DC, MC, V* Ⓜ*6 to 77th St.* ✛*5:F3*

$$
BRASSERIE

✗**Café d'Alsace.** Unusually comfortable burgundy banquettes, huge antiqued mirrors, and low lighting that makes everyone look fabulous characterize this Alsatian gem. Start with a house cocktail— say, L'Alsacien, in which the aperitif Belle de Brillet meets cognac, pear, and fresh lemon in a happy union.

Standouts include the *tarte flambé*, a *fromage-blanc*–topped flat bread scattered with tawny caramelized onions and hunks of bacon. The *choucroute garnie* entrée comes in a cast-iron kettle that keeps it piping hot for the entire meal. Sausages, smoked pork breast, and pork belly are so carefully braised that everything comes out in perfect harmony. Delicious bread pudding is studded with strawberries. ⊠*1695 2nd Ave., at E. 88th St., Upper East Side* ☏*212/722–5133* ⊕*www.cafedalsace.com* ⊟*AE, MC, V* Ⓜ*4, 5, 6 to 86th St.* ✛*6:G6*

$$$$
FRENCH

✗**Daniel.** Celebrity-chef Daniel Boulud has created one of the most elegant dining experiences in Manhattan today. The prix-fixe–only menu (there are à la carte selections in the lounge and bar) is predominantly French, with such modern classics as slow-baked Atlantic halibut with radishes, curried asparagus marmalade, and pepper jus; and quartet of Vermont veal, with chanterelle tenderloin, peppered quenelles, cheek with layered pasta, and crispy sweetbreads. Equally impressive are the professional service and primarily French wine list. Don't forget the decadent desserts and overflowing cheese trolley. A three-course vegetarian menu is available. ⊠*60 E. 65th St., between Madison and Park Aves., Upper East Side* ☏*212/288–0033* ⊕*www.danielnyc.com/daniel* ⚠*Reservations essential, jacket required* ⊟*AE, DC, MC, V* ⊗*Closed Sun. No lunch* Ⓜ*6 to 68th St./Hunter College.* ✛*5:F5*

$$$$
NEW AMERICAN

✗**David Burke Townhouse.** Don't be surprised if you spot the Queen of Hearts perched above tables of lunching ladies and dapper businessmen in this formal yet stylish modern American restaurant. Deck-of-cards themed lithographs punctuate the serious atmosphere and foreshadow the whimsical stylings of chef David Burke, perhaps best known for his cheesecake lollipops served with bubble-gum-flavor whipped cream. Standouts include Dover sole with zucchini chips and tomato-mint butter, and homemade cavatelli with braised short ribs, wild mushrooms, mushroom chips, and truffle mousse. During colder months, smokers can visit the adjacent "smoking room"—a white stretch limo that idles in front of the restaurant all evening long. ⊠*133 E. 61st St., between Lexington and Park Aves., Upper East Side* ☏*212/813–2121* ⊕*www. dbdrestaurant.com* ⚠*Reservations essential* ⊟*AE, D, MC, V* ⊗ *No lunch Sat.* Ⓜ*N, R, W to 59th St.; F to Lexington Ave.* ✛*5:G6*

$ ✕ **Le Pain Quotidien.** This international Belgian chain brings its home-
CAFÉ   land ingredients with it, treating New Yorkers to crusty organic breads,
Multiple jams, chocolate, and other specialty products. You can grab a snack to
Locations go or stay and eat breakfast, lunch, or dinner at communal or private
ⓒ   tables with waiter service. Come for a steaming latte and croissant
in the morning, a tartine (open-faced sandwich) or salad at noon,
and a glass of wine and Tuscan cheese-and-meat platter for a late
afternoon snack. For a quick lunch or a refueling treat, this bakery-
café can't be beat. ✉ *252 E. 77th St., near 2nd Ave.,* ☎ *212/249–
8600* Ⓜ *6 to 77th St.* ✛ *5:G2* ✉ *38 E. 19th St., between Broadway
and Park Ave. S* ☎ *212/673–7900* Ⓜ *R, W, 6 to 23rd St.* ✛ *3:F3*
✉ *124 7th Ave., between W. 17th and 18th Sts.* ☎ *212/255–2777*
Ⓜ *1 to 18th St.* ✛ *3:D3* ✉ *1270 1st Ave., at 68th St.Upper East Side*
☎ *212/988–5001* Ⓜ *6 to 68th St.* ✛ *5:H4* ✉ *100 Grand St., at Mercer
St.* ☎ *212/625–9009* ⊕ *www.lepainquotidien.com* ⌦ *Reservations
not accepted* ▭ *AE, DC, MC, V* Ⓜ *N, Q, R, W to Canal St.* ✛ *2:E4*
✉ *60 W. 65th St., near Columbus Ave.* ☎ *212/721–4001* Ⓜ *1 to 66th
St.* ✛ *5:C5* ✉ *922 7th Ave., at 58th St.* ☎ *212/757–0775* Ⓜ *N, Q, R,
W to 57th St.* ✛ *4:C1* ✉   ✉ *50 W. 72nd St., near Central Park W*
☎ *212/712–9700* Ⓜ *B, C to 72nd St.* ✛ *5:C4* ✉ *10 5th Ave., at 8th
St.* ☎ *212/253–2324* Ⓜ *R, W to 8th St.* ✛ *2:D1* ✉ *833 Lexington
Ave., near 64th St.* ☎ *212/755–5810* Ⓜ *F to 63rd St.* ✛ *5:G5* ✉ *801
Broadway, between E. 11th and E. 12th Sts.* ☎ *212/677–5277* Ⓜ *4,
5, 6, L, N, Q, R, W to 14th St./Union Sq.* ✛ *3:F4 .*

$$$ ✕ **Maya.** The upscale-hacienda appearance of this justifiably popular
MEXICAN restaurant showcases some of the best Mexican food in the city. Begin
with a fresh mango margarita, then tuck into delicious roasted corn
soup, stuffed poblano peppers, and smoky butterflied beef tenderloin
marinated in lime. Finish with caramel crepes and cinnamon ice cream
and you'll leave wearing a big grin. ✉ *1191 1st Ave., between E. 64th
and E. 65th Sts., Upper East Side* ☎ *212/585–1818* ⊕ *www.modern
mexican.com/mayany* ⌦ *Reservations essential* ▭ *AE, D, DC, MC, V*
ⓢ *No lunch* Ⓜ *6 to 68th St./Hunter College.* ✛ *5:H5*

$$$ ✕ **Park Avenue Summer/Autumn/Winter/Spring.** New York's most self-con-
AMERICAN sciously seasonal restaurant swaps out much more than its menu as tem-
peratures change. Four times a year the restaurant—the formerly staid
Park Avenue Café—shuts its doors for a head-to-toe makeover, switching, for instance, from a summery blond-wood beach-house motif to
dark-wood-and-copper fall-foliage tones. Chef Craig Koketsu's seasonal
food lives up to the striking surroundings. Summer brings a bounty of
fresh-shucked corn, with a big, juicy veal chop and heirloom tomatoes.
Come autumn the kitchen turns its focus to mushrooms, truffles (on
a flaky John Dory fillet), and game (local quail, big venison chops).
Desserts, by award-winning pastry chef Richard Leach, include hard-
to-resist elegant-homey creations like caramelized banana crepes with
sweet crumbled bacon. ✉ *100 E. 63rd St., at Park Ave., Upper East
Side* ☎ *212/644–1900* ⊕ *www.parkavenyc.com* ▭ *AE, DC, D, MC,
V* Ⓜ *F to Lexington Ave.-63rd St.; 4, 5, 6 to 59th St.; N, R, W to 5th
Ave.-59th St.* ✛ *5:F6*

18

$$$

BISTRO

✗**Payard Pâtisserie & Bistro.** Pastry chef François Payard is the force behind this combination bistro and pastry shop. Snazzy local luminaries come here in droves, and you'll quickly discover why. The wine list is particularly fine and focused. Start with an intensely rich and delicious upside-down cheese soufflé with Parmesan-cream sauce and white truffle oil. Follow with sautéed red snapper with English pea puree, morels, local ramps, and oven-dried grape tomatoes in a sorrel-cured lemon sauce. Payard's tarts, soufflés, and other French pastries are simply unforgettable. ✉*1032 Lexington Ave., between E. 73rd and E. 74th Sts. Upper East Side* ☎*212/717–5252* ⊕*www.payard.com* ⚲*Reservations essential* ▭*AE, DC, MC, V* ⊘*Closed Sun.* Ⓜ*6 to 77th St.* ✛*5:G3*

> **WORD OF MOUTH**
>
> "A great sushi place on the UES Is Sushi of Gari. This is a serious sushi place, however, and not trendy; it ranks among the best in the city for innovative sushi. You must reserve ahead. Also, there is not much atmosphere. It is a pretty plain, small place, as are many of the top sushi spots in the city.   —ekscrunky

$$$

ITALIAN

✗**Sfoglia.** Veiled from the street by linen curtains, this tiny Manhattan offshoot of its Nantucket namesake does a fine impression of a shabby-chic Tuscan farmhouse. The fastidious decor includes big wooden communal tables, plush pillows, vintage posters of Italian food, and Murano glass chandeliers. The food, too, has an air of photo-styled perfection. A complimentary bowl of plump glistening olives comes artfully tossed with lemon and herbs. A too-quickly devoured basket of crusty bread arrives fresh from the oven sprinkled with sea salt. The oft-changing menu might include amaretto-cookie-topped feather-light gnocchi or parchment-steamed whole orata exposed at the table in a cloud of heady aromas. The baked-to-order *torta del giorno*—a seasonal buttery fruit tart—is a showstopping finale that feeds a crowd. ✉*1402 Lexington Ave., at 92nd St., Upper East Side* ☎*212/831–1402* ⊕*www.sfoglia restaurant.com* ▭*AE, MC, V* ⊘*Closed Sun. No lunch Mon.* Ⓜ*4, 5, 6 to 86th St.* ✛*6:G5*

$$

JAPANESE

Multiple

Locations

✗**Sushi of Gari.** Options at this popular sushi restaurant range from the ordinary (California roll) to such exotic items as tuna with creamy tofu sauce, miso-marinated cod, or Japanese yellowtail with jalapeño. Japanese noodles (udon or soba) and meat dishes such as teriyaki and negimaki (scallions rolled in thinly sliced beef) are well prepared. Reservations are recommended. ✉*402 E. 78th St., at 1st Ave.,Upper East Side* ☎*212/517–5340* ⊕*www.sushiofgari.com* ▭*AE, D, MC, V* ⊘*Closed Mon. No lunch* Ⓜ*6 to 77th St.* ✛*5:H2* ✉*370 Columbus Ave., between 77th and 78th Sts.* ☎*212/362–4816* Ⓜ*1 to 79th St.; B, C to 81st St.-Museum of Natural History.* ✛*5:B2*

UPPER WEST SIDE AND HARLEM

HARLEM

$

BARBECUE

✗**Dinosaur Bar-B-Que.** New York's reputation for inferior barbecue improved instantly when John Stage opened the third outpost of his Syracuse-based joint in 2004, installing it in a riverside meatpacking warehouse in Harlem. Here, the city's friendliest waitstaff serves piled-high plates of pulled pork, ribs, chicken, brisket, and knockout wings; a well-stocked bar corrals the Columbia students. ⊠ *646 W. 131st St., at 12th Ave.,Harlem* ☎ *212/694–1777* ⊕ *www.dinosaurbarbque.com* ⊟ *AE, D, DC, MC, V* Ⓜ *1 to 125th St.* ✛ *6:A2*

UPPER WEST SIDE

$$$$
ASIAN

✕ **Asiate.** The unparalleled view is reason enough to visit Asiate's pristine dining room, perched on the 35th floor of the Time Warner Center in the Mandarin Oriental Hotel. Artfully positioned tables and minimalist decor help direct eyes to the windows, which peer over Central Park. At night crystalline lights reflect in the glass, creating a magical effect. Chef Toni Robertson creates contemporary dishes with an Asian influence. One of Robertson's signature dishes is the crispy

> **WORD OF MOUTH**
>
> "Our splurge lunch was at Asiate, high up in the Mandarin Oriental at Columbus Circle. We were disappointed not to get the window seats we had requested when we booked a month ago. . . . but our food was delicious and we were pleasantly surprised by very fair prices for drinks and good wines by the glass." —NeoPatrick

suckling pig croquette and tenderloin with black truffle and pork jus. Professional, attentive service helps foster an atmosphere of dreamlike luxury. The restaurant offers prix-fixe menus only. ⊠ *Time Warner Center, 80 Columbus Circle, 35th fl., at W. 60th St., Upper West Side* ☎ *212/805–8881* ⊕ *www.mandarinoriental.com/newyork/dining/asiate* ⊟ *AE, D, DC, MC, V* Ⓜ *A, B, C, D, 1 to 59th St.–Columbus Circle.* ✛ *5:C6*

18

$$
FRENCH
Fodor's Choice
★

✕ **Bar Boulud.** Acclaimed French chef Daniel Boulud, known for upscale New York City eateries Daniel and Café Boulud, brings diners his most casual venture yet with this lively contemporary bistro. The long narrow space accommodates 100 people and has a 14-seat round table for special tastings. An additional level has three rooms for larger parties. The menu emphasizes charcuterie including terrines and pâtés designed by Parisian charcutier Gilles Verot, as well as traditional French bistro dishes like steak frîtes and *poulet rôti à l'ail* (roast chicken with garlic mashed potatoes). The 500-bottle wine list is heavy on wines from Burgundy and the Rhône Valley. Wallet watchers won't feel left out: a pretheater three-course menu starts at $39, and weekend brunch has two hearty courses for $28. ⊠ *1900 Broadway, between 63rd and 64th Sts.,Upper West Side* ☎ *212/595–0303* ⊕ *www.barboulud.com* ⊟ *AE, DC, MC, V* Ⓜ *1 to 66th St./Lincoln Center; 1, A, C, B, D to 59th St./Columbus Circle* ✛ *5:B5*

$
DELI

✕ **Barney Greengrass.** At this New York Jewish landmark, brusque waiters send out stellar smoked salmon, sturgeon, and whitefish to a happy crowd packed to the gills at small Formica tables. Split a fish platter with bagels, cream cheese, and other fixings, or get your fish with scrambled eggs. If you're still hungry, go for a plate of cheese blintzes or the to-die-for chopped liver. Beware: the weekend brunch wait can exceed an hour. ⊠ *541 Amsterdam Ave., between W. 86th and W. 87th Sts., Upper West Side* ☎ *212/724–4707* ⊕ *www.barneygreengrass.com*

⚓Reservations not accepted ▭No credit cards ◷Closed Mon. No dinner Ⓜ1, B, C to 86th St. ✚6:B6

$ ✕**Big Nick's.** This cramped neighborhood diner is decorated with pho-
DINER tographs of the celebrities who've visited, but the primary draw is the burgers, which are huge and juicy. The endless menu lists every conceivable burger topping, from avocado and bacon to Greek tzatziki sauce. The classic Bistro Burger has mushrooms, cheddar, and fried onions on toasted challah bread. Nick's is open later than most burger joints—until 5 AM. ✉2175 Broadway, between W. 76th and W. 77th Sts., Upper West Side ☎212/362–9238 ⊕www.bignicksnyc.com ▭MC, V Ⓜ1 to 79th St.; 1, 2, 3 to 72nd St. ✚5:A3

$ ✕**Bouchon Bakery.** Never mind that you're in the middle of a shopping
CAFÉ mall under a Samsung sign, soups and sandwiches don't get much more luxurious than this. Acclaimed chef Thomas Keller's low-key lunch spot (one floor down from his extravagant flagship, Per Se) draws long lines for good reason. Share a mason jar of salmon rillettes—an unctuous spread of cooked and smoked salmon folded around crème fraîche and butter—then move onto one of the fork-and-knife open-faced tartines, like the tuna niçoise. When a sandwich has this much pedigree, $13 is actually a bargain. Grab dessert to go, a fresh macaroon or éclair, from the nearby bakery window. ✉10 Columbus Circle, 3rd fl., at 60th St., Upper West Side ☎212/823–9366 ⊕www.bouchonbakery.com ▭AE, MC, V Ⓜ1, A, B, C, D to 59th St./Columbus Circle ✚5:C6

$$$$ ✕**Café Luxembourg.** The old soul of the Lincoln Center neighborhood
BRASSERIE seems to inhabit the tiled and mirrored walls of this lively, cramped restaurant, where West End Avenue regulars are greeted with kisses, and musicians and audience members pack the room after a concert. The menu (served until 11:45 PM) includes dishes like steak tartare and lobster roll alongside dishes with a more contemporary spin like harissa-glazed duck with cumin-scented yogurt. ✉200 W. 70th St., between Amsterdam and West End Aves., Upper West Side ☎212/873–7411 ⊕www.cafeluxembourg.com ⚓Reservations essential ▭AE, DC, MC, V Ⓜ1, 2, 3, B, C to 72nd St. ✚5:A4

$$ ✕**Carmine's.** Savvy New Yorkers line up early for the affordable family-
ITALIAN style meals at both branches of this large, busy eatery. There are no
Multiple reservations taken for parties of fewer than six people after 7 PM, but
Locations those who wait are rewarded with mountains of such popular, tooth-
ↄ some items as fried calamari, linguine with white clam sauce, chicken parmigiana, and veal saltimbocca. The Upper West Side dining room has dark woodwork and black-and-white tiles; outdoor seating is available in the front. The Midtown West location can be a zoo. Although it's impossible not to order too much, everything tastes just as satisfying for leftovers the next day. ✉2450 Broadway, between W. 90th and W. 91st Sts., Upper West Side ☎212/362–2200 ⊕www.carminesnyc. com ▭AE, D, DC, MC, V Ⓜ1, 2, 3 to 96th St. ✚6:A5 ✉200 W. 44th St., between Broadway and 8th Ave. ☎212/221–3800 ⊕www. carminesnyc.com ▭AE, D, DC, MC, V Ⓜ A, C, E, N, Q, R, W, S, 1, 2, 3, 7 to 42nd St./Times Sq. ✚4:C4

$$$ ✕**'Cesca.** This rambling but highly stylish space showcases chef Kev-
ITALIAN in Garcia's foray into southern Italian cuisine, with comforting-yet-

sophisticated flavors. Start with spicy, gooey Parmesan fritters, then tuck into braised duck ravioli with balsamic-brown butter and sage. Follow with a hefty grilled pork chop with smoked bacon and crisp broccoli rabe. Finish with cannoli piped full of ricotta and mascarpone, and topped with chocolate sauce and a scattering of pistachios. ✉ *164 W. 75th St., at Amsterdam Ave., Upper West Side* ☎ *212/787–6300* ⊕ *www.cescanyc.com* ▭ *AE, D, DC, MC, V* ⊗ *No lunch Mon.–Sat.* Ⓜ *1, 2, 3 to 72nd St.* ✛ *5:B3*

$$$
AMERICAN

✕ **Dovetail.** Inside Dovetail, chef-owner John Fraser's subdued town house and restaurant, cream-color walls, and maple panels create a warm, soothing atmosphere. The menu, which changes daily, features refined but hearty dishes. Seek solace from winter temperatures with the earthy gnocchi topped with veal short-rib ragout and foie gras butter. Tender lamb is heightened by exotic Indian spices, yogurt, and winter tabbouleh. The savory feast continues with pastry chef Vera Tong's salty but sweet bacon bread-and-butter pudding. ✉ *103 W. 77th St., at Columbus Ave., Upper West Side* ☎ *212/362–3800* ⊕ *www.dovetail nyc.com* ▭ *AE, DC, MC, V* ⊗ *No lunch Mon.–Sat.* Ⓜ *1 to 79th St.; B, C to 81st St./Museum of Natural History* ✛ *5:B3*

$$$$
MODERN
AMERICAN

✕ **Eighty One.** The entrance to Ed Brown's ambitious restaurant is through an inviting bar and lounge, an elegant spot to sip swanky cocktails such as the Wandering Poet (gin, sake, litchi, ginger, and lime) or to order off of Brown's unabashedly sophisticated New American menu. In fact, dining in the bar may not be a bad option: the large, bright dining room lacks the intimacy of the bar area, though its moderate decibel level will please noise-weary diners. Highlights of the menu include a creamy pumpkin risotto that makes a mouthwatering, shareable starter; tender lamb three ways with sheep's ricotta gnocchi, wild mushrooms, and braised lettuce; and cod dressed in a sake and black bean broth. The entrée prices may leave you wondering whether you have been sufficiently blown away, though. No matter what, save room for the mille-feuille dessert, a delightful work of architecture in chocolate and hazelnut. ✉ *45 W. 81st St., between Columbus Ave. and Central Park W, Upper West Side* ☎ *212/873–8181* ⊕ *www.81nyc.com* ▭ *AE, MC, V* ⊗ *No lunch* Ⓜ *1 to 79th St.; B, C to 81st St./Museum of Natural History* ✛ *5:B2*

18

$$$$
FRENCH

✕ **Jean Georges.** This culinary temple focuses wholly on *chef celebre* Jean-Georges Vongerichten's spectacular creations. Some approach the limits of the taste universe, like foie gras brûlée with spiced fig jam and ice-wine verjus. Others are models of simplicity, like slow-cooked cod with warm vegetable vinaigrette. Exceedingly personalized service and a well-selected wine list contribute to an unforgettable meal. For Jean Georges on a budget, try the prix-fixe lunch in the front room, Nougatine. ✉ *1 Central Park W, at W. 59th St., Upper West Side* ☎ *212/299–3900* ⊕ *www.jean-georges.com* ⌁ *Reservations essential, jacket required* ▭ *AE, DC, MC, V* ⊗ *Closed Sun.* Ⓜ *A, B, C, D, 1 to 59th St./Columbus Circle.* ✛ *5:C6*

$
GREEK

✕ **Kefi.** Michael Psilakis's homage to his grandmother's Greek cooking occupies the space that once housed the chef's haute Hellenic spot, Onera. Though the menu, decor, and price points have changed, the cuisine remains stellar. Among the mezes, the meatballs with roasted garlic, olives, and tomato is a standout, and the flavorful roast chicken, potatoes, red peppers, garlic, and thyme makes for a winning entrée. Reasonable prices—appetizers are no more than $9.95, and main courses max out at $15.95—make it easy to stick around for a piece of traditional walnut cake with walnut ice cream. ✉*505 Columbus Ave., at W. 84th St., Upper West Side* ☎*212/873–0200* ▤*No credit cards* ◷*No lunch* Ⓜ*1 to 79th St.* ⊹*5:B1*

¢ ✕**Ollie's Noodle Shop.** This local chain offers Chinese fare in a no-frills setting. Fans rave about the Cantonese-style barbecued meats (duck, pork, chicken), steamed dumplings and buns, and Mandarin noodle soups. The locations in the Theater District and near Lincoln Center are great for patrons in search of a quick budget meal. The portions are generous, but don't expect any culinary revelations. If you order a noodle bowl, you can get out of here for under $10. But if you want to splurge a little, try the fried filet of sea bass with spicy salt, spicy eggplant in garlic sauce, steamed little juicy buns, and BBQ spare ribs. It's a feast that—with beer or cocktails—comes in under $20 a person. ✉*1991 Broadway, at W. 68th St., Upper West Side* ☎*212/595–8181* ⚅*Reservations not accepted* ▤*AE, MC, V* Ⓜ*1 to 66th St./Lincoln Center* ⊹*5:B4* ✉*2315 Broadway, at W. 86th St.* ☎*212/362–3111* Ⓜ*1 to 86th St.* ⊹*5:B1* ✉*2957 Broadway, at W. 116th St.* ☎*212/932–3300* Ⓜ*1 to 116th St./Columbia Univ.* ⊹*6:A1* ✉*200B W. 44th St. near Broadway* ☎*212/921–5988* Ⓜ*1, 2, 3, 7, N, Q, R, W, S to Times Sq./42nd St.* ⊹*4:C4*

CHINESE
Multiple
Locations

$$$$ ✕**Per Se.** Thomas Keller, who gave the world butter-poached lobster and the Napa Valley's French Laundry restaurant, has given New York Per Se, which serves his witty, magical creations to well-heeled diners. Come with an open mind and open wallet, and discover his inventive combinations of flavors reduced to their essences. Waiters can, and may, recite the provenance of the tiniest turnip. For reservations, call exactly two months in advance of your hoped-for dining date. ✉*Time Warner Center, 10 Columbus Circle, 4th fl., at W. 60th St., Upper West Side* ☎*212/823–9335* ⊕*www.perseny.com* ⚅*Reservations essential, jacket required* ▤*AE, MC, V* ◷*No lunch Mon.–Thurs.* Ⓜ*A, B, C, D, 1 to 59th St./Columbus Circle.* ⊹*5:C6*

AMERICAN
Fodor's Choice
★

$$$$ ✕**Picholine.** Terrence Brennan's classic French restaurant has a dignified and hushed atmosphere. His kitchen maintains a strong emphasis on contemporary Mediterranean cuisine and relies conspicuously on artisanal farmers and food producers. The menu is divided into four relatively small sections: Preludes, Pastas, Day Boats, and the Land, and you are invited to construct your own tasting by selecting from two to four sections. Some of the dishes are given confusing names. "Roquefort Parfait" is no such thing: it's a heap of grassy endive shards fluttered over a gentle sauterne gelée. The kitchen's spin on chicken Kiev is particularly brilliant: an heirloom chicken breast is pressed into a fat juicy tube and rolled in crushed cornflakes before it is deep-fried. Slice into the soft cylinder and it spills its luscious "liquid foie gras" filling. Don't miss the famous cheese course, which was practically invented here. ✉*35 W. 64th St., between Broadway and Central Park W, Upper*

MEDITERRANEAN

West Side ☎212/724–8585 ⊕*www.picholinenyc.com* ⌖*Reservations essential* ▭*AE, DC, MC, V* ⊘*No lunch* Ⓜ*1 to 66th St./Lincoln Center* ⊹*5:C5*

$$$$
STEAKHOUSE

✕**Porter House.** With clubby interiors by Jeffrey Beers and an adjoining lounge area, Porter House marks the splashy return to the scene of former Windows on the World chef Michael Lomonaco. Filling the meat-and-potatoes slot in the Time Warner Center's upscale "Restaurant Collection," the masculine throwback highlights American wines and pedigreed super-size meat. The neighborhood, long underserved on the steak-house front, has quickly warmed to Lomonaco's simple solid American fare. Begin with his smoky clams casino or rich tarragon-kissed oyster pan roast. Steaks are huge and expertly seasoned and come with the usual battery of à la carte sides—creamed spinach, roasted mushrooms, and mashed potatoes. ✉*10 Columbus Circle 4th fl., at 60th St., Upper West Side* ☎*212/823–9500* ⊕*www.porterhousenewyork.com* ▭*AE, MC, V* Ⓜ*1, A, B, C, D to 59th St./Columbus Circle* ⊹*5:C6*

$$
AMERICAN
Multiple
Locations

✕**Sarabeth's.** Lining up for brunch here is as much an Upper West Side tradition as taking a sunny Sunday afternoon stroll in nearby Riverside Park. Locals love the bric-a-brac–filled restaurant for sweet morning-time dishes like lemon ricotta pancakes, as well as for the comforting dinners. The afternoon tea includes buttery scones with Sarabeth's signature jams, savory nibbles, and outstanding baked goods. Dinner entrées include chicken potpie and truffle mac and cheese. ✉*423 Amsterdam Ave., at W. 80th St., Upper West Side* ☎*212/496–6280* ⊕*www.sarabeth.com* ▭*AE, D, DC, MC, V* Ⓜ*1 to 79th St.* ⊹*5:B2* ✉*1295 Madison Ave., at 92nd St.* ☎*212/410–7335* ⊕*www.sarabeth.com* ▭*AE, D, DC, MC, V* Ⓜ*6 to 96th St.* ⊹*6:F5* ✉*40 Central Park S, near 6th Ave.* ☎*212/826–5959* ⊕*www.sarabeth.com* ▭*AE, D, DC, MC, V* Ⓜ*N, R, W to 5th Ave./59th St.* ⊹*5:E6* ✉*Whitney Museum of American Art, 945 Madison Ave., at 75th St.* ☎*212/606–0218* ⊘*Closed Mon.* ⊕*www.sarabeth.com* ▭*AE, D, DC, MC, V* Ⓜ*6 to 77th St.* ⊹*5:F3* ✉*Chelsea Market, 75 9th Ave.* ☎*212/989–2424* ⊕*www.sarabeth.com* ▭*AE, D, DC, MC, V* Ⓜ*A, C, E to 14th St.; L to 8th Ave.* ⊹*3:B4*

¢
BURGER
Multiple
Locations
Fodor's Choice
★

✕**Shake Shack.** Local restaurant legend Danny Meyer has gone a little low-brow with his fast-ish food venture, Shake Shack—and New Yorkers are loving it. The Upper West Side Shack is an eat-in joint located just across Columbus Ave. from the American Museum of Natural History. While the lines may be long at lunchtime, the grub is good and well priced. Fresh steer burgers are ground daily, and a single will run you from $3.75 to $4.75, depending on what you want on it. They're not the best or the biggest burgers in the city, but they're decidedly tasty. For a few more bucks you can also order doubles and stacks or a vegetarian 'Shroom Burger—a melty muenster and cheddar cheese-stuffed portobello, topped with lettuce, tomato, and Shack sauce. The Shake Shack also offers beef and bird (chicken) hot dogs, French fries and fries drizzled with Shack-made cheddar and American cheese sauce, and a variety of delicious frozen custard desserts and—of course—shakes! ✉366 Columbus Ave., at W. 77th St., *Upper West Side* ☎646/747-

18

8770 ⊕*www.shakeshacknyc.com* ═*AE, D, MC, V* Ⓜ*B, C to 81st St.*
✛*5:B3* ⊠Madison Square Park near Madison Ave. and E. 23rd St.
☎*212/889-6600* ⊕*www.shakeshacknyc.com* ═*AE, D, MC, V* Ⓜ*N,*
R, W, 6 to 23rd St. ✛*3:F2*

$$$ ✕**Tavern on the Green.** As you might expect, given the kitchen's near-
AMERICAN impossible task of accommodating more than 500 guests at once, the
food and service vary wildly. Nonetheless, people throng (on foot, by
taxi, even by horse and carriage) to this fantastical maze of dining
rooms in Central Park. In good weather (May through October), try for
a spot in the lovely garden area under a canopy of lighted trees. Think
of the place as an elaborately catered wedding party, and you'll do fine
by sticking to simple dishes like crab cakes and prime rib, the two best
dishes on the menu, and actually as good as any in town. Or skip the
food and grab a drink at the charming upstairs bar. ⊠*In Central Park*
at W. 67th St.Upper West Side ☎*212/873–3200* ⊕*www.tavernon*
thegreen.com ⌔*Reservations essential* ═*AE, D, DC, MC, V* Ⓜ*1 to*
66th St.–Lincoln Center; B, C to W. 72nd St. ✛*5:C5*

$$$ ✕**Telepan.** Chef-owner Bill Telepan's menu is divided into three courses:
AMERICAN appetizers of salads, light fish dishes, and soups; middle courses of
eggs, pasta, or vegetables; and main courses of meat and fish. House-
smoked brook trout heads the menu. The fish is flaked and mounted on
a celery-root blini with green-apple sour cream. Robiola cheese–stuffed
tortellini are set in a Parmesan-infused chicken broth with shards of
Swiss chard and tiny veal meatballs. Halibut comes encrusted with
lemon thyme. For dessert, the dark-chocolate almond tart is sublime.
⊠*72 W. 69th St. between Columbus Ave. and Central Park W, Upper*
West Side ☎*212/580–4300* ⊕*www.telepan-ny.com* ═*AE, D, MC,*
V ☾*No lunch Mon.–Tues.* Ⓜ*1 to 66th St.-Lincoln Center; 1, 2, 3 to*
72nd St.; B, C to 72nd St. ✛*5:B4*

New York City Dining & Lodging Atlas

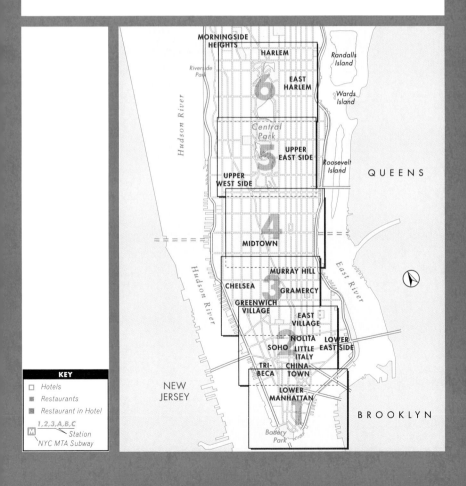

MORNINGSIDE
HEIGHTS

HARLEM

Riverside
Park

Randalls
Island

EAST
HARLEM

Wards
Island

Hudson River

Central
Park

6

UPPER
EAST SIDE

Roosevelt
Island

5

QUEENS

UPPER
WEST SIDE

4

MIDTOWN

East River

MURRAY HILL

CHELSEA

3

GRAMERCY

Hudson River

GREENWICH
VILLAGE

EAST
VILLAGE

NOLITA

LOWER
EAST SIDE

SOHO

LITTLE
ITALY

TRI-
BECA

2

CHINA-
TOWN

NEW
JERSEY

LOWER
MANHATTAN

1

Battery
Park

BROOKLYN

KEY

☐ Hotels
■ Restaurants
■ Restaurant in Hotel

M 1,2,3,A,B,C
Station
NYC MTA Subway

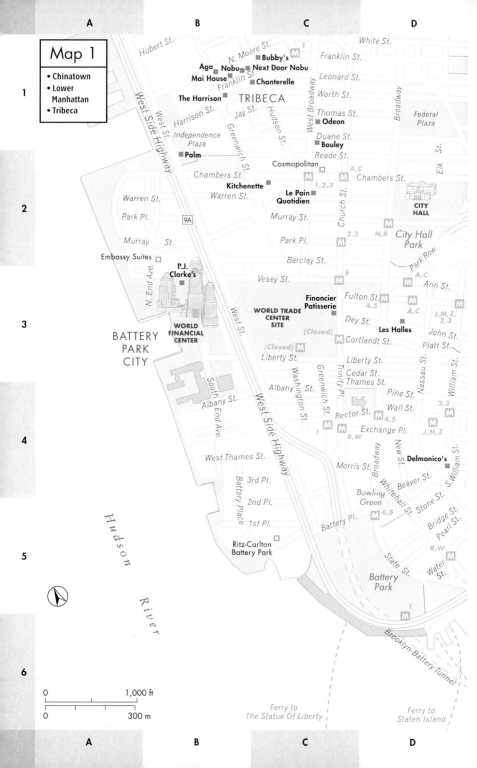

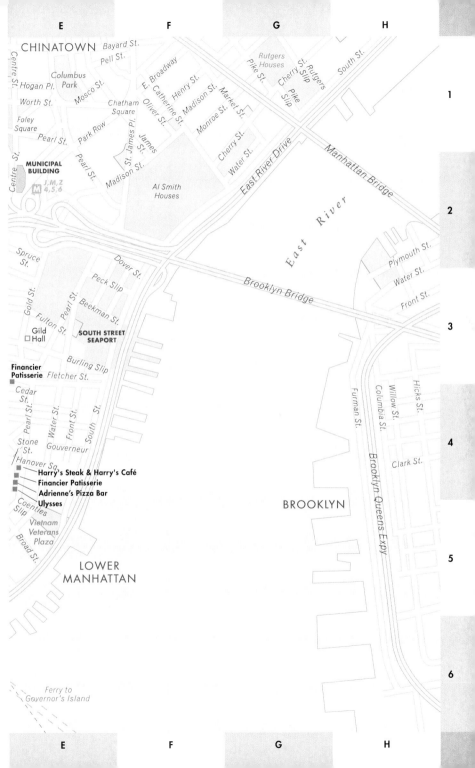

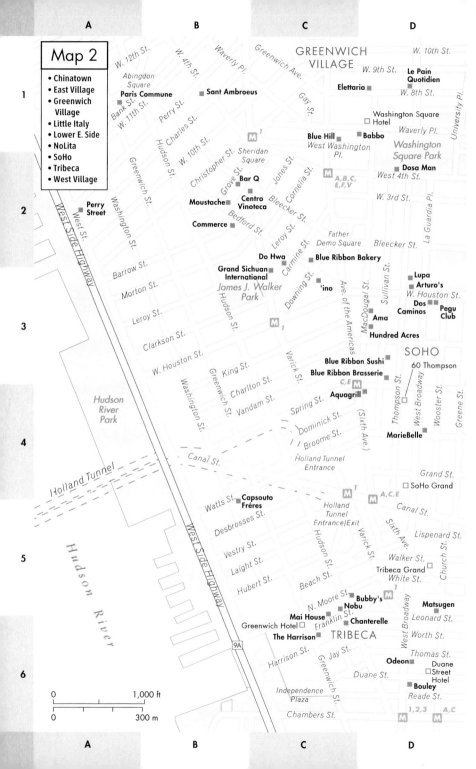

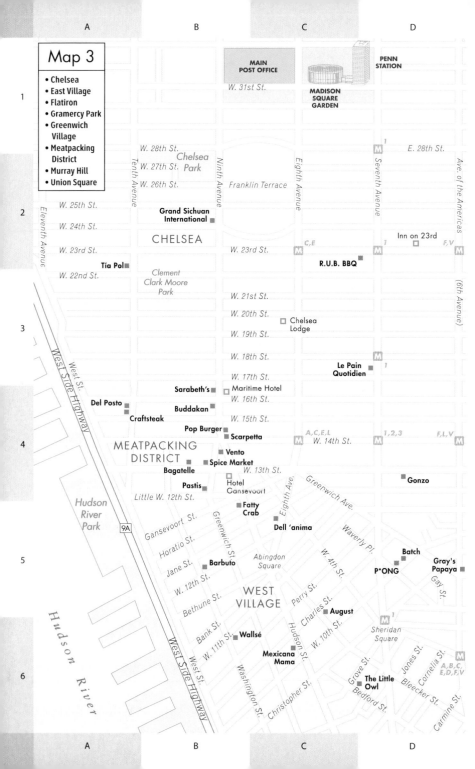

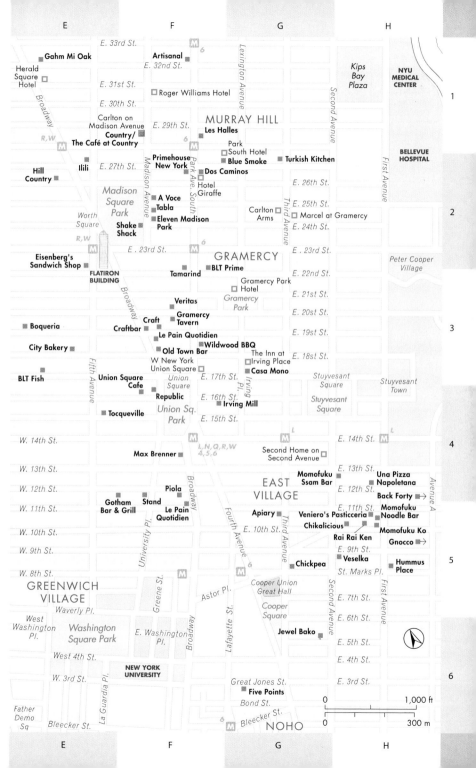

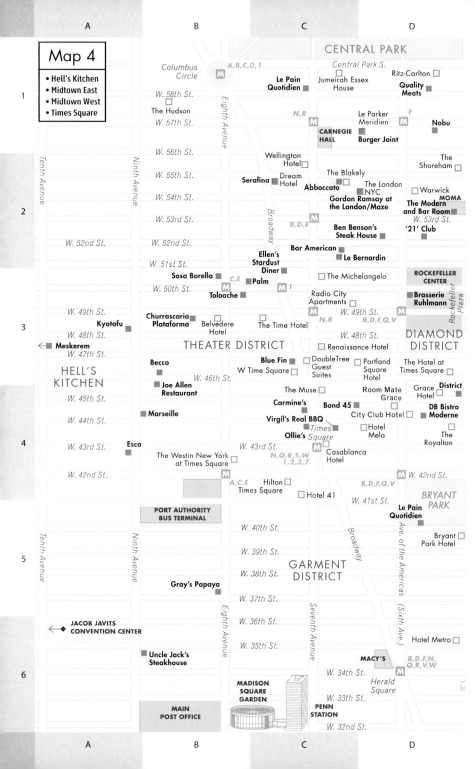

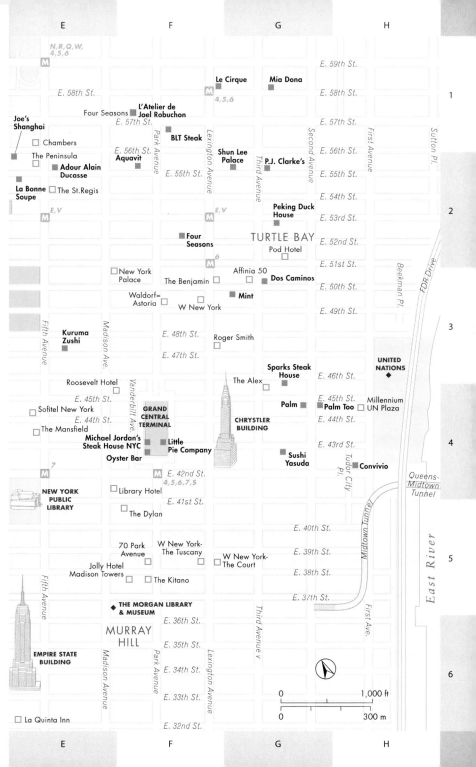

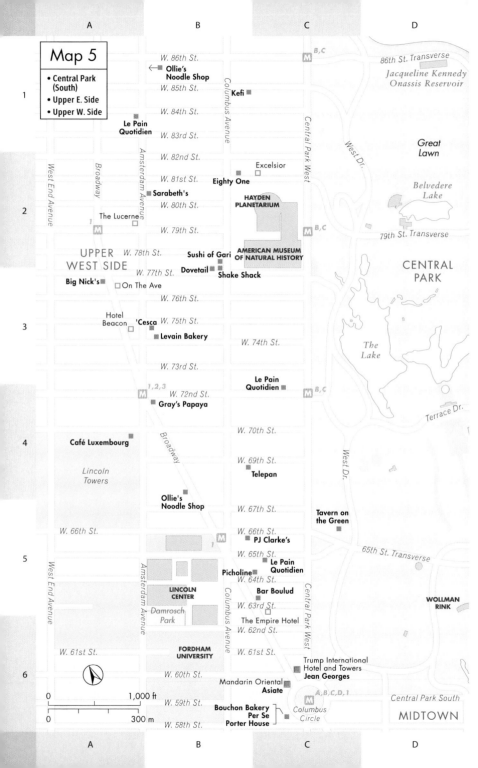

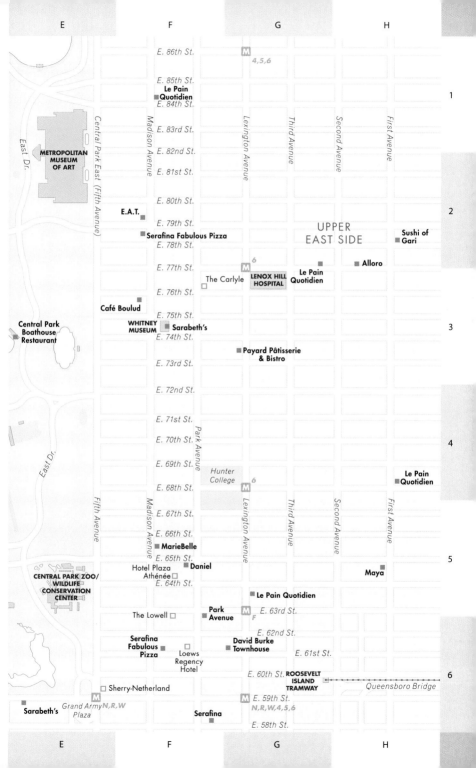

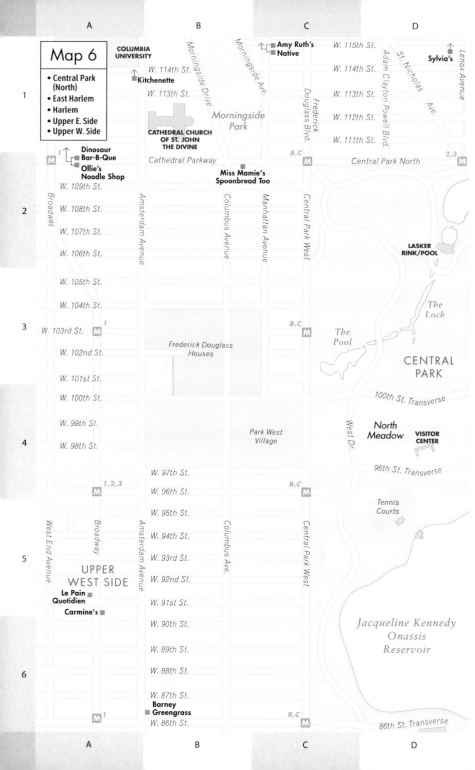

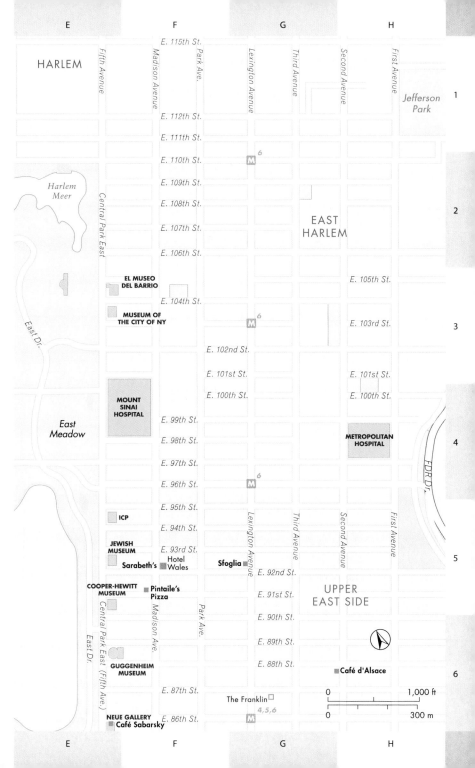

Where to Stay

WORD OF MOUTH

"We just returned from a three-night stay at the Michelangelo Hotel. The feel is European with a comfortable lobby and bar. On our second night we had a basket of Godiva chocolates delivered, which I thought was a nice touch."

—cindymal

Updated by
Alexander
Basek

Consider yourself lucky. Finding a hotel room in New York used to be a challenge, with high prices echoing high demand. That's history. Welcome to a new buyers market, where the deals are plentiful.

Those savings mean you'll have some extra spending money for your trip—or the ability to splurge a little. (Did someone say room service?) Maybe those 400-thread-count sheets were out of your league before, but chances are today there's a sweet weekend rate in Gotham that includes Egyptian cotton bedclothes you can actually afford. It may still require a little hunting and planning, but that's where we can help.

The first thing to consider is location (check out our "Where Should I Stay?" chart on the following page). Many New York City visitors insist on staying in the hectic Midtown area, but other neighborhoods are often just as convenient. Less-touristy areas, such as Gramercy, the Lower East Side, the Upper West Side—even Brooklyn—offer a far more realistic sense of New York life.

Also consider timing: the least expensive months to book rooms in the city are January and February. If you're flexible on dates, ask the reservationist if there's a cheaper time to stay during your preferred traveling month—that way you can avoid peak dates, like Fashion Week and the New York marathon. And be sure to ask about possible weekend packages that could include a third night free. (The Financial District in particular can be a discount gold mine on the weekend.)

Another source of bargains? Chain hotels. Many have moved into the city, offering reasonable room rates. In addition to favorites like the Sheraton, Hilton, and Hyatt brands, there are Best Westerns, Days Inns, and Comfort Inns. These rates aren't quite the same as the low prices you'll find outside Manhattan, but they're certainly getting closer.

WHERE SHOULD I STAY?

	Neighborhood Vibe	Pros	Cons
Lower Manhattan (below Canal St., with TriBeCa)	Mostly skyscraper hotels in an area that buzzes with activity during weekday hours, but can be eerily quiet at night.	Low crime area; easy subway access to Uptown sights; great walking paths along the waterfront and in Battery Park.	Construction and ...tion near World Trade Center site; limited choice of restaurants and shopping.
SoHo, NoLita, and Little Italy	Swanky, high-end hotels with hip restaurants and lounges patronized by New Yorkers and travelers alike.	Scores of upscale clothing boutiques and art galleries nearby; safe area for meandering walks; easy subway access.	Not budget friendly; streets are crowded on weekends; few major monuments nearby.
Greenwich Village (with West Village and Meatpacking)	More hotels are opening, in the city's trendiest restaurant and nightlife area.	Easy subway access to anywhere in town; great shopping, dining, and drinking venues.	Winding streets can be tough to navigate; most hotels are on the pricey side.
Union Square (with Gramercy, Murray Hill, and Flatiron)	A residential area where you'll get a feel for what it's really like to live in the city.	Patches of calm respite from the hustle-and-bustle of downtown and Midtown; low crime area.	Limited subway access; Gramercy or Murray Hill area may be too quiet for some.
East Village and Lower East Side	The epicenter of edgy New York, great for travelers looking to party.	Great low-cost options for twenty-somethings. Excellent chef-owned restaurants and independent boutiques nearby.	One of the least subway-accessible Manhattan neighborhoods; expect late-night noise.
Midtown East and Upper East Side	Business travelers flock to Midtown for its central location and its power-dining restaurants.	Easy regional rail and subway access; near tourist attractions like Central Park and several museums.	Most hotels here are expensive; the streets are quiet after 9 PM; few budget dining options.
Midtown West and Chelsea	Mostly big-name hotel chains and luxury business suites in the area around Times Square, where out-of-towners tend to congregate.	Near Broadway theaters; easy access to regional trains and most subway lines; budget options are available in chain hotels and indies alike.	Streets are often packed with pedestrians; restaurants are chain-owned and often overpriced; area around Port Authority can feel gritty.
Upper West Side	High-priced hotels in a residential neighborhood near Central Park, Lincoln Center, and several museums.	Low crime area; tree-lined streets; great delis and laid-back neighborhood eateries.	The 1 train can be dreadfully slow; most hotels are on the pricey side.

19

NEW YORK CITY LODGING PLANNER

Strategy

With hundreds of Manhattan hotels, it may seem like a daunting question. But fret not—our expert writers and editors have done most of the legwork. The 120-plus selections here represent the best this city has to offer—from the best budget motels to the sleekest designer hotels. Scan "Best Bets" on the following pages for top recommendations by price and experience. Or find a review quickly in the listings—search by neighborhood, then alphabetically. Happy hunting!

Need a Reservation?

Hotel reservations are an absolute necessity when planning your trip to New York—although rooms are easier to come by these days. Competition for clients also means properties undergo frequent improvements, especially during July and August, so when booking ask about any renovations, lest you get a room within earshot of construction. In this ever-changing city travelers can find themselves temporarily, and most inconveniently, without commonplace amenities such as room service or spa access if their hotel is upgrading.

Services

Unless otherwise noted in the individual descriptions, all the hotels listed have private baths, central heating, air-conditioning, and private phones. Almost all hotels have data ports and phones with voice mail, as well as valet service. Many now have wireless Internet (Wi-Fi) available, although it's not always free. Most large hotels have video or high-speed checkout capability, and many can arrange babysitting. Pools are a rarity, but most properties have gyms or health clubs, and sometimes full-scale spas; hotels without facilities usually have arrangements for guests at nearby gyms, sometimes for a fee.

Parking

Bringing a car to Manhattan can significantly add to your lodging expenses. Many properties in all price ranges do have parking facilities, but they are often at independent garages that charge as much as $20 or more per day, and valet parking can cost up to $60 a day. The city's exorbitant 18¾% parking tax can turn any car you drive into the Big Apple into a lemon.

Family Travel

New York has gone to great lengths to attract family vacationers, and hotels have followed the family-friendly trend. Some properties provide such diversions as Web TV and in-room video games; others have suites with kitchenettes and fold-out sofa beds. Most full-service Manhattan hotels provide roll-away beds, babysitting, and stroller rental, but be sure to make arrangements when booking the room, not when you arrive.

Does Size Matter?

If room size is important to you, ask the reservationist how many square feet a room has, not just if it's big. A hotel room in New York is considered quite large if it's 500 square feet. Very large rooms, such as those at the Four Seasons, are 600 square feet. To stay anywhere larger you'll have to get a multiroom suite. Small rooms are a tight 150 to 200 square feet. Very small rooms are less than 100 square feet; you'll find these at inns and lodges and they're sold as a single for only one person. There are studio apartments in the city that are 250 square feet and include a kitchen; 1,000 square feet is considered a huge abode in this very compact and crowded urban playland.

Prices

There's no denying that New York City hotels are expensive, but rates run the full range. For high-end hotels like the Mandarin Oriental at Central Park, prices start at $745 a night for a standard room in high season, which runs from September through December. At the low end of the spending spectrum, a room at Chelsea Lodge starts at $129 for a single. But don't be put off by the prices printed here—many hotels slash their rates significantly for promotions and Web-only deals.

The price ratings we've printed are based on standard double rooms at high season, excluding holidays. Although we list all of the facilities that are available at a property, we don't specify what is included and what costs extra. Those policies are subject to change without notice, so it's always best to ask what's included when you make your reservation.

WHAT IT COSTS FOR TWO PEOPLE

$$$$	$$$	$$	$	¢
over $600	$450–$599	$300–$449	$150–$299	under $150

Prices are for a standard double room, excluding 13.625% city and state taxes.

In This Chapter

BEST BETS FOR NEW YORK CITY LODGING

Fodor's offers a selective listing of quality lodging experiences in every price range, from the city's best budget motel to its most sophisticated luxury hotel. Here, we've compiled our top recommendations by price and experience. The very best properties—in other words, those that provide a particularly remarkable experience in their price range—are designated in the listings with the Fodor's Choice logo.

Fodor's Choice ★

The Carlyle
Gramercy Park Hotel
Hotel on Rivington
Inn at Irving Place
Inn on 23rd
Library Hotel
Mandarin Oriental
The Peninsula
Pod Hotel
Ritz-Carlton Central Park South
SoHo Grand
The St. Regis

By Price

¢

Carlton Arms
La Quinta Inn
Pod Hotel
Second Home on Second Avenue

$

Casablanca Hotel
Herald Square Hotel
Hotel Beacon
Hotel 41
Hotel Metro
Nu Hotel

$$

Grace Hotel
Holiday Inn SoHo
Hotel on Rivington
Inn at Irving Place
Inn on 23rd
Library Hotel
The Mansfield
Maritime Hotel

$$$

Gramercy Park Hotel
The Mercer
The Michelangelo
SoHo Grand
W Hotel New York

$$$$

The Carlyle
Mandarin Oriental
The Peninsula
Ritz-Carlton Central Park South
The St. Regis

By Experience

BEST AFTERNOON TEA

The Carlyle
Four Seasons
Inn at Irving Place
The London NYC
The St. Regis

BEST BEDS

Four Seasons
Hotel on Rivington
Inn at Irving Place
The Mansfield
Ritz-Carltons

BEST FOR BUSINESS

Bryant Park Hotel
The Peninsula
Ritz-Carlton, Battery Park
The St. Regis
Trump International Hotel and Towers

BEST CELEBRITY RETREAT

Hotel Gansevoort
The Lowell
Mandarin Oriental
Maritime Hotel
The Mercer

BEST CONCIERGE

Four Seasons
Le Parker Meridien
The London NYC
Mandarin Oriental
Ritz-Carlton Battery Park

BEST GYM

Le Parker Meridien

The London NYC

Trump International Hotel and Towers

BEST FOR JOGGING BUFFS

Le Parker Meridien

The Ritz-Carlton Battery Park

The Ritz-Carlton Central Park South

Trump International Hotel and Towers

BEST HIPSTER HOTELS

Bowery Hotel

Gramercy Park Hotel

Hotel Gansevoort

The Mercer

60 Thompson

BEST FOR HISTORY BUFFS

The Carlyle

Inn at Irving Place

The St. Regis

The Waldorf=Astoria

BEST HOTEL BAR

Bemelmans Bar at The Carlyle

King Cole Bar at St. Regis

Lobby Bar at the Bowery Hotel

Rose Bar at Gramercy Park Hotel

BEST HOTEL RESTAURANT

Asiate at Mandarin Oriental

Country at Carlton on Madison Avenue

Gordon Ramsay and Maze at The London NYC

Jean Georges at Trump International Hotel and Towers

L'Atelier de Joel Robuchon at Four Seasons

BEST FOR KIDS

Affinia 50

Embassy Suites New York

Le Parker Meridien

Omni Berkshire Place

BEST LOBBY

Four Seasons

Gramercy Park Hotel

Hudson Hotel

Mandarin Oriental

The Peninsula

The St. Regis

BEST NEIGHBORHOOD EXPERIENCE

The Carlyle

The Franklin

Inn at Irving Place

Washington Square Hotel

BEST NEW HOTELS

The Bowery

Gramercy Park Hotel

Hotel Mela

The London NYC

Nu Hotel

On the Ave

BEST FOR PETS

The Carlyle

Loews Regency

Ritz-Carlton Battery Park

Ritz-Carlton Central Park South

70 Park Avenue

BEST POOL

Hotel Gansevoort

Mandarin Oriental

Millennium UN Plaza

The Peninsula

Trump International Hotel and Towers

BEST-KEPT SECRET

The Franklin

Inn at Irving Place

Inn on 23rd

The Lowell

Second Home on Second Avenue

BEST SERVICE

The Carlyle

Four Seasons

The Peninsula

Ritz-Carlton Battery Park

SoHo Grand

BEST TOILETRIES

Gramercy Park Hotel

Hotel Gansevoort

The Peninsula

SoHo Grand

The St. Regis

Tribeca Grand

BEST VIEWS

The Carlyle

The Ritz Carlton Battery Park

The Ritz Carlton Central Park South

Trump International Hotel and Towers

MOST ROMANTIC

Inn at Irving Place

Library Hotel

Ritz-Carlton Battery Park

W New York

19

BROOKLYN

$$ 🍴 **New York Marriott at the Brooklyn Bridge.** Don't rule out Brooklyn; you may not save money at particular hotel, but you will get bang for your buck. What Manhattan hotel has room for an Olympic-length lap pool, an 1,100-car garage, and even a dedicated kosher kitchen? Rooms are classic Marriott—large, comfortable, plain guest rooms enhanced by niceties such as high ceilings, massaging showerheads, and rolling desks. If you're looking to explore, some of the country's best neighborhoods—Brooklyn Heights, Cobble Hill, Carroll Gardens, and DUMBO, as well as the Brooklyn Bridge pedestrian path—are just a five-minute walk, and if you need to get to Manhattan, major subway lines are a block away or a few short minutes by taxi. **Pros:** near New York's new, hip neighborhoods; full-service hotel; clean, new rooms. **Cons:** on a busy street in downtown Brooklyn. ✉ *333 Adams St., between Johnson and Willoughby Sts., Downtown Brooklyn* 🕿 *718/246–7000 or 888/436–3759* 🌐 *www.marriott.com/nycbk* 🛏 *666 rooms, 25 suites* ⚐ *In-room: safe, Internet. In-hotel: restaurant, room service, bar, pool, gym, laundry service, concierge, public Wi-Fi, parking (fee), no-smoking rooms* ☱ *AE, D, DC, MC, V* Ⓜ *2, 3, 4, 5 to Borough Hall.*

$ 🍴 **Nu Hotel.** The hip-yet-affordable Nu is perfect for visitors seeking a manageable taste of outer borough New York. Sitting atop Smith Street, one of Brooklyn's main drags for nightlife and shopping, the Nu's staff is eager to highlight the neighborhood's charms to guests. Flat-screens, complimentary Wi-Fi, and AV hook-ups for your iPod or laptop make the above-average size rooms livable, though the minimalist white-and-grey color scheme (punctuated with eco-friendly flourishes like cork floors, organic cotton sheets, and lead-free paint) can feel chilly at times. Just off the small check-in area downstairs, a quiet bar serves small plates of Spanish food at night and free pastries with Starbucks coffee come morning——but more fun can be had outside the front door. **Pros:** great Brooklyn launching pad; knowledgeable staff; fitness center open 24-hours. **Cons:** It's subway or cab ride to anything in Manhattan; bar area can be a little too quiet; limited in-room amenities. ✉ *85 Smith St., Brooklyn* 🕿 *718/852–8585* 🌐 *www.nuhotelbrooklyn.com* 🛏 *3 rooms, 16 suites* ⚐ *In-room: Wi-Fi, safe. In-hotel: bar, gym, parking (fee), public Internet* ☱ *AE, MC, V* Ⓜ *F to Bergen St.; A,C, G to Hoyt-Schermerhorn*

LOWER MANHATTAN—BELOW CANAL STREET, INCLUDING TRIBECA

FINANCIAL DISTRICT

$$ 🍴 **Gild Hall.** Captains of Industry, meet your first financial district boutique hotel. Operated by the owners of the successful, chic 60 Thompson Hotel in SoHo, Gild Hall aggressively courts clientele with a Y chromosome: beds have padded leather headboards and tartan throw blankets. The rooms are small but come replete with custom-made wood desks and tables. Todd English's restaurant, the Libertine, doubles down on the vibe the hotel also strives to achieve, sort of English gentlemen's club meets high-roller. The Gold Street location, though

slightly hard to find, is a short walk from downtown's central banks and business, as well as two blocks from South Street Seaport and City Hall. **Pros:** central financial district location; eye-popping lobby; excellent restaurant. **Cons:** small rooms for the price; untraditional location. ⊠*15 Gild Hall, at Platt St., Financial District* ☎*212/232–7700 or 800/268–0700* ⊕*www.wall streetdistrict.com* ⊅*126 rooms*

⚷*In-room: safe, Wi-Fi. In-hotel: restaurant, room service, bar, laundry service, public Internet, public Wi-Fi* ▭*AE, D, DC, MC, V* ⦿*CP* Ⓜ*2, 3, 4, 5, 6, A, C to Fulton St. Broadway-Nassau.* ✢*1:E3*

TRIBECA

$ ☷**Cosmopolitan.** Surprisingly, there's no *Sex and the City* affiliation at the Cosmo, but for those saving for Jimmy Choos (or just on a budget) it's a steal. Rooms are rather plain, but at least they are all modern and clean. The hotel is situated on a busy TriBeCa intersection, and is an ideal launching pad for exploring downtown neighborhoods like Chinatown, Little Italy, and SoHo. The building dates to 1850—Abraham Lincoln slept here. Repeat clientele come for the "miniloft" rooms, with a bed on an upper level and bath downstairs. **Pros:** spotlessly clean; friendly staff. **Cons:** noisy location; spartan rooms. ⊠*95 West Broadway, at Chambers St., TriBeCa* ☎*212/566–1900 or 888/895–9400* ⊕*www. cosmohotel.com* ⊅*125 rooms* ⚷*In-room: Wi-Fi. In-hotel: public Wi-Fi, no-smoking rooms* ▭*AE, DC, MC, V* Ⓜ*1, 2, 3, A, C to Chambers St.* ✢*1:C2*

$$ ☷**Duane Street Hotel.** Amid TriBeCa's historic warehouses and trendy art galleries sits the Duane Street Hotel, a fashionable addition to the neighborhood. Comfortable rooms are painted in shades of soft lilac or green apple while light pours through loft-like windows. Hardwood floors, flat-screen TVs, and compact fold-up desks give rooms a modern, playful feel, and cashmere throws and fresh flowers add touches of romance. Sophisticated bathrooms have slate floors and "We Live Like This"–brand amenities. Guests can use complimentary passes to work out at a nearby Equinox or relax at 'beca, the hotel's equally swanky restaurant. Be warned: the restaurant and the rooms facing the street are both loud. **Pros:** great location; in-room spa treatments available through Euphoria Spa TriBeCa; turndown service with Jacques Torres chocolates. **Cons:** noisy; small restaurant. ⊠*130 Duane St., TriBeCa* ☎*212/964–6400* ⊕*www.duanestreethotel.com* ⊅*45 rooms* ⚷*In-room: safe, Wi-Fi. In-hotel: restaurant, room service, bar, executive floor, public Wi-Fi, no-smoking rooms* ▭*AE, DC, MC, V* Ⓜ*1, 2, 3 to Chambers St.; A,C to Chambers St.* ✢*2:D6*

$$ ☷**Embassy Suites New York.** With a convenient downtown location near a waterfront park and the World Financial Center, this flashy Embassy Suites has a lot to offer to families and business travelers. The hotel is part of a complex with a six-screen movie theater and a 20,000-square-

19

foot health club. As the name suggests, every one of the modern rooms here is at least a one-bedroom suite, with a living area that includes a pull-out double bed sofa, dining table, and microwave oven. The hotel has an attractive lobby, with a 14-story center atrium and a colorful Sol LeWitt mural running down its entire length. You'll have a relatively long walk to the subway, but there is a complimentary evening cocktail reception and the trademark Embassy Suites breakfast bonanza to make up for it. **Pros:** good for families; movie theater downstairs. **Cons:** a schlep to the subway; far from Midtown; nearby construction. ✉*102 North End Ave., at Murray St., TriBeCa* ☎*212/945–0100 or 800/362–2779* ⊕*www.newyorkcity.embassysuites.com* ⤢*463 suites* ⌂*In-room: safe, refrigerator, Wi-Fi. In-hotel: restaurant, room service, bar, concierge, laundry service, public Internet, public Wi-Fi, parking (fee), no-smoking rooms* ☰*AE, D, DC, MC, V* Ⓜ*R, W to Cortlandt St.; A, C, E to Chambers St.* ✛*1:A2*

$$$$ 🏨 **Greenwich Hotel.** You talkin' to me? Yes, Robert DeNiro is a financial backer behind the Greenwich Hotel in TriBeCa, DeNiro's backyard. Despite the big name behind it, the Greenwich flies under the radar, with an unmarked entrance leading to a jumbled lobby without a discernable theme. Upstairs, rooms have an internationalist souk theme with Moroccan tile, rugs covering floors made from reclaimed oak, and French doors. No two rooms are decorated alike. The hotel's big-name restaurant Ago, an import from Los Angeles, couldn't find its stride in NYC and was shuttered. At this writing, a new restaurant is in the works. The spa is done in a traditional Japanese style, as is the hotel pool. **Pros:** varied yet clever room decoration; efficient staff. **Cons:** restaurant situation unknown; odd lobby. ✉*377 Greenwich St., TriBeCa* ☎*212/941–8900* ⊕*www.thegreenwichhotel.com* ⤢*88 rooms, 16 suites* ⌂*In-room: safe, Wi-Fi, DVD. In-hotel: restaurant, room service, spa, pool, gym, parking (fee), public Internet* ☰*AE, MC, V* Ⓜ*1 to Franklin St.* ✛*2:C6*

$$ 🏨 **Ritz-Carlton New York, Battery Park.** If you're staying this far downtown, the Ritz is your top choice. The hotel provides the classic Ritz-Carlton experience—you'll be greeted by at least one staffer each time you walk into the hotel or enter the lobby from your room—and the big rooms boast sweeping views of the Statue of Liberty and Ellis Island. West-facing rooms come with telescopes. Happily, the rooms diverge from the typical fussy Ritz-Carlton decor, with designer touches like marble baths and modern wood desks. The superlative staff includes a bath butler who can fill your soaking tub with anything from rose petals to rubber duckies. There's steak-house fare at 2 West and a hopping post-work scene at the outdoor Rise Bar on the 14th floor, but neither are exceptional, considering the markup. **Pros:** NYC's only waterfront luxury hotel; best base for downtown exploring; pet- and kid-friendly; Liberty views. **Cons:** removed from Midtown tourist sights; limited nighttime activities; few neighborhood options for dining and entertainment. ✉*2 West St., at Battery Park, TriBeCa* ☎*212/344–0800 or 800/241–3333* ⊕*www.ritzcarlton.com* ⤢*254 rooms, 39 suites* ⌂*In-room: refrigerator (some), DVD (some), Internet, Wi-Fi. In-hotel: 2 restaurants, room service, bars, laundry service, concierge, executive*

floor, public Internet, public Wi-Fi, parking (fee), some pets allowed, no-smoking rooms ⊟*AE, D, DC, MC, V* Ⓜ*1, R, W to Rector St.* ✛*1:C5*

$$ Ⓣ**Tribeca Grand.** A fabulous, suburban-style eight-story atrium in the middle of one of New York's hippest hotels? All part of the wild fun. Movie- and music-industry celebs hang out at the Church Lounge— a bar, café, and dining room at the base of the atrium—well into the night, sometimes to the dismay of serenity-seeking guests (a white-noise filter in rooms helps keep the peace to some extent). Even if you're not a celeb, it's a great place to meet friends without straying too far from the twin glass elevators that whisk you up and away. Comfortable and stylish rooms with a retro nod have low platform beds and podlike bathrooms with aluminum consoles reminiscent of those in airplanes, complete with Malin + Goetz amenities. The special "iStudios" are premium rooms kitted with the latest gadgets from Apple. Pets are welcome with open arms; you can even request goldfish brought to your room. **Pros:** great dining and bar scene; iPods in each room; fun social atrium; pet-friendly. **Cons:** rooms get noise from restaurant below; bathroom has slightly cold design. ⊠*2 Ave. of the Americas (6th Ave.), between Walker and White Sts., TriBeCa* ☎*212/519–6600 or 800/965–3000* ⊕*www.tribecagrand.com* ⇖*197 rooms, 6 suites* ⌂*In-room: safe, refrigerator, Wi-Fi. In-hotel: restaurant, room service, bar, gym, laundry service, concierge, parking (fee), public Wi-Fi, public Internet, some pets allowed, no-smoking rooms* ⊟*AE, D, DC, MC, V* Ⓜ*A, C, E to Canal St.* ✛*2:D5*

SOHO, NOLITA AND LITTLE ITALY

SOHO

$$ Ⓣ**Holiday Inn SoHo.** Guests here are the hippest you'll find at any Holiday Inn. If that doesn't interest you, stay here for the cheapest rates in SoHo. Like so many formerly budget options in the city, plans are in the works to convert this property into a swank boutique hotel, so get in on the savings while you can. Historical features that remain in this former bank building include oversize arched windows, high ceilings, and a classic exterior. Rooms are standard-issue, but clean and well maintained, with touches like in-room coffeemakers and CD players. Bustling Canal Street is on the corner for bargain shopping. **Pros:** cheap SoHo solution; well-trained staff. **Cons:** hotel won't be around much longer; nothing stylish; standard-issue rooms. ⊠*138 Lafayette St., near Canal St., SoHo* ☎*212/966–8898 or 800/465–4329* ⊕*www.hidowntown-nyc.com* ⇖*215 rooms, 12 suites* ⌂*In-room: safe, Wi-Fi. In-hotel: restaurant, room service, bar, gym, laundry service, concierge, public Internet, public Wi-Fi, parking (fee), no-smoking rooms* ⊟*AE, D, DC, MC, V* Ⓜ*6, M, N, Q, R, W to Canal St.* ✛*2:E5.*

$$$ Ⓣ**The Mercer.** Owner Andre Balazs, known for his Chateau Marmont in Hollywood, has a knack for dating Hollywood starlets and channeling a neighborhood sensibility. Here it's SoHo loft all the way. It's superbly situated in the heart of SoHo's shopping district, although you wouldn't know it once you're inside the lobby, a minimalist oasis created by acclaimed French designer Christian Liagre. Most guest

19

rooms are generously sized with long entryways, high ceilings, and walk-in closets, but the lowest-priced rooms are a slightly snug 250 square feet. Dark African woods and custom-designed furniture upholstered in muted solids lend serenity with sophistication.

Some bathrooms feature decadent two-person marble tubs surrounded by mirrors. Downstairs is the always happening Mercer Kitchen, and the submercer bar, with a separate entrance, is one of the city's hottest doors. Beware the inconsistent service, which runs the gamut from friendly to indifferent. **Pros:** great location; sophisticated design touches; celebrity sightings in lobby. **Cons:** service inconsistent. ⊠*147 Mercer St., at Prince St., SoHo* ☎*212/966–6060 or 888/918–6060* ⊕*www.mercerhotel.com* ⤳*67 rooms, 8 suites* ⟳*In-room: safe, DVD, Wi-Fi. In-hotel: restaurant, room service, bars, concierge, public Internet, public Wi-Fi, some pets allowed, no-smoking rooms* ⊟*AE, D, DC, MC, V* Ⓜ*R, W to Prince St.* ✛*2:E3*

$$$ 🛏 **60 Thompson.** The success of this hotel spurred its owners to replicate the hotel's vibe in three new hotels elsewhere in the city. There is much to admire here. It's one of the hippest hotels in New York, offering a range of dining and bar choices. Kittichai, the chic Thai restaurant on the ground floor, has patio dining and a gold-suffused bar. The rooftop lounge A60 is a guests- and members-only warm-weather haven for hipsters. Thom bar, the second-floor lobby is a dark space filled with contemporary art. Rooms feature a dramatic, spare design. The generous use of dark woods and full-wall leather headboards gives the rooms welcoming warmth. **Pros:** hip, cosmopolitan scene; lots of nightlife options; access to private rooftop club; good gym; some rooms have balconies. **Cons:** can be sceney; not family oriented; no pets allowed. ⊠*60 Thompson St., between Broome and Spring Sts., SoHo* ☎*212/431–0400 or 877/431–0400* ⊕*www.thompsonhotels.com* ⤳*82 rooms, 8 suites* ⟳*In-room: safe, DVD, Internet, Wi-Fi. In-hotel: restaurant, room service, bars, concierge, parking (fee); public Internet, public Wi-Fi, no-smoking rooms* ⊟*AE, D, DC, MC, V* Ⓜ*C, E to Spring St.* ✛*2:D4*

$$$

Fodor's Choice
★

🛏 **SoHo Grand.** The SoHo Grand defines what SoHo is today—cosmopolitan, creative, and a bit hard on your cash flow. When it opened in 1996, it had been a century since a new hotel debuted in the neighborhood. Today, as new hotels crowd the field, the Grand's low-key sophistication stands out more clearly. The Grand Bar & Lounge is sometimes called SoHo's Living Room for its comfortable, social atmosphere. Public spaces as well as guest rooms use an industrial-chic design to mimic the architecture of the neighborhood, though this can come across as spartan to some. Comfortable contemporary rooms are mainly focused on the view out the ample windows; bathrooms are stark but have deep soaking tubs. A great seasonal pleasure is The Yard—a large outdoor space where you can have a drink or meal and then spread out on the grassy lawn—the only one of its kind in the city. The staff here is professional, polished, and more experienced than you'll find at other fashionable hotels. **Pros:** fashionable, laid-back sophistication; great service; surprisingly discreet setting; diverse eating and drinking options. **Cons:** closer to Canal Street than prime SoHo; rooms on small side. ⊠*310 West Broadway, at Grand St., SoHo* ☎*212/965–3000 or 800/965–3000* ⊕*www.sohogrand.com* ↪*365 rooms, 2 suites* △*In-room: safe, refrigerator, VCR, Internet, Wi-Fi. In-hotel: restaurant, room service, bars, gym, laundry service, concierge, parking (fee), some pets allowed, no-smoking rooms* ⊟*AE, D, DC, MC, V* Ⓜ*6, J, M, N, Q, R, W to Canal St.* ✛*2:D4*

EAST VILLAGE AND LOWER EAST SIDE

EAST VILLAGE

ℂ ⏏**Second Home on Second Avenue.** If you like the East Village, reserve your room now, because these eight rooms are the only way to experience the neighborhood like a local. A loyal core of regular patrons, mainly Europeans, keeps it booked at least five months in advance. Far from the tourist traps, it's easy to blend into the scene here. A punctilious owner keeps the large rooms spotless and the prices cheap. Two caveats: you have to walk up to the third or fourth floor, and the bar downstairs can be noisy, especially on weekends. The six largest rooms are themed: two are modern plus Caribbean, Peruvian, skylight, and tribal. Guests have use of a communal kitchen. **Pros:** spacious rooms; very clean; rare East Village rooms. **Cons:** walk-up building; two rooms share a bath. ⊠*221 2nd Ave., between 13 and 14th Sts., East Village* ☎*212/677–3161* ⊕*www.secondhomesecondavenue.com* ↪*8 rooms, 3 with bath* △*In-room: no phone, safe, Wi-Fi. In-hotel: no elevator, public Wi-Fi, no kids under 5* ⊟*AE, D, DC, MC, V* Ⓜ*4, 5, 6, L, N, Q, R, W to 14th St./Union Sq.; L to 3rd Ave.* ✛*3:G2*

LOWER EAST SIDE

$$$ ⏏**The Bowery Hotel.** The principal pleasure in a stay at the Bowery Hotel is lounging in the ground-floor lobby, skimming the tabloids left out for guests. Full of old-world dark wood and leather chairs, it's an English hunting lodge in Manhattan, warmed by rich floor-to-ceiling tapestries, fireplaces, and chandeliers. Sadly, rooms upstairs don't maintain the richness of the lobby—they're on the minimalist side, with the big console desks and old-school windows the only grand flourishes. Still, the mood created by the attractive red-coated doormen, the clubby bar, and the trendy former-flophouse address makes this one of the hottest hotels—and scenes–of the moment. **Pros:** quirky, fun location; ravishing bar and lobby-lounge area; celebrity sightings; interesting views. **Cons:** gritty neighbors; rooms aren't luxurious; may be too trendy for some. ⊠*335 Bowery, at 3rd St., Lower East Side* ☎*212/505–9100* ⊕*www. theboweryhotel.com* ↪*117 rooms, 18 suites* △*In-room: safe, Wi-Fi. In-hotel: restaurant, room service, bar, laundry service, concierge, public Internet, public Wi-Fi, parking (fee), some pets allowed, no-smoking rooms* ⊟*AE, D, DC, MC, V* ⦿|*CP* Ⓜ*6 to Bleecker; B, D, F, V to Broadway/Lafayette.* ✛*2:F2*

19

Hotel on Rivington

The Carlyle

Library Hotel

$$ ☃**Hotel on Rivington.** The rooms here have something completely origi-
Fodor'sChoice nal and breathtaking—when you hit a button on a remote control, your
★ curtains slowly open to reveal floor-to-ceiling glass windows. Seen that
trick before? Well, this is the only tall building in the area, and the views
of the Lower East Side and Midtown are unadulterated New York. The
bathrooms aren't for the modest or faint of heart—you'll either want to
shower with your glasses on, or you'll blush at being completely naked
before the entire city (privacy curtains can be requested). Downstairs,
the hotel bar is pure excess—it and the jumping restaurant are velvet-
roped mayhem on weekends. (Staying here also gives you access to a
small VIP bar next door.) The mezzanine bar–art library–billiard room
is a hangout you can call your own. **Pros:** superhip location and vibe;
huge windows with wonderful New York views; happening bar and
restaurant. **Cons:** feels like a club on weekends; spotty service; small
rooms and suites. ✉*107 Rivington St., between Ludlow and Essex Sts.,
Lower East Side* ☎*212/475–2600 or 800/915–1537* ⊕*www.hotelon
rivington.com* ↝*110 rooms* ⌂*In-room: safe, refrigerator, Internet,
Wi-Fi. In-hotel: restaurant, room service, bar, laundry service, con-
cierge, parking (fee), some pets allowed* ▭*AE, D, DC, MC, V* Ⓜ*F, J,
M, Z to Delancey/Essex Sts.* ✛*2:G3*

GREENWICH VILLAGE WITH MEATPACKING DISTRICT AND WEST VILLAGE

GREENWICH VILLAGE

$ ☃**Washington Square Hotel.** Across
from Washington Square Park's
magnificent arch, this low-key
European-style hotel right in the
heart of New York University and
Greenwich Village is popular with
visiting NYU parents. One block
from the very central West 4th

WORD OF MOUTH

"The Washington Square Hotel is
ideally located in the Village. It's a
small European-type hotel, but the
location is lovely."   —mclaurie

19

Street subway station, it's easy to get to the rest of Downtown's sights.
Some rooms are cheerfully decorated—deluxe rooms have a snazzy
Hollywood art-deco style, while the standard rooms are plainer with
pastel florals and limited amenities. Deluxe rooms come with pillow-top
mattresses and complimentary high-speed Internet access. The intimate
Deco Room has mosaic floors, elegant mirrors, and a wrought-iron-
and-glass brass gate from Paris. North Square restaurant has a jazz
brunch and surprisingly sophisticated fare. **Pros:** park-front location;
deluxe rooms are charming; convenient to nearly every subway. **Cons:**
NYU students everywhere; rooms are small. ✉*103 Waverly Pl., at
MacDougal St., Greenwich Village* ☎*212/777–9515 or 800/222–0418*
⊕*www.wshotel.com* ↝*160 rooms* ⌂*In-room: safe, Internet (some).
In-hotel: restaurant, bar, gym, public Wi-Fi* ▭*AE, MC, V* ⦿*CP* Ⓜ*A,
B, C, D, E, F, V to W. 4th St./Washington Sq.* ✛*2:D1*

CLOSE UP

Hotel Hot Spots

Some of the city's most stylish bars and lounges are located in hotels. These stylish boîtes occasionally require traversing a velvet-roped entrance, but most extend automatic entry to guests of the hotel.

Mega-hotelier Ian Schrager's properties are design temples, with chic lounges favored by jet-setters and locals alike. The new "haute Bohemian" **Gramercy Park Hotel** (⇨Union Square/Gramercy) is Schrager's latest offering, with its popular—and pricey—Rose Bar and Jade Bar. The hotel also features a private members- and guests-only Roof Club. **The Hudson** (⇨Midtown West and Chelsea) houses several hip hangouts, including the chic Hudson Bar, with its lighted glass floors and fanciful ceiling mural, as well as an enclosed garden lounge. The rooftop Sky Terrace is an exclusive feature just for guests. At the **Royalton** (⇨Midtown West and Chelsea), the immense lobby lounge is a perennial favorite of music and film industry scenesters as well as magazine publishing types.

In the Meatpacking District, **Hotel Gansevoort** (⇨Greenwich Village/Meatpacking) has a happening bar scene on the rooftop deck. At street level, wander through the lobby into scene-stealing Ono. Not only are the sushi and *robatayaki* (grilled meats made tableside) excellent, but the outdoor lounge here is an urban oasis, with reflecting pools and private cabanas, with curtains, to shut out the crowds.

Down in SoHo, some of the chicest hotels in the city have rock-star-worthy scenes. Movie stars and their hangers-on imbibe into the wee hours at cool Mercer Bar in the **Mercer Hotel** (⇨SoHo) or the even trendier and more exclusive Submercer bar—come in through a hidden entrance just outside the hotel. **60 Thompson**'s (⇨SoHo) rooftop lounge is one of the hottest tickets in town on warm evenings; hotel guests get automatic entrance. There's also the less manic Thom bar, just one floor up.

In Midtown, the trippy **Dream Hotel** (⇨Midtown West) has a rooftop bar that swings into action as soon as the weather warms, and three other bars, including a subterranean lounge under the swanky Mediterranean restaurant Amalia. Hotel guests get priority entrance into all the trendy spots.

The **Grace Hotel** (⇨Midtown West and Chelsea) in Times Square has a bar that's adjacent to a lobby-level pool; you can see all the underwater action through voyeur windows above the bar. Just make sure to pay attention at the end of the evening, or you might be the hotel's next swimming sensation.

MEATPACKING DISTRICT

$$$$ 🖥 **Hotel Gansevoort.** Like a statuesque blonde in a red dress, the Gansevoort is a glamorous, aloof beacon in the trendy Meatpacking District. The rooftop deck is the place to be, and not only for the free breakfast: there's a heated 45-foot pool, myriad terraces, and a swank lounge filled with late-night scene-seekers. Sleek, sexy rooms have sweeping views of the city or the Hudson River; slate-and-marble bathrooms have unique showers that double as steam rooms. However, at these prices, there could be a bit more emphasis on quality over looks in the

furnishings. Downstairs, the Japanese-influenced restaurant Ono has a vibrant Asian interior and a large outdoor bar and lounge space, and there's the G-Spa, a full-service spa and salon. It may not be tasteful, but it's all very representative of the Meatpacking District. **Pros:** stylish; great salon; rooftop pool; wonderful art collection. **Cons:** highly fashion-conscious clientele; bar-restaurant always packed; slipshod service. ⊠*18 9th Ave., at 13th St., Meatpacking District* ☎*212/206–6700 or 877/426–7386* ⊕*www.hotelgansevoort.com* ⊐*166 rooms, 21 suites* ⚐*In-room: safe, Wi-Fi. In-hotel: restaurant, room service, bars, pool, gym, spa, laundry service, concierge, parking (fee), public Internet, some pets allowed* ═*AE, MC, V* ⊙|*CP* Ⓜ*A, C, E, L to 14th St. and 8th Ave.* ✛*3:B4*

UNION SQUARE WITH FLATIRON DISTRICT, GRAMERCY PARK AND MURRAY HILL

GRAMERCY PARK

$$$ 🔲**Gramercy Park Hotel.** The GPH is on such a different plane of cool Fodor'sChoice in comparison to all other NYC hotels, it might as well have its own ★ hospitality category. Ian Schrager, who forged the boutique-hotel concept just over a decade ago, turned the design reins of this hotel over to famed painter and director Julian Schnabel. Embracing a spirit of High Bohemia, the property has a rock-and-roll baroque feel. Works by Cy Twombley, Andy Warhol, and Jean-Michel Basquiat mark the lobby and the two exclusive, ground-level bars that have become key components in the city's nightlife. Only guests, however, enjoy access to the rooftop deck and its interesting lounges—no small privilege. Rooms are an assemblage of specific tastes: opulent velvets; studded leathers; moodily dark bathrooms and showers; photo prints from the famed Magnum collective. If it's your thing, you've just found your new favorite hotel, but some find the hipper-than-thou aspects uncool. **Pros:** great discreet city location, near all but private; radical design; superhip bars and lounges. **Cons:** if you don't like the moody design it will be hard to be comfortable here; dark bathrooms; tiny spa; inconsistent service. ⊠*2 Lexington Ave., at Gramercy Park, Gramercy Park* ☎*212/920–3300* ⊕*www.gramercyparkhotel.com* ⊐*140 rooms, 40 suites* ⚐*In-room: safe, refrigerator, DVD, Internet. In-hotel: restaurant, room service, bars, gym, laundry service, parking (fee), no-smoking rooms* ═*AE, D, DC, MC, V* Ⓜ*6 to 23rd St.* ✛*3:F3*

$$ 🔲**Inn at Irving Place.** Fantasies of old New York—Manhattan straight Fodor'sChoice from the pages of Edith Wharton and Henry James, an era of genteel ★ brick town houses and Tiffany lamps—spring to life at this discreet 20-room inn, the city's most romantic. There is no sign outside the 1830 town house, a hint of the somehow small-town qualities of Irving Place, a lightly trafficked street on the south side of Gramercy Park. One of the city's most famous tea salons, Lady Mendyl's, is run on the lobby level. Rooms have ornamental fireplaces, four-poster beds with embroidered linens, wood shutters, and glossy cherrywood floors. The room named after Madame Olenska (the lovelorn Wharton character) has a bay window with sitting nook—this is one of the most memorable spots in New York; reserve it for anniversaries. **Pros:** romantic;

19

quaint; big rooms; excellent breakfast and tea service; Mario Batali's Casa Mono is downstairs; martini bar. **Cons:** dainty; rooms aren't flawless, with imperfections like older grouting. ⊠*56 Irving Pl., between E. 17th and E. 18th Sts., Gramercy Park* ☏*212/533–4600 or 800/685–1447* ⊕*www.innatirving.com* ↻*5 rooms, 6 suites* ⛶*In-room: refrigerator, VCR. In-hotel: restaurant, room service, bar, laundry service, no kids under 8* ═*AE, D, DC, MC, V* ⍾○⎮*CP* Ⓜ*4, 5, 6, L, N, Q, R, W to 14th St./Union Sq.* ✛*3:G3*

$ ⛌ **Marcel at Gramercy.** A fall 2008 redesign has transformed the Marcel into a chic, yet affordable stay providing guests with both style and substance. The small lobby is outfitted in a dark palette of black, gray, and blue, giving it swanky nightclub vibe; rooms are modernized with flat-screen TVs, iPod docking stations, Frette linens, and Gilchrist & Soames bath amenities. The 10th-floor lounge with its complimentary computer and Wi-Fi access, free coffee, and connecting outdoor patio offers respite from the bustling city below. The Italian restaurant 'inoteca is located on the ground floor and provides room service to hotel guests. **Pros:** outdoor patio offers great space and spectacular views of the city; good value. **Cons:** elevators are slow; poor TV reception; complimentary wine-and-cheese reception could run longer. ⊠*201 E. 24th St., Gramercy Park* ☏*212/696–3800* ⊕*www.themarcelatgramercy. com* ↻*133 rooms, 2 suites* ⛶*In-room: safe. In-hotel: restaurant, room service, public Wi-Fi, laundry service, public Internet, no smoking rooms* ═*AE, D, MC, V* Ⓜ*6 to 23rd St.* ✛*3:G2*

MURRAY HILL

¢ ⛌ **Carlton Arms.** Europeans and students know about the chipper, winning attitude of this friendly, no-frills hotel. For most rooms you have to be willing to share a bathroom (there are two unisex bathrooms per floor), and to carry your bags up a few flights of stairs. If you're fine with that, and don't mind rooms with minimal furnishings, then let the fun begin: every wall and ceiling in this bohemian dive is covered with a mural. Even individual rooms have a theme, such as the Versailles Room, with its outré symphony of trompe-l'oeil trellises and classical urns. The English Cottage room decorated in the Tudor style with vine-covered walls. Despite the great designs, rooms do not have TVs or phones. They do have consistent prices: $130 including tax for a private bath, $110 to share. **Pros:** rock-bottom prices; chipper attitude; quieter residential Murray Hill location. **Cons:** no elevator; few furnishings; many shared baths. ⊠*160 E. 25th St., at 3rd Ave., Murray Hill* ☏*212/684–8337, 212/679–0680 for reservations* ⊕*www. carltonarms.com* ↻*54 rooms, 20 with bath* ⛶*In-room: no phone, no TV. In-hotel: no elevator, public Internet, some pets allowed* ═*MC, V* Ⓜ*R, W to 28th St.* ✛*3:G2*

$$ ⛌ **Carlton on Madison Avenue.** A five-year, $60 million renovation has turned a nearly invisible old dowager into a modern scene-stealer. The Carlton's makeover includes many a happy detail, from the two-story lobby designed by David Rockwell to the still-intact, original 1904 Beaux-Arts details such as the Tiffany-style stained-glass dome (created by workers from the venerable factory but not by Louis Comfort himself). The rooms are done up in a cottage-y style, with fabric-framed

Pod Hotel

19

The Peninsula

The St. Regis

beds, Frette linens, and plenty of mahogany, though the free Wi-Fi and iPod docks are modern enough to balance things out. Country, the restaurant adjacent to the lobby, was joined by a steak house in March 2009; both offer impressive fare and dizzying prices. **Pros:** spectacular lobby; spacious rooms; great restaurant. **Cons:** expensive bar; small rooms. ⊠ *88 Madison Ave., between 28th and 29th Sts., Murray Hill* ☎ *212/532–4100 or 800/601–8500* ⊕ *www.carltonhotelny.com* ↝ *294 rooms, 22 suites* ⟳ *In-room: safe, Wi-Fi. In-hotel: 2 restaurants, room service, bar, laundry service, concierge, public Internet, public Wi-Fi, parking (fee), some pets allowed, no-smoking rooms* ⊟ *AE, D, MC, V* Ⓜ *6 to 28th St.* ✛ *3:F1*

$ 🔟 **Herald Square Hotel.** The sculpted cherubs on the facade and vintage magazine covers adorning the common areas hint at the Herald's previous incarnation as *Life* magazine's headquarters. The hotel is a great value. Rooms are basic and clean; all have TVs and phones with Wi-Fi; some were renovated with flat-screens. Shabby chic fixtures and white-on-white bedspreads round out the look. There's no concierge and no room service, but the staff is friendly, and nearby restaurants will deliver. It's a great bargain for the convenient neighborhood. **Pros:** cheap; centrally located. **Cons:** unattractive lobby; readers report inconsistent service. ⊠ *19 W. 31st St., between 5th Ave. and Broadway, Murray Hill* ☎ *212/279–4017 or 800/727–1888* ⊕ *www.heraldsquarehotel. com* ↝ *120 rooms* ⟳ *In-room: safe, Wi-Fi. In-hotel: airport shuttle, public Internet, public Wi-Fi, some pets allowed* ⊟ *AE, D, MC, V* Ⓜ *B, D, F, N, Q, R, V, W to 34th St./Herald Sq.* ✛ *3:E1*

$$$ 🔟 **Hotel Giraffe.** Inspired by the colors and sleek lines of European moderne, this retro-glam property aspires to the sophisticated style of the 1920s and '30s. Guest rooms with 10-foot ceilings are adorned with antique-rose velveteen armchairs, sorbet-hue sheer curtains, and marble-topped desks. Deluxe rooms have French doors opening onto private balconies from which you can survey Park Avenue. For the ultimate in entertaining (or an exorbitant romantic getaway), reserve the spectacular penthouse suite with baby grand piano and rooftop garden. The civilized service here includes complimentary breakfast, coffee, and weekday evening champagne reception. The staff is exemplary. **Pros:** high-quality linens: rooftop terrace for guests; quiet hotel. **Cons:** street noise near lower levels; pricey for the quality you get. ⊠ *365 Park Ave. S, at E. 26th St., Murray Hill* ☎ *212/685–7700 or 877/296–0009* ⊕ *www. hotelgiraffe.com* ↝ *52 rooms, 21 suites* ⟳ *In-room: safe, DVD, Wi-Fi. In-hotel: restaurant, room service, bars, laundry service, concierge, public Internet, public Wi-Fi, parking (fee), no-smoking rooms* ⊟ *AE, DC, MC, V* ⦿*CP* Ⓜ *6 to 28th St.* ✛ *3:F2*

$ 🔟 **Jolly Hotel Madison Towers.** Italians flock to this hotel operated by Jolly Hotels, the largest hotel chain in Italy. In this U.S. flagship you can expect native Italians, or at least Italian-speaking staff at the front desk and the breakfast room. The chain brings a European air to this friendly hotel on a residential Murray Hill corner, combining an Italian aesthetic with an art-deco design. Deluxe rooms on the top floors have a sleek, contemporary design, grand bathrooms with separate soaking tubs, and views of the Empire State Building. The standard rooms are a bit cramped, and the decor, despite the snazzy cherrywood furniture, can be blah—for an Italian hotel, anyway. The cozy Whaler Bar has a fireplace and a wood-beam ceiling. A separate concession on the premises offers shiatsu massage and a Japanese sauna. **Pros:** Italian influence creates a unique New York hotel experience; good value for location and service; attractive bar. **Cons:** no restaurant; no gym; not contemporary in feel. ⊠*22 E. 38th St., between Madison and Park Aves., Murray Hill* ☎*212/802–0600 or 800/225–4340* ⊕*www.jolly madison.com* ⚲*238 rooms, 6 suites* ⌂*In-room: safe, Wi-Fi. In-hotel: bar, laundry service, concierge, parking (fee), public Internet, public Wi-Fi, some pets allowed, no-smoking rooms* ▭*AE, DC, MC, V* Ⓜ*6 to 33rd St.* ✛*4:F5*

\$ ☷**The Kitano.** This Japanese-owned property, a few blocks from Grand Central, is an oasis of tranquillity. The austere Asian-influenced airy marble lobby is centered around a Botero sculpture of a chunky puppy that you can rub for good luck. Handsome cherry and mahogany furnishings, tea makers, and watercolor still lifes decorate the large rooms; soundproof windows make them among Manhattan's quietest. Hakubai is perhaps the most authentic Japanese dining in the city, with authentic sushi and Kaiseki cuisine. The Garden Café features American fare. The cozy mezzanine-level lounge features live jazz Wednesday through Saturday. Vacationers can take advantage of discounted weekend rates on standard guest rooms and suites larger than those at trendier hotels. **Pros:** big, tranquil rooms; cute mezzanine bar area; guest pass to great local gym; good value. **Cons:** lower floor views are limited. ⊠*66 Park Ave., at E. 38th St., Murray Hill* ☎*212/885–7000 or 800/548–2666* ⊕*www.kitano.com* ⚲*149 rooms, 18 suites* ⌂*In-room: safe, refrigerator, Internet. In-hotel: 2 restaurants, room service, bar, laundry service, concierge, parking (fee), no-smoking rooms* ▭*AE, D, DC, MC, V* Ⓜ*6 to 33rd St.* ✛*4:F5*

\$ ☷**Park South Hotel.** In this beautifully transformed 1906 office building, restful rooms feel smartly contemporary though they've retained some period details. Watch out for rooms that overlook noisy 27th Street or are too close the bar on the ground floor; ask instead for a view of the Chrysler Building. Historic New York flavor is the design focus in the mezzanine library, with black-and-white photos of city scenes from the 1880s through 1950s. The Black Duck bar and restaurant warms patrons with its wood-burning fireplace, though the decor is better than the average food. Luckily, several excellent Indian restaurants are just around the corner. The square Murray Hill location may disappoint hipster guests. **Pros:** free breakfast and Internet; turndown service; good value. **Cons:** small elevators; tame location; spotty service. ⊠*122 E. 28th St., between Lexington and Park Aves., Murray Hill* ☎*212/448–0888 or 800/315–4642* ⊕*www.parksouth hotel.com* ⚲*139 rooms, 2 suites* ⌂*In-room: safe, Internet. In-hotel: restaurant, bar, gym, laundry service, public Wi-Fi, public Internet, concierge* ▭*AE, D, DC, MC, V* ⍥*CP* Ⓜ*6 to 28th St.* ✛*3:F2*

\$\$ ☷**Roger Williams Hotel.** Vibrant colors, bold architecture, and an informal, residential vibe are keystones of this Murray Hill neighborhood hotel. The hotel lobby's "living room" features 20-foot-high windows

19

and a comfortable seating area stocked with newspapers. Rooms are comfortably appointed with playfully colored down comforters, robes, and Aveda bath products, as well as candles, books, and flat-screen plasma TVs. In-room work areas feature wireless Internet. The $14 breakfast buffet features local delicacies like croissants from Balthazar, smoked salmon from Petrossian, and bagels from H&H. It's served in the comfortable "breakfast pantry." Fifteen rooms have private, land-scaped terraces facing Midtown. **Pros:** colorful room decor; easygoing vibe; good value. **Cons:** no room service. ⊠ *131 Madison Ave., at E. 31st St., Murray Hill* ☎*212/448–7000 or 877/847–4444* ⊕*www. rogerwilliamshotel.com* ⤴*193 rooms, 2 suites* ⌂*In-room: Wi-Fi. In-hotel: restaurant, room service, bar, gym, concierge, parking (fee), public Internet, public Wi-Fi, no-smoking rooms* ⊟*AE, D, MC, V* ⏐◯⏐*CP* Ⓜ*6 to 33rd St.* ✛*3:F1*

$$$ ⌂ **70 Park Avenue.** Kimpton hotels have something of a cult following with design enthusiasts, but 70 Park is a low-key, slightly disappointing offering that's more for road-warrior business types than style hounds. The lobby, with its limestone fireplace and thick-pillowed couches, looks like a contemporary living room, and you'll find people parked here with their laptops for hours—a couple of laptops are even set out here for guest use. The rest of the hotel channels a prosperous Park Avenue abode with a conservative, rather unexciting look, with neutral-palette scheme, Ultrasuede chairs and couches, and plasma TVs. This hotel is a casual, comfortable, safe choice in this quiet neighborhood a couple of blocks form Grand Central. Some suites have hot tubs and terraces with Empire State Building views. Silverleaf Tavern serves modern-American small plates, and the bar is comfortable even if you're alone. **Pros:** week-day wine reception; polite service; simple, unobtrusive rooms and hotel layout. **Cons:** bland design; no gym. ⊠ *70 Park Ave., at 38th St., Murray Hill* ☎*212/973–2400 or 800/707–2752* ⊕*www.70parkave.com* ⤴*201 rooms, 4 suites* ⌂*In-room: safe, DVD, Internet, Wi-Fi. In-hotel: restau-rant, room service, bar, laundry service, concierge, some pets allowed, no-smoking rooms* ⊟*AE, D, DC, MC, V* Ⓜ*6 to 33rd St.* ✛*4:F5*

$$$$ ⌂ **W New York–The Court and W New York–The Tuscany.** Just 800 feet away from each other are these technically separate but very similar hotels. Both are boutique properties run by the W brand, with more discreet entrances and a calm residential presence in Murray Hill, a few blocks from Grand Central. The hotels have larger-than-typical rooms, as they were formerly residential apartments. With richly colored bedding and cranberry accents, and ottomans with chenille throws, they're not quite as edgy as other W properties—you'll have to go to Times Square or Union Square for that. However, they uphold the W chain's hip nightlife standards with Tuscany's Cherry Lounge, a rock-and-roll vision in red, and the Court's popular Wet Bar and excellent Icon restaurant. **Pros:** quiet, residential neighborhood; near Grand Central. **Cons:** not for hard-core W guests; 39th Street rooms are noisy; underwhelming lobby. ⊠ *130 E. 39th St., between Lexington and Park Aves., Murray Hill* ☎*212/685–1100 or 877/946–8357* ⊕*www.whotels.com* ⤴*Court: 150 rooms, 39 suites; Tuscany: 122 rooms, 12 suites* ⌂*In-room: safe, DVD, VCR, Internet. In-hotel: restaurant, room service, bar, gym,*

spa, laundry service, concierge, public Internet, public Wi-Fi, some pets allowed, no-smoking rooms ▭*AE, D, DC, MC, V* ✉*Tuscany, 120 E. 39th St., near Lexington Ave., Murray Hill* ☎*212/779–7822, 800/223–6725 for reservations* Ⓜ*4, 5, 6, 7, S to 42nd St./Grand Central.* ✛*4:F5*

UNION SQUARE

$$$$ 🏨**W New York Union Square.** This W Hotel is the most geographically desirable of the brand's many Big Apple branches. It's also the most elegant, utilizing the grand spaces of the landmark Guardian Life building at Union Square's northeast corner. Both the interior and exterior of the 1911 Beaux-Arts–style building retain many original granite and limestone details, including the grand staircase that leads to the Great Room lobby. Rooms are traditional W spaces, including velvet armchairs, Bliss bathroom amenities, and leather headboards. Todd English's Olives anchors the ground floor with a fine, bustling restaurant. Generally, the service staff look as though they just stepped out of a photo shoot, and at times it feels like that's where they'd rather be. **Pros:** fashionable location and staff; great restaurant and exploring neighborhoods. **Cons:** trendy decor; noisy lobby; dim lighting. ✉*201 Park Ave. S, at E. 17th St., Union Square* ☎*212/253–9119 or 877/946–8357* ⊕*www. whotels.com* ⤵*254 rooms, 16 suites* ♿*In-room: safe, refrigerator, DVD, VCR, Wi-Fi. In-hotel: restaurant, room service, bars, gym, spa, laundry service, concierge, parking (fee), some pets allowed, no-smoking rooms* ▭*AE, D, DC, MC, V* Ⓜ*4, 5, 6, L, N, Q, R, W to 14th St./ Union Sq.* ✛*3:F3*

MIDTOWN WEST AND CHELSEA

CHELSEA

¢ 🏨**Chelsea Lodge.** On a quiet neighborhood street near the galleries of Chelsea and the nightlife of the Meatpacking District, this country-inn-style brownstone is a great budget option if you don't need a lot of services or amenities. The majority of the petite rooms share a toilet, but have their own sink and shower in the room. There are small bedrooms with reach-in closets, no phones, and small TVs. However, meticulous attention to cleanliness, lovely period detailing such as decorative wainscoting, and truly helpful staff make a visit here worthwhile. A few doors past the main building are "suites," really small apartments with kitchens and kitchenettes. At $195, these are a great option if you're planning an extended stay or want to take advantage of the gourmet wares at nearby Chelsea Market. **Pros:** on a gorgeous Chelsea block; great bang for the buck; good subway proximity. **Cons:** not romantic; shared bathrooms not right for everyone. ✉*318 W. 20th St., between 8th and 9th Aves., Chelsea* ☎*212/243–4499* ⊕*www.chelsealodge. com* ⤵*22 rooms, 2 with bath; 4 suites* ♿*In-room: kitchen (some), no phone, Wi-Fi. In-hotel: no elevator, public Wi-Fi, no-smoking rooms* ▭*AE, D, MC, V* Ⓜ*C, E to 23rd St.; 1 to 18th St.* ✛*3:C3*

19

$$ 🏨**Inn on 23rd.** Charming and friendly innkeepers Annette and Barry Fisherman will welcome you to this five-floor, 19th-century building in the heart of Chelsea. They took care to make each guest room spacious

Fodor'sChoice
★
☾

and unique. One exotic and elegant room is outfitted in bamboo, another in the art moderne style of the 1940s. Although it's small and homey, the inn provides private baths and satellite TV in all rooms. Dorothy, the house cat, is very friendly, and has an endearing quirk: she loves to ride the elevator. A big continental breakfast is cooked daily by famous-chefs-to-be: members of New School University's culinary program, who use the kitchen in the mornings as a laboratory. If you're a B&B person, you've found your New York retreat. **Pros:** charming innkeepers; comfy and relaxed library; affordable for location. **Cons:** few services for businesspeople; some older amenities; beware if you have cat allergies. ⊠*131 W. 23rd St., between 6th and 7th Aves., Chelsea* ☎*212/463–0330* ⊕*www.innon23rd.com* ↘*13 rooms, 1 suite* ⌂*Inroom: DVD (some), Internet, Wi-Fi. In-hotel: laundry service, public Internet, public Wi-Fi, no-smoking rooms* ⊟*AE, D, DC, MC, V* ❍|*CP* Ⓜ*F, V to 23rd St.* ✛*3:D2*

$$ Ⓣ**Maritime Hotel.** In just about any other city, the Maritime would constitute a major entertainment and cultural epicenter. The hotel houses the 800-room Hiro Ballroom nightclub; Matsuri, the cavernous Japanese restaurant below the hotel that is one of the city's most extravagant dining experiences; and La Bottega, a delightful plaza level bar complex. You wouldn't need to leave the hotel for a full dose of nightlife. But this is New York, and the Meatpacking District is two blocks away, so you're near the throbbing center of New York's sceniest, priciest clubs and boutiques. The Maritime's white-ceramic tower was the first luxury hotel in the heart of the Chelsea gallery scene. The warm, small rooms resemble modern ship's cabins, with burnished teak paneling, sea-blue drapes and bed accents, and 5-foot-tall porthole windows that face the Hudson River skyline. **Pros:** nightlife options galore; great restaurants; fun rooms with big portal windows. **Cons:** all nightlife all the time; street noise. ⊠*363 W. 16th St., at 9th Ave., Chelsea* ☎*212/242–4300* ⊕*www.themaritimehotel.com* ↘*120 rooms, 4 suites* ⌂*In-room: safe, DVD, Internet, Wi-Fi. In-hotel: 2 restaurants, room service, bars, laundry service, public Internet, public Wi-Fi, gym, some pets allowed, no-smoking rooms* ⊟*AE, MC, V* Ⓜ*A, C, E to 14th St.* ✛*3:B3*

MIDTOWN WEST

$$ Ⓣ**Belvedere Hotel.** Guests choose the Belvedere more for the central location, adjacent to Times Square, and less for the rooms, which lack life (and light). Exceptions are the executive rooms, which raise the bar considerably with chandeliers, cream-color carpets, and leather chairs. Still, even standard rooms are spacious and offer kitchenettes with microwave, mini-refrigerator, and coffeemakers. The helpful desk staff and location convenient to theaters make this a great affordable choice. **Pros:** good rates available; renovated rooms are good value. **Cons:** can be loud with street noise; slow elevators. ⊠*319 W. 48th St., between 8th and 9th Aves., Midtown West* ☎*212/245–7000 or 888/468–3558* ⊕*www.belvederehotelnyc.com* ↘*328 rooms, 1 suite* ⌂*In-room: safe, kitchen, refrigerator, Wi-Fi. In-hotel: restaurant, laundry facilities, laundry service, concierge, public Internet, public Wi-Fi, parking (fee)* ⊟*AE, D, DC, MC, V* Ⓜ*C, E to 50th St.* ✛*4:B3*

$$$ ◫ **The Blakely.** The cozy English clubhouse–like lobby sets the tone for this hotel, with plenty of maple and cherry paneling, large library chairs, and leather-bound books along the walls. The rooms also have that English lived-in quality, at 310 square feet with fully equipped kitchenettes, large work areas, and

CD and DVD players. The dark-wood touches and rich fabrics add a stylish touch. Abboccato, the well-reviewed Italian restaurant, provides room service. **Pros:** central location; good-size rooms; free Internet. **Cons:** rooms facing 54th Street can be noisy; some rooms have little natural light. ✉ *136 W. 55th St., between 6th and 7th Aves., Midtown West* ☎ *212/245–1800 or 800/735–0710* ⊕ *www.blakelynewyork.com* ⬐ *57 rooms, 54 suites* ♿ *In-room: safe, kitchen, refrigerator, DVD, Wi-Fi. In-hotel: restaurant, room service, bar, gym, laundry service, concierge, parking (fee), public Internet, public Wi-Fi, no-smoking rooms* ⊟ *AE, DC, MC, V* Ⓜ *N, Q, R, W to 57th St.* ✛ *4:C2*

$$$$ ◫ **Bryant Park Hotel.** A New York landmark in brown brick towering over the New York Public Library and Bryant Park, this sleekly modern hotel is fashioned from the bones of the former American Radiator Building. Rooms are minimalist chic with sumptuous travertine bathrooms, hardwood floors covered by Tibetan rugs, and killer views. Since it's at the busy hive of Fashion Week activities, expect a designer-filled crowd and a runway feel in the stark red lobby during those times, though normal-size guests are welcomed year-round. Both Koi, the restaurant, and the two bars are popular with the after-work crowd. This is one of the best locations in the city, set off the park (one of New York's most vibrant spaces), near Times Square, Grand Central, and 5th Avenue shopping. **Pros:** gorgeous building; fashionable crowd and setting; across from Bryant Park. **Cons:** expensive; Cellar Bar frequently booked for events. ✉ *40 W. 40th St., between 5th and 6th Aves., Midtown West* ☎ *212/869–0100 or 877/640–9300* ⊕ *www. bryantparkhotel.com* ⬐ *112 rooms, 17 suites* ♿ *In-room: safe, Wi-Fi, Internet. In-hotel: restaurant, room service, bars, gym, laundry service, concierge, public Wi-Fi, parking (fee), no-smoking rooms* ⊟ *AE, DC, MC, V* Ⓜ *B, D, F, V to 42nd St.; 7 to 5th Ave.* ✛ *4:D5*

19

$ ◫ **Casablanca Hotel.** The Casablanca remains one of New York's great hotel bargains. It's hard to believe you're a stone's throw from all the Times Square hoopla when you enter the lobby. Evocative of a locale straight out of its namesake film, a sultry Mediterranean feel permeates throughout the hotel, with mirrors and mosaics in public spaces ceiling fans, wooden blinds, and dainty little bistro tables. Huge tiled bathrooms, many with windows, feature Baroness Cali amenities. On the second floor, classical music plays while guests linger in the spacious library-like Rick's Café for the complimentary breakfast buffet and wine-and-cheese evenings. **Pros:** great access to the theater district; all rooms are smoke-free. **Cons:** exercise facilities at nearby New York Sports Club, not on premises; heavy tourist foot traffic. ✉ *147*

Romantic Retreats

As English poet Sir Walter Raleigh once wrote, "Romance is a love affair in other than domestic surroundings." Indeed, many high-end hotels seem custom-built for romance with their plush feather beds, silky linens, and ultrasoft robes. But some properties go above and beyond in catering to couples, offering services like bath butlers and in-room massage services. Here's our pick of the city's best spots for an intimate getaway.

At the **Ritz-Carlton, Battery Park** (⇨Lower Manhattan) your wish is their command. Take advantage of lower-than-normal weekend rates to book a Liberty Suite, with sweeping views of the Statue of Liberty. With a quick call to the concierge you can arrange to have champagne and strawberries waiting in your room when you arrive. A bath butler can then fill your marble tub with a potion of bath oils and flower petals. If you're here in February, don't miss a trip to the penthouse Chocolate Bar with its aphrodisiac chocolate-and-champagne buffet.

The Inn at Irving Place (⇨Union Square/Gramercy) does romance the old-fashioned way, with four-poster beds, fireplaces, fur throws, and plenty of privacy in an elegant 1800s brownstone. The complimentary breakfast is served on fine bone china either in the cozy sitting room or in bed.

The renovated, 23,000-square-foot Bliss Spa at **W New York** (⇨Midtown East and Upper East Side), on Lexington Avenue, is an urban oasis with men's and women's lounges, a gym, and a full menu of facial and body treatments, massage, waxing, and nail services. Couples can spend a full day being pampered and pedicured in the spa or unwind in their rooms with an in-room massage, offered 24 hours a day.

All of the rooms at the **Library Hotel** (⇨Midtown East and Upper East Side) have a certain inviting charm that makes them a good choice for a romantic weekend away, but if you're looking for a little mood reading, ask for the Erotic Literature room or the Love Room, curated by Dr. Ruth.

W. 43rd St., Midtown West ☎212/869–1212 ⊕*www.casablanca hotel.com* ⌨*48 rooms* ⌂*In-room: safe, DVD, Wi-Fi. In-hotel: restaurant, room service, bar, laundry, concierge, public Wi-Fi, no-smoking rooms* ☰*AE, MC, V* Ⓜ*1, 2, 3, 7, N, Q, R, W, S to Times Sq.-42nd St.* ✛*4:C4*

$$$ 🛏**Chambers.** If you love contemporary art, this might be your favorite Midtown hotel. More than 500 works of art, mainly contemporary paintings, from one of the owners' private collection, hang in rooms, hallways, and public spaces. Loftlike rooms with hand-troweled concrete walls are warm with additional decorations, and the bathroom floors are covered with reflective glass mosaic tiles. Push through the heavy teak doors and you'll find yourself in a soaring lobby. Rooms boast excellent showers with Bumble and Bumble amenities and mod touches all around, though some wear is visible in the carpeting and paint. Town, a rather posh American restaurant downstairs, provides room service. **Pros:** artsy, fun, lighthearted style; great art abounds;

free wireless; wonderful central location. **Cons:** no gym; rooms slightly worn. ✉*15 W. 56th St., off 5th Ave., Midtown West* ☎*212/974–5656 or 866/204–5656* ⊕*www.chambershotel.com* ⤢*72 rooms, 5 suites* ♨*In-room: safe, DVD, Internet, Wi-Fi. In-hotel: restaurant, room service, bar, laundry service, concierge, parking (fee), public Internet, public Wi-Fi, some pets allowed, no-smoking rooms* ▭*AE, D, DC, MC, V* Ⓜ*F, V to 57th St.* ✛*4:E1*

$$ 🖥 **City Club Hotel.** City Club's ocean-liner-inspired rooms are brisk, bright, and masculine, with Jonathan Adler ceramics. They are also about the same size as a room on a cruise ship—that means tight quarters, matey. All rooms have city-oriented photos from the '50s, Bigalow bathroom products, and "City Club" monogrammed wool blankets. Privacy, not publicity, is the emphasis at this luxe boutique property owned by young man-about-town Jeff Klein and designed by celebrity decorator Jeffrey Bilhuber. The lobby is tiny, and guests who wish to drink are sent across the street to the Royalton. Top chef Daniel Boulud opened his db bistro moderne downstairs, making for delicious room service. **Pros:** free wireless; great restaurant; personal service. **Cons:** no gym; some guests find lighting substandard; no real lobby. ✉*55 W. 44th St., between 5th and 6th Aves., Midtown West* ☎*212/921–5500* ⊕*www.cityclubhotel.com* ⤢*62 rooms, 3 suites* ♨*In-room: safe, DVD, Wi-Fi. In-hotel: restaurant, room service, bar, parking (fee), public Internet, public Wi-Fi, some pets allowed, no-smoking rooms* ▭*AE, D, DC, MC, V* Ⓜ*B, D, F, N, R, V, W, 1, 2, 3, 9 to 42nd St.; 7 to 5th Ave.* ✛*4:D4*

$$ 🖥 **DoubleTree Guest Suites Times Square.** A just-completed renovation of ⟳ its public spaces has transformed this Fodorite favorite into a sleek, modern contender for Times Square top dog. Fans of the property have long called it a "very comfortable hotel" in an "ideal location." Now it's a stylish spot with WiFi-enabled lobby lounge, outfitted in sleek gray leather, mirrored surfaces, blue-fringed chandeliers, and an all-day bar/café menu. Typical room layouts are spacious, 1-bedroom suites of about 400 square feet with double vanities, mini refrigerators, microwaves, and wet bars. The comfortable lobby lounge is a great place to relax with a cocktail or grab a quick bite from the bar menu. **Pros:** free 24-hour gym; extremely helpful, informed concierge; free WiFi in public areas; clock radio compatible with iPod and portable music players. **Cons:** paid WiFi in guest rooms; some Fodorites say rooms are "tiny" for the price. ✉*1568 Broadway, at 47th St., Midtown West* ☎*212/719-1600* ⊕*doubletree1.hilton.com* ⤢*460 rooms* ♨*In-room: safe, refrigerator, DVD, Wi-Fi. In-hotel: 1 restaurant, room service, 1 bar, laundry service, Internet terminal, Wi-Fi, parking (fee), some pets allowed.* ▭*AE, D, DC, MC, V.* 🍽*EP.* Ⓜ*B, D, F, V to 42nd St.* ✛*4:C3*

$ 🖥 **Dream Hotel.** Part hotel, part Kafkaesque dream, this Midtown experience is brought to you by hotelier Vikram Chatwal, and it specializes in style over comfort. The lobby combines an enormous two-story cylindrical neon-lighted aquarium, an unsettling two-story photograph of a tattooed woman, and a copper sculpture of Catherine the Great. Step off the elevator onto your floor and you'll be met with a jarring

19

Fodor'sChoice ★

Mandarin Oriental

Inn on 23rd   Ritz-Carlton New York, Central Park South

neon photograph; rooms are almost as disquieting—stark white walls, black furniture, and light-box desks that glow from within. Stay here if you love things modern: plasma TVs, complimentary iPod use, a Deepak Chopra spa, and a velvet-rope rooftop bar scene. Despite the over-the-top qualities—and noise from the scenesters headed to the rooftop bar—it's quite livable. **Pros:** Ava Lounge penthouse bar; big spa; up-to-the-minute electronics. **Cons:** small rooms; spotty service; trendier-than-thou atmosphere. ⊠*210 W. 55th St., at Broadway, Midtown West* ☎*212/247–2000 or 866/437–3266* ⊕*www.dreamny.com* ⇖*208 rooms, 20 suites* ⟳*In-room: safe, refrigerator, Internet. In-hotel: restaurant, room service, bars, spa, laundry service, concierge, parking (fee), some pets allowed* ⊟*AE, D, DC, MC, V* Ⓜ*N, Q, R, W to 57th St.* ✛*4:C2*

$$ ⌖**Grace Hotel.** Giving budget a good name is this Times Square hotel founded by Andre Balazs as the Hotel QT a few years ago. (He's since passed the property along to new operators.) The unique lobby centers on a raised pool with peep-show-like windows that overlook the bar. Upstairs, rooms are modern, dorm-room in size, but have upscale hotel touches such as feather-pillow-topped mattresses, rain-head showers, and DVD players to accompany the flat-screen TVs. There's no work space, no bathtubs, and double rooms have bunk beds sprouting out of the wall. Still, you can't beat the price—rooms start at just $225, including continental breakfast—and the location is as central as they come. **Pros:** free wireless; cheap rates; complimentary breakfast. **Cons:** little natural light in some rooms; expensive for amount of space. ⊠*125 W. 45th St., between 5th and 6th Aves., Midtown West* ☎*212/354–2323* ⊕*www.room-matehotels.com* ⇖*139 rooms* ⟳*In-room: safe, refrigerator, DVD, Wi-Fi. In-hotel: bar, pool, gym, laundry service, some pets allowed, no-smoking rooms* ⊟*AE, DC, MC, V* ⍐*CP* Ⓜ*B, D, F, V to 42nd St.; 7 to 5th Ave.* ✛*4:D4*

$$$ ⌖**Hilton Times Square.** The Hilton Times Square sits atop a 335,000-square-foot retail and entertainment zone on a bustling section of 42nd Street that includes a 25-theater movie megaplex and Madame Tussaud's Wax Museum. The building has a handsome Mondrian-inspired facade, though the room decor has a case of the chain hotel blahs. Nonetheless, the rooms are comfortable and larger than many in the city, with amenities such as in-room coffeemakers and bathrobes, though charges for Internet access are staggering. The hotel is efficiently run and the staff is pleasant. Guest rooms are above the 21st floor, affording excellent views of Times Square and Midtown while keeping noise at bay. Restaurant Above is off the "sky lobby" on the 21st floor. **Pros:** lovely views from restaurant; immediate access to entertainment; convenient to public transportation. **Cons:** impersonal feel; nickel-and-dime charges; overpriced food and drink. ⊠*234 W. 42nd St., between 7th and 8th Aves., Midtown West* ☎*212/642–2500 or 800/445–8667* ⊕*www.hilton.com* ⇖*444 rooms, 15 suites* ⟳*In-room: safe, Wi-Fi, Internet. In-hotel: restaurant, room service, bar, gym, laundry service, concierge, parking (fee), some pets allowed, no-smoking rooms* ⊟*AE, D, DC, MC, V* Ⓜ*1, 2, 3, 7, N, Q, R, W, S to 42nd St./Times Sq.* ✛*4:C4*

19

$ ☎**Hotel 41.** Bamboo in the window beckons guests to the warmly lighted lobby of the Hotel 41. This stylish hotel is not meant for family visits; rooms are tiny, even for two people. Most standard rooms face a brick wall, but if you can get past the size and not-so-thrilling views, it's a cozy place to stay, with a bed showing off crisp linens and a TV hanging above the closet. Bathrooms are elegant, with half-glass showers, original tile on the floor, and Aveda amenities. Downstairs, Bar 41 is a dark sports bar–like hangout with rock music loudly playing. Find serenity in the intimate back room wine cellar. **Pros:** DVD player in rooms; some rooms have refrigerators. **Cons:** lack of queen-size beds; small rooms; no view. ⊠*206 W. 41st St., Midtown West* ☎*212/703–8600* ⊕*www.hotel41nyc.com* ⤵*47 rooms* ⚷*In-room: safe, refrigerator (some), DVD, Internet. In-hotel: restaurant, room service, bar, concierge, laundry, parking (fee) no-smoking rooms* ⊟*AE, MC, V* Ⓜ*1, 2, 3, 7, N, Q, R, W, S to Times Sq.-42nd St.; A, C, E to 42nd St.-Port Authority Bus Terminal.* ✛*4:C4*

$ ☎**The Hotel at Times Square.** Yes, there really is a Super 8 in Times Square—though it no longer goes by that name. The rooms are motel plain with an unfortunate sea-foam color scheme, but most are well maintained and clean. However, if you're an unfussy traveler who wants to be in the thick of the madness, it's not a bad option. This small prewar hotel shares its block with a plethora of Brazilian restaurants and is near many theaters and Rockefeller Center. The peculiar lobby has a narrow corridor that snakes off around a corner and is decorated with some rather handsome art-deco Bakelite lamps. **Pros:** free breakfast; free wireless; free local calls. **Cons:** peremptory, low-frills service; noisy area. ⊠*59 W. 46th St., between 5th and 6th Aves., Midtown West* ☎*212/719–2300 or 800/848–0020* ⊕*www.applecorehotels.com* ⤵*209 rooms* ⚷*In-room: Wi-Fi. In-hotel: bar, gym, parking (fee), public Internet, no-smoking rooms* ⊟*AE, D, DC, MC, V* Ⓜ*B, D, F, V to 47th–50th Sts./Rockefeller Center.* ✛*4:D3*

$ ☎**Hotel Mela.** You get an undisguised whiff of trendiness entering this swanky hotel. European lounge music pulses to the beat in the lobby, and there is a subtle scent of guava coming from the candles. The concierge, you learn, is referred to as an "Agent of Desires." Ah, yes: this feels like South Beach—where the management team runs three other hotels. The mellifluous name is Italian for "apple," and the hotel draws a good number of Italians and other Europeans who like the beat and the new rooms, which are stylish and contemporary with their straightforward lines, light colors, and simplicity. Fill out the hotel guest preference questionnaire in advance and get a complimentary snack and drink upon arrival. **Pros:** stylish, clean new rooms; guest preference program. **Cons:** slow and small elevator; no glasses in bathroom. ⊠*120 W. 44th St., between 6th Ave. and Broadway, Midtown West* ☎*212/710–7000 or 877/452–6352* ⊕*www.hotelmela.com* ⤵*223 rooms, 6 suites* ⚷*In-room: safe, Wi-Fi. In-hotel: restaurant, room service, bar, gym, laundry service, concierge, parking (fee), public Internet, public Wi-Fi, some pets allowed, no-smoking rooms* ⊟*AE, D, DC, MC, V* Ⓜ*N, R, W, 1, 2, 3 to 42nd St./Times Sq.* ✛*4:C4*

$ 🛏 **Hotel Metro.** With its mirrored columns and elegant black-and-white photos in the lobby, the Hotel Metro has a distinctive retro feel. Guests tend to hang out in the lounge, where coffee and tea are served all day, or in the adjacent library, a quiet nook with sofas and a desk. Upstairs, restrained, tasteful rooms with leather headboards and cushioned art-deco chairs include bathrooms with Gilchrist & Soames products and double-height ceilings. In summer the Metro Grill rooftop bar promises outstanding Empire State Building views. **Pros:** renovated exercise room has flat-screen TVs; iHome in rooms. **Cons:** noise seeps from outside; rooms are tasteful but spartan. ✉45 W. 35th St., Midtown West ☎212/279–1310 ⊕www. hotelmetronyc.com ⇱179 rooms ♿In-room: safe, Wi-Fi (no fee). In-hotel: restaurant, room service, bar, executive floor, public Wi-Fi, no-smoking rooms ☰AE, DC, MC, V Ⓜ B, D, F, N, Q, R, V, W to 34th St.-Herald Sq. ✛ 4:D6

> ### WORD OF MOUTH
>
> "For a first-time visitor, I think [Midtown] is an ideal location. You'll be able to walk to Central Park, 5th Avenue, Rockefeller Center, St. Patrick's Cathedral, and Times Square. Trendier neighborhoods are definitely worth a visit, but are too far away from a lot of the things first-timers would want to see." —NewbE

$$$ 🛏 **The Hudson.** From the bower-draped lobby to the dark-wall rooms with their whiter-than-white furnishings, the Hudson is yet another extravaganza from the team of Ian Schrager and Philippe Starck. They manage to cram one thousand rooms into the building—some as small as 150 square feet—over 23 floors; the service is as minimalist as the decor. Tight quarters are balanced by comparatively low (by Manhattan standards) rates, but if you're staying here, it's for the atmosphere, not the accommodations. Some bathrooms have see-through shower walls, and all have a supply of candles. The garden-lounge remains one of the more coveted outdoor spaces in town. **Pros:** fabulous, elegant bar; gorgeous Clemente fresco in lobby; breathtaking Sky Terrace. **Cons:** staff can be condescending; slightly cold-feeling rooms. ✉356 W. 58th St., between 8th and 9th Aves., Midtown West ☎212/554–6000 ⊕www. hudsonhotel.com ⇱1,000 rooms, 2 suites ♿In-room: safe, Wi-Fi. In-hotel: restaurant, room service, bar, gym, concierge, laundry service, public Internet, public Wi-Fi, parking (fee), no-smoking rooms ☰AE, D, DC, MC, V Ⓜ1, A, B, C, D to 59th St./Columbus Circle. ✛4:B1

$$$ 🛏 **Jumeirah Essex House.** New managers Jumeirah Hotel Group aimed high with a $90 million refurbishment program for this famed property; both common areas and guest rooms have been recently updated. The lobby of this stately Central Park South property is an art-deco masterpiece, with inlaid marble floors and bas-relief elevator doors. Dreaming of Central Park? It's across the street. Reproductions of Chippendale or Louis XV antiques decorate guest rooms, all of which have marble bathrooms and luxuriously comfortable beds. Afternoon tea in the lobby lounge is elegantly arranged. Kerry Heffernan's South Gate draws a European crowd to its design-y interior with an extensive wine list. **Pros:** great service; amazing views; freshly renovated head to toe. **Cons:**

19

overly complex room gadgetry; very expensive bar. ✉ *160 Central Park S, between 6th and 7th Aves., Midtown West* ☎ *212/247–0300 or 800/937–8461* ⊕ *www.jumeirahessexhouse.com* ↝ *515 rooms, 70 suites* ♿ *In-room: safe, Internet, Wi-Fi. In-hotel: 2 restaurants, room service, bar, gym, spa, laundry service, concierge, public Internet, public Wi-Fi, parking (fee), some pets allowed, no-smoking rooms* 🚭 *AE, D, DC, MC, V* Ⓜ *F, N, R, Q, W to 57th St.* ✛ *4:C1*

ȼ   🏨 **La Quinta Inn.** The name may conjure a cheapie siesta spot, but don't dismiss it: smack in the middle of Koreatown and close to Penn Station, this budget-friendly hotel in a cheerful old Beaux-Arts building may be one of the best deals in town. Never mind the drab green and burgundy decor when your room features treats like free Wi-Fi, an iPod plug-in, and a bathtub. In the morning the free continental breakfast goes beyond the usual fare with granola and oatmeal. Perhaps the best part about staying here is access to Mé Bar. In the evening both guests and locals head up to this year-round mellow rooftop bar for a cocktail in the shadow of the Empire State Building. **Pros:** self-check-in machines; gift shop on the premises for necessities. **Cons:** no room service; no frills. ✉ *17 W. 32nd St. , between 5th Ave. and Broadway, Midtown West* ☎ *212/736–1600* ⊕ *www.lq.com* ↝ *182 rooms* ♿ *In-room: safe, Wi-Fi (no fee). In-hotel: bar, gym, laundry, public Wi-Fi, parking (fee), no-smoking rooms* 🚭 *AE, D, DC, MC, V* Ⓜ *B, D, F, N, Q, R, V, W to 34th St.-Herald Sq.* ✛ *4:E6*

$$$ 🏨 **Le Parker Meridien.** No hotel in New York is as lighthearted as the ☽ Parker. Despite the Meridien marketing affiliation, this is the largest privately owned hotel in the city, which means the hotel freely uses a refreshingly wry approach: Tom & Jerry cartoons in the elevators, a $1,000 omelet on the breakfast menu at Norma's, and door privacy signs that read FUHGETTABOUDIT. At the same time, it's also quite sleek. The lobby's striking atrium combines cherry paneling, hand-painted columns, and contemporary art. Crisp, modern rooms include low platform beds, supercool rotating ceiling-to-floor entertainment units, Aeron chairs, and Central Park or skyline views (ask for the Park rooms). Gravity, a 15,000-square-foot health club with a glass-enclosed rooftop pool and spa services, is, by far, the best hotel gym facility in New York. Norma's serves the morning meal from 6:30 AM to 3 PM, with a famous brunch. The wonderful, discreetly hidden Burger Joint has—if you haven't heard—possibly the best burger in the city just beyond its velvet curtain. **Pros:** lively, animated spirit; best hotel gym in the city; fun eating options; tech-friendly rooms. **Cons:** lobby is a public space; building heat spotty in transitional seasons. ✉ *118 W. 57th St., between 6th and 7th Aves., Midtown West* ☎ *212/245–5000 or 800/543–4300* ⊕ *www.parkermeridien.com* ↝ *484 rooms, 249 suites* ♿ *In-room: safe, refrigerator, DVD, VCR, Internet. In-hotel: 3 restaurants, room service, bar, pool, gym, spa, concierge, laundry service, parking (fee), no-smoking rooms* 🚭 *AE, D, DC, MC, V* Ⓜ *B, D, E, N, Q, R, W to 57th St.* ✛ *4:D1*

$$$ 🏨 **The London NYC.** Boasting the design expertise of David Collins and the decadent cuisine of Britain's most celebrated chef Gordon Ramsay in his first eponymous stateside restaurant, the London NYC merges

the style and flair of both of its namesake cities. Each of the 561 spacious, tech-savvy suites features custom furniture like an embossed-leather desk and Egyptian-cotton bedding in a style that combines modern sleek with art-deco chic. Bathrooms are equally well styled, featuring a Waterworks double-head shower and mosaic tiles. For the ultimate splurge, the 54th-floor penthouse London Atrium suite is the highest hotel room in New York. The exclusive British concierge service, Quintessentially, attends to your every whim with tireless charm. **Pros:** posh atmosphere without prissiness; Gordon Ramsay restaurant; great fitness club. **Cons:** service reported as pretentious and inconsistent; no bathtubs in most rooms. ⊠ *151 W. 54th St., between 6th and 7th Aves., Midtown West* ☎*212/307–5000 or 866/690–2029* ⊕*www.thelondonnyc.com* ⤵*562 suites* ⌂*In-room: safe, Internet, Wi-Fi. In-hotel: restaurant, room service, bar, gym, laundry service, concierge, parking (fee), some pets allowed, no-smoking rooms* ▭*AE, D, DC, MC, V* Ⓜ*B, D, E to 7th Ave.; N, Q, R, W to 57th St.* ✛*4:C1*

$$$$
Fodor's Choice
★

🏨**Mandarin Oriental.** The Mandarin brings some Asian style to a rather staid corner of New York. Its cavernous lobby sizzles with energy from the 35th floor of the Time Warner Center. Here you'll find two wonderful lounges, and the restaurant Asiate, from which to soak in the dramatic views above Columbus Circle and Central Park. On the higher floors, silk throws abound on plush beds, and the marble-clad bathrooms prove the Mandarin's commitment to excess. That said, contrasted with the monumental frame created by floor-to-ceiling glass, and the view it presents, regular rooms feel small. Suites are really what set this hotel apart, by creating enough stage space to make the hotel's Asian-influenced decor, and the views, really dazzle. The swimming pool is one of the city's best in a hotel, with panoramic Hudson River views. The elaborate spa is impressive. **Pros:** a vibrant urban hotel; luxury all the way; fantastic pool with views; best spa in the city. **Cons:** Trump hotel blocks portion of park views; expensive; mall-like environs. ⊠*80 Columbus Circle, at 60th St., Midtown West* ☎*212/805–8800* ⊕*www.mandarinoriental.com* ⤵*203 rooms, 46 suites* ⌂*In-room: DVD, refrigerator, Internet. In-hotel: restaurant, room service, bar, pool, gym, spa, laundry service, concierge* ▭*AE, D, DC, MC, V* Ⓜ*A, B, C, D, 1 to 59th St./Columbus Circle.* ✛*5:C6*

19

$$

🏨**The Mansfield.** The Mansfield has the best small details of any New York hotel. For instance, attractive key cards with old New York scenes, the lovely elongated leather guest services catalog, or the gilt-script font on black leather privacy cards that read "Kindly Service My Room." This attitude can be found throughout the hotel: built in 1904 as lodging for distinguished bachelors, the small, clubby property has an Edwardian sensibility from the working fireplace in the lounge to the lobby's coffered ceiling and marble-and-cast-iron staircase. The intimate M Bar, lined with books and leather banquettes, is one of the nicer hotel bars in the city. One quirk: standard rooms have much bigger bathrooms than suites, which are comically small. **Pros:** complimentary wireless; business center; 24-hour gym; great bar; breakfast included. **Cons:** suites have tiny bathrooms; air-conditioners are window units. ⊠*12 W. 44th St., between 5th and 6th Aves., Midtown*

Kids in Tow

Many New York hotels go out of their way to accommodate families with special amenities and family-size rooms. However, a hotel claiming that it's child friendly doesn't always translate to true kid-welcoming style. Ask if cribs come with linens, whether there are high chairs and children's menus in the dining room, and if there are in-house babysitters. Some hotels will even clear out the minibar (for bottle or baby-food storage), baby-proof a room, or provide baby-proofing materials. Here are some of the top picks for traveling with kids.

SUITE LIFE. Space is at a premium in New York hotels, and if you have more than two people in a standard room, you'll really start to feel the squeeze. The answer? A suite, where you can spread out in style. The **Embassy Suites New York** (⇨ Lower Manhattan), a tried-and-true family option, is even more kid friendly in New York since it's in the same building as a multiplex movie theater and several reasonably priced dining options. With renovated, spacious suites, **Affinia 50** (⇨ Midtown East and Upper East Side) is the family hotel of choice on the residential East Side.

PURE PAMPERING. Just because you have children in tow doesn't mean your dream of a pampering vacation needs to go down the drain. Several top New York hotels go out of their way to accommodate families. The

Ritz-Carlton's two hotels (⇨ Lower Manhattan and Midtown West and Chelsea) offer special healthful children's menus, rubber-duck-filled baths, and toy menus from FAO Schwarz. The Battery Park location has children's etiquette classes the first Saturday of the month; the Central Park branch holds special teddy bear teas.

FUN FLAVOR. Grace Hotel (⇨ Midtown West and Chelsea) might make the perfect respite if you have teens in tow. There's a funky lobby pool; a kiosk that stocks sweets with which to fill the in-room refrigerators; and rooms with bunk beds that levitate out of the walls and have their own plasma TVs. At the hip **Hotel on Rivington** (⇨ East Village and Lower East Side), a special family suite has two full bedrooms, one with two sets of bunk beds and a big bin of toys, two full baths, and a Japanese tub. Bonus points: the hotel is across from Economy Candy.

KID KARMA. Family-friendly **Le Parker Meridien** (⇨ Midtown West and Chelsea) has a large pool, a restaurant that serves decadent breakfast foods such as chocolate French toast until 3 PM, and another dining spot that serves nothing but burgers and shakes. Upon check-in at the **Omni Berkshire Place** (⇨ Midtown East and Upper East Side), kids get a goodie bag and a loaner backpack.

West ☎212/944–6050 *or* 800/255–5167 ⊕*www.mansfieldhotel.com* ⮑*124 rooms, 25 suites* ⚭*In-room: safe, Wi-Fi. In-hotel: restaurant, room service, bar, laundry service, concierge, parking (fee), public Wi-Fi, public Internet, some pets allowed, no-smoking rooms* ▭*AE, D, DC, MC, V* Ⓜ*B, D, F, V to 42nd St.* ✣*4:E4*

$$$ ▦ **The Michelangelo.** Italophiles will feel that they've been transported to the good life in the boot at this deluxe hotel, whose long, wide

lobby lounge is clad with multihue marble and Veronese-style oil paintings. Upstairs, the decor of the relatively spacious rooms (averaging 475 square feet) varies. You can choose contemporary, neoclassic, art deco, or French country—all have marble foyers and marble bathrooms equipped with bidets and oversize 55-gallon tubs. (The different styles are mainly manifested in bedspreads and different colored furniture.) Complimentary cappuccino, pastries, and other Italian treats are served each morning in the baroque lobby lounge. The hotel is located a few blocks from Rockefeller Center and 5th Avenue shopping. Insieme, Marco Canora's exemplary modern Italian restaurant, is on the ground floor. **Pros:** good location; fantastic restaurant; spacious rooms. **Cons:** noisy air-conditioning units; some rooms have limited views; small closets. ⊠ *152 W. 51st St., at 7th Ave., Midtown West* ☎ *212/765–1900 or 800/237–0990* ⊕ *www.michelangelohotel.com* ⤷ *123 rooms, 56 suites* ⌂ *In-room: Internet. In-hotel: restaurant, room service, bar, gym, laundry service, concierge, public Internet, parking (fee), no-smoking rooms* ▭ *AE, D, DC, MC, V* ⊚ *CP* Ⓜ *B, D, E to 7th Ave.; 1 to 50th St.; B, D, F, V to 47th–50th Sts./Rockefeller Center.* ⊹ *4:C3*

$$$$ ⊤ **Muse Hotel.** If you're determined to find ostrich leather headboards in a stylish Midtown hotel, your troubles are over. A makeover in summer 2007 reimagined rooms from head to toe: black and cream contemporary carpets, Eames-style chairs, and the most whimsical bathrobes in the city (they're leopard print). Stylish throws, smartly folded over comfy beds, have Greek letter forms, as do the attractive custom carpets. A bust of a muse in the room is a nice touch to continue the theme, even if the lobby ceiling painted with the muses is over the top. The rooms and location are great, so in a way, the flourishes are beside the point, though the Times Square location can be a bit stressful for some. Six rooms have balconies, and three spa suites have deep hot tubs and separate showers. **Pros:** contemporary interiors; good Midtown location; Spacious rooms. **Cons:** service sometimes great, sometimes lacking; no gym. ⊠ *130 W. 46th St., between 6th and 7th Aves., Midtown West* ☎ *212/485–2400 or 877/692–6873* ⊕ *www.themusehotel.com* ⤷ *200 rooms, 19 suites* ⌂ *In-room: safe, Wi-Fi. In-hotel: restaurant, room service, bar, gym, laundry service, concierge, parking (fee), public Internet, public Wi-Fi, some pets allowed, no-smoking rooms* ▭ *AE, D, DC, MC, V* Ⓜ *Subway: B, D, F, V to 47th–50th Sts./Rockefeller Center.* ⊹ *4:C4*

19

$ ⊤ **Portland Square Hotel.** You can't beat this no-frills theater district old-timer for value, given its clean, simple rooms that invite with wooden headboards and cream bed linens. James Cagney once lived in the building, and—as the story goes—a few of his Radio City Rockette acquaintances lived upstairs. *Life* magazine used to have its offices here, and the original detailing evokes old New York. All rooms are no-smoking. Rooms on the east wing have oversize bathrooms, though cheaper rooms require you to share bath facilities. Rates are low, but there are caveats, including some rooms that are down-at-the-heels, indifferent staff, and windows with bars. On the plus side, Wi-Fi is free throughout the hotel. **Pros:** good theater district location; cheap for the area. **Cons:** poor lighting; some shared bathrooms; average-to-disappointing service. ✉*132 W. 47th St., between 6th and 7th Aves., Midtown West* ☎*212/382–0600 or 800/388–8988* ⊕*www.portlandsquarehotel.com* ⤵*147 rooms, 112 with bath* △*In-room: Wi-Fi. In-hotel: gym, public Internet, public Wi-Fi* ▭*AE, MC, V* Ⓜ*R, W to 49th St.* ✛*4:C3*

$ 🈂 **Radio City Apartments.** If you can tolerate tired furniture and dim ☺ lighting, this suite hotel is one of the best bargains in midtown. The property is a converted apartment building, with layouts ranging from studios (350 square feet and up) to two-bedroom apartments. All apartments have full kitchens (including oven) with pots, tableware, and utensils. Fodorites describe the service as "friendly and efficient," noting that rooms are "meticulously kept." Fans also cite the central location, right off Broadway near Times Square, as a top selling point. Be sure to book far in advance, as the property fills up quickly. **Pros:** free WiFi; easy subway access; spacious rooms excellent for traveling with family. **Cons:** allergy-sufferers beware—smoking is allowed in most rooms. ✉*142 W. 49th St. , Midtown West* ☎*212/730-0728* ⊕*www. radiocityapartments.com* ⤵*110 suites* △*In-room: kitchen, refrigerator, Wi-Fi. In-hotel: laundry facilities, Wi-Fi, parking (fee).* ▭*AE, D, DC, MC, V.* ⓘⓞⓛ*EP. m N, R, W to 49th St.; 1 to 50th St.* ✛*4:C3*

$$$ 🈂**Renaissance Hotel.** After a massive $26 million renovation completed in early 2008, you can experience contemporary New York style in a big hotel in the heart of Times Square. The renovation, headed by designer Jordan Mozer, who is known for his audacious curves and funky shapes, has radically transformed this formerly staid business hotel. The all-glass view from the new ground-floor lobby entrance makes Times Square a theatrical event; look for a new restaurant to replace the recently departed Chop Suey on the third floor soon. Refreshed guest rooms feature a palette of gold, sand, and terra-cotta; all have flat-screen TVs. **Pros:** contemporary design; latest in-room technology. **Cons:** in the heart of the Square: pandemonium isn't for everyone; some may find design over-the-top. ✉*714 7th Ave., between W. 47th and W. 48th Sts., Midtown West* ☎*212/765–7676 or 800/628–5222* ⊕*www.renaissancehotels.com* ⤵*300 rooms, 5 suites* △*In-room: safe, Internet, Wi-Fi. In-hotel: restaurant, room service, bars, gym, concierge, laundry service, parking (fee), public Internet, public Wi-Fi, some pets allowed, no-smoking rooms* ▭*AE, D, DC, MC, V* Ⓜ*R, W to 49th St.; 1 to 50th St.* ✛*4:C3*

$$$$ 🈂**Ritz-Carlton New York, Central Park.** A luxurious retreat with stellar
Fodor'sChoice views of Central Park, the former St. Moritz hotel is easily one of the
★ top properties in the city. No request is too difficult for the superlative
☺ Ritz staff, one reason the hotel is a favorite of celebrities and royalty. Even the regular rooms are the size of a small New York apartment, boasting a marble bath and shower, Wi-Fi, flat-screens, Frédéric Fekkai amenities, and 400-thread count linens. Chef Laurent Tourondel opened a BLT Market here in late 2007, featuring a seasonal menu that changes monthly. For getting around town in style, Bentley car service is available upon request. The club level features six food servings a day, including a champagne-and-caviar reception overlooking the park from the second floor. **Pros:** great concierge; personalized service; stellar location; views. **Cons:** pricey; limited common areas. ✉*50 Central Park S, at 6th Ave., Midtown West* ☎*212/308–9100 or 800/241–3333* ⊕*www.*

Inn at Irving Place

19

SoHo Grand

Gramercy Park Hotel

ritzcarlton.com ⤵*259 rooms, 47 suites* ♨*In-room: safe, DVD (some),
Internet, Wi-Fi. In-hotel: restaurant, room service, bar, gym, spa, laundry service, concierge, executive floor, no-smoking rooms, parking (fee),
some pets allowed* ⊟*AE, D, DC, MC, V* Ⓜ*F, V to 57th St.* ✛*4:D1*

$$ 🖵 **Room Mate Grace.** A favorite of European visitors and business travel-
🕑 ers in fashion and entertainment, Grace offers high-design lodgings on
a budget. The decor is modern and playful—Jonathan Adler reflective
wallpaper, bright geometric patterns, and a check-in desk that doubles
as a newsstand. Guests and locals gravitate to the lobby bar and swim-
ming-pool lounge (a real glassed-in pool, with sauna and steam room)
for cocktails and eye candy. Rooms are smallish, around 230 square feet
to 300 square feet, but smartly designed (comfortable beds are elevated
on platforms so luggage can be stored underneath) and well-insulated
from street noise. Room capacity varies from two to four people (in
a quad bunk-bed layout—each bed with its own TV and headset),
convenient for traveling with teenagers or kids. **Pros:** free, ample con-
tinental breakfast; friendly, helpful staff. **Cons:** Tiny rooms; little in-
room privacy (no door separating shower from main room). ✉*125 W.
45th St., Midtown West* ☏*212/354-2323* ⊕*www.room-matehotels.
com* ⤵*139 rooms* ♨*In-room: safe, refrigerator, DVD, Wi-Fi. In-hotel:
1 bar, pool, gym, laundry service, Wi-Fi, parking (fee).* ⊟*AE, D, DC,
MC. V.* 🍽*BP.* Ⓜ*B, D, F, V to 42nd St.* ✛ *4:D4*

$$$ 🖵 **The Royalton.** During the 1990s the Royalton's dramatic lobby started
the craze of local A-listers meeting and greeting in hotel boîtes. The
space has since been completely redesigned by Roman and Williams
and is attracting a new generation of movers and shakers to congregate
around its sumptuous sofas and the warm glow of its massive cast-
bronze fireplace. Brasserie 44 is also an excellent locale for a quick bite.
Alas, before you can get to your room, you'll have to run the gauntlet
of this bustling hipster lounge, but the efficient check-in and helpful
staff ensure that things go smoothly. Updated guest rooms, designed
by Charlotte Macaux, are all comfortably sleek and elegantly outfitted
with atmospheric lighting, fresh flowers, and candles changed daily.
Some of the rooms have working fireplaces, and all have plasma-screen
TVs. Bathrooms have been sumptuously renovated with huge circular Roman soaking tubs and rainfall showers. **Pros:** hip lobby scene;
luxe beds and bathrooms; helpful service. **Cons:** dark hallways; lighting
verges on eye-straining. ✉*44 W. 44th St., between 5th and 6th Aves.,
Midtown West* ☏*212/869–4400 or 800/635–9013* ⊕*www.royalton
hotel.com* ⤵*141 rooms, 27 suites* ♨*In-room: safe, Internet, Wi-Fi.
In-hotel: restaurant, room service, bar, gym, laundry service, concierge,
parking (fee), public Internet, public Wi-Fi, no-smoking rooms* ⊟*AE,
D, DC, MC, V* Ⓜ*B, D, F, V to 42nd St.* ✛*4:D4*

$$ 🖵 **The Shoreham.** If you're looking for a taste of chic New York in Mid-
town, the Shoreham comes through with flying colors. You're welcomed
with a glass of champagne at check-in inside a trendy little waiting area
with interesting flat-screen art animation. To the side is a hip little bar
and café that also serves an eclectic, light menu of sandwiches and sal-
ads. The Shoreham is a miniature, low-attitude version of the ultracool
Royalton—and it's comfortable to boot. Amenities in the rooms run

the gamut; all have pillow-top mattress and slate bathrooms; suites have massage chairs. Tech touches are a bonus, with complimentary wireless everywhere and even the occasional Xbox 360. **Pros:** great location; suave doormen; stylish throughout. **Cons:** not designed for families; headboards prevent you from sitting up in bed. ⊠*33 W. 55th St., between 5th and 6th Aves., Midtown West* ☎*212/247–6700 or 877/847–4444* ⊕*www.shorehamhotel.com* ↘*174 rooms, 37 suites* ♿*In-room: safe, DVD, Wi-Fi. In-hotel: restaurant, room service, bar, public Internet, public Wi-Fi, laundry service, concierge, parking (fee), some pets allowed, no-smoking rooms* ▭*AE, D, DC, MC, V* ⍾*CP* Ⓜ*E, V to 5th Ave.* ✛*4:D2*

$$ Ⓣ **Sofitel New York.** The French hotel group's property is a dramatic, contemporary 30-story curved tower overlooking 5th Avenue. The place has international sophistication that manages to be unfussy, with a gracious lobby, an elegant French restaurant (Gaby, named for a Parisian model who made a name for herself in the Big Apple in the 1920s), and courteous staff, always on hand with a friendly "Bonjour." Guest rooms are European modern with blond-wood headboards, silver wall sconces, and plush seating. Spacious bathrooms have separate stall showers and bathtubs. Room views vary; the best ones have balconies and overlook the Chrysler Building. Ask for a Sofitel "privilege card" and get a 4 PM checkout. **Pros:** central location; great beds. **Cons:** pricey; room views vary. ⊠*45 W. 44th St., between 5th and 6th Aves., Midtown West* ☎*212/354–8844* ⊕*www.sofitel.com* ↘*346 rooms, 52 suites* ♿*In-room: safe, Wi-Fi. In-hotel: restaurant, room service, bar, gym, laundry service, concierge, public Internet, public Wi-Fi, parking (fee), no-smoking rooms* ▭*AE, D, DC, MC, V* Ⓜ*B, D, F, V to 42nd St.* ✛*4:E4*

$$ Ⓣ **The Time Hotel.** One of the neighborhood's first boutique hotels, this spot half a block from the din of Times Square tempers trendiness with a touch of humor. A ridiculously futuristic glass elevator—eggshells line the bottom of the shaft—transports guests to the second-floor lobby. In the adjoining bar, nature videos lighten up the low-slung, serious, gray-scale furnishings while homegrown New York City DJs spin a fresh selection of music in the trendy Time Lounge. The smallish guest rooms, each themed on one of the primary colors—red, yellow, or blue—have mood lighting and even specific "color" aromas that create a unique, if contrived, hotel experience. Whatever your primary color, they boast iPod docks, large flat-screens, and modern, if not especially comfortable, beds and couches. **Pros:** acclaimed and popular Serafina restaurant downstairs; surprisingly quiet for Times Square location; good turndown service. **Cons:** decor makes the rooms seem a little dated; service is inconsistent; water pressure is lacking. ⊠*224 W. 49th St., between Broadway and 8th Ave., Midtown West* ☎*212/320–2900 or 877/846–3692* ⊕*www.thetimeny.com* ↘*164 rooms, 29 suites* ♿*In-room: safe, Internet. In-hotel: restaurant, room service, bar, gym, laundry service, concierge, public Internet, parking (fee), no-smoking rooms* ▭*AE, D, DC, MC, V* Ⓜ*1, C, E to 50th St.* ✛*4:C3*

$$$$ Ⓦ **W Times Square.** This supersleek 57-floor monolith is no shrinking violet: with a neon exterior and an entrance that shoots you up a

19

glass-enclosed elevator through cascading water, it fits right into the flashy environs of Times Square. You emerge onto the seventh-floor lobby, where Michael Kors–clad "welcome ambassadors" await. The contemporary Jetsons experience continues in the space-age, white-on-white lobby backed with a huge, hot-pink wall. Rooms are just as over-the-top, with a floor-to-ceiling mirrored headboard, featherbeds with goose-down duvets, and a stern, gray color scheme. The bi-level Blue Fin restaurant with its sushi bar and floor-to-ceiling windows caps the architectural wonderment. **Pros:** bustling nightlife and happy-hour scene; brash design. **Cons:** if you want quiet, head elsewhere. ✉ *1567 Broadway, at W. 47th St., Midtown West* ☎ *212/930–7400 or 877/946–8357* ⊕ *www.whotels.com* ↘ *464 rooms, 43 suites* ♿ *In-room: safe, DVD, VCR, Internet. In-hotel: restaurant, room service, bar, gym, spa, laundry service, concierge, public Internet, public Wi-Fi, some pets allowed, no-smoking rooms* ▭ *AE, D, DC, MC, V* Ⓜ *1, 2, 3, 7, N, Q, R, W, S to 42nd St./Times Sq.* ✛ *4:C3*

$$$ 🖵 **Warwick.** Astonishingly, this palatial property was built by William Randolph Hearst in 1927 as a private hotel for his friends and family. A Theater District favorite, it is well placed for most of Midtown's attractions. The marble-floor lobby buzzes with activity; the Randolph Bar is on one side and Murals on 54, a continental restaurant, offers a pre-theater dinner menu. The spacious rooms are rather plain—some would even say worn—though the free wireless, marble bathrooms, and suites with terraces compensate for the limited amenities and dated furnishings. The Cary Grant suite was the actor's New York residence for 12 years, and encapsulates a more refined moment in New York glamour. **Pros:** gorgeous entrance with historic hotel feel; central location. **Cons:** scratched, slightly dated furniture; rooms vary in size. ✉ *65 W. 54th St., at 6th Ave., Midtown West* ☎ *212/247–2700 or 800/223–4099* ⊕ *www. warwickhotelny.com* ↘ *359 rooms, 66 suites* ♿ *In-room: safe, refrigerator, Wi-Fi. In-hotel: 2 restaurants, room service, bar, gym, laundry service, concierge, parking (fee), no-smoking rooms* ▭ *AE, DC, MC, V* Ⓜ *E, V to 57th St.; N, Q, R, W to 57th St.* ✛ *4:D2*

$ 🖵 **Wellington Hotel.** A few blocks south of Central Park and Columbus ☮ Circle, the Wellington is a fine jumping-off point for visitors who want to see the sights both in Midtown and the Upper West Side. The vibe in the rooms is more classic New York than edgy or modern, with floral patterns and dark-wood headboards and chests. The bathrooms don't have much to recommend them, as they are both small and dark. Suites, however, are spacious and include fold-out couches and extra beds—great for large families. Molyvos, a boisterous Greek restaurant in the hotel, is an excellent dining option, and the breakfast area doubles as a classic diner the rest of the day. The staff is quite amenable to requests. The hotel runs clever themed packages during holidays. **Pros:** central location; chipper staff; good for big families. **Cons:** dark bathrooms; limited breakfast. ✉ *871 7th Ave., at W. 55th St., Midtown West* ☎ *212/247–3900 or 800/652–1212* ⊕ *www.wellingtonhotel.com* ↘ *600 rooms, 100 suites* ♿ *In-room: Wi-Fi. In-hotel: restaurant, bar, laundry facilities, laundry service, public Internet, public Wi-Fi, park-*

ing (fee), no-smoking rooms ⊟*AE, D, DC, MC, V* Ⓜ*N, Q, R, W to 57th St.* ✛*4:C2*

$ 🏨**Westin New York at Times Square.** The Westin changed the skyline of Midtown with this soaring skyscraper that subtly mimics the flow of the city—look for subway patterns in the carpets and the city reflected on the building's exterior. A thoughtful staff helps make the cavernous lobby and throngs of guests tolerable. Exceptionally large rooms are blissfully quiet and built to give you optimal views, which will probably be the most memorable part of your stay. Try especially for the light-filled corner rooms. Decor is sleek and amenities like flat-screen TVs are up to the latest standards. Bathrooms are stylish, with two-tone tiling, and have fun double showerheads. For even more comfort, spa-floor rooms come with massage chairs, aromatherapy candles, and other pampering pleasures. **Pros:** busy Times Square location; big and stylish rooms and baths. **Cons:** busy Times Square location; small bathroom sinks. ✉*270 W. 43rd St., at 8th Ave., Midtown West* ☎*212/201–2700 or 866/837–4183* ⊕*www.westinny.com* ⬎*737 rooms, 126 suites* ♿*In-room: safe, refrigerator, Wi-Fi. In-hotel: restaurant, room service, bars, gym, spa, laundry service, concierge, public Internet, public Wi-Fi, parking (fee), some pets allowed, no-smoking rooms* ⊟*AE, D, DC, MC, V* Ⓜ*A, C, E to 42nd St./Times Sq.* ✛*4:B4*

MIDTOWN EAST AND UPPER EAST SIDE

MIDTOWN EAST

$$ 🏨**Affinia 50.** This extremely popular hotel has a distinctly businesslike
☺ mood, but it's also supremely comfortable for families or leisure travelers. Most studios and all suites have plenty of space to stretch out in, with full kitchens and a clean, playful design including oversize chairs and couches. The second-floor club lounge provides business services and has board games for guest use. Those aren't the only quirky amenities, either. There's an "evening cheer" reception with complimentary wine and cheese Monday through Thursday, complimentary fruit and iced tea at reception, and a six-choice pillow menu. All rooms have a mini-refrigerator and microwave, and suites have countertop stoves. **Pros:** apartment-style living; good value; kid- and pet-friendly. **Cons:** ugly lobby; occasionally chintzy decor; unattractive room color scheme. ✉*155 E. 50th St., at 3rd Ave., Midtown East* ☎*212/751–5710 or 800/637–8483* ⊕*www.affinia.com* ⬎*56 rooms, 151 suites* ♿*In-room: safe, kitchen (some), refrigerator, Internet. In-hotel: room service, gym, laundry facilities, laundry service, concierge, public Internet, public Wi-Fi, parking (fee), some pets allowed, no-smoking rooms* ⊟*AE, D, DC, MC, V* Ⓜ*6 to 51st St./Lexington Ave.; E, V to Lexington–3rd Aves./53rd St.* ✛*4:G3*

$$$ 🏨**The Alex.** The goal of the David Rockwell–designed Alex is to create a soothing, Zen-like environment for travelers, enhanced by impeccable service. Unobtrusive sliding panels with nature prints hide the rooms' many gadgets. The focus remains on a clean, calm, sophisticated space where you can appreciate details in suites like kitchenettes with Gaggenau range tops, Poggenpohl cabinetry, and Sub-Zero refrigerators;

19

nightstands that turn into leather desktops; and flat-screen bathroom TVs that you can watch from the impressively deep bathtubs. Comfortable beds feature Frette linens. Award-winning chef Marcus Samuelsson runs Asian-inflected Riingo restaurant, which also provides room service. **Pros:** most rooms have kitchens; good service; on-site fitness facilities. **Cons:** cramped lobby; small bathrooms; no in-room Wi-Fi. ✉*205 E. 45th St., between 2nd and 3rd Aves., Midtown East* 🕾*212/867–5100* ⊕*www.thealexhotel.com* ⊷*73 rooms, 130 suites* ♿*In-room: kitchen (some), refrigerator (some), DVD, Internet. In-hotel: restaurant, room service, bar, gym, laundry service, public Internet, public Wi-Fi, parking (fee), some pets allowed, no-smoking rooms, concierge* ⊟*AE, MC, V* Ⓜ*4, 5, 6, 7, S to 42nd St./Grand Central.* ✛*4:G4*

$$$ 🛏 **The Benjamin.** This property prides itself on selling a great night's sleep. Guests consult with the "sleep concierge" to select from 13 styles of pillows (most popular: Swedish memory), white-noise machines, and other sleep aids before they hop into plush, 400-thread-count bedding. Beyond a superb slumber, many Fodorites stay at the property for its "excellent service" and "great location" across the street from the 6-line subway, one stop from Grand Central Terminal. Although the hotel caters largely to a business clientele, it is a popular choice for travelers with kids and teens, as most of the rooms are suites, primarily studio layouts of about 300 square feet and 1-br. suites of about 550 square feet. **Pros:** spacious by Manhattan standards; suites have kitchenette with microwave; personalized service. **Cons:** paid Internet and WiFi. ✉*125 E. 50th St., at Lexington Ave., Midtown East* 🕾*212/715-2500* ⊕*www.thebenjamin.com* ⊷*200* ♿*In-room: safe, refrigerator, Internet, Wi-Fi. In-hotel: 1 restaurant, room service, bar, gym, spa, laundry service, Internet terminal, Wi-Fi, parking (fee), some pets allowed.* ⊟*AE, D, DC, MC, V.* ⦿*EP.* Ⓜ*6 to 51st St./Lexington Ave.; E, V to Lexington–3rd Aves./53rd St.* ✛*4:F3*

$$$ 🛏**The Dylan.** New owners and complete room renovation make this boutique hotel worth a look, even though the service is more perfunctory than welcoming. Business travelers like the location a block from Grand Central, and the Benjamin, its grand steak house within. The 1903 Beaux-Arts–style building includes ornate plasterwork on the facade and a stunning marble staircase spiraling up its three floors. The 11-foot ceilings (the lower the floor, the higher the ceilings) give the modern guest rooms a touch of grandeur, and the beakers that serve as glasses in the bathrooms are a clever nod to the building's past as home of the Chemists Club. Alas, some of the rooms remain small and dark, even post-reconstruction. **Pros:** central location; free Internet; new room furnishings. **Cons:** inattentive service; small fitness center; pricey for limited amenities. ✉*52 E. 41st St., between Park and Madison Aves., Midtown East* 🕾*212/338-0500* ⊕*www.dylanhotel.com* ⊷*107 rooms, 5 suites* ♿*In-room: safe, Internet, Wi-Fi. In-hotel: restaurant, room service, bar, gym, public Wi-Fi* ⊟*AE, D, DC, MC, V* Ⓜ*4, 5, 6, 7, S to 42nd St./Grand Central.* ✛*4:E5*

$$$$ 🛏**Four Seasons Hotel.** Want to see what ascending to modernist heaven is like? Just walk up the towering lobby steps from 57th Street—past the rigid refinement of austere limestone, the legion of polished blond

wood. Now you stand at the foot of the altar: the best and most imposing concierge desk in America, the prototype for the much-revered Four
Seasons service. Indeed, everything at this hotel comes in monumental
proportions—including rooms starting at 600 square feet and a cost of
$915 in high season. They all have 10-foot-high ceilings, silk-covered
walls, large plasma TVs, English sycamore walk-in closets, and blond-
marble bathrooms with tubs that fill in 60 seconds. But even with the
whiz-bang frills, the rooms feel sterile at times, and not au courant,
design-wise. In addition to the restaurant's famous lunch, dinner at
the counter of esteemed restaurant L'Atelier de Joël Robuchon is a
can't-miss splurge. **Pros:** spacious and comfortable rooms; perfect concierge and staff service; afternoon tea in the lobby lounge. **Cons:** pricey;
design can feel a bit lifeless. ⊠ *57 E. 57th St., between Park and Madison Aves., Midtown East* ☎ *212/758–5700 or 800/487–3769* ⊕ *www.
fourseasons.com* ⤳ *300 rooms, 68 suites* ⚷ *In-room: safe, DVD, Internet, Wi-Fi. In-hotel: restaurant, room service, bar, gym, spa, laundry
service, concierge, parking (fee), public Internet, public Wi-Fi, some
pets allowed, no-smoking rooms* ☰ *AE, D, DC, MC, V* Ⓜ *4, 5, 6, N,
Q, R, W to 59th St./Lexington Ave.* ✛ *4:F1*

$$
Fodor'sChoice
★

Ⓣ **Library Hotel.** Bookishly handsome, this stately landmark brownstone,
built in 1900, is inspired by the New York Public Library. Each of its
10 floors is dedicated to one of the 10 categories of the Dewey Deci-
mal System; undersize modern rooms are stocked with art and books
relevant to a subtopic such as erotica, astronomy, or biography—let
your interests guide your choice. Either way, many of the rooms are
surprisingly big and offer a good value to "check out." The staff is very
hospitable, and the whole property is old-leather-armchair comfortable,
whether you're unwinding in front of the library fireplace, partaking of
the complimentary wine and cheese or continental breakfast, or relaxing
in the roof garden. **Pros:** fun rooftop bar; playful book themes; stylish
rooms. **Cons:** rooftop often reserved for events; more books in rooms
themselves would be nice. ⊠ *299 Madison Ave., at E. 41st St., Mid-
town East* ☎ *212/983–4500 or 877/793–7323* ⊕ *www.libraryhotel.
com* ⤳ *60 rooms* ⚷ *In-room: safe, refrigerator, DVD, Internet, Wi-Fi.
In-hotel: restaurant, room service, bar, laundry service, concierge, park-
ing (fee), no-smoking rooms* ☰ *AE, DC, MC, V* ⑩ *CP* Ⓜ *4, 5, 6, 7, S
to 42nd St./Grand Central.* ✛ *4:E4*

$$$

Ⓣ **Loews Regency Hotel.** The snazzy lobby displays the focus of this Park
Avenue hotel: service and space. The modern guest rooms have lush
details like silk wallpaper and mahogany accents, but more importantly,
are rather large for the price point and come kitted with flat-screens
and high-speed Internet. That space comes at the expense of the bathrooms, which are on the small side. Goose-down duvets and ergonomic
leather desk chairs reinforce the pleasingly modern feel. Feinstein's at
the Regency hosts some of the hottest (and priciest) cabaret acts in
town, and 540 Park has become a destination in its own right among
restaurant-savvy locals. The Loews Regency accepts pets. **Pros:** friendly
and helpful staff; relatively quiet; good for pets. **Cons:** Rooms are pretty
but not a great value; overpriced room service. ⊠ *540 Park Ave., at E.
61st St., Midtown East* ☎ *212/759–4100 or 800/233–2356* ⊕ *www.*

19

loewshotels.com ⤴*266 rooms, 87 suites* ⌂*In-room: safe, kitchen (some), refrigerator, VCR, Internet. In-hotel: restaurant, room service, bar, gym, laundry service, concierge, parking (fee), no-smoking rooms, some pets allowed* ⊟*AE, D, DC, MC, V* Ⓜ*4, 5, 6, N, Q, R, W to 59th St./Lexington Ave.* ✚*5:F6*

$ 🖵**Millennium UN Plaza.** This sky-high tower near the United Nations begins on the 28th floor. Rooms have breathtaking views (get one facing west towards Manhattan) and make generous use of warm woods and neutral tones. The multilingual staff caters to a discerning clientele that includes heads of state. The views also dazzle from the elegant 27th-floor pool and health club, and the indoor rooftop tennis court attracts name players. Service throughout the hotel is first-rate, though the common areas have seen better days. **Pros:** unbeatable East River and city views; discreet decor; great front-door and bell staff. **Cons:** a walk to the subway; pricey Internet access. ⊠*1 United Nations Plaza, at E. 44th St. and 1st Ave., Midtown East* ☎*212/758–1234 or 866/866–8086* ⊕*www.millenniumhotels.com* ⤴*382 rooms, 45 suites* ⌂*In-room: safe, Internet. In-hotel: restaurant, room service, bar, tennis court, pool, gym, laundry service, concierge, public Internet, public Wi-Fi, parking (fee), no-smoking rooms* ⊟*AE, D, DC, MC, V* Ⓜ*4, 5, 6, 7, S to 42nd St./Grand Central.* ✚*4:H4*

$$$ 🖵**New York Palace Hotel.** Want the privileged *Gossip Girl* experience? Stay at these connected mansions, built in the 1880s by railroad baron Henry Villard and populated by Serena van der Woodson, circa 2009. The lobby, with its sweeping staircases, golden chandeliers, and arched colonnades is host to the acclaimed New American restaurant Gilt. Standard rooms in the main section of the hotel are done up in warming beige and marble, but they are hardly exceptional. The better option is rooms in the tower: these are either modern or classic, depending on the floor, have more luxe decor and bathrooms, separate check-in, and more-attentive service with a dedicated concierge and a butler. Many hotel rooms, as well as the 7,000-square-foot health club, have terrific views of St. Patrick's Cathedral. **Pros:** gorgeous courtyard with 15th Italian style motifs; great service; unmatched views of St. Patrick's Cathedral. **Cons:** overpriced; harried service from staff. ⊠*455 Madison Ave., at E. 50th St., Midtown East* ☎*212/888–7000 or 800/697–2522* ⊕*www.newyorkpalace.com* ⤴*804 rooms, 88 suites* ⌂*In-room: safe, refrigerator (some), Internet. In-hotel: 2 restaurants, room service, bars, gym, spa, laundry service, concierge, public Internet, public Wi-Fi, parking (fee), some pets allowed, no-smoking rooms* ⊟*AE, D, DC, MC, V* Ⓜ*6 to 51st St./Lexington Ave.; E, V to Lexington–3rd Aves./53rd St.* ✚*4:E3*

$$$$ 🖵**The Peninsula.** Stepping through the Peninsula's Beaux-Arts facade
Fodor'sChoice onto the grand staircase overhung with a monumental chandelier, you
★ know you're in for a glitzy treat. Service here is world-class, and personalized: Expect to be referred to by name as you make your way through the hotel. Rooms have the latest touches in luxury comfort. The views are stunning: see the northward sweep up 5th Avenue to Central Park past church steeples; or look east toward the beautiful St. Regis across the street. The high-tech amenities are excellent, from a bedside console

that controls the lighting, sound, and thermostat for the room to a TV mounted over the tub for bath-time viewing (in all but standard rooms). The rooftop health club, with indoor pool, is monumental. The Salon de Ning, a rooftop bar bedecked with chinoiserie, has dazzling views of Midtown. **Pros:** brilliant service; fabulous rooms, including best room lighting of all city hotels (good angles, easy to use); unforgettable rooftop bar. **Cons:** expensive. ⊠ *700 5th Ave., at 55th St., Midtown East* ☎ *212/956–2888 or 800/262–9467* ⊕ *newyork.peninsula.com* ⇨ *185 rooms, 54 suites* ⚭ *In-room: safe, refrigerator, dial-up, Wi-Fi. In-hotel: restaurant, room service, bars, pool, gym, spa, laundry service, concierge, parking (fee), some pets allowed, no-smoking rooms* ⊟ *AE, D, DC, MC, V* Ⓜ *E, V to 5th Ave.* ✛ *4:E2*

¢ 🏨 **Pod Hotel.** This is the hotel that made bunk beds cool again. By offering spotless stainless-steel bunks with pull-out flat-screen TVs, the Pod makes tiny, tiny rooms tolerable. If you can handle cramped quarters, this is one of the best deals in Midtown. About half the rooms come with standard queen beds and private bath. The rooms, starting at a meager 100 square feet, borrow space-saving ideas from mass transit, with sink consoles like those in an airplane restroom, and built-in shelves tucked under the beds. But you may be willing to trade space for the convenient location and modern amenities like in-room iPod docking stations and free Wi-Fi. Families take note, five new suites of 336 square feet can give you a little more breathing room. The common areas are cheerful and modern, with an outdoor bar-café and a stylish roof deck. Don't expect luxe linens or fab toiletries. Do expect to book well in advance, as budget-minded hipsters and stylish thrifty folk of all ages are sure to keep this hotel hopping. **Pros:** an inexpensive and fun way to save money. **Cons:** many will hate the small rooms; some shared bathrooms. ⊠ *230 E. 51st St., between 2nd and 3rd Aves., Midtown East 10022* ☎ *212/355–0300 or 800/874–0074* – ⊕ *www.thepodhotel. com* ⇨ *347 rooms, 195 with bath* ⚭ *In-room: Wi-Fi. In-hotel: Wi-Fi* ⊟ *AE, DC, MC, V* Ⓜ *6 to 51st St./Lexington Ave.; E, V to Lexington– 3rd Aves./53rd St.* ✛ *4:G2*

Fodor'sChoice
★

$ 🏨 **Roger Smith.** One of the better budget buys in the city, the Roger Smith is a quirky and inexpensive choice. The art-filled rooms, matched by the murals in the lobby, are homey and comfortable, including down pillows and quilts on the beds. Some have stocked bookshelves and fireplaces. Suites have kitchenettes. Bathrooms are small but do have tubs. An eclectic mix of room service is provided by five local restaurants, and guests have access to the nearby New York Sports Club ($10 fee). Rates can drop by as much as $75 per night in winter and summer, so ask when booking. A complimentary continental breakfast is included. **Pros:** good location near Grand Central; intimate atmosphere; free Wi-Fi. **Cons:** street noise; small bathrooms. ⊠ *501 Lexington Ave., between E. 47th and E. 48th Sts., Midtown East* ☎ *212/755–1400 or 800/445–0277* ⊕ *www.rogersmith.com* ⇨ *102 rooms, 28 suites* ⚭ *In-room: kitchen (some), refrigerator, Internet, Wi-Fi. In-hotel: restaurant, room service, bar, laundry service, parking (fee), some pets allowed, no-smoking rooms* ⊟ *AE, D, DC, MC, V* ⏹ *CP* Ⓜ *6 to 51st St./Lexington Ave.; E, V to Lexington–3rd Aves./53rd St.* ✛ *4:F3*

19

$ 🛏 **Roosevelt Hotel.** Named after Teddy, not Franklin, this Midtown icon steps from Grand Central has plenty of elbow room for stretching out in. A Gilded Age lobby with cushy couches and old-school bar with heavy wood detailing makes the Roosevelt feel like it's from another time, and it should—the property dates from 1924. Happily, the amenities do not hark back to that era, though rooms are a little tired: the carpeting shows some wear, the art on the walls is chain-generic, and the bedding is blah. However, the beds come with pillow-top mattresses and the bathrooms are nice and big. The impressive banquet areas are lavish to the point of being over the top. **Pros:** great public areas; big bathrooms. **Cons:** dated decor; limited in-room amenities. ⊠*45 E. 45th St., at Madison Ave., Midtown East* ☎*888/TEDDY–NY* ⊕*www.theroosevelthotel.com* ⊷*1,015 rooms, 24 suites* ⟳*In-room: Wi-Fi. In-hotel: room service, restaurant, gym, parking (fee)* ☰*AE, MC, V* Ⓜ*4, 5, 6 to Grand Central/42nd St.* ✥*4:F4*

$$$$ 🛏 **The St. Regis.** World-class from head to toe, the St. Regis comes as

Fodor's Choice close to flawless as any hotel in New York. Even without the hive

★ of activity in its unparalleled public spaces, this 5th Avenue Beaux-Arts landmark would rank near the top of any best-of list. You can dine in two dining rooms—including a new Alain Ducasse restaurant, Adour—as well as the legendary King Cole Bar, a dimly lighted institution with its famously playful Maxfield Parrish murals. Guest rooms feature the best technology in the city, including easy-to-use bedside consoles (developed by an in-house R&D team) that control lighting, audio, and climate; and huge flat-screen TVs that rise via remote control from the foot of your bed. Each floor is serviced by its own butler, a touch no other hotel here can match. Rooms have high ceilings, crystal chandeliers, silk wall coverings, Louis XVI antiques—though even in this price range, you're not guaranteed a stellar view. Still, if you require the best, the St. Regis delivers. **Pros:** rooms combine true luxury with helpful technology; easy-access butler service; superb in-house dining; prestigious location. **Cons:** expensive; too serious for families seeking fun. ⊠*2 E. 55th St., at 5th Ave., Midtown East* ☎*212/753–4500 or 877/787–3447* ⊕*www.stregis.com* ⊷*164 rooms, 65 suites* ⟳*In-room: safe, refrigerator, DVD, Internet. In-hotel: restaurant, room service, gym, laundry service, concierge, parking (fee), no-smoking rooms* ☰*AE, D, DC, MC, V* Ⓜ*E, V to 5th Ave.* ✥*4:E2*

$$$$ 🛏 **Sherry-Netherland.** With its iconic sidewalk clock on the southeast corner of Central Park and a captivating finial spire atop its slender form, the Sherry is a stately part of the New York landscape. So it may come as a surprise to learn that it's essentially a tall, luxurious apartment building. The 50 guest rooms on offer come decorated in the fashion of their individual owners, but the standards are kept very high throughout. With a marble-lined lobby, crystal chandeliers, and wall friezes from the Vanderbilt mansion, its historic glamour is undeniable. The luxurious suites—reached via elevator operated by a white-gloved attendant—have separate living and dining areas. Many have decorative fireplaces, antiques, and glorious marble baths. You should use the private hotel entrance to have a complimentary breakfast at Harry Cipriani's. (You might even stay for lunch for some of the best people-watching in town.) **Pros:** gorgeous lobby; commanding, impeccable location; Cipriani access. **Cons:** rooms vary in taste and decor; nonsuites are on the small side; interior rooms lack views. ⊠*781 5th Ave., at E. 59th St., Midtown East* ☎*212/355–2800 or 800/247–4377* ⊕*www.sherrynetherland.com* ⟋*30 rooms, 20 suites* ⚸*In-room: safe, refrigerator, VCR, Internet. In-hotel: restaurant, room service, bar, gym, laundry service, parking (fee), concierge* ☰*AE, D, DC, MC, V* ❙⚬❙*CP* Ⓜ*N, R, Q, W to 5th Ave.* ⟊*5:E6*

$$$ 🏨**Waldorf=Astoria.** The lobby of this landmark 1931 art-deco masterpiece, full of murals, mosaics, and elaborate plaster ornamentation, features a grand piano once owned by Cole Porter and still played daily. Standard rooms top out at a cozy 250 square feet with marble bathrooms and wood headboards to balance the extensive floral patterns. Downstairs, the Bull and Bear Bar is a 1940s throwback complete with miniature soda bottles and no-nonsense barkeeps. The ultra-exclusive Waldorf Towers (the 28th floor and above) has a separate entrance and management. The Waldorf is famous for its former residents; besides Porter, these have included Herbert Hoover and Nikola Tesla; presidents usually stay here thanks to the security of the drive-in entrance. The new Guerlain spa is an impressive and much needed addition. **Pros:** historic art-deco building filled with NYC's aristocratic, gangster, and jazz histories; best Waldorf salad in town; knowledgeable doormen. **Cons:** rooms not contemporary; more about the name than the experience. ⊠*301 Park Ave., between E. 49th and E. 50th Sts., Midtown East* ☎*212/355–3000 or 800/925–3673* ⊕*www.waldorfastoria.com* ⟋*1,176 rooms, 276 suites* ⚸*In-room: safe, Internet. In-hotel: 4 restaurants, room service, bars, gym, laundry service, concierge, executive floor, parking (fee), public Wi-Fi, public Internet, some pets allowed, no-smoking rooms* ☰*AE, D, DC, MC, V* Ⓜ*6 to 51st St./Lexington Ave.; E, V to Lexington–3rd Aves./53rd St.* ⟊*4:F3*

$$$ 🏨**W Hotel New York.** This was the first of the W hotels to open in New York, and after a decade rooms got a much-needed overhaul in 2008. Window boxes filled with grass, bowls heaped with green apples, flowing curtains, and vast floor-to-ceiling windows that pour sunlight into the airy lobby all conjure up a calming outdoor vibe here—quite a trick considering a hopping bar and a sunken lounge flank the reception area. The rooms hew to the classic W formula: they're small and they look great—especially thanks to the overhaul, which added LED lights around the windows and beds, wooden desks topped with swiveling panes of glass, and amethyst wall coverings in the bathroom. Of course the party-hearty clientele also means you're likely to hear your neighbors partying heartily through the night. Downstairs, Heartbeat Restaurant serves heart-healthy foods; the attached Whiskey Blue draws a young, hip, and moneyed crowd; and the Bliss Spa flagship draws legions of beauty devotees. **Pros:** central location; great-looking rooms. **Cons:** thin walls; inconsistent service. ⊠*541 Lexington Ave., between E. 49th and E. 50th Sts., Midtown East* ☎*212/755–1200 or 877/946–8357* ⊕*www.whotels.com* ⟋*629 rooms, 62 suites* ⚸*In-room: safe, DVD, Internet. In-hotel: restaurant, room service, bar, gym, spa, laundry service, concierge, public Internet, public Wi-Fi, some pets*

19

allowed, no-smoking rooms ⊟*AE, D, DC, MC, V* Ⓜ*6 to 51st St./Lexington Ave.; E, V to Lexington–3rd Aves./53rd St.* ✛*4:F3.*

UPPER EAST SIDE

$$$$

Fodor's Choice

★

The Carlyle, A Rosewood Hotel. On the well-heeled corner of Madison Avenue and 75th Street, this hotel's fusion of venerable elegance and Manhattan swank is like entering a Chanel boutique: walk in chin high, wallet out, and ready to be impressed. As you might expect, everything about this Upper East Side landmark suggests cultivated refinement: rooms decorated with fine antique furniture, vast Central Park views, white-gloved operators working the elevators 24 hours a day. It's all overwhelmingly grand—almost to the point of diminishing comfort. The range of the hotel's dining and entertainment options impresses: Cabaret luminaries take turns holding court at the Café Carlyle (and yes, Woody Allen still visits once a week). Bemelmans Bar may never lose its title as greatest old-school cocktail spot in New York. The polished black key slots behind the reception desk are the old guest key deposits, though now they're a fashionable reminder of the hotel's storied history as host to presidents and celebrities. **Pros:** perhaps NYC's best Central Park views; refined service; delightful array of dining and bar options. **Cons:** removed from tourist Manhattan; stuffy vibe may be inappropriate for families. ⊠*35 E. 76th St., between Madison and Park Aves., Upper East Side* ☎*212/744–1600* ⊕*www.thecarlyle.com* ⤸*122 rooms, 57 suites* ♿*In-room: safe, kitchen, refrigerator, DVD, Internet. In-hotel: restaurant, room service, bar, gym, spa, laundry service, parking (fee), concierge, no-smoking rooms, some pets allowed* ⊟*AE, DC, MC, V* Ⓜ*6 to 77th St.* ✛*5:F3*

$$

The Franklin. The Franklin is the best luxury boutique hotel north of 57th Street. And it's way north of 57th Street in spirit, firmly ensconced in the youthful residential area of the Upper East Side, where there's nary another hotel to be seen. Though quite small, rooms are well appointed with name brand knickknacks, including Bulgari toiletries, iHome stations, free wireless, and Frette linens. The lobby of this nine-story town house feels comfortable and lived-in, with newspapers laid out on comfortable couches and a free 24-hour cappuccino machine behind it. The generous complimentary breakfast uses a local bakery for all goods, and the hotel hosts a wine-and-artisanal-cheese reception on weekday evenings. You can meet (sweaty) locals with a comp pass to New York Sports Club. **Pros:** neighborhood-y location; free Wi-Fi. **Cons:** far from many NYC tourist sights except Museum Mile; small rooms. ⊠*164 E. 87th St., between Lexington and 3rd Aves., Upper East Side* ☎*212/369–1000 or 877/847–4444* ⊕*www.franklinhotel. com* ⤸*50 rooms* ♿*In-room: safe, Wi-Fi. In-hotel: room service, bar, laundry service, public Internet, public Wi-Fi, some pets allowed, no-smoking rooms* ⊟*AE, D, DC, MC, V* ⦿I*CP* Ⓜ*4, 5, 6 to 86th St.* ✛*6:G6*

$$$$

Hôtel Plaza Athénée. It's easy to be seduced by this luxurious hotel positioned discreetly by Central Park on the Upper East Side. The key is finding the right room—they come in a cavalcade of layouts and design schemes. Some even have small patios. Service is stellar, with a personal sit-down check-in to the side of the lobby, and extravagant room service. The hotel may seem stuffy to younger visitors. To others, touches like the lobby tapestries depicting forest scenes will be a welcome old-school luxury. The Bar Seine is a dark and secretive hideaway, one of the best bars in the city, and surely the only one with a floor made of leather. Arabelle is a much-touted, if not particularly well-loved restaurant. **Pros:** discerning service; exotic bar. **Cons:** hoity-toity; nonstandarized rooms hit-or-miss. ⊠ *37 E. 64th St., at Madison Ave., Upper East Side* ☎ *212/734–9100 or 800/447–8800* ⊕ *www.plaza-athenee.com* ⤴ *115 rooms, 35 suites* ♿ *In-room: safe, kitchen (some), refrigerator, Internet. In-hotel: restaurant, room service, bar, gym, concierge, laundry service, parking (fee), no-smoking rooms, some pets allowed* ▭ *AE, D, DC, MC, V* Ⓜ *6 to 68th St./Hunter College* ✛ *5:F5.*

> **WORD OF MOUTH**
>
> "Something I have learned about hotels in NYC—the rooms are often small. It is very common to get a room in NYC that is smaller than you would normally expect. Sure there are hotels with larger rooms, but I have found that they are the exception to the rule. Even a NYC room that is labeled a "suite" may be smaller than you are hoping for."   —Shandy1977

$$ ☎ **Hotel Wales.** Every effort has been made to retain the turn-of-the-20th-century mood of this 1901 Carnegie Hill landmark—from the cavernous lobby to the Pied Piper parlor, where vintage children's illustrations cover the walls. A complimentary European-style breakfast is served in the parlor; on a nice day head up to the rooftop terrace with your treats. Guest rooms are small, but they do have fine oak woodwork, and all come with CD players. Most of the suites face Madison Avenue; unfortunately, soundproof windows are not de rigueur, making for some noisy evenings, especially when coupled with the loud air-conditioning units. The lovely Sarabeth's Restaurant, a local favorite for brunch, is in the hotel, as is the recently reopened Joanna's restaurant. **Pros:** on-site fitness facilities; good restaurant; charming decor. **Cons:** can be noisy; expensive Internet access; cramped rooms. ⊠ *1295 Madison Ave., between E. 92nd and E. 93rd Sts., Upper East Side* ☎ *212/876–6000 or 877/847–4444* ⊕ *www.waleshotel.com* ⤴ *46 rooms, 42 suites* ♿ *In-room: safe, kitchen (some), refrigerator (some), DVD (some), VCR (some), Wi-Fi. In-hotel: restaurant, room service, bar, gym, laundry service, concierge, parking (fee), some pets allowed, no-smoking rooms* ▭ *AE, D, DC, MC, V* ❘○❘ *CP* Ⓜ *4, 5, 6 to 86th St.* ✛ *6:F5*

$$$ ☎ **The Lowell.** This old-money refuge was built as an upscale apartment hotel in the 1920s and still delivers genteel sophistication and pampering service in an unbeatable location. Steps away from Madison Avenue shopping and the Museum Mile, the Lowell is tucked away on a leafy residential block. The lobby may be small and cramped, but guest rooms have all the civilized comforts of home, including stocked bookshelves, luxe bathrooms, and even umbrellas. Thirty-three of the suites, all decorated in different themes such as the "Hollywood Suite" and the "Garden Suite," have working fireplaces, and 11 have private terraces, the better for spying on posh neighboring abodes. Most of the

19

Lodging Alternatives

APARTMENT RENTALS VS. SUITE HOTELS

For your trip to New York, you may want a little more space than the city's typically tiny hotel rooms provide. Some travelers consider apartment rentals, but we tend to recommend hotel suites instead. Why? Unfortunately, apartment rental scams are prevalent. In some published reports, potential guests have arrived to find that the apartment they rented does not exist, or that they are paying for an illegal sublet. In some cases, travelers have lost their deposit money, or their pre-paid rent (note: never wire money to an individual's account).

There are a few reputable providers of short term rentals, noted below. But many Fodorites have turned to suite hotels and B&Bs with apartment-like accommodations to guard themselves from possible scams. We've noted some of their most enthusiastic recommendations.

Local rental agencies include: **Abode Limited** (⬚ *Box 20022, New York, NY 10028* ☎ *800/835–8880 or 212/472–2000* ⊕ *www.abodenyc.com*) arranges rentals of furnished apartments. **Manhattan Getaways** (⬚ *Box 1994, New York, NY 10022* ☎ *212/956–2010* ⊕ *www.manhattangetaways.com*).

Suite suggestions from **Fodor's Forums** (⊕ www.fodors.com/forums)

"For a week or less, there's no need to risk being scammed or renting something illegal by renting a private apt. There are LOADS of suite hotels and B&B's at all price levels that will provide the space and convenience of an apartment, many with the amenities of a hotel including the ability to be able to read reviews of them before you book and know what

you're getting. **Affinia** (⊕ www.Affinia. com) is a group of seven suite hotels at various prices that's well regarded. **Radio City Apartments** (⊕ www. radiocityapartments.com), **Milburn Hotel** (⊕ www.milburnhotel.com), and **The Salisbury Hotel** (⊕ www.nyc-salisbury.com) are some of the more popular independent budget options." —mclaurie

BED-AND-BREAKFASTS

B&Bs booked through a service may be either hosted (you're the guest in someone's quarters) or unhosted (you have full use of someone's vacated apartment, including kitchen privileges). Reservation services include: **All Around the Town** (⊠ *270 Lafayette St., Suite 804, New York, NY* ☎ *212/675–5600 or 800/443–3800* ⊕ *www.newyorkcitybestbb.com*). **Bed-and-Breakfast Network of New York** (⊠ *134 W. 32nd St., Suite 602, between 6th and 7th Aves., New York, NY* ☎ *212/645–8134 or 800/900–8134* ⊕ *www.bedandbreakfastnetny. com*). **City Lights Bed-and-Breakfast** (⬚ *Box 20355, Cherokee Station, New York, NY 10075* ☎ *212/737–7049* ⊕ *www.citylightsbedandbreakfast.com*).

"**West Eleventh** (⊕ www.west-eleventh.com) and **Abingdon Guest House** (⊕ www.abingdonguesthouse. com) are two of many B&B's in the village with some charm, but are only good for two people." —mclaurie

"Also try **B&B Manhattan** (⊕ www. bandbmanhattan.com) which has very nice studio and 1-bed apartments in Chelsea and GV. A friend stayed with them last year and liked it a lot." —tomassocroccante

nonsuite rooms have been redecorated in a more modern, streamlined style with less chintz and no patterns. The Pembroke Room serves a fine afternoon tea, and the Post House serves some of the best steaks in town. The in-room iPods (on-request) and *New York Times* delivered to the room are particularly nice touches. **Pros:** great location; service with a personal touch; charming decor. **Cons:** unimpressive cramped lobby; some rooms need updating. *⊠28 E. 63rd St., between Madison and Park Aves., Upper East Side ☎212/838–1400 or 800/221–4444 ⊕www.lowellhotel.com ⋑23 rooms, 47 suites ⚫In-room: safe, kitchen, refrigerator, DVD, VCR, Internet. In-hotel: 2 restaurants, room service, bar, gym, laundry service, concierge, parking (fee), some pets allowed ⊟AE, D, DC, MC, V Ⓜ 4, 5, 6, N, R, W to 59th St./Lexington Ave.; F to 63rd St./Lexington Ave. ✛5:F6*

UPPER WEST SIDE

$$ 🛈**The Empire Hotel.** This historic Upper West Side spot, which officially reopened in June 2008 after an extensive redesign, offers a dizzying number of amenities. When you first enter the hotel, you'll be drawn to the sophisticated, bi-level lobby with floor-to-ceiling silk drapes, high-back banquettes with animal-print accents, and the dimly lighted bar. That's before you soak up the sun and enjoy the breathtaking views from the rooftop pool and lounge area underneath the hotel's iconic red neon sign. Guest rooms, which are small (in keeping with their original construction), provide a comfortable and chic escape from the bustle of the city. A soothing palette of varying shades of brown is complemented with animal-print chairs, dark-wood accents, and luxurious amenities such as flat-screen TVs, iPod docking stations, and Frette linens. **Pros:** prime location, situated next to Lincoln Center and just blocks from Central Park; beautiful rooftop pool and bar; complimentary issues of *Time Out New York* magazine; fresh apples left at your bedside at turndown. **Cons:** elevators are beautifully redecorated but still feel rickety; although nicely designed; bathrooms are tiny; pool is quite small. *⊠44 W. 63rd St., at Columbus Ave., Upper West Side ☎212/265–7400 ⊕www.empirehotelnyc.com ⋑50 suites, 370 rooms ⚫In-room: safe, refrigerator, Wi-Fi In-hotel: room service, bars, pool, laundry service, public Wi-Fi ⊟AE, MC, V Ⓜ1, A, B, C to 59th St/ Columbus Circle ✛5:C5*

$ 🛈**Excelsior.** Directly across the street from the American Museum of Natural History, this well-kept spot rubs shoulders with fine prewar apartment buildings (make sure to spring for a room with museum views). The frilly, faux-Victorian rooms with cushy beds have modern comforts like satellite television and Wi-Fi—the hotel even lends wireless cards for guests without it on their computer. The second-floor breakfast room serves a good, if slightly pricey for the neighborhood, breakfast. The library lounge, with leather sofas, a cozy fireplace, and tables with built-in game boards, is an unexpected plus. On the minus side is a staff that seems to be too busy to focus on customer service. **Pros:** unique Upper West Side location near Central Park; closest hotel in NYC to foodie mecca Zabar's; tranquil environment. **Cons:** guests report unfriendly front-desk staff; rooms can use updating.

19

✉ *45 W. 81st St., between Central Park W and Columbus Ave., Upper West Side* ☎ *212/362–9200 or 800/368–4575* ⊕ *www.excelsiorhotelny.com* ⤢ *118 rooms, 80 suites* ♿ *In-room: safe, Wi-Fi. In-hotel: gym, laundry service, concierge, public Internet, public Wi-Fi, some pets allowed, no-smoking rooms* ▭ *AE, D, DC, MC, V* Ⓜ *B to 81st St.* ✛ *5:C2*

WORD OF MOUTH

"The Beacon is on the Upper West Side—a lively mid/upscale residential area with tons of great inexpensive/moderate restaurants. You're right near Central Park and several of the major museums. There are two subway lines to carry you to other areas of the city quickly." —nytraveler

$ ⊡ **Hotel Beacon.** The Upper West Side's best buy for the price is three blocks from Central Park and Lincoln Center, and footsteps from Zabar's gourmet bazaar. All of the generously sized sea-green rooms and suites include marble bathrooms, kitchenettes with coffeemakers, pots and pans, stoves, and microwaves. Closets are huge, and some of the bathrooms have Hollywood dressing room–style mirrors. High floors have views of Central Park, the Hudson River, or the Midtown skyline; the staff here is especially friendly and helpful. The Hotel Beacon makes a nice choice for exploring a different corner of New York in a safe, exciting residential neighborhood. **Pros:** kitchenettes in all rooms; heart of UWS location; affordable. **Cons:** rooms emphasize comfort over style. ✉ *2130 Broadway, at W. 75th St., Upper West Side* ☎ *212/787–1100 or 800/572–4969* ⊕ *www.beaconhotel.com* ⤢ *120 rooms, 110 suites* ♿ *In-room: safe, kitchen, refrigerator. In-hotel: laundry facilities, parking (fee), no-smoking rooms* ▭ *AE, D, DC, MC, V* Ⓜ *1, 2, 3 to 72nd St.* ✛ *5:A3*

$ ⊡ **The Lucerne.** The landmark facade of this exquisite building has more pizzazz than the predictable guest rooms, with their requisite dark-wood reproduction furniture and chintz bedspreads. Health-conscious adults might like the gym on the top floor, with its city views, and children may be glued to the in-room Nintendo games. Service is the hotel's strong suit, and their popular Mediterranean restaurant Nice Matin is one of the better ones on the Upper West Side. The affluent residential neighborhood is filled with an impressive array of boutiques and gourmet food shops, and the American Museum of Natural History is a short walk away. **Pros:** free wireless; clean; close to Central Park. **Cons:** Inconsistent room size; some report uncomfortable pillows. ✉ *201 W. 79th St., at Amsterdam Ave., Upper West Side* ☎ *212/875–1000 or 800/492–8122* ⊕ *www.thelucernehotel.com* ⤢ *142 rooms, 42 suites* ♿ *In-room: kitchen (some), refrigerator (some), Wi-Fi. In-hotel: restaurant, room service, bar, gym, laundry service, concierge, parking (fee), public Internet, public Wi-Fi, no-smoking rooms* ▭ *AE, D, DC, MC, V* Ⓜ *1 to 79th St.* ✛ *5:A2*

$ ⊡ **On the Ave Hotel.** This tranquil Upper West Side property is a foodie's delight, as it's home to a new brunch spot from Tom Valenti and the Upper West Side branch of Zak Pelaccio's beloved (and tiny) Fatty Crab. Inside, the hotel is tasteful and modern with the occasional swath of color from a red chair or green drapes. Rooms aren't especially big in relative terms—they start at 240 square feet—but for the price, they are quite spacious. Plus, they're kitted out with Aeron chairs, flat-screen TVs, and Trump-style black marble bathrooms. Nickel-and-dime charges for Internet, valet parking, and the use of a mini-refrigerator are a bit frustrating, however. Suites and lofts have impressive views of Central Park, and the proximity to Lincoln Center is another plus. **Pros:** great dining options; excellent value. **Cons:** small charges add up; location not ideal for all NYC visitors. ✉*2178 Broadway, at W. 77th St., Upper West Side* ☎*800/509–7598* ⊕*www.ontheave-nyc.com* ⤳*250 rooms, 32 suites* ♿*In-room: Internet, Wi-Fi, safe. In-hotel: 2 restaurants, room service, parking (fee)* ═*AE, MC, V* Ⓜ*1 to 79th St.* ✛*5:A3*

$$$$ ⌂**Trump International Hotel and Towers.** Go figure: Donald Trump has created a very discreet hotel. An inconspicuous lobby immediately introduces you to the hotel's fine service, which continues throughout your stay with available personal assistants. What is showy is the building, a black skyscraper jutting high above Columbus Circle presenting unobstructed views of Central Park from floor-to-ceiling windows. Suites that corner the park and circle have some of the most compelling urban views in the world. Rooms and suites resemble mini-apartments: all have fully equipped kitchens with dishwashers. Room decor is slightly outdated in that razzle-dazzle Trump style—gold fixtures!—like a luxury apartment form a decade ago. Personalized stationery and business cards are provided on request. The restaurant, Jean Georges, is one of the city's finest, and for a price a Jean Georges's sous-chef will prepare a meal in your kitchenette. That's luxury. **Pros:** fine service; stellar views; discrete treatment. **Cons:** somewhat outdated luxury furnishings. ✉*1 Central Park W, between W. 59th and W. 60th Sts., Upper West Side* ☎*212/299–1000 or 888/448–7867* ⊕*www.trumpintl.com* ⤳*37 rooms, 130 suites* ♿*In-room: safe, kitchen, refrigerator, DVD, VCR, Internet. In-hotel: restaurant, room service, bar, pool, gym, spa, laundry service, concierge, parking (fee), no-smoking rooms* ═*AE, D, DC, MC, V* Ⓜ*1, A, B, C, D to 59th St./Columbus Circle.* ✛*5:C6*

19

Travel Smart
New York City

WORD OF MOUTH

"I loved having the unlimited metro pass (one per person)—that way we could hop on a subway even for a short distance without thinking twice. Of course, last time we were there it was cold and short hops on the subway were warranted!"

—sf7307

GETTING HERE & AROUND

Made up of five boroughs, New York City packs a staggering range of sights and activities into just under 7,000 square mi. You'll probably want to focus most of your visit in Manhattan, a compact island of attractions. To experience the most from the city, you need to think like a New Yorker: explore the city with your eyes open to everything around you; every city block offers new and unexpected sights.

If you're flying into one of three major airports that service New York, pick your mode of transportation for getting to Manhattan before your plane lands. The typical route is to hire a car or wait in the taxi line. Looking to save? Pick from the shuttle or public transportation options we've outlined.

Once you're in Manhattan, getting around can be a breeze when you get the hang of the subway system. You can hop in and out of neighborhoods, each with its own completely different vibe, in minutes. When you're not in a rush, just walk—it's the best way to discover true New York. Not quite sure where you are or how to get where you're headed? Ask a local. You just may be surprised how friendly the city's inhabitants are, especially when it's not rush hour. In the same getting-there-is-half-the-fun spirit, find water, land, and air journeys to see the city from a whole new perspective.

■ AIR TRAVEL

Generally, more international flights go in and out of Kennedy Airport, more domestic flights go in and out of LaGuardia Airport, and Newark Airport serves both domestic and international travelers.

Airlines & Airports Airline and Airport Links.com (⊕ *www.airlineandairportlinks.com*) has links to many of the world's airlines and airports.

Airline Security Issues Transportation Security Administration (⊕ *www.tsa.gov*) has answers for almost every question that might come up.

AIRPORTS

The major air gateways to New York City are LaGuardia Airport (LGA) and JFK International Airport (JFK) in the borough of Queens, and Newark Liberty International Airport (EWR) in New Jersey. Cab fares are generally higher to and from Newark. LaGuardia is closer to Manhattan and easier to navigate than JFK. The AirTrain link between Newark Airport and New Jersey transit makes the journey in less than 15 minutes; then you must transfer to NJ Transit to Penn Station.

Airport Information JFK International Airport (☏ *718/244–4444* ⊕ *www.panynj. gov*). **LaGuardia Airport** (☏ *718/533–3400* ⊕ *www.laguardiaairport.com*). **Newark Liberty International Airport** (☏ *973/961–6000 or 888/397–4636* ⊕ *www.newarkairport.com*).

TRANSFERS—CAR SERVICES

Car services can be a great deal because the driver will often meet you on the concourse or in the baggage-claim area and help you with your luggage. The flat rates and tolls are often comparable to taxi fares, but some car services will charge for parking and waiting time at the airport. To eliminate these expenses, other car services require that you telephone their dispatcher when you land so they can send the next available car to pick you up. New York City Taxi and Limousine Commission rules require that all car services be licensed and pick up riders only by prior arrangement; if possible, call 24 hours in advance for reservations, or at least a half day before your flight's departure. Drivers of nonlicensed vehicles ("gypsy cabs") often solicit fares outside the terminal in baggage-claim areas. Don't take them:

even if you do have a safe ride you'll pay more than the going rate.

For phone numbers, see Taxi Travel.

TRANSFERS—TAXIS & SHUTTLES

Outside the baggage-claim area at each of New York's major airports are taxi stands where a uniformed dispatcher helps passengers find taxis (⇨ *Taxi Travel)*. Cabs are not permitted to pick up fares anywhere else in the arrivals area, so if you want a taxi, take your place in line. Shuttle services generally pick up passengers from a designated spot along the curb.

New York Airport Service runs buses between JFK and LaGuardia airports, and buses from those airports to Grand Central Terminal, Port Authority Bus Terminal, Penn Station, Bryant Park, and hotels between 31st and 60th streets in Manhattan. Fares cost between $12 and $15 one way and $21 to $27 round-trip. Buses operate from 6:15 AM to 11:10 PM from the airport; between 5 AM and 10 PM going to the airport.

SuperShuttle vans travel to and from Manhattan to JFK, LaGuardia, and Newark. These blue vans will stop at your home, office, or hotel. There are courtesy phones at the airports. For travel to the airport, the company recommends you make your requests 24 hours in advance. Fares range from $13 to $22 per person.

Shuttle Service New York Airport Service (☏ *718/875–8200* ⊕ *www.nyairportservice. com).* **SuperShuttle** (☏ *212/258–3826* ⊕ *www.supershuttle.com).*

TRANSFERS FROM JFK INTERNATIONAL AIRPORT

Taxis charge a flat fee of $45 plus tolls (which may be as much as $6) to Manhattan only, and take 35–60 minutes. Prices are roughly $20–$55 for trips to most other locations in New York City. You should also tip the driver.

AirTrain JFK links to the A subway line's Howard Beach station, and to Long Island Railroad's (LIRR) Jamaica Station, which is adjacent to the Sutphin

Boulevard/Archer Avenue E/J/Z subway station, with connections to Manhattan. The light rail system runs 24 hours, leaving from the Howard Beach and the LIRR stations station every 4–8 minutes during peak times and every 12 minutes during low traffic times. From Midtown Manhattan, the longest trip to JFK is via the A train, a trip of less than an hour that costs $2 in subway fare in addition to $5 for the AirTrain. The quickest trip is with the Long Island Railroad (about 30 minutes), for a total cost of about $12. When traveling to the Howard Beach station, be sure to take the A train marked FAR ROCKAWAY or ROCKAWAY PARK, not LEFFERTS BOULEVARD.

JFK Transfer Information AirTrain JFK (⊕ *www.airtrainjfk.com).* **Long Island Railroad** (*Jamaica Station* ✉ *146 Archer Ave., at Sutphin Ave.* ☏ *718/217–5477* ⊕ *www.mta.info/lirr).*

TRANSFERS FROM LAGUARDIA AIRPORT

Taxis cost $21–$30 plus tip and tolls (which may be as high as $6) to most destinations in New York City, and take at least 20–40 minutes.

For $2 you can ride the M-60 public bus (there are no luggage facilities on this bus) to 116th Street and Broadway, across from Columbia University on Manhattan's Upper West Side. From there, you can transfer to the 1 train to Midtown. Alternatively, you can take Bus Q-48 to the Main Street subway station in Flushing, where you can transfer to the 7 train. Allow at least 90 minutes for the entire trip to Midtown.

TRANSFERS FROM NEWARK AIRPORT

Taxis to Manhattan cost $40–$65 plus tolls ($5) and take 20 to 45 minutes. "Share and Save" group rates are available for up to four passengers between 8 AM and midnight—make arrangements with the airport's taxi dispatcher. If you're heading to the airport from Manhattan, a $15 surcharge applies to the normal taxi rates and the $5 toll.

AirTrain Newark is an elevated light rail system that connects to New Jersey

Transit and Amtrak trains at the Newark Liberty International Airport Station. Total travel time to Penn Station in Manhattan is approximately 20 minutes and costs $15. AirTrain runs every 3 minutes from 5 AM to midnight and every 15 minutes from midnight to 5 AM.

The AirTrain to Newark's Penn Station takes five minutes. From Newark Penn Station you can catch PATH trains, which run to Manhattan 24 hours a day. PATH trains run every 10 minutes on weekdays, every 15 to 30 minutes on weeknights and weekends. After stopping at Christopher Street, one line travels along 6th Avenue, making stops at West 9th Street, West 14th Street, West 23rd Street, and West 33rd Street. Other PATH trains connect Newark Penn Station with the World Trade Center site. PATH train fare is $1.75.

Coach USA with Olympia Trails buses leave for Grand Central Terminal and Penn Station in Manhattan about every 15 to 30 minutes until midnight. The trip takes roughly 45 minutes, and the fare is $15. Between the Port Authority or Grand Central Terminal and Newark, buses run every 20 to 30 minutes. The trip takes 55 to 65 minutes

Newark Airport Information AirTrain Newark (☎ 888/397–4636 ⊕ www.airtrain newark.com). **Coach USA** (☎ 877/894–9155 ⊕ www.coachusa.com). **PATH Trains** (☎ 800/234–7284 ⊕ www.pathrail.com).

▌BOAT TRAVEL

The Staten Island Ferry runs across New York Harbor between Whitehall Street next to Battery Park in Lower Manhattan and St. George terminal in Staten Island. The free 25-minute ride gives you a view of the financial district skyscrapers, the Statue of Liberty, and Ellis Island.

New York Water Taxi, in addition to serving commuters, shuttles tourists to the city's many waterfront attractions between the West and East sides and Lower Manhattan, the South Street Seaport, and Brooklyn's waterfront parks. The hop-on, hop-off one-day pass ticket is $20; the two-day pass is $25.

Information New York Water Taxi (*NYWT* ☎ 212/742–1969 ⊕ *newyorkwatertaxi.com*). Staten Island Ferry (*www.siferry.com*).

▌BUS TRAVEL

Most long-haul and commuter bus lines feed into the Port Authority Bus Terminal, on 8th Avenue between West 40th and 42nd streets. You must purchase your ticket at a ticket counter, not from the bus driver, so give yourself enough time to wait in a line. Several bus lines serving northern New Jersey and Rockland County, New York, make daily stops at the George Washington Bridge Bus Station from 5 AM to 1 AM. The station is connected to the 175th Street Station on the A line of the subway, which travels down the West Side of Manhattan.

Most city buses follow easy-to-understand routes along the Manhattan street grid. Routes go up or down the north–south avenues, or east and west on the major two-way crosstown streets: 96th, 86th, 79th, 72nd, 57th, 42nd, 34th, 23rd, and 14th. Usually bus routes operate 24 hours, but service is infrequent late at night. Traffic jams can make rides maddeningly slow, especially along 5th Avenue in Midtown and the Upper East Side. Certain bus routes provide "limited-stop service" during weekday rush hours, which saves travel time by stopping only at major cross streets and transfer points. A sign posted at the front of the bus indicates that it has limited service; ask the driver whether the bus stops near where you want to go before boarding.

To find a bus stop, look for a light-blue sign (green for a limited bus) on a green pole; bus numbers and routes are listed, with the stop's name underneath.

Bus fare is the same as subway fare: $2 MetroCards *(⇨ Public Transportation Travel)* allow you one free transfer between buses or from bus to subway; when using coins on the bus, you can ask the driver for a free transfer coupon, good for one change to an intersecting route. Legal transfer points are listed on the back of the slip. Transfers generally have time limits of two hours. You cannot use the transfer to enter the subway system.

Route maps and schedules are posted at many bus stops in Manhattan and at major stops throughout the other boroughs. Each of the five boroughs of New York has a separate bus map; they're available from some station booths, but rarely on buses. The best places to obtain them are the MTA booth in the Times Square Information Center, or the information kiosks in Grand Central Terminal and Penn Station.

Pay your bus fare when you board, with exact change in coins (no pennies, and no change is given) or with a MetroCard.

Buses in New York Metropolitan Transit Authority (MTA) Travel Information Line (☎ *718/330–1234, 718/330–4847 for non–English speakers* ⊕ *www.mta.info*). MTA Status information hotline (☎ *718/243–7777 or 718/330–1234*), updated hourly.

Buses to New York Adirondack, Pine Hill & New York Trailways (☎ *800/225–6815* ⊕ *www.trailways.com*). Coach (☎ *800/631–8405* ⊕ *www.coachusa. com/shortlinebus*).Greyhound Lines Inc. (☎ *800/231–2222* ⊕ *www.greyhound.com*). New Jersey Transit (☎ *973/275–5555* ⊕ *www.njtransit.com*). Peter Pan Trailways (☎ *413/781–2900 or 800/237–8747* ⊕ *www.peterpanbus.com*). Vermont Transit (☎ *800/552–8737* ⊕ *www.vermonttransit.com*).

Bus Stations George Washington Bridge Bus Station (✉ *4211 Broadway, between 178th and 179th Sts., Washington Heights* ☎ *800/221–9903* ⊕ *www.panynj.gov*). Port Authority Bus Terminal (✉ *625 8th Ave., at 42nd St., Midtown West* ☎ *212/564–8484* ⊕ *www.panynj.gov*).

▌ CAR TRAVEL

If you plan to drive into Manhattan, try to avoid the morning and evening rush hours and lunch hour. The deterioration of the bridges to Manhattan, especially those spanning the East River, means that repairs will be ongoing for the next few years. Listen to traffic reports on the radio before you set off, and don't be surprised if a bridge is partially or entirely closed.

Driving within Manhattan can be a nightmare of gridlocked streets, obnoxious drivers and bicyclists, and seemingly suicidal jaywalkers. Narrow and one-way streets are common, particularly downtown, and can make driving even more difficult. The most congested streets of the city lie between 14th and 59th streets and 3rd and 8th avenues.

GASOLINE

Gas stations are few and far between in Manhattan. If you can, fill up at stations outside the city, where prices are anywhere from 10¢ to 50¢ cheaper per gallon. The average price of a gallon of regular unleaded gas is between $2.50 and $1.75, at this writing. In Manhattan, you can refuel at stations along the West Side Highway and 11th Avenue south of West 57th Street and along East Houston Street. Some gas stations in New York require you to pump your own gas; others provide attendants.

PARKING

Free parking is difficult to find in Midtown and on weekday evenings and weekends in other neighborhoods. n the other hand, parking lots charge exorbitant rates—as much as $23 for two hours (this includes an impressive sales tax of 18.625%). If you do drive, use your car sparingly in Manhattan. Instead, park it in a guarded parking garage for at least several hours; hourly rates decrease somewhat if a car is left for a significant amount of time. If you find a spot on the street, check parking signs carefully. Before leaving your car, scour the curb for that bane of every motorist's existence, the painted yellow line that's so faded you had better look twice to ascertain both its existence and range.

CAR RENTALS

When you reserve a car, ask about cancellation penalties, taxes, drop-off charges (if you're planning to pick up the car in one city and leave it in another), and surcharges (for being under or over a certain age, for additional drivers, or for driving across state or country borders or beyond a specific distance from your point of rental). All these things can add substantially to your costs. Request car seats and extras such as GPS when you book.

Rates are sometimes—but not always—better if you book in advance or reserve through a rental agency's Web site. There are other reasons to book ahead, though: for popular destinations, during busy times of the year, or to ensure that you get certain types of cars (vans, SUVs, exotic sports cars).

■TIP➜Make sure that a confirmed reservation guarantees you a car. Agencies sometimes overbook, particularly for busy weekends and holiday periods.

Rates in New York City are around $75–$125 a day and $250–$400 a week for an economy car with air-conditioning, automatic transmission, and unlimited mileage. This includes the state tax on car rentals, which is 13.62%. Rental costs are lower just outside New York City, specifically in such places as Hoboken, New Jersey, and Yonkers, New York. The Yellow Pages are also filled with a profusion of local car-rental agencies, some renting secondhand vehicles. If you're traveling during a holiday period, make sure that a confirmed reservation guarantees you a car.

CAR-RENTAL INSURANCE

If you own a car and carry comprehensive car insurance for both collision and liability, your personal auto insurance will probably cover a rental, but read your policy's fine print to be sure. If you don't have auto insurance, then you should probably buy the collision- or loss-damage waiver (CDW or LDW) from the rental company. This eliminates your liability for damage to the car. Some credit cards offer CDW coverage, but it's usually supplemental to your own insurance and rarely covers SUVs, minivans, luxury models, and the like. If your coverage is secondary, you may still be liable for loss-of-use costs from the car-rental company (again, read the fine print). But no credit-card insurance is valid unless you use that card for *all* transactions, from reserving to paying the final bill.

You may also be offered supplemental liability coverage; the car-rental company is required to carry a minimal level of liability coverage insuring all renters, but it's rarely enough to cover claims in a really serious accident if you're at fault. Your own auto-insurance policy will protect you if you own a car; if you don't, you have to decide whether you are willing to take the risk.

U.S. rental companies sell CDWs and LDWs for about $15 to $25 a day; supplemental liability is usually more than $10 a day. The car-rental company may offer you all sorts of other policies, but they're rarely worth the cost. Personal accident insurance, which is basic hospitalization coverage, is an especially egregious rip-off if you already have health insurance.

■TIP➜You can decline the insurance from the rental company and purchase it through a third-party provider such as Travel Guard (www.travelguard.com)—$9 per day for $35,000 of coverage. That's sometimes just under half the price of the CDW offered by some car-rental companies.

■ PUBLIC TRANSPORTATION TRAVEL

When it comes to getting around New York, you have your pick of transportation in almost every neighborhood. The subway and bus networks are extensive, especially in Manhattan, although getting across town can take some extra maneuvering. If you're not pressed for time, take a public bus *(Bus Travel)* ⇨; they generally are slower than subways, but you can also see the city as you travel. Yellow cabs *(⇨ Taxi Travel)* are abundant, except during the evening rush hour, when many drivers' shifts change. Like a taxi ride, the subway *(⇨ Subway Travel)* is a true New York City experience; it's also often the quickest way to get around. But New York is really a walking town, and depending on the time of day and your destination, hoofing it could be the easiest and most enjoyable option.

During weekday rush hours (from 7:30 AM to 9:30 AM and 5 PM to 7 PM) avoid the jammed Midtown area, both in the subways and on the streets—travel time on buses and taxis can easily double.

Subway and bus fares are $2, although reduced fares are available for senior citizens and people with disabilities during nonrush hours.

You pay for mass transit with a MetroCard, a plastic card with a magnetic strip. As you swipe the card through a subway turnstile or insert it in a bus's card reader, the cost of the fare is automatically deducted. With the MetroCard, you can transfer free from bus to subway, subway to bus, or bus to bus. You must start with the MetroCard and use it again within two hours to complete your trip.

MetroCards are sold at all subway stations and at some stores—look for an "Authorized Sales Agent" sign. The MTA sells two kinds of MetroCards: unlimited-ride and pay-per-ride. Seven-day unlimited-ride MetroCards ($25) allow bus and subway travel for a week. If you will ride more than 13 times, this is the card to get.

The one-day unlimited-ride Fun Pass ($7.50) is good from the day of purchase through 3 AM the following day. It's sold only by neighborhood Metro-Card merchants and MetroCard vending machines at stations (not through the station agent).

When you purchase a pay-per-ride card worth $7 or more, you get a 15% bonus. For example, $20 gives you $23 on your card, which is 11 rides for the price of 10 plus $1. Unlike unlimited-ride cards, pay-per-ride MetroCards can be shared between riders. (Unlimited-ride Met-roCards can be used only once at the same station or bus route in an 18-minute period.)

You can buy or add money to an existing MetroCard at a MetroCard vending machine, available at most subway station entrances (usually near the station booth). The machines accept major credit cards and ATM or debit cards. Many also accept cash, but note that the maximum amount of change they will return is $6.

Schedule & Route Information Metropolitan Transit Authority (MTA) Travel Information Line (☎ 718/330–1234, 718/596–8585 travelers with disabilities ⊕ www.mta.info).

SUBWAY TRAVEL

The subway system operates on more than 840 mi of track for 24 hours a day and serves nearly all the places you're likely to visit. It's cheaper than a cab, and during the workweek it's often faster than either taxis or buses. The trains are well lighted and air-conditioned. Still, the New York subway is hardly problem-free. Many trains are crowded, the older ones are noisy, the air-conditioning can break, and platforms can be dingy and damp. Homeless people sometimes take refuge from the elements by riding the trains, and panhandlers head there for a captive audience. Although trains usually run frequently, especially during rush hours, you never know when some incident somewhere on the line may stall traffic. In addition, subway construction sometimes causes delays or limitation of service, especially on weekends.

Most subway entrances are at street corners and are marked by lampposts with an illuminated Metropolitan Transit Authority (MTA) logo or globe-shape green or red lights—green means the station is open 24 hours and red means the station closes at night (though colors don't always correspond to reality). Subway lines are designated by numbers and letters, such as the 3 line or the A line. Some lines run "express" and skip stops, and others are "locals" and make all stops. Each station entrance has a sign indicating the lines that run through the station. Some entrances are also marked "uptown only" or "downtown only." Before entering subway stations, read the signs carefully. One of the most frequent mistakes visitors make is taking the train in the wrong direction. Maps of the full subway system are posted in every train car and usually on the subway platform (though these are sometimes out-of-date). You can usually pick up free maps at station booths.

For the most up-to-date information on subway lines, call the MTA's Travel Information Center or visit its Web site. The Web site Hopstop is a good source for figuring out the best line to take to reach your destination. (You can also call or text Hopstop for directions.) Alternatively, ask a station agent.

Subway fare is the same as bus fare: $2. You can transfer between subway lines an unlimited number of times at any of the numerous stations where lines intersect. If you use a MetroCard (⇨ *Public Transportation Travel*) to pay your fare, you can also transfer to intersecting MTA bus routes for free. Such transfers generally have time limits of two hours.

Pay your subway fare at the turnstile, using a MetroCard bought at the station booth or from a vending machine.

Subway Information Hopstop (☎ 888/2–HOPSTOP ⊕ www.hopstop. com;). **Metropolitan Transportation Authority (MTA) Travel Information Line** (☎ 718/330–1234, 718/330–4847 for non-English speakers ⊕ www.mta.info). **MTA Lost Property Office** (☎ 212/712–4500). **MTA Status information hotline** (☎ 718/243–7777), updated hourly.

TAXI TRAVEL

Yellow cabs are in abundance almost everywhere in Manhattan, cruising the streets looking for fares. They are usually easy to hail on the street or from a cab stand in front of major hotels, though finding one at rush hour or in the rain can take some time. Even if you're stuck in a downpour or at the airport, do not accept a ride from a gypsy cab. If a cab is not yellow and does not have a numbered aqua-color plastic medallion riveted to the hood, you could be putting yourself in danger by getting into the car.

You can see if a taxi is available by checking its rooftop light; if the center panel is lighted and the side panels are dark, the driver is ready to take passengers. Once the meter is engaged (and if it isn't, alert your driver; you'll seldom benefit from negotiating an off-the-record ride) the fare is $2.50 just for entering the vehicle and 40¢ for each unit thereafter. A unit is defined as either 0.20 mi when the cab's cruising at 6 mph or faster or as 60 seconds when the cab is either not moving or moving at less than 12 mph. A 50¢ night surcharge is added between 8 PM and 6 AM and a much-maligned $1 weekday surcharge is tacked on to rides after 4 PM and before 8 PM.

One taxi can hold a maximum of four passengers (an additional passenger under the age of seven is allowed if the child sits on someone's lap). There is no charge for extra passengers. You must pay any bridge or tunnel tolls incurred during your trip (a driver will usually pay the toll himself to keep moving quickly, but that amount will be added to the fare when the ride is over). Taxi drivers expect a 15% to 20% tip.

To avoid unhappy taxi experiences, try to know where you want to go and how to get there before you hail a cab. You should assist your driver, however, by directing him to the specific cross streets of your destination (for instance, "5th Avenue and 42nd Street"), rather than the numerical address, which means nothing to drivers. Also, speak simply and clearly to make sure the driver has heard you correctly. A quick call to your destination will give you cross-street information, as will a glance at a map marked with address numbers. When you leave the cab, remember to take your receipt. It includes the cab's medallion number, which can help you track the cabbie down in the event that you lose your possessions in the cab or, if after the fact, you want to report an unpleasant ride.

Taxis can be extremely difficult (if not impossible) to find in many parts of Brooklyn, Queens, the Bronx, and Staten Island. As a result, you may have no choice but to call a car service. Always determine the fee beforehand when using a car service sedan; a 10%–15% tip is customary above that.

Taxi Companies Carmel Car Service (☎ *212/666-6666 or 800/922-7635* ⊕ *www. carmelcarservice.com*). **Dial 7 Car Service** (☎ *212/777-7777 or 800/222-9888* ⊕ *www. telavivlimo.com*).

London Towncars (☎ *212/988-9700 or 800/221-4009* ⊕ *www.londontowncars.com*).

TRAIN TRAVEL

Metro-North Commuter Railroad trains take passengers from Grand Central Terminal to points north of New York City, both in New York State and Connecticut. Amtrak trains from across the United States arrive at Penn Station. For trains from New York City to Long Island and New Jersey, take the Long Island Railroad and New Jersey Transit, respectively; both operate from Penn Station. The PATH trains offer service to Newark and Jersey City. All of these trains generally run on schedule, although occasional delays occur.

Information Amtrak (☎ *800/872-7245* ⊕ *www.amtrak.com*). **Long Island Rail Road** (☎ *718/217-5477* ⊕ *www.mta.info/ lirr*). **Metro-North Commuter Railroad** (☎ *212/532-4900* ⊕ *www.mta.info/mnr*). **New Jersey Transit** (☎ *800/772-2222* ⊕ *www. njtransit.com*). **PATH** (☎ *800/234-7284* ⊕ *www.pathrail.com*).

Train Stations Grand Central Terminal (✉ *Park Ave. at E. 42nd St., Midtown East* ☎ *212/340-2555* ⊕ *www.grandcentral terminal.com*). **Penn Station** (✉ *W. 31st to W. 33rd Sts., between 7th and 8th Aves., Midtown West* ☎ *212/630-6401*).

ESSENTIALS

■ COMMUNICATIONS

INTERNET

You can check your e-mail or surf the Internet at cafés, copy centers, libraries, and most hotels. By far the best equipped and probably most convenient is Cyber Café in Times Square, which has a staggering 650-plus computer terminals; it's open from 8 AM to 11 PM on weekdays and 11 AM to 11 PM on weekends. The organization NYCwireless keeps track of free Wi-Fi hot spots in the New York area. The Web site JiWire allows you to find Wi-Fi hot spots in hotels, libraries, parks, and other locations throughout the city.

Contacts JiWire (⊕ www.jiwire.com).

Internet Cafés Cyber Café (⊠ 250 W. 49th St., between 8th Ave. and Broadway, Midtown West ☎ 212/333–4109 ⊕ www.cyber-cafe.com). **www.web2zone** (⊠ 54 Cooper Sq., East Village ☎ 212/614–7300 ⊕ www.web2zone.com).

Other Internet Locations New York Public Library–Mid-Manhattan Library (⊠ 455 5th Ave., at E. 40th St., Midtown East ☎ 212/930–0800 ⊕ www.nypl.org). **NYCwireless** (⊕ www.nycwireless.net).

■ DISABILITIES & ACCESSIBILITY

New York has come a long way in making life easier for people with disabilities. At most street corners curb cuts allow wheelchairs to roll along unimpeded. Many restaurants, shops, and movie theaters with step-up entrances have wheelchair ramps. And though some New Yorkers may rush past those in need of assistance, you'll find plenty of people who are more than happy to help you get around.

Hospital Audiences maintains a Web site with information on the accessibility of many landmarks and attractions. A similar list, "Tourist and Cultural Information for the Disabled," is available from New

York City's Web site. Big Apple Greeters has tours of New York City tailored to visitors' personal preferences. The Andrew Heiskell Braille and Talking Book Library houses an impressive collection of braille, large-print, and recorded books in a layout designed for people with vision impairments.

Local Resources Andrew Heiskell Library (⊠ 40 W. 20th St., between 5th and 6th Aves., Flatiron District Ⓜ F, V to 23rd St. ☎ 212/206–5400 ⊕ www.talkingbooks. nypl.org). **Big Apple Greeters** (⊠ 1 Centre St., Suite 2035, Lower Manhattan ☎ 212/669–8159 ⊕ www.bigapplegreeter.org). **Hospital Audiences** (☎ 212/575–7676 ⊕ www.hospaud.org). **New York City** (☎ 311 in New York City, 212/639–9675 [212/NEW-YORK] outside New York ⊕ www.nyc.gov).

LODGING

Despite the Americans with Disabilities Act, the definition of accessibility seems to differ from hotel to hotel. Some properties may be accessible by ADA standards for people with mobility problems but not for people with hearing or vision impairments, for example.

If you have mobility problems, ask for the lowest floor on which accessible services are offered. If you have a hearing impairment, check whether the hotel has devices to alert you visually to the ring of the telephone, a knock at the door, and a fire/emergency alarm. Some hotels provide these devices without charge. Discuss your needs with hotel personnel if this equipment isn't available, so that a staff member can personally alert you in the event of an emergency.

If you're bringing a guide dog, get authorization ahead of time and write down the name of the person with whom you spoke.

RESERVATIONS

When discussing accessibility with an operator or reservations agent, ask hard questions. Are there any stairs, inside *or* out? Are there grab bars next to the toilet *and* in the shower/tub? How wide is the doorway to the room? To the bathroom? For the most extensive facilities meeting the latest legal specifications, opt for newer accommodations. If you reserve through a toll-free number, consider also calling the hotel's local number to confirm the information from the central reservations office. Get confirmation in writing when you can.

SIGHTS & ATTRACTIONS

Most public facilities in New York City, whether museums, parks, or theaters, are wheelchair-accessible. Some attractions have tours or programs for people with mobility, sight, or hearing impairments.

TRANSPORTATION

Other than at major subway exchanges, most stations are still all but impossible to navigate; people in wheelchairs should stick to public buses, most of which have wheelchair lifts and "kneelers" at the front to facilitate getting on and off. Bus drivers will provide assistance.

Reduced fares are available to all disabled passengers displaying a Medicare card. Visitors to the city are also eligible for the same Access-a-Ride program benefits as New York City residents. Drivers with disabilities may use windshield cards from their own state or Canadian province to park in designated handicapped spaces.

The U.S. Department of Transportation Aviation Consumer Protection Division's online publication *New Horizons: Information for the Air Traveler with a Disability* offers advice for travelers with a disability, and outlines basic rights. Visit DisabilityInfo.gov for general information.

Information & Complaints Aviation Consumer Protection Division (⊕ *airconsumer. ost.dot.gov/publications/horizons.htm* for airline travel advice and rights). **Departmental**

Office of Civil Rights (☎ *202/366–4648, 202/366–8538 TTY* ⊕ *www.dotcr.ost.dot.gov*). **Disability Rights Section** (☎ *202/514–0301 ADA information line, 800/514–0301, 202/514–0383 TTY, 800/514–0383 TTY* ⊕ *www.ada.gov*). **U.S. Department of Transportation Hotline** (☎ *800/778–4838 for disability-related air-travel problems, 800/455–9880 TTY*).

■ GAY & LESBIAN TRAVEL

Attitudes toward same-sex couples are very tolerant in Manhattan and many parts of Brooklyn. Chelsea, Greenwich Village, and Hell's Kitchen are the most prominently gay neighborhoods, but gay men and lesbians feel right at home almost everywhere. The world's biggest gay-pride parade takes place on 5th Avenue the last Sunday in June.

For details about the gay and lesbian scene, consult *Fodor's Gay Guide to the USA* (available in bookstores everywhere).

PUBLICATIONS

For listings of gay events and places, check out *HX, Next, New York Blade News,* and the *Gay City News,* all distributed free on the street and in many bars and shops throughout Manhattan. Magazines *Paper* and *Time Out New York* have a gay-friendly take on what's happening in the city.

Local Information Gay & Lesbian Switchboard of NY (☎ *212/989–0999 or 888/843–4564* ⊕ *www.glnh.org*). **Lesbian, Gay, Bisexual & Transgender Community Center** (✉ *208 W. 13th St., between 7th and 8th Aves., Greenwich Village* ☎ *212/620–7310* ⊕ *www.gaycenter.org*).

Gay Publications Gay City News (⊕ *www. gaycitynews.com*). **HX** (⊕ *www.hx.com*). **New York Blade News** (⊕ *www.nyblade.com*). **Next** (⊕ *www.nextmagazine.net*).

Gay- & Lesbian-Friendly Travel Agencies Different Roads Travel (☎ *760/325–6964, 800/429–8747 Ext. 14* ✉ *lgernert@tzell.com*). **Skylink Travel and Tour/Flying Dutchmen**

Travel (☎ *707/546–9888 or 800/225–5759*), serving lesbian travelers.

▌ KIDS IN NEW YORK

For listings of children's events, consult *New York* magazine. The Friday *New York Times* "Weekend" section also includes children's activities. Other good sources on happenings for youngsters are the monthly magazines *New York Family* and *NY Metro Parents*, both available free at toy stores, children's museums, and other places where parents and children are found. The Web site Parents Connect includes listings of what's going on. If you have access to cable television, check the local all-news channel New York 1, where you'll find a spot aired several times daily that covers current and noteworthy children's events. *Fodor's New York City with Kids* (available in bookstores everywhere) can help you plan your days together.

Publications & Web Sites NY Metro Parents (⊕ *www.nymetroparents.com*). Parents Connect(⊕ *www.parentsconnect.com*).

LODGING

Before you consider using a cot or fold-out couch for your child, ask just how large your hotel room is—New York City rooms tend to be small. Most hotels in New York allow children under a certain age to stay in their parents' room at no extra charge, but others charge for them as extra adults; be sure to find out the cutoff age for children's discounts.

PUBLIC TRANSPORTATION

Children shorter than 44 inches ride for free on MTA buses and subways. If you're pushing a stroller, don't struggle through a subway turnstile; ask the station agent to buzz you through the gate (the attendant will ask you to swipe your MetroCard through the turnstile nearest the gate). Keep a sharp eye on your young ones while on the subway. At some stations there is a gap between the train doors and the platform. Unfortunately New York riders are not known to give up their seats for children, for someone carrying a child, or for anyone else.

▌ MONEY

CREDIT CARDS

Throughout this guide, the following abbreviations are used: **AE**, American Express; **D**, Discover; **DC**, Diners Club; **MC**, MasterCard; and **V**, Visa.

Record all your credit-card numbers—as well as the phone numbers to call if your cards are lost or stolen—in a safe place, so you're prepared should something go wrong. Both MasterCard and Visa have general numbers you can call if your card is lost, but you're better off calling the number of your issuing bank, since MasterCard and Visa usually just transfer you to your bank; your bank's number is usually printed on your card.

Reporting Lost Cards American Express (☎ *800/992–3404 in U.S., 336/393–1111 collect from abroad* ⊕ *www.americanexpress. com*). **Diners Club** (☎ *800/234–6377 in U.S., 303/799–1504 collect from abroad* ⊕ *www. dinersclub.com*). **Discover** (☎ *800/347–2683 in U.S., 801/902–3100 collect from abroad* ⊕ *www.discovercard.com*). **MasterCard** (☎ *800/622–7747 in U.S., 636/722–7111 collect from abroad* ⊕ *www.mastercard.com*). **Visa** (☎ *800/847–2911 in U.S., 410/581–9944 collect from abroad* ⊕ *www.visa.com*).

TRAVELER'S CHECKS & CARDS

Both Citibank (under the Visa brand) and American Express issue traveler's checks in the United States, but Amex is better known and more widely accepted; you can also avoid hefty surcharges by cashing Amex checks at Amex offices. Whatever you do, keep track of all the serial numbers in case the checks are lost or stolen.

American Express now offers a stored-value card called a Travelers Cheque Card, which you can use wherever American Express credit cards are accepted, including ATMs. The card can carry a minimum of $300 and a maximum of $2,700, and it's a very safe way to carry your funds.

Although you can get replacement funds in 24 hours if your card is lost or stolen, it doesn't really strike us as a very good deal. In addition to a high initial cost ($14.95 to set up the card, plus $5 each time you "reload"), you still have to pay a 2% fee for each purchase in a foreign currency (similar to that of any credit card). Further, each time you use the card in an ATM you pay a transaction fee of $2.50 on top of the 2% transaction fee for the conversion—add it all up and it can be considerably more than you would pay when simply using your own ATM card. Regular traveler's checks are just as secure and cost less.

Contacts American Express (☎ *888/412–6945 in U.S., 801/945–9450 collect outside of U.S. to add value or speak to customer service* ⊕ *www.american express.com*).

▌ RESTROOMS

Seinfeld fans might recall George Costanza's claim that if you named any given coordinates in New York City, he could instantly name the closest and most worthy public restroom in the vicinity. Regrettably, unless you're traveling with your own George or a potty training–toddler who can drive even the most hardened retailers to share their private bathrooms, public restrooms in New York are few and far between. Plans are in the works to add coin-operated street toilets at several locations. (at press time, the first toilet was operating in Madison Square Park with 20 more on the way).In the meantime, when looking for a restroom, head for Midtown department stores, museums, or the lobbies of large hotels to find the cleanest bathrooms. Public atriums, such as those at the Citicorp Center and Trump Tower, also provide good public facilities, as do Bryant Park and the many Barnes & Noble bookstores and Starbucks coffee shops in the city. If you're in the area, the Times Square Information Center, on Broadway between 46th and 47th streets, can be a godsend.

Find a Loo The Bathroom Diaries (⊕ *www. thebathroomdiaries.com*) is flush with unsanitized info on restrooms the world over—each one located, reviewed, and rated.

▌ SAFETY

New York City is one of the safest large cities in the country. However, do not let yourself be lulled into a false sense of security. As in any large city, travelers in New York remain particularly easy marks for pickpockets and hustlers.

After 9/11 security was heightened throughout the city. Never leave any bags unattended, and expect to have yourself and your possessions inspected thoroughly in such places as airports, sports stadiums, museums, and city buildings.

Ignore the panhandlers on the streets and subways, people who offer to hail you a cab (they often appear at Penn Station, the Port Authority, and Grand Central), and limousine and gypsy cab drivers who (illegally) offer you a ride.

Keep jewelry out of sight on the street; better yet, leave valuables at home. Men should carry their wallets in their front pants pocket rather than in their back pockets. When in bars or restaurants, never hang your purse or bag on the back of a chair or put it underneath the table.

Avoid deserted blocks in unfamiliar neighborhoods. A brisk, purposeful pace helps deter trouble wherever you go.

The subway runs around the clock and is generally well trafficked until midnight (and until at least 2 AM on Friday and Saturday nights), and overall it is very safe. If you do take the subway late at night, ride in the center car, with the conductor, and wait on the center of the platform. Watch out for unsavory characters lurking around the inside or outside of stations.

When waiting for a train, stand far away from the edge of the subway platform, especially when trains are entering or leaving the station. Once the train pulls into the station, avoid empty cars. While on the train don't engage in verbal exchanges with aggressive riders, who may accuse others of anything from pushing to taking up too much space. If a fellow passenger makes you nervous while on the train, trust your instincts and change cars. When disembarking, stick with the crowd until you reach the street.

Travelers Aid International helps crime victims, stranded travelers, and wayward children, and works closely with the police.

Information Travelers Aid (✉ *JFK International Airport, Terminal 6* ☎ *718/656–4870* ✉ *Newark International Airport, Terminal B* ☎ *973/623–5052* ⊕ *www.travelersaid.org*).

▌ SENIOR-CITIZEN TRAVEL

The Metropolitan Transit Authority (MTA) offers lower fares for passengers 65 and over. On the subway, show your Medicare card to the station agent, and for the standard fare ($2) you will be issued a MetroCard and a return-trip ticket; on the bus, show your Medicare card to the bus driver and a cash fare of $1 can be made. (Payment must be made in coins.)

To qualify for age-related discounts, mention your senior-citizen status up front when booking hotel reservations (not when checking out). Be sure to have identification on hand. When renting a car, ask about promotional car-rental discounts, which can be cheaper than senior-citizen rates.

Educational Programs Elderhostel (☎ *877/426–8056, 978/323–4141 international callers, 877/426–2167 TTY* ⊕ *www.elderhostel.org*).

Information MTA Reduced Fare hotline (☎ *718/243–4999* ⊕ *www.mta.info*).

▌ SPORTS & THE OUTDOORS

The City of New York's Parks & Recreation division lists all of the recreational facilities and activities available through New York's Parks Department. For information about athletic facilities in Manhattan as well as a calendar of sporting events, visit the Web site or pick up a copy of *MetroSports* at sporting-goods stores or health clubs. The sports section of *Time Out New York,* sold at most newsstands, lists upcoming events, times, dates, and ticket information.

Contact Information *MetroSports* (⊕ *www. mctrosportsny.com*). **Parks & Recreation division** (☎ *311 in New York City, 212/639–9675, 212/NEW–YORK outside New York City* ⊕ *www.nyc.gov/parks*).

BASEBALL

The subway will get you directly to stadiums of both New York–area major-league teams. A fun alternative, the *Yankee Clipper* cruises from Manhattan's East Side and from New Jersey to Yankee Stadium on game nights. The round-trip cost is $22. The regular baseball season runs from April through September.

The New York Mets recently moved from Shea Stadium to the neighboring, newly constructed CitiField, at the next-to-last stop on the 7 train, in Queens; the New York Yankees also got a new home at the new Yankee Stadium. Founded in 2001, the minor-league Brooklyn Cyclones are named for Coney Island's famous wooden roller coaster. A feeder team for the New York Mets, they play 38 home games at KeySpan Park, next to the boardwalk, with views of the Atlantic over the right-field wall and views of historic Astroland over the left-field wall. Most people make a day of it, with time at the beach and amusement rides before an evening game. Take the D, F, or Q subway to the end of the line, and walk one block to the right of the original Nathan's Famous hot dog stand.

For another fun, family-oriented experience, check out the Staten Island Yankees, one of New York's minor-league teams, which warms up many future New York Yankees players. The stadium, a five-minute walk from the Staten Island Ferry terminal, has magnificent panoramic views of Lower Manhattan and the Statue of Liberty.

Contact Information Brooklyn Cyclones (✉ *1904 Surf Ave., at 19th St., Coney Island* ☎ *718/449-8497* ⊕ *www.brooklyncyclones. com* Ⓜ *D, F, Q to Stillwell Ave.).* **CitiField** (✉ *Roosevelt Ave. off Grand Central Pkwy., Flushing* ☎ *718/507-8499* ⊕ *www.mets. com* Ⓜ *7 to Willets Pt./Shea Stadium).* **Staten Island Yankees** (✉ *Richmond County Bank Ballpark at St. George, Staten Island* ☎ *718/720-9265* ⊕ *www.siyanks.com).* **Yankee Clipper** (☎ *800/533-3779* ⊕ *www.ny waterway.com).* **Yankee Stadium** (✉ *161st St. at River Ave., Bronx* ☎ *718/293-6000* ⊕ *www. yankees.com* Ⓜ *B, D to 167th St.; 4 to 161st St.–Yankee Stadium).*

BASKETBALL

The New York Knicks arouse intense hometown passions, which means tickets for home games at Madison Square Garden are hard to come by. The New Jersey Nets play at the Meadowlands in the Continental Airlines Arena but have plans to relocate and become the Brooklyn Nets. Tickets are generally easy to obtain. The men's basketball season runs from late October through April. The New York Liberty, a member of the Women's NBA, had its first season in 1997; some of the team's more high-profile players are already legendary. The season runs from Memorial Day weekend through August, with home games played at Madison Square Garden.

If the professional games are sold out, try to attend a college game where New York stalwarts Fordham, Hofstra, and St. John's compete against national top 25 teams during invitational tournaments.

Contact Information Madison Square Garden (⊕ *www.thegarden.com).* **New**

Jersey Nets (☎ *201/935-3900 box office, 800/765-6387* ⊕ *www.nba.com/nets).* **New York Knicks** (☎ *212/465-5867* ⊕ *www. nba.com/knicks).* **New York Liberty** (☎ *877/962-2849 tickets, 212/564-9622 fan hotline* ⊕ *www.wnba.com/liberty).*

BICYCLING

Central Park has a 6-mi circular drive with a couple of decent climbs. It's closed to automobile traffic from 10 AM to 3 PM (except the southeast portion between 6th Avenue and East 72nd Street) and 7 PM to 7 AM on weekdays, and from 7 PM Friday to 7 AM Monday. On holidays it's closed to automobile traffic from 7 PM the night before until 7 AM the day after.

The bike lane along the Hudson River Park's esplanade parallels the waterfront from West 59th Street south to the esplanade of Battery Park City. The lane also heads north, connecting with the bike path in Riverside Park, the promenade between West 72nd and West 110th streets, and continuing all the way to the George Washington Bridge. From Battery Park it's a quick ride to the Wall Street area, which is deserted on weekends, and over to South Street and a bike lane along the East River.

The 3.3-mi circular drive in Brooklyn's Prospect Park is closed to cars year-round except from 5 PM to 7 PM on weekends and 7 AM to 9 AM on weekdays except holidays. It has a long, gradual uphill that tops off near the Grand Army Plaza entrance. (Biking around Manhattan streets next to the dense traffic is best left to messengers and seasoned cyclists.)

Bike Rentals Bicycle Rentals at Loeb Boathouse (✉ *Midpark near E. 74th St., Central Park* ☎ *212/517-2233).* **Hub Station** (✉ *73 Morton St. , between Hudson. and Greenwich Sts., West Village* ☎ *212/965-9334* Ⓜ *A, C, E to Canal St.).***Larry & Jeff's Bicycles Plus** (✉ *1400 3rd Ave., between E. 79th and E. 80th Sts., Upper East Side* ☎ *212/794-2929* Ⓜ *4, 5, 6 to 86th St.).* **Pedal Pusher** (✉ *1306 2nd Ave., between E. 68th and E. 69th Sts., Upper East Side* ☎ *212/288-5592*

⊕www.pedalpusherbikeshop.com Ⓜ6 to 68th St./Hunter College). **Toga Bike Shop** (⊠110 West End Ave., at W. 64th St., Upper West Side ☎212/799–9625 ⊕www.togabikes.com Ⓜ1 to 66th St.).

GROUP BIKE RIDES

For organized rides with other cyclists, call or e-mail before you come to New York. Bike New York runs a five-borough bike ride in May. The Five Borough Bicycle Club organizes day and weekend rides. The New York Cycle Club sponsors weekend rides for every level of ability. Time's Up!, a nonprofit environmental group, leads free recreational rides at least twice a month for cyclists as well as skaters; the Central Park Moonlight Ride, departing from Columbus Circle at 10 PM the first Friday of every month, is a favorite.

Contact Information Bike New York (⊠891 Amsterdam Ave., at W. 103rd St., Upper West Side ☎212/932–2453 ⊕www.bikenewyork.org). **Five Borough Bicycle Club** (⊠891 Amsterdam Ave., at W. 103rd St., Upper West Side ☎212/932–2300 Ext. 115 ⊕www.5bbc.org). **New York Cycle Club** (⊠Box 4541, Grand Central Station, 10163 ☎212/828–5711 ⊕www.nycc.org). **Time's Up!** (☎212/802–8222 ⊕www.times-up.org).

BOATING & KAYAKING

Central Park has rowboats (plus one Venetian gondola for glides in the moonlight) on the 22-acre Central Park Lake. Rent your rowboat at Loeb Boathouse, near East 74th Street, from March through October; gondola rides are available only in summer. In summer at the Pier 96 Boathouse in Midtown West you can take a sturdy kayak out for a paddle for free on weekends and weekday evenings from mid-May through mid-October. Beginners learn to paddle in the calmer embayment area closest to shore until they feel ready to venture farther out into open water. More experienced kayakers can partake in the three-hour trips conducted every weekend and on holiday mornings. Sign-ups for these popular tours end at 8 AM. Due to high demand, names are entered

into a lottery to see who gets to go out each morning. No reservations are taken in advance. **Manhattan Kayak Company** runs trips (these are not free) and gives lessons for all levels.

Contact Information Loeb Boathouse (⊠Midpark near E. 74th St., Central Park ☎212/517–2233 ⊕www.centralparknyc. org). **Manhattan Kayak Company** (⊠Chelsea Piers, Pier 66, W. 26th St. at the Hudson River, Chelsea ☎212/924–1788 ⊕www.manhattan kayak.com Ⓜ C, E to 23rd St.).**Pier 96 Boathouse** (⊠56th St. at the Hudson River, Midtown West ☎646/613–0740 daily status, 646/613–0375 information ⊕www.downtownboathouse.org Ⓜ1, A, C, E to 59th St.).

FOOTBALL

The football season runs from September through December. The enormously popular New York Giants play at Giants Stadium in the Meadowlands Sports Complex. Most seats for Giants games are sold on a season-ticket basis—and there's a long waiting list for those. However, single tickets are occasionally available at the stadium box office. The New York Jets also play at Giants Stadium. Although Jets tickets are not as scarce as those for the Giants, most are snapped up by fans before the season opener.

Contact Information New York Giants (☎201/935–8222 for tickets ⊕www.giants. com). **New York Jets** (☎516/560–8200 for tickets, 516/560–8288 for fan club ⊕www. newyorkjets.com).

ICE-SKATING

The outdoor rink in Rockefeller Center, open from October through early April, is much smaller in real life than it appears on TV and in movies. It's also busy, so be prepared to wait—there are no advance ticket sales. Although it's also beautiful, especially when Rock Center's enormous Christmas tree towers above it, you pay for the privilege: rates are $13.50–$17.50 and skate rentals are $9.

The city's outdoor rinks, open from roughly November through March, all have their own character. Central Park's beautifully situated Wollman Rink offers skating until long after dark beneath the lights of the city. Be prepared for daytime crowds on weekends. The Lasker Rink, at the north end of Central Park, is smaller and usually less crowded than Wollman. Prospect Park's Kate Wollman Rink borders the lake, and has a picture-postcard setting. Chelsea Piers' Sky Rink has two year-round indoor rinks overlooking the Hudson. Rentals are available at all rinks. The Pond at Bryant Park offers free skating, not including the cost of skate rental, from late October through January, from 8 AM to 10 PM from Sunday through Thursday and from 8 AM to midnight Friday and Saturday.

Contact Information Bryant Park (⊠ *6th Ave. between 40th and 42nd Sts., Midtown West* ☎ *866/221–5157* ⊕ *www.bryantpark. org* Ⓜ *B, D, F, V to 42nd St.).* **Kate Wollman Rink** (⊠ *Ocean and Parkside Aves., Prospect Park, Brooklyn* ☎ *718/287–6431* Ⓜ *2, 3 to Grand Army Plaza; B, Q to Prospect Park; F to 15th St./Prospect Park).* **Lasker Rink** (⊠ *Midpark near E. 106th St., Central Park* ☎ *917/492–3875* ⊕ *www.laskerskatingrink. com* Ⓜ *B, C to 103rd St.).* **Rockefeller Center** (⊠ *50th St. at 5th Ave., lower plaza, Midtown West* ☎ *212/332–7654* ⊕ *www.therinkat rockcenter.com* Ⓜ *B, D, F, V to 47th–50th Sts./Rockefeller Center; E, V to 5th Ave.–53rd St.).* **Sky Rink** (⊠ *Pier 61, W. 23rd St. at the Hudson River, Chelsea* ☎ *212/336–6100* ⊕ *www.chelseapiers.com* Ⓜ *C, E to 23rd St.).* **Wollman Rink** (⊠ *North of 6th Ave., between 62nd and 63rd Sts., north of park entrance,* ☎ *212/439–6900* ⊕ *www. wollmanskatingrink.com).*

JOGGING

In Manhattan, Central Park is the busiest spot, specifically along the 1.6-mi path circling the Jacqueline Kennedy Onassis Reservoir, where you jog in a counterclockwise direction. A runners' lane has been designated along the park roads. A good 1.75-mi route starts at Tavern on the Green along the West Drive, heads south around the bottom of the park to the East Drive, and circles back west on the 72nd Street park road to your starting point; the entire loop road is a hilly 6 mi. Riverside Park, along the Hudson River bank in Manhattan, is glorious at sunset. You can cover 4.5 mi by running from West 72nd to 116th Street and back, and the Greenbelt trail extends 4 more mi north to the George Washington Bridge at 181st Street. Other favorite Manhattan circuits are the Battery Park City esplanade (about 2 mi), which connects to the Hudson River Park (about 1.5 mi), and the East River Esplanade (just over 3 mi from East 59th to East 125th streets).

❚ TAXES

A sales tax of 8.375% applies to almost everything you can buy retail, including restaurant meals. However, clothing and footwear are exempt as are prescription drugs and nonprepared food bought in grocery stores. For clothing and footwear items over $110, there is no city sales tax, although there is a 4.375% state sales tax.

❚ TIPPING

The customary tipping rate for taxi drivers is 15%–20%, with a minimum of $2; bellhops are usually given $2 per bag in luxury hotels, $1 per bag elsewhere. Hotel maids should be tipped $2 per day of your stay. A doorman who hails or helps you into a cab can be tipped $1–$2. You should also tip your hotel concierge for services rendered; the size of the tip depends on the difficulty of your request, as well as the quality of the concierge's work. Waiters should be tipped 15%–20%, though at higher-end restaurants, a solid 20% is more the norm. Tip $1 per drink you order at the bar.

❚ VISITOR INFORMATION

The Grand Central Partnership (a sort of civic Good Samaritans' group) has installed a number of information booths in and around Grand Central Terminal (there's one near Vanderbilt Avenue and East 42nd Street). They're loaded with maps and helpful brochures on attractions throughout the city and they're staffed by friendly, knowledgeable, multilingual New Yorkers.

NYC & Company's Times Square Visitors Center is decked out with lots of fun and helpful tools like multilingual kiosks. The bureau also has a midtown visitors center on 7th Avenue and runs kiosks in Lower Manhattan at City Hall Park and at Federal Hall National Memorial at 26 Wall Street; in Chinatown at the triangle where Canal, Walker, and Baxter streets meet; and in Harlem at the Apollo Theater at 253 West 125th Street.

The Downtown Alliance has information on the area encompassing City Hall south to Battery Park, and from the East River to West Street. For a free booklet listing New York City attractions and tour packages, contact the New York State Division of Tourism.

THE FODORS.COM CONNECTION

Before your trip, be sure to check out what fellow travelers are saying in Talk on www.fodors.com.

CONTACTS

City Information Brooklyn Information & Culture Inc. (BRIC) (✉ 647 Fulton St., 2nd fl., Brooklyn ☎ 718/855-7882 ⊕ www.briconline.org). **Downtown Alliance** (✉ 120 Broadway, Suite 3340, between Pine and Thames Sts., Lower Manhattan ☎ 212/566-6700 ⊕ www.downtownny.com). **Grand Central Partnership** ☎ 212/883-2420 ⊕ www.grandcentral-partnership.org). **NYC & Company Convention & Visitors Bureau** (✉ 810 7th Ave., between W. 52nd and W. 53rd Sts., 3rd fl., Midtown West ☎ 212/484-1222 ⊕ www.nycgo.com). **Times Square Information Center** (✉ 1560 Broadway, between 46th and 47th Sts., Midtown West ☎ 212/768-1560 ⊕ www.timessquarenyc.org).

Statewide Information New York State Division of Tourism (☎ 518/474-4116 or 800/225-5697 ⊕ www.iloveny.com).

INDEX